Mimetic Theory and World Religions

STUDIES IN VIOLENCE, MIMESIS, AND CULTURE

SERIES EDITOR

William A. Johnsen

The Studies in Violence, Mimesis, and Culture Series examines issues related to the nexus of violence and religion in the genesis and maintenance of culture. It furthers the agenda of the Colloquium on Violence and Religion, an international association that draws inspiration from René Girard's mimetic hypothesis on the relationship between violence and religion, elaborated in a stunning series of books he has written over the last forty years. Readers interested in this area of research can also look to the association's journal, *Contagion: Journal of Violence, Mimesis, and Culture.*

Mimetic Theory and World Religions

Edited by Wolfgang Palaver and Richard Schenk

Michigan State University Press · *East Lansing*

∞ The paper used in this publication meets the minimum requirements
of ANSI/NISO Z39.48-1992 (R 1997) (Permanence of Paper).

Michigan State University Press
East Lansing, Michigan 48823-5245

Printed and bound in the United States of America.

27 26 25 24 23 22 21 20 19 18 1 2 3 4 5 6 7 8 9 10

LIBRARY OF CONGRESS CATALOGING-IN-PUBLICATION DATA
Names: Palaver, Wolfgang, 1958- editor.
Title: Mimetic theory and world religions / edited by Wolfgang Palaver and Richard Schenk.
Description: East Lansing : Michigan State University Press, 2017. | Series: Studies in violence, mimesis, and culture | Includes bibliographical references and index.
Identifiers: LCCN 2016057848| ISBN 9781611862621 (pbk. : alk. paper) | ISBN 9781609175443 (pdf) | ISBN 9781628953138 (epub) | ISBN 9781628963137 (kindle)
Subjects: LCSH: Girard, René, 1923-2015. | Memetics. | Religion. | Religious pluralism. | Religions.
Classification: LCC B2430.G494 M46 2017 | DDC 200—dc23 LC record available at https://lccn.loc.gov/2016057848

Book design by Charlie Sharp, Sharp Des!gns, East Lansing, Michigan
Cover design by David Drummond, Salamander Design, www.salamanderhill.com.
Cover image is *Le Sacrifice d'Isaac* (1960–65) oil on canvas, 230 × 235 cm
by Marc Chagall (1887–1985), located at Musée National Marc Chagall,

green press INITIATIVE

Michigan State University Press is a member of the Green Press Initiative and is committed to developing and encouraging ecologically responsible publishing practices. For more information about the Green Press Initiative and the use of recycled paper in book publishing, please visit *www.greenpressinitiative.org*.

Visit Michigan State University Press at *www.msupress.org*

Contents

Introduction

Our globalized world of today brings with it a unity of humankind such as never experienced before. Opportunities to fight hunger and poverty on a worldwide level and to act globally against the threats of climate change have come within the reach of humankind. Globalization, however, also brings with it terrorist threats and related apocalyptic dangers. Concerning religion, the world of today faces two important challenges. We need to overcome an all too simple secularism that reduces religion to a solely private matter, and we have to acknowledge the plurality of religions at the local as well as at the global level.

After the terrorist attacks in Paris in January 2015, two quite divergent thinkers criticized the secularism that aims at the privatization of religion. The French philosopher Pierre Manent, who delivered Imitatio's Girard Lecture in Paris in Fall 2016, called in his book *Beyond Radical Secularism*, which he wrote in reaction to the Charlie Hebdo shootings, for a new union between religion and politics, forfeiting the separation of church and state.[1] Pankaj Mishra, an Indian essayist and novelist familiar with Girard's work, claimed after these terrorist attacks in an essay in the British newspaper *The Guardian* that the world of today can no longer rely on the modernist opposition between secularism and religion. According to Mishra, we need a new enlightenment. Voltaire's disrespect for religion is no longer a viable option for the twenty-first century: "We may have to retrieve the Enlightenment, as much as religion, from its fundamentalists."[2] These criticisms of secularism find a parallel in insights by politicians like the former U.S. secretary of state Madeleine Albright, who emphasized that we need to study spiritual matters far more seriously, because "religion is perhaps the single largest influence in shaping the human conscience, and yet it is also a source of conflict and hate."[3] She claimed in her book *The Mighty and the Almighty* that the neglect of religion in the world of today impairs politics: "In the future, no American ambassador should be assigned to a country where religious feelings are strong, unless he or she has a deep understanding of the faiths commonly practiced there."[4]

It is, however, not enough to overcome radical secularism. We also need to come to terms with the fact that today we face a plurality of religions on the global and most often on the local level as well. Our globalized world shows a universal interdependence that characterizes our lives. In earlier times, many people lived just among their own, with seldom a chance to meet strangers coming from different cultural or political backgrounds. Today we are moving toward a global family on the one hand, while on the other we have cultural or religious "strangers" as our neighbors.[5] We desperately need an awareness of this cosmopolitan plurality that characterizes the world of today. Knowledge about other religions has become as important as interreligious dialogue.

This collection of essays explores the scope of René Girard's mimetic theory in view of a world that can no longer neglect the public role of religion as well as its plurality. Regarding secularism, Girard never gave in to its radical privatization of religion. Mimetic theory belongs definitely to the Enlightenment, for example in its attempt to disclose the founding murder that builds the foundation of the archaic sacred.[6] This, however, does not mean that Girard ever succumbed to the temptations of a radical secularism.[7] It is mostly due to his reading of great European novelists like Gustave Flaubert, Marcel Proust, and Fyodor Dostoyevsky that he distanced himself from the modern secularization thesis that predicted the disappearance of religion from the modern world. According to Girard, human beings are essentially religious beings. He recalled Max Scheler's words in the motto for his first book: "Man believes either in a God or in an idol. There is no third course open!"[8] Girard maintained that position throughout his unfolding of mimetic theory. Against Marcel Gauchet's thesis that Christianity will lead to the "exit of religion," he claimed that "our celebrated humanism will turn out to have been nothing but a brief intermission between two forms of religion."[9] In his discussion with Gianni Vattimo he also insisted that "religion forms part of human nature."[10]

Girard has convincingly distanced himself from secularism. His take on the plurality of religions, however, is less clear and more problematic. There is a tendency in some of Girard's writings that seems to suggest that only Christianity overcame the archaic sacred stemming from the foundational murder. An example in this direction is the interview with Nathan Gardels from 2005 in which Girard emphasized the singularity and superiority of Christianity among all other religions: "All of my work has been an effort to show that Christianity is superior and not just another mythology. . . . This revelation of collective violence as a lie is the earmark of Christianity. This is what is unique about Christianity. And this uniqueness is true."[11] While this position does rightly reject the danger of relativism, it remains too narrow, because it limits rashly the universal potential of mimetic theory. In response to Girard's interview, the Indian essayist Pankaj Mishra expressed his admiration of Girard's insight into the nonviolent message of the Gospels, which he recognized as a significant source of inspiration for Mahatma Gandhi's political-spiritual vision and method. With this reference to Gandhi, however, Mishra also criticized Girard's emphasis on the superiority of Christianity: "I wonder if it is not more relevant to try to find traditions—in Buddhism, Hinduism, Islam—which chime with the truth of the Gospels."[12] Similarly, some younger Girardians have also claimed that mimetic theory should be taken into interreligious dialogue.[13]

Girard's emphasis on the uniqueness of Christianity, however, should not lead us to identify this claim with mimetic theory's take on other world religions in general. From the very beginning of his work, Girard repeatedly showed an openness toward other religions. We can discover such an opening already in the mystic core at the end of his first book.[14] In it he claims that the great novelists were only able to write their masterpieces insofar as they were able to overcome their own egoism and pride. Recalling an expression of the French mystic and philosopher Simone Weil that articulated a kenotic understanding of God, Girard named this personal transformation of the great novelists "creative renunciation."[15] The death of the prideful ego led to the birth of the novelistic masterpieces. Girard distinguished therefore two radically different types of death: "one death which is an extinction of the spirit and one death which is spirit."[16] The second type of death consists in a spiritual transformation and a rebirth. By going in this direction, Girard—like Weil—opens up to mysticism in general and to other religious traditions connected to it. After his description of genuine conversion as the death of pride, he refers to a traditional Asian tale: "The conclusions of all the novels are reminiscent of an oriental tale in which the hero is clinging by his fingertips to the edge of a cliff; exhausted, the hero finally lets himself fall into the abyss. He expects to smash against the rocks below, but instead he is supported by the air: the law of gravity is annulled."[17] Leo Lefebure, a theologian familiar with Girard's mimetic theory as well as with Asian religions, refers to this passage to show how this type of renunciation or letting go comes close to practices of Buddhist meditation.[18] Creative renunciation as discussed by Weil and Girard is also part of the Muslim tradition. We need only refer to Sufism and its emphasis on a purported Hadith, "Die before you die!," that also aims at the overcoming of a limited and self-centered ego in order to receive a true self from God.[19]

Although Girard used a concept of Simone Weil in the concluding chapter of his first book, he did not mention the philosopher. One of the reasons for this peculiar omission is surely her sharp criticism of the Old Testament that Girard saw as a severe weakness and that he attributed mainly to her teachers who were "hellenizing humanists," like the French philosopher Alain.[20] Despite his strong identification with Christianity, Girard emphasized a continuity between the Hebrew Bible and the New Testament. He saw Judaism as an integral part of the Judeo-Christian revelation that disclosed the foundational murder. In an interview with James G. Williams, Girard sides in this regard with Friedrich Nietzsche, who "was the first thinker to see clearly that the singularity of Judeo-Christianity was that it rehabilitates victims that myths would regard as justly immolated."[21] According to Girard, there is a "uniqueness of the Bible."[22] It is not by chance that Sandor Goodhart, one of the first doctoral students of Girard, could easily connect his own Judaism with mimetic theory.[23]

Simone Weil's mysticism enabled her to reach out to the Eastern religions, building an important bridge between the West and the East.

Although Girard did not follow her directly in this outreach to the East, he also looked for openings in this direction. In 1979 when he was working on his book *The Scapegoat*, he wrote to the Swiss Jesuit and theologian Raymund Schwager that he now wanted to include Eastern religions as well in his mimetic theory. He mentioned particularly the Brahmanas, the "great Hindu reflection on sacrifice . . . which is exceptional, but which never takes the prophetic direction toward the revelation of the scapegoat. It has everything except the truth."[24] In his response from August 19, 1979, Raymund Schwager explicitly encouraged Girard to reach out toward Hinduism.[25] It took, however, more than twenty years until in 2002 Girard gave a lecture at the Bibliothèque nationale de France in Paris on the topic of sacrifice in the ancient Indian Vedas and different forms of transformation developing out of this sacrificial culture. This lecture was published in 2003 under the title *Le sacrifice*, later also translated into English.[26] Compared to his letter from 1979 Girard's view of the Eastern religions had become milder, as he now recognized certain parallels between the biblical exodus from the archaic sacred and similar developments within Buddhism and the Vedānta. It was also in 2002 that Girard relativized his position on the absolute superiority of the Bible in an interview with Sandor Goodhart by referring to Eastern religions: "I don't want to privilege the Bible absolutely."[27] In this and another interview, he added the Upanishads and Jainism as further examples for moving out of the archaic sacred.[28]

The most difficult question that Girard's mimetic theory has to address, however, is its relationship with Islam. After the terrorist attacks of 9/11 this question also became an urgent question for Girard himself. In an interview with the French newspaper *Le Monde* some two months after 9/11, Girard did not blame Islam as an essentially violent religion, but he emphasized global mimetic rivalry as the main cause of terrorism.[29] He soon started to focus more directly on Islam and tried to read the Qur'an.[30] For the octogenarian, however, it was too difficult to enter this new field of scholarly inquiry. As he himself admitted, he was no longer able to struggle with the different translations and interpretations that would be needed to interpret Islam properly from the perspective of mimetic theory. Repeatedly he told his interview partners who asked him about jihadism that he was not an expert in this field and was not able to contribute much. He nevertheless started to express more and more concerns about issues that he missed in Islam or that he found problematic. Drawing on a book by Jacques Ellul, Girard remarked critically that for Islam "God is essentially power," whereas the Christian God is "non-power."[31] Moving in a similar direction was his accusation that Islam "makes violence totally divine."[32] He missed especially the Passion of Christ in the Qur'an and complained that "Islam excludes the possibility that God could accept to suffer."[33] This corresponds to Girard's insistence that only the cross on which Jesus died was able to finally overcome the scapegoat mechanism of the archaic past: "In Islam, the most important thing is missing: a Cross. As in Christianity, Islam rehabilitates the innocent victim, but it does so in a militant way. The Cross, on the contrary, puts an end to the ancient and violent myths. The Cross is the symbol of the inversion of violence, of the resistance to lynching."[34] All these remarks did not claim to stem from a deep and systematic engagement with Islam but were rather offhand remarks offered to discussion partners who asked what Girard as an expert on violence and religion would have to say about jihadist terrorism. Some of these responses were summarized in the epilogue to Girard's last book, *Battling to the End*. There he claimed that Islam is a religion that "has used the Bible as a support to rebuild an archaic religion that is more powerful than all the others."[35] This recondite thesis remains quite isolated in this book and stands in tension to his claim that there are "no longer any archaic religions" in today's modern world.[36] Despite all of his criticism of Islam, Girard is at the same time very much aware of the danger of being mimetically drawn into a Western opposition against Islam without coming to a genuine understanding of it. According to Girard, we need to avoid explanations that "often belong to the province of fraudulent propaganda against Muslims."[37]

A last important issue has to be addressed in this systematic overview of how Girard's mimetic theory relates to other religions. It is the relationship between the biblical religions and the archaic sacred. A superficial reading of Girard's work could assume that these two types of religions are completely opposed to each other. Such a radical contraposition is dangerous and characterizes especially contemporary fundamentalist positions, be they secular or religious. The Canadian philosopher Charles Taylor clearly understood the threat that such a break with the archaic past entails. According to Taylor, the "recreation of scapegoating violence both in Christendom . . . and in the modern secular world" results from attempts of reform that try to break entirely with the past: "It is precisely these claims fully to supercede the problematic past which blinds us to the ways in which we are repeating some of its horrors in our own way."[38] Girard was aware of this problem and emphasized very early on in his unfolding of mimetic theory that these "religions of violence" were "always in search of peace."[39] In his last book on Carl von Clausewitz, Girard turned for this reason to the work of Friedrich Hölderlin to demonstrate that there is not only a "fundamental discontinuity" but also a "continuity between the Passion and archaic religion."[40] Whereas the earlier Girard often emphasized the fundamental difference between Dionysus and the Crucified in reversing Nietzsche, the mature Girard complements this important insight with Hölderlin's emphasis on the connection between Dionysus and Christ—"you are the brother also of Evius"—without hiding the truth that "Dionysus is violence and Christ is peace."[41]

With Hölderlin Girard touched again the mystical side of his own thought, because the German poet sides in his later Christian hymns with Christ's kenosis in ways similar to Simone Weil, who had influenced Girard's first book.[42] Mysticism enables different religions to come closer to one another without needing to end in mimetic rivalries. Georges Anawati, an Egyptian Dominican and Islam expert who helped the Catholic Church to find an opening toward Islam at the Second Vatican Council, understood the importance of mysticism in this regard.[43] With Hölderlin—who recently has been called the "Sufi of German literature"[44]—Girard's mimetic theory may find a new approach toward Islam. In the future, this will be one of mimetic theory's main tasks.

The present book results from a conference on "René Girard and World Religions" that was convened by the Dominican theologian and philosopher Richard Schenk and the Austrian theologian Wolfgang Palaver at the Graduate Theological Union at Berkeley (California) in spring 2011. Berkeley was an ideal location for this meeting, because this city is known for its cultural and religious diversity and for its ongoing scholarly engagement with it. The Graduate Theological Union is a consortium of schools and centers dedicated to the study and interrelation of the various Christian traditions and significant non-Christian religions. We brought together experts on mimetic theory and experts on different world religions who were willing to engage Girard's insights. All participants received for their consideration an advance copy of Girard's book *Sacrifice* that was just being published in English.

This book presents the papers of the conference systematically. Its first part comprises those essays that discuss mimetic theory and its approach toward religion more generally. In his essay "Neither Dawkins nor Durkheim," Jean-Pierre Dupuy situates Girard's theory of religion by discussing his relation on the one hand to the anthropological tradition represented by Durkheim and on the other to representatives of the currently favored cognitivist approach found among scientists like Dawkins. Against the cognitivist turn, Dupuy emphasizes that Girard, like Durkheim, underlined the importance of rituals to understand archaic religion as a morphogenetic force that created all human institutions. Girard also differs, however, from Durkheim, who did not understand the morphogenetic power of religion and who focused in his understanding of Christianity too strongly on its morality. According to Dupuy, reducing Christianity to morality overlooks its place in history as an epistemology that disclosed the violence of the archaic sacred and thereby deprived it of its creative power.

Anselm Tilman Ramelow discusses Girard's understanding of sacrifice in light of Hegel, who via Kojève was one of the philosophers who had a significant impact on the unfolding of mimetic theory. This close reading of Hegel is enriched by comparing his view of sacrifice with Kierkegaard, Schiller, and Bataille. Ramelow attributes to Hegel the understanding of sacrifice as an anthropological constant, whereas Girard seems to be too critical of transient, archaic sacrifice. According to Ramelow, both Hegel and Girard regard the cross only as a cognitive event. This observation leads him to question the absence in Girard's theory of important theological matters like redemption, prayer, sacraments, or the church, which could lead to a more constructive approach. Ramelow, however, admits at the same time that these theological issues may necessarily be outside the scope of Girard's anthropology.

John Ranieri discusses the relationship between reason and revelation by comparing Girard's mimetic theory with the political philosopher Voegelin. Whereas Girard discovers in the biblical revelation a corrective of reason insofar as it sees it as an offspring of the foundational murder, Voegelin dismisses a distinction between reason and revelation. The political philosopher did not recognize practices of victimization as sustaining the political order. Despite the fact that Voegelin dealt intensively with different cultures and religions, it is his very dissolution of the distinction between reason and revelation, according to Ranieri, that prevents his intentionally philosophical method from providing a common language across different religious traditions.

Benoît Chantre compares Girard with the French philosopher Bergson and his important distinction between a closed religion and an open one. Chantre claims that Girard's view of archaic religions treats them as a prefiguration of Judeo-Christianity. Chantre criticizes Bergson's misrecognition of sacrificial institutions, especially the scapegoat mechanism. A better understanding of the scapegoat mechanism would have made possible a better comprehension of the Christian transformation of sacrifice on the cross and led to an open religion. Chantre ends his contribution by referring to Girard's siding with Hölderlin, who regarded the essence of the divine as consisting in the withdrawal from the world. This withdrawal is connected to a new type of imitation that was already recognized by Bergson but for which Girard forty years later provided a solid theoretical explanation.

Otto Kallscheuer discusses Girard's take on religion in an age of secularism. Comparing Girard's approach with different secularization narratives, Kallscheuer finds missing a coherent vision of secularization in the work of the anthropologist. Girard seems to be undecided if his theory is a secular scientific hypothesis or an eschatological prophecy. Kallscheuer is especially irritated by Girard's apocalyptic book, *Battling to the End*. He recognizes a certain affinity to great reactionary writers like de Maistre, Bonald, and Donoso-Cortés regarding their cultural sensibilities, even without siding politically with them. According to Kallscheuer, one may finally dare to ask if Girard identifies secularization with apocalypse.

Jeremiah Alberg uses Girard's mimetic theory to explain why Rousseau cannot laugh. He follows Girard's interpretation of Clausewitz and tries a religious interpretation of the work of the French philosopher leading to a new rationality. According to Alberg, Rousseau is seeking a place of mastery at the place of the victim, an impossible task because the place of the victim is essentially the place of nonmastery. Ultimately, the difference between Rousseau and Girard depends on their views of original sin. Rousseau rejected it and founded his philosophy on the natural goodness of humans. Girard, on the contrary, follows Pascal and recognizes original sin as being fundamental without being foundational. By taking original sin seriously, Girard does not create an intellectual cage to imprison everyone but himself and therefore can welcome laughter about one's own failings.

In the final essay of this part of the book, Martha Reineke compares Girard with the feminist critique developed by Kristeva. Her thesis is that mimetic theory lacks sensory experience and could be enhanced if feminism's emphasis on such experience were taken seriously. Girard's last book, *Battling to the End*, with its apocalypticism and its quietism, following the pattern of Hölderlin's withdrawal, results, according to Reineke, from an anthropological dualism marginalizing bodily experiences. With Kristeva and the young Girard, Reineke returns to Proust and the spiritual life of Ignatius of Loyola, who were both very aware of the importance of bodily activity. Ignatius in particular avoids dualism and quietism and evidences an opening toward an anthropology that could enrich mimetic theory.

The second part of this book comprises those essays that take the privilege that mimetic theory grants Christianity as a starting point investigating, nevertheless, its scope in regard to interreligious dialogue. The conference in Berkeley was not the first gathering that discussed the relationship of Girard's mimetic theory to other world religions.[45] In the year 2000, Robert J. Daly had organized a conference at Boston College that focused on "Violence and Institution in Christianity, Judaism, Hinduism, Buddhism, and Islam." His contribution to this volume summarizes the results of this meeting and ends with a list of important issues that require further reflection. In his contribution to the present volume, Michael Kirwan provides a review of the several conferences of the Colloquium on Violence & Religion that have reflected on different world religions and related questions. He starts with the conference at Boston College and adds Purdue University (2002: Judaism/Christianity), Amsterdam (2007), Riverside (2008), and London (2009), where vulnerability, tolerance, Islam, and jihadism were discussed. Kirwan relates these discussions to the opening of the Catholic Church toward other religions during the Second Vatican Council and compares them with still other approaches, such as comparative theology.

One of the aims of the Berkeley conference was to position Girard's relation to the world religions in the broader context of the Western philosophical and theological tradition. Richard Schenk refers to the Dominican theologian Kilwardby, who contrary to many of the theologians before him was able to recognize graceful workings of rites in all ages, including the rites of pre-Abrahamic religions. Kilwardby minimalizes the differences between the religions. Schenk, however, shows by drawing on the work of Waldenfels that it is also the recognition of the abiding strangeness and limitation within one's own religion that helps to overcome mimetic rivalries between different religions. The capacity for self-critique is therefore an important criterion to evaluate religions and a measure of their adequacy. According to Schenk, it is Girard's more nuanced later understanding of sacrifices, recognizing both continuity and discontinuity with the archaic past, that allowed him to develop a greater appreciation of non-Christian religions.

Nikolaus Wandinger addresses the concept of sacrifice by referring to its seminal discussion in the exchange of letters between Girard and Schwager and by asking about its significance for interreligious dialogue in light of Lonergan's work. It was a process of conversion within the Judeo-Christian tradition that led both, Girard and Schwager, to a deeper understanding of the transformation of the concept of sacrifice in Judaism and Christianity. It is in particular Lonergan's understanding of religious conversion that Wandinger brings to the discussion of interreligious dialogue. He emphasizes that a religious conversion can be fostered by interreligious dialogue, which leads more to a conversion within one's own tradition than it aims at changing the religious affiliation of the dialogue partners.

Wolfgang Palaver calls the overcoming of the human sacrifices that characterizes the three Abrahamic religions an "Abrahamic Revolution." He illustrates this exodus from archaic religions with the help of Girard's interpretation of the story of the Binding of Isaac and of the story of Joseph in Genesis and adds to it a mimetic reading of the Qur'anic versions of these stories. A final part of this contribution shows how the Abrahamic religions can avoid the temptation of a cult of the victim by becoming aware of our common human weakness.

Ann Astell explores the "Hellenic" rationality of interreligious dialogue by relating Girard's work to Simone Weil and Pope Benedict XVI. The Regensburg lecture of Pope Benedict with its critique of dehellenization helped Girard to emphasize that faith and reason need to support each other. This is also true for Weil who likewise underscored the closeness of Greek philosophy and the New Testament. For all three thinkers it is, however, crucial that philosophy is understood in the light of religion and not the reverse. Seen in this way, Judeo-Christian Hellenism means a broadly defined rationality that can bridge the gap between the sciences and religious faith and between the different world religions.

The third part of this book addresses more directly the relationship between mimetic theory and world religions. An important part of the conference dealt with Eastern religions, especially concerning Girard's little book *Sacrifice* and its implications for a discussion of sacrifice in the older Indian religions. Brian Collins's essay reflects on the role of fire and its understandings in Hindu and Buddhist traditions. He establishes significant intersections between mimetic theory and Indian religions. The functions of fire in Vedic religion, for instance, support Girard's understanding of the violent sacred as the root of human community.

Noel Sheth's contribution to this volume deals with the relationship between mimetic theory and Hindu sacrifice. He confirms at first Girard's interpretation of Vedic sacrifice, but he also criticizes Girard's thesis, pointing to examples in the Vedic tradition where the innocence of the victim is exposed in ways similar to key narratives in the Bible. In a supplementary part, Sheth also shows that Girard's thesis is not universally applicable to all Vedic sacrifices, most notably as regards selfless and altruistic sacrifices.

Jacob Dalton and Alexander von Rospatt bring Buddhism into conversation with Girard's mimetic theory. They do not so much apply mimetic theory to the study of Buddhism, but rather draw on Buddhism to situate and interpret mimetic theory. In a first part, they address the psychology of the individual and the central role of mimetic desire in constituting it. Secondly, their interpretation of the "liberation rite" of tantric Buddhism finds parallels in Girard's analysis of sacrifice. Thirdly, they also show how this ritual can be read as a critique of sacrificial violence, confirming that there is a renunciation of sacrifice outside the realm of Christianity.

Ted Peters looks into the relation between mimetic theory and world religions from the point of view of a Lutheran theology. By distinguishing between the rituals of sacrifice within religious traditions and scapegoating, Peters claims that Girard's theory illuminates the latter more than the former. According to Peters, the main value of mimetic theory is its insight into human nature in general. Through the revelation in Jesus Christ Girard provides an explication of sin within anthropology.

Sandor Goodhart explores the exodus from archaic religion in Judaism. He identifies Judaism with this exodus and names it the law of anti-idolatry. By Judaism, he especially means its prophetic tradition that emerged with the destruction of the Temple in Jerusalem and the Babylonian exile. Goodhart claims that Judaism is "Girardianism before the fact" and proves it by referring to Jesus as the mediator of Girard and to Isaiah as the mediator of Jesus: "Girard articulates what is at the core of Isaiah's reading of Judaism, which is at the core of Jesus's reading, which is thus at the core of Judaism itself."

Two essays address relations between Girard's mimetic theory and Islam. Adam Ericksen reflects on Islamic monotheism and the desire for the good. Against claims that Islam is a return to archaic religions Ericksen maintains that it is itself a critique of the violent sacred. Tawhid, the oneness of God in Islam, criticizes the ambivalent nature of archaic gods and means essentially God's grace and mercy. By orienting human desires toward God, Islam seeks to lead the people from the hell of accusations toward God's mercy. Ericksen finally introduces three Muslim scholars who have advocated nonviolence: Maulana Wahiddudin Khan, Abdul Ghaffar Khan, and Jawdat Sa'id.

Rüdiger Lohlker discusses law and violence in Islam. Though not himself a Girardian, Lohlker agrees with Girard's claim that religious violence is first and foremost a human question. By distinguishing between traditional teachings on jihad and contemporary jihadism, he maintains that the latter is essentially a modern concept. The same is true for the interpretations of martyrdom by jihadist terrorists that stem from nationalism, because in traditional Islam death is not a witness for the truth of God. In Islam sacrifice is demythologized, recommending piety instead. A final section addresses ways out of violence and refers like Ericksen to Jawdat Sa'id and his reading of the Qur'anic Cain and Abel story, which underlines the willingness to break with mimetic contagion.

As a coda to the whole book we present James Alison's essay that nicely concludes all these reflections on how Girard's anthropology relates to different religions. As a Christian theologian committed for many years to mimetic theory, he reflected on Girard's understanding of how desire and idolatry are interrelated. With his careful reading of two passages in the New Testament (Matthew 6:43–45, and Galatians 2:19–20), Alison shows how hostility can be overcome with the help of God's grace. By referring to St. Paul, he explains that it was Christ's belief in Paul that enabled the apostle to break out of his own enmity against God and all those followers of Christ that he persecuted. Through Christ Paul was healed from within. The kenotic understanding of grace found here comes close to the mysticism that we can discover in Girard's work.

The editors are grateful to all the presenters who shared with us their readings of mimetic theory, to the Graduate Theological Union at Berkeley for hosting our conference, and to Imitatio for the financial support that allowed us to bring together all these scholars. We would also like to thank Bill Johnsen and the MSU Press for publishing this volume in their series "Studies in Violence, Mimesis, and Culture."

NOTES

1. Pierre Manent, *Beyond Radical Secularism: How France and the Christian West Should Respond to the Islamic Challenge*, trans. Ralph C. Hancock (South Bend, IN.: St. Augustine's Press, 2016).
2. Pankaj Mishra, "After the Paris Attacks: It's Time for a New Enlightenment," *The Guardian*, January 20, 2015.
3. Madeleine Albright, *The Mighty and the Almighty: Reflections on America, God, and World Affairs* (New York: HarperCollins, 2006), 95.
4. Ibid., 75.
5. Zygmunt Bauman, *Strangers at Our Door* (Malden, MA: Polity, 2016).
6. René Girard, *Violence and the Sacred*, trans. Patrick Gregory (Baltimore: Johns Hopkins University Press, 1977).
7. Wolfgang Palaver, *René Girard's Mimetic Theory*, trans. Gabriel Borrud (East Lansing: Michigan State University Press, 2013), 15–32.
8. René Girard, *Mensonge romantique et vérité romanesque* (Paris: Grasset, 1961); Max Scheler, *On the Eternal in Man*, trans. Bernard Noble (New York: Harper, 1961), 399.
9. René Girard and Michel Treguer, *When These Things Begin: Conversations with Michel Treguer*, trans. Trevor Cribben Merrill (East Lansing: Michigan State University Press, 2014), 120–21; Marcel Gauchet, *The Disenchantment of the World: A Political History of Religion*, trans. Oscar Burge (Princeton, NJ: Princeton University Press, 1999).
10. Gianni Vattimo and René Girard, *Christianity, Truth, and Weakening Faith: A Dialogue*, trans. William McCuaig (New York: Columbia University Press, 2010), 31.
11. René Girard, "Ratzinger Is Right: Interview with Nathan Gardels," *New Perspectives Quarterly* 22, no. 3 (2005): 46.
12. Pankaj Mishra, "What Would the Buddha Think?," *New Perspectives Quarterly* 22, no. 3 (2005): 53.
13. Frederiek Depoortere, *Christ in Postmodern Philosophy: Gianni Vattimo, René Girard and Slavoj Žižek* (London: T & T Clark, 2008), 147; Jacob Nordhofen, *Durch das Opfer erlöst? Die Bedeutung der Rede vom Opfer Jesu Christi in der Bibel und bei René Girard* (Vienna: LIT, 2008), 243–48.
14. Wolfgang Palaver, "Creative Renunciation: The Spiritual Heart of *Deceit, Desire, and the Novel*," in *Mimesis, Desire, and the Novel: René Girard and Literary Criticism*, ed. Pierpaolo Antonello and Heather Webb (East Lansing: Michigan State University Press, 2015).

15. René Girard, *Deceit, Desire, and the Novel: Self and Other in Literary Structure*, trans. Yvonne Freccero (Baltimore: Johns Hopkins University Press, 1965), 307; Simone Weil, *Waiting for God*, trans. Emma Craufurd (New York: Perennial, 2001), 99.

16. Girard, *Deceit, Desire, and the Novel*, 291.

17. Ibid., 294.

18. Leo D. Lefebure, "Mimesis, Violence, and Socially Engaged Buddhism: Overture to a Dialogue," *Contagion* 3 (1996): 136.

19. William C. Chittick, *Sufism: A Beginner's Guide* (Oxford: Oneworld Publications, 2008), 43–45, 108–9, 79–80; Toshihiko Izutsu, *Sufism and Taoism: A Comparative Study of Key Philosophical Concepts* (Berkeley: University of California Press, 1984); Rob Baker and Gray Henry, eds., *Merton & Sufism: The Untold Story. A Complete Compendium* (Louisville, KY: Fons Vitae, 2005).

20. René Girard, *Things Hidden since the Foundation of the World*, research undertaken in collaboration with with J.-M. Oughourlian and G. Lefort, trans. Stephen Bann and Michael Metteer (Stanford, CA: Stanford University Press, 1987), 245; Girard, *Evolution and Conversion: Dialogues on the Origin of Culture with Pierpaolo Antonello and João Cezar de Castro Rocha* (London: Continuum, 2008), 150–51; Girard, "Simone Weil (Entretien)," in *Simone Weil*, ed. Emmanuel Gabellieri and François L'Yvonnet (Paris: Éditions de l'Herne, 2014), 27–34; Phil Rose, "A Conversation with René Girard (August 2006/May 2007)," *Contagion* 18 (2011): 26–27.

21. René Girard, *The Girard Reader*, ed. James G. Williams (New York: Crossroad, 1996), 272.

22. René Girard, *I See Satan Fall Like Lightning*, trans. James G. Williams (Maryknoll, NY: Orbis, 2001), 103–20.

23. Sandor Goodhart, "Literature, Myth, and Prophecy: Encountering René Girard," in *For René Girard: Essays in Friendship and in Truth*, ed. Sandor Goodhart et al. (East Lansing: Michigan State University Press, 2009); Goodhart, *The Prophetic Law: Essays in Judaism, Girardianism, Literary Studies, and the Ethical* (East Lansing: Michigan State University Press, 2014).

24. René Girard and Raymund Schwager, *René Girard and Raymund Schwager: Correspondence 1974–1991*, trans. Chris Fleming and Sheelah Treflé Hidden (New York: Bloomsbury Academic, 2016), 76–77 (letter from August 1, 1979).

25. Ibid., 79.

26. René Girard, *Sacrifice*, trans. Matthew Pattillo and David Dawson (East Lansing: Michigan State University Press, 2011).

27. René Girard, "Mimesis, Sacrifice, and the Bible: A Conversation with Sandor Goodhart," in *Sacrifice, Scripture, and Substitution: Readings in Ancient Judaism and Christianity*, ed. Ann W. Astell and Sandor Goodhart (Notre Dame, IN: University of Notre Dame Press, 2011), 64.

28. Girard, *Evolution and Conversion*, 212–13.

29. René Girard and Henri Tincq, "Ce qui se joue aujourd'hui est une rivalité mimétique à l'échelle planétaire," *Le Monde*, November 6, 2001; Girard, Henri Tincq, and Thomas C. Hilde, "What Is Happening Today Is Mimetic Rivalry on a Global Scale," *South Central Review* 19, nos. 2–3 (2002): 22–27.

30. René Girard, Laurent Linneuil, and Guillaume de Tanoüarn, "Entretien avec René Girard," *La nouvelle revue Certitudes*, no. 16 (2003 [2004]): 42.

31. René Girard and David W. Gill, "A Conversation with René Girard," *The Ellul Forum*, no. 35 (2005): 20; Jacques Ellul, *What I Believe*, trans. Geoffrey William Bromiley (Grand Rapids, MI: W. B. Eerdmans, 1989), 179.

32. Robert Doran, "Apocalyptic Thinking after 9/11: An Interview with René Girard," *SubStance* 37, no. 1 (2008): 28.

33. René Girard and Wolfgang Palaver, "The Bloody Skin of the Victim," in *The New Visibility of Religion: Studies in Religion and Cultural Hermeneutics*, ed. Michael Hoelzl and Graham Ward (London: Continuum, 2008), 65.

34. René Girard and Giulio Meotti, "René Girard's Accusation: Intellectuals are the Castrators of Meaning," *Modern Age* 50, no. 2 (2008): 184.

35. René Girard, *Battling to the End: Conversations with Benoît Chantre*, trans. Mary Baker (East Lansing: Michigan State University Press, 2010), 214.

36. Ibid., 212, 14.

37. Ibid., 215.

38. Charles Taylor, *A Secular Age* (Cambridge, MA: Belknap Press, 2007), 772.

39. Girard, *Things Hidden since the Foundation of the World*, 401.

40. Girard, *Battling to the End*, xv.

41. Ibid., 127, 30.

42. Wolfgang Palaver, "Girard und Hölderlin: Die Bedeutung der *kenosis* für Girards apokalyptisches Denken," in *Eskalation zum Äußersten? Girards Clausewitz interdisziplinär kommentiert*, ed. Wilhelm Guggenberger and Wolfgang Palaver (Baden-Baden: Nomos, 2015), 135–55.

43. Georges C. Anawati, *Ich liebe die Muslime, weil sie Gott lieben: Aufforderungen zum Dialog*, trans. Hoda Issa (Freiburg im Breisgau: Herder, 2014), 50.

44. Navid Kermani, *Über den Zufall: Jean Paul, Hölderlin und der Roman, den ich schreibe*. Frankfurter Poetikvorlesungen (Munich: Hanser, 2012), 50.

45. James G. Williams, *Girardians: The Colloquium on Violence and Religion, 1990–2010* (Vienna: LIT, 2012), 125–28, 85–90, 214–23.

PART 1

Mimetic Theory and Religion

Neither Dawkins nor Durkheim: On René Girard's Theory of Religion

Jean-Pierre Dupuy

From Religious to Cognitive Anthropology

The Religious Anthropological Tradition

The greatest disservice that could be done to Girard would be to claim that he invented his theory from scratch. Girard belongs to the great Franco-German-British tradition of religious anthropology that was brought to a premature halt in 1939 by decades of structuralism and poststructuralism: in particular, the French sociological school, with the works of Numa Denis Fustel de Coulanges, Émile Durkheim, and Marcel Mauss; the British anthropological school, with James Frazer, William Robertson-Smith, and the Belgo-British anthropologist Arthur Hocart; not to forget Friedrich Nietzsche and Sigmund Freud who gave these traditions a new momentum.

If Girard's theory is right, Girard himself invented nothing: those "things hidden since the foundation of the world" have become an open secret. The fact that they have is itself a remarkable feature that needs to be accounted for.

Before passing away, religious anthropology had reached the following basic conclusions (most of them were later reversed, or just forgotten, by the subsequent paradigms):

1. All human institutions (e.g., family, power, money, war, the judicial system, the state) stem from religion.
2. Among the three dimensions of all religious systems—Rituals (Practice), Myths (Beliefs), Prohibitions and Obligations (Morals)—the most fundamental, since the most originary, is the ritual.
3. All rituals stem from sacrificial rituals.

Those findings were far-reaching, but the general picture was tainted with a series of serious contradictions. For instance, authors like Robertson-Smith would liken the sacrificial ritual to an offering, a kind of exchange between the god and the offerer, as if some kind of reciprocity could exist between the divine and the human levels. The objection was obvious: it is easy to understand why human beings would owe everything to God, but why would God expect anything from the humans? Then came Durkheim, who solved the enigma elegantly. Durkheim believed that religion is the collective in symbolic form. Divinity is society transformed and conceived symbolically. Society commences with the birth of religion, more precisely with the totem as a symbolic, religious representation of the community. As Durkheim puts it rhetorically, if the totem is at once the symbol of the god and of the society, "is that not because the god and the society are only one?" Religion, then, according to Durkheim, is a set of beliefs and practices by which society represents itself to itself. God and society are one—or rather, God is a figurative expression of society. If we feel dependent on God, that is but a symbolic representation of our dependency on society. We depend on society, but at the same time society depends on us, the individuals. If society were not embodied in the individuals and their mental representations, it would amount to nothing. Here we find a reciprocity of sorts between two hierarchical levels: the encompassing and the encompassed.

Durkheim's account had its own shortcomings, and British anthropologist E. E. Evans-Pritchard cruelly brought them out. Durkheim's reputation as an anthropologist suffered a lot as a consequence. This is indeed quite a crucial point in the intellectual history of French social thought. For Durkheim (as for Louis Dumont and all holistic thinkers), the social whole is transcendent in relation to its individual constituents. The problem is that Durkheim accounted for this transcendence in two opposite ways. First, by the fact that we are the products of our cultures, institutions, languages, symbols, etc.: they make us, we don't make them. Second, by the fact that in a group "in effervescence"—during a ritual or a festivity like carnival, for instance—the individual disappears and fuses with the crowd. Religion emerges from the cauldron of collective effervescence, a sort of social electricity generated by the collectivity. First the transcendence of the collective level is brought about by social order, then by social disorder and chaos.

As we know too well here, Girard was able to unravel this paradox. The paradox, as he put it, is that a process of social totalization appears at times infinitely close to a process of social decomposition—as if social order *contained* social disorder, in the two senses of the word "contain."

The Cognitivist Turn

After the Second World War, the structuralist break operated by Claude Lévi-Strauss, Girard's major mimetic rival after Freud, paved the way for the cognitivist takeover. Consequently, there was a return to a former conception of religion as a system of ideas, beliefs, and concepts. Durkheim had already shown that this conception was completely erroneous but, as I said, by that time he was already banned from the anthropological community.

If you are a cognitivist like Richard Dawkins who construes cognition in an evolutionary framework, the challenge for you is to understand how human beings can believe unbelievable things, such as the existence of a mountain that is alive and feeds on animals that are sacrificed to it. Two questions arise. First, how can such ideas, held by you to be absurd, actually be conceived and maintained in a person's mind? Second, how can they then spread, like an epidemic, passing from the mind of one person to another?

What you then forget is that religion is first and foremost an *activity* that is practiced *collectively*, in the company of others, and that it is in this active, social context that religious ideas are formed simultaneously in the mind of each person. Dawkins sees ritual as the product of myth, and as something still more enigmatically ridiculous than myth itself. "Why do humans fast, kneel, genuflect, self-flagellate, nod maniacally towards a wall, crusade, or otherwise indulge in costly practices that can consume life and, in extreme cases, terminate it?"[1] he asks, apparently sincerely—and pathetically, in view of his confessed incomprehension. For the theory of evolution, which serves as the theoretical basis for cognitive psychology and anthropology, explaining ritual presents an even more formidable challenge than accounting for the origin of religious ideas. Indeed, Darwinian selection acts in the same way as Occam's razor: hating wastefulness, it eliminates the superfluous and, like a utilitarian judge, ruthlessly punishes everything that strays from the optimum. How could the grotesque extravagance of religious practices have been allowed to pass through its selective filter? That cognitivists should find no satisfactory response to a question that arises only because they have approached the problem the wrong way around comes as no surprise. Their failure is a consequence of this very mistake.

In *The Elementary Forms of Religious Life* (1912), Durkheim identified the same misapprehension:

> Most often, the theorists who have endeavoured to express religion in rational terms have seen it, above all, as a system of ideas that correspond to a definite object. This object has been conceived in different ways: nature, the infinite, the unknowable, the ideal, and so on. But these differences are unimportant. In all cases, it was ideas and beliefs that were considered the essential element of religion. As for rites, they seem from this point of view to be merely an external, contingent, and material expression of these inner states that were singled out as having intrinsic value. This conception is so widespread that, for the most part, debates about religion revolve around the question of knowing whether it can be reconciled with science or not, that is, if there is a place next to scientific knowledge for another form of thought that would be specifically religious.[2]

Durkheim's explanation of religion and of the preponderant place that ritual plays in it is well known: the reality to which mythologies and religious experience refer, without knowing it, is society. Now,

> Society can make its influence felt only if it is in action, and it is in action only if the individuals who compose it are assembled and act in common. It is through common action that it becomes conscious of itself and affirms itself; it is above all an active cooperation. . . . Therefore, action dominates religious life for the very reason that society is its source.[3]

This explanation is not itself without serious problems, to which I am going to return. But one cannot help but be impressed by the force of conviction one finds in a passage such as this one:

> A philosophy can indeed be elaborated in the silence of inner meditation, but not a faith. For faith is above all warmth, life, enthusiasm, the exaltation of all mental activity, the transport of the individual beyond himself. Now, without leaving the self, how could one add to the energies he has? How could he surpass himself with his forces alone? The only source of heat where we might warm ourselves morally is that formed by the society of our peers; the only moral forces with which we might sustain and increase our own are those [lent to us by] others. . . . Beliefs work only when they are shared. One can certainly maintain them for a time through wholly personal effort; but they are neither born nor acquired in this way. It is even doubtful that they can be preserved under these conditions. In fact, the man who has real faith has an irrepressible need to spread it; to do this, he leaves his isolation, approaches others, and *seeks to convince them, and it is the ardour of their convictions that sustains his own. His faith would quickly [wilt] if it remained alone.*[4]

In the light of this remarkable passage, in which one recognizes the fundamental mimetic pattern that Girard called *double mediation*, it becomes clear that the laboratory experiments conducted by cognitivist researchers to make religious beliefs grow in the mind of an isolated individual have as much chance of succeeding as the attempt to make roses grow on Mars.

The Ethical Fallacy

In July 1898, at the height of the controversy surrounding the Dreyfus affair, Durkheim published an article that is no less fresh and pertinent today than it was then. Titled "Individualism and the Intellectuals," it was a rejoinder to charges made by the anti-Dreyfusard Ferdinand Brunetière, who, in an article published several months earlier under the title "After the Trial: Replies to a Few Intellectuals," had castigated individualism—the "disease" peculiar to those who were not yet called social scientists, and that led them, in the name of the scientific spirit and respect for truth, to challenge the verdict brought by the authorities competent to rule in the matter, thus imperiling the survival of the nation.

The interesting question is how Durkheim—one of the first Dreyfusards, and an active member of the League for the Defense of the Rights of Man and of the Citizen—managed to defend the intellectuals against the charge of individualism. He did this by showing that *individualism was a religion*, the sole guarantor of the social order and, what is more, a religion issued from Christianity.

Durkheim contrasted two types of individualism. The one that served as a target for the attacks of the anti-Dreyfusards, as though it were the only imaginable kind of individualism, is "the narrow utilitarianism and utilitarian egoism of Spencer and the economists."[5] This individualism, which rests on the unleashing of selfish interests, is in fact incompatible with the common good. "However, there exists another individualism over which it is less easy to triumph. It has been upheld for a century by the great majority of thinkers: it is the individualism of Kant and Rousseau and the spiritualists, that which the Declaration of the Rights of Man sought, more or less successfully, to translate into formulae, which is now taught in our schools and which has become the basis of our moral catechism."[6] The ideal sought by this individualism, which Durkheim connects with the great tradition of eighteenth-century liberalism, "goes so far beyond the limit of utilitarian ends that it appears to those who aspire to it as having a religious character. The human person is considered as sacred, in what can be called the ritual sense of the word. It has something of that transcendental majesty that the churches of all times have accorded to their gods. Whoever makes an attempt on a man's life, on a man's liberty, on a man's honor, inspires us with a feeling of revulsion, in every way comparable to that which the believer experiences when he sees his idol profaned. Such a morality is not simply a hygienic discipline or a wise principle of economy. It is a religion of which man is, at the same time, both believer and god."[7]

The anti-Dreyfusards criticized the individualism of the intellectuals in the name of a conservative Christian morality. "But are those who take this position unaware," Durkheim objects, "that the originality of Christianity has consisted precisely in a remarkable development of the individual spirit?"[8] And if, he goes on to say, "that restricted individualism which constitutes

Christianity was necessary eighteen centuries ago, it seems probable that a more developed individualism should be indispensable today; for things have changed in the interval. It is thus a singular error to present individualist morality as antagonistic to Christian morality; quite the contrary, it is derived from it. By adhering to the former, we do not disown our past; we merely continue it."[9]

In his reply to Brunetière, Durkheim relies heavily on the idea that this religion of humanity, by which "man has become a god for man,"[10] is absolutely indispensable to social cohesion. Speaking of the Dreyfusards, he writes:

> If every attack on the rights of an individual revolts them, this is not solely because of sympathy for the victim. Nor is it because they fear that they themselves will suffer similar acts of injustice. Rather it is that such outrages cannot rest unpunished without putting national existence in jeopardy. . . . A religion which tolerates acts of sacrilege abdicates any sway over men's minds. The religion of the individual can therefore allow itself to be flouted without resistance, only on penalty of ruining its credit; since it is the sole link that binds us to one another, such a weakening cannot take place without the onset of social dissolution. Thus the individualist, who defends the rights of the individual, defends at the same time the vital interests of society.[11]

Here we reach the limits of Durkheim's theory of religion, for which "the idea of society is the soul of religion."[12] At the same time we find ourselves in a position to appreciate the magnitude of the error that Durkheim commits with regard to Christianity.

Durkheim's moral individualism defends mankind in general, mankind in abstracto. He is less troubled by the torments of actual individuals than by attacks on what he takes to be the universal and transcendent values of liberty, truth, justice, and reason. Durkheim himself had made this unmistakably clear when, at the beginning of his essay on individualism and intellectuals, published only a few months after Commandant Ferdinand Walsin Esterhazy's acquittal and Émile Zola's trial, while Alfred Dreyfus was rotting away on Devil's Island, he wrote, "Let us forget the Affair itself and the melancholy scenes we have witnessed." No doubt a great many Dreyfusards joined Durkheim in judging that the scapegoat, Captain Alfred Dreyfus, a graduate of the École Polytechnique, was unworthy of the noble cause they upheld.

Christianity, as I understand it, stands in complete opposition to this. Neither mankind in general nor some set of supreme values deserve to be divinized, on pain of idolatry. The person who suffers, the lost sheep of the flock, must be saved, even if it means endangering the ninety-nine others. This is the only thing that counts. Far from being the ultimate guarantor of the social order, Christianity acts as a lethal agent of disruption, a source of turmoil whose purpose and ultimate effect is to destroy all humanly constituted authority. If it is destined to triumph, this will be at the expense of everything that makes up our world today.

There is a great irony in this, for the cognitivists have arrived today, though by a quite different route, at the very same error committed by Durkheim. All of them devalue religion, to the advantage of morality, by denying the religious foundation of human societies. Religion for Durkheim has no morphogenetic power: it is an interpretation—a "collective representation"—of a unique and preexisting reality, namely, society; it does not create society. Instead, and particularly in the case of Christianity and the morality that flows from it, this interpretation serves to strengthen the social order. As for the cognitivists, in making morality the offspring of biology, they are condemned to see religion as a purely illusory illustration of moral intuitions. Ultimately the same impulse of denial is at work, the same blindness in the face of two disconcerting truths. The first truth is that it is not biology but rather the sacred that gives birth to human societies. The second is that Christianity is not a morality but rather an epistemology: it conveys the truth of the sacred and, by virtue of just this, deprives it of creative power—for better or for worse. Only human beings will decide.

NOTES

1. Richard Dawkins, *The God Delusion* (Boston: Houghton Mifflin Company, 2006), 166.
2. Emile Durkheim, *The Elementary Forms of Religious Life*, trans. Carol Cosman (Oxford: Oxford University Press, 2001), 311.
3. Ibid., 313.
4. Ibid., 320. Emphasis added.
5. Emile Durkheim, "Individualism and the Intellectuals," in *Durkheim on Politics and the State*, ed. Anthony Giddens (Stanford, CA: Stanford University Press, 1986), 79–83, 79.

6. Durkheim, "Individualism and the Intellectuals," 80.

7. Ibid., 81.

8. Steven Lukes, "Durkheim's 'Individualism and the Intellectuals,'" *Political Studies* 17, no. 1 (1969): 14–30, 26.

9. Ibid., 27.

10. Ibid., 26.

11. Ibid., 27.

12. Durkheim, *The Elementary Forms of Religious Life*, 314.

Sacrifice in Hegel and Girard

Anselm Tilman Ramelow

A comparison between G. W. F. Hegel and René Girard on the notion of sacrifice might seem far-fetched; at least it is not immediately clear how to identify the points of contact between both theories. And yet, in a recent text (*Battling to the End*) as well as in conversation, Girard recalls the great influence Hegel had had early on in his thought. Similar to many other French intellectuals in the 1930s, 1940s, and 1950s, Hegel's influence seems to have come to him by way of Alexandre Kojève. It is noteworthy that an important essay by Georges Bataille connected Kojève's thought very explicitly with the notion of sacrifice. We will have a look at this possible influence on Girard in the second part of this paper, before concluding with a comparison between Girard and Hegel. In a first part, however, we have to outline Hegel's thought on the subject of sacrifice.

Hegel on Sacrifice

There is very little study on the notion of sacrifice in Hegel. Most of it focuses on Hegel's use of sacrifice in the *Phenomenology of the Spirit*.[1] This is indeed a work of fundamental importance, especially in the light of its later use by

Kojève. So I will begin with the *Phenomenology* as well; I will then, however, turn to his more neglected *Lectures on the Philosophy of Religion*.[2] In both works, sacrifice as a cultic and ritual event is not prominent; yet in the form of death and negation, sacrifice plays, literally, a crucial role in the makeup of Hegel's thought.

Phenomenology

We usually distinguish appearance from reality, and this distinction has been a continuous feature of philosophy since the pre-Socratics. However, when we consider our very own nature, the nature of a self-conscious being, then that which we are is both appearance and reality at once.[3] What we are cannot be separated from how we appear to us, because our identity also depends on who we take ourselves to be, even if mistakenly so. While appearance is not everything we are, who we are for ourselves is nevertheless coconstitutive of our being and identity. There is a certain facticity to us, but the truth about ourselves is not independent from who we take and make ourselves to be, simply because we *are* self-conscious beings (in this sense one might say: *verum et factum convertuntur*). In Hegel's terminology, we are what we are not only *in* ourselves but also *for* ourselves. The way our reality is constituted depends on this interplay, and this interplay has its own history; this is the very topic of the *Phenomenology of the Spirit*.

What we are for ourselves—how we identify ourselves—has to do with negation. In fact, the very distinction between appearance and reality is its own kind of negation. This negation is the reason why we have the kind of history that the *Phenomenology* describes: it is a history because, unlike natural beings, we never simply are what we are but always transcend, that is, negate, our present state by being conscious of it, by taking it to be something, and this self-conceptualization is never at its end until it has reached a higher kind of identity in which subject and object are identical, that is, the Absolute in which appearance and reality are one.

In the meanwhile, we identify who we are by demonstrating what we are not—*omnis determinatio est negatio*. This demonstration of nonidentity is, for Hegel, a matter of practical consciousness: in the merely theoretical and contemplative attitude of the first chapters of the *Phenomenology*, self-consciousness does not emerge. We develop ourselves in practical opposition to things, rather than in their theoretical assimilation. Self-consciousness is practical reason—this is Johann Gottlieb Fichte's anti-Cartesian heritage: the primordial self is a fact-act, *Tathandlung*.[4] Because of this, the negation that constitutes our identity is a practical negation; it is a sacrifice.

While the word "sacrifice" might not play a major terminological role in Hegel's work, sacrifice is in many ways ubiquitous because of the crucial role of negation as a form of death—something that has been picked up particularly by Kojève and his followers. Cultic sacrifice as a form of religion is a telling subspecies of these kinds of sacrifices. Negation and otherness are implied in Hegel's notion of practical reason; cult therefore emerges whenever history and consciousness make a turn to practical reason; it typically involves self-consciousness over against another.[5] Thus, practical reason, death, and self-consciousness emerge together in the second part of the *Phenomenology*. Sacrifice plays a major role for who or what self-consciousness takes itself to be. We are not a self without sacrifice. For example, sacrifice implies a certain commitment that elevates us beyond mere animal desire, by sacrificing mere biological desires for a higher goal. In some way we commit ourselves to and identify with what we are sacrificing for.

But even more fundamentally, we identify ourselves not by what we sacrifice *for*, but by what we sacrifice, pure and simple. And the most fundamental thing we can sacrifice is our very life. To use an example of Robert Brandom's: what it means to be a samurai is demonstrated by the requirement to commit ritual suicide under a daunting variety of circumstances. By doing so, one would identify with an ideal code of conduct, a code that elevates one above the animal kingdom. Failure to commit suicide would indeed be the true death of the samurai, who is then only survived by an animal, or rather, who has never been anything else but an animal in the first place. In other words, ritual self-sacrifice is what demonstrates to us our elevation over the brute biological realm of animals.[6]

While death plays a similar role in Hegel's *Phenomenology*, there are also fundamental differences. Hegel, first of all, notices that there is, obviously, death in the animal realm as well. Yet animals do not thereby achieve consciousness and ever new self-conceptions. Animals, too, sustain their identity by dying, but they survive only in the species: every dog will be like its ancestors; they all correspond to the same concept, that of the species. The species is their universal, but this universal does not exist as anyone's concept. It is an abstraction, but an abstraction by death: the universal species abstracts from this or that dog by its death. Hence there is a concept of "dog," but it is not a concept that is had by the dog itself; Fido does not know that he is a dog. The universal is outside the individual and achieved only by its survival in another individual.

This is different for man. "A dog / that dies / and that knows / that it dies / like a dog // and that can say / that it knows / that it dies / like a dog / is a man."[7] Man is the animal that knows that he has to die. This means that we have internalized our death. Death is a negation, and negation is involved in the formation of a universal: we are negating this or that accidental feature in order to arrive at the universal concept of a species. The animal has this negation outside of itself, but we have it internalized. We are a species unto ourselves.[8] We are a living negation, that is, an abstraction from and for ourselves; we conceptualize ourselves. We never simply are, but we take ourselves to be something.

This picture, however, is incomplete, because it leaves out that self-consciousness is practical. We take ourselves to be something by positing ourselves practically. Practical activity is a striving that aims at arriving at an image of itself in the objects of these strivings. As striving, however, it *is not* what it strives for. Already on the animal level there is striving and its corresponding "notness." An animal strives for food, and hunger is the presence of the absence of food. It is not absence plainly and simply, but the absence of something that ought to be there, akin to what tradition calls a privation. Subjectivity and selfhood therefore open up in the animal realm as drive, *Trieb* (Fichte), which draws a distinction into reality. It is a distinction different from the distinction between two natural objects; rather, it is the distinction between subject and object. This distinction, however, is not conscious of itself. And it will consequently disappear with the achievement of its goal: the animal devours its food and will simply sink back into the stupor of satisfaction.

How do we, then, achieve self-consciousness? Merely eating would leave us, too, on the level of animals—a level of which Ludwig Feuerbach says "man is what he eats" (*Der Mensch ist, was er ißt*). Our practical consciousness rather aims at self-consciousness, that is, at an object that is another self, not a natural object that is to be devoured and then forgotten. And we do not achieve self-consciousness on our own, but only through this other self: neither Fichte nor Hegel know of a Cartesian cogito that could know itself apart from an Other that reflects its selfhood back to itself.

Hence the example of the samurai might be insufficient: while there is a social element in the samurai's code of conduct, it does not seem to involve other selves, but rather primarily the negative relation to the animal world (provided this example is a sufficient description of the historic reality, which I am unable to discern).

For Hegel, then, we know ourselves only in another self that we recognize as such. But if we recognize it, that is, if we take it as another self, we take it to be itself a taker, that is, a recognizer. The other self must also be someone who conceptualizes who he or she is by recognizing me. As a result, we have our self-consciousness only outside of ourselves: we are an "I" only in so far as we are a "We." Self-consciousness is the whole of these two selves; in Hegel's famous phrase: *an I that is a We, and a We that is an I.*

All of this might seem to have led us far away from sacrifice in Hegel. But here is where it reemerges: both of these selves, in order to have this recognition, have to demonstrate to each other that they are such beings, namely that they are not animals, but beings that have internalized their own death and therefore superseded it. As a matter of fact, they are not even sure of it for themselves, until they have demonstrated it to each other.[9] What they therefore need to demonstrate to each other is that they are willing to sacrifice their lives. Moreover, they do not demonstrate this by merely one of them committing suicide in front of the other; they also want to know that the other is also someone who is not attached to mere animal life; hence they must risk not only their own life, but *each other's* lives. Only then is this recognition the recognition of selves and worth anything. This is how the struggle for life and death ensues, which will lead to one side beginning to fear death and becoming the bondsman to the other who will be the master; he will be the master, not because he is physically stronger, but because he has not feared death and is therefore more truly a self.

The further famous master/slave dialectic that emerges from this does not need to concern us here. What is important, however, is that the locus of sacrifice in Hegel is therefore social. While there is no question of myth and ritual on this level yet, it is already fundamentally intersubjective and has to do with relationships of recognition and with our very identity, with who we take ourselves to be. Who we appear to be, how we conceptualize ourselves, might not take the form of myth and ritual, but it nevertheless involves sacrifice. It might be worth pointing out that, contrary to the

Girardian analysis, this is not the sacrifice of an innocent victim, but a form of a (mutual) self-sacrifice. Not unlike Girard, however, it does have to do with practical consciousness and desire, and with how this desire is, if not mimetic, then at least in some way intersubjective and, unlike animal desire, underdetermined if it remains on its own.

If the social sphere is constituted in and with sacrifice or rather with the willingness to sacrifice one's life, then the subsequent enactments of sacrifice will take more social and less fundamental forms. Yet these, too, are sacrifices that demonstrate and constitute our identity. Thus, we might identify ourselves by being willing to sacrifice our good name or our jobs; for example, we might identify ourselves as Catholics by sacrificing jobs that do not allow for conscience clauses in certain morally neuralgic areas; or we might risk our freedom where there are no such escapes—which is still less than risking our lives: in other words, it might not require us to become martyrs by sacrificing our lives, but something less than that.

Thus, in the following stages of Hegel's *Phenomenology*, less fundamental sacrifices surface. And in these contexts Hegel begins to use the term *Opfer* more specifically, and more often the term *Aufopferung* and its derivatives—a use that seems to imply a *self*-sacrifice, as Paolo Diego Bubbio points out.[10] According to Bubbio, this is, however, also the problem: if it is a self-sacrifice, then it implies the sacrifice of one's own absoluteness. Typically, the individual is to sacrifice himself in order to achieve union with something greater, that is, with the universal.[11] This is truly to be achieved only as Spirit, that is, in the realm of intersubjectivity, a realm that Hegel likes to characterize in terms of "fluidity," in which the I is the We and the We the I. In the meanwhile, various attempts at this "Aufopferung" fail because the self-sacrifice of the individual is disingenuous or involves various contradictions.

For example, Stoicism, the first stage after the master/slave dialectic, is again a stage of theoretical consciousness, in which typically the otherness of practical consciousness is absorbed. The whole relationship between master and slave is superseded by a consciousness of independence for which it does not matter whether it is the master or the slave; the Stoic philosopher can be either Marcus Aurelius or Epictetus. There is a simple union of oneself in reason and thought, which "lives in accordance with reason," keeping itself independent and immune from challenge by sacrificing individual interests in advance, acquiescing the universal fear and bondage of the culture of the

Roman Empire. This will, however, imply a certain emptiness of what truth or "accordance with reason" is meant to be. It is indeed compatible with everything, the situation of the slave as well as the emperor. Consequently, the insights of stoic wisdom tend toward empty generalizations and platitudes. This appears to undermine the true universality and rationality for the sake of which the individual pretended to sacrifice itself.[12]

The next stage, skepticism, retains the individual independence of this stage of consciousness, preserving the self as immune, but it does this now in an antirationalistic way: if Stoic reason fails, then it cannot challenge the individual. This universal Stoic logos, however, does not simply disappear, it is merely skeptically declared to be in an unreachable beyond.

This will lead to the Hegel's stage of "unhappy consciousness" in which sacrifice is again an important theme. Here again, individuality forgoes trying to impose itself on reality, but rather sacrifices itself to the beyond that skepticism had established.

This, however, it does not do by laying down its life, but by practices that sound suspiciously like a Protestant caricature of Catholic religious life, including practices like prayer, work, sacraments, penance, and religious vows. The first is a sacrifice in feeling only, literally in "smells and bells," a kind of "musical thinking" that does not reach its objective, but only stretches itself out to the universal in an infinite longing, in which the distance is felt with pain.[13] Perhaps Hegel was thinking of faith as merely seeking understanding, and at any rate, it is the elevation to the universal Beyond in a mere movement toward thinking, *An-dacht* (a term that Martin Heidegger will later restore to a positive connotation). The notion of work seems to have connotations of the good works, which are at the same time the effect of the universal, that is, of grace, and that therefore are internally broken. Hegel seems to allude to Eucharistic imagery to make this point: the Eucharist is a product of our own work, which as bread is meant to be an enjoyment (including of ourselves who are its producers), but it is a broken reality, uniting the particular work and the universal meaning. The Eucharist would then be the thanksgiving for the activity of the universal in our works, which, however, is at the same time the activity of the thanks-giver. Unlike for Catholic thought, to Hegel's mind this is a contradiction and contributes to the unhappiness of a split consciousness. To overcome this split, the unhappy consciousness has finally recourse to penitence, that is, it sacrifices its feeling for its self as individual in its enjoyments. The more it is attacking the body as their source, the more this individual body becomes a focus; rather than allowing the bodily functions to be the trifles they are, it makes them the center of attention, if not obsession, over which the individual is brooding. This means that rather than elevating the individual to the universal, this sacrifice only serves to enclose it in itself. In order to break this self-enclosement it hands itself over to a minister, who, for Hegel, is a false kind of mediation in the syllogism of universal and individual.[14] Hegel is here thinking of the aspect of penitence that is the forgiveness of sins, but also of religious vows of obedience, poverty, and chastity, the handing over of one's decisions, property, and enjoyment. This is the opposite of the freedom that Hegel is seeking as the ultimate result of sacrifice: the state in which we are at one with ourselves in the other of ourselves (and all the others of ourselves), freedom as the opposite of alienation. Here, however, the sacrifice does not lead to free selfhood, but to making oneself into an object, a thing. It is not itself even in its very own doings, which it does not understand, but which are rather the result of blind obedience, nor are the fruits of its labor its own to enjoy. It is alienated from everything that might count as its actualization. However, at the end Hegel also sees that this sacrifice makes this more internal devotion real, and through this discipline, universal reason in the form of the counsel of the minister or superior is becoming real as well. It does achieve a union of individual and universal that will become "observing reason."[15]

Generally, while the individual might achieve a kind of certainty by self-annihilation before the universal, this is in fact not the true union of universal and individual that a sacrificial system of mutual recognition would aim at. Perhaps because the individual is really left behind as a mere thing, perhaps also because in all of this the individual actually tries to preserve its independence from both external things as well as from God; in other words: *independence* gets in the way of the *interdependence* that is to be achieved by true forms of sacrifice.

This entails that sacrifice as a form of interdependence cannot be the act of an individual. In a later chapter, *Virtue and the Way of the World (Weltlauf)*, virtue tries to overcome the way of the world, which resembles Jean-Jacques Rousseau's social state, which, against Thomas Hobbes, really is the beginning and not the end of a war of all against all. Against this universal selfishness, the virtuous individual tries to respond in a sacrificial way. But this sacrifice as mere negation remains unsubstantial, because it is separated from the social fabric that it wants to transform, but to which it has nothing concrete to oppose. Thus it falls back into a deficient unity with the universal *Weltlauf*, identifying its virtue with the selfish pursuits of the world, declaring private vices to be public benefits (i.e., Bernard Mandeville and Adam Smith).[16]

Sacrifice therefore depends on being part of the social fabric; it is a concrete, reflective social practice. This should not be surprising, if its telos is interdependent recognition. This is true for *Culture (Bildung) and Its Realm of Actuality* and the subsequent chapters. Here it also becomes apparent that true forms of sacrifice ultimately do not happen by sacrificing life, money, or the like, but in the medium of language, because this is the medium of mutual recognition of selves, in which the self knows itself to be for another, is an I as a We, and therefore is the embodiment of the sacrifice of independence for the sake of interdependence. Historically, Hegel sees this emerging with Absolutism, which thereby undermines itself, paving the way for the Enlightenment: in the age of feudalism the aristocracy was still a warring class and, like the master, willing to risk their lives. This potential sacrifice implied honor and service as identity-conferring commitments. Their honor was derived from service to the universal or common good. However, this failed to achieve real union: disagreement and fighting about what the public interest or common good really was led to internal battles and duels among "haughty vassals." Nor was there real sacrifice unto death, but the vassal survived with his particular interests. Consequently, Absolutism as a resolution forced all of them to submit to the universal, while allowing them to keep their privileges; that is, they now sacrifice not their lives but their independence. But this leaves the "noble consciousness" self-alienated, sacrificing their very action and thought. At the same time, sacrifice is now linguistic, even if one-sided: it is the linguistic sacrifice of flattery for the monarch. The one-sidedness implies no true recognition: flattery gives apparent recognition while keeping something else in one's heart, despising the monarch as just another self-serving individual. This awareness of duplicity comes out in another linguistic form of intersubjectivity: the nihilistic wit that articulates this duplicity (e.g., Denis Diderot's *Rameau's Nephew*; perhaps one might also think of the French moralists), and the sneering bon mot that now replaces battles and duels. The Enlightenment will use this linguistic medium to promote its particular form of reason. It is in this language that it will criticize the very notion of sacrifice as foolish superstition. It will not try to improve on sacrifice, but rather see it as opposed to reason itself, because reason is measured by bourgeois utility; and there is nothing useful about sacrificing one's property. Reason does not need to demonstrate its superiority over nature by sacrifice; it claims to be superior to it, although it is only instrumental reason and as such serves only the fulfillment of these natural biological enjoyments. The Enlightenment will also point out that religious sacrifice is a mere sign or token anyway, the believers are not really serious in their sacrifices, retaining most of the enjoyment. While the Enlightenment might spot a problem with dishonest sacrifice, it will soon make this sacrifice of the religious believer more serious by means of the guillotine. It does, however, also fail to see that the higher forms of sacrifice are unbloody: if they are mere tokens, then this might rather imply that they have entered the realm of symbolic representation, that is, the realm of a linguistic medium. This linguistic medium is what will ultimately be used for mutual recognition and reconciliation (e.g., between the beautiful soul and the hard-hearted judge), which is itself a representation of the Absolute as intersubjectivity.[17]

The first explicit connection of sacrifice with religion happens only after all of this, in the last chapters of the *Phenomenology* (although unhappy consciousness had some religious connotations). It occurs on two pages in the section on "art religion,"[18] that is, the Greek form of religion, in which the gods have the form of self-conscious beings, rather than mere beings of light, plants or animals or the dead. This will therefore be the first time that there can be a form of recognition between the gods and the protagonist-consciousness of the *Phenomenology*, between the universal and the particular.[19] This will also be the first time that gods as self-conscious beings can speak. Initially, however, the artist, even though he tries to let the Muses speak through him, will produce sculptures, of which he (unlike the people) knows that they are the work of his hands, that is, deaf and dumb idols.

Language enters religion as oracle as well as linguistic forms of divine law. Both seem to form a dialectic unity: the law only gives general rules, while the oracle addresses particular concerns; they represent the universal and the particular respectively in a linguistic medium. However, they do not come together in one self-conscious articulation. The particular is rather achieved by abandoning self-consciousness, for example, in the vapors of the Pythia or in the throwing of dice or in natural phenomena like the flight of birds.

The mediation of self-consciousness, on the other hand, is again achieved in a practical form of consciousness, namely the cult. The fundamental form of the cult is the hymn, that is, a subjective collective, uttering itself before the statue of the god. It is a form of self-consciousness, spirit being present to itself in a living voice, but only in its immediate feeling for itself, in its empty purity. It remains secret, that is, unreal. (Hegel apparently thinks of the mystery religions; he also mentions washings and white garments.)

The one thing that makes it real and establishes actual recognition between the divine and the people is sacrifice. It is important to notice that this first mention of sacrifice as a cultic act comes late not only in the *Phenomenology*; even within religion it comes late, after the establishment of a linguistic medium of recognition.

In sacrifice, the inner immediacy of the collective self becomes practically actualized by the pouring out of something or by burning it in fact and reality. (And perhaps the hymn is already a form of *Lobopfer*.) Hegel does not mention the animal sacrifices of Greek religion, but rather the sacrifices of Ceres and Bacchus,[20] which apparently he identifies with the offering of grain and wine. What is important about this is that the offering, even if real, is only symbolic: not only do the offerers receive something back for their enjoyment (and usually the best part), but bread and wine are really signs of the gods themselves. In other words, what is sacrificed here are the gods. While this might sound like Girard's theory of the gods as divinized victims, it is not what Hegel has in mind. Rather, the institution of these signs is the initiative of the gods themselves; the universal divine being has given itself an individual being, so that it then can become one with the individual sacrificing consciousness. This happens in the subsequent meal, which consequently is a form of communion with the divine. What distinguishes this sacrifice from the earlier, failed stages is that here, even though there is a return, there is no deception, because what is returned is the universal, not a particular interest. There is a real sacrifice of the particular for the universal, and the universal gives itself back. This kind of communion is a sacrificial recognition between god and man, a human–divine intersubjectivity. Again, one should note that this happens through sacred signs, which presuppose a linguistic medium, without which there is no intersubjectivity. It is the linguistic medium that allows the god to be invoked and to appear. Already in the hymn this medium is, in a way, the mediation of individual and universal, self and other, and sacrifice is what (as practical) makes real this union of individual and universal in its othering (sacrifice) and gathering (enjoyment). It is the soul of the community of the polis that finds its self-consciousness in what it dedicates to its god; his honor is their honor, his treasure is theirs, and their worship is therefore its own reward, here and now.[21]

All of this is not yet the final stage of religious sacrifice, but prepares for it. Not accidentally the bread and wine of Bacchus and Ceres are reminiscent of the Eucharistic species. The pre-Christian, mythological sacrifices are related to the Christian sacrifice, not so much as their undoing, but as their fulfillment. In fact, it is only now that it becomes a true human sacrifice:[22] the bread and wine have to become flesh and blood. Bread and wine only signify Bacchus and Ceres as mere things rather than self-conscious beings; it is the spirit as nature, the universal as bacchantic indifferentiation. The performers of the sacrifices of bread and wine are self-conscious, but the victim is not; it is a mere thing of enjoyment, like food eaten up by animals. They are not a divine universal in which we can recognize ourselves, and there is something of a lack of true self-sacrifice as well. It is only in Christ's sacrifice that the victim is a self, appearance and reality at once.

At this point, however, there is also a reversal; Christianity is the absolute, the consummate, the revealed religion. It is revealed and manifest (*offenbar* as well as *geoffenbart*): this means that it is not man who in his religious consciousness tries to find symbolic ways to bridge the chasm between man and god, between individual and universal. Here the universal itself takes the initiative. Yet God does not reveal himself as a completed being. God himself becomes a self only in the very act of his incarnation and death; on the cross God sacrifices himself, which is to say, he sacrifices his own divinity, universality, and absoluteness! This does not mean that God demands atonement and gets it by sacrificing his Son. In the *Lectures*, Hegel explicitly rejects this idea.[23] Rather, God becomes himself only by sacrificing himself. As the universal, as the abstract Being, he would remain "das leblose Einsame" (the lifeless lonely one). He might be substance, but not subject, because he has not appeared to himself. Appearance and reality, *Sein und Schein*, have not been differentiated. In other words: God has not appeared to himself; he is not a Self. For God to become real, it takes his death on the cross and his resurrection into the (Holy) Spirit of the community. God as the absolute is real only in the linguistic intersubjectivity of the community, and this is achieved through his sacrifice on the cross. God must die in order to become himself. As for human selves death had become an internal negation or abstraction, so for Hegel there needs to be death and negation in God himself (even though from his side he sets out as a universal, not as a particular); without sacrifice, God is not a Self. Even God achieves his identity only by sacrifice and commitment, which is ultimately achieved in the identity of appearance and reality as the intersubjective recognition of the community.[24]

Hegel points out that Spirit is to know one's negative or one's limit. And this negation is an *Aufopferung* as externalization and *Darstellung*, representation or appearance of the Spirit for itself. Since this is, in a sense, the whole process of the *Phenomenology*, this book is in its own way an entire sacrificial system, a "speculative Good Friday," a Golgotha and Calvary of the Spirit, as Hegel says.[25] Toward the end of the book we find the following passage:

> The self-knowing Spirit knows not only itself but also the negative of itself, or its limit: to know one's limit is to know how to sacrifice oneself [*aufzuopfern*]. This sacrifice [*Aufopferung*] is the externalization in which Spirit displays [*darstellt*] the process of its becoming Spirit in the form of free contingent happening.[26]

Sacrifice in this sense is self-representation, not only for determining one's identity, but in order to produce the split of appearance and reality in the first place, which is constitutive of recognition as divine self-sacrifice. Even if for Hegel philosophy finally supersedes religion as well, this philosophy remains, in this sense, a *sacrificial* philosophy, just as it remains a Trinitarian philosophy.[27]

In Christ, then, human and divine nature meet in the sense of (1) a human self-sacrifice, in which the individual offers himself up to the universal, and (2) a divine self-sacrifice, in which the universal offers itself up to become a particular. It is the complete union of universal and particular that will then be only further unfolded, in order to be finally explicated in Hegel's philosophy.

All of this is a far cry from orthodox Christian theology, and might also be slightly preposterous as a theory. But it certainly is impressive as a comprehensive system, which sheds light on a variety of phenomena, even if it might not at times do justice to them; and it has sacrifice at its heart.

Before we enter into a comparative discussion of this system, we need to have a look at Hegel's *Lectures on the Philosophy of Religion*. I will make use especially of the penultimate version of his lectures, that of 1827.

Lectures on the Philosophy of Religion

For Hegel, philosophy of religion is not to be contrasted with theology as the study of what God is in himself, while religion would be only our consciousness of or relation to God. Rather, God is our developing consciousness of who he is, and is himself becoming real in this process. Appearance and reality, religion and God are one, the rational is the real, epistemology is ontology, and knowledge of what is real is part of the reality that it knows. Revelation as manifestation is nothing but the manifestness of God in the other of himself. This is the logical consequence of what has been said above about the *Phenomenology of the Spirit*. The history of religion is therefore a history of God's unfolding self-consciousness in us, in which various shapes of consciousness supersede one another and are in a sense sacrificed for higher stages. In such a scheme of things, the beginnings will have a particular significance: the sacrifice of the second Adam is anticipated in that of the first Adam; both are part and parcel of our very hominization. In the history of religions, God explicates himself not only in the incarnation and the cross, but he does so already in the first Adam, particularly in his fall. Thus, evil is part of God's very own history. These beginnings are therefore crucial for an understanding of religion. These beginnings, however, are only beginnings of what begins to unfold in history. Hegel repeatedly rejects the notion of a primordial revelation, of which all later religions would be splinters and products of decay. Rather, his story is one of growth.[28] At the same time, in the system of sciences, religion presupposes that we have already arrived at the existence of a God who is already a concrete universal, that is, the Trinity as Hegel understands it. And so we do already begin on the level of spirit. Still, every beginning as beginning is a state of immediacy. The immediacy of the starting point is, in Hegel, usually analogous to the immediacy of the senses (for example, the "sense-certainty" of the *Phenomenology*). Only that in the case of religion this is the immediacy of the concept, that is, it is Religion, it is Spirit.[29] Thus Hegel makes clear that even the early religions of nature do not worship sensual things but a spiritual presence within them—it is only that they have an unclear and confused placement of what is implicitly already spiritual: form and content do not yet match. It will be part of the history of religion to develop this more adequately.

This original state is the state of Adam and Eve, and this is just what their original "innocence" means. Innocence is nothing but the unexplicated immediacy, which religious picture thinking envisions as Adam and Eve and projects into the past (2:422). That this paradise is lost is an indication that it was not the fulfillment, let alone divine; it was innocent, but not good.[30] Accordingly, their fall is pictured as something sensual, the eating from the tree, and paradise itself is something of an animal state (as Hegel points out, "paradeisos" means a kind of zoo). Because this is sensuality on the level of spirit, it is something that qua immediacy cannot last: animals in their sensual state are neither good nor evil, but we in our "natural," sensual state are evil: we are by nature not what we ought to be. We are by nature evil, and this is what "original sin" means; that original sin is inherited is merely the popular picture-thinking version (2:424). Therefore it is good that we fall, because consciousness implies a cleavage, an *Ur-teil*, a judgment on the state of nature. History of religion is not a descent from pristine origins, but an ascent through a necessary fall. This might be in contrast to Rousseau's desire to go back to nature, but it is also contrary to traditional understandings of the fall, including the biblical text itself. For example, for Hegel, work is not a punishment for sin; rather it is a necessary part of our purification from our pseudo-sensual particularity. Labor is part of our higher nature, culminating ultimately in Hegel's own "labor of concepts" (*Arbeit des Begriffes*). Innocence does not possess the universality of goodness; it needs to be elevated to it through education—a mediation that happens through work and through sacrifice. Hegel therefore does not call this a fall; rather, the refusal to leave the state of nature would be what is evil. We are not by nature good, but we become good by leaving the state of nature. This rather odd reversal of the actual story line finds additional explanations in the earlier lectures of 1824. Here he locates the source of this progression in the contradiction that human nature is: as rational it is universal, but as embodied it has particular desires. This is the heritage of Immanuel Kant: the universality of the categorical imperative implies an "ought," while the fact of our particular desires is therefore tantamount to evil. It is our very finitude and particularity that is evil; as one might say: it is not merely a *malum metaphysicum*, but itself ipso facto a moral evil. While Hegel will disagree with Kant, he does accept this scenario as a stage, and one that is there from the beginning (2:144–45). Our nature therefore has this ambiguity of good qua rational universality and evil qua particularity. The fall is nothing but the cleavage and explication of their more immediate union in the state of plantlike "innocence." It is part of our nature to abandon our nature and bring this to a higher resolution. This higher resolution will require a sacrificial integration of our individuality in the universal, but also the other way around: a cleavage or fall of the particular from the universal.[31] Similar things are said in the *Phenomenology*, where this fall is thematized only at the very end, because there the religious state is a result, not the beginning point.

Even here, however, it is not just the story of the past as which religious imagination takes it. It is the inner reality of the present concept, with which we are always already acquainted (presumably in some kind of intellectual intuition) (e.g., 2:146–49). As Hegel says elsewhere: "Common fancy puts the Absolute far away in a world beyond. The Absolute is rather directly before us, so present that so long as we think, we must, though without express consciousness of it, always carry it with us and always use it."[32] Even Adam, therefore, knows the inner nature of things or the heart of things,[33] although only implicitly. (Hegel does not mention Adam's naming of things at this point.)[34] But it is part of our nature to leave this state of nature. In this eternal, timeless story (and in each of us)[35] there will therefore necessarily be a fall, a cleavage, and the judgment (*Ur-teil*) passed on Adam and Eve is itself part of this fall, because it is this primordial cleavage (*Ur-teilung*)[36] that indeed leads to the knowledge of good and evil, and the very knowledge of God himself.[37] What is in fact evil in this result is that we now have thematized our contradictory nature as being both evil and good, but as such we seem indifferent against either side. The indifference between good and evil is itself evil and will only subsequently be overcome.[38] So, the snake did not lie, and God subsequently seems to confirm this, as Hegel points out: "behold, Adam has become like us, knowing good and evil" (2:427). The assumption that Adam and Eve could have known God's commandment before the fall therefore appears as "absurd"; they were dumb and dull as well as "zurechnungsunfähig."[39] What remains unclear in Hegel's analysis is how this fall can be a sin, if it is both necessary and committed in ignorance.

One of the consequences of the fall is death—the precondition of sacrifice. For Hegel, in the lectures of 1821, our mortality is both a consequence of sin, but also natural.[40] Since sin and the fall are part of the necessary unfolding of our nature (and ultimately of God himself!),[41] death itself is part of this unfolding. It is that internal negation that we still have to integrate sacrificially. Ours is a spiritual union with nature, which can be achieved only through fall and reconciliation (*Versöhnung*) (2:149).

The subsequent history of religions is not just a history of errors, superstitions, idolatries, or foundational murders. They are ways in which the rational becomes real and the real becomes rational. While Hegel struggles with the necessary historical sequencing and intelligibility of the considerable knowledge he has of the then known history of religions, he does maintain that these are not contingent happenings, but unfoldings of the original diremption of the concept. What unfolds is the elevation from immediacy into reflexive freedom, an internal cleavage in which spirit learns to relate to spirit.

In the earliest stage of mere magic, there is still an immediate involvement with nature that does not even achieve the freedom of tool use yet. The individual is individuated by the power of will and decision, but one with the universal powers of nature, which imbue special individuals with an immediate power of magic, which is used without thought and reflection (2:436–39).[42] With Herodotus, Hegel sees these practices of shamans and others especially prevalent in Africa, but also among Eskimos. In Africa this goes a step further by using dead ancestors for magic: dead people are removed from the here and now and enjoy a rudimentary state of universality. Rudimentary, because they are still imagined with sensual and evil desires. They are invoked to possess the magician, who proceeds to remedy bad situations by human sacrifice. Cannibalism as well as random mass murder (for the sake of "shock and awe," it seems) are also ways in which religions try to participate in the life of the dead. Hegel does not get too analytic in this very descriptive collection of curiosities. For reasons of its very nature, he does not attribute much intelligibility to it (2:433–45). Over all it is the magician and the dead who function as a link between the universal powers of nature and particular situations.

In the Chinese religion, according to Hegel, the only one who can perform sacrifices is also the only one who is free: the emperor. He is the only one who mediates the universal and the particular: the universal Thian[43] and the particular magical superstitions of the people do not really connect (2:457–58). Connection apparently is made by sacrifice, and this is the source of reflective freedom. As pure negation and cutting off of this particularity, the "sect" of Daoism goes into itself in a form of immediacy with the universal as substance or essence (2:453–65)—a form of thought that characterizes India. Here the universal is simply identified with the individual, but as the nothingness or nirvana of the individual. This is achieved cultically by asceticism, concentration, indifference, thoughtlessness, but also in forms of sacrifice: Hegel quotes the burning of widows, forms of sacrificing parents and children and oneself (by throwing oneself into the sources of the Ganges in the mountains of the Himalayas) (2:497). He points out that these are not sacrifices of atonement (which would have to correspond to and atone for the acts of free subjectivity), but the "elevation into the universal"; they are ways in which the individual gives itself significance (2:497). The same can be said for acts of penance and asceticism: they have nothing to do with notions of sin and atonement.[44] There is a lack of true mediation between universal and individual: individuality is seen as accidental in reincarnation (which, however, rightly identifies us with thought and freedom); on the other hand, the various incarnations of the universal, the lamas, are disconnected and do not know of each other; there is no recognition in the universal for them. The universal itself does not have the form of subjectivity, is not really for-itself, does not appear to itself, but lives unconsciously in its particulars, like the species in animals, like the soul animating the body, or like the law of nature, the *nous* of Anaxagoras or even Friedrich Schelling's intellectual intuition; in other words it still has all the marks of immediacy and is a form of unreflective pantheism (2:468–69).

While the Persian stage (moving westward) distributes this universal into a dualism that is personified, that is, concretely individualized (Ormuzd and Ahriman), these remain superficial personifications (2:510–11) by being apart from one another; they are accordingly identified with material elements like fire and matter. Only when mediation and reconciliation become a felt need does sacrifice emerge, namely in the cult of Mithras (with its sacrifice of a steer) (2:513). But it is only the Syrian religion in which both sides will really engage in a mixture, namely in the form of a battle, in pain and death. It is now one subject that experiences death and rising in itself. It has internalized the death and negation that the animal (as well as the individual of the Indian religion) has outside of itself. While Hegel does not mention cultic sacrifice, the notion of death as the articulation of the union and cleavage of universal and individual is obvious (2:514–18).

This death is at the heart of the Egyptian religion: the individual subject now survives its death (Osiris).[45] Embalming and pyramids are shrines to this fact. But so is the realm of signs, hieroglyphs: if death is a form of abstraction, then something can be abstracted in the form of a representation; a representation or an image makes something present by negating its physical presence, abstracting from its here and now. A linguistic medium depends on the death of what it signifies. Letters are indeed pyramids or tombs of their meaning. It is, again, noteworthy that the linguistic system, even though it might be based on the experience of death, is not the product of sacrifice. For Hegel, the cult avails itself of this linguistic medium and therefore presupposes it. The main sacrifice of the Egyptians, however, is work: work in irrigation, and work on the pyramids. But the universal cannot come to full self-consciousness in this cult: the work remains a riddle (cf. the Sphinx) (2:525–32).

While the signs of the Egyptian religion are still the riddles of hieroglyphs and of the Sphinx (combinations of man and animal), the riddle is solved in the Greek world: it is the individual subjectivity of the artist, engaging the free subjectivity of the anthropomorphic gods of his imagination. This free subjectivity has, first, the character of natural immediacy, and therefore an immediate union of both gods and worshipper. Athena is the city, which embodies her in individual athletic achievements (the athlete as living sculpture) and collective processions. It does not require the negativity of asceticism and penance, but only athletic discipline; even the sacrifices are no form of self-negation; most of what is sacrificed is also enjoyed—if not stolen from the gods: Prometheus stole not only the fire for the sacrifices, but also the meat from Zeus, and gave it to man for his natural needs (as a Titan, he was not concerned with man's ethical needs) (2:541–42). The cult of Bacchus and Demeter (the Greek for the Roman Ceres of the *Phenomenology*) includes eating as the positive assimilation of the sacrifice. Man is free and with himself in the object of his *cultus*. This is the Greek *Heiterkeit* (2:554–56). Human sacrifices for the appeasement of the gods, as Agamemnon's daughter, are seen as unusual archaisms (2:394–95), comparable perhaps to the magic and frenzied practices of natural religions.[46] Otherwise, Greek sacrifice is this free exchange with the gods.

Yet there is still that universal negativity of fate and necessity above it all. It is mediated in tragedy, when the individual protagonists identify with parts of the universal ethical powers (Creon and Antigone); the conflict is tragic because it is a split between two necessities and their gods (which are thereby delegitimized). The individual hero is in the middle, splitting these universal powers, but also reconciling them in his death. The hero therefore embodies the unity of universal and individual through his death. As a result, universal fate ceases to be blind and takes on self-conscious, reasonable forms. Unlike in the *Phenomenology*, the oracle takes on the features of not only contingent particulars, but also fateful necessity. Oedipus, like Greek religion, knew the answer to the riddle of the Sphinx: individual man. But he had not understood universal fate yet, as announced by the oracle. His tragedy attempts to integrate both. Fate and its oracle will eventually become providence, that is, they will take on the features of free and reasonable subjectivity. In Socrates, who also begins with an oracle, the oracle is internalized in the individual as *daimonion*, but still remains negative (2:556–60).

In the meanwhile, the Jewish religion begins from the other end: the absolute subjectivity of God and his providence, an infinite subject, the One that leaves the Many demythologized and outside itself, organizing them by an unreflective positive law. Not the Greek imagination but pure thought is the principle, banning all images. God reveals himself as spiritual unity, as subject, not substance, in thought, wisdom, and holiness (2:561–63). As free subjectivity over against the world, he is the creator (and not a source of theogonies or emanations: 2:626, 1831 version) and also the free worker or miracles (2:568–69).[47] However, he is only the beginning, not the end, he is not result and return yet; that is, he is not yet Trinity, as Hegel understands it.

The individual subject unites with this universal in praise (located in human consciousness rather than in things),[48] in faith, and in obedience to the law. The failure of this obedience leads to contrition, a new kind of interiority that will also lead to the true cult and sacrifice as contrition of the heart (2:570–74). But as such, sacrifice is again the middle and mediation between universal and particular, the universal law and the individual that tries to fulfill it. In the lectures from 1824, he sees some sacrifices as forms of negating particular property before the universal, and others as sacrifices of atonement as a manifestation of the nothingness that the particular sinner has acquired and that would have otherwise cost him the negation of his life. Instead, the blood, that is, the life, of an animal is sacrificed, either by the shedding of the blood or by sending a living scapegoat into the desert (2:351–52). Not dead possessions are sacrificed, but the highest possession: life.[49]

The Roman religion unites universal (Jewish) and particular (Greek) in a false universal: its own particular tribal power is universalized in an external empire.[50] Its quasi-divine universal purposivity and teleology subjects all the particular deities of all other tribes (they become images for its cultural entertainment), while its own gods serve the particular needs of the state (*Jupiter Capitolinus* etc.) or the "gray" prosaic needs of the individuals in it (*Jupiter pistor*, *Juno moneta*) (2:582–88). "The need is the universal theogony from which the gods originate" (2:588–89). What mediates between universal and particular besides need are various forms of death: the "cold patriotism" and the wars of the empire, the slaughters of the circus, which replaces the Olympic games, and the cold death of the Stoic philosopher (Seneca). The Stoic philosophers also provide the abstract personality that is the basis of Roman law, for the juridical person and its purposivities (i.e., at this stage only property rights of the person). It is a world of pure natural pragmatism, combined with pure skepticism regarding the meaning of the external world: in other words, a very modern world (2:589–91).

Over all, the Roman religion is a religion of despair that prepares the ground for Christianity, the true reconciliation between universal and particular. While the Roman religion is the pure affirmation of the purposive subject over against a meaningless world, Jewish interiority and contrition is the pure negation of the subject that cannot find justification before God. Both prepare for the intersubjectivity of love, which arises out of infinite anguish, the great equalizer (2:641–42, 1831 version).

Christianity is the justification and reconciliation of the individual with the universal, but in the starkest contrasts and most absolute contradictions. It is God's own eternal story in time; the immanent Trinity is the economic Trinity (3:251). This incarnation of the universal cannot happen in an accidental manifold, as with the many lamas, but as spiritual and therefore unique event (3:283, 1831 version). Jesus's death is God's own sacrifice, but only in externality. Yet it is precisely his death that allows the resurrection as internalization into the spirit of the community.[51] What in Jesus is only sensual immediacy is mediated in the intersubjective recognition of the Christian community. It is noteworthy that for Hegel this is the *only* reason why Jesus has to die. His death does not add anything essential to his mission. As a form of martyrdom it is a mere "addition," and otherwise it is completely natural to die.[52] His death is salvific only as a Pentecostal sublation of the universal and the individual in the fluidity of the community. It makes the merely sensual and human presence of Jesus into a presence of God in our intersubjectivity. God has to shed the garment of this individual humanity again.[53] This death is a double negation: the incarnation itself is already a negation and the sacrifice of the universal; the death on the cross and the Resurrection are the death of this death. The highest pain in God, God's very own death, the death of all higher aspirations and hopes, turns out to be the death of all death (3:247–51). In the 1831 version, it is the death of humanity as finite. Our finite humanity as such is evil in its difference from the infinite; it needs to die, and that is what Jesus's death accomplishes; at the same time it is the death of the Father in the Son (a form of *patripassianism*, it seems), because he gives up his abstraction. In other words, death needs to be involved as a double negation: the incarnation is the first step of the immediate union of God and man, and it is a form of negation; the crucifixion is the second step, which negates the sensual immediacy of this union so as to sublate it in the Spirit of the community.

This explanation is also the reconciliation of two further, opposed explanations: Jesus as a moral teacher as opposed to an understanding of his death as an extrinsic vicarious atonement. Jesus is not a mere moral teacher, but indeed God himself speaking in an immediate union of man and God. But Hegel also agrees with Kant that vicarious atonement does not make sense, because moral imputation applies only to the one who has done the act. Atonement is not accomplished by Christ but revealed: it is nothing but the reconciliation of finite and infinite in those two steps. His preaching makes it present in the sensual immediacy; his death and resurrection make it present in the reconciled community. In this way, however, reconciliation is indeed real, and it is even vicarious: it is *our* sacrifice. And precisely because of this, it does not dispense from appropriating this sacrifice by sacrificing our natural will to the infinite love (3:65 and 251–52).[54] This does not seem to imply a need for atonement or penance, though: it is realized in the mere insight that it has already happened. Bad deeds remain only as a memory that is already sublated by reason; evil is merely external, but God sees the heart, where we have already overcome our individuality, even if we have not realized it cognitively (3:259–60).

This does not mean that Jesus rose only "into the faith of the community" rather than literally. Hegel does not deny that Jesus appeared to the disciples; it is not just a story for the believers, but it was real, so as to strengthen the faith of the disciples. Faith begins, however, already with Jesus's death: here a decision is to be made, whether one reads the life of Jesus as believer or unbeliever, that is, whether one sees him as a mere moral teacher of charity or a mere martyr like Socrates, or rather as the presence of the Absolute and its death and resurrection. Either one reads this story already in the Spirit or merely sensually "like profane history" (3:240–51).

Over all, Jesus's death and Resurrection is as real as Hegel can make it against Enlightenment skepticism; yet the redemption it offers is largely a cognitive process, not an ontological change. This remains largely true for Hegel's understanding of the life of the Christian community; the Eucharist has sacrificial aspects, but as a mere representation of an eternal (rather than historical) process. More importantly, it is, even if sensual, a conscious personal and active appropriation of the achieved reconciliation and resurrection; the consecration happens cognitively, in faith.[55] Ultimately, however, all of this still needs to be realized not in the shape of the church—which is still a mere realization in the heart only—but as the political reconciliation and recognition that is the state. The state is the true march of the Spirit through history, with its own sacrifices of warfare and revolution, the labor pains of its realization.[56] Its form of consciousness is philosophy, not religion; it is reason, not faith. This philosophy, however, is Trinitarian, because only in this way can the universal and the individual be reconciled. Other forms of religion tend to mere feeling and irrationalism and, with this, ultimately to fanaticism and terror (Hegel is thinking of Rousseau, pietism, and Islam).[57]

Generally, even if sacrifice is not frequently thematized by Hegel, it does seem to be an anthropological constant, part of life as human life. In the *Manuscript* of the lectures, Hegel sees it involved in every human enjoyment, insofar as eating (paradigmatically) destroys its object: "Essen heißt Opfern, und Opfern heißt Selbstessen" (2:81). It is the freedom and spirituality of ordinary life, its poetry. What that might mean is that our eating is different from that of animals. It is *conscious* negation, and therefore double negation.

It is recognition of the universal (divine) in the eating and enjoying of the particular. This happens in sacrifices of *purification*, which have nothing to do with sin, nor are they a matter of inner or moral conversion.[58] Rather, it is the acknowledgement of the finitude of all one's doings; Hegel seems to think of sacrifices at harvest time, in which I am indicating over against the universal that the appropriation of the fruits as mine is not serious. Perhaps this could be taken to mean something as simple as table manners and thanksgiving before meals; they constitute the "poetry of life" by contrast with particular animals devouring particular food stuff without reference to the universal. There is no economic rationale for this: none of these sacrifices is to enrich the receiver; they are similar to the sacrificial custom of giving gifts to oriental monarchs (who do not need them either). These are mere tokens, similar to sacrifices of praise—both of which are therefore joyful, because they do not cost much (1:255). Hegel also considers punishment as a form of sacrifice, namely as a civil restitution for damage done (but as external, in contrast with moral penitence). A more profound form of sacrifice he finds in human labor, because it, like all sacrifices, relates the particular to the universal, the finite to the infinite, by shaping it according to a concept.[59] It is more than giving up merely natural things, but rather presenting things that are already shaped by human consciousness, beginning from pure action (like dancing and ritual) and culminating in colossal architecture (pyramids) as well as genuine artwork (Greek religion); according to Hegel, all of these are forms of sacrifice (1:257). The more immediate, natural forms of sacrifices have a pleasant, celebratory character. Yet there is an unknown power of fateful necessity looming over them; it will reveal itself to be the power of death, fate as devouring us all. Its cult will first be the cult of the dead, but more importantly it will eventually become the death of sin, which means that a fall from immediacy and the "breaking of the heart" will emerge and with it the realization of a need for reconciliation (1:258–64). Its form of sacrifice is the most interior form: penance, an inner purification by contrition; and it can be found only in higher religions. More natural religions, on the other hand, sacrifice what is particular by sacrificing particular external property; taken in this sense, sacrifices have no place in higher religion, except in a symbolic mode.[60] The history of sacrifice, Hegel seems to say, is a history of ever greater interiorization and ethical seriousness. Ultimately, however, *all* human activity is sacrifice, insofar as one gives up one's internal subjectivity to a universal purpose.[61] The one true cult is therefore *Sittlichkeit*, the ethical life.[62] Yet, even this is superseded by the theoretical realization that it has always already been accomplished: the one true sacrifice, the one true cult is philosophy. Thought itself is an elevation above one's particularity to the universal by the labor of concepts.[63]

Overall, sacrifice in its explicit, cultic form does not play a great role in Hegel's thought, while various forms of death and negation do. Sacrifice is the cultic form of such kinds of negativity. It typically serves to elevate the particular to the universal and spiritualize it in some way ("'to sacrifice' means to sublate the natural, to sublate otherness");[64] particularity that insists on its particularity is the very definition of evil that needs reconciliation.[65] On the other hand, particularity is in turn necessary as a kenotic self-sacrifice of the universal; it therefore involves ways in which the divine gives itself to finite consciousness, most prominently when the Father sacrifices his abstractness in the incarnation. Sacrifice is constitutive of God himself;[66] the Trinity is an eternal sacrifice,[67] and for us not to sublate ourselves into this Trinitarian sacrifice means to be "evil."[68] Our forgiveness and our reconciliation as a community of self-consciousnesses is the way in which God gives himself existence.[69] As such, sacrifices are forms of religious mediation between universal and particular and therefore an important feature, even if not in their cultic form.

Kierkegaard, Hegel, and the Fall

It is always instructive to compare Hegel's views on religion with those of Søren Kierkegaard. Not only does Kierkegaard restore the rights of faith and religion over against reason and state, refusing the sublation of faith into philosophy, he also rejects the sublation of the individual life into the linguistic intersubjectivity of the community (but rather practicing "indirect communication"). His peculiar rediscovery of celibacy and poverty is very much in contrast with Hegel's rejection of a separate and vowed religious life for the sake of bourgeois labor and its professional place in society. For Kierkegaard, individual existence is not "evil" but rather refuses its sublation into the universal essence.

For Kierkegaard, just as for Hegel, sacrifice is at the heart of the matter. But rather than sacrifice being a sublation into the linguistic rationality of universal intersubjectivity, the sacrifice of Isaac establishes Abraham as an individual, and not rationally so, but in pure obedience to God's authority. The obedience of faith cannot be sublated into reason, and therefore not communicated to others: the knight of faith can communicate only indirectly. Who we are is established in an act of sacrifice indeed, but it does not establish our union with the other of ourselves, but a relationship with the radical otherness of God.

In complete opposition to Hegel, sacrifice for Kierkegaard is first and foremost a *sacrificium intellectus*. Whatever the merits of such a notion are, there is one place in which it has a proper application, one that escapes Hegel, and that is the fall of Adam. Why did Adam fall? Hegel's suggestion that this was the necessary fall of the divine substance and that knowledge of good and evil do not precede it is not compatible with the story line (even if not taken for its literal historicity). If the fall was necessary and the result of ignorance, then it was not a sin, not a fall. It does not explain what it pretends to explain.[70] Nor does it suffice to explain it as a result of natural desires, because before the fall there was no concupiscence in Adam and Eve.[71] Friedrich Schiller, whom Hegel quotes at the end of the *Phenomenology* as compatible with his own views on the origin of the community from the divine substance, does have a different view of the fall nevertheless. For Schiller, the sublime vocation of man cannot be realized unless it is challenged by a commandment that he cannot anticipate in the natural structure of his desires. This commandment is not against the desires, but exceeds them.[72] This, however, might still not be sufficient. Kierkegaard agrees with Thomas Aquinas that this vocation can be realized only if the challenge goes not only beyond natural desires, but even beyond natural reason itself.[73] Similar to the challenge of faith as being *supra rationem* (although not *contra rationem*), the will needs to be actualized by a challenge to do at least once something simply for the reason that it has been commanded. This is not a crippling of human nature but its unfolding, because only this opens up a relationship with God as truly other than ourselves, with a will of his own, capable of free commandments, of revelation, of the free gift of grace, of acceptance and love. In such a relationship the telos of our will is actualized and not stifled. If this is a *sacrificium intellectus*, then it is one that leads to knowledge, namely the knowledge of recognition: the recognition of our creaturely finitude before God—the very recognition that, according to tradition, was refused by the fallen angels.[74] It is only in this recognition of obedience that not only our inclinations but even our reason functions properly—all of which, however, is lost after the fall. The "knowledge of good and evil" promised by the snake is not the knowledge of the commandment, but knowledge of a *reason for* the commandment—which is precisely what the commandment asked them to sacrifice. While for Hegel it is the fall that gets us out of the state of nature, it is in fact the refusal of obedience to God's transcendence that leaves us in a warped kind of immanence of nature and its desires.[75]

This has immediate implications for the notion of sacrifice. For, if sacrifice is what redeems us from this warped state, then Hegel and Kierkegaard do present us with two opposed views. For Hegel, the fall was a necessary cognitive process that God himself needed in order to come to a reflective self-awareness. The sacrificial death of the second Adam is therefore nothing but the completion of this process: reconciliation as completed reflection. Revelation is meant to help us participate in this eternal process but is in other ways also the very history of God himself.

Kierkegaard's view, on the other hand, might imply an understanding that is compatible with St. Paul's hymn from the letter to the Philippians: sacrifice as "obedience unto death," rectifying what Adam got wrong, who "grasped at" his divine calling and sonship, rather than receiving it as the gift of obedience. Far from being mythological and murderous, this notion of sacrifice is one that allows us to understand our own death and sufferings as redemptive participation in this sacrifice, rectifying our wills so as to be in a renewed relationship with God. This is why the punishment and curses of the old law now can become sources of blessings:[76] blessed are those who suffer, mourn, hunger and thirst, or are poor and persecuted, for they will be called children of God.[77] By contrast, it is Hegel's view of sacrifice that might remythologize sacrifice—not in spite of his rationalism, but because of it. The necessity of the unfolding of the divine essence makes death and sacrifice part of God's nature himself and thereby justifies suffering, rather than making it an outcome of a contingent history.

Kojève and Bataille

Before considering René Girard's relationship with Hegel, we have to provide the missing link for the French reception of Hegel's thought, and this is, famously, Alexandre Kojève, whose lectures on Hegel's *Phenomenology* in the 1930s (at the École Pratique des Hautes Études) were attended by many intellectuals who became leading figures later on, among them, Georges Bataille, Maurice Merleau-Ponty, André Breton, Jacques Lacan, Raymond Aron, Jean Hyppolite, Jean-Paul Sartre (probably), Louis Althusser, and Hannah Arendt.[78] Kojève himself did his doctorate under Karl Jaspers and was influenced by German thought, particularly that of Heidegger. And it is Heidegger's understanding of death that colors Kojève's reading of the role of death—and consequently sacrifice—in Hegel's *Phenomenology*.[79] Heidegger emphasizes our finitude: human consciousness is not only consciousness of our mortality, it is also limited by death and its negativity, while for Hegel we supersede this limitation reflexively, even if intersubjectively, in a double negation. For Kojève, who gave particular attention to the chapters leading up to the struggle on life and death and the master/slave dialectic, this negation appears to remain a simple negation. It is this negation that is the decisive feature that makes us free subjects and individuates us[80]—something that will reappear particularly in J. P. Sartre's thought. While natural entities and animals are just a brute fact, unchangingly the same throughout the ages, we by contrast are not beings, we are "negatings," and this negation is our death. The death of animals is in some way already a beginning of consciousness, transcending its here and now. But it is we who truly are the "deathly sickness of nature." Man is a prolonged death; war and revolution are therefore essential to us. As human beings we negate that which is and therefore generate the temporality characteristic of history, as opposed to the unchanging returns of the cosmos. Thinking is negating (and conceiving is a form of killing); but the result of negating being, according to Hegel's logic, is becoming, time. *Geist ist Zeit*, and we are time. We abstract the essence (*Wesen*) by negating the presence and making it a past (*Gewesen*), in the form of a decision for the future. This labor of concepts is therefore a temporally and historically unfolding activity.[81] For Kojève that means that we are essentially temporal and finite, and therefore mortal. The kind of incarnate logos that we are needs to die and needs to be willing to die and to be recognized as such.[82] Sacrifice is intrinsic to spirit, because spirit is negation. For Kojève, however, this negation does not sublate the natural world and does not culminate in the absolute spirit or a theological totality. As a double negation, this would be tantamount to returning to the mindless positivity of the natural world.

Insofar as this is envisioned as the end of history, it would leave us in an undifferentiated state of mindlessness.[83] The resulting pure welfare state that does not lead to war anymore—that does not give its citizens the opportunity to die for the common good (the universal) and obtain the consequent recognition—might be a mere animal kingdom, not a state.[84] While there seems to be a sense in which we transcend death by thinking it,[85] taken to its consequence this would indeed also be the end of history, perhaps even of individuation—the abolition of man and his reduction to a "species-being."[86] If, however, this were the realization of the Absolute or God, then this god would in the end exist only in and as the linguistic medium itself, that is, as Hegel's philosophy. And this philosophy, according to Kojève, is a philosophy of death.[87]

With this analysis, Kojève certainly highlights the notion of negation and death, abstraction and temporality that can indeed be found in Hegel. However, freedom and individuality are features that seem to receive greater emphasis than in Hegel. Even if negation lifts us out of the animal world, it does not seem to be the elevation into the universal essence that Hegel envisions as the result of sacrifice, but rather leads to more radical individuation.[88]

It is precisely these features that seem to be extended in an essay by Bataille (1955), who applies them to the notion of sacrifice—something Kojève himself was not interested in.[89] Furthermore, while Kojève still had an important place for the social rivalries of recognition and prestige in the master/slave situation, Bataille's sacrifices appear to be solitary. And indeed, they appear to take the place of the Hegelian recognition: if in Hegel we could not become conscious of who we are without intersubjective recognition, for Bataille we become aware of our essential negativity, that is, of our death, in an act of sacrifice. We are the animal that knows of its mortality, but how do we know this? When we have died, it is too late for us to recognize anything. How then can death become a cognitive object for us? This can happen only in the death of a substitute-victim with which we identify and that is sacrificed in our stead.[90] No other subjects are involved—except, perhaps, for the victim itself. Hegel's term for the effect of the negative as "dismemberment" (*Zerissenheit*) of nature seems to lend itself to this interpretation, and it aims at man's very own nature.[91] That animal sacrifices precede human sacrifices, as Bataille assumes, would show that sacrifices aim at destroying the animal nature in us. This sacrifice constitutes who man is and can therefore be found practically everywhere.[92] Sacrifice is the "marvelous magic of death" that touches us even before we die—in a spectacle, a representation, rituals and performances and literature. This means that language and literature are derivative from the ritual representation of sacrifice (which is indeed "*the* primary theme of representation"), just as later in Girard. In seeing a tragedy, we identify with the hero as the victim. But since it is not really our own death, it remains a "subterfuge," a comedy by which we deceive ourselves.[93] Yet in this there is an intentional excitement about sacrifice that escapes Hegel, the Protestant; it is the "sacred horror" that raises the curtain and destroys all limited meaning in bright daylight (apparently as the sublation of the limitations that the night of negation has introduced). Hegel did not see that sacrifice includes the whole movement of the *Phenomenology*; he limited it to the negative side of death, to its sadness, presumably also as opposed to its comical side.[94] Yet, the "naïve" subterfuge-customs of a "wake," which celebrates death (as one can find it in Mexican customs or in "Finnegan's Wake") is the image of one's own death in the death of another. And these customs show better than Hegel that there is a kind of exhilaration in death (as "gay anguish").[95] Bataille therefore claims that sacrifice harmonizes with pleasure, especially the pleasure of eroticism, which for him cannot be without sin and death, without defilement and irregularities like nudity; women would be the primary victim of this kind of sacrifice.[96] As we have seen earlier, for Hegel sacrifice is indeed essential to a truly human enjoyment, elevating it into cultural universals; but for Hegel this would be rather the opposite of transgression, sin, or defilement. For Bataille on the other hand, pleasure is an expression of the negativity of our freedom; pleasure is that man does as he pleases. The sacrificial pleasure of transgression would do this better than the bourgeois labor that Hegel, Marx, and Kojève find important. Labor, including the labor of concepts, would establish the meaning of the world and of our words along the lines of pragmatic utility. It ultimately leads to the homogeneity of the animal kingdom at the end of history, the state of reciprocal equilibrium that Kojève envisioned and Bataille hated. Nor can this nominalist, pragmatic world be redeemed by the bourgeois art religion of beauty. Poetry does not dissolve the utilitarian meanings of ordinary discourse. It needs the stronger measure of sacrifice and its transgressions. Of course, sacrifice itself has been made vulgar (e.g., by James Frazer's *Golden Bough*) and associated with all sorts of utility (e.g., as sacrifice for rain or the city's well-being), while in truth it is destructive of any meaning, revealing man to himself as sovereign over all meanings. Hegel, by contrast, is still trying to discover meaning, affirming the emerging linguistic medium as revelatory of the spirit, thus subordinating sacrifice to wisdom. For Hegel, the dismemberment of sacrifice is only a temporary disruption of the ascent toward meaning and intersubjective discourse.[97] Bataille, on the other hand, seems to favor a nondiscursive, asocial, existentialist, or Nietzschean subject of sacrifice, an individual that does not need other people for recognition, but only as lower-level subterfuges, while the ultimate goal is to experience one's sovereignty over all meaning in sacrificial destructions.[98]

René Girard

All of this seems far away from the notions of sacrifice in Girard. However, in his interview book *Battling to the End* Girard acknowledges Hegel's influence on his early thought. The battle for recognition between master and slave is reminiscent of the sacrificial crisis as an escalation of false differences into false identities. Accordingly, after *Deceit, Desire, and the Novel* in 1961, people saw Girard as the successor to Kojève, replacing the Hegelian desire for recognition with mimetic desire.[99] According to his own admission, Girard fought this association, without being able to deny that Hegel was in the background; self-consciousness as a recognition by the consciousness of the other did influence his reading of novels. Mimetic desire is indeed what Hegel (or perhaps rather Kojève) characterizes as the desire for the desire of another, a double desire.[100] The ensuing "bad infinity" of rivalry makes the rivals more and more alike; they are never as close to reconciliation as when they are at war.[101] Yet Girard feels a little more prosaic than Hegel. This is true in the sense that he does not want to bypass the contingencies of history, where not only Hegelian tragedy and reconciliation rules, but possibly catastrophe and the escalation to extremes. According to Girard, General Carl Philipp Gottfried von Clausewitz, confronted with the same Napoleonic wars as Hegel, saw this more clearly and articulated it as a dynamic of dueling rivals.[102] But Girard is more prosaic not only historically, but even structurally, in that mimetic desire does not primarily have to do with a struggle for recognition, but rather for real material objects (perhaps a somewhat Feuerbachian (re)turn: religion as the product of frustrated desire).[103] It is not desire *for* another desire, but desire *according to* the other's desire (although this, too, can be found in Kojève);[104] still, in the unfolding of this rivalry there emerges a more "metaphysical" desire: a desire for the being of the model (i.e., what he is, when he possesses this object). The notion of an ensuing "double mediation," in which the rivals become twins, does sound Hegelian insofar as the self is constituted by the other, and vice versa. However, the resulting subjection of one to the other, and the murderous resentment of the one subjected, are not Hegel's master and slave; nor is there any equivalent to the (almost) unanimous victimization of a third in Hegel: in a sense, Hegel remains in a twinning stage.[105] Likewise, Hegel's event of recognition is much more conciliatory, because it depends on the survival of both (if one dies, there is nobody to do the recognizing); mimetic rivalry with its more radical notion of violence on the other hand, can indeed be the bloody end; it is, in fact, always a reconciliation built on that bloody third, which Hegel would have forgotten.[106]

If we try to locate Girard among the previous authors, then he will reject Hegel's rationalism of the universal essence for the sake of real history, of which we never get a God's-eye view: "Hegel's *Phenomenology of the Mind* introduced an impressive philosophical illusion that we are finally managing to discard."[107] Even Kojève's desire for recognition and intersubjectivity might still be too rational. Desire is a rather physiological affair, and it is still directed at a material and very contingent object, as in animal desire, even if it is pursued with technological rationality.[108] For Kojève, the difference from animal desire is human freedom as a negation of the particular being. For Girard, it is our lack of instinctual determination, our indifference with regard to the objects of desire, which finds determination only in the desire of the other and hence is mimetic desire. In that sense, Girard is more prosaic than Kojève, but he is also less self-centered than Bataille, with whom he nevertheless shares an interest in the dynamics of sacrifice, including human sacrifice.[109] While for Hegel as well as for Kojève sacrifice is primarily or ultimately self-sacrifice, for both Bataille and Girard sacrifice is primarily the sacrifice of the other.[110] In Bataille's case it is to establish the mystical experience of one's own death and the sovereignty over established meanings, while in Girard's case it is the reverse: the sacrifice of the other establishes all meaning and structure in the first place.[111] Both, however, see language and representation as the outcome of ritual sacrifice, be it as "subterfuge" or as the enactment of myth. Hegel, on the other hand, seems to see language and signification as a *presupposition* of cultic sacrifice, and itself already established by recognition and other developments.[112] The linguistic medium will, for Hegel, also be the place where sacrifice and death are sublated, while for Bataille sacrifice is rather meant to destroy language and its meaning. For Girard, in turn, language begins as ritual, myth, and deceit,[113] but can develop into a "text in travail" that eventually can bring the truth to light. Unlike Hegel and Kojève, both Bataille and Girard have a sense for the mystical power of the numinous and for sacred horror, though for Girard these experiences are inherently evil. Consequently, while for Bataille sacrifice is the revelation of human greatness and enjoyment, for Girard it is bad in almost every sense of the word (although possibly a necessary evil for a time). The same is true for funeral and mourning rituals, which Bataille appreciates as related to sacrificial dynamics, while Girard is suspicious of them for the very same reasons.[114] Likewise, while Hegel and Girard would agree that Christianity has understood and articulated the true nature of sacrifice, they would disagree on its evaluation.[115] While Hegel certainly rejects human sacrifices as crude, he regards their intelligible essence as something we can still understand and appreciate today.[116]

Much of the philosophy of religion is about redemption; but what redemption is depends on what the original state and fall are conceived to be. Bataille and Kojève do not have too much to say about this. But both Hegel and Girard do, by connecting the first and the second Adam. Girard is quite explicit about this, even regarding the very role of sacrifice in it: "The 'second Adam,' to use Saint Paul's expression, revealed to us how the 'first' came to be. The Passion teaches us that humanity results from sacrifice, is born with religion."[117] In this statement, Girard is quite explicit that hominization requires the fall. In this regard, he is quite in agreement with Hegel,[118] for whom the contradiction, which human nature is, can only unfold by the fall, explicating the universal and the individual. For Hegel, however, it is unanimity *plus* one: the concrete universal posits the particular outside of itself, differentiates itself in a first sacrifice of its universality. For Girard, on the other hand, it is not only man but also the gods who originate with sacrifice: the gods are a product of the scapegoat mechanism, and they are part of our hominization.

For both, the state of nature is something that ought to be left behind. While Hegel would say this as a criticism of Rousseau, Girard might rather agree with Rousseau that the beginnings are mimetic rivalries over property: the first fencing-in creates society by creating rivalries.[119]

For Girard, however, this rivalry is as unavoidable as its sacrificial solution, a solution that creates religion as based on mimetic desire and necessary for the avoidance of violence. For Hegel, on the other hand, this is unavoidable for cognitive reasons: the fall creates religious relationships as based in reflection and re-cognition.

For both Hegel and Girard, the stage preceding religion is a state of immediacy and fluidity. For Girard it is the flood of mimetic frenzy out of which a world emerges at the beginning of Genesis, and into which it can again be submerged (as in Noah's time).[120] For Hegel this might be the liquidity of something like Friedrich Schleiermacher's and Feuerbach's religious "feeling," with which religion might begin but according to Hegel should not end.[121] Feeling needs to have or generate a rational object or representation, like the Bacchantic "Taumel" in the *Phenomenology*.[122] Perhaps more clearly, Bataille characterizes the state of the "holy" as fluid, watery immanence, immediacy, and an intimacy with itself, that is, before the profaning split between subject and object, which is then undone by sacrifice.[123] Likewise, Girard's mimetic frenzy eventually finds its object, and although it is less connected to reason, it will play a cognitive role. In either case, the beginning is a state of indifferentiation and of dissolute immediacy, feeling, or desire. I believe that this is important, because if redemption is to restore an original state, then redemption will be conceived analogously. What the second Adam is going to accomplish by his sacrifice is then likewise a state of indifferentiation and liquidity. For Girard, Christ unleashed a mimetic frenzy, which afterwards cannot be contained anymore; while it contains the possibility of an epiphany of peaceful identity, it in fact leads to the identity of violence,[124] a dissolution of all human sacrificial institutions (and there do not seem to be any other) into the chaos of the Apocalypse, the escalation of universal and global contagion, beyond which not much of redemptive value is envisioned. For Hegel, on the other hand, it is the establishment of a rational, language-based community of recognition; it is the reality of the Spirit. It might be worth noticing, however, that those in the Spirit appear drunk at Pentecost, and speaking in many languages. The medium of language that the Spirit inspires is a cognitive medium, yet in Hegel it is one that is repeatedly characterized by fluidity, and even by "universal contagion" (*allgemeine Ansteckung*); it sublates feeling and its cognitive object into the higher fluidity of intersubjectivity.[125] While Hegel's political state is a differentiated organism, a number of differences are dissolved as well, most notably the difference between the community and God, and certainly between church and state. As it was more apparent in Kojève, the question arises whether this double negation is not a return to the animal kingdom, a reestablished equilibrium with a consequent loss of individuation. The *eschaton* or end of history resembles its beginning in both cases, but in Girard with negative connotations. The reason is that there is nothing else, nothing positive to return to. There was no hominization, nothing positive before the fall that could be recovered. What starts with indifferentiation ends with indifferentiation.[126]

But does this not ignore the biblical story line? Since Adam was naming things before the fall, in response to God's creative word, was there not reason, knowledge, and language before the fall?[127] Was there not a commandment appealing to our already existing ability to understand and obey? Was language not even presupposed in Satan's lie (lies being parasitic on truth)? Were there not at least rudimentary kinds of institutions that were good rather than the work of Satan's sacrificial systems?[128] Was there not the whole positive order of creation, which precedes the fall? Was this not a differentiation and an order of elements that was the outcome of a covenant, which was not sealed with a sacrifice, but with a Sabbath? Was there not at least one human relationship preceding the fall, namely that between Adam and Eve, on which John Paul II could so profoundly reflect? What is that positive excitement that Adam experienced when he saw Eve?[129] Was there not even the possibility of making a sacrifice in the positive sense, namely by sacrificing one's self-will in an act of love and obedience?[130] Could there be a fall without this, that is, without something to fall *from*?[131] Can all this really be hidden from the foundation of the world? And the question that one can pose to Hegel can be asked of Girard as well: How could this fall be a sin, if there was no knowledge and if it was necessary for our hominization? Girard has more to say about subsequent scenarios (e.g., about Cain and Abel) than about the fall. What he does say about the fall, however, is rather puzzling: the expelled victim here is Adam (and Eve), and the victimizer appears to be

God, who builds the new world order on this expulsion.[132] Perhaps one might say that this is a text in travail, and this is actually Satan posturing as God (as Marcion might have said). Yet the snake is subject to similar punishments, after all. I do not see a particular need to mistrust the narrative here. What becomes clear is rather that Adam and Eve are not innocent victims.[133] Original sin does mean guilt; or else, if Adam and Eve are not guilty then God must be the guilty victimizer in order to lay the "foundations of the world."

Ironically, this might rather be a remythologization of the biblical narrative, treating God rather like the gods who are punishing Prometheus. The early Nietzsche saw that difference quite clearly: for him the conflict between god and man is the entrance into every culture, and cultures will vary according to this conflict. Prometheus stands for the "Aryan" culture, Adam for the Semitic culture. Prometheus's crime was a necessary sacrilege,[134] whereas Adam's misstep is characterized as contingent, as a sin in response to a temptation; Prometheus's act is an active deed of sublime defiance, whereas Adam is characterized by affectivity and curiosity, with an effeminate or female element (Eve) that is missing from the masculine Prometheus. The result is accordingly: the gods take *revenge* on Prometheus, whereas Adam is *punished*. While Nietzsche prefers Prometheus's heroism, he does see the difference clearly.[135] There is no necessary or tragic fall in Adam; the only necessary aspect that was important for hominization is the actualization of the will in an act of sacrificial obedience. And this act did not have to go the way it did.

What Girard says about the first Adam is not quite what he says about the second Adam. God does not expel or punish the second Adam (it only appears to be what he does with the "suffering servant").[136] Rather, he is sacrificed by the mechanisms of contagion.[137] Although God is on the cross, thereby guaranteeing that the victim is innocent, he does not do much else. What the cross effects is mostly cognitive—and as such not so different from Hegel; although Hegel's God is much more active, and in fact it is part of his own development, he is also not one to sacrifice his son for atonement's sake, but rather effecting a cognitive reversal as well. In Hegel, the cognitive developments of the history of religions are so many dialectic reversals, the breaking down of preconceptions, which in this sense turn out to be something like myths. This labor of concepts might be compared to the cognitive process of the text in travail. For Hegel, however, there might be even more of a continuity between the "sacrifice" of Christ and the preceding religions; it is in fact an evolution leading up teleologically to this event. For Girard there might be anticipations of the truth in the Old Testament, but he would otherwise agree with Augustine's assessment that all the gods of the pagans are demons. While for Hegel they might be cognitively necessary stages, for Girard they are just the expression of the hardened heart of the sacrificial mechanism; they do not even have the partial truth that Hegel might concede to them. Hegel can find Christ's sacrifice anticipated in the bread and wine of Ceres and Bacchus, whereas for Girard all these similarities only point to the same sacrificial mechanism that has always sacrificed innocent victims.

Dialectical reversals play a role in both Girard and Hegel. For Girard there is indeed even a place for the "ruse of reason" on the cross.[138] But this is in tune with the Greek church fathers more than with Hegel: it is about God duping the devil and putting him on display in a cognitive reversal.[139] It is a revelation by destruction, in a reversal in which the victim as such is the victor.[140] Still, the mechanics of sacrifice do display certain dialectics that are reminiscent of Hegel: double mediations, double transferences, models as mediators or go-betweens between subject and object.[141] These constitute false mediations of universal and particular: they proceed from universal frenzy and panic[142] to an individual scapegoat as a mediation of both that only produces a false universal, unanimity minus one.

What both Hegel and Girard have in common is that the cross is primarily a cognitive event. It does not effect anything but these cognitive reversals. It might change the mind of a community (eventually), but it does not effect forgiveness or atonement,[143] nor does it merit grace for our sake; it just reveals what already is the case (in Hegel's case, an already existing reconciliation; in Girard's case, the evil of the sacrificial mechanism). Nor does Jesus seem to have an abiding role in all of this; he is either sublated or just leaves the ripple effect of the cross to itself. There is no sense in which redemption forgives sins; it only deals with the causes of sin, not with their effect.[144] Nor is there a sense in which our response to these revelations would require a grace that is gained for us on the cross, and then given to us by divine agency as an ontological reality changing the soul. Grace can at best be the influence of the display itself, with its subversion of the mechanism (Girard) or as starting point for our cognitive realization of the Absolute (Hegel). There is no further sense in which Jesus died for the victims and their victimizers. If the sin that Jesus died for is therefore structural rather than moral, then the forgiveness of the moral sins might still need to be addressed otherwise; moral sin in this sense does not seem to be in the scope of Girard's theory—perhaps similar to Adam's sin, which within the theory would be a structural necessity, that is, a sin that can be neither regretted nor forgiven. Perhaps an anthropological theory does not aim at explaining theological matters; after all, Girard (to my knowledge) nowhere pretends to explain why there should be a Eucharist or any of the sacraments, or what the role of and need for prayer should be,[145] or how a personal God interacts with us.[146] Perhaps this is simply outside of his theory.

And perhaps that is also the reason why the suggestions of mimetic theory are largely negative: unveiling the evil of violence and victimization, without being able to say what should take its place. Every positive proposal therefore comes under suspicion; if all institutions, and perhaps even ethics, laws, and philosophy are as such the invention of the devil and founded on the violence of Cain,[147] then the approach becomes reminiscent of Theodor Adorno's negative dialectic—which is another honorable form of anti-Hegelian Hegelianism, declaring Hegel's Whole to be a false whole, a kind of unanimity minus one as well (in spite of itself). Yet, are all wholes false? If all institutions are dissolving today, including the family, is this good?[148] Methodologically, anthropology provides an essentially negative framework and might not offer many resources for a constructive theology.

There are, of course, elements that could be used more positively. There is a way in which there can be positive mimesis, as when Girard says that Jesus models our desire for the Father.[149] One might extrapolate from this and point out that we can indeed participate in the metaphysical being of God (i.e., the fullness of being possessed by the mediator Christ, a model who is not an obstacle), without any kind of competition and rivalry:[150] God does not lose anything, and our fellow Christians do not lose anything either; according to traditional wisdom, they rather gain by having more people involved.[151] Rivalry only emerges when it takes lesser models (and models it will indeed always need) to be that fullness. Or if a part takes itself for the whole, that is, when that which part-icipates in being wants to exist by its nature and take the place of God himself: *eritis sicut Deus*.[152] (According to

R. Schwager, the ultimate violence that we harbor is the grudge that we bear against God himself. This is why it needed a God-man to reveal it.)[153]

Without these positive elements the historical end times will look even bleaker than they are: Both Hegel and Girard do agree that historical Christianity was wrong in its understanding of itself and that the true message of Christianity has now become manifest to them.[154] And both feel that they live in the end times, either as the end of history inaugurated by Napoleon or as the approaching apocalypse (Girard).[155] For Hegel the end times are rather positive, whereas for Girard the escalation is not increasingly rational, but rather the reverse.[156] There is nothing to be done to stop this escalation but simply to cope with total dissolution and violence, kept in check only by absolute deterrence and the promises of the modern market.[157] It is something that cannot even be stopped by coming to know it (for there is no bird's-eye view of it, neither for Hegel, nor for mimetic theory, nor does revelation provide it). All that is left is Friedrich Hölderlin's silence as the only possible imitation of the withdrawal of Christ the suffering servant, a withdrawal from the systems of rivalry.[158] The only positive note appears to be a religious hope for "*peaceful* reciprocity," but this is only apparent in a *via negativa*: it is simply the only alternative, for we can only destroy each other or love each other.[159]

Realistic though this picture is, one might wonder where the church and the Holy Spirit are, which might not be victorious, but still operative, witnessing and making present the kingdom of God in a lived anticipation of the heavenly Jerusalem.

Again, all of this might be outside of the scope of an anthropological approach, but it is not incompatible with it—which is why I offer it here as a friendly amendment.

NOTES

1. E.g. the essays of G. Bataille, Robert Brandom, and Paulo Diego Bubbio, as quoted later. In the German discussion, however, Wölfle's valuable contribution rather starts from the *Lectures*, with only a concluding look at the *Phenomenology*. Gerhard Wölfle, *Kult und Opfer in Hegels Religionsphilosophie* (Tübingen: Attempto, 1999).
2. The references are to the Jaeschke edition: G. W. F. Hegel, *Vorlesungen über die Philosophie der Religion*, ed. Walter Jaeschke, vols. 1–3 (Hamburg: Meiner, 1993–95); I will quote them in the text with volume and page number.
3. In the following, I am taking some inspiration from R. B. Brandom, "The Structure of Desire and

Recognition: Self-Consciousness and Self-Constitution," *Philosophy & Social Criticism* 33, no. 1 (2007): 127–50.

4. I.e., where *verum et factum* are indeed at one, even though this has not yet appeared.

5. E.g., very clearly, Hegel, *Vorlesungen über die Philosophie der Religion*, 1:330–31, but also 1:248; practical reason expels its content as an external (i.e., as not yet achieved) and therefore objective purpose. The sacrifice, however, is also to be consumed, i.e., the reunion is to be enjoyed.

6. Brandom, "Structure of Desire and Recognition," 130.

7. "Ein Hund, / der stirbt/ und der weiß, / daß er stirbt/ wie ein Hund, / und der sagen kann, / daß er weiß, / daß er stirbt / wie ein Hund, / ist ein Mensch." Erich Fried, "Definition," in *Warngedichte* (Munich: Carl Hanser, 1964), 120 (my translation).

8. Kojève points out that killing a species is a crime: while it is not true for an individual lion (unlike a human individual), it would ("almost") be a crime to exterminate the whole species of lions. Being a species (by negation) demands recognition. A. Kojève, *Hegel: Eine Vergegenwärtigung seines Denkens*, ed. I. Fetscher (Stuttgart: Kohlhammer, 1958), 169–70.

9. In a complicated analysis, Robert Brandom shows that recognition is an equivalence relation, i.e., only if it is symmetric as well as transitive does it logically entail the desired reflexivity of self-consciousness. "Structure of Desire and Recognition," 140.

10. Paolo Diego Bubbio, "Sacrifice in Hegel's Phenomenology of Spirit," *British Journal for the History of Philosophy* 20, no. 4 (2012): 797–815. In the following I am indebted to Bubbio's article for pointing out the occurrences in Hegel's *Phenomenology*.

11. One example might be the "Reich der Sittlichkeit of the Greek" *polis*; G. W. F. Hegel, *Phänomenologie des Geistes* (Hamburg: Meiner, 1986), 265–66.

12. Ibid., 156–59.

13. At a preliminary stage the beyond is sought with longing in the Holy Sepulcher, for which the Crusades consequently fight, but mistakenly so, because it is just another particular.

14. Apparently this would not be true for Christ: he is the true *terminus medius* in this syllogism.

15. Hegel, *Phänomenologie*, 159–77.

16. Ibid., 283–91.

17. Ibid., 324–440.

18. Ibid., 523–24. G. Bataille testifies that these two pages have been part of the conversation in the twentieth-century French reception. See G. Bataille, "Hegel, la Mort et le Sacrifice," *Deucalion* 5 (1955): 21–43. For a translation of this article see, G. Bataille, "Hegel, Death and Sacrifice," trans. J. Strauss, *Yale French Studies* 78 (1990): 9–28, at 18.

19. Hegel, *Phänomenologie*, 512–44.

20. There is an early mentioning of these also in the chapter on sense-certainty, which, however, has not yet "learned to eat bread and drink wine," as something that cannot yet be understood, namely as total despair over the nothingness of the sensual world, which is simply eaten up, as by an animal. Ibid., 91.

21. There are, of course, further conflicts that will play out in tragedy, only to obliterate the gods in comedy as mere platonic universals or mere images and masks, if not caricatures of picture thinking, as our productions, over against which we have a hilarious certainty of ourselves as

the true reality (ibid., 540–44). The universal essence has now become a predicate of the self (cf. "person," state of right), rather than vice versa. Comic consciousness is happy, yet unhappy (experiencing the absence of the universal): "god is dead." It becomes mere eclectic remembering and presentation, its celebration merely frivolous entertainment or *Schwärmerei*, projecting itself back into ancient religions (perhaps like some forms of New Age). But this will set the stage for the true universal to come: the Absolute as self, rather than the self as absolute; ibid., 545–52.

22. Bloody sacrifices seem to occur only in the violent tribal battles, which, however, are the expression of animal gods.

23. "The sacrificial death offers occasion for representing God as a tyrant who demands sacrifice; this is untrue. On the contrary, the nature of God is spirit, and that being so, negation is an essential moment." G. W. F. Hegel, *Lectures on the Philosophy of Religion*, ed. and trans. Peter C. Hodgson, 3 vols. (Oxford: Oxford University Press, 1996–2008), 3:220.

24. The light of the spirit is in some way taken from the fire of sacrifice; Joseph Cohen, *Le sacrifice de Hegel* (Paris: Galilée, 2007), 47.

25. One might speculate how the chapter on phrenology aims at this in its own peculiar way.

26. I owe this quote to Bubbio, "Sacrifice in Hegel's Phenomenology of Spirit," 811; Hegel, *Phänomenologie*, 590: "Das Wissen kennt nicht nur sich, sondern auch das Negative seiner selbst oder seine Grenze. Seine Grenze wissen heißt sich aufopfern wissen. Diese Aufopferung ist die Entäußerung, in welcher der Geist sein Werden zum Geiste in der Form des *freien zufälligen Geschehens* darstellt" (i.e., as nature and history). Cf. also Cohen, *Le sacrifice de Hegel*, 50: "Toute la *Phénoménologie de l'esprit* sera la diction médiatrice de cette mort, du sacrifice qui 'deporte' le Soi-même hors de soi-même."

27. One thing it does sacrifice is religion itself as "picture thinking"—death and negation as a form of radicalized negative theology, which then is superseded by a negation of the negation: the total affirmation of the historically real (including sin, fall, and evil) as rational and as identical with God himself.

28. E.g., Hegel, *Vorlesungen über die Philosophie der Religion*, 2:428 and 144–49. Hegel likes to point out that too much is made of the ancient wisdom of the Indians, as recent research would show; e.g. 2:154.

29. Hegel should therefore not have identified Schleiermacher's "feeling of absolute dependency" with the feelings of a dog (in the *Vorrede zu Hinrichs' Religionsphilosophie* [1822]); it could be understood as precisely this immediacy. Schleiermacher does, however, seem to refuse to go beyond this starting point conceptually.

30. Even children *ought* to "lose their innocence" in this sense (Hegel, *Vorlesungen über die Philosophie der Religion*, 2:149).

31. Similar also in 1827 (ibid., 2:423). Both are cases of practical reason, producing a cleavage, as well as its reelevation by sacrifice.

32. Georg Wilhelm Friedrich Hegel, *The Logic of Hegel*, translated from the *Encyclopedia of Sciences*, by William Wallace (Oxford: Clarendon Press, 1874), 42 (preliminary notion, § 24).

33. "es hat sich noch nicht geschieden das Fürsichsein seiner und der Dinge; er sieht den Dingen ins Herz" (Hegel, *Vorlesungen über die Philosophie der Religion*, 2:145 [1824 version]). It is similar to somnambulism or *Hellsehen* (clairvoyance), an *inner* intuition (2:146).

34. He does allow for an intuitive knowledge of specific properties, comparing it to the "signatura

rerum" of medieval philosophy or the instinct of animals for what is harmful and useful (ibid., 2:150).

35. This is still the case for Kierkegaard; but for him it is also clear that this leaves us with a dilemma: How do we know that everybody falls? As a fall, it must be free; but if free then contingent and cannot be known a priori. Or else we know it (as Hegel thinks), and then it is not free, not a sin, not a fall. If this story is timeless, then Hegel's whole take on history might need to be taken with a grain of salt.

36. This etymology has been introduced precisely in this sense by Hölderlin (in the fragment "Urteil und Sein"); the first act of the mind is not synthesis (Kant), but cleavage; and only in this way can a self/ego emerge (against Fichte).

37. Hegel, *Vorlesungen über die Philosophie der Religion*, 2:425–26. It might in fact seem that Adam and Eve's innocence is God's very own state before the fall, because he is the (merely implicit and immediate) union of universal and particular as Trinity. Both creation and Adam's fall are the original cleavage of God himself, coming to a knowledge of good and evil, and indeed of himself. Creation is part of his own eternal story, which achieves self-consciousness (i.e., beatific vision) for God (3:189–204).

38. Ibid., 2:426–27. Already in the *Phenomenology* this is a process of the *Insichgehen* of the absolute, a reflection of the immediacy into itself, producing otherness, good and evil, which religious picture thinking makes into the story of Adam and Eve.

39. Ibid., 2:424. It is the "Vorstellung des Paradieses, dieser dumpfen, bewußt- und willenlosen Unschuld" (2:427).

40. Thomas Aquinas would not disagree with that; immortality is a preternatural gift for Adam; by nature, soul and body are separable, and we are therefore mortal.

41. Paradise is just a "moment" of the divine totality, one which is not the truth and has to be lost (Hegel, *Vorlesungen über die Philosophie der Religion*, 2:148).

42. Trance states, achieved by dancing, music, screaming, and sexual activity, are typical for this (ibid., 2:202); cf. Wölfle, *Kult und Opfer*, 31.

43. Hegel, *Vorlesungen über die Philosophie der Religion*, 2:446–47; the Thian's heaven is empty and does not rule; the souls of the dead belong to the emperor who rules them; ibid.

44. In the 1831 version (ibid., 2:621).

45. Ibid., 2:519–21. Precisely because death as negation has entered the godhead itself (Osiris): it is subject, not substance. Wölfle, *Kult und Opfer*, 38–39.

46. Cf. Hegel's detailed descriptions ibid., 2:433–45, including human sacrifice and cannibalism.

47. Unlike his successors, Hegel does not deny the reality of miracles. He agrees with David Hume that they cannot be proven; they are sensual and contingent and therefore unessential. But once the Gospels are accepted as God's own story, they are to be expected and believable (e.g. 1831 [these are D. Fr. Strauß's notes!]; 3:285–86); taking Jesus as a mere teacher of morality, as the Enlightenment did, is for Hegel pure unbelief. Miracles make sense, once we believe that in Jesus God himself speaks and that the Incarnation and Passion is God's own story (3:240 and 284).

48. It also leads to complaint—which is not an attitude that one would have over against fate, but only over against a personal God, as Hegel astutely observes.

49. What has not been realized is that even life is subordinate to concrete freedom (Hegel, *Vorlesungen über die Philosophie der Religion*, 2:351–52).

50. A "relative totality" (ibid., 2:579–80).

51. He dies "Einer für Alle, Einmal ist Allemal" (ibid., 3:69). His death is the transformation of his external, particular, and sensual presence into an internal, universal, and spiritual presence; this movement is repeated in Eucharistic communion, which in Hegel's scheme is neither external (Catholic) nor mere *Er-innerung*, internal memory (Reformed).

52. This and the following: ibid., 3:244–50.

53. It seems to remain something external; ibid., 3:247–48.

54. Cf. also Wölfle, *Kult und Opfer*, 65.

55. Hegel, *Vorlesungen über die Philosophie der Religion*, 3:260–61. "What is represented in the sacrament is that Christ is eternally sacrificed and rises again in the heart; this is correct. The eternal sacrifice is the process through which single individuals make themselves their own, the process by which their implicit being passes away" (Hegel, *Lectures*, trans. Hodgson 3:236; similar: 3:152–53).

56. Hegel, *Vorlesungen über die Philosophie der Religion*, 3:262–65. "Der Staat ist die wahrhafte Weise der Wirklichkeit." Das Verhältnis der Religion zum Staat, nach der Vorlesung von 1831 (1:339–47).

57. The French Revolution is the theoretical Indian asceticism put into practice; a self-consciousness that actualizes and feels itself only in the fury of destruction. In his description of Hindu sacrifices, Hegel uses the same term he employs in the *Phenomenology* for the guillotine: human life is not worth more than "ein Schluck Wassers." Hegel, *Vorlesungen über die Philosophie der Religion*, 2:497.

58. "das Subjekt kann das Geschehene nicht ungeschehen machen und auch nicht bereuen, daß es so gehandelt habe" (Ibid., 1:255). Perhaps one might think of R. Swinburne's example: accidentally knocking over the precious vase of a friend: there is no fault, yet a need for restitution. Richard Swinburne, *Responsibility and Atonement* (Oxford: Oxford University Press, 1989), 74.

59. Cf. the *Manuscript* (Hegel, *Vorlesungen über die Philosophie der Religion*, 2:18–26).

60. Ibid., 1:250 and 254–55. For the early stage: "nicht das Herz ist zu durchbohren, sondern die Natürlichkeit des Menschen"; ibid.

61. In the *Manuscript* (ibid., 2:18–26).

62. "Insofern ist Sittlichkeit der wahrhafteste Kultus" (ibid., 1:334–35) This might sound like Kant, but unlike Kant, for Hegel there is a real continuity with the cult of religion.

63. "Philosophie [ist] ein beständiger Kultus" (ibid., 1:334–35). It is the one true relation to God; religion as cultic has its own kind of knowledge of God (especially in Christian dogmatic theology, which has no parallel in other religions), but philosophy is the "knowledge of this knowledge" ("ist das Wissen dieses Wissens. Das ist die wahre Religion."); 1:335–38.

64. Hegel, *Lectures*, trans. Hodgson, 3:327. It is the elevation from the finite to the infinite; e.g. Cohen, *Le sacrifice de Hegel*, 176.

65. Cf. also Wölfle, *Kult und Opfer*, 27, who rightly points out that Hegel does not sufficiently distinguish between finitude and evil; ibid., 64.

66. "the nature of God is spirit, and that being so, negation is an essential moment." Hegel, *Lectures*, trans. Hodgson, 3:220.

67. "This is not a single act, but the eternal divine history: it is a moment in the nature of God himself; it has taken place in God himself." Ibid., 3:327–28. "For it is *this* suffering and death, this sacrificial death of the individual for all, that is the nature of God, the divine history." Ibid., 3:219. For Cohen, this is a double sacrifice (i.e., a double negation): the sacrifice of the sacrifice is the very nature (*quiddité*) of the Self, which cannot itself be sacrificed without loss of the Self. It is ultimately the act of love and gift of oneself and finding oneself in the other. Cohen, *Le sacrifice de Hegel*, 178 and 47. The sacrifice sacrifices by sacrificing sacrifice itself; ibid., 187. Cohen's equation of *Aufhebung* and *Aufopferung* (196), however, blurs the distinction between double and simple negation. For Cohen, sacrifice is an act of love, because it is a sacrifice for another—in the sense of an act of the witness of one's own irreplaceable death as a gift of recognition, which establishes an infinite presence; ibid., 45–46. This would appear to be a very free association, based on Hegel's text.

68. "For the personality that does not sacrifice itself in the divine idea is evil." Hegel, *Lectures*, trans. Hodgson, 3:194.

69. Wölfle, *Kult und Opfer*, 76–77.

70. Let alone that it would explain creation and the origin of the many as such; dissatisfaction with such a view might be found also in Schelling's appeal to a primordial *will* rather than intellect in God.

71. Even less would this explain the fall of the angels (although Tertullian seems to attribute concupiscence to them).

72. Cf. Robert Spaemann, "Über einige Schwierigkeiten mit der Erbsündenlehre," in *Das unsterbliche Gerücht*, ed. R. Spaemann (Stuttgart: Klett-Cotta, 2007), 185–211, 202–3. This might combine features of Kant's moral philosophy with his aesthetics of the "dynamically sublime."

73. Reason itself might have been actualized in Adam's naming of things, as well as in the understanding of God's commandment. But while reason is a necessary condition for free will, it is not a sufficient condition. It requires a different kind of challenge for its actualization. For Aquinas, however, disobedience itself results from Adam's disordered desire for his own spiritual excellence; Aquinas, *Summa theologiae*, II-II, 163, 1c and ad 1; this excellence could have been the very power of the will itself (ibid., II-II, 163, 2c), whose disorder consists in that very disobedience.

74. That might be the relationship of recognition that Job had to learn; it required more than conventional wisdom. Hegel himself sees that the recognition of God's power was more than mere following of the law (Wölfle, *Kult und Opfer*, 48). It was this relationship of obedience on which Abraham had to rely already when he left Ur.

75. Spaemann, "Über einige Schwierigkeiten mit der Erbsündenlehre," 200–203. Hence the quest for natural immortality in fertility cults, of which the snake might be a symbol; cf. Joseph Ratzinger, *Im Anfang schuf Gott* (Munich: Erich Wewel Verlag, 1986). Refusal of obedience leads back to the zoo of the animal kingdom, but now with added labor pains.

76. Death itself might have redemptive functions as a memento mori, or in a secularized form: as a call to authenticity. Eating from the tree of life in paradise would have prevented this remedy; this was the reason for the expulsion of Adam and Eve, not their victimization. Perhaps even the old law with its "obsessive differentiations" (René Girard, *Things Hidden since the Foundation of the World*, research undertaken in collaboration with with J.-M. Oughourlian and G. Lefort, trans. Stephen

Bann and Michael Metteer [Stanford, CA: Stanford University Press, 1987], 154) in some of its arbitrariness (the abominations of Leviticus?) is pedagogical in requiring an obedience for its own sake—maybe so as to overcorrect the original mistake.

77. Had Adam not fallen, our relationship with God would still have exceeded our natural powers, but it would have been without the pain of sacrifice, but a pure, unbloody act of devotion. There would have been no labor pains, not even for the philosophical labor of concepts. Now, however, we have to grow, mature in painful decision-makings and renunciations, reinforcing our commitments in spite of ourselves. These sacrifices are a good thing. They might prove the fall in retrospect even to be a felix culpa.

78. Even Carl Schmitt's notion of the enemy, at least in *Ex Captivitate Salus*, was influenced by Kojève; cf. the interesting quote (including the fraternal rivalry between Cain and Abel) in Wolfgang Palaver, *René Girard's Mimetic Theory* (East Lansing: Michigan State University Press, 2013), 112.

79. For Kojève, the *Phenomenology of the Spirit* is truly understood only through *Being and Time*. Kojève, *Hegel*, 190. However, for Kojève, Heidegger might not quite have understood the importance of history; ibid., 234. All of this complements the additional influence of Karl Marx. Kojève's influence in America includes Allan Bloom, Stanley Rosen, and Francis Fukuyama.

80. Kojève, *Hegel*, 173–83. Both freedom and individuality (as a result of free decision and conversion) emerge radically only with Christianity; ibid., 196–97.

81. Ibid., 95–109. Kojève mentions that according to Kant, concepts are applied to things only by way of the temporal schematisms—something that was of interest to Heidegger as well; ibid., 105–6. Labor itself is a form of negation of what is natural; labor is therefore always forced; ibid., 162.

82. Ibid., 110; cf. also 198–99, explicating Hegel, of course. Being willing to die might imply most consequently suicide. But what is most interesting for Kojève is the nihilist who stays alive. Ibid., 53–54.

83. This state is capitalistic rather than communist; it does imply universal recognition in a global, homogeneous society, dominated by absolute knowledge and abstract art (Kandinsky was Kojève's uncle). Kojève consequently stops, within the *Phenomenology*, at the master/slave dialectic (as the beginning of history), and with the Being-Nothingness-Becoming triad in the *Logic*. The same is true for Sartre (*Being and Nothingness*); cf. Robert R. Williams, *Hegel's Ethics of Recognition* (Berkeley: University of California Press, 2000), 366–71.

84. Kojève, *Hegel*, 222. We might be less inclined to attribute such spiritual benefits to war: PTSD has preplaced recognition for soldiers. Girard might be less surprised by this development. In an odd way it is particularly totalitarian states that appear to take their citizens seriously enough to kill them—which would then be their peculiar act of recognition. Ibid., 208 and 212–17.

85. Something that distinguishes us from animals, which is the level on which Epicurus envisions it; ibid., 186.

86. Ibid., 186–90, 223. Apparently, Kojève changed his thought about the terminus a quo of this end of history from Napoleon (with his *wars*), to Stalin, to the West (Palaver, *René Girard's Mimetic Theory*, 116); the rest is administration—he consequently became a bureaucrat.

87. Kojève, *Hegel*, 200–201.

88. That essence is rather, with Feuerbach and Marx, a form of alienation that man needs to reclaim.

89. Bataille, "Hegel, la Mort et le Sacrifice." Bataille, "Hegel, Death and Sacrifice." Bataille, however, shared this interest with the "College of Sociology" and the Surrealists.

90. Bataille, "Hegel, Death and Sacrifice," 19.

91. Ibid., 14–15.

92. Ibid., 18.

93. Ibid., 20.

94. Ibid., 21–22. This would also be true for Kojève, where it remains unclear how the mere negativity of dismemberment relates to the satisfaction of recognition. Ibid., 22–23.

95. Ibid., 24–25. This might be compared to Girard's analysis of mourning rituals as inherently sacrificial.

96. Ibid., 23. He almost makes it sound as if the only truly human enjoyment is rape-murder.

97. It is really still servile meaning (rather than its sovereign sacrifice), fleeing absolute negation and death; it is the repressed slave, subsequently becoming the master in Hegel's philosophy, as Derrida points out with reference to Bataille; cf. Williams, *Hegel's Ethics of Recognition*, 404–5.

98. Something like a Nietzschean revaluation of all values might be the goal, i.e., a new, personal mythos, based on the violence of a sacrifice.

99. R. Schwager later observes "surprising parallels" as well, although according to Schwager, Hegel never gets to the other as the other, but only to mimetic doubles; Raymund Schwager, *Must There Be Scapegoats? Violence and Redemption in the Bible*, trans. Maria L. Assad (San Francisco: Harper & Row, 1987), 39.

100. E.g. René Girard, *I See Satan Fall Like Lightning*, trans. James G. Williams (Maryknoll, NY: Orbis, 2001), 16.

101. René Girard, *Battling to the End: Conversations with Benoît Chantre*, trans. Mary Baker (East Lansing: Michigan State University Press, 2010), 30.

102. Ibid., 28–29. For both, however, Napoleon is, in varying ways, the beginning of the end of history.

103. Girard, *Things Hidden since the Foundation of the World*, 320.

104. Cf. Palaver, *René Girard's Mimetic Theory*, 114–15.

105. Girard, *Battling to the End*, 30–31.

106. Ibid., 32.

107. Ibid., 27. This is also an articulation of Girard's understanding that philosophy as such is still complicit with sacrifice and mythos; logos and mythos are *not* opposed; Heraclitus's logos is the same kind of thing (Girard, *Things Hidden since the Foundation of the World*, 263–66). Perhaps one would therefore need to amend St. Anselm: *fides quaerens anthropologiam?* But what is the status of anthropology?

108. E.g. by the war machinery of Clausewitz; Girard, *Battling to the End*, 34.

109. An interest in human sacrifice inspired the foundation of the secret society "Acéphale" (its symbol was a decapitated man). "According to legend, Bataille and the other members of Acéphale each agreed to be the sacrificial victim as an inauguration; none of them would agree to be the executioner. An indemnity was offered for an executioner, but none was found before the dissolution of Acéphale shortly before the war" ("Georges Bataille," New World Encyclopedia,

http://www.newworldencyclopedia.org/entry/Georges_Bataille). They celebrated the decapitation of Louis XVI, an event that prefigured the "chiefless crowd" targeted by "acéphalité."

110. Girard is even opposed to Christian notions of self-sacrifice as self-divinizations: *Things Hidden since the Foundation of the World*, 236–37.

111. Sacrifice establishes identity (even collectively) in the sense that R. Brandom found in Hegel; see above. Furthermore, the victim is the scapegoat, the expelled third, cast out from the binary oppositions, the system regulated by the play of sacred difference. Ibid., 50. Lévi-Strauss is the myth without the skeleton in the closet; ibid., 64. This skeleton turns out to be the first real signifier.

112. Indeed, religion is a very late stage altogether for Hegel, at least systematically, if not historically.

113. E.g. Girard, *Things Hidden since the Foundation of the World*, 103–4.

114. E.g. ibid., 80–83.

115. In a sense, for Hegel Christianity is the only religion that has made sacrifice its inner law. Cohen, *Le sacrifice de Hegel*, 182.

116. He disclaims any justification of child sacrifices and the like; they remain "schauderhaft" and "abgeschmackt" (Hegel, *Vorlesungen über die Philosophie der Religion*, 1:107–8); cf. also Wölfle, *Kult und Opfer*, 11.

117. Girard, *Battling to the End*, xv.

118. I would consider it less important that Hegel does not know about animal mimesis (i.e., *pace* Palaver, *René Girard's Mimetic Theory*, 119).

119. The original state would be characterized by isolation—something that ideally might be restored in the voting cabin (avoiding mimesis, perhaps making us into "so many little Descartes" [Girard, *I See Satan Fall Like Lightning*, 88], entering rationally into social contracts behind the veil of ignorance), or else completely reversed in the unanimity of the *volonté générale*, which one might suspect of sacrificial overtones.

120. E.g. Girard, *Things Hidden since the Foundation of the World*, 143 and 148.

121. And this was also, against the Enlightenment, Hegel's early understanding of religion; Walter Jaeschke, "Speculative and Anthropological Criticism of Religion: A Theological Orientation to Hegel and Feuerbach," *Journal of the American Academy of Religion* 48 (1980): 348–51. Feeling is also the starting point for his psychology in the *Encyclopedia* (G. W. F. Hegel, *Enzyklopädie der philosophischen Wissenschaften* [Hamburg: Meiner, 1975], 361–62.). This might be akin to "stream of consciousness" theories in W. James or Edmund Husserl and others, a kind of neutral monism, preceding the subject/object split (Bertrand Russell, perhaps still under the influence of his early Hegelianism?), comparable perhaps also to Lacan's "Real" (Lacan got his Hegelianism through Kojève as well).

122. Hegel, *Phänomenologie*, 528. It remains the right of the subject, however, to experience religion in this immediacy, testifying to his heart; on the other hand, the heart cannot discriminate between good and evil, just as Adam cannot; it needs representation and cognitive education; only if the heart knows what its master is doing, is it truly free (Hegel, *Vorlesungen über die Philosophie der Religion*, 1:285–98).

123. Cf. Wölfle, *Kult und Opfer*, 14–16.

124. Girard, *Battling to the End*, 46. Also René Girard, *Violence and the Sacred* (Baltimore: Johns Hopkins University Press, 1977), 188–89.

125. "Das Kunstwerk erfordert daher ein anderes Element seines Daseins, der Gott einen andern Hervorgang als diesen, worin er aus der Tiefe seiner schöpferischen Nacht in das Gegenteil in die Äußerlichkeit, die Bestimmung des selbstbewußtlosen *Dinges* herabfällt. Dies höhere Element ist die *Sprache*—ein Dasein, das unmittelbar selbstbewußte Existenz ist. Wie das *einzelne* Selbstbewußtsein in ihr da ist, ist es ebenso unmittelbar als eine *allgemeine* Ansteckung; die vollkommne Besonderung des Für-sich-seins ist zugleich die Flüssigkeit und die allgemein mitgeteilte Einheit der vielen Selbst; sie ist die als Seele existierende Seele. Der Gott also, der die Sprache zum Elemente seiner Gestalt hat, ist das an ihm selbst beseelte Kunstwerk, das die reine Tätigkeit, die ihm, der als Ding existierte, gegenüber war, unmittelbar in seinem Dasein hat." Hegel, *Phänomenologie*, 518–19. (*Das abstrakte Kunstwerk*).

126. Monistic philosophies tend to be antisacrificial. Where the Godhead is seen as a "Monad," as the Neoplatonic "One," the mystical entry into the One is not a sacrifice. Plotinus criticizes the notion of sacrifice precisely for this reason; likewise, where the ultimate "reality" is Nothing, as in Arthur Schopenhauer, sacrifice does not play a role either; for Christianity as Trinitarian, on the other hand, sacrifice seems to be the essential way to relate to God; cf. the comment of Theo Kobusch, in *Zur Theorie des Opfers*, ed. by Richard Schenk (Stuttgart: Frommann-Holzboog, 1995), 170.

127. For Aquinas Adam was created as an adult not just physically but also mentally (including infused knowledge); *Summa theologiae* I, 94, 3. Adam and Eve were not even deceived by the snake, except by way of the already beginning sinful inclinations of pride; I, 94, 4 ad1.

128. Thomas Aquinas, for example, envisions a social state, in case the fall had not happened (*Summa theologiae* I, 96). Adam would not have ruled as a victim with a suspended sentence, unlike Girard's "sacred kingship" (*Things Hidden since the Foundation of the World*, 51–57).

129. Similar: Gil Bailie, "Raising the Ante: Recovering an Alpha and Omega Christology," *Communio* 35 (2008): 83–106, especially 94–95. Could this be something like a positive "catharsis"? As a form of disclosure of the other?

130. For Aquinas, sacrifice is part of the natural virtue of religion, which in turn is part of the virtue of justice, which gives to everyone, including God, what is his own. As such it belongs not primarily to the doing of penance but to holiness (*Summa theologiae*, II-II, 85). Christ completed all the sacrifices, including those of atonement; but the most generic sense is, with St. Augustine, "every good work done in order that we might cling to God in holy fellowship, yet referred to that consummation of happiness wherein which we can truly be blessed." Cf. Matthew Levering, *Christ's Fulfillment of Torah and Temple* (Notre Dame: University of Notre Dame Press, 2002), 55. According to Augustine every consecrated person (and even the whole city of God) is a sacrifice; Augustine, *The City of God*, 10, 6 (New York: Modern Library, 1994), 309–10. According to Thomas, there would have to be sacrifices, even apart from original sin and only according to natural law. In the order of things the lower things are exhibiting honor and subjection to the higher things. And for human beings this has to be expressed by material signs, because of our incarnational structure. It is an offering of one's soul to God; *Summa theologiae*, II-II, 85, 1 and 2. In it "anima seipsum offert Deo sicut principio suae creationis, et sicut fini sui beatificationis" (*Summa theologiae*, II-II, 85, 2). Elsewhere he mentions also that sacrifice is offered "ad hoc quod spiritus hominis perfecte Deo uniatur," and this "maxime erit in gloria" (*Summa theologiae*, III, 22, 2).

131. This is also the critique of Robert Spaemann, "Bemerkungen zum Opferbegriff," in Schenk, *Zur Theorie des Opfers*, 15 and 18. In Girard, aggression and the act of killing are something *primary*;

R. Schwager, *Der wunderbare Tausch: Zur Geschichte und Deutung der Erlösungslehre* (Munich: Kösel, 1986), 225.

132. Girard, *Things Hidden since the Foundation of the World*, 142. Of this, H. U. v. Balthasar has been rightly critical; *Theodramatik* (Einsiedeln: Johannes Verlag, 1980), 3:282.

133. The expulsion of Adam and Eve, unlike that of the falling Satan himself, is a medicinal one.

134. It is necessary, because in order to know nature, you have to violate nature; the same can be said for Oedipus; cf. Friedrich Nietzsche, *Die Geburt der Tragödie aus dem Geist der Musik*, § 9 (Leipzig: C.G. Naumann, 1907), 68–72.

135. Ibid.

136. Girard, *Things Hidden since the Foundation of the World*, 157.

137. Girard, *I See Satan Fall Like Lightning*, 21.

138. Ibid., 149–52. Typically he will be rather suspicious of those ruses of reason that go on behind our backs.

139. "The powers are not put on display because they are defeated, but they are defeated, because they are put on display." Ibid., 143–44.

140. Ibid., 143.

141. Ibid., ix. Perhaps one might consider the whole of history as a double negation: from animal stage through the negation of a victim, to the double negation of the contemporary victimization of the victimizers, in which we are most interested in those victims that allow us to accuse/victimize our neighbors, with Christianity (and the biblical text; Girard, *Things Hidden since the Foundation of the World*, 177–78) itself as the "scapegoat of the ultimate resort" (*I See Satan Fall Like Lightning*, 164) and mimetic rivalry in concern for victims (ibid., 167–68), which also produces a return of pagan practices: abortion, euthanasia, sexual undifferentiation, circus games (even if without real victims); ibid., 181. Another double negation: the divinization of the victims of myth is negated/does not happen in the Old Testament, but reoccurs on the cross; ibid., 121.

142. Ibid., 69.

143. According to R. Schwager, God simply forgives unconditionally: Schwager, *Must There Be Scapegoats?*, 241.

144. Yet Jesus did not merely die from our sins, but for our sins (1 Corinthians 15), as is noticed also by Balthasar, *Theodramatik*, 3:247–48. Otherwise this might also trivialize the death of Christ, since everybody dies from somebody's sin (including the sin of Adam).

145. Among other aspects, one might wonder, whether prayer is something like an offering (sacrifice) that is owed to God. "Keep burning continually the sweet-smelling incense of prayer. Take up the sword of the Spirit. Let your heart be an altar. Then, with full confidence in God, present your body for sacrifice. God desires not death, but faith; God thirsts not for blood, but for self-surrender; God is appeased not by slaughter, but by the offering of your free will." Peter Chrysologus, *Sermo* 108, in *Patrologiae Cursus Completus, Series Latina*, ed. by Jacques-Paul Migne, 221 vols. (Paris: Migne, 1844–64), 52, cols. 499–500.

146. Accordingly, while in Hegel the relationship between Father and Son is crucial (even if not as atonement), for Girard it does not seem to play a role. Although in *I See Satan Fall Like Lightning*, 15 he does say that Jesus models our desire for the Father, and there is therefore a true "imitation of Christ." Yet not as self-sacrifice: *Things Hidden since the Foundation of the World*, 236–37. More

recently this seems to have been revised: René Girard, *The Girard Reader*, ed. James G. Williams (New York: Crossroad, 1996), 272 and 282.

147. Girard, *I See Satan Fall Like Lightning*, 83–94, and *Things Hidden since the Foundation of the World*, 144–48. In a sense, the law provokes the desire for what it forbids (*I See Satan Fall Like Lightning*, 14); it sets up an obstacle; in a sense the law itself becomes a rival, making us want to "possesses what is on the other side of the fence" and resent that "melior est conditio possidentis."

148. For Girard this includes the family as well as the church hierarchy; Girard, *Things Hidden since the Foundation of the World*, 208.

149. Girard, *I See Satan Fall Like Lightning*, 13. We choose to imitate either God or Satan, *tertium non datur*; ibid., 42. It is not quite clear why the mimesis of art, or the imitation by which children learn, should be rejected (both, of course, can be found in Aristotle). Are we not indeed made to transcend ourselves toward a universal good, possessing a soul which is *quodammodo omnia*, being able to imitate everything? And so, Girard does indeed acknowledge that mimetic desire is intrinsically good; it is responsible for the best and the worst in us (ibid., 15–16). However, the good mimesis remains secondary to the bad one: Girard, *Reader*, 268–69.

150. Unlike material goods, spiritual goods grow by being shared (e.g., knowledge), although there might be exceptions, as for example fame.

151. Someone to explore possibilities of a preceding positive communion, from which the fall would have occurred, is Bailie, "Raising the Ante," 94–95. This would be only the fleeting moment of recognition between Adam and Eve, however.

152. Attempting to exist by one's own nature, and therefore unrestrictedly; unanimity as one minus the rest. That might be the mimetic rivalry that made Satan fall like lightning; anticipating the incarnation of the second Adam as a rival might be reason enough to tempt the first Adam.

153. Schwager, *Must There Be Scapegoats?*, 193–200. All scapegoats had therefore already something of God, which makes for their "sacred" character in a legitimate sense. Ibid., 199–200. This seems to imply that all sacrifices are ultimately satanic, directed against God. Sacrifices do not try to offer something to God, but rather try to kill him.

154. For Girard, the churches as well as their enemies are mistaken in their sacrificial reading of the text; *Things Hidden since the Foundation of the World*, 185; and even the text is infected with minor defects (ibid., 188), especially the letter to the Hebrews (ibid., 227–31).

155. While Girard does reject Hegelian notions of the "end of history" (Palaver, *René Girard's Mimetic Theory*, 119), he does envision an apocalyptic end.

156. Girard, *Battling to the End*, 48. It is now an escalation of competition among victims, somehow victimizing their victimizers; ibid., 111.

157. By "the bomb"—in the singular: mimetic rivals becoming identical twins; at the same time they are named after Greek gods, and adoring its own destructive power; Girard, *Things Hidden since the Foundation of the World*, 256–58. The de-differentiated desires can attach to just any object, and the promise is to satisfy them all without rivalry—through technology and the market.

158. Girard, *Battling to the End*, 46–47.

159. Girard, *Battling to the End*, 48. Strictly speaking this might be more optimism than hope, because hope has to do with eternal salvation, whereas the revealed promises for the end of history are no reason for optimism.

Reason and Revelation: An Important Distinction?

John Ranieri

Among twentieth-century political philosophers, Eric Voegelin stands out; not only for his insistence on the relevance of religion for political philosophy, but for the attention he gave to analyzing the kinds of experiences that underlie both religious and political phenomena. The most decisive shift in his thought occurred when he abandoned an approach based upon an analysis of political ideas and adopted a method that sought to gain access to the experiences out of which ideas emerged.[1] This change in orientation enabled him to penetrate ever more deeply to a level of experience where apparent differences in ideas were discovered to be experientially similar. After this turn in his thought, much of his theoretical work was focused on an attempt to articulate a set of terms and relations that could encompass the most varied kinds of experience. During this process Voegelin displayed a remarkable openness and willingness to revise his terminology in light of his examination of data, advances in scholarship, and his own best insights. This pursuit of a common, experientially grounded language was for him inseparable from his aims as a political philosopher. Ever attentive to the violent consequences that so frequently follow the hardening of political ideas into positions that must be defended at any cost, he understood his life work to be in part an attempt to get beyond ideological posturing by means of the articulation of a language rooted in experiences recognizable to those of seemingly disparate traditions. Voegelin took his role as public philosopher with the utmost seriousness. In a lecture entitled "Theology Confronting World Religions?" this attitude comes through strongly:

> The possibility of effective dialogue depends on the existence of a common medium of experience and of language in which to talk. If there is no common experience and no common language, one does not get very far. Sometimes, too, what looks like a common language isn't one at all. It actually hides the differences.[2]

Of course, the desire for a common language does not guarantee that it actually exists or that it could even be developed. For some, Voegelin's efforts might well be regarded as an exercise in nostalgia, a longing for a time in which people of various faiths and philosophies could at least communicate by means of a shared metaphysical vocabulary. In addition, pertinent questions can be asked as to whether the development of such a language is at all desirable or useful. One danger is that in order to accommodate the diversity of "wisdom" traditions, this language would have to be so generic as to be practically meaningless. Another possible problem would be that any self-described "common" terminology runs the risk of presenting as universal what is in fact only a particular, limited perspective. It is this latter possibility that interests me here. In particular, I wish to consider whether Voegelin's development of a common experiential language leads to a method that is adequate for handling biblical texts. More specifically, I am interested in whether his mature theory is able to do justice to the distinction between reason and revelation that has emerged in those religious traditions that have developed under biblical influence. What is at stake in this question will be considered through an examination of the approach taken by René Girard; making use of his insights to illuminate and critique Voegelin's position.

We will begin to approach the issue by considering a point made by philosopher and theologian Bernard Lonergan in his essay "Natural Knowledge of God." Lonergan concludes the essay with the following observation: "I do not think that in this life people arrive at natural knowledge of God without God's grace, but what I do not doubt is that the knowledge they so attain is natural."[3] Lonergan is here arguing for the relevance of the doctrine concerning natural knowledge of God affirmed by the First Vatican Council.

He reminds his readers how Vatican I, in defending natural knowledge of God, was speaking of a *quaestio iuris* rather than *quaestio facti*, a matter of possibility rather than a matter of fact. In his reading, the relevant conciliar document, *Dei Filius*, "does not commit itself either to saying that the possibility ever was realized or to predicting that it ever would be realized." He then goes on to specify some of the conditions that would have to be fulfilled in order for people to reach such knowledge. Among them, "[they] must have succeeded in avoiding all the pitfalls in which so many great philosophers have become entrapped," and "[they] must resist their personal evil tendencies and not be seduced by the bad example of others."[4] In other words, the exercise of natural reason, while in principle able to come to knowledge of God, is beset with difficulties that either weaken or, more drastically, even render inoperative this natural capacity. The conditions under which we think and act frequently impair the natural exercise of our reason.

Girard understands this well. By showing the ways in which we, as members of any given culture, are already shaped (or more accurately, distorted) by the effects of the scapegoating mechanism, he describes the factual situation in which the pursuit of knowledge (including knowledge of God) occurs. We operate within societies already structured by the effects of mimetic rivalry and the single-victim mechanism. Girard shows how profoundly these practices skew every aspect of culture and society. They quite literally constitute the horizon within which human life unfolds. What we take to be normal, even rational, is already twisted by the effects of scapegoating. If at the origins of every culture there is an act of victimization, then every area of human endeavor will bear traces of this violent origin, including human understanding.

It is within this context that the following claim must be understood: "Our own rationality cannot reach the founding role of mimetic victimage because it remains tainted with it. Narrow rationality and victimage lose their effectiveness together. Reason itself is a child of the foundational murder."[5] Girard is not here dismissing the role of intelligence and reasonableness in human life. He is arguing that appeals to "reason" that seek to justify a particular course of action must themselves be subject to critical scrutiny in light of the disclosure of how the single-victim mechanism functions within societies. He calls our attention to the fact that any given understanding of "reason" arises within a particular cultural context and that those operating within that context are for the most part unaware of their involvement with scapegoating practices. For Girard, this is the pervasive illusion of all those who would justify their own acts of victimization by an appeal to reason. It is difficult, if not impossible, to argue with those who are convinced that, unlike their opponents, they alone follow the dictates of reason.

Girard in no way disparages reason, but he cautions us that reason needs to become aware of its own involvement with scapegoating in order to be faithful to the exigencies of its own reasonableness. This is not a matter of liberating a Cartesian "thinking thing" from the tangle of mimetic desire. Humans remain mimetic creatures, constituted in their selfhood by borrowing the desires of others. The image of the autonomous, solitary self drawing out rational principles through reflection on its own cognitional activity is itself a dangerous distortion. This is one of the illusions from which reason must be freed in order to operate authentically. If Girard is correct in his account of how humanity's reliance on victimizing practices distorts all aspects of culture, then reason is both unaware of and thus powerless to do anything about its predicament. Enmeshed in a culture, it takes as normative the dictates of that culture. Reason, as concretely operating within a community, shares, however unwittingly, in the lie involved in the "misremembering" of the community's victimary foundations.[6] Thus imprisoned, it needs to be freed in order to exercise its inherent, "natural" capacities. Reason, thus liberated, would then become more capable of operating in accordance with its own innate tendencies.

James Alison makes a similar point:

> Humans constituted by and living in the world of rivalistic mimetic desire are no less mimetically constituted in alterity than the revealer of the divine beneficent mimesis: his human nature is the same as ours. This means that humans do not need to cease to be the sort of animal that they are in order to see the lie which has constituted us. Put in other words: we are capable of recognizing that we are wrong.[7]

To say that we are *capable* of recognizing that we are wrong is to maintain that human intelligence, despite the aberrations to which it is subject due to the effects of the ongoing operation of structures of victimization, retains enough of its original integrity to be able to understand its own distortions when confronted with them. In line with this insight, to say that *we* are capable of recognizing that we are wrong is to argue that our identity as persons is not canceled out by the process of liberation from the lies in which we have been ensnared. The process of conversion transforms; it does not annihilate the self. To misunderstand ourselves and to be able to recognize this implies that we, at least in principle, possess the capacity for developing into persons whose humanity is not so distorted and that there is a continuity of identity between the person who can be brought to this recognition and the person who is transformed through this process.

The crucial question then becomes how people come to know that they are wrong. The effectiveness of the scapegoating mechanism depends upon it remaining unrecognized. Blindness on the part of those who scapegoat is an essential element in successful victimization. The more pervasive the lie, the more communities and individuals become incapable of understanding the truth. What is in fact a distortion at the heart of the cultural and social order comes to be understood as not only normal, but praiseworthy. For according to the self-understanding of scapegoaters, only the guilty are punished. Utterly convinced of the justness of their actions, human beings become prisoners of their own solution to the problem of the violence, unaware of their bondage to the single-victim mechanism and thus incapable of imagining an alternative. Such a predicament requires a liberating insight that eludes us. Humanity is in need of the grace of revelation.

Girard acknowledges this need when he says that "the idea of grace in Christianity or Judaism is precisely that the truth cannot be known by human means because it is always buried by the mechanism of Satan."[8] "Satan," for Girard, is the New Testament's way of speaking about violent contagion and the means by which it brings about order through the mechanism of victimization—hence Satan's titles as the sower of discord, the accuser, the prince of this world, and the father of lies. If humanity is indeed imprisoned in falsehood, then revelation is necessary if we are to understand our plight. In the conclusion of *I See Satan Fall Like Lightning* Girard writes:

> Until now I have been able to find plausible responses to the questions posed in this book within a purely commonsensical and "anthropological"

> context. This time, however, it is impossible. To break the power of mimetic unanimity, we must postulate a power superior to violent contagion. If we have learned one thing in this study, it is that none exists on earth. It is precisely because violent contagion was all-powerful in human societies, prior to the day of Resurrection, that archaic religion divinized it. . . . The Resurrection is not only a miracle, a prodigious transgression of natural laws. It is the spectacular sign of the entrance into the world of a power superior to violent contagion.[9]

From Girard's perspective, the anthropological insights contained in the Judeo-Christian scriptures point beyond themselves toward an intelligence that explains their presence in the biblical text:

> There is an irreducible supernatural dimension to the Gospels that I do not wish to deny or denigrate. . . . The rationality I am disclosing, the mimeticism of human relations, is too systematic in principle, too complex in its effects, and too visibly present, both in the "theoretical" passages on scandal and in the accounts entirely controlled by it, to be there by accident. Nevertheless this rationality was not completely devised or created by those who put it there. . . . At the text's origin there must have been someone outside the group, a higher intelligence that controlled the disciples and inspired their writings. As we succeed in reconstituting the mimetic theory in a kind of coming and going between the narratives and the theoretical passages, the words attributed to Jesus, we are disclosing the traces of that intelligence, not the reflections of the disciples.[10]

Understood in this fashion "revelation" is not contrary to reason, but is itself a higher form of intelligibility that does not displace, but heals and illuminates the human reality in which it occurs. In Girard's thought there is clearly continuity between nature and grace, reason and revelation. James Alison explains the implications of this approach:

> What role is left for human reason within mimetic theory? Let us start by conceding that the understanding of original sin I have developed is radical. It posits that human culture was born from and tends to maintain its order by means of a lie—the *meconnaissance* of its victimary foundations.

> Furthermore, this lie was only really completely revealed for what it is by the death and resurrection of Christ. So far we seem to have a highly "supernaturalist" position.

However, Alison argues that such a conclusion does not follow from Girard's claims. It is the Christ event that enables us to understand how wrong we have been about ourselves:

> Another way of saying this is that, having been able to see, thanks to the coming of Christ, what we were and what we are to become, we can also see that it has been within the abstract possibility of all (adult) humans everywhere to have come, no doubt through an arduous and incomplete process, to the perception of the victim and to have sided with him or her. . . . Girard has, notoriously, shown that such an insight did occur from time to time in certain great works of theater and literature. . . . His thought is able to be entertained within rational discourse by nonbelievers, because its anthropology and the embryonic theology which emerged in later works (to the annoyance of some who then accused Girard of crude apologetics) form a seamless robe.[11]

In a Girardian context then, Christian formulations of the nature/grace and reason/revelation distinction are transposed in terms of the relationship between anthropology and theology, with Girard being content (for the most part) to leave the work of transposition to the theologians. The narrative that animates mimetic theory accords with the Christian narrative of creation and redemption. We find in this narrative a humanity that has fallen into patterns of behavior that it imagines it cannot do without, but that in fact are a distortion of what humans are capable of becoming (in theological terms, humanity is trapped in sin). Into this situation the biblical message comes as a genuine revelation, since it offers us insights that we would not have come to on our own, imprisoned as we are in a horizon largely constituted by the practice of victimization. That Girard's theory is in harmony with the biblical story of salvation is in no way surprising, since he has been quite clear in recent years that his is a biblically inspired anthropology.[12] It is also fair to say that his approach to the relationship between reason and revelation is compatible with that of the Catholic theological tradition.[13] In this tradition, insights derived from revelation serve to correct, modify, and restrain the pretensions of reason where necessary. Revelation, so conceived, is understood to be therapeutic with reference to a natural reason mired in a culture shaped by victimizing practices. The role of revelation in this context is not to replace reason but to free it to become more truly reasonable. With regard to reason, revelation is restorative rather than destructive.

In the work of Eric Voegelin, the relationship between reason and revelation is treated very differently. From the beginning to the end of his career, Voegelin was concerned with the problem of political and social order; and it is the need to address questions arising from the manifest disorder and violence of the last century that shapes his treatment of the reason/revelation distinction. Compared to Girard, he is far more ambivalent in his attitude toward the biblical legacy—in particular with regard to the effects of biblical revelation.

Essentially, Voegelin's understanding of revelation becomes more critical over time. His work is not easily divided into sharply distinguishable periods, but there are certain recognizable shifts and changes. Roughly speaking, Voegelin's development as a thinker can be said to unfold in two phases. The first phase begins in the 1920s and runs through the 1940s, culminating in his posthumously published *History of Political Ideas*. As indicated earlier, it was during the writing of *History of Political Ideas* that he became increasingly dissatisfied with the study of ideas as the means to gain access to political reality. He realized that, in order to adequately study what it is that constitutes the political, he would need to go more deeply into the primary sources than a focus on "ideas" would allow. Years later, Voegelin noted the breakthrough that occurred while working on the Friedrich Schelling chapter of the *History of Political Ideas*, which prompted the new direction his thought would take:

> Because Schelling was an intelligent philosopher, and when I studied the philosophy of myth, I understood that ideas were nonsense: There are no ideas as such, and there is no history of ideas; but there is a history of experiences that can express themselves in various forms, as myths of various types, as philosophical development, theological development, and so on. One has got to get back to the analysis of experience.[14]

The analysis of experience would occupy Voegelin for the rest of his career, developing into a theory that would move from the symbols created by individuals and societies to express their sense of participation in the encompassing reality within which they find themselves, to the underlying experiences of which the symbols are an articulation. At the basis of this method was the principle that "*the reality of experience is self-interpretive.*" For Voegelin this required the development of a theory of consciousness that would emphasize the reality of participation rather than a model based upon a division between subject and object:

> This understanding of the In-Between [*metaxy*, a term derived from Plato] character of consciousness, as well as of its luminosity—which is the luminosity not of a subjective consciousness but of the reality that enters into the experience from both sides—results furthermore in a better understanding of the problem of symbols: symbols are the language phenomena engendered by the process of participatory experience. . . . [A symbol] is engendered by the divine–human encounter and participates, therefore, as much in divine as in human reality.[15]

These developments in Voegelin's thought would certainly impact his understanding of the relationship between reason and revelation; but equally if not more important in shaping his treatment of this relationship is his evaluation of the political effects of biblical religion, particularly Christianity. It should be emphasized that his concern with the problem of political order and the changes in his theoretical framework are inseparable in the unfolding of his mature philosophical perspective. It is not as if he develops his theory of consciousness and experience independently of his political preoccupations. The issue of reason and revelation bridges both of these areas of his thought; so changes in his theory of consciousness as well as his evolving perception of Christianity will dovetail harmoniously in his handling of the issue.

The topic of reason and revelation is hardly prominent in Voegelin's work prior to the 1950s. However, his ambivalence with regard to Christianity's effects already shows itself in his 1938 work, *The Political Religions*. Thomas Aquinas's appropriation of Aristotle, when joined to the idea of the subordination of the temporal to the spiritual power, is said to destroy the central meaning of the Greek philosopher's work. With the division of society into two realms, it is only a matter of time until the political sphere will assert its autonomy, thus bringing into existence the first "inner-worldly political religion." He also notes how:

> As a result of the Christian monastic movements since Benedict and above all, the development of mendicant orders . . . within Christianity, the spiritual view of the renewal of the soul and the partaking in the perfection of the Christian ideal of existence are considered part of this world.

This bringing of the Christian ideal into the world has contributed, in Voegelin's view, to the false notion of the perfectibility of human reason, to the idea of humankind's progressive perfection, to Freemasonry, communism, and National Socialism.[16] A similar charge is leveled against Francis of Assisi and Franciscanism in the *History of Political Ideas*. As Voegelin sees it, by bringing the gospel to the poor and suffering and by discerning the presence of God in nature (things for which Voegelin certainly admires him), Francis also brought the Christian message down to earth in a way that dislocates the carefully worked out hierarchical structure of the institutional church, thereby subverting civilizational order and turning the gaze of believers from heaven to earth. According to Voegelin, this furthers the unfortunate immanentization of the Christian vision.[17]

Despite his reservations about the political implications of certain developments in Christianity, Voegelin was well aware that it was senseless to discuss the problems confronting Western civilization without taking its positive influence into account. While the Christian message contains socially disruptive elements, he also thought that, in the form of the institutional church and some of the peaceful evangelizing movements, Christianity acted as a politically stabilizing force. To account for these opposed tendencies within the tradition, he is led to distinguish between what he describes as "essential" Christianity and "eschatological" Christianity. The latter is part of the prophetic, messianic legacy of Israel that emphasizes the need to strive as much as possible to establish the kingdom of God on earth; the former identifies the core of Christian belief with supernatural fulfillment beyond this world. In Voegelin's dualistic rendering, these understandings of Christianity are largely incompatible. Eschatological Christianity, in this view, is associated with the historical roots of the Christian movement, but it is something to be overcome and suppressed whenever it asserts itself. Essential Christianity, on the other hand, is the genuine version of the faith; it is acutely conscious of human limits in bringing about a relatively better world, and it focuses on the soul's relationship to God and its fulfillment through grace in death.[18]

It is within this context (i.e., the development of his theoretical framework and his attitude toward Christianity) that we can best understand Voegelin's handling of the reason/revelation distinction. Voegelin's break with an analysis based upon "ideas" and his move toward a theory revolving around differentiations of consciousness occurred during the time he was offering the 1951 series of lectures that would become his most well-known work, *The New Science of Politics*.[19] In *The New Science* he had not yet developed the specific language of noetic and pneumatic differentiation; at this stage he differentiates between the "anthropological truth" discovered by the Greek philosophers and the "soteriological truth" of Christianity. Both of these developments go beyond "cosmological truth" (in which the divine, the human, and the social are viewed as dimensions within an encompassing whole) by more clearly delineating the various aspects of reality in which humans participate. Anthropological truth focuses on the "psyche as the sensorium of transcendence," whereas the soteriological truth illuminates the divine reality toward which the soul is oriented and from which it takes its bearings.[20] Commenting on the difference between these two truths, Voegelin notes the limits of Platonic-Aristotelian philosophy in comparison to Christian revelation:

> The impossibility of *philia* between God and man may be considered typical for the whole range of anthropological truth. The experiences that were explicated into a theory of man by the mystic philosophers had in common the accent on the human side of the orientation of the soul toward divinity. The soul orients itself toward a God who rests in his immovable transcendence; it reaches out toward divine reality, but it does not meet an answering movement from beyond. The Christian bending of God in grace toward the soul does not come within the range of these experiences—though, to be sure, in reading Plato one has the feeling of moving continuously on the verge of a breakthrough into this new dimension. The experience of mutuality in the relation with God, of the *amicitia* in

> the Thomistic sense, of the grace that imposes a supernatural form on the nature of man, is the specific difference of Christian truth. The revelation of this grace in history, through the incarnation of the Logos in Christ, intelligibly fulfilled the adventitious movement of the spirit in the mystic philosophers.[21]

Here Voegelin operates with what is for the most part a Thomistic, Catholic understanding of the relation between reason and revelation. Human wonder, expressing itself through the philosophical life, is oriented toward divine transcendence but is incapable of achieving its final end. By the grace of God, revelation is granted, as God bends toward the questioner in love, elevating human nature toward its supernatural goal. Yet at the same time he was affirming this distinction between reason and revelation, Voegelin clearly brings out just how seriously he intends the term "mystic philosophers" to be applicable to Plato and Aristotle:

> Through the opening of the soul the philosopher finds himself in a new relation with God; he not only discovers his own psyche as the instrument for experiencing transcendence but at the same time discovers the divinity in its radically nonhuman transcendence. Hence, the differentiation of the psyche is inseparable from a new truth about God. . . . The validity of the standards developed by Plato and Aristotle depends on the conception of a man who can be the measure of society because God is the measure of his soul.[22]

So even though Voegelin is willing to concede that compared to the soteriological differentiation there are limits to the anthropological truth with regard to the articulation and grasp of divine reality, it is clear that he views them both as revelatory. *Philia* between God and human may not fall within the range of the philosophers' experience, but Voegelin has no reservations in claiming that Plato and Aristotle possess standards by which to order society precisely because they are aware that "God is the Measure."[23] In terms of theory the two truths are equal and complementary. At the very least, he makes clear that philosophy is no handmaiden. Nor can the anthropological differentiation be judged to be in any way inferior to the soteriological in terms of its ability to provide for the ordering of society—quite the contrary.

The "revolutionary substance" in Christianity, with its "uncompromising, radical, de-divinization of the world" is more than enough to disqualify it as a civil religion. In light of this warning, it becomes increasingly clear that, for Voegelin, it is the anthropological principle of the philosophers that is best suited to ordering the world.[24] It will only be a matter of time before he begins to draw out fully the consequences of the position articulated in *The New Science of Politics.*

With the publication of the first three volumes of *Order and History* (1956–57), Voegelin's articulation of the reason/revelation question does not change significantly. While the entire first volume, *Israel and Revelation*, argues that Israel was itself constituted through revelation, Voegelin opens the second volume, *The World of the Polis*, with the following assertion:

> The Hellenic experience of God as the unseen measure of man is neither a sequel to the Israelite experience of the God who reveals himself from the thornbush to Moses and from Sinai to his people, nor even an intelligible advance beyond it in the sense in which both of these experiences differentiate a new truth about the order of being beyond the compact truth of the myth. The leap in being, the epochal event that breaks the compactness of the early cosmological myth and establishes the order of man in his immediacy under God, . . . occurs twice in the history of mankind, at roughly the same time, in the Near Eastern and the neighboring Aegean civilizations. The two occurrences, while they run parallel in time and have in common their opposition to the Myth, are independent of each other; and the two experiences differ so profoundly in content that they become articulate in the two different symbolisms of Revelation and Philosophy.[25]

Once again we find Voegelin emphasizing the parallelism between philosophy and revelation. Much like his account in *The New Science of Politics*, he calls attention to the profound difference in content between the two ways of truth. That he still understands this difference as he had in *The New Science of Politics* becomes clear toward the end of the third volume of *Order and History*, *Plato and Aristotle*:

> There remained in Aristotle the fundamental hesitation which distinguished the Hellenic from the Christian idea of man, that is, the hesitation

> to recognize the formation of the human soul through grace; there was missing the experience of faith, the *fides caritate formata* in the Thomistic sense. . . . The Aristotelian position does not allow for a *forma supranaturalis*, for the heightening of the immanent nature of man through the supernaturally forming love of God. . . . Although the noetic self is the *theiotaton* in man, and though its actualization is conceived as an immortalization, human nature finds its fulfillment immanently. Transcendence does not transform the soul in such a manner that it will find fulfillment in transfiguration through Grace in death.[26]

Despite the similarity with *The New Science of Politics*, it is already possible to detect some of the features that will come to the fore in Voegelin's subsequent formulations of the reason/revelation relationship. There is, first of all, the recognition that the important breakthroughs in consciousness cannot be neatly arranged on a timeline. This insight will eventually contribute to Voegelin's decision to break with the original plan for *Order and History*. Of greater consequence for understanding the reason/revelation question is Voegelin's underlining of the fact that while philosophy and revelation may differ in content, they are equal in bringing about an awareness of humanity's immediacy under God.

Simultaneous with the publication of the first three volumes of *Order and History*, Voegelin's criticisms of biblical religion become more frequent and more pointed. The preface to *Israel and Revelation* contains a warning that metastatic faith (which has its origins in Israelite prophecy) is one of, if not the greatest source of, disorder in the contemporary world. The biblical and Christian roots of gnosticism and its modern ideological offspring are increasingly emphasized. The intensity of the pneumatic differentiation of consciousness, characteristic of Israelite religion and Christianity, is said to frequently lead to an imbalance in consciousness that overflows into socially destructive behavior. This tendency toward imbalance is contrasted with the balance of consciousness maintained by the Greek philosophers.[27] When these reservations about the influence of the Bible are considered alongside Voegelin's conviction that both philosophy and revelation disclose humanity's existence in immediacy under God, it is easily anticipated that it will be just a matter of time before the distinction between reason and revelation also becomes questionable. For of what relevance is such a distinction, if philosophers are equally recipients of divine revelation as any saint or prophet? And what becomes of the previously articulated difference in "content" between philosophy and revelation, when both are emphasized to be forms of life that unfold in immediacy before God? This latter question becomes especially relevant when we recall Voegelin's warnings that the distinctive "content" of biblical revelation is a frequent source of social disorder.

It is a tribute to Voegelin's integrity as a thinker that he did not hesitate to draw out the conclusions implicit in his evolving perspective. As late as 1967 he still retains the distinction between reason and revelation, but his manner of speaking about it has altered. His philosophy of "experience" is developing, and his approach to this question changes as well:

> In the case of philosophy you have an experience that we might call the "noetic" experience, because its center, the area in which the immediacy under God is experienced, is the differentiation of *nous* or "reason." In the other case, of revelation, you might speak of a pneumatic experience, because the *pneuma* is again the area in which the immediacy is experienced. . . . We now have two types, a noetic and a pneumatic type, or philosophy and revelation . . . or you may call it the distinction between reason and revelation. . . . You might say in the noetic type . . . you get a tendency toward exploring the structure of experience. . . . In the pneumatic, or revelatory, type you have the substance so strongly predominant that an analysis of its structure is never done, at least not in the Israelite and Judaic context.[28]

This is a fascinating transitional text. The language that would distinguish between philosophy and biblical religion by attributing a merely "natural" reason to the former and the supernatural dimension of grace to the latter has been abandoned. The distinction is now drawn in terms of structure and substance. Both differentiations are focused on divine transcendence; both emerge from the experience of immediacy under God. Instead of understanding the difference between philosophy and revelation in terms of distinct content, the two major differentiations of consciousness come to be understood as dimensions or facets within one encompassing experience of reality. Given the direction in which his thought was already developing on this question, it would not be long before Voegelin discarded this terminology of structure/substance when referring to reason and revelation. In the final phase of his thought he would retain the idea of the noetic (philosophical) differentiation as focused on the search and on articulating the structure of the experience as simultaneously seeking and being drawn by divine reality. But in the case of the pneumatic differentiation, the language of "substance" is dropped and replaced with language that emphasizes the divine dimension or "pole" within the experience of transcendence. The pneumatic emphasis is focused on the divine "Beyond" that is experienced as drawing us into the quest for truth, and whose entering into human experience is often best expressed as an inrushing of the spirit rather than as a noetic quest for truth. This change in emphasis is not surprising; Voegelin is simply developing the insight already found in *The New Science of Politics*, where Plato and Aristotle are referred to as mystic philosophers. To distinguish between reason and revelation in terms of structure and substance makes no sense when the "substance" or content behind the two symbolisms is in fact the same. The experience of living in immediacy before God may be articulated differently by philosophers and prophets, but the difference does not lie in the latter's having access to a revelation denied to the philosopher.

By 1970 Voegelin had accepted this conclusion, and he consequently abandons the distinction between reason and revelation:

> In Christian theology there is the encrusted conception that revelation is revelation and that classic philosophy is the natural reason of mankind unaided by revelation. That is simply not true empirically. Plato was perfectly clear that what he is doing in the form of a myth is a revelation. He does not invent it by natural reason; the God speaks. The God speaks just as in the prophet or in Jesus. So the whole conception which is still prevalent today—not only in theological thinking but penetrating our civilization: "on the one hand we have natural reason and on the other hand revelation"—is empirically nonsense.[29]

From this point onward Voegelin insisted that there was a theophany at the core of both the noetic and pneumatic differentiations. These were parallel revelations, and the task now became one of explaining how and why they differed.[30] He continued to maintain that the encounter with the divine Beyond was articulated with greater clarity and intensity within the pneumatic differentiation; but increasingly this very intensity came to be understood as a source of imbalance and social disruption.[31] Since the distinction between reason and revelation is "empirically nonsense," it remained for Voegelin to account for its origin. One explanation was that the difference was simply the result of the same type of experience manifesting itself in two disparate ethnic cultures, where the particular variations in language, religion, and cultural attitude shaped the manner in which the revelations were expressed. But this explains very little, since it overlooks the possibility that it might very well be the differences in the content of revelation that account for the cultural differences in the first place. More strikingly, Voegelin came to the conclusion that the reason/revelation distinction reflected a struggle for power; natural reason was distinguished from and subordinated to revelation in order to assert the superiority of the Judeo-Christian tradition:

> Thus we are dealing here with the categories of two ethnic cultures, both of which are in pursuit of the truth but in very different forms. These differing forms were then transformed into the form of a natural seeking of truth and into the godly revelatory form, with the intention of letting the Jewish-Christian form predominate.[32]

Essentially then, the distinction between reason and revelation represents an attempted power grab on the part of revealed religion. Understood in this fashion, it would seem eminently sensible to abandon it as part of the residue from an age when Christian theology sought to subordinate philosophy and place it in the service of Christian cultural and political dominance. With this understanding in mind, Voegelin decided that the distinction needed to be cleared away.[33]

▪ ▪ ▪

Girard has not been especially concerned with the theological question of nature and grace, but he does share with Catholic tradition the idea that revelation can serve as a healing corrective to reason (as it operates in the concrete). While he reads the Bible in an anthropological way, he more than suggests that the exposure of the scapegoating mechanism contained therein is not the product of the merely human intellect. This is not a positive attempt to prove the existence of divine revelation, but an inference based upon the observation that human reason conditioned by and in a serious sense in thrall to scapegoating practices is unlikely to discover its own complicity in these practices. That does not mean that insights approximating those of the Bible have not occurred outside the orbit of biblically inspired cultures. Premonitions of what is disclosed with maximum clarity in the biblical text are to be found in Greek tragedy, in philosophy, and throughout the range of humanity's wisdom traditions.

In Voegelin's narrative, the situation is largely reversed, with philosophy increasingly playing a corrective role in light of the disorder too easily unleashed by revelation. Certainly in his work up to and including the 1950s he still saw a place for the revelatory traditions of Judaism and Christianity as antidotes to the excesses of modern ideological movements. Religion (or at least certain forms of religion) is seen as a social force that can enable people to deal with societal problems in a temperate, respectful, and nonideological fashion.[34] But even when he is able to praise the social benefits of revealed religion, he tended to see it as exercising its moderating function alongside reason—never as a corrective to reason.

Eventually though, this respect for religion as a stabilizing influence gives way in his thought to a growing concern about the dangerous side effects of Judeo-Christian revelation. Increasingly there appears in his writings a cleavage between a "good" religion that supports and preserves order and a "bad" religion that disrupts it. True Christianity becomes identified with an Augustinian pessimism that emphasizes the limits to transformation of this world. The church likewise comes to be conceived as an institution that does not so much proclaim the kingdom as moderate its demands in accordance with the ontological structure of human existence. In Voegelin's view, the "laws of mundane existence" cannot be changed by human effort, and to the extent that biblical religion has encouraged people to believe otherwise it is to be repudiated. The influence of biblical tradition on Western civilization cannot be ignored by the political philosopher, but it needs to be interpreted in a way that better accords with the more balancing influence of classical philosophy. As we have seen in the case of Christianity, Voegelin begins to distinguish between an essential Christianity (which recognizes the constraints governing human efforts in this world and keeps its sight focused on the heavenly realm) and an eschatological Christianity (mainly of biblical origin) that is a menace to social order.

By distilling the "essential" form of Christianity from what he considers to be its unstable and dangerous eschatological roots, Voegelin also is able to more easily assimilate this genuine Christianity to his evolving theory of consciousness. Once the essence of Christianity has been extracted from the deforming elements that seek to transform the world in accordance with the demands of the kingdom of God, it can be understood within the framework of the kinds of experiences that constitute the epochal differentiations of consciousness. Consequently, revelation comes to be understood increasingly as an event within consciousness, as a part of the process of differentiation of consciousness. In *The Ecumenic Age* and the work that follows he takes special pains to underline the fact that the great differentiations of consciousness do not alter the order of things as governed by the "laws of mundane existence." With this accommodation of biblical revelation to a theory of consciousness derived largely from Plato, there is little point in continuing to distinguish between reason and revelation. As an event within consciousness, the pneumatic differentiation characteristic of the biblical tradition can now be evaluated from the perspective of the noetic differentiation. By distinguishing between natural reason and revelation Voegelin thinks that the Judeo-Christian tradition tries to assert its superiority over philosophy. But in rejecting this distinction, Voegelin asserts a superior role for philosophical criteria in judging revelation. The noetic differentiation may suffer in comparison with the pneumatic in terms of the intensity of the experience of divine transcendence, but this is more than offset by its superior degree of balance and moderation, a point Voegelin returns to frequently in his later work. Given the development of his philosophy, his rejection of the reason/revelation distinction is practically inevitable.

The disappearance of this distinction, the approximation/absorption of biblical thinking into a framework in which a philosophy of consciousness serves as the criteria for evaluating what is to be considered order and disorder, and the suppression of the eschatological dimension of biblical religion are not without serious consequences. Perhaps the most significant consequence is to obscure that which is distinctively biblical. Voegelin therefore deprives himself of insights that might help to illuminate the limitations of the Platonic vision he adopts. Among those limitations is an approach to the problem of political and social order that is not sufficiently cognizant of the practices of victimization that underpin and sustain that order. In Voegelin's case this shows itself in his wariness with regard to early Christianity's inability to serve as a proper civil religion. With its radical de-divinization of the political sphere, Christianity (along with the prophetic traditions of Israel) erodes the important function of civil religion in providing the cohesiveness of order.[35] Voegelin, like Plato, perceives the importance of civil religion, and just like Plato he is wary of those forces that weaken it. If for Plato these forces were embodied in the work of Homer and the other poets, for Voegelin they are to be found in the eschatological traditions of the Bible. Plato expels the poets, and Voegelin expels the prophets. Hence we find in his work a series of selective expulsions geared to salvaging from the biblical legacy that which can serve to preserve society from disruption, while ridding the world of those elements perceived to be responsible for the germination of disruptive ideologies. Essential Christianity is praised, while eschatological Christianity is condemned. Methodists earn Voegelin's approval (because they helped to preserve the English working classes from revolution), but Puritans are heaped with scorn. Augustine is extolled for his realism and wisdom, while Joachim of Fiore is denounced as the precursor of National Socialism. Nor should we forget the dangerous influence of Francis of Assisi in turning people's eyes from heaven to the needs of this world.

Voegelin's treatment of reason and revelation is of one piece with his attempt to eliminate what he takes to be the destructive tendencies of biblical religion. But in doing so he misses something tremendously important. Girard is quite aware of how biblical revelation undermines social structures, but this awareness is accompanied by the even more crucial insight that the structures so undermined rest themselves on mechanisms of victimization. What Girard takes to be central to the biblical message—the defense of victims—receives scant attention from Voegelin. This is not because he is insensitive to the plight of victims; in many ways his whole philosophical enterprise is motivated by a desire to prevent the victimization wrought by political violence.[36] Girard is not naive. He is well aware that where the biblical message begins to take root, previous forms of order become questionable and that there is no guarantee that their dissolution will be peaceful. Revelation is indeed a disruptive force in this sense. Voegelin likewise understands the disruption and excesses associated with the biblical message, but unlike Girard he has far less of an appreciation as to how this dis-ordering is part of the dissolution of political/social/cultural practices of victimization.

I have argued at greater length elsewhere that Girard allows the biblical text to disclose its intelligibility in a way that Voegelin's interpretation does not.[37] As counterintuitive as it might seem to those who would regard any appeal to the Bible as parochial and sectarian, Girard's anthropological approach to the text actually comes closer to achieving the kind of common language that Voegelin sought to develop. For those accustomed to equating "philosophical" with "universal" or "nonsectarian," this may be an insight that is difficult to accept. But as noted earlier, if Girard is correct, a method derived from an anthropological reading of the Bible holds a good deal of promise as a means of evaluating the claims of reason, for reason itself needs to be freed from its association with the violence that it can too easily seek to justify. With Voegelin it is otherwise. He adheres to the myth that by means of a Platonically inspired form of reason it might be possible to limit and moderate the destruction inspired by the biblical legacy. But as Girard reminds us, myths are not innocent—and this one is no exception.

With this observation in mind it is possible to suggest an answer to a question raised toward the beginning of this essay—whether the experientially grounded language developed by Voegelin achieves its aim of being able to serve as a common language among world religions and other "wisdom" traditions, or whether it remains a limited perspective claiming to be universal. To the extent that Voegelin's philosophical method leads him to dissolve the distinction between reason and revelation, it is difficult to conceive how it could serve as a common language for any conversation involving religious traditions in which this distinction is affirmed. As open as he is to the varieties of religious experience in all their manifestations, the language he developed remains far too dependent upon classical Greek philosophy to serve as an adequate basis for interreligious dialogue.

The problem is not just that a theory whose fundamental terms and relations are derived from Plato is inadequate to analyze the Bible. The difficulties engendered by Voegelin's use of Greek philosophy to interpret texts extend beyond the application to biblical material, as the following rather testy exchange makes clear:

> D. SALMAN: What would you say if somebody told you that you seem, from outside, very culture bound, proclaiming that your tradition is the tradition, the good one, the only one, the more general. . . .

E. VOEGELIN: I would not be impressed in the least, because the term *culture bound* is an ideological term which assumes that there are cultures as absolutes. . . . Culture is not an absolute. That is bad methodology. When you go back to Plato—

D. SALMAN: But they [Buddhists, Muslims, Chinese religions] don't go back to Plato—

E. VOEGELIN: But you have to. If you refuse, there is no basis for anything, and we are again at the point of: Who pulls the gun first?

D. SALMAN: Do you believe in Plato?

E. VOEGELIN: No, I don't. This objection—that I believe in Plato—is a demagogic insinuation that I am an ideologist like everybody else. But I am not. We talk in signs about reality. You are free *not* to talk about existential tension. But *if* you talk about it, you must talk about it in the language developed by the persons who have discovered existential tension; there is no other.[38]

Admittedly, views expressed during a question-and-answer period following a talk may be delivered in a less nuanced way than in an essay written under conditions more conducive to reflection, but Voegelin's insistence that the Greek philosophers discovered and articulated the notion of "existential tension," and that those who choose to speak about this tension must employ this language, is a point he affirmed on numerous occasions in his writings. Of course for the purposes of this essay the relevant question is not whether the Greek philosophers developed the language of existential tension, but rather whether such language adequately captures what is central and/or common to the world's great wisdom traditions. As applied to those traditions in which reason and revelation are carefully distinguished, Voegelin's theoretical framework (with its rejection of this distinction) fails to do justice to much that is essential. But if that is so, then its usefulness as a common language for a dialogue among world religions is called into question as well.

NOTES

1. Eric Voegelin, "Autobiographical Statement at Age Eighty-Two," in *The Collected Works of Eric Voegelin*, vol. 33, *The Drama of Humanity and Other Miscellaneous Papers, 1939–1985* (Columbia: University of Missouri Press, 2004), 442.

2. Eric Voegelin, "Conversations with Eric Voegelin at the Thomas More Institute for Adult Education in Montreal," in *The Drama of Humanity and Other Miscellaneous Papers, 1939–1985*, 244.
3. Bernard Lonergan, "Natural Knowledge of God," in *A Second Collection* (Philadelphia: Westminster Press, 1974), 133.
4. Ibid.
5. René Girard, *A Theater of Envy: William Shakespeare* (Leominster: Gracewing, 2000), 208.
6. James Alison, *The Joy of Being Wrong* (New York: Crossroad, 1998), 304.
7. Ibid.
8. Markus Müller, "Interview with René Girard," *Anthropoetics* 2, no. 1 (Spring/Summer 1996): 5.
9. René Girard, *I See Satan Fall Like Lightning*, trans. James G. Williams (Maryknoll, NY: Orbis, 2001), 189.
10. René Girard, *The Scapegoat*, trans. Yvonne Freccero (Baltimore: Johns Hopkins University Press, 1986), 162–63. See also Thomas F. Bertonneau, "The Logic of the Undecidable: An Interview with René Girard," *Paroles Gelees* 5 (1987): 15–16.
11. Alison, *The Joy of Being Wrong*, 304–5.
12. Girard, *I See Satan Fall Like Lightning*, 3, 182.
13. Alison, *The Joy of Being Wrong*, 269–310.
14. Voegelin, "Autobiographical Statement," 442.
15. Eric Voegelin, *Autobiographical Reflections* (Baton Rouge: Louisiana State University Press, 1989), 73–74.
16. Eric Voegelin, *The Political Religions* in *The Collected Works of Eric Voegelin*, vol. 5, *Modernity without Restraint* (Columbia: University of Missouri Press, 2000), 49, 51–52.
17. Eric Voegelin, *The Collected Works of Eric Voegelin*, vol. 20, *History of Political Ideas; The Middle Ages to Aquinas* (Columbia: University of Missouri Press, 1997), 2:142–43.
18. Eric Voegelin, "On Christianity," in *The Philosophy of Order*, ed. Peter J. Opitz and Gregor Sebba (Stuttgart: Klett-Cotta, 1981), 452; Voegelin, "The Spiritual and Political Future of the Western World," in *The Drama of Humanity and Other Miscellaneous Papers 1939–1985*, 79–80.
19. Voegelin, *Autobiographical Reflections*, 64.
20. Eric Voegelin, *The New Science of Politics* in *Modernity without Restraint*, 149–52.
21. Ibid., 150.
22. Ibid., 141, 143.
23. Ibid., 142.
24. Ibid., 152, 169.
25. Eric Voegelin, *Order and History*, vol. 2, *The World of the Polis* (Baton Rouge: Louisiana State University Press, 1957), 1.
26. Eric Voegelin, *Order and History*, vol. 3, *Plato and Aristotle* (Baton Rouge: Louisiana State University Press, 1957), 364.

27. John J. Ranieri, *Disturbing Revelation: Leo Strauss, Eric Voegelin, and the Bible* (Columbia: University of Missouri Press, 2009), 48–102, 131–57.

28. Eric Voegelin, "The Drama of Humanity," in *The Drama of Humanity and Other Miscellaneous Papers 1939–1985*, 198–99.

29. Voegelin, "Conversations," 301.

30. Voegelin, *Autobiographical Reflections*, 109–10.

31. Eric Voegelin, "The Gospel and Culture," in *The Collected Works of Eric Voegelin*, vol. 12, *Published Essays, 1966–1985* (Columbia: University of Missouri Press, 1990), 189; Eric Voegelin, *Order and History*, vol. 4, *The Ecumenic Age* (Baton Rouge: Louisiana State University Press, 1974), 27; Ranieri, *Disturbing Revelation*, 48–102, 131–57.

32. Eric Voegelin, "The Meditative Origin of the Philosophical Knowledge of Order," in *The Drama of Humanity and Other Miscellaneous Papers, 1939–1985*, 386.

33. Ibid., 388.

34. Eric Voegelin, "Democracy and Industrial Society," in *The Collected Works of Eric Voegelin*, vol. 11, *Published Essays, 1953–1965* (Columbia: University of Missouri Press, 2000), 213, 218–19, 221–22; Eric Voegelin, "Democracy in the New Europe," in *Published Essays, 1953–1965*, 61–62; Eric Voegelin, "Freedom and Responsibility in Economy and Democracy," in *Published Essays, 1953–1965*, 72–74.

35. Voegelin, *The New Science of Politics*, 169–74.

36. Voegelin, "Autobiographical Statement," 440.

37. Ranieri, *Disturbing Revelation*, 186–248.

38. Voegelin, "Conversations," 267–70.

The Messianic Moment: Bergson and Girard

Benoît Chantre

Translated by Trevor Cribben Merrill

For Frédéric Worms

The title of the conference session in which this contribution was originally presented—"Beyond Archaic Religion"—was very well suited to the hypothesis that I would like to defend. Archaic religion, as defined by René Girard in *Violence and the Sacred*, is indeed conceived—even if this conception is only hinted at in 1972—as a prefiguration of Judeo-Christianity. This interpretation of archaic religion, grounded in the description of the scapegoat mechanism, is the first stage in a new approach to the study of Judeo-Christian revelation. Girard positions himself in the lineage of thinkers who have attempted to describe the *prophetic rupture* and the upheavals that it causes in the structure of religion. The structure remains, but the revelation of which it is the object gives it a final twist.

This idea of an "open religion" obliges me to bring René Girard face to face with Henri Bergson, who was the first to use this concept in France, thus renewing our understanding of religion. In *The Two Sources of Morality and Religion*, published in 1932, Bergson identifies two *vital* origins of morality and religion: one natural, social, mythical, "closed"; the other individual, heroic, mystical, "open." He then shows how the two are linked, inasmuch as every religion has at once a "closed" and an "open" dimension. I will try to show that this undeniable progress in our understanding of religious phenomena comes at the cost of an almost total misrecognition of what would become, forty years later, the object of René Girard's research, namely sacrificial institutions.

This point is not without significance. By focusing his attention on the "oddity" of sacrifices, which Bergson is too quick to reduce to a superstition confined to "stagnant societies," Girard brings an important discovery to the Bergsonian framework, and thus to the question of the openness of one form of religion to another: that of the "double substitution" (substitution of the "emissary victim"—or "scapegoat"—and of the "sacrificial victim"). This description of the scapegoat mechanism, which is lacking in Bergson, makes it possible to better understand the Christian event and the new model that it brings into existence. Affirming by his analysis of the collapse of the sacrificial institution that *the essence of the divine consists in its tendency to withdraw from the world*, Girard asks with Friedrich Hölderlin the fundamental question of our time: How is it possible to hold back the departing gods except by positing a "God that is drawing near"? I will suggest that this synthesis of the two forms of religion constitutes a new kind of imitation. This is an intuition that Bergson was already developing in 1932, and for which Girard provided the solid theoretical foundations forty years later.

The Two Sources of Religion

One of the interesting things about *Battling to the End* in 2010 was that it invoked the author's early, traumatic experience: the French defeat of 1940. Girard made this event the subject of his doctoral dissertation in 1950, and it is to this event that he came back sixty years later. It was as if he had to write his entire oeuvre before being able to understand that inaugural moment. The question of war is, in fact, the central question of his work, and it was also a central question for Bergson in his last book in 1932. The author of *The Two Sources of Morality and Religion* sees armed conflict as the decisive ordeal in the shift from a "closed society" to an "open society," and from a "static religion" to a "dynamic religion." Between the "morality of pressure" proper to societies closed in on themselves, and the "morality of aspiration" proper to exceptional individuals, there is the extreme figure of the enemy, which is at once collective and individual and which only heroes and saints can apprehend as a fraternal figure. The scandalous character of adversity—its status as an "obstacle," to use a term that appears in both Bergson and Girard—is thus what makes it impossible to imagine the shift from "closed" to "open" as a simple expansion. Bergson says that there must be a "forward bound" or a "quantum leap" because the difference between the two poles is not one of degree but of essence. Emmanuel Levinas later takes up this intuition when he posits war as the obstacle that must be surmounted in order to move from the legal-political "totality" to the "infinity" of moral relationship.

But how can this leap forward be made, how can the obstacle be surmounted, and how can one religion "open" onto another? Bergson never makes this clear. He is content to observe that a few exceptional beings have enabled humanity to conceive of something beyond war. These beings are heroes and saints. But each time, the opening up that they made possible was closed up again in the tumult of armed conflict: "static religion," the "machine for making gods," once again gave "closed morality" (or "social morality") the hallucinations that it needed to close ranks in the face of adversity, to come together against the enemy necessary to the group's cohesion. In France, our monuments to the dead are tragic totems of the work of the "myth-making function," the proof that the twentieth-century European apocalypse revealed deep layers that were only covered up by the varnish of civilization. Bergson adds that this nature becomes all the more *insistent* when the call to move beyond it is made: the fate of the prophets is to be ignored or, worse still, to provoke nature into a "defensive reaction." The anger of the prophets, like the supereffective acts of the heroes and the saints, were moments of opening, unpredictable "creations." The closure of human societies appeared in the light of this opening. Thus history amounts to the striving of humanity, which draws energy from its vital impetus, its "*élan vital*," to go beyond the limits imposed by nature. The long process of hominization unfolds in the constant movement of expansion and contraction that constitutes the fundamental internal polarity of all human relationships, between the two vital sources of morality and religion, the one natural, the other mystical, the one always ready to break through the varnish of culture, the other brought forth from beneath nature by the deeper call of the prophets and the saints.

Far from being a fiction of static religion, that is to say a form of false transcendence, Bergson's "dynamic" God is one with the *élan vital*.[1] The acts of the heroes and the saints, made possible by the indignation of the prophets and by the rupture accomplished by the "Christ of the Gospels," draws its energy from the very principle of life, discovered by the mystics as "love and object of love." Without telling us anything more about the means of subverting the figure of the enemy, that central obstacle between "closed moralities" and "open moralities," Bergson merely observes that there were exceptional individuals who were capable of making humanity take this "forward bound" or this "quantum leap," heroes who half opened the door of the closed societies. Let us listen to the author of the *Two Sources* on this point:

> In whatever light we view the transition from relative to absolute justice, whether it took place by stages or all at once, there has been creation. Something has supervened which might never have existed, which would not have existed except for certain circumstances, certain men, perhaps one particular man.[2]

That sums up in a word both the moment and the essential problem that Bergson is trying to understand. In order to move from "closed societies" to an "open society," from the tribe to humanity, a certain period of time had to elapse during which several individualities appeared and disappeared in succession, and this until the coming of a "certain man"; farther on, he specifies that for this movement to happen the lineage that goes from the "prophets of Israel" to the "Christ of the Gospels" had to emerge. It was to this fundamental event, inscribed in the substance of time, that numerous "heroes" of "open morality" inwardly conformed, even if they are necessarily but the "incomplete continuers" of Christ. I will call this period the *messianic moment*. It is the moment of a gradual opening up of religion, or, to cite Vladimir Jankélévitch's very beautiful expression in his commentaries on Bergson, the advent of a "half-open religion."[3] Thus "closed" and "open" religions were but the extreme poles of a decisive experience, a fundamental movement. For the open that comes after the closed is never irreversible and can quite easily close up again. As we know, there is an ideology of opening as there is an ideology of conservation. Even love can become a dogma and it is then that the opening out of the self to the other closes up again. It is thus in this intermediary moment that, according to Bergson, the link between "static religion" and "dynamic religion" is played out, and it could be said that the whole book is one long variation on the theme of this "in-between."

But Bergson nonetheless goes to the heart of the problem, so much so that in his text he touches upon what would become René Girard's sole object of inquiry forty years later. It is significant that this insight should appear at the very moment that the philosopher cites the famous question that Ivan Karamazov poses to his brother Alyosha:

> Let us dwell on this point, put to ourselves the famous question: "What should we do if we heard that for the common good, for the very existence of mankind, there was somewhere a man, condemned to suffer eternal torment?" Well, we should perhaps agree to it on the understanding that some magic philter is going to make us forget it, that we shall never hear anything more about it; but if we were bound to know it, to think of it, to realize that this man's hideous torture was the price of our existence, that it was even the fundamental condition of existence in general, no! a thousand times no! Better to accept that nothing should exist at all! Better let our planet be blown to pieces.[4]

What the "[pre-Socratic] philosophers just missed," namely "the community of essence" among all human beings sharing the same rights (Simone Weil would have called this a "pre-Christian insight") is brought into being by the messianic moment. Christ crowns (but does not close) the prophetic moment, which was a movement of indignation and protestation against the injustice of sacrifices, and a very concrete movement for social justice. But Christ, writes Bergson, is the one in whom the fundamental event occurs, the one whose denunciation of the scandal of injustice opens the city to a "universal republic": the prophetic form is finished off by the Christian matter that it called for. But how did this rupture happen? What was the context in which it was made possible? Bergson is content to cite the Sermon on the Mount, as if strong words and a few parables were enough to transform the course of the world.

It is hard to understand why the philosopher skips over the Passion. Could it be that the Cross closes up what prophetic indignation had begun to open? That the total gift manifested here contained within itself the threat of an imminent dogmatic closure? Bergson implies that this is the case. Yet it is undeniable that he comes extremely close to what would later constitute the central object of René Girard's research. But he is turned away at once by an instinctive allergy and a secret modesty: allergy with regard to sacrifice, which is revealed explicitly in *The Two Sources*, and modesty with regard to his own conversion to Catholicism, which came to light only in his will.[5] Does Bergson want to remain a philosopher at the moment that the realities touched upon in his text would necessitate either an extensive anthropological inquiry or a profession of faith? I would put it a bit differently: it seems to me that Bergson the philosopher, having entered into the messianic moment, holds back from acknowledging his conversion, *as if he wanted to make that moment last*. It is as if the moment when Bergson, in solidarity with all of the persecuted ones of the Jewish people, glimpsed the reality of the Cross would also coincide with the moment of his own death.

Let us then linger for a moment over this admirable passage from *The Two Sources*, where the Cross is not cited but is nonetheless present. Here we can see the emergence of themes that Girard would seize upon after the Second World War. Thus the power of myth, fruit of the "myth-making function," Bergson tells us, nature's defensive reaction against the effects of intelligence—"depressing for the individual" and "vitiating for society"—this binding hallucination of the morality of "stagnant societies," is described in terms that the author of *Violence and the Sacred* might easily have used himself:

> we should perhaps agree to it [to having an innocent suffer "eternal torment" for the salvation of a people] *on the understanding that some magic philter is going to make us forget it, that we shall never hear anything more about it.*[6]

What does Bergson glimpse here if not that mythological representation deliberately erases all trace of the sacrifice that has been committed? That it is this erasure that constitutes myth's power, guaranteeing the order of the group "turning in place" in the forgetting of the founding murder? There is an eternal suffering of the innocent that cannot, that can no longer, after the messianic rupture, go unmentioned. Nonetheless, human beings, Bergson suggests in the second movement of the sentence, prefer the "magic philter," for they are incapable of bearing apocalyptic revelation:

> but if we were bound to know it, to think of it, to realize that this man's hideous torture was the price of our existence, that it was even the fundamental condition of existence in general, no! a thousand times no! Better to accept that nothing should exist at all! Better let our planet be blown to pieces.

Here, Bergson and Girard speak as one. Only the Cross, which reveals the secret of the founding murder, makes it possible to "know" that flagrant injustice exists, but also to "realize that this man's hideous torture was the price of our existence." Only the Cross makes it possible for us to formulate the very idea that our existence might depend on the sufferings of an innocent. Nature immediately responds to this dazzling but nonetheless unbearable insight with the magic potion of the "myth-making function." It is undeniable that Bergson is touching upon the idea that man is the fruit of sacrifice and still owes his existence to the sacrifice of innocents. This knowledge of injustice can only appear in the opening of a "transcendent" justice, which Bergson recognizes is the fruit of the messianic moment.

The tone and the style of this passage could be read as a strikingly inverted version of aphorism 125 of *The Gay Science*, in which Friedrich Nietzsche, deliberately activating what Bergson calls the "myth-making function," calls on us to become gods so as to rise to the challenge of the "divine decomposition." The author of *The Two Sources* does not complain about this retreat of the gods—on the contrary—but with startling serenity invokes the spirit of the prophets:[7]

> Now what has happened? How has justice emerged from social life, within which it had always dwelt with no particular privilege, and soared above it, categorical and transcendent? Let us recall the tone and accents of the Prophets of Israel. It is their voice we hear when a great injustice has been done and condoned.[8]

There is no panic here, as there is in Nietzsche's writings, before the "divine decomposition" (or the collapse of sacrificial institutions). Bergson remains the thinker of the in-between stage, the shift from closed to open societies. This "half-opened opening" is filled with hope. In fact, it cannot be denied that it is under the influence of the messianic moment that an absolute monopoly of the state where justice is concerned was slowly put into place in the West, ensuring little by little, within the framework of each gradually unified territory, internal peace, social justice, and the impossibility of vengeful reprisals. This messianic impulse has continued to shape history, giving rise to the hope that peace and justice will finally be achieved in the "concert of nations." Such is the slow process of hominization, accelerated by the Christian event. But this victory is never assured, because it presents at once its "open" side and its "closed" side. Thus "categorical and transcendent" justice, which no longer accepts the idea that an innocent should be sacrificed to the state, maintains the essential ambivalence of the crucifix that was once hung on the walls of courtrooms: at once the closed transcendence of stagnant societies (a veritable "theology of sacrifice" writes Girard in 1972), and the open transcendence of absolute innocence, which, little by little, in the way a tenacious but nonetheless vital illusion is gradually dissipated, exceptional figure by exceptional figure and creation by creation, outlines the true face of man and the true face of God.

The Double Substitution

Between closed and open societies there is thus an obstacle to be overcome. And only religion, in its double form, provides examples of the elimination or overcoming of this obstacle, of the closure or the opening of these societies: static religion compensates for the "depressing and vitiating" effects of intelligence with mythological fictions,[9] and dynamic religion gives rise to exceptional individuals, *for whom the obstacle does not exist*, who pay no heed to the social pressures of nature and see a potential brother in every enemy. It is very interesting to note that Bergson evokes the elimination or the overcoming of this double obstacle—the obstacle of the intelligence that hesitates to kill the enemy and the obstacle of the enemy transfigured by love—just after having evoked the reality of human sacrifices with particular disgust. Indeed, Bergson refuses to linger over this oddity of societies that "pivot on themselves." Nature prescribes murder; supernature calls on us to love. That is all Bergson has to say about the question. But what about the sacrificial act itself, that meticulous management of human violence? And what about the Cross, which operates the shift from sacrifice of the other to self-sacrifice? On this point, Bergson remains quite vague:

> As to sacrifice, it was, doubtless, to begin with, an offering made with a view to buying the favour of the god, or turning aside his wrath. If so, the greater the cost and the more valuable the thing sacrificed, the more acceptable it was likely to be. This is probably the explanation, at least in part, of the custom of human sacrifice, a custom to be found in most ancient religions, perhaps in all, could we trace them back far enough. There is no limit to the extent of error, or of horror, to which logic may lead, when it is applied to matters not pertaining to pure intelligence.[10]

Thus is inaugurated, with *The Two Sources*, a philosophical refusal to see the reality of sacrificial institutions. From Bergson to Claude Lévi-Strauss there is a decisive shift, where ritual and sacrifice, in a word archaic religion, prove to be less important for understanding the primitive mentality than myths and the imaginary.[11] True, it cannot be denied that Bergson quite clearly glimpses the breach opened up by the "prophets of Israel" and the "Christ of the Gospels." But we cannot avoid recognizing that he forswears himself when it comes to the reality of sacrifice and the Cross. It is this very silence that René Girard dispels forty years later when he makes the tragic observation that the "errors and horrors" of World War II make it necessary to oppose the reduction of primitive religion to some "myth-making function." If myth is an "ideomotor" force, to use Bergson's expression, the latter does not reflect on its own genesis. Girard, however, reveals in very convincing fashion that myth hides what ritual brings into the open: the scapegoat mechanism as the morphogenetic principle of all human societies.[12]

Bergson thus contributes an important distinction for thinking about the link between the static and the dynamic and also the essential polarity of religious phenomena, but he refuses all the same to examine the ordeal specific to this shift, the transformation of sacrifice of the other into self-sacrifice, which culminates in the Cross. This reluctance contributed to the eclipse of religious anthropology over the following four decades. Neither the gesticulations of the College of Sociology nor Georges Bataille's apologies of sacrifice—which bear witness to a fascination with sacrifice that Bergson never displayed—make possible a systematic study of the function of ritual and sacrifice. It would not be until 1972 that the question would find a new currency, and a new answer, with the description of the "scapegoat mechanism" provided by René Girard. Allow me to stress that *Violence and the Sacred* appears in a precise context: that of the Cold War and the nuclear threat. The author was therefore not only interested in devoting his energies to an analysis of archaic religion, but was also seeking to understand both the structure of sacrificial religion and the cause of its disintegration; in other words, the apocalyptic end of all sacrificial protections—law, from this point of view, being but an avatar of sacrifice. What is true for primitive societies is equally true, writes Girard in the wake of Bergson, for civilized societies; nature always reemerges beneath the varnish of civilization.

In the first chapter, titled "Sacrifice," Girard gives his definition of primitive society and touches upon the idea of "essential violence," which will run throughout the book and reappear on its last page, a threat that all rituals and sacrifices seek precisely to ward off:

> A *primitive* society, a society that does not possess a legal system, is vulnerable, as we have said, to the escalation of vengeance, the pure and simple annihilation that we will henceforth refer to as *essential violence*; it is forced to adopt certain attitudes toward this violence that appear incomprehensible to us. . . . Considered in their entirety, the ritual precautions directed against violence, as absurd as some of them may appear, have nothing illusory about them. We already observed the same thing with regard to sacrifice. If sacrificial *catharsis* manages to prevent the disordered propagation of violence, it is really a kind of *contagion* that it succeeds in stopping.[13]

"Primitive," "essential violence," "contagion": the terms that Girard stresses here all speak to the same reality, what he calls elsewhere the "fundamental identity" "between vengeance, sacrifice, and legal punishment,"[14] in other words the "undifferentiation" of "bad violence" (or "illegal violence") and "good violence" (or "legal violence"), insofar as ritual ceaselessly repeats the latter so as to ward off the former. From this point of view, the "sacrificial crisis" is nothing other than the confusion of sacrifice and crime. In this passage, Girard is explicitly targeting the reduction of ritual to the "myth-making function."[15] "The ritual precautions directed against violence, as absurd as some of them may appear to us," he writes, "have nothing illusory about them." But in the same movement, he also suggests a precise definition of primitive society: "a society that does not possess a legal system [and that] is vulnerable . . . to the escalation of vengeance." Sacrifice in archaic societies is thus nothing other than that which regularly vaccinates these societies against the risk of vengeful reprisals.

Between the sacrificial rites of primitive societies, which aim to prevent violence that has not yet been committed, and the judicial retributions of civilized societies, which aim to remedy violence that has already taken place, there is the trial and error of primitive thought, distancing itself little by little from the sacred at the same time as sacrifice stops being effective and risks becoming indistinguishable from crime. This is René Girard's discovery, which brings the others along in its wake. Legal violence ends up becoming confused with illegal violence. The illusory transcendence of archaic religion is dissipated, and with it the formidable protection that it gave to early societies. How does this decadence of sacrifice happen? Through the shift from one victim to another: from the "external victim" of ritual to the "internal victim" of the founding murder. The preventive ritual regresses toward the primordial scene and all of the risks that it implies for the society's survival, toward what Girard calls the return of "essential violence."

The victim of legal sacrifice, which primitive societies immolate at regular intervals, is a victim external to the group. It is either "higher" or "lower" than the rest of the community, writes Girard: a king or a slave, it is a sacred victim set apart and thus expendable, equivalent to any other sacrificial victim. Selected for sacrifice from birth or after being taken in a raid, its ritual immolation leads to no vengeful reprisals. On the contrary, it offers the community an ideal outlet, an endlessly renewable "vaccine" for nipping violence in the bud. This external victim must be contrasted with the victim internal to the group, a random victim whose immolation is always very risky: immolating a member of the group "at random" always risks causing an escalation. In this way Girard seeks to make apparent the structuring role of the "scapegoat." The latter, unlike the ritual victim, is chosen by the group in extremis from among its own. This internal victim is the victim of the "founding murder" that will then be repeated by the external victims of ritual.

Armed with a lot of empirical descriptions, Girard can then formulate his theory by making an essential distinction: the internal victim or the "scapegoat" is the one that provides the secret basis for the effectiveness of the external or "sacrificial" victim. The second repeats the first without those who participate in the sacrifice being aware of it, but also without them being completely unaware of it. There is a fundamental and founding ignorance and failure to recognize that is responsible for all the technical effectiveness of ritual. This is why the external victim must also not be "too external" and maintain a certain likeness to the members of the community that it is going to purge of its violence. Thus, writes Girard, "the minor catharsis of the sacrificial act is derived from that major catharsis circumscribed by collective murder."[16]

All rites originate in this primordial scene in which each group must remedy its own violence in a curative fashion, that is, in a very risky fashion, by immolating one of its own. The internal victim, or scapegoat, is nonetheless hidden behind the external victim of ritual. It is this half erasure that neutralizes the consciousness of the crime and makes ritual repetition possible; it is this misrecognition that neutralizes illegal violence and makes legal violence possible: thus does the transcendence of sacrificial institutions become established as the mechanism by which differences within the group are guaranteed. This erasure, of which there remains just enough of a trace not to be pure and simple forgetting, is what makes it possible to "persuade men of the fundamental difference between sacrifice and revenge."[17] Such is the origin of religious belief. It is thus less a question of an illusion (or of a "defensive reaction of nature," as Bergson thought), than of a ruse that draws its effectiveness from an obscure awareness.

René Girard sums up his discovery under the name "double substitution":

> Ritual sacrifice is founded on a double substitution. The first, which passes unperceived, is the substitution of one member of the community for all, brought about through the operation of the surrogate victim. The second, the only truly "ritualistic" substitution, is super-imposed on the first. It is the substitution of a victim belonging to a predetermined sacrificial category for the original victim. The surrogate victim comes from inside the community, and the ritual victim must come from outside; otherwise the community might find it difficult to unite against it.[18]

"Might find it difficult to unite against it," which is to say that the process is not a spontaneous, automatic one, but works only in a secondary way, by way of the selection of the victim. Thus "the second substitution graft[s] itself onto the first," writes Girard, thus "founding violence succeed[s] in imposing a centrifugal force on the rite,"[19] and expels from the community the violence that would otherwise contaminate the group. This preventive repetition of a curative violence, this "*minor* catharsis derived from a *major* catharsis," formerly effected at great peril for the entire group, makes it possible for the latter to avoid taking on such risks. It would be obliged to take them on, on the other hand, if it were to stop choosing its victims according to the protocol of ritual, if it were to stop choosing the place and time of their immolation, throwing itself spontaneously on a victim internal to the community. Ritual thus knows very well what it is doing, even as it fails to grasp the workings of the transcendence that it obeys. Sacrifice corresponds to a "normal" situation, while the founding murder remedies an "abnormal" situation. That is why only a well-established legal system has the luxury of striking at the heart of violence, of punishing the guilty party without being afraid that the punishment will have harmful consequences for the whole group. The sacrifice that strikes off to one side of the target is essentially myopic, and the legal apparatus that strikes the bull's eye is essentially lucid. But, as Girard constantly stresses, there was a form of lucidity in misrecognition, just as there is a form of misrecognition in lucidity. There is always a risk in striking violence: the risk of waking up the sleeping tiger, of causing an escalation that will once again erase every difference between legal and illegal violence. The transcendence of justice is every bit as precarious as the transcendence of sacrifice.

Such is the unsettling light that *Violence and the Sacred* sheds on our time. And we must thank Paul Dumouchel for having extrapolated the contemporary consequences of the theory of "double substitution" in his book, *The Barren Sacrifice: An Essay on Political Violence*,[20] in which he analyzes what happens when the state, instead of designating external enemies, designates internal ones, as is the case in genocides or mass murders: the expendable victim is among us, and exterior and interior merge together. The state that was formed by designating the enemy on the exterior and the friend on the interior ends up disappearing by devouring its own children. Thus the scapegoat mechanism endures in societies that have abolished "sacrificial institutions": there is a difference not of nature but of degree between the death penalty and the slide into genocidal violence. The legal-political order is every bit as precarious as the strictly sacrificial order. This self-destruction of politics bears witness to a return of the "essential violence" or the "sacrificial crisis" that inattentive readers of Girard were too quick to associate exclusively with the archaic origins of culture. The crisis of undifferentiation is valid for all institutions.

After this detour by way of *Violence and the Sacred*, it is thus time to come back to what I called the messianic moment, and more precisely to the project for which Girard's second book sets the stage: a new interpretation of the Cross as the only possible remedy to the flood of violence. I will have only to deduce the implications of this encounter between Girard and Bergson to obtain some interesting results. Earlier I cited a passage from *The Two Sources*, in which Bergson evokes the emergence of the idea of "absolute justice" with the prophets of Israel. René Girard's contribution consists in joining to this event the contribution of the Greek tragic playwrights, which in his opinion is just as decisive. Indeed, it is at the intersection of the Jewish experience and the Greek experience that the event of the Passion takes on its full meaning:

> Historians seem to agree that Greek tragedy belonged to a period of transition between the dominance of an archaic theocracy and the emergence of a new, "modern" order based on statism and laws. Before its decline the archaic order must have enjoyed a certain stability; and this stability must have reposed on its religious element—that is, on the sacrificial rites.
>
> Although they predate the tragedians, the pre-Socratics are often regarded as the philosophers of classical tragedy. In their writings we can find echoes of the religious crisis we are attempting to define. The fifth fragment of Heraclitus quite clearly deals with the decay of sacrificial rites, with their inability to purify what is impure. Religious beliefs are compromised by the decadent state of the ritual. . . . The difference between blood spilt for ritual and for criminal purposes no longer holds. The Heraclitus fragment appears in even sharper relief when compared to analogous passages in the Old Testament. The preexilian prophets Amos, Isaiah, and Micah denounce in vehement terms the impotence of the sacrificial process and ritual in general. *In the most explicit manner they link the decay*

> *of religious practices to the deterioration of contemporary behavior.*[21] Inevitably, the eroding of the sacrificial system seems to result in the emergence of reciprocal violence. Neighbors who had previously discharged their mutual aggressions on a third party, joining together in the sacrifice of an "outside" victim, now turn to sacrificing one another.[22]

The difference in tone between Bergson's text and Girard's stems from the fact that Girard comes to the subject by way of a precise study of sacrificial institutions and their historical breakdown. Such is the context that makes it possible to understand the Christian event. According to Girard, "the decay of religious practices" and "the deterioration of contemporary behavior" are one and the same thing. The crisis of sacrifice is a mimetic crisis, that is to say a crisis of models. It corresponds to the moment at which each of us becomes an obstacle for the other, when relationships are no longer regulated by rites in which "group members sacrifice victims together"; when the scapegoat mechanism, the mechanism by which victims are selected, no longer functions. The closest person can then become an enemy, an obstacle to be destroyed. The legal-political order, avatar of sacrificial institutions, attempted to combat this sacrifice of the other that characterizes the breakdown of ritual regulations, while waiting for the new order announced by the prophets. This wait for the kingdom anticipates the collapse of the "Powers and Principalities," to use St. Paul's expression. It is apocalyptic inasmuch as it perceives the commonality of structure between sacrifice and the state. That is why the kingdom is prefigured by the Cross and by the new model that it both induces and produces. It is with the Cross that we move from an exterior model, or a social model, to an interior model, or an intimate model; that we move, in other words, from one god to another.

The Two Forms of Imitation

"The Greeks never sought to imitate gods. It was not until Christianity that the mimetic perspective imposed itself as the only possible form of redemption, given the revealed madness of humanity," writes René Girard in *Battling to the End*,[23] picking up the thread of the most fraught pages of *Violence and the Sacred*. The question of the model implied by the Christian event, which operates a shift from an exterior to an interior model, from a visible to an invisible model, is thus decisive, and we can be legitimately surprised that neither Bergson nor Girard expanded any further on their description. Both of them even admit to having encountered problems of formulation when dealing with this matter.[24] I would thus like to indicate, in a few concluding remarks, the benefit of comparing and contrasting the two thinkers' perspectives on this particular point. The question remains open and calls for further clarification and development.

For the stakes are not small. Indeed, it is a question of understanding how the Christian event attempts to remedy the ravages brought about by the collapse of sacrificial institutions. It suffices for an absolute innocent to exonerate all of the scapegoats immolated instead of the true guilty parties, and a new response to human violence takes hold, a response that the state will be obliged to take charge of with terrible effectiveness. But the Christian event, even as it makes a legal, that is to say a curative, solution to violence possible, is also the invention of a new preventive model, the only one that enables us to confront the truth about the founding murder without, in Bergson's words, "letting the planet be blown to pieces." This new model is paradoxical because it draws its force from its invisibility: the Christian event can be defined as a destruction of all ancient models, a destruction of their very ability to dazzle or to produce veneration. It is because it has discovered and described the scapegoat mechanism as the principle of archaic societies (and of their structuring models) that the mimetic theory sheds new light on the constitution of the Christian model, whose genesis Bergson understood perhaps less well than its function.

It is in the first chapter of *The Two Sources*, which is literally pre-Girardian, that the philosopher goes straight to the subject that concerns us, while distinguishing between the two moralities, "closed" and "open," "incomplete" and "complete." The moral imperative is a mixture of social obligation and individual aspiration. It draws its compelling force from these two sources. Social morality prefigures individual morality such as it is incarnated in exceptional beings. The latter have become good models: they are no longer idolized gods or demigods, but individuals who can be imitated without any danger. In opposition to the social model divinized by his glorious actions, the interior model is, in the image of Christ, divinized by his refusal of glory. He is a hero transformed by his refusal to remain a hero. The imitation of the interior image of these singular beings, freed from glory, makes it possible to move societies forward, to open them up, instead of becoming attached to their conservation in the way that the bee is attached to the conservation of the hive.

This "common imitation of a model" is a good definition of the "ideal society," or the invisible society, that is constructed thanks to the imitation of interior models. Each of us must ask ourselves, at such and such moment in our lives, what a "great moral figure . . . would expect from us in such a situation." "In our imaginations," we then submit our conduct to the judgment of this intimate guide. Who or what is this model? It can be a family member, a friend, "a man whose life we have been told about," in a deeper way it can even be "a personality that is born in us." And Bergson concludes:

> As a matter of fact this personality takes shape as soon as we adopt a model; the longing to resemble, which ideally generates the form, is an incipient resemblance; the word which we shall make our own is the word whose echo we have heard within ourselves.[25]

How was this radical interiority opened up? By the Christian event, Bergson and Girard suggest with one voice. The mystical being, the interior model or the "hero of open morality," following in imperfect fashion the path opened by the "Christ of the Gospels," has surmounted the obstacle of social pressure, constitutive of the figure of the enemy. He may have undergone the pressures that come with any social obligation, he may, for example, have waged war, but he has not been satisfied with the glory that war brings and has found the way to open his group up to the universal.[26] He has thus managed to go beyond the limits of the human species and to merge with the creative impulse. The mystical being does not use mimetic energies, as would a demagogue or a military leader, fascinating models in whom society idolizes itself, but he "puts society back in motion again" by the new imitation that he brings into existence. It is this visionary capacity that heroes and saints possess. We must therefore adhere to their model: we must know how to imitate so as to be able to draw people along with us. The interior effort required to conform to the model is a contraction, and the superactive action that results from it is release. It falls to us, then, to know how to hear this interior voice. But mere wisdom is not enough, because it loves humanity in too abstract a way: the Stoics, for example, writes Bergson, "did not succeed in drawing humanity after them."[27] Only the Christian event was able to produce a good model, the one that communicates an "enthusiasm which spreads from soul to soul, unceasingly, like a conflagration."[28]

It is in addressing the notion of "self-respect" as a "social sentiment" that Bergson comes close to what would later become one of the pillars of the mimetic theory. The admiration that every person feels "for a Man eminent among men" is at the origin of the "sentiment of honor." Self-respect here coincides "with the group's self-love." This is not far from what Girard would later call, in 1961, "external mediation," or veneration for exterior models. The latter constitute a framework for each individual's actions: they are "ideomotors," to use one of Bergson's expressions. Exemplary war heroes or sages contribute, by the prestige of their image, to the education of citizens. Coming after the gods or demigods of antiquity, who were produced by the scapegoat mechanism and venerated for the order that they made it possible to maintain, social models draw the subject into the "circular movement" of closed societies; they model the subject's behavior so as to make it serve the conservation of society.

Every society adores itself in the mirror of its eminent models: to kill the enemy that nature prescribes, it is necessary to be drawn along by the adoration of a demigod or the prestige of a leader, to obey what Bergson calls the "somnambulistic imperative" generated by all closed societies. The messianic event takes humanity out of this vital torpor by recharging it, at an even deeper level, in the very impulse of life. This event overturns the very logic by which these societies were formed. In *Deceit, Desire, and the Novel*, René Girard thus sheds light on the destruction of social models that characterizes the opening up of modern societies: mimetic pathology is inscribed in the veneration of external models; the shift from "external mediation" to "internal mediation,"[29] from the admiration of a distant model to the idolatry of a model close at hand, is inherent to the structure of "triangular desire." It is this instability of desire that characterizes modern societies shaken by the Christian event and that makes it impossible to reconstitute the sacrificial order.

This event brings with it a revelation of desire. The model that it offers us is nothing other than the resistance to mimetic crisis, which is the pathology proper to the collapse of the old sacrificial system. The content of this revelation is simple: the moral effect of the exempla depends on the gaze that we level at them. There can either be an exterior gaze or an interior gaze, a "closed" gaze or an "open" gaze. Such is the central phenomenological impact of this event. From now on, it is the quality of the admiration that presides over the choice of a good model, but also the existence of good models that makes open admiration possible. Judeo-Christian revelation "opened up" admiration by interiorizing it. As long as they remain social models, that is to say as long as they are not individualized and interiorized, exterior models lack the mystical impulse necessary to society's forward progression. The Bergsonian method makes it possible to distinguish between two forms of imitation, or two forms of admiration. There is in "open" imitation, which corresponds to an interior gaze, an inventiveness that does not exist in "closed" imitation, which aims only to coincide with a social model.[30] Girard has devoted his work to pointing out the danger in this coincidence: the trust that we put in the "external model" (closed imitation or the external gaze) carries within itself the seeds of mimetic crisis. That is why in St. Paul's thought, faith intervenes in advance to remedy the possible fetishism of the law.[31] Mimetic desire is not what Bergson calls the "desire to resemble"; it is the desire to appropriate either an object desired by the Other or else the very being of the Other, who stands as an obstacle: to "possess" a model is to be possessed by that model, which is to say that the model has not been interiorized. Bergson does not evoke the danger of the model's proximity, the fact that it can enter into rivalry with the subject. This crisis of imitation is the same thing, according to Girard, as the rise of nihilism or egalitarianism and corresponds to a realm of "internal mediation." Thus the crisis of desire, which is at the origin of the "degradation of human relationships," corresponds to the crisis of closed societies that are in the process of opening up. The erosion of all the old models would urgently call for a final model.

There is, Bergson tells us, a positive contagion proper to the "ideal society," in which we can all participate if we engage in introspection, descending into ourselves beneath our social nature, to the place where interior models are calling to and waiting for us. The attraction that the interior model exerts on the subject, and the trust or faith that the subject has in this image, does not involve the risks associated with the exterior model, who is always likely to become a rival, that is to say a veritable object of fascination. Here we have the elements of a theory of *the imitation of the interior model*, the only imitation capable of stimulating civilized societies by keeping them immersed in the life impulse. It is significant that Bergson ventures onto the terrain of anamnesis in order to define this opening. If external models correspond to a social pressure, interior models correspond to a mystical aspiration. They have an "aura," a "mysticity" that constitutes their force of attraction. We aspire to become one with this image, "like the copy with the model," but without the risk of sliding down the slippery slope of self-love. Between these two kinds of imitation, Girard tells us, between exterior imitation and interior imitation, there is a slow decadence of all institutions, the irreversible rise of nihilism. The crisis of Western civilization is one with the shift from one kind of imitation to the other; and hominization is nothing other than the long and painful interiorization of our models. Now that we know the content of Christian revelation, we can decide either to remain possessed by our models or to liberate ourselves from this enslavement.

René Girard enlightens us as to the sacrificial genesis of these ideomotor fictions that are our external models, these exempla that culture provides and that are the "derivatives" of the scapegoat mechanism. But what does he have to say about the genesis of the interior model, whose "open" imitation puts us back in the life stream? This genesis, more than the Sermon on the Mount, is sacrificial, since it and the Cross are one. I will do no more than summarize the contributions of mimetic theory with regard to this point. The Christian model, the only remedy to the flood of violence, appears against the backdrop of what Nietzsche calls the "divine decomposition" and what Girard calls the end of sacrifice (or "the return of essential violence"). Regardless of whether Judeo-Christian revelation was the cause or sanction of this sacrificial decadence, it remains the case that this revelation took place. It is because Christ removed himself as an obstacle, because he refused to be divinized by the fascination of men, that he withdrew from this possible fascination and joined the Father in His silence. Only Christ is capable of inhabiting this "divine decomposition": mediating between an absent Father and mankind, henceforth orphan of the gods, he becomes the single model, or rather the prototype of all good models, because he averted the dangers of imitation. Here we can detect the inspiration of the poet Hölderlin, who had already been discussed at length in *Violence and the Sacred* and to whom Girard comes back in *Battling to the End*. At the very moment he decides to go into retirement forever in his tower in Tübingen, the poet understands that only the imitation of Christ can save us from the imitation of other human beings, that only conforming to this interior model keeps us at a healthy distance from the divine. Bergson suggests nothing else when he describes the saints, those "heroes of open morality," as the "incomplete continuers" of Christ, an eminent model in his very discretion and his withdrawal from the world.

Let us very provisionally bring these reflections to a close. At the moment at which the archaic is eroding and the legal system is emerging, the moment at which a shift occurs from a misrecognition that is no longer effective to a lucidity that is not yet blinding, a truth about violence, the presentiment of which appears in the prophets of Israel and the Greek tragic playwrights, is finally spoken to mankind. At this precise moment, between the erosion of sacrifice and the advent of law, a crucified figure reveals the innocence of all emissary victims. The question of this innocence is thus posed only with the Cross, which has something of both archaic sacrifice and legal punishment about it. But this sacrifice is useless and this legal punishment is unfair. The Cross thus reveals the precariousness of these institutions, one moribund, the other being born, and the persistent problem of the distinction between legal and illegal violence. The Cross thus disqualifies all self-transcendence, all adoration of the social. Whence the absolute urgency of a new model, and of a new definition of God. Girard makes it possible for us to hazard some theological formulations: only the absolute innocence of the Son leads us to the absolute transcendence of the Father. Refusing to be a "model-obstacle," removing himself as an obstacle, Christ becomes the only mediator between the orphans of the gods and the absent Father. Intervening in the heart of "divine decomposition," Christ reveals the nature of man, constituted by sacrifice, and the nature of God, which is not a product of the scapegoat mechanism. The Passion thus points toward this withdrawal of God that is both self-effacement and enticement, toward the essence of the divine that consists in withdrawing so as to make the vital and creative impulse possible.

The messianic event is one and the same thing as a transformation of sacrifice, which it turns inside out rather than nullifying: the true models, the interior models, are "transformed heroes," Bergson would say. They are inscribed in the Christian opening, which they make it possible to take hold of. The messianic event and the new model that it produces thus appear historically between the archaic and the legal orders, but they aim at once this side of the scapegoat mechanism and beyond it. The Passion of the Christ alerts us to the end of sacrifice, for Christ is a useless victim, incapable of reconciling the group; and it alerts us to the dangers of all legal-political orders, for Christ is an innocent victim, denouncing the arbitrariness that is always potentially present in legal punishment. This is why René Girard finishes his oeuvre with a salute to the poet Hölderlin secluded in Tübingen. Conscious of the need for holding together the two natures of God: the one that comes *from* mankind and the one that comes *to* mankind, the poet stops just short of this synthesis and of the new experience that it makes possible. It is to this experience that we are called today, even if we are only the "incomplete continuers" of Christ, this "brother" of the archaic gods.

NOTES

1. Frédéric Worms, "Dieu dans la philosophie de Bergson," in *L'Évolution Créatrice e il problema religioso* (Milan: Mimesis, 2007), 51–60. See also, Worms, *Bergson ou les deux sens de la vie* (Paris: Presses Universitaires de France, 2004); and for the subject that concerns us: "Le clos et l'ouvert dans *Les Deux Sources de la morale et de la religion*: Une distinction qui change tout," in *Bergson et la religion: Nouvelles perspectives sur "Les Deux Sources e la morale et de la religion,"* ed. Ghislain Waterlot (Paris: Presses Universitaires de France, 2008).
2. Henri Bergson, *The Two Sources of Morality and Religion*, trans. R. Ashley Audra and Cloudesley Brereton, with the assistance of W. Horsfall Carter (London: MacMillan, 1935), 57.
3. Vladimir Jankélévitch, "Bergson et le judaïsme," in *Henri Bergson* (Paris: Presses Universitaires de France, 1989).
4. Bergson, *The Two Sources of Morality and Religion*, 60–61.
5. Bergson writes in his will: "My reflections led me closer and closer to Catholicism, in which I saw the complete achievement of Judaism. I would have been converted had I not been aware for years of the beginnings of . . . the immense wave of anti-semitism that was to break over the world. I wanted to remain among those who were to be the persecuted of tomorrow. But I hope that a Catholic priest will come say prayers at my funeral. In the event that this authorization is not granted, a rabbi should be called upon, but without hiding from him or from anyone else my moral adherence to Catholicism, as well as my initial desire to have the prayers of a Catholic priest" (cited by Philippe Soulez and Frédéric Worms, *Bergson*, coll. "Biographies" (Paris: Flammarion, 2002), 277).
6. Bergson, *The Two Sources of Morality and Religion*; my emphasis.
7. "What expiatory rites, what sacred games will we be forced to invent? The greatness of this act is too great for us. Must we not become gods ourselves, simply to appear worthy of it? . . . God is dead! God is dead! And we have all killed him" (Nietzsche, *The Gay Science*, section 125).
8. Bergson, *The Two Sources of Morality and Religion*, 61.
9. "indefinite in number also are the forms of superstition, or rather of static religion . . . But the complexity vanishes if we place man back in nature as a whole, *if we consider that intelligence is apt*

to be an obstacle to the serenity we find everywhere else, and that the obstacle must be surmounted, the balance restored. . . . Unrest and myth-making nullify each other" (ibid., 177, my emphasis).

10. Ibid., 172.

11. The deliberate setting aside of sacrifice and ritual, along with the notion of the "myth-making function" used to understand "static" religions, makes it possible to understand the importance of the *scheme* in Lévi-Strauss, who is much closer to Bergson than one would think a priori: no longer an ideomotor scheme (as the "fables" of static religion still are), but a scheme that structures language. I thank Frederick Keck for having made it possible for me to articulate this idea.

12. See Lucien Scubla, "René Girard et la renaissance de l'anthropologie religieuse," in *Girard*, ed. Mark Anspach (Paris: Cahiers de l'Herne, 2008).

13. René Girard, *La Violence et le sacré*, in *De la violence à la divinité* (Paris: Grasset, 2007), 332. Translator's note: In this particular case, the official Gregory translation of *Violence and the Sacred*, while no doubt smoother than my own, fails to render a few key words in the French text. For the sake of comparison, I give it in its entirety here: "A primitive society, a society that lacks a legal system, is exposed to the sudden escalation of violence. Such a society is compelled to adopt attitudes we may well find incomprehensible. . . . Considered all together, the ritual precautions against violence are firmly rooted in reality, absurd though some of them may appear to our own eyes. If the sacrificial catharsis actually succeeds in preventing the unlimited propagation of violence, a sort of *infection* is in fact being checked" (*Violence and the Sacred*, trans. Patrick Gregory [London: Continuum, 2005], 31).

14. Girard, *Violence and the Sacred*, 25.

15. Henri Bergson is not cited in René Girard's oeuvre before *Battling to the End: Conversations with Benoît Chantre*, trans. Mary Baker (East Lansing: Michigan State University Press, 2010), in which the latter acknowledges having read *The Two Sources* with interest, but not having derived any precise information, not surprisingly, given that his object of study is the very one that Bergson refuses to examine.

16. *Violence and the Sacred*, op. cit., 107.

17. Ibid., 25.

18. Ibid., 107.

19. Ibid.

20. Paul Dumouchel, *The Barren Sacrifice. An Essay on Political Violence* [Michigan State University Press, 2015 ; *Le Sacrifice inutile. Essai sur la violence politique*, Flammarion, 2011.]

21. Translator's note: the French original refers more precisely to the deterioration of human relationships: "Ils lient de façon très explicite à cette décomposition religieuse la détérioration des rapports humains" (Girard, *La Violence et le sacré*, 348).

22. Girard, *Violence and the Sacred*, 45; my emphasis.

23. Girard, *Battling to the End*, 122.

24. "The first morality is comparatively easy to formulate, but not the second," writes Bergson (*The Two Sources of Morality and Religion*, 45).

25. Ibid., 24.

26. That is why the French writer Charles Péguy turned to Corneille in order to understand more fully the transformation from heroism to holiness.

27. Bergson, *The Two Sources of Morality and Religion*, 47.

28. Ibid. Girard's thought makes it possible for us to temper Bergson's enthusiasm by making a necessary distinction between possession and interiorization, enthusiasm and inspiration. The "intimate mediation" implied by the interior dialogue (or the opening up of interiority made possible by the intimate model) is a source of communion more than it is a source of "enthusiasm." This is one of the reasons the distinction between hero and saint, patriotic fervor and mystical communion, is not very clear in Bergson. From this point of view, the radical critique of heroism made by Girard in *Battling to the End* brings a necessary distinction.

29. Whence the need that René Girard and I felt to invent the term "intimate mediation" in *Battling to the End*, in order to define the third type of imitation proper to interior models.

30. I owe this distinction between the two imitations to a discussion with Frédéric Worms.

31. On this point, see my essay "Le clocher de Combray: René Girard ou la dernière loi," in *René Girard: La théorie mimétique; de l'apprentissage à l'apocalypse*, ed. Charles Ramond (Paris: Presses Universitaires de France, 2010).

Girard and Religion in the Age of Secularism

Otto Kallscheuer

Christianity is the only religion that foresaw its own failure.

—René Girard, *Achever Clausewitz*

Let me begin with a warning. It might also be read as a plea for excuse: I am neither a true believer in mimetic theory/theology nor a connoisseur of Girardian methodology and its recent developments (if there are any).[1] My reading of René Girard's oeuvre has been rather sporadic and even somewhat naive. I always took (and after consideration, I still take) the Girardian approach for a general (but also generic) suspicion; I don't read his theory as a specific (scientific) hypothesis. In the end René Girard's "big" and iconoclastic thesis—about the scapegoat mechanism as the very origin and essence (function, telos, secret) of sacrificial religion in human history—is probably better understood as a kind of metascientific challenge than as a testable anthropological or social-scientific theory. And it may be a very useful exercise to answer this challenge—at least for a clarification of our concepts.[2]

In other words, I am tempted to classify René Girard (and especially the later Girard) as a "religious critique"—more or less in the sense in which Harold Bloom has coined this term for himself: Religious criticism is concerned with the specific ("*spiritual*") dimensions of religion, its "spirituality that survives every reduction," in the same way as literary criticism is concerned with literature's aesthetic dimensions.[3]

But what does this mean for the rather explicit truth-claims that René Girard himself is making about the real, factual, empirical ("extraritual and extratextual"[4]) existence of the foundational murder of innocent scapegoats at the origins of society?[5] For the time being they remain just claims, until they have been verified—as other truth-claims, other theories of culture, society, religion, should be tested too. (And in the next two paragraphs I shall indeed have a look on what kind of results such a factual "check" of Girardism might yield.)

But from my point of view Girard's general antimythos of the "foundational murder" as the secret origin of humanity and society itself (the city of Cain!) looks much more like a universalistic provocation than like a precise hypothesis (to say nothing about its scientific testability). In other words, I read Girard's reconstructions of the "bloody origins"[6] of every society, religion, and culture in very much the same spirit as I read also Sigmund Freud's *Totem and Taboo* or Friedrich Nietzsche's *Anti-Christ*: as a memento concerning the rather uncivil origins of civilization, as a healthy invitation to incredulity toward our own modern historical myths or "narratives," as an antidote to our own historicist ideas about *perfectibilité* and progress in human affairs.[7]

Such skepticism should be welcome also to (self-)critical modernists. Many of the familiar (self-)portraits of our present benign modernity are themselves very far from having been tested empirically.[8] What does this mean for the perspective of our future progress—classically conceived as increasingly peaceful *commercium* in human affairs? Therefore, with the critical and self-critical sides of our modern mind, we might conclude that even the antidote to our modernist illusions might need some "mythical" elements as well. And in this function also the Girardian antimythos should be welcome. Didn't even the great Thomas Hobbes, himself more a rationalist in the style of René Descartes, announce his own project of the pacifying role of state power in mythological and biblical terms?[9] Whether mimetic theory in itself, conceived by its author as a general revelation of "things hidden since the foundation of the world," is empirically true or false, well, that might be another affair. Without final revelation the question "What is truth?" (John 18:38) shall remain open.

Mimetic Theory as Hypothesis?

What is mimetic theory? Can we understand René Girard's approach in the same way as we treat other theoretical approaches in anthropology and/ or theory of religion too? Well, then mimetic theory would be another hypothesis about the function and origin of religion. This hypothesis took shape first in René Girard's literary studies, then in his anthropological comparative analyses (1); and it might be combined with some (rather rough) methodological hint (2):

1. "Girardism" is sustaining a general thesis: The neuralgic core of (any) religious ritual, taboo, and symbolism lies in the containment of otherwise inevitable collective murderous violence. This genealogical origin in murderous violence makes for its "realism." (And *this* is also Girard's basic objection to any structuralist or moralist interpretation of religious symbolism.)
2. Does mimetic theory also offer us a theoretical "tool-set" to check its validity? Well, I think it does so: René Girard indeed gives us something like a hermeneutical "instrument" apt to test his general, rather elementary, but far-reaching hypothesis—at least a rough framework for theoretical verification. This is obviously no formal tool, more a theoretical ideal-type or archetype, by which we can reduce the extraordinary variety of archaic religious and ritual symbolism to one recurrent structure: to the circular "dramatic" model of mimetic rivalry.[10]

The "mimetic circle" begins with the mutual contagion of *mimetical desire* between (usually) the men of a given community, then its drama continues with the *reciprocal escalation* and generalization of mimetic rivality, until it culminates in a general *mimetic crisis*. Now the whole community risks breaking down in general chaos and violence. But how can this crisis end? For Girard this crisis cannot but find its solution in sacrifice: first in the real sacrifice or "foundational murder" of a human scapegoat; and then, later, in its "ritual" recurrence, repetition, or evocation through animal sacrifice. So, the maximum version of the Girardian hypothesis "G" would be the following: [G] There is, at the hidden origins of each and every religious message (symbolism, ritual code, doctrine) always—inevitably and "in the last instance"[11]—the collective murder of an innocent victim, which then sooner or later—thereafter and therefore—was inevitably totemized or divinized.

As it is obvous, in this maximal version the mimetic hypothesis of the murderous/sacrificial origin of all human culture (or, to humanity as such)[12] will never be proven. It would be impossible, because no proposition with an all-quantifier can ever be verified—it can only be falsified. And for a strict follower of Karl R. Popper's "logic of falsifiability," mimetic theory may have already been disproved by finding just one single counterexample.[13] But could the finding of just one archaic religious system without any (ritual or symbolic) reference to sacrifice refute the whole Girardian enterprise? I don't think so. Besides, we have also to take into account that according to Girard within traditional religious symbolism the nonreference to the foundational killing of the first victim is rather probable or even necessary: It is the ignorance about this first murder and/or the glorious transfiguration of its victim that we should expect in mythology, not its bloody trace or any smoking gun.[14] But this nonverifiability and its difficult falsifiability does not make the foundational Girardian thesis a useless hypothesis (or transform it into an article of faith). A big hypothesis may very well serve precisely when (or because) its maximum version will be falsified—thereby retaining a reduced but more precise explanatory power. In order to understand this rather simple truth I propose a mental experiment with our big (or universal) Girardist hypothesis "G."

Conjectures and Specifications

Let us suppose that we could get access to a "God's-eye view" platform: from here we could have an overview of the whole process of anthropogenesis and/or the origins of human culture, overlooking the one hundred thousand (or perhaps more)[15] years of human/social/cultural history. And now let's suppose that a serious empirical survey undertaken from our universal celestial observation-point would come to the following, empirically corroborated conclusions: The big thesis of Girardism (G) concerns only a relevant but minor part of world prehistory (big G is thereby becoming a small g_1

or g_2, just one among other big hypotheses as V, F, B, T etc.—proposed by Giambattista Vico, Sigmund Freud, Walter Burkert, Victor Turner, and others—to be tested).

- [g_1] Only 20 percent of the (former) primate-gatherings[16] or "*Urhorden*" (Sigmund Freud) that in prehistoric periods had developed a "human culture" did so by first committing a *foundational murder* (as in the Girardian hypothetical "mimetic cycle") and then ritualizing it, and so only for these 20 percent of prehistoric mankind[17] was it ritually transformed human sacrifice that caused humanization, culture, and the development of society.
- [b_1] For some other 20 percent of protohuman gatherings the sacrificial rituals originated in the anthropological shock caused by the development of *hunting* (Walter Burkert), that is, the killing of nonhuman animals by *homines necantes*.[18]
- [v_1] Still other primitive religions, another 20 percent of the total, might just have arisen out of the experience of *fear*, stimulating also the sense of *curiosity* (Giambattista Vico)—especially after the natural catastrophes connected with the end of the Ice Age about ten thousand years ago: After the Great Flood, isolated primitive men, having grown giants in the wilderness, were fleeing from the wild beasts in the forests,[19] and at a certain point for the first time experienced thunder and lightning. They were "frightened and astonished by the great effect whose cause they did not know, and [they] raised their eyes and became aware of the sky. And because in such a case the nature of human mind leads to attribute its own nature to the effect, and because in that state their nature was that of men all robust bodily strength, who expressed their passions by shouting and grumbling, they pictured the sky to themselves as a great animated body, which in that aspect they called *Jove* . . . who meant to tell them something by the hiss of his bolts and the clap of his thunder."[20] Thereafter these hominid giants began to interpret nature as *gran corpo animato*, ordered by a will, and in searching to understand his signs and orders, they engage specialists, *divinatori* and priests, and they develop archaic religion, poetic fantasy, poetic science, and metaphysics.
- [m_1] Other elements of religious anthropogenesis might have had been

caused by the mysteries of *life-giving*, motherhood, childbirth, and the numinous powers of procreation.[21]

- [t_1] Still other religious rituals could have to do with the collective *identity formation* of early protohuman communities, stabilizing their sense of belonging, of inside/outside differentiation, by egalitarian *communitas*-rituals (Victor Turner), in which the threshold of being socially "born" (or reborn) as member of the group is performed and confirmed, renewed and stabilized for newcomers.[22]

And perhaps upon more detailed analysis of our celestial survey we may discover that in some of these rituals (t_2, t_3, t_4 . . .) also various other elements of former religious hominization or group-formation have been preserved and combined, accumulated and/or transformed: for example, some removed experiences of foundational killing (g_2, g_3, g_4 . . .); some unresolved mysteries of human fertility (m_2, m_3 . . .); various shamanistic powers dealing with the collective memory of past hunting societies and their anxieties (b_2, b_3, b_4 . . .), perhaps ritually reenacted in societies already touched by the agricultural technology of the "neolithical revolution."[23] Some religious rituals and myths might contain different mixtures of various foundational experiences or functional narratives (g, m, t, or others). So instead of one big G-story, one single explanation, the religious map of early human societies would contain a rather complex, even sometimes contradictory mosaic (e.g., of $g_2 + b_3$–rituals here, of $m_3 + v_4$–mythologies there, and so on).

Now let us come to our evaluation: What would this general picture of early human societies, obtained from our God's-eye view of the genealogies of religion(s), mean for the usefulness of Girardism, here understood as hypothesis? Would the empirical downgrading of the validity of mimetical theory (from the one and only universal big G to some minor percentage of $g_{1,2,3}$ . . .) be a problem? To my opinion—not at all. On the contrary. Because that's exactly what hypotheses are for: they can never be totally verified, so they shall remain hypotheses. And their method of falsification—especially in cultural and historical sciences—cannot be the Popperian way of refutation either (with the falsification rule: one mismatch and you're out). But in our case we can use the model of a hypothetical "dramatic circle" of mimetic desire and foundational violence that Girard has developed out of his anthropological reading of Marcel Proust, William Shakespeare, and various Holy Scriptures. We take historical documents and ethnological evidence about the plurality of religions, we adopt the Girardian ideal-typical "mimetic cycle" as a heuristic pattern of reconstruction for this or that religion, and then we check and see:

- How/where/when it fits;
- Where/when/why it doesn't fit;
- If/how it may be modified, specified (in order to fit), or even combined with other hypotheses;
- If/how the archetypical story of human sacrifice in itself may be part of another story explaining it (or of another drama): of paleontology? of theology?

By the way, isn't this exactly what René Girard himself is trying to do in his little book on *Sacrifice* in the Vedic texts? "By recognizing that the Vedic tradition can also [sc. like the Bible and like Buddhism] lead to a revelation that discredits sacrifice, mimetic theory locates within sacrifice itself a paradoxical power of quiet reflection that leads in the long run to the eclipse of this violent institution that is nevertheless fundamental for the development of humanity."[24]

Secularization, Secularism, Secularity

I have also been asked to review René Girard's approach to religion in its relation to secularization, but secularization in itself is a rather complex concept. It may be understood as historical process: as constitutive element of modern (Western) state-formation,[25] or as global trend (with many countertendencies) toward the growing disentangling of religion and politics.[26] It may be understood as social theory explaining this process (or justifying it), and even as ethical-political program (as secularism, aiming at the reduction of any political or social impact of religion).[27] And whether we count René Girard among secular anthropologists or among religious thinkers *tout court*, he is thinking and writing under the epistemological, cultural, and political conditions of our secularity—of Western modernity.

In his recent opus magnum *A Secular Age* Charles Taylor has shown convincingly how the social and cultural conditions of the plausibility of religion have changed radically over the last four hundred years. Compared to the premodern and early modern societies in Europe, modern Western societies live under a secular heaven: "The shift to secularity . . . consists, among other things, of a move from a society where belief in God is unchallenged and indeed, unproblematic, to one in which it is understood to be one option among others, and frequently not the easiest to embrace."[28]

This common cultural and epistemological horizon obviously influences believers and nonbelievers alike, and it has an undeniable impact on both religious and antireligious thinkers, on anthropologists of religion as well as religious critics.[29] This state of affairs might indeed facilitate an agnostic state of mind, but it could also provoke the conscious reaffirmation of an endangered "old-time religion" (and then, obviously, this "born-again" religion will never be the same as the old one). So the secular age does not determine any specific answer to religious questions or theological quarrels, but the secular horizon of social plausibility might render difficult some forms of religious question(ing) and facilitate others, especially under the conditions of an increasingly pluralistic public sphere for religious and nonreligious worldviews. This new situation of religious pluralism could privilege a rather problematic and possibly reflexive understanding not just of religion, but of one's own religious identity, of our own thinking about religion (or about our reasons to believe).[30] Consequently all contemporary thinkers are aware of the fact that religion cannot be taken for granted any longer. This kind of awareness is shared today by secularists and clericalists, by religious fundamentalists and religious liberals alike.

As to René Girard, he obviously is not a secularist thinker at all—at least not in the antireligious understanding of secularism shared by many contemporary philosophers or social theorists, especially in the French tradition of *laicité*. This, however, does not mean that we should understand René Girard's writings simply as testimony of his personal religious convictions, as another theological elaboration of the Christian revelation—even if in recent years a certain apocalyptical tone and a somewhat doctrinary style did indeed show up in Girard's oeuvre (and I will come to this latest Girard later; see "A Short Resumé" below). Be that as it may, his first books did present a purely secular account of literature, mythology, or religion; at least they pretended to do so. *La violence et le sacré* (1972), Girard's first great synthesis of religious anthropology, has even been described by contemporary critics as "the first atheist theory of religion."[31] For a certain period the author himself seems to have understood his own work as purely secular scientific research—respecting contemporary methodological standards in social science,[32] arguing in the name of anthropological "realism" not only against any positivist sociology or ethnology, but also against prevailing trends in late twentieth-century cultural analysis and French theory to see fiction everywhere (especially in the structuralist interpretation of foundational myths).[33]

Only in a second time (so it seems)[34] did Girard come to recognize that in working out his own mimetic theory of violence he might already have been—somehow "anonymously"[35]—a religious thinker all the time: his own cultural-anthropological work could be understood as an apology of the existential truth of the Christian message. And now also his self-interpretations change: his own mimetical realism in anthropology might have been already, from the beginning, an unconscious apology of the biblical revelation.[36] Of course, this later interpretion of his own early works leaves us with a special kind of puzzle: How far may "anthropological apologetics"—first only unconsciously Christian, later consciously so—be understood as a purely secular theory? I will come back to this puzzle at the end.

Four Secularization Narratives

But let us consider possible correspondences or oppositions between Girardism and secularization: Is there within the framework of mimetical theory also a space for secular modernity itself? And how does René Girard's own mimetic reconstruction of the sacrificial origins of religion relate to the different versions of the modern secularization narrative (from G. W. F. Hegel to Max Weber)—or to its critics (from Joseph de Maistre to Friedrich Nietzsche)? A new discussion about the explanatory force of the secularization thesis and its normative consequences has been inaugurated by Charles Taylor's *A Secular Age*.[37] In this debate José Casanova has proposed a useful fourfold classification of secularization narratives:

> (1) the triumphant secularist and anthropocentric progressive stories of enlightenment and emancipation of the secular spheres from religious institutions and norms; (2) the inverse negative philosophies of history, counter-Enlightenment narratives, and mainly Catholic traditionalist defenses of the lost normative age; (3) the positive, mainly Protestant postmillenial identifications of Western modernity and Christian civilization that tend to interpret secular modernity as a process of internal secularization and progressive institutionalization of Christian principles and norms; and (4) their opposite, Nietzschean-derived critical genealogies of modernity, which question the legitimacy of the modern secular age and its disciplinary and civilizing project precisely brecause of its bastard Christian lineage.[38]

Our following short confrontation will show the paradoxical position of mimetic theory with respect to these dominant narratives of (Western) secularism.[39] I will call them versions (1) to (4). As we will see, René Girard may very well share, up to a certain extent, some element in the diagnosis of one or another of these reconstructions of the Western secularization process(es). But his judgment cuts across them all, his questions and answers arising from a totally different horizon. This should be evident especially for the two positive secularization narratives in Casanova's list: version (3) and version (1), roughly corresponding to two dominant progressive (self-) interpretations of Western Enlightenment, whereas versions (2) and (4) in some respect represent their negative, reactionary counterpart. Even when Girard joins (some of) the conclusions of these positive secularization stories (3) and (1), his diagnosis shares many elements with their critical antagonists (2) and (4).

Enlightenment as Christian Liberty?

Casanova's version (3) sees secular Enlightenment as benificial consequence and/or continuation of Christianity. In the history of European thought this story has been told by rationalist or historicist philosophers, usually thinkers of Protestant culture: in Germany from G. E. Lessing's *Education of the Human Race* (1777) over Immanuel Kant's *Religion within the Limits of Pure*

Reason (1793), up to G. W. F. Hegel's *Lectures* on the Philosophy of History, on the Philosophy of Religion, and on the Philosophy of Law (1822–31). For Immanuel Kant and later for other "culturally Protestant" thinkers in Germany,[40] the element of continuity between Christian religion and secular Enlightenment could be found in Jesus's moral message.

G. W. F. Hegel's "theory of secularization" went even further.[41] Indeed Hegel, a former student of theology in the famous Tübingen Convict, took theology (and here, Christology) much more seriously than other Enlightenment thinkers. For Hegel it was only as the consequence of God's incarnation in human history that the realization of an "ethical life" (*Sittlichkeit*) in freedom became possible for all. And while the young Hegel had imagined this Christian freedom realizing itself in the form of community (*die Gemeinde*), the late philosopher of the "objective spirit" saw the realization of general freedom as result of the institutionalization of reason (i.e., the reform of the state). In Hegel's political philosophy it is the constitutional state that realizes Christian liberty through civil *Sittlichkeit* and the rule of law: Secular civil liberty is the realiziation of Christian freedom. *Quod erat demonstrandum*.

These and other versions of the classical positive Protestant thesis of the fundamental continuity between Christianity and liberal secularism can be completed today by newer interpretations of the subsequent and/or parallel Catholic modernization processes in European history, from the Catholic Reform in the sixteenth century to the Second Vatican Council in the twentieth century. In the end Protestant Reformation and Catholic Reform may have delivered analogous results: Charles Taylor has identified in the "Providential Deism" of the early modern Christian philosophers (Catholic and Protestant alike) a hermeneutical link in the transition from the personal Christian God to an impersonal, theologically more and more "disembedded" natural order.[42]

So at least objectively the intellectual outcome of both reforms has contributed to the construction of a secular, scientific worldview and a secularized institutional polity: a world from which the personal God of Christian faith has more and more retreated. And if the passage to modernity has meant leaving the spiritually "thick," supranaturally "embedded," medieval imaginary behind—in order to build the impersonal, objectivated modern worldview[43] as seen by disengaged rational subjects—then we may also put the macrosociological interpretation of Christianity as "the very religion of the exit from religion" (Marcel Gauchet) in the same family or version (3) of secularization narratives.[44]

What is then Girard's attitude to this kind of secularization theory (3)? He shares, obviously, its positive valutation of "the modern evolution away from violence" when he writes: "Our world has abolished serfdom and slavery. Our penal legislation has become more humane, the status of women has been raised, and we protect children and the aged. We have invented such things as the hospital, free medical care, and various forms of social protection for the weak and the handicapped. However feeble these mitigations of violence may seem compared with our aspirations, they are without precedent in all of human history. Our world has become progressively more aware of arbitrary victimization . . . we are rewriting history from the standpont of the victims." Girard also recognizes the roots of this evolution "quite directly" in the "non-violent side of the biblical inspiration."[45]

But Girard does not believe in any direct or linear genealogy between the revealed Christian truth and a secular civil order. For his mimetic theory there is no continuity between the biblical demystification of traditional religion, based on sacrificial violence, and the secular limitation of violence by state monopoly and the rule of law. It would even, so Girard maintains, be a very dangerous attitude to put our trust (as Hegel and liberal Protestantism have done) in this continuity—seeing secular reason, rational law, and civic morality as a successful continuation of the Christian revelation by other means.[46] In philosophy Girard's anthropological "realism" of mimetic theory stands with Friedrich Nietzsche's "vitalism" against both the idealistic philosophies of history of the nineteenth century and the normativistic stance of the present day's liberal political theory. And contrary to (post)Christian idealism and historicism, Girard's mimetic anthropological realism is no optimistic outlook at all.

And what about secular humanism and the liberal rule of law (as consequences of the Christian revelation, according to the genealogy of secularization theory version 3)? For Girard they can only weaken sacrificial violence, destroying its legitimation, but they cannot prevent the "tremendous increase in violence and in the threats of violence," which in the eyes of Girard is the other, the "dark" side, of all the humanitarian progresses of the last two centuries or so (in the West).[47] The point of view of the innocent victims is not—and will perhaps never be—the point of view of the victorious party.

What Christ's Passion has shown, performed, embodied is nothing else but the innocence of all victims, the arbitrariness of any justification for violence. But the violence continues, nonetheless—without reason, and also with less and less containment by sacrificial religion. So from Girard's point of view biblical revelation offers no viable political alternative—no alternative short of general religious conversion of all participants:[48] without universal *metanoia*, without a "changing of the heart" of all mankind, there will be no salvation. But this religious perspective of salvation has no anthropological necessity as its driving force: the truth of the "universal victim" Jesus might well be defeated in the end.[49] Revelation does not garantee salvation.

But wait a minute: doesn't this point of view correspond to the perspective of the Anti-Christ? Doesn't mimetic theory with this fatalism of violence recognize the anthropological superiority of Friedrich Nietzsche's realism or tragic vitalism: his apology of life under the permanent condition of violence and struggle (without reason), of death and rebirth (without afterlife)?—Well, it does.

Indeed we find in Girard's oeuvre strong elements of the last, negative secularization narrative (or version 4 of Casanova's list): of the "Nietzschean-derived" criticism of Western modernity "precisely because of its association with Christianity."[50] In Girard's view (as, for that matter, in Nietzsche's) the Christian delegitimation of sacrificial violence does not eliminate violence at all; it only destroys or weakens its legitimation, concealment, or rationalization.[51] Against Christian morals and against secular humanism in versions (3) and (1) of the dominant secularization narratives, it is Nietzsche/Dionysos—as René Girard reads him—who maintains the anthropological truth, that (any) civilization continues to rely on (sacrificial) violence.

It is impossible to treat this crucial relation between Girard and Nietzsche in just a few remarks. So let me just make one point. Girard's (intellectually, not morally) sympathetic look on Nietzsche's struggle against dominant social morality rightly focuses on Nietzsche's very contradictions.[52] But in doing so Girard underestimates the performing elements of Nietzsche's paradoxical identification of the author (*Ecce homo* = Dionysos = Zarathustra) with the crucified. Indeed (and that is Girard's point), the last Nietzsche identifies Dionysos and "the Crucified" by their both being victims of sacrifice.[53] Thereby (and here also Girard is following Nietzsche's provocation) Nietzsche is criticizing the idealism or moralism of the liberal *imitatio Christi*. But is Nietzsche, in writing his last aphorisms, also pursuing a realist anthropology? Are his changing identifications with Dionysos and Jesus (not to speak of Zarathustra) really to be read as anthropological axioms? Is Nietzsche trying to grasp the transcultural or metahistorical identity of any murderous violence, whether occuring in pagan myths or in the stories of the Bible? Or is he looking for heroic violence (or, for that matter, heroic martyrdom) as esthetic antipode to any moralism, liberal or Christian (especially Protestant) alike?[54]

Heinrich Detering has recently proposed another interpretation, in his brillant study on Nietzsche's last writing process as philosopher (in the years from 1882 to 1889).[55] According to this reading, Nietzsche in his last texts is more and more performing roles. This struggling author, *Ecce homo*, "the philosopher with the hammer," is (re)searching and (re)writing role models for his self-understanding (and self-creation) as artist and avantgardist. So Nietzsche's famous last contrast and identification between Dionysos and "the Crucified" might rather express the contradictions of modern identity and authorship than reveal (as Girard maintains) a profound anthropological insight into the nature of sacrificial violence.

False Consciousness and the Apocalypse

As for the remaining two versions of secularization theory, version (1) of Casanova's list represents more or less the standard secularist interpretation of Western modernity. Modernity proceeds hand in hand with the political defeat of the church and/or the loss of social influence of religion; its sense of victory over superstition is usually combined with an anticlerical understanding of Enlightenment. Culturally speaking this militant attitude of secularism is typical for (formerly) Catholic countries, but not limitied to them: getting rid of religion, dismantling its clerical apparatus, for this family of secularists means emancipation, as religion is seen as false consciousness, moral repression, and social oppression. Such crude realist, often materialist versions of Enlightenment present a classical example for "subtraction stories" of secularism, as Charles Taylor has called them in *A Secular Age*: Take away false consciousness, remove religious mystification or superstition, and what remains after this subtraction is the real thing, the unrestricted view of reality—so this kind of diagnosis goes. Theirs is a rather optimistic narrative: in the long run we're all better off without superstition.

Now to our question: Can we find within Girardian theory elements or argumentative patterns that might (cor)respond to this demystificatory interpretation or version (1) of Enlightenment? The answer is: yes—not in the sense of atheism, obviously, but in Girard's spirit of anthropological realism. René Girard too has identified a core element of mystification within traditional/sacrificial religion, a basic ideological mechanism of "delusion" or *méconnaissance*.[56] His argument is rather simple, and Girard reproposes it in nearly all his writings—sometimes with different examples from literature, from cultural memory, from pagan or biblical mythology, but without any substantial variation.[57]

We know the argument already; grosso modo it goes like this. In order to be effective the original scapegoat mechanism (i.e., the "foundational murder" at the origins of culture, society, religion) presupposes that all its participants must ignore its very driving force: mimetic contagion of rivalry. *Mimetic rivalry* is contagious, setting in motion a *mimetical cycle* that then will culminate in a generalized *mimetic crisis* that can only be resolved by the (virtually collective) assassination of a real victim.[58] The reciprocal escalation of mimetic rivalry leads inevitably to a collective outbreak (*emballement mimétique*)[59] of rage, hatred, and murder that threatens every society with chaos and distruction—a violent entropy of social order and differentiation that then, in turn, can only be resolved by the arbitrary choice of a sacrificial victim. This victim, the scapegoat, becomes the substitute for all other possible victims, thus rescuing the society from total breakdown.[60] The reason for this turn from chaos to order at the peak of the mimetic cycle lies in the "mimetical paradox": human beings cannot share pacifically an object desired by all of them, whereas it is much easier (and according to Girard always possible) for them to share their hate of a common enemy—and then to join in his assassination. So only this common victim can reconcile the divided community—at least for a while.[61]

In the foundational myths of archaic religion this original reconciliation by murder has to be symbolically perpetuated/ignored/transformed: the victim will be divinized as heroic founder, ancestor, or mythical lawgiver of cosmos and city.[62] And, if we follow Girard, the same argument about the necessary *méconnaissance* (ignorance/distortion) of the real origin and sense of religion holds also for the later elaboration of foundational myths in archaic religions and societies. The substitution of a human victim by animal sacrifice is nothing else but a ritual repetition of the hidden foundational murder; according to mimetic theory ritual and mythos permanently reenact this original sin, concealing it and reconciling with it at the same time. Thus the social order founded, upheld, and structured by archaic religion is based on systematic ignorance.

Both the antireligious secularism of version (1) and Girard's mimetic theory are proposing (or pretending) the demystification of archaic religion. The difference between materialist Enlightenment and Girardian realism lies in the causes and motives of this demystificatory process. For secularist modernists the liberating forces of demystification lie in natural or social science—it is human reason dissolving the *idola* of religious imagination by showing the real forces of order and change in nature and history, thereby furthering the general progress of human knowledge and welfare. As I said before, theirs is an optimistic outlook.

But for mimetic theory the driving force of the modern demystification of mythology cannot lie in science at all. The withering away of the mythical illusion can only be the indirect outcome of biblical revelation: the innocence of the victim, from Abel to Jesus, that is, the innocence of all victims—definitively revealed through the Passion of the Christ. René Girard is very explicit about this point: Even the undeniable progresses of secular science (and their undeniable beneficial results) for him are just byproducts of the historical process initiated by biblical revelation.[63] Once the bloody origin of every ritual, mythology, religious/social order has been revealed—and once the foundational murder has been shown as arbitrary killing of innocent victims—archaic religion shall undergo inevitably a process of decay, corrosion, loss of credibility. This evolution might well take more or less time, but the outcome of this process is inevitable: the end of the mythical order, of the *aion* of sacrificial religion, has already begun with the announcement of biblical revelation, with its enactment in the Passion of Christ. From now on historical time itself has changed—and here also Girard's writing is changing tone: becoming more prophetic, demanding, less indulgent (and less scientific). With eschatological time approaching, the time of decision has come: either toward the conversion of all mankind to the point of view of Christ, by identification with the victim, without any mimetical revenge; or toward apocalypse, approaching a terrible, catastrophic "end of history."[64]

Girard's diagnosis of the consequences of demystification of mythical religion are far from optimistic: After Christ's Passion/revelation there are no credible founding myths left. So either mankind will be converted to the message of Christ's Passion—to the point of view of the victim—or the destruction of all social order by unrestrained mimetical desire and extremization of murderous rivalry shall prevail. Without sacrificial religion (and without any other functionally equivalent social mechanism that might hold back the outbreak of collective violence) the apocalypse is inevitable.

But what happened after Jesus Christ's Passion was neither general *metanoia* nor the apocalypse. History went on, even after the Passion—after the demystification of the scapegoat mechanism in all religions, after any possible rationalization of violence had been destroyed on the cross, once and for all. How was this possible? For René Girard a sacrificial misreading of the Bible must have taken place. Only a distortion of the Christian message could have transformed the biblical message into a new foundational myth of social order and political stability—but exactly this had been the development of historical Christianity.[65] Instead of announcing the imminent breakdown of social order founded on sacrificial violence (and of the empire as horizon of political legitimacy) Christianity itself was transformed into a new founding myth;[66] it became a new universalistic code for the legitimation of order.[67] So it could even function as state religion of the Roman Empire and constitute the code of legitimacy for its later "translations."[68]

For René Girard it must have been this sacrificial distortion of Christianity that in fact delayed the outbreak of the apocalypse—even if "the mystery of the lawlessness [was] already at work." Christendom, organized as church, became the very *katechon* that (or, who) "withholdeth that he might be revealed in his time"—as mentioned by St. Paul in the Second Letter to the Thessalonians (2:6–7).[69] And if historical Christianity—that is, the Roman church as the religious continuation/transformation of the Roman Empire—has contained apocalyptic violence until now, then the anti-Roman secularization process, destroying this *katechon*, will inevitably lead to apocalypse.

In his last writings and interviews René Girard is adopting the thesis of the (more or less) imminent apocalyptic chaos or entropy as the ultimate truth of history. It is not our business here to judge this kind of prophecy. Girard's prognostic might still turn out right, but his theory cannot prove it; blurring all differences between empire and church, between sacrificial paganism and sacrificial Christianity—all of them are holding back the apocalypse. (And by the way: why can another *katechon* be excluded?) It is even difficult to classify René Girard's last interventions within the debates of anthropology, religious studies or social science at all. As a general theory of (Western) religious history this type of diagnosis is colorful, emotionally demanding, but analytically much too vague.[70]

Unless it is just the reproposal of an older story. Somehow René Girard with his apocalyptic diagnosis of secularization is also taking up some elements of the antimodern secularization narrative of the nineteenth century, from version (2) in José Casanova's list quoted above. The story of secularization as apocalyptic destruction of God-given order has been told over and over again by Catholic legitimists, traditionalists, reactionaries opposing the social and symbolic consequences of the French Revolution first and liberal constitutionalism later. Indeed in the crisis of the European Catholic monarchies after the French Revolution (symbolized by the nationalization of the clergy in Napoleonic France)—and later with the crisis of the Spanish monarchy in 1848—Joseph de Maistre, Louis Gabriel Ambroise de Bonald, Louis Veuillot, and Juan Donoso-Cortés had identified secularization with the end of the political power of the Catholic Church, preceded by the Protestant contestation of its symbolic monopoly of the sacred. Their "ultramontanism" saw Protestantism, Enlightenment, and secularization as one continuously degenerating chain of corrosion: all three poisons were destroying the normative order of social authority by undermining the truth monopoly of the Holy Roman Church. In their grim prophetic spirit those great Spanish and French antirevolutionaries of the nineteenth century have designed their catastrophic version of secularization theory as the very center of their critique of modernity, democracy, market economy, and civil society.[71] In doing so J. de Maistre and company were presenting another kind of subtraction theory of secularization[72]—with a very simple, clear-cut thesis: If social order and political legitimacy can only be guaranteed by one unquestioned Christian hierarchy in church and state, then the crisis of religious hierarchy must inevitably produce chaos, stasis, disorder. But even if René Girard sometimes seems to share some of the cultural sensibilities of these great reactionary writers and cultural and religious critics,[73] nothing in his writings speaks for any political affinity to their outlook.[74]

A Short Resumé

This paper, analyzing the relations between mimetic theory and secular modernity, could not find a coherent vision of secularization in Girardism. The main reason for this incoherence lies in the systematic ambivalence of Girard's oeuvre itself, and especially of his latest writings. René Girard remains undecided whether his theory is to be understood (and used) as a (secular) scientific hypothesis or as a (revealed) eschatological prophecy.

- We may try to reconstruct Girardism as a contribution to secular social science. We can use his theory of the "mimetic circle" culminating in the "foundational murder" as a fundamental anthropological or social-scientific hypothesis for the study of the origins, patterns, and functions of religion. (We have to admit: the question of its testability is not very well defined by René Girard.)
- If this hypothesis turns out to be true, then according to Girard all social institutions are—in the last instance—product of a "slow process of secularization," coinciding with some kind of "rationalization and functionalization."[75] But what would be rationalized or civilized in this historical process? If it is the original violence of the foundational murder (as Girard assumes here), then the positive mechanism of secularization consists in the cumulative effect of its ritual repetition or transformation, that is, of sacrificial religion.[76] In short: *secularization is religion* (a not very helpful terminology).
- But Girard is also using "secularization" in the usual, common understanding of the term: as process in which Christian religion is losing its political power, social influence, cultural plausibility. Here secularization has a more negative connotation, at least from the point of view of traditional Christian thought and church hierarchy: as known from the famous *Syllabus* of Pope Pius IX or from the writings

of Catholic reaction in the nineteenth century (a rather too well-known view on secularization).

- Now Girard does not see the institutional church and traditional dogma as coherent realizations of the revelation of Christ. For him historical Christendom is (or has been) rather a "katechontic" institution preventing social chaos and normative anomy. But when secularization means the retreat or defeat of this normative institution, then the outcome will be the same: the same apocalyptic chaos that traditionalist Christians were fearing and predicting all the time along—the outbreak of general violence that according to Girard "sacrificial" Christendom has prevented until the present day. In short: *secularization is apocalypse* (a "gothic" prophecy—be it ultramontanist or fatalist, reactionary or impolitical).

NOTES

1. In this paper I will use "Girard(ism)" and "mimetic theory" as synonyma.
2. See the remarks of Renato Rosaldo, in Hamerton-Kelly 1987 (239–44), and the following debate between the participants of the colloquium.
3. "Literary criticism, as I have learned to practice it, relies finally upon an irreducibly *aesthetic* dimension in plays, poems, and narratives. Analogously, religious criticism must seek for the irreducibly *spiritual* dimension in religious matters or phenomena of any kind" (Bloom 1992, 21)—René Girard probably might prefer the diction "the irreducibly *real* dimension in religious matters or phenomena of any kind" (see the title of Girard 2002, 2005).
4. Girard stresses: "il faut affirmer l'existence *réelle* du meurtre fondateur. Il ne faut pas diluer sa specificité extra-rituelle et extra-textuelle. Il ne faut pas ramener cet événement à une espèce de cas limite plus ou moins idéal, à un concept régulateur, à un effet de langage, à quelque tour de passe-passe symbolique sans répondant véritable sur le plan des rapports concrets" (Girard 1972, 463).
5. Of every society in history? Or only of some? I shall come back to this question.
6. See the debates in Girard 2011a.
7. "It would be a good idea" was the proverbial answer of Mahatma Gandhi to the question of what he thought about Western civilization.
8. As the recent debate about Steven Pinker's theory of the world-historical decline of violence in (and between) human societies has shown (Pinker 2011).
9. His image of the great *Leviathan* refers to the biblical God's final speeches in the book Job (chaps. 38–41), where JAHWE recycles older Mesopotamian and Egyptian mythical monsters of chaos and order; but this image of the absolutist state as "mortall god" within Hobbes's theory evokes also the apocalyptic *katechon* in St. Paul's second letter to the Thessalonians (2 Thessalonians 2:6–8) the restraining power holding back the omnipresence of war and chaotic violence. See Palaver 1995.

10. But for Girard "religion" includes more than just its mimetic/sacrificial core-structure or archetype. Otherwise Girard would already define "religion" by the "mimetic circle," thereby committing a mortal sin for any critical methodology: validation by definition or *petitio principii.*

11. To borrow the term from Friedrich Engels, another exponent of anthropological "realism" (and follower of Morgan).

12. "When future human beings became too mimetic to live as animals do, their dominance patterns collapsed and the resulting crisis triggered the mimetic victimage mechanism around which the first systems of prohibition and sacrificial rites coalesced" (Girard 2004, 13).

13. See Popper 1963, 33–39.

14. This Girardian argument of necessary *méconnaissance* would—obviously!—be seen by a strictly observant Popperian as mere theoretical immunization. See also below, the section "A Short Resumé."

15. If we take the use of language as indication of human culture, the estimations about the age of language are between fifty thousand and one hundred thousand years. See Nicholas Wade (2011), referring to research on the phonemic development of human languages conducted by Quentin D. Atkinson.

16. The appearance of large multimale/multifemale aggregations of primates is estimated by recent studies as having occured about fifty-two million years ago (connected perhaps with the change from nocturnal to diurnal hunting activity that then implied a much increased predation risk for these primates); the pattern of stable pair-living systems (titi monkeys) or single-male harem systems (gorillas) seems to have showed up much later (sixteen million years ago). See Schultz, Opie, and Atkinson 2011.

17. These (and the following) percent numbers are celestial, so we should not discuss them.

18. See Burkert, in Girard 2011a, 117–59, and the following debate with Girard and others.

19. See Vico 1953/1984, No. 369.

20. See Vico 1953/1984, No. 377.

21. See van Gennep 1981, chap. 4.

22. See van Gennep 1981, chap. 3; Turner 1969.

23. This seems to be the hypothesis of archeologist Klaus Schmidt who is directing the excavations/reconstructions of the neolithical "temple district" of Göbekli Tepe in southeast Turkey (Prepottery Neolithic Age, ca. 9,500–8,500 BCE) with its sacral buildings containing megalithic sculptures and steles with awe-inspiring animal (and human-animal) representations. (There is even the representation of a "scapegoat"—but in the biblical, not Girardian meaning of the term; see Schmidt 2006, 119–21.) The cooperation necessary for the construction of such a monumental holy site might even have been one causal element in the transition from hunting to agricultural societies (see Schmidt 2006, 216–20, 247–48).

24. Girard 2011a, xii. I will not consider this lecture of Girard here, as other contributions in this volume are discussing the usefulness of mimetic theory for an understanding of Vedic, Buddhist, and Hinduist traditions. For a more pluralist vision of sacrifice in the Vedic tradition, see Doniger 2009, chaps. 4–6.

25. See Böckenförde 1967.

26. See Norris and Inglehard (2004).

27. The classical secularization thesis had, obviously, been put forward by Max Weber. Today there is a whole family of not always consonant secularization theories. Important conceptual and historical differentiations within the concept/process of secularization have been proposed by José Casanova and Charles Taylor in their recent work, to which I am referring here.

28. Taylor (2007, 3) is distinguishing this more general and existential "secularity^3" from the more political or constitutional "secularity^1," i.e. the secularization of the state and/or "public reason" (in the Rawlsian sense) in Western liberalism, and from the more sociological or cultural "secularity^2," i.e. the falling off of religious practice or belief, of church-going and widespread identification with the Christian churches in Western culture.

29. Religious critic Harold Bloom acknowledges quite explicitly these epistemic plausibilities of our "secular age"; according to Bloom literature and religion are "both conceptual orphans, stumbling around in our cosmological emptiness that stretches between the unattainable poles of meaning and of truth" (Bloom 1992, 21).

30. The classical analysis of the effects of religious pluralism on religious (and antireligious) identities remains Peter Berger's study on the "heretical imperative" (1979). Charles Taylor (2007, part 3) speaks of a "nova-effect."

31. See Benoît Chantre 2010, 170, quoting a review of Girard's book in the leading French intellectual newspaper *Le Monde*. Recently René Girard has even been defined—by an Australian Jesuit website (Kirkwood 2011)—as the "Charles Darwin of the human sciences," whatever that may mean. Girard himself, in his last book, stesses that the "Darwinian perspective" cannot take into account the complete "humanisation" of mankind—as from the perspective of evolution the last step must be missing: the arrival of Christ's Passion. "Cet achèvement est avènement." See Girard 2011a, 212–13.

32. Girard 1972; Girard 1977, 92.

33. See Girard's criticism of Levi-Strauss in Girard 2005, 16–21. In the introduction to a collection of his essays, René Girard characterizes his own work retrospectively: His essay on laughter, e.g., pretends to be nearer to the spirit of Charles Darwin and Charles Baudelaire than to Henri Bergson; an essay on Nietzsche takes Nietzsche's side against positivist anthropology; against structuralist anthropology Girard argues for a "realistic" (i.e., not merely symbolic, allegoric, fictional) reading of the scapegoat mechanisms in myths of origin; see Girard 2005, 7–9, 93–97, 180–201.

34. Girard's explicit awareness of the "evangelical" message of his own anthropological hypothesis becomes evident in the 1980s. (see Girard 1986, esp. chap. 15, 198–212); probably also as a result of Girard's confrontation with the theology of Raymund Schwager. See Girard 2014 and his conversations with Giuseppe Fornari, "La lotta fra Gesù e Satana" (Girard 1998, 149–67), and with Wolfgang Palaver (Girard 2010, 33–83).

35. In the sense of Karl Rahner's "anonymous Christianity."

36. See the introduction of Girard 1999, 19–20 [2001, 3]; see also Girard 2011b, 18, 330.

37. Taylor 2007, 2011; cf. Warner, VanAntwerpen, and Calhoun (2010); see also the useful monographical issue "Rethinking Secularism" of the Vienna-based review *TRANSIT* (2010).

38. Casanova 2010, 266.

39. I regret, but I must leave aside here the question of the peculiarity or exclusivity of the Western path of secularization. It has been posed—not least in confrontation with Charles Taylor's *A Secular Age* (2007; see also Taylor 2011, chap. 13, 303ff.)—by scholars like Rajeev Bhargava, Tariq

Modood, Akeel Bilgrami, Talal Assad, and others. See the useful thematical issue of *TRANSIT* (2010).

40. The German term "Kulturprotestantismus" usually refers to the twentieth-century version of politically progressive and theologically liberal Protestant thinkers in the Lutheran context.

41. See Kallscheuer 2009b.

42. See Taylor 2007, part 2. The leading British sociologist of religion David Martin stresses more the differences between the paths to modernity not only in Protestant and Catholic countries, but also between the various families of Protestant spirituality—between Lutherans, Presbyterians, Anglicans, Pentecostals, etc. But this is not the place to go into these discussions.—*Nota bene*: It is also not my intention here to discuss the impact of Girardian mimetic theory (which has been rather important) on Taylor's own work. The diagnosis of both thinkers about the "crisis of modernity" has been the subject of a recent study by Andrew O'Shea (2010). Unfortunately I came to know of its existence only after having written this paper.

43. Or world-*picture*, see Heidegger 1938.

44. See Gauchet 1985.

45. Girard 2004, 17.

46. So it comes as no surprise that Girard in his last work (a somewhat theological reading of the political-philosophical antagonism between German and French culture in the last two hundred years) prefers a "catastrophic" interpretation of Clausewitz's "logic of escalation" dubbing the Hegelian research of rationalization, institutionalization, resolution as pure illusion. See Girard 2007, esp. chaps. 2 and 3.

47. This is the leitmotif of Girard's recent writings: Girard 2004, 2010; Doran 2008.

48. See Gonzales 2010, 133–37.

49. One of the most impressive theological books of the end of the twentieth century, written by the Italian lay-theologian Sergio Quinzio, treated "the defeat of God" (Quinzio 1992).

50. Casanova 2010, 266.

51. For Nietzsche this (Jewish or Christian) delegitimation of heroic violence is then in itself the result of the "Ressentiment" of the weak.

52. Girard 1999, chap. 14, 263–79 [2001, 170–81]; 2008, 213–26; see also Girard 2003; 2005, 88–113.

53. "Dionysos gegen den 'Gekreuzigten': Da habt ihr den Gegensatz. Es ist nicht eine Differenz hinsichtlich des Martyriums,—nur hat dasselbe einen anderen Sinn." Nietzsche 1906, no. 1052.

54. Charles Taylor has written on various occasions about this nexus between Nietzsche's criticism of morality and the (post)modern "ethics of authenticity."

55. Detering 2010.

56. Girard 1972, 156; 1977, 103–4.

57. For a useful overview, see Palaver 2013, chap. 4; cf. Girard's own short presentation in Girard 2010; Girard 1987, 73–105.

58. Girard 1999, 38–35; Girard, "Generative Scapegoating," 126–29.

59. Girard 1999, 44–45.

60. See Girard 1986, chaps. 2 and 10.

61. See Girard 2011a, 82–90.

62. An argument obviously known already from Sigmund Freud's "Totem and Tabou."

63. "The invention of science is not the reason that there are no longer witch-hunts, but the fact that there are no longer witch-hunts is the reason that science has been invented. The scientific spirit, like the spirit of enterprise in an economy, is a by-product of the profound action of the Gospel text" (Girard 1986, 204–5).

64. Benoît Chantre has tried to spell out these apocalyptic versions (or dimensions) of Girardism—whether already contained in Girard's original approach or as possible consequence of his outlook. See Girard 2007; Chantre 2010. See also Doran 2010.

65. *Nihil novum sub sole*: A somewhat analogous diagnosis of the historical development of Christianity had already been made, at the beginning of the twentieth century, by the dissident Protestant theologian of Basel university Franz Overbeck (*nota bene*: a colleague and close friend of Friedrich Nietzsche!).

66. This point also had already been made by Hannah Arendt (1961, 125–26): By transforming the church into a public institution, founded by Christ (the Apostles, witnesses of this founding, thereby became the "founding fathers"), Christianity "could be transformed into a new mundane beginning to which the world was bound back once more [*religare*] in a curious mixture of new [Christian] and old [Roman] religious awe."

67. See Veyne 2007.

68. I obviously refer to the *translatio imperii* as classical form of legitimation in the post-Roman Christian world. See Kallscheuer 2009a, 17–46.

69. Here I am following Palaver 1995.

70. *Achever Clausewitz*, Girard's last book, written with B. Chantre (2007), shortcuts back and forth between the biblical time of revelation, the French/German political and philosophical antagonism in the nineteenth century with Napoleon and Clausewitz, Hölderlin and Mme de Stael, the extremization of violent mimetic reciprocity in the wars of the twentieth century, and the twenty-first century with its terrorism and tsunami. This picture can be rather impressive, but the argument is fuzzy.

71. See Schmitt 1934, 69–84; 1950; Gonzales 2010.

72. Which obviously is the exact opposite of the laicist secularization theory, of version (1) discussed above.

73. Their view is then sometimes sociologically underscored by a Toquevillian diagnosis of modern equality as the reign of unsatisfiable mimetic desire—a mechanism that Girard himself had analyzed so brillantly in his first book (Girard 1961). Cf. the contributions of Benoît Chantre, Domingo Gonzales, and Christian Lazzeri in Ramond 2010.—I must refrain here from discussing this view.

74. The political consequences of their diagnosis are well known: Juan Donoso-Cortés opted for the dictatorship as political answer to the social entropy of democracy.

75. Girard 1999; 2008, 122–23.

76. "Turning this murder into ritual is the first institution and the most fundamental one. It is the

mother of all the others, the decisive development in the invention of human culture." (Girard 1999; [2001, 93–94]).

WORKS CITED

Arendt, Hannah. 1961. *Between Past and Future: Six Exercises in Political Thought*. New York: Viking.

Berger, Peter L. 1979. *The Heretical Imperative: Contemporary Possibilities of Religious Affirmation*. Garden City, NY: Doubleday.

Bloom, Harold. 1992. *The American Religion: The Emergence of the Post-Christian Nation*. New York: Simon and Schuster.

Böckenförde, Ernst-Wolfgang. 1967. *Die Entstehung des Staates als Vorgang der Säkularisation*. Stuttgart: Kohlhammer.

Casanova, José. 1994. *Public Religions in the Modern World*. Chicago: University of Chicago Press.

———. 2009. "The Secular and Secularisms." *Social Research* 74, no.4 (Winter): 1049–66.

———. 2010. "A Secular Age: Dawn or Twilight?" In *Varieties of Secularism in a Secular Age*, edited by Michael Warner, Jonathan VanAntwerpen, and Craig J. Calhoun, 265–81. Cambridge, MA: Harvard University Press.

Chantre, Benoît. 2010. "Le clocher de Combray: René Girard ou la dernière loi." In *René Girard: La théorie mimétique; de l'apprentissage à l'apocalypse*, edited by Charles Ramond, 147–201. Paris: Presses Universitaires de France.

Detering, Heinrich. 2010. *Der Antichrist und der Gekreuzigte: Nietzsches letzte Texte*. Göttingen: Wallstein.

Doniger, Wendy. 2009. *The Hindus: An Alternative History*. Oxford: Oxford University Press.

Doran, Robert. 2008. "Apocalyptic Thinking after 9/11: An Interview with René Girard." *SubStance* 37, no. 1: 20–32.

Gauchet, Marcel. 1985. *Le désenchantement du monde*. Paris: Gallimard.

Girard, René. 1961. *Mensonge romantique et vérité romanesque*. Paris: Grasset.

———. 1972. *La violence et le sacré*. Paris: Grasset.

———. 1977. *Violence and the Sacred*. Baltimore: Johns Hopkins University Press.

———. 1986. *The Scapegoat*. Baltimore: Johns Hopkins University Press.

———. 1987. "Generative Scapegoating." In *Violent Origins: Walter Burkert, René Girard, and Jonathan Z. Smith on Ritual Killing and Cultural Formation*, edited by Robert G. Hamerton-Kelly, 73–105. Stanford: Stanford University Press.

———. 1998. *La vittima e la folla: Violenza del mito e cristianesimo*. Edited by Giuseppe Fornari. Treviso: Ed. Santi Quaranta.

———. 1999. *Je vois Satan tomber comme l'éclair*. Paris: Grasset.

———. 2001. *I See Satan Fall Like Lightning*. Translated by James G. Williams. Maryknoll, NY: Orbis Books.

———. 2002. *La voix méconnue du réel*. Paris: Grasset.

———. 2003. "Nietzsche Versus the Crucified." In *The Girard Reader*, edited by J. G. Williams, 243–61. New York: Crossroad, .

———. 2004. "Violence and Religion: Cause or Effect?" *The Hedgehog Review* 6, no. 1 (Spring): 8–20.

———. 2005. *Die verkannte Stimme des Realen*. Munich: Carl Hanser Verlag.

———. 2010. *Gewalt und Religion: Usache oder Wirkung?* Edited by Wolfgang Palaver. Berlin: Matthes & Seitz).

———. 2011a. *Sacrifice*. Translated by Matthew Pattillo and David Dawson. East Lansing: Michigan State University Press.

———. 2011b. *Achever Clausewitz*. Entretiens avec Benoît Chantre. Paris: Flammarion.

———. 2014. "Mimetic Theory and Theology." In *The One by Whom Scandal Comes*, 33–44. East Lansing: Michigan State University Press.

Gonzales, Domingo. 2010. "Théologie politique et théologie impolitique: Juan Donoso Cortés et René Girard." In *René Girard: La théorie mimétique; de l'apprentissage à l'apocalypse*, edited by Charles Ramond, 105–45. Paris: Presses Universitaires de France.

Hamerton-Kelly, Robert G., ed. 1987. *Violent Origins: Walter Burkert, René Girard, and Jonathan Z. Smith on Ritual Killing and Cultural Formation*. Stanford: Stanford University Press.

Heidegger, Martin. 1938. "Die Zeit des Weltbildes." In *Heidegger Gesamtausgabe*. Vol. 5. *Holzwege*, 75–114. Frankfurt am Main: Vittorio Klostermann 1977.

Kallscheuer, Otto. 2009a. *Zur Zukunft des Abendlandes*. Springe: zu Klampen Verlag.

———. 2009b. "Hegels Theorie der Säkularisierung." In *Staat und Religion in Hegels Rechtsphilosophie*, edited by Andreas Arndt, Christian Iber, and Günter Kruck, 109–20. Springe: Zu Klampen Verlag.

Kirkwood, Peter. 2011. "The 'Charles Darwin' of Human Sciences." http://www.eurekastreet.com.au. July 28.

Nietzsche, Friedrich. 1906. *Der Wille zur Macht*. Edited by Peter Gast and Elisabeth Förster-Nietzsche. Frankfurt am Main: Insel Verlag.

Norris, Pippa, and Inglehart, Ronald. 2004. *Sacred and Secular: Religion and Politics Worldwide*. Cambridge: Cambridge University Press.

O'Shea, Andrew. 2010. *Selfhood and Sacrifice: René Girard and Charles Taylor on the Crisis of Modernity*. New York: Continuum.

Palaver, Wolfgang. 1995. "Hobbes and the Katechon." *Contagion* 2:57–74.

———. 2013. *René Girard's Mimetic Theory*. Translated by G. Borrud. East Lansing: Michigan State University Press.

Pinker, Steven. 2011. *The Better Angels of Our Nature: Why Violence Has Declined*. New York: Penguin.

Popper, Karl R. 1963. *Conjectures and Refutations*. London: Routledge and Keagan.

Quinzio, Sergio. 1992. *La sconfitta di Dio*. Milano: Adelphi.

Ramond, Charles, ed. 2010. *René Girard: La théorie miméthique; de l'apprentissage à l'apocalypse*. Paris: Presses Universitaires de France.

Schmidt, Klaus. 2006. *Sie bauten die ersten Tempel: Das rätselhafte Heiligtum der Steinzeitjäger*. Munich: C. H. Beck.

Schmitt, Carl. 1934. *Politische Theologie*. Berlin: Duncker & Humblot.

———. 1950. *Juan Donoso Cortés in gesamteuropäischer Interpretation*. Cologne: Greven Verlag.

Schultz, Susanne, Christopher Opie, and Quentin D. Atkinson. 2011. "Stepwise Evolution of Stable Sociality in Primates." *Nature* 479 (November 10): 219–22.

Taylor, Charles. 2007. *A Secular Age*. Cambridge, MA: Belknap Press.

———. 2011. *Dilemmas and Connections: Selected Essays*. Cambridge, MA: Belknap Press.

TRANSIT: European Review 39 (2010), thematical issue: "Den Säkularismus neu denken" [Rethinking Secularism].

Turner, Victor. 1969. *The Ritual Process, Structure and Anti-Structure*. New York: Aldine.

van Gennep, Arnold. 1981. *Les rites de passage*. Paris: Éditions A. et J. Picard.

Veyne, Paul. 2007. *Quand notre monde est devenu chrétien*. Paris: Albin Michel.

Vico, Giambattista. 1953. *Principi di scienza nuova* [= Scienza Nuova Seconda, 1744]. Edited by Fausto Nicolini Milano:Mondadori.

———. 1948. *The New Science of Giambattista Vico*. Translated by Thomas G. Bergen and Max H. Fisch. Ithaca, NY: Cornell University Press..

Wade, Nicholas. 2011. "Phonetic Clues Hint Language Is Africa-Born."*New York Times*, April 15, A1–A3.

Warner, Michael, Jonathan VanAntwerpen, and Craig J. Calhoun, eds. 2010. *Varieties of Secularism in a Secular Age*. Cambridge, MA: Harvard University Press.

Why Rousseau Cannot Laugh: Structuring Motif—"Achever"

Jeremiah Alberg

I begin with a quote from the introduction to René Girard's *Achever Clausewitz*.[1] I want to use this quote to extract a kind of operational definition of what it means to "achever," or, according to the English translation, "to complete," a thinker and then use this as a programmatic outline for this attempt to understand Rousseau and his status as a religious thinker. Girard writes:

> completing [the *achever* of the title] the interpretation of [Carl von Clausewitz's] *On War* is to say that its meaning is religious and that only a religious interpretation has a chance of reaching what is essential in it. Clausewitz conceives relations among men as mimetic [*pense les relations mimétiques entre les hommes*], in spite of the fact that his philosophical approach was that of Enlightenment rationalism. . . . Clausewitz and his commentators were hampered by their rationalism. This is as good a proof as any that a different kind of rationality is needed to understand the reality of what he glimpsed. (*BE*, xii–xiii)

So Girard defines "achever" as involving three interrelated claims about a text and its interpretation: the author being interpreted must think human relations mimetically; when an author thinks thus, then the text's "meaning is religious," and so only a religious interpretation will grasp what is essential in it; and another kind of rationality is needed to reach this religious interpretation. This last point further implies that the rationality used by the author, in this case Enlightenment rationalism, will not be sufficient for understanding "what is essential" in the text. Its own essence lies beyond the rationality that produced it. In another place Girard puts it this way: "*Completing* what he [Clausewitz] only glimpsed means rediscovering what is most profound in Christianity" (*BE*, 81).

There is a leap between the first claim that the necessary condition for completing a text is that it treats human relations mimetically, and the second claim that the text's meaning is religious. Girard could plausibly claim that the whole of his oeuvre serves to fill the gap between the two claims and justifies his simple assertions of them in the introduction. It is an oeuvre that is meant to connect a mimetic conception of human relations with religion.

Thus a text's meaning is religious when it follows out, with greater or lesser explicit awareness, the mimetic dynamism of human relations and shows how this leads, through a kind of idolatry of the other with its attendant ascesis, to a deviated transcendence.[2] In the novels of our greatest writers, that is, those with the most explicit awareness of the mimetic dynamism, this process ends in a conversion—a moving beyond the mimetic rivalry. All that I have said in these last two sentences is established by Girard in his first work, *Deceit, Desire, and the Novel*, a work of literary criticism.[3] The religious dimension is already very present in this early work. We could even expand the above to include the apocalyptic without leaving the framework of *Deceit, Desire, and the Novel.*[4]

What Girard's later works make clearer is that a text's meaning is religious when the reader is led to understand that mimetic desire results not simply in mimetic rivalry and deviated transcendence but that at the heart of this rivalry and transcendence is violence; violence as the "heart and the secret soul of the sacred."[5] This sacred violence itself is mimetic, and so it escalates into more and more of a crisis until it is resolved through some sort of violent expulsion. This violent expulsion develops into rituals of sacrifice so that religion is understood to be the whole phenomenon as contained in the myths, rituals, and prohibitions that are both grounded in the mimetic phenomenon and that then envelop this violent contagion with a sacred aura.

> *Religion* in its broadest sense, then, must be another term for that obscurity that surrounds man's efforts to defend himself by curative or preventative means against his own violence. It is that enigmatic quality that pervades the judicial system when that system replaces sacrifice. This obscurity coincides with the transcendental effectiveness of a violence that is holy, legal, and legitimate successfully opposed to a violence that is unjust, illegal, and illegitimate. (*VS*, 23)

At the same time Girard's use of "religious" in the opening quotation from *Battling to the End* is deliberately underdetermined. It means more than the violent sacred of primitive religions because it also includes the continuity/discontinuity of this archaic religious phenomenon with the Judeo-Christian tradition that subverts this whole phenomenon from within.

An interpretation of this kind, that is, a religious interpretation of a text, reaches what is essential, then, when it shows the relationship between the human relations and the eventual violence and expulsion of the scapegoat. That is, as *The Scapegoat* makes clear, an interpretation is religious when it is done from the viewpoint of the victim.[6] In this sense the religious dimension of the interpretation can be different from the religious dimension of the text being interpreted. The text may be informed by primitive religious thinking and thus may be a "text of persecution." The religious interpretation that shows it to be such is done from the viewpoint of the victim. Thus, the different kind of rationality to which Girard refers could be called the "rationality of the victim."[7]

This form of rationality can be traced back to the scriptures and to Christ himself. "Christ, the last prophet, then places humanity before a terrible alternative: either continue to refuse to see that the duel is the underlying structure of all human activities, or escape from that hidden logic by means of a better one, that of love, of positive reciprocity" (*BE*, 63). The two logics, one of "negative" and the other of "positive" reciprocity, are alternatives that resemble each other. "Almost the same form of undifferentiation is involved in both cases, but what is at stake is the salvation of the world." Girard calls the "better" logic "*religious rationality*" and claims that it enables one to understand the "oscillation that is always possible between one form of undifferentiation and the other" (*BE*, 82). He continues: "Only religious rationality can enable us to understand what I have grasped through study of the forms of archaic religion, namely that a victim who has been made into a devil is thereafter made a god. This transmutation is in no way rational, in the sense of Enlightenment rationality, but it is not superstition either. The same logic prevails in what we are trying to think about now. It forces us to change how we reason" (*BE*, 82).

Does Rousseau Think Mimetically

To begin to understand Jean-Jacques Rousseau as a religious thinker is to ask this question: Does Rousseau think human relations mimetically? Some scholars, remembering Girard's early distinction in *Deceit, Desire, and the Novel* between those few great novelists who reveal mimetic desire and the many lesser novelists and even, for that matter, the lesser novels of the great novelists that merely reflect mimetic desire, would answer no. That is, Rousseau never achieved the kind of distance on mimetic desire that someone like Fyodor Dostoyevsky evinces. But Girard's latest work on Clausewitz expands the categories a little. Girard writes the following about Clausewitz and his relationship with Napoleon.

> Clausewitz had a vehement passion for Napoleon; he was, to use my own concepts, in a relationship of *internal mediation* with the emperor. . . . Internal mediation supposes a nearness of the model in time and space, which was precisely the case of Clausewitz with respect to Napoleon. . . . Clausewitz is more profound and interesting from my point of view, because he is much more mimetic. He thought *against* Napoleon in both senses of the word. See how fruitful resentment can be, and how it can make one theorize. (*BE*, 12)

Clausewitz is mimetic and therefore thinks mimetically without ever really mastering the mimetic situation or articulating the theory. In the above quote we could substitute the name Rousseau for Clausewitz and the name Jean-Baptiste le Rond d'Alembert or Voltaire for Napoleon and nothing would be lost. Rousseau presents human relations as mimetic "by travelling along the system of" mimetic relations "with a blind infallibility, and the sure foot of the sleepwalker," to borrow what Jacques Derrida said about him in reference to the system of supplementarity.[8]

To clarify the way in which Rousseau both understands and misunderstands mimeticism, let us look at one of his most famous distinctions: between *amour de soi* and *amour-propre*. Rousseau sees self-love or *amour de soi* as the desire for self-preservation. It precedes *amour-propre*. This desire is natural. In one of the notes attached to the *Discourse on Inequality among Humans* (1755) Rousseau writes that as *amour de soi* gets directed "by reason and modified by pity, [it] produces humanity and virtue."[9] In the "genuine state of nature" only this form of love exists, because the man in the state of nature is not capable of making comparisons, which are the source of the *amour-propre* (*CW*, 3:91). The presence of this nonmimetic and therefore innocent desire for self-preservation is one great difference between Rousseau and Girard.

Amour-propre is the serpent in the state of nature that allows for such feelings as honor. It allows one to interpret the actions of others as intending harm or offense and thus makes possible the desire for revenge to emerge. *Amour-propre* is responsible for the emotions of insolence and spite. As Tzvetan Todorov remarks parenthetically: "the mimetic desire of Girard is only another name for the amour-propre of Rousseau."[10]

If we look at Rousseau's description of actual man, that is, social man, the similarities between Rousseau and Girard are striking. The former's description of man in society is, in fact, thoroughly mimetic. It is society that "necessarily brings men to hate each other in proportion to the conflict of their interests, to render each other apparent services and in fact do every imaginable harm to one another" (*CW*, 3:74).

In fact, Rousseau's most penetrating reflections on the effects of *amour-propre* are stated before he has properly introduced the concept itself. Earlier in the *Discourse on Inequality*, again in a footnote, he reflects on the specifically human trait of perfectibility, the tragic flaw in human beings that at one and the same time raises him above and casts him below all the other animals on the face of the earth. Rousseau writes at length in this note about human wickedness. Human wickedness is social, or, better, societal. It springs up and follows its own dialectical development in the context of society. The development runs along these lines:

> it is first of all a question of providing for the necessary, and then for the superfluous; next come delights, then immense wealth, and then subjects, and then Slaves; he does not have a moment of respite. What is most singular is that the less natural and urgent the needs, the more the passions augment, and, what is worse, the power to satisfy them; so that after long prosperity, after having swallowed up many treasures and desolated many men, my Hero will end by ruining everything until he is the sole master of the Universe. Such in brief is the moral picture, if not of human life, at least of the secret pretensions of the Heart of every Civilized man. (*CW*, 3:75–76)

This is also the description of the person consumed by mimetic rivalry.

Rousseau poses this question: "What is to be thought of intercourse in which *the reason of each individual* dictates to him maxims directly contrary to those that *public reason* preaches to the body of Society, and in which each man finds his profit in the misfortune of others?" (*CW*, 3:74; emphasis mine). He thus implies, in a way analogous to Girard, that there are two kinds of reason: a reason that goes along with *amour-propre* and a "public reason." The former is implanted in the "bottom of the heart in a state of things where all men are forced to flatter and destroy one another, and where they are born enemies by duty and swindlers by interest" (*CW*, 3:75).

For Rousseau this reason directed at the benefit of the individual finds its source in the desire to distinguish oneself. As Rousseau says in his *Preface to Narcissus: Or the Lover of Himself*, "every man who occupies himself with agreeable talents wants to please, to be admired, and he wants to be admired *more than the others*" (*CW*, 2:192; emphasis mine). It is this last phrase that shows how Rousseau thinks mimetic relations among men. "He does everything to obtain it [public applause], if he did not do still more to deprive his rivals of it" (*CW*, 2:193).

For Rousseau, the truth "most cruel" is that society itself has

> made it impossible for men to live among themselves without being prejudiced against supplanting, betraying, mutually destroying each other! Henceforth, humans must beware of letting ourselves be seen as we are: for two men whose interest agree a hundred thousand can be opposed to them and there is in this case no other means to succeed than to deceive

> or ruin all these people. This is the deadly source of violence, treachery, perfidy, and all the hours necessarily demanded by a state of things in which each—pretending to work for the fortune and reputation of the others—seeks only to raise his own above them and at their expense. (*CW*, 2:193)

Nevertheless, it would seem that Rousseau grants himself an exception. He is not like others. His heart is different, still "natural," that is, nonmimetic. He begins his *Confessions* by writing:

> I wish to show my fellows a man in all the truth of nature; and this man will be myself.
>
> Myself alone. I feel my heart and I know men. I am not made like any of the ones I have seen; I dare to believe that I am not made like any that exist. If I am worth no more, at least I am different. Whether nature has done well or ill in breaking the mode in which it cast me, is something which cannot be judged until I have been read. (*CW*, 5:5)

Certainly, this qualifies Rousseau in terms of revealing the mimetic truth. In this sense he is a true romantic, holding out the illusion of being an autonomous self. And yet it is precisely this point that makes his thinking not less mimetic, but more; more dominated by it than dominating it.

Eric Gans shows us how this claim to uniqueness is perhaps the most mimetic and therefore the most religious of them all. According to Gans, it is significant that Rousseau belongs to the second generation of the philosophes. Voltaire belongs to the first generation, his fame "was founded on the distinction between the author's presence in society and his representational presence in his works."[11] But at this point in the changing relations between the writer and society the noncentrality of society to the writers' writing is formal; "the private space in which they are written—and read—does not affect their content." Already with Rousseau this changes: "if society must now center itself around those whose primary function requires them to reject it, the next stage can only be the thematization of this rejection."[12] The only place where Rousseau can maintain his triumph would be "that of the outcast whose writings, addressed only to himself, only accidentally fell into the public domain." The society of Rousseau "called forth a new formula of self-centralization that would reestablish social relations around a new concept of individuality. Rousseau was to become the Christ of this time of crisis."[13] Gans lays it out in this way:

> Although many would rather have it otherwise, it seems no exaggeration to affirm that since the time that Jesus (or one of his disciples) applied to his individual self the "suffering servant" role of deutero-Isaiah, the most successful mechanism for self-maintenance in the center of the human universe has been that devised by Jean-Jacques Rousseau. Such mechanisms are rare, and although their significance comes from the fact that they can be used by virtually anyone, a particular prestige attaches to their inventors who acquire, for good or ill, the status of mimetic models.[14]

Rousseau invented "a variant of the Christic mechanism." Rousseau, who claimed to be the most unmimetic creature of all, turns to be hypermimetic and thus, by a kind of logical extension, hyperreligious.

The Letter to d'Alembert on the Theater

Having established that Rousseau thinks human relations mimetically, I want to turn now to the specific text I wish to treat and to address the three questions that emerge from the initial quotation from Girard. The text is titled *The Letter to d'Alembert on the Theater*.[15] It was published in August 1758. It is a response to the entry "Geneva" in volume 7 of the *Encyclopedia*, which appeared in October 1757. The entry was, of course, written by Jean-Baptiste le Rond d'Alembert, coeditor, along with Denis Diderot, of the *Encyclopedia*. So now I ask: (1) In this particular text does Rousseau think about human relations mimetically? (2) Does my interpretation "achever" the *Letter to d'Alembert*, that is, does the religious interpretation reach what is essential in that text? Is the essential in this text the relationship between arts and politics, as most commentators have held, or is the text a manifestation of the search for self-mastery? Later we will ask whether my interpretation shows anything that can help us to further specify the "different kind of rationality."

Does Rousseau Think Human Relations Mimetically?

The above considerations concerned Rousseau's thought in general and so they also apply to this text. But we can be more specific. There are historical and biographical details concerning this text that are highly relevant.

In his "Preface" to the *Letter*, Rousseau states the cause that occasioned it. He quotes in full the passage from the entry in the *Encyclopedia* dedicated to the city of Geneva in which d'Alembert proposes the establishment of a theater in that city. This would allow Geneva, so writes d'Alembert, to "join the prudence of Lacedaemon with the urbanity of Athens" (*CW*, 10:253). The other relevant facts are that Voltaire had settled on the outskirts of Geneva in 1755. He very much wanted to be able to stage plays there. Allan Bloom in the introduction to his translation of the *Letter* writes that "Voltaire persuaded d'Alembert . . . to insert a passage in an otherwise laudatory presentation suggesting that Geneva should have a theater."[16] Rousseau responds with this *Letter* that is ostensibly addressed to d'Alembert, but is also explicitly addressed to the public and to the Genevan public in particular.

Bloom does an excellent job of showing the mimetic nature of the situation in which the *Letter* was written. He writes:

> The particular circumstances which provided the occasion for this book—which constituted his definitive break with the Encyclopedists—are reminiscent of a drama whose particular events are all meant to epitomize general issues; it is like a morality play, entitled "The Spirit of the Enlightenment against the Spirit of Republican Virtue." The *dramatis personae* are Rousseau, the protagonist; d'Alembert, the editor of *l'Encyclopédie* and the author of its plan; and behind him, unmentioned but nevertheless the key figure, the genius of the Enlightenment incarnate, Voltaire.[17]

Thus, the historical context is a drama for a letter on drama. Two sides are lined up against each in opposition. Certainly for Bloom, as well as Patrick Coleman and Mark Hulliung, there are real differences between the protagonists, especially differences regarding religion.[18] Hulliung sees the issue in this way: "In a larger sense the aim of the philosophes was to induce Geneva to break with its Calvinist past by embracing the theater, long accused of exciting the most sinful passions."[19] For the philosophes the stage should supplant the pulpit for the "dissemination of philosophical messages," but not so for Rousseau.[20] But this does not mean that the two sides were actually opposed in getting Geneva in particular or Europe in general to break from Christianity.

To show that it is not improper to consider these biographical and historical facts as they bear on this text, it is good to remember that Rousseau himself writes that he is acting mimetically. He writes that he "is speaking my opinion in imitation of your [d'Alembert's] example" (*CW*, 10:262). The *Letter* itself is an imitation.

The main topic of the *Letter* is the spectacle or theater, perhaps the most mimetic of the arts, both in the sense that, as Rousseau writes, "the stage [*scene*] is, in general, a painting of the human passions, the original of which is in every human heart" (*CW*, 10:263). But also in the sense that his main motivation for writing is the concern that, as Christopher Kelly, puts it, "the essence of this experience is one of identification with the characters portrayed on the stage and forgetting about oneself" (*CW*, 10:xxiii). Human beings in society are highly mimetic. In fact, Rousseau claims "nothing appears good or desirable to individuals which the public has not judged to be such, and the only happiness which most men know is to be esteemed happy" (*CW*, 10:300).

Rousseau is exercised about d'Alembert's proposal for a theater because the mimetic effect that theater has is always negative for a virtuous republic. The damage comes from the bad examples on the stage and also from the mimetic rivalry that will develop in what one wears to the theater, and extends to the bad example of the actors and actresses outside the theater. Almost every issue raised by Rousseau in the *Letter* has to do with mimeticism. Thus, it can hardly be considered accidental that while preparing to write the *Letter*, Rousseau composed another work, unpublished in his lifetime, titled *On Theatrical Imitation*. It consists of extracts and translations from Plato's *Republic* dealing with mimesis.[21]

Meaning Is Religious

So let us turn now to the second claim: Given that the text thinks human relations mimetically, how is its meaning religious? How does it call forth a religious interpretation? Recall that one definition that Girard gives for religion is the "obscurity that surrounds man's efforts to defend himself by curative or preventative means against his own violence" (*VS*, 23).

Girard's cryptic remarks on "achever" hold that an interpretation that would *achever On War* is one whose meaning is religious because "only a religious interpretation has a chance of reaching what is essential in it." This evaluation of religious interpretation rests on Girard's own mimetic theory:

> My hypothesis is mimetic: because humans imitate one another more than animals, they have had to find a means of dealing with contagious similarity, which could lead to the pure and simple disappearance of that society. The mechanism that reintroduces difference into a situation in which everyone has come to resemble everyone else is sacrifice. Humanity results from sacrifice; we are thus the children of religion. (*BE*, ix)

Thus, the fundamental meaning of "religious" when talking about this kind of religious interpretation is that it does not cover up but rather brings out the mimetic element in human relations. In so doing it also brings out the violence, since mimetic behavior leads almost necessarily to violence. This violence leads, again almost necessarily, to sacrifice as a way of containing the violence. And this leads to religion. We can say then that it is an interpretation that follows what Girard calls the "implacable logic of the sacred," the logic by which innocent victims are killed "to enable their fellow humans to live together" (*BE*, ix).

But this is in effect only half of what a "religious interpretation" would entail, because the "logic of the sacred" must include for us another "decisive point" (*BE*, ix). That point is Christian revelation. "Christianity demystifies religion" (*BE*, x). In effect, Christianity is what allows us to see the logic of the sacred in the first place. The fundamental truth of this revelation, according to Girard, is "*about the identity of all humans*" (*BE*, x). It is a truth that we do not want to hear, "instead we hang ever more frantically onto our false differences" (*BE*, x).

Rousseau's *Letter* is certainly meant to be a preventative measure to ensure the preservation of the sacred order of society. Even a cursory reading allows one to see that Rousseau is upset because a theater will ruin the republican virtues that keep Genevan society intact. With a theater it will, gradually perhaps but certainly, degenerate into violent conflict. And yet the obscurity is also there: What is so upsetting about a theater? Why this issue? What is it about drama that could be so dangerous?

Girard on Comedy

To understand the danger, we have to deepen our understanding not just of theater in general but of comedy as well. Girard's repeated engagement with tragedy and especially with Sophocles' tragedy *Oedipus Rex* is well known and documented.[22] Less well known is the fact that Girard finds parallels between this classic tragedy and modern comedy. In fact, Girard has deconstructed the distinction between these two art forms in an essay called "Perilous Balance: A Comic Hypothesis."[23] In this essay Girard looks, as usual, first at the continuities and identities between tragedy and comedy, as between tears and laughter. Tragedy produces tears.

> Tears suggest that tragic emotion really has something to do with a process of purification and evacuation that is certainly present in the medical *katharsis* and that I strongly believe to be present in the religious *katharsis*. Ideas of religious purification are inseparable from sacrifice, and other forms of ritual always refer, in my view, to an original scapegoating process, to a holy lynching truly capable of restoring the order and peace of the city because it reunifies all the citizens against a single victim. The ritual expulsion of this victim is the expulsion of violence itself. (*DBB*, 123)

Comedy, on the other hand, produces laughter. Once again we find the body trying to expel or ward off something. "Laughter . . . seems to be asserting, exactly like tears, that it must get rid of something; there is more of that something, and laughter must get rid of it more promptly than mere crying" (*DBB*, 124). Extreme laughter and extreme crying or sobbing are practically indistinguishable. Girard's conclusion is that "the crisis element is *more acute* in laughter than in tears. Laughter seems *closer* than tears to a paroxysm that would turn it into actual convulsions, to a climatic experience of rejection and expulsion. Laughter is *further along* toward a total negative response to a threat considered overwhelming" (*DBB* 125; emphasis mine).

Tragedy and comedy are both sacrificial institutions that help society to ward off or expel something. Tragedy tends to emphasize the individual character, the hero, and to assert his difference over against his opponents, while comedy brings the structural similarities to the fore in order to make it amusing. Girard uses a parallel reading of Molière's *Le Bourgeois gentilhomme* and Sophocles' *Oedipus Rex* to make his point. In each drama characters come onto the stage in the midst of something that is in the nature of a conflict—a plague or a dispute—and try to intervene. In Molière's comedy the Doctor of Philosophy wants to mediate the dispute between the music master, the dancing master, and the fencing master over which discipline is superior. Instead of settling the dispute he simply falls into it by saying that all three are nothing compared to philosophy. The illusion of superiority enjoyed by the Doctor of Philosophy lasted only so long as he was a pure spectator, and that led to an eagerness to arbitrate the conflict. But in fact the conflict engulfs the character that felt so superior. The same dynamic can be seen in the disputes between Oedipus, Creon, and Tiresias. The difference lies in how clearly the underlying structure is brought out. In tragedy it remains in the background; in comedy it is part of the joke. Comedy makes this explicit by deemphasizing the individual and emphasizing the structure. To use Girard's own example: Two men are standing on ice, one of them slips and falls. The second one begins to laugh at him, but the laughter causes him to lose his balance and he falls. The second man is funnier than the first. A third would be even funnier, unless it happens to be me.

> We are really laughing at something that could and, in a sense, should happen to anyone who laughs, not excluding ourselves. This, I believe, clearly shows the nature of the threat, unperceived yet present that laughter is always warding off, the still unidentified object it has to expel. The man who laughs is just about to be enveloped into the pattern of which his victim is already a part; as he laughs he both welcomes and rejects the perception of the structure into which the object of his laughter is already caught; he welcomes it insofar as it is someone else who is caught in it and he tries to keep it away from himself. (*DBB*, 128)

Laughter, as a manifestation of our self-mastery over the other, destroys that same self-mastery in that it robs us of our autonomy as a spectator. This is the paradox. "As an assertion of superiority, in the more intellectual forms of the comic, laughter really means a denial of reciprocity." The person who causes laughter has tried and in the very effort failed to deny reciprocity between himself and others. When I laugh at him, I "mimic and repeat the whole process" (*DBB*, 128). I feel superior to him and I am aware that I am now trapped in a similar dynamic of attempted mastery and its failure.

Rousseau on Comedy

This gives us some clues as to what Rousseau might be afraid of. He inscribes the *Letter* within the theoretical space of the principle of his system of thought: "the state of nature" or "natural goodness." He holds that he has proven that "man is born good" (*CW*, 9:267). Thus, "the heart of man is always right concerning that which has no personal relation to himself" (*CW*, 9:267–68). That is, insofar as one is free from *amour-propre*, from the mimetic influence of society, then one will naturally tend toward the good and the just. It is only when one's interests are involved that the sentiments get corrupted and a person can prefer evil to "the good that nature makes us love" (*CW*, 9:268). Laughter, it would seem, is an indication that the person is in danger of losing his position outside or above the fray.

Rousseau holds that as long as we are "pure Spectators, we immediately take the side of justice" (*CW*, 9:268). As long as we can maintain the observational stance and thus take the side of justice, then "there is no act of viciousness which does not give us a lively sentiment of indignation" (*CW*, 9:268). And it is here that laughter becomes dangerous. Girard has shown that laughter destroys our stance as the "pure Spectator." According to Rousseau also, it cannot be combined with the sentiment of indignation. "There is nothing less funny or laughable than virtue's indignation" (*CW*, 9:270). Girard acknowledges what Rousseau refuses to countenance: that laughter can be a way of asserting one's distance from and superiority over the other. Rousseau implicitly understands what Girard has made explicit: to laugh at the moment of indignation at another's evil is to wipe out the insistence on nonreciprocity that the indignation indicates. But Rousseau does not go far enough. Even without the laughter, the assertion of nonreciprocity in indignation establishes reciprocity because, as I would paraphrase without, I hope, distorting Rousseau: for the virtuous man there is no act of viciousness that does not inspire him to an act of viciousness against the vicious. This is mimeticism at its purest.

Rousseau's most serious criticism of the theater occurs, then, not in his discussion of tragedy but of comedy. Rousseau finds the latter more harmful to society than the former.

> Happily, the tragedy such as it exists is so far from us, it presents Beings so enormous, so bloated, so chimerical, that the example of their vices is hardly more contagious than that of their virtues is useful; and, to the extent that it wants to instruct us less, it does us also less harm. But it is not so with comedy, the morals of which have a more immediate relationship with ours, and whose characters resemble men more. It is all bad and pernicious; every aspect strikes home with the Audience. And since the very pleasure of the comic is founded on a vice of the human heart, it is a consequence of this principle that the more the comedy is amusing and perfect, the more its effect is disastrous for morals. (*CW*, 10:275)

It is a principle, then, that the pleasure afforded by the comedic is "founded on a vice of the human heart." According to this principle, the more perfect a comedy is, the more disastrous it is for morals. To understand this Rousseau tells us that we must turn to what he had to say about the "nature" of comedy (cf. *CW*, 10:275).

In the first place Rousseau argues against anyone who thinks that simply by "depicting" morals one has corrected them. "An ugly face does not appear ugly to him who wears it" (*CW*, 10:269; a remark that seems to veer dangerously close to being comic). If someone should argue that comedy does not merely depict, it caricatures these bad morals, then Rousseau holds that one has left "the realm of probability and nature, and the picture no longer produces an effect" (*CW*, 10:269). For caricature does not render its objects "hateful," it renders them ridiculous.

At this point in the text Rousseau makes his main argument against comedy based on its nature. First, he claims that it is "by dint of fearing what is ridiculous" that "vices . . . are no longer frightening" (*CW*, 10:270, translation emended). He then claims that one cannot "remedy" or "cure" what is ridiculous without "fomenting" those vices that are no longer frightening.[24]

How does the correcting of the ridiculous lead to vices that are no longer frightening? Rousseau says it is a "necessary opposition"—one cannot remedy the ridiculous without encouraging vices. Rousseau gives us a clue on how to interpret what he means here. A little later in the text, in the context of criticizing Molière, he writes: "He did not, then, pretend to form a decent man but a man of the world. Consequently, *he did not wish to correct the vices, but what is ridiculous*" (*CW*, 10:277; emphasis mine).[25] The necessary opposition means that when one intends to correct the ridiculous, one is necessarily not correcting vices. Rather, one is encouraging them because, in order to avoid being ridiculous in this world, one must have the vices of this world. Molière's comedy was created with an aim at remedying or correcting the ridiculous rather than vices (which Rousseau has already shown to be impossible anyway), and so it produces men of the world. But the vices of the men of the world do not frighten people, least of all those who have them.

Rousseau is saying that this necessary opposition between the correction of the ridiculous and the correction of vice is a duel fought by adversaries armed with different weapons. Virtuous men do not use ridicule; "the good do not make evil men the object of derision" (*CW*, 10:270). The good see nothing ridiculous in vice. They cannot laugh at it and laughing at it would be a cause of shame. As we saw above, it is a principle for Rousseau that "nothing is less funny or laughable than virtue's indignation" (*CW*, 10:270).

On the other hand, the correction of the ridiculous is accomplished by ridicule, and ridicule is an attack on virtue used by vice. In fact it is its "favorite weapon" (*CW*, 10:270). This finding and naming of the ridiculous attacks the "respect that the heart owes to virtue" and finally extinguishes the "love that is felt for it" (*CW*, 10:270).

The only real remedy for what is ridiculous is ridicule, and ridicule is the weapon vice uses to exterminate virtue. Thus, one corrects what is ridiculous at the cost of virtue. Without virtue vice is no longer frightening. The virtuous but ridiculous man necessarily becomes vicious in being delivered from his ridiculousness.

Molière is thus in some ways an evil man: "His greatest care is to ridicule goodness and simplicity and to present treachery and falsehood so that they arouse our interest and sympathy" (*CW*, 10:275). For Rousseau, this world is already too full of the reality of virtuous fools being the victims of the vicious for it to be an excuse for putting it on stage, "as if to excite perfidious souls to punish under the name of folly, the candor of good men" (*CW*, 10:276). Rousseau's criticism grows in intensity:

> See how this man, for the sake of multiplying his jokes, shakes the whole order of society; how scandalously he overturns all the most sacred relations on which it is founded; how ridiculous he makes the respectable rights of fathers over their children, of husbands over their wives, of masters over their servants! He makes us laugh, it is true, and for that he is all the more guilty, in forcing, by an invincible charm, even the wise to lend themselves to jests which ought to call forth their indignation. (*CW*, 10:276)

The comedy of Molière is so dangerous that we have to look in detail at how he accomplishes this effect. Only then we will be convinced that the "seductions of vice" represented there are so effective as to deserve banishment (*CW*, 10:285).

Interpretations of *The Misanthrope*

Both Rousseau and Girard interpret Molière's play *The Misanthrope*. A comparison of their interpretations brings into relief the way in which Girard's approach is able to "achever" Rousseau.

Rousseau finds in this "masterpiece" the true aims of Molière's comedy: he wished to correct not what was evil or vicious but what was ridiculous. In particular, he wanted to expose to "public derision all the failings opposed to the qualities of the likable man—the man of Society" (*CW*, 10:277). So he put on the stage the man who is ridiculous precisely because he is virtuous. Here we see concretely the "necessary opposition" between remedying the ridiculous and promoting vices that no longer frighten. In curing the ridiculous through ridicule, Molière is necessarily ridiculing virtue and to avoid the ridicule the man will have to adapt vices.

For Rousseau, Alceste is a "righteous man, sincere, worthy, truly a good man" (*CW*, 10:277). Alceste is not really a misanthrope at all; he is the "victim" (*CW*, 10:281). "Precisely because he loves his fellow creatures, [he] hates in them the evils they do to one another and the vices of which these evils are the product" (*CW*, 10:277). He is filled with indignation at the evils that he sees. Indignation is practically a mark of virtue. For Rousseau it is "natural" that his anger degenerates into fury. So that Rousseau concludes, "if there were neither knaves nor flatterers, he would love all humankind" (*CW*, 10:278).

Rousseau criticizes Molière for some of the characteristics with which he presents Alceste. The misanthrope's character is determined by "the nature of his dominant passion. This passion is a violent hatred of vice, born of an ardent love of virtue and soured by the continual spectacle of men's viciousness" (*CW*, 10:279). He has then a "great and noble soul" (*CW*, 10:279). He is filled with contempt for vice, and this contempt keeps the vices at bay. He has a "pride of character which leaves room in his soul only for sentiments worthy of occupying it" (*CW*, 10:279).

Rousseau acknowledges that the misanthrope can in fact be "weak, unjust, unreasonable" (*CW*, 10:279). Still, according to Rousseau's conception of the character, the misanthrope would only rage at disorders of which he is a witness, not those that touch his person. Each time that Molière disfigures the misanthrope by making him rage at something that concerns his own self, Rousseau says Molière does it because "he had to make the audience laugh" (*CW*, 10:280–81).

We have already seen that Rousseau holds it as a principle that "nothing is less funny or laughable than virtue's indignation" (*CW*, 10:270). He is, then, most critical of Molière precisely because he makes the audience laugh, that is, when he forces, "by an invincible charm, even the wise to lend themselves to jests which ought to call forth their indignation" (*CW*, 10:276). But there is one more principle of Rousseau, again given in a footnote, that we must consider. He holds that "in things that dishonor, no one laughs with good grace at his own expense" (*CW*, 10:281n). As the text makes clear, Rousseau is arguing by this principle that if one put on a play with the intention of making the audience laugh "at the expense of the man of the world," the play would fail because the men in the audience would, in effect, be laughing "at their own expense" (*CW*, 10:281n).

Rousseau's conclusion: "since the intention of the author is to please corrupt minds, either his morality leads to evil, or the false good that he preaches is more dangerous than the evil itself; in that it seduces by an appearance of reason" (*CW*, 10:280). Thus, the play and the author must be expelled *instead* of Alceste being figuratively expelled as a misanthrope.

For Girard, the other hand, *The Misanthrope* is the most powerful critic of French intellectualism. French intellectualism is defined by Molière as "the pure spirit of contradiction dreaming of distinguishing itself" (*BE*, 160). In the play, the "crucial duel" is neither between contempt and ridicule, nor between the virtuous and the vicious, as Rousseau would have it. Rather it is "between persons who have distinguished themselves and those who have failed, between those who have understood the rules of society and those who claim to be their victim" (*BE*, 161). Célimène, a character almost ignored by Rousseau, becomes the key to the play for Girard because she has "discovered Alceste's secret, and will suffer as a result at the end of the play" (*BE*, 160). She will suffer the same result as the play suffers at Rousseau's hands. The core to her insight is contained in a few lines.

> And is not this gentleman [Alceste] bound to contradict? Would you have him subscribe to the general opinion; and must he not everywhere display the spirit of contradiction with which Heaven has endowed him? Other people's sentiment can never please him. He always supports a contrary idea, and he would think himself too much of the common herd, were he observed to be of any one's opinion but his own. The honour of gainsaying has so many charms for him that he very often takes up the cudgels against himself; he combats his own sentiments as soon as he hears them from other folks' lips.[26]

It is because he can find no other way of distinguishing himself that Alceste pretends to disdain the company of others. Célimène is the only character in the play who points out Alceste's resentment. Girard's surprising conclusion is that "Célimène suffers the consequences [of the disintegration of the salon] since she ends up in a convent" (*BE*, 161).[27]

> The denouement of the play is literally a lynching. Because she is the most spiritual, Célimène pays the price in a world of conversation that goes to extremes and that contains a bitterness that follows a movement towards greater violence in society. As soon as it stops being superficial, the conversation explodes into violence. Alceste is not a scapegoat: he has failed to distinguish himself but he does not want to admit it. He is already a creature of resentment. (*BE*, 161)

At the conclusion of the play one character after another makes a statement and leaves the stage. In glaring contradiction to the reigning theatrical conventions of the time only Célimène is given no line, no stage direction for how or when to leave the stage. She is left, bereft, having been expelled from society.

Conclusion

Years ago Girard wrote "no philosophy in the classical sense can understand laughter or account for it because philosophy tries to establish our mastery as human beings or individuals on unshakeable grounds" (*DBB*, 133). I have already pointed out that it is a principle for Rousseau that "no one laughs with good grace at his own expense" (*CW*, 10:281). The virtuous are indignant at vice, and ridicule itself is a kind vice, so one cannot laugh when one is being ridiculed. I believe that Rousseau argues in this way because he recognized what Girard had also seen: the comic is rooted in the ultimate failure of individualism. And thus Rousseau hates it.

Rousseau can't laugh. Girard explains why. Rousseau cannot laugh because he needs to occupy the place of mastery. His brilliance was to understand that if such a place were to exist, it could only be the place of the victim. His failure, his moral and intellectual obtuseness, was to fail to see that precisely such a place does not exist. The place of the victim is precisely the place of nonmastery.

Girard turns to Charles Baudelaire to understand the deeper meaning of laughter. He sees in Baudelaire indications that Baudelaire also understood laughter as a sign of the mimetic crisis. "In his few admirable pages on *De l'essence du rire*, Baudelaire clearly perceives the difference between the mocker and the mocked as a disintegrating and vanishing difference, as creeping identity" (*DBB*, 129). Girard's attraction to Baudelaire's analysis is that he recognizes laughter

> can weaken as well as strengthen the barriers that separate each of us from the others. Laughter will erupt when we see our long-cherished prejudices confirmed and also when we see them finally crumble into dust. Baudelaire . . . is among the few who recognize the existence of a truly superior

> laughter, the one that welcomes its own downfall. Unlike so many of our peevish "demystifiers," he was not building intellectual cages in which to imprison everyone but himself. He read laughter in a Pascalian light, as a sign of contradiction pointing both to the "infinite mercy" and the "infinite greatness" of man. (*DBB*, 130)

This Pascalian light, with which Baudelaire read laughter, casts a long shadow. Our repeated attempts to establish our mastery as human beings or individuals on unshakeable grounds seem like a version of Friedrich Nietzsche's eternal recurrence. The difference between Girard and Rousseau is precisely the difference of the kind of unshakeable ground upon which they try to build a system. For Rousseau the putative foundation is the natural goodness of humans with a concomitant rejection of the doctrine of original sin. The real foundation is the rejection of grace or forgiveness, a rejection that also takes away the light by which one sees original sin for what it is. Everything, including the expulsion of theater, of comedy, and of Molière, comes out of that. For Girard, in contrast, original sin as what defines man is "fundamental" (*BE*, 22). At the same time he recognizes that this foundation is not like others. Girard appeals to Blaise Pascal because Pascal "saw and immediately understood the 'abysses' of foundation" (*BE*, 22). Original sin is fundamental without being foundational. It is so because it is not an intellectual cage designed "to imprison everyone but himself" (*BE*, 22). Girard is implicated in his own analysis in a way that Rousseau could never be. This is a new type of rationality.

NOTES

1. René Girard, *Achever Clausewitz: Entretiens avec Benoît Chantre* (Paris: Carnetsnord, 2007). The book is translated as *Battling to the End: Conversations with Benoît Chantre*, trans. Mary Baker (East Lansing: Michigan State University Press, 2010). Hereafter *BE* and cited in the text. My reason for using the French title at this point is to underline the centrality of the concept I am using. It bears mentioning that "achever" carries with it at least the double meaning of to end and to complete. The longer quote is found on page 15 of *Achever Clausewitz*.

2. Mimetic desire is Girard's earliest concept. We desire something not so much because the object is somehow in itself desirable but because someone else desires it. Someone else shows us that it is desirable, normally by possessing it or by desiring it himself.

3. Originally published as *Mensonge romantique et vérité romanesque* (Paris: Grasset, 1961), it was translated by Yvonne Freccero and published in 1965 by Johns Hopkins University Press as *Deceit, Desire, and the Novel: Self and Other in Literary Structure*.

4. Chapter 11 is titled "The Dostoyevskian Apocalypse."

5. René Girard, *Violence and the Sacred*, trans. Patrick Gregory (Baltimore: Johns Hopkins University Press, 1977), 31. Hereafter *VS* and cited in the text.

6. René Girard, *The Scapegoat*, trans. Yvonne Freccero (Baltimore: Johns Hopkins University Press, 1986). See especially chapter 2, "Stereotypes of Persecution."

7. Beginning with his early work, *Knowing Jesus* (London: Society for Promoting Christian Knowledge, 1993), James Alison calls it "the intelligence of the victim." This is the title of chapter 2 of that work. Andrew McKenna refers to "the victim, whose epistemological privilege is paramount," in his introduction to *René Girard and the Bible*, special issue, *Semeia* 33, no. 4 (1985): 4.

8. Jacques Derrida, *Of Grammatology*, trans. Gayatri Chakravorty Spivak (Baltimore: Johns Hopkins University Press, 1974), 203.

9. A note on the references to Rousseau's texts: For the French text of J. J. Rousseau's works I have used *Oeuvres completes*, vols. 1–5 (Paris: NRF-Edition de la Pléiade, 1959–95). All translations are taken from *Collected Writings of Rousseau*, ed. Roger D. Masters and Christopher Kelly, 13 vols. (Hanover, NH: University Press of New England, 1991–2010). Here, 3:91. Hereafter *CW* and cited in the text.

10. Tzvetan Todorov, *Life in Common: An Essay in General Anthropology*, trans. Katherine Golsan and Lucy Golson (Lincoln: University of Nebraska Press, 2001), 38.

11. Eric Gans, "The Victim as Subject: The Esthetico-Ethical System of Rousseau's *Rêveries*," in *Jean-Jacques Rousseau*, ed. Harold Bloom (New York: Chelsea House, 1988), 220.

12. Ibid.

13. Ibid.

14. Ibid., 215.

15. The *Letter to d'Alembert on the Theater* is contained in volume 10 of the *CW*. The introduction provides some historical background for the *Letter*. More information can be found in Allan Bloom's *Politics and the Arts: Letter to M. d'Alembert on the Theatre* (Ithaca, NY: Cornell University Press, 1960).

16. Bloom, *Politics and the Arts*, xvi.

17. Ibid., xv.

18. Patrick Coleman, *Rousseau's Political Imagination: Rule and Representation in the* Lettre à d'Alembert (Geneva: Librairie Droz, 1984); Mark Hulliung, *The Autocritique of Enlightenment: Rousseau and the Philosophes* (Cambridge, MA: Harvard University Press, 1994).

19. Hulliung, *The Autocritique of Enlightenment*, 126.

20. Ibid., 127.

21. The piece is published in vol. 5 of the *Oeuvres completes*, 1195–212, and in *CW*, 7:337–50. For some historical background please consult the introduction to that volume, especially xxxv–xxxvi.

22. See in particular René Girard, *Oedipus Unbound: Selected Writings on Rivalry and Desire*, ed. Mark R. Anspach (Stanford, CA: Stanford University Press, 2004).

23. René Girard, *"To Double Business Bound": Essays on Literature, Mimesis, and Anthropology*

(Baltimore: Johns Hopkins University Press, 1978), 121–35. Hereafter referred to as *DBB* and cited in the text.

24. The French text is "c'est qu'à force de craindre les ridicules, les vices n'effrayent plus, et qu'on ne sauroit guèrir les premiers sans fomenter les autres" (*Oeuvres completes*, 5:24). The English translation in the *Collected Works* is: "afraid of being ridiculous, men are no longer afraid of being vicious. The former cannot be remedied without promoting the latter" (*CW*, 10:270). I think this translation reflects an interpretation that would say if you remedy the "former," that is, men who are afraid of being ridiculous, you will promote the "latter," men who are no longer afraid of being vicious. This would mean that the remedy is to make the men less afraid of being ridiculous and the concomitant result is also less fear of vice. But this is not a "necessary opposition"; rather it is a reciprocal relation and so it cannot be what Rousseau means.

25. The French text is: "il n'a point voulu corriger les vices, mais les ridicules" (*Oeuvres completes*, 5:35).

26. *The Misanthrope*, act 2, scene 5. *Battling to the End* uses a different translation. Mine is taken from *Plays by Molière* (New York: Modern Library, 1950), 198.

27. Surprising because there is no textual evidence for Célimène entering the convent. Still, I would argue that Girard's conclusion is true to the spirit of the ending of the play, as my subsequent analysis makes clear.

Girard and the Feminist Critique of Religion: Intimate Mediation in Kristeva and Girard

Martha Reineke

After thirty years, as feminist theories in the philosophy of religion, theology, and religious studies approach middle age, on what basis can we reflect on Girard and that feminist critique? Surely, we would most productively move forward were we to home in on aspects of feminist theorizing about religion that have maintained the most saliency. Moreover, feminist theorists of religion would most productively engage Girard in dialogue were they to share with him a sense of urgency about the world that he has conveyed in his most recent works, especially in *Battling to the End*. On both counts, an observation on feminism offered by Julia Kristeva is most suggestive: Taking a retrospective measure of feminism and expressing fears that "we may have reached the point of no return" for a human community leaning toward destruction, Kristeva writes,

> I am convinced that after all the more or less reasonable and promising projects and slogans the feminist movement has promulgated over the past decades, the arrival of women at the forefront of the social and ethical scene has had the result of revalorizing the sensory experience. . . . The immense responsibility of women in regard to the survival of the species . . . goes hand in hand with this rehabilitation of the sensory.[1]

In this essay, I want to explore Kristeva's assertion that close attention to sensory experience is among the most lasting legacies of feminism and one that offers important lessons for our times even as I also suggest that mimetic theory would be enhanced were it to take from feminist theory the impetus to rehabilitate sensory experience.[2]

But does mimetic theory actually need to rehabilitate sensory experience? After all, such experience lies at the heart of Girard's early work. In *Deceit, Desire, and the Novel*, Girard argues that affective memory and sensory experience are the "source of the true and the sacred" and the "salvation" of Marcel Proust.[3] Understanding that mimetic desire runs through the body, Girard finds in sensory experience the mechanism of spiritual conversion. Unfortunately, even as Girard breaks through to mimetic theory with Proust, he breaks away from "Merleau-Ponty and all the authors related to phenomenology" whose philosophical reflections on sensory experience he says he found "fascinating" when he was a young scholar.[4] In *Violence and the Sacred* and *Things Hidden since the Foundation of the World*, as well as in more recent works, sensory experience and associated terminology figure not at all.[5]

As a consequence, if mimetic theory is to attend to sensory experience, that which Girard set aside as he developed his mimetic theory will need to be recovered. In what follows, I argue for the importance of such a move even as I suggest that Girard's dismissal of sensory experience as a key component in his theory has come at great cost. For sensory experience establishes *the* pathway humans take from acquisitive to positive mimetic desire. The deleterious consequences of Girard's move away from sensory experience have festered largely unnoticed; in *Evolution and Conversion* and in *Battling to the End*, they are palpably manifest. In these works, an immeasurably deep chasm separates bad and good mimesis, the apocalypse and the kingdom. Attesting to a dualism in Girard's thought, these oppositions put in doubt how humans might pass from destruction and sin to healing and grace.

Dualism in Girard's Theological Anthropology

Reflecting on problematic features of Girard's anthropology, I want to consider the polarities that split Girard's theory.[6] I begin by examining Girard's notion of apocalyptic violence. Girard emphasizes that scapegoating is an effective tool for limiting societal violence only when persons agree on the guilt of a victim; a society capable of recognizing that a victim of mob violence is innocent can no longer use scapegoating as an instrument of social control. Because the scapegoat mechanism has been desacralized, exposing its mainspring, it has been stripped of its power to diffuse violence. Generative violence multiplies; for, as Girard laments, "after the decomposition of the sacrificial order there is nothing standing between ourselves and our possible destruction."[7] For Girard, Matthew captures the "purely apocalyptic" contours of the present: at the end of the age, individuals will hate each other and nations will turn against nations. Matthew's warning—"where the corpse lies, the vultures shall gather"—attests to the "decomposition of the mimetic mechanism." I quote Girard: it remains visible, but "it doesn't work."[8]

Especially in *Battling to the End*, despair prevails: "violence, which produced the sacred, no longer produces anything but itself."[9] Here, Girard directly counters statements he makes in *Things Hidden since the Foundation of the World*. There, he counsels patience as humans make their way along a developmental trajectory to reach a spiritual adulthood that will enable them to understand the subversive and shattering truth contained in the Gospels.[10] Girard now asserts that Christianity has not labored forward to a time when mature humans will embrace Christianity's antisacrificial message. To the contrary, Christianity has itself "provoked the escalation to extremes" we currently face.[11] Girard still advises patience, but not because growth into adult spirituality is a centuries-long journey. Instead, patience before one's own desire is needed, lest one rise to contest "Powers and Principalities that will be destroyed anyway." Girard avers: "Christ will have tried to bring humanity into adulthood, but humanity will have refused." He expressly asks his readers to notice his use of the future perfect tense because he wants them to appreciate the profundity of the "deep failure" he is describing.[12] In *Battling to the End* the violence of acquisitive desire no longer can be checked; the apocalypse already has arrived.

But Girard does not wholly abandon the other pole of his dualism. Rather than consign humanity to the apocalypse, Girard asserts that we are left "only the choice between total destruction and realization of the Kingdom."[13] The route to the latter is through "positive imitation."[14] Elsewhere in

Battling to the End, Girard typifies such imitation as an "innermost mediation" experienced through the imitation of Christ that transforms mimeticism and "opens the door to the other side of violence."[15]

But what does Girard mean when he suggests that, on the other side of violence, the kingdom can be accessed? In order to understand what might count for Girard as an opening of the door and to identify the agency involved, I want to examine assumptions about the structure of mimetic desire that undergird Girard's notions of negative as well as positive mimesis. In *I See Satan Fall Like Lightning*, Girard asserts that desire has "no essential goal."[16] Animal desire does have an end, for instinct guides the animal toward its goals, as cows seek out grass on which to graze. But with freedom comes an elevation of the human outside of need, an elevation that renders desire aimless. With no end toward which it intrinsically tends, desire in the human is always borrowed desire: "truly to desire, we must have recourse to people about us."[17] Thus, desire comes into being only as one imitates a model; in the absence of that model "human desire, lacking its own proper object, cannot come into being."[18] Desire—good or bad—is an outcome of having good or bad models. In itself, desire is neutral.[19]

That Girard understands human desire to be without aim is of significant import as we seek to understand how a door might be opened to the kingdom that Girard claims is the sole alternative to the apocalypse. Girard indicates that humans experience an "almost instantaneous" conversion that transfers them from a kingdom of violence to the kingdom of grace through imitation of Christ.[20] Not only is entry sudden and asynchronous with all that has preceded it, but also, because Girard understands that positive mimetic desire aims toward no end,[21] the recipients of conversion are wholly passive in their transfer to the kingdom. Writes Girard of the disciples' own experience of this transformation: "The Spirit takes charge of everything." The disciples have done nothing in their own right; rather, "it is the Spirit of God that possesses them and does not let them go."[22]

Of course imitation does play a critical role in this conversion experience. When humans imitate Christ, they are offered personal salvation "through the spirit of Christ and his Father."[23] However, even as positive mimesis plays a role in conversion, positive mimetic desire does not. No, for Girard, Jesus has no "desire proper, a desire 'of his very own'" that humans can imitate. Instead, his desire is the desire of his Father: "his goal is to become the perfect image of God." Christ invites us to imitate him, thus to "imitate his own imitation."[24] Nor does God provide humans with a model of positive mimetic desire. Even God is without desire, for God acts in a mode of "detached generosity."[25]

In *Battling to the End*, Girard makes explicit what he means by Christ's imitation of God in God's mode of detachment. He states, "*The aspect of Christ that has to be imitated is his withdrawal* to be with his father.[26] Coinciding with the "advent of the Kingdom," Christ's withdrawal is linked too with God's "absence."[27] When humans engage in positive imitation of Christ, their actions take the form of renunciation. In a time of a "corrupted sacred," humans escape sacrifice and enter the kingdom only along a route characterized by silence. Indeed, Girard states that Christ's silence and God's absence are "the new face of the divine."[28]

Girard's theological quietism, which goes hand in hand with his dualism, is born of two influences. Girard states that he has become ever more acutely aware that mimeticism, even in its positive form, is unstable. Humans always are too close to or too far from others. Christ, in his mode of withdrawal, which models God's own detachment, frees humanity from "the mimetic whirlpool" in which we are drowning. Thus, access is granted to the kingdom, the alternative to destructive engulfment, only as others remain at a distance.[29] Influencing Girard also is Friedrich Hölderlin whom Girard describes as "the central thinker" of *Battling to the End*.[30] Girard credits Hölderlin with alerting him to shortcomings in his earlier reflections on generative violence and calls on us "to take the measure" of Hölderlin's silence and "to measure up to it."[31] Embracing Hölderlin's discovery of the dangers of proximity, whether of gods or humans, Girard avers that positive imitation of Christ must be enacted through withdrawal.[32] Hölderlin points the way for his solitary existence for forty years in a tower consists of "a mysterious relationship to the absence of God, an imitation of his withdrawal."[33]

When Girard confirms that the two worlds whose features he sketches—that of an impending apocalypse and that of the kingdom—"do not bespeak each other" except in the silence "of which Hölderlin showed the importance,"[34] he offers an impoverished metaphor of redemption that highlights key issues with his dualism and quietism. Girard says that "one cannot escape from bipolarity unless one undergoes a conversion which involves reversing time."[35] But in juxtaposing rather than relating two epochs of human existence—the time of sin and the time of redemption—Girard misrepresents the condition of human finitude. As Paul Ricoeur observes, "finitude is neither evil nor sinful, but a creative limit meant to orient and protect freedom rather than repress it."[36] Because Girard's dualism precludes him from treating finitude as a dimension of human experience that is part of the goodness of creation, a lacuna emerges in his anthropology. As Stephen Duffy suggests, any anthropology that speaks about Christian grace should account for structures of finitude out of which that goodness can be brought to expression. When an anthropology does so, it tracks human potential for graceful re-creation. Grace can be seen to home in on that which is estranged from God, not on that which is alien to God.[37] Especially in *Battling to the End*, Girard's anthropology, preoccupied with the deadly contagion of mimeticism, consigns humanity to historical time isolating those who are constrained by finitude from the time of redemption.

Girard's quietism also creates other problematic regions of silence in his anthropology. Possessed of no positive mimetic desire, humans are utterly passive in a transformative process that affords agency only to the Spirit. As Rebecca Adams observes, when Girard "*tells us* that we can take on this new perspective," he does not show us how humans relinquish roles of victim and persecutor in a system of acquisitive mimesis and assume new roles in imitation of God.[38] With divine absence and silence providing the sole frame for positive mimesis, we do not learn from Girard how humans become graceful.

Sensory Experience and the Path to Intimate Mediation

Even so, contained within the work of the young Girard are elements of a theological anthropology missing from his later work. Moreover, Girard's early work shows how access to positive mimetic desire is through sensory experience. When Girard set aside his early phenomenological explorations, he eliminated from view within mimetic theory the means by which humans move from acquisitive mimesis and its violent manifestations toward our true end: the intimate mediation to which he briefly alludes in *Battling to the End*. When we reconsider embodied practices of mimesis and positive desire, we can hold to the course from which Girard diverged and retrieve for mimetic theory insights that remain vital to it. Drawing our attention to this course, Kristeva enables us to move away from dualism and quietism as we seek with her the times and spaces of sensory experience that open onto redemption. With Kristeva, I return to Proust and to *In Search of Lost Time*, which played a critical role in the formation of Girard's theory. With Kristeva, I also consider the spiritual life of Ignatius of Loyola, who offers a powerful metaphor of redemption. In drawing on Proust and Ignatius to retrieve for mimetic theory the transformative resources of sensory experience, a feminist critique of religion, exemplified by Kristeva, secures hope as the most important legacy of Girard's mimetic theory.

Proust's attention to sensory experience reveals how the damaging aspects of mimetic desire, so visible in Girard's musings on apocalyptic violence, can be surpassed. As Kristeva explains, desire that separates us from each other is countered by sensation that exists "at the interface of the world and the self." Not oriented in respect to a lack of being, as are our desires, sensation offers access to being that is "nourished by the essence of things."[39] Proust acknowledges that in our efforts to experience being, we initially are blocked, for our lack of being and our immersion in a world of desire means that we can only imagine what is absent. Although we live in spaces crowded with others, we feel completely alone. Swept up in mimetic desire that is fueled by a lack of being, our lives are devoid of affective connection.[40] But the cure for our dis-ease, Proust shows, is not further withdrawal from the world. Proust holds out an alternative—experiencing life as a metaphor. What would it mean to experience being, not as lack, but as metaphor?

Kristeva's study of the Proustian metaphor is compelling. On her reading, Proust acknowledges that violence is the inescapable reverse side of the inconsistency of being, but room remains for an alternative vision. Exploring sensation, Proust understands that past and present sensations are "magnetized by the same desire."[41] As an association of sensations is forged, sensation becomes fixed as an impression. As such, it has something of the generality of an idea; however, instead of becoming an abstraction, sensation is incarnate. It is anchored in the world.[42] Yes, those we love are the occasion for suffering, and desire is caught up in that suffering. But impressions—hieroglyphs, palimpsests, figured truths—enable us to depart from pain.[43] Impressions can annihilate, depriving persons of their identity; however, by restoring persons to places and time through the work of affective memory, a new truth can be transcribed on sensations of long ago. In Proust's novel, that truth is grafted onto the actual body of the narrator.[44] Not consigning erotic excess, violence, and jealousy to the margins of the text, the narrator holds in balance the contradictions of human experience by threading through the text suffering and joy, profanation and redemption.

Proust's acute awareness of bodily suffering is testimony to this truth. But Proust shows that desire need not end in suffering or withdrawal. The unity of the Proustian experience—sensual, artful, and blasphemous—always escapes us. Yes, we are always only intermittently in the presence of Being, incapable of capturing it; nevertheless, we experience Being.[45] As Kristeva notes, Proust is drawn to the incarnation because "it wove into the figure of the Passion the indissociable symbiosis between the sensible and the sensed, between the Word and flesh.[46] Christ is an exemplary Proustian metaphor, for Christ's journey of the flesh tracks human violence to its depths and articulates from the midst of Being transformation and connection with others. In this way, Proust shows how humanity tends toward an end: the graceful re-creation of human existence. As Kristeva observes, in his embrace of metaphor, Proust's narrator is "neither in the *status corruptionis* of sin, nor the *status integratatis* of conceptual understanding, but remains in the intermediate stage of *status gratiae*."[47]

The Tears of Ignatius and the Hope of Mimetic Theory

Grace, suspended within the space of a metaphor, is, for Proust and for those who hear his words, testimony to the full contours of our journey of desire. Tending toward communion rather than apocalypse, we can draw on the Proustian metaphor so that we may anchor hope at the heart of mimetic theory. In order to see how this may be so, I follow Kristeva in further explorations of the truth that is grafted onto the body of one who experiences grace. My focal point is intimacy, a category of experience Kristeva takes neither from Jacques Lacan nor from Sigmund Freud, the two primary inspirations for her work, but from Augustine and Ignatius of Loyola. Interestingly, in their respective appeals to intimacy, Girard and Kristeva share terminology and a source of influence. For when Girard describes as intimate mediation processes that "transform mimeticism and open the door to the other side of violence," he specifically links this innermost mediation with Augustinian theology (*Deos interior intimo meo*).[48] With Kristeva's concept of intimacy, I suggest that Kristeva sketches the contours of what Girard would recognize as positive mimesis, even as she grounds intimacy in a sensory experience that surpasses the dualism on which Girard's mimetic theory is seen to falter. Indeed, Girard's evocation of Augustine, with its hopeful affirmation of an alternative to violent mimesis, is placed back-to-back in Girard's text with a contrasting assertion: Girard claims that mimeticism cannot be thwarted and that we live in times in which we must "abandon all optimism."[49]

When Kristeva discusses intimacy, she distinguishes intimacy from elements of privacy that typically feature in our closest personal relationships. Instead, as Cecilia Sjöholm suggests, for Kristeva "intimacy is a function of subjectivity that always appears to touch the truth of ourselves."[50] Linked with affect—sensation, mood, feeling—the intimate is not so much a function of a psychic interior as it is a "discourse of corporeality" that joins language with sensibility.[51] For Kristeva, intimacy also is associated with revolt. Rehabilitating revolt from its current confinement within the narrow constraints of political action, Kristeva returns to the etymological roots of revolt in order to name it as unveiling and returning, a movement of retrospection that Kristeva associates with Proust and Augustine, suggesting that the theologian's fundamental questioning (*questo mihi factus sum*) finds expression in a "remembrance of things past."[52] Characterizing "re-volt" as a "gestation of psychic space," Kristeva finds exemplary Stéphane Mallarmé's expression of revolt, which targets previous investments by a unitary subject who now advances through a "musicalization of meaning" to an interrelating of differences through which the subject and Being are reconstituted.[53]

Kristeva's revolt is not that of the slave against its master, a battle Girard would typify in terms of two subjects caught in mimetic desire. For Kristeva, revolt contrasts with violence, foregrounding instead renewal and regeneration. Specifically, intimate revolt is a process by which the subject opposes distortions in human relationships through an experience of love felt through a sensorial activity of the body. As such, revolt does not transgress the law, which from Girard's perspective in *Battling to the End* is the law of war, but displaces the authority of violent mimesis within the psychic economy.[54] Intimacy structures desire as cause rather than as goal.[55] Writing of this structure, Cecilia Sjöholm traces it to Lacan. However, so sure is Lacan that access by the subject to that through which it is constituted is experienced only as symptom, that he actually walls off intimacy and marks its inaccessibility with the term "extimacy." By contrast, Sjöholm reminds us that Kristeva sees openings to intimacy that Lacan disavows. Kristeva agrees with Lacan that the Symbolic order does not grant access to the intimate. Drawing expressly on Girard, she earlier has aligned that Symbolic with sacrifice.[56] But Kristeva understands that sensory experience opens us to intimacy beyond the constraints of law and sacrifice.

Ignatius's *Spiritual Exercises* and *Spiritual Diary* offer compelling testimony to intimacy as a focal point of Kristeva's anthropology. Kristeva acknowledges that Ignatius describes the goal of the *Exercises* to "make one's sensual nature obedient to reason."[57] But standing out for Kristeva in Ignatius's exercises is not a dualistic confrontation between law and the body, reason and the senses; rather, Kristeva perceives a continuity "beyond division" in the very exercises themselves.[58] As a consequence, Ignatius offers a compelling counterpoint to Hölderlin, the mystic to whom Girard has asked that we "measure up."

Attested to by Ignatius's life are familiar themes in mimetic theory. The young Iñigo exhibits all features of acquisitive desire—aggression, bellicosity, and narcissism—in his interactions with others. Hailing from a clan of fierce fighters, Iñigo is highly competitive with other men, kin and nonkin, and committed to a chivalrous ideal. Iñigo battles the French army. Consumed with bravado, he is a risk taker. After he is struck by a cannonball at Pamplona in 1521, he almost dies. His journey back to life is marked by ongoing violence, this time directed against himself as he battles against desire by means of extreme asceticism. His transformation into one of the great mystics of the Christian tradition does initially portray conversion in accord with the Girardian model of passive reception, for Iñigo is offered "consolation without previous cause" and avers that it "belongs to the creator to enter into the soul, to leave it, and to act upon it."[59] However, in key respects Iñigo, now Ignatius, attests to a spiritual life in which dualism and quietism do not figure, thus suggesting an anthropology that aligns with Girard's but sidesteps that anthropology's shortcomings. Features of Ignatius's exercises in intimacy link Ignatius with the Christian passion cited by Kristeva as a model for Proust. For Ignatius's journey of the flesh plumbs human violence to its depths and articulates from the midst of Being transformation and connection with others.

Engaging in these exercises in intimacy, Ignatius encounters a graceful truth through sensory impressions that, run through with pain, also prove restorative. The *Spiritual Exercises*, suggests Kristeva, "plunge us into . . . a sensorial anamnesis." When Ignatius meditates on the martyred body of Christ or on the experience of hell, he draws on the five senses to create a topography of suffering.[60] Reacting to dead words he re-creates sacred texts as living language. Ignatius's tears flow across the pages of his *Spiritual Diary*: "Saturday, July 5—Tears. Sunday, July 6—No tears. Monday, July 7—No tears. Tuesday, July 8—Many before and during Mass."[61] As Ignatius marks page after page after page with tears, he cannot be understood to home in on an obsession; rather, he encounters the truth of affect. And what is this truth? In the same *Diary*, Ignatius records also the *loquela*. Words and sounds that do not signify, the *loquela* are "infralinguistic marks" at the "exact border between the outpouring of tears and the appearance of words."[62] Linked by Kristeva with the semiotic, which previously she has sketched in young children's babbling and in the glossolalia of symbolist poetry, the *loquela* show Ignatius at the boundaries of meaning, at the border of affect and signification. In the *loquela*, truth unfolds. But again, we ask with Ignatius, what truth? In the "material traces of a body" suggests Kristeva, "divine indices take on meaning." A divine code that is corporeal-sensorial and infralinguistic, at the zero degree of the sign, the silence of God meets the plenitude of Being.[63] The harsh frame of Ignatius's life—obsession, discipline, judgment—is, at the very limits of meaning, matched by a receptive unfolding, an endlessly suspended code, an undecidable narrative, in a word—truth.[64] Thus, as for Proust so also for Ignatius, with tears and *loquela*, the truth of conversion is grafted onto the actual body of the one who narrates his conversion in his spiritual exercises and diary.

In the course of this intimate mediation, rather than dualistically oppose the epochs of his life, pre- and postconversion, Ignatius can be seen to continually balance suffering and joy, separation and redemption, that are proper to one who has assumed *status gratiae*. As a consequence, Ignatius is no quietist, no Hölderlin. True, in the wake of a mimetic crisis, he does withdraw from the world to engage in rigorous ascetic practices at Manresa; however, he leaves his cave to journey on in faith, studying, serving the poor, establishing the Society of Jesus. As William Meissner suggests, "In some profound sense, the transvaluation of identity that transformed

Iñigo de Loyola into Ignatius was a process of evolution. . . . It does not seem accurate to envision that process as the elimination of an old identity and its replacement with a new one. The identity of Iñigo was not destroyed; it was transformed."[65]

Meissner—Jesuit, psychiatrist, professor of religion, and author of two massive and definitive works on Ignatius—inquires about the relation between grace and the psychic substratum of human life and argues that grace interplays with psychic structure. Ignatius's life offers profound testimony to that assertion. One can read in Ignatius's life obsession, aggression, narcissism, and an authoritarian personality built over a fragile ego structure of a child who lost his mother while still an infant or toddler. But Ignatius, in the possible throes of psychosis in the cave at Manresa, rebuilds a psychic structure from the ground up even as a graceful truth heals him. No longer consumed by mimetic rivalries so well practiced by his clan or threatened by a loss of subjectivity while floundering in the abyss of maternal absence, Ignatius becomes someone to whom Girard could suggest we measure up.

Ignatius and Proust, focal points for Kristeva's analysis and for mine, show how the feminist critique of religion can enrich mimetic theory. Kristeva's sensitivity to the importance of sensory experience, supported by three decades of feminist theorizing, has alerted her to features of Proust's and Ignatius's lives I have highlighted here. As a consequence of her engagement with feminist theory, Kristeva has noted that women's rehabilitation of sensory experience, a transformation undertaken in spite of women's centuries-long circumscription by patriarchal culture within a domestic sphere in which women have been linked more closely with the body than men, offers hope to a world bent on destruction. Where Girard's theory still remains vulnerable to cultural and spiritual dualisms that have opposed body and mind, affect and signification, Kristeva has shown how these dualisms can be surpassed. Her insights demonstrate also how quietism can open out onto engagement in the world. To the extent that a divide of cultural history that has made men and women rivals of each other can be bridged, enhanced awareness of the healing potential of sensory experience and affect can be matched with attentiveness to the grounding of signification in a psychic space that opens out onto a world of relationship with others. Grace lived as Ignatius has recorded it suggests that we need no longer view the world as hopelessly divided among dueling mimetic rivals bent on destruction who must withdraw from each other if they are to experience God. Ignatius offers a model for renewed hope.

NOTES

1. Julia Kristeva, *Intimate Revolt: The Powers and Limits of Psychoanalysis*, trans. Jeanine Herman (New York: Columbia University Press, 2002), 5.

2. A review of the history of feminist scholarship in religion confirms Kristeva's argument. Applying a magnifying glass to three decades of that history, sensory experience appears as a thread woven through the fabric of that scholarship. For example, contributing to second-wave feminist theory in religion (1968–83), feminist philosophers trained in analytic philosophy (e.g., Grace Jantzen) or in process thought (Margorie Suchocki, Rita Brock, Catherine Keller) offered feminist critiques of the problem of God that focused critical attention on divine attributes and explored the embodied relationality of God and panentheism. Theorists contributing to third-wave feminist theory in religion (1983–98) drew on psychoanalysis (Jacques Lacan, Melanie Klein) to explore the Imaginary as fundamental to religious expression. For instance, with their insights informed by Girard's mimetic theory, Luce Irigaray and Julia Kristeva argued that sacrifice lies at the foundation of religious practice in the West and that the body at the foundation of that sacrifice is the maternal body. More recent developments in third-wave feminist theory (1998 to the present) home in on colonial and postcolonial subject positions in which embodied experience emerges as a theme at the intersection of feminist theorizing with other critical theories. Links are forged between concerns about life-threatening environmental degradation and a widespread loss of personal and social meaning. As this essay demonstrates, Kristeva continues to contribute critically to the concerns of third-wave feminist theory.

3. René Girard, *Deceit, Desire, and the Novel: Self and Other in Literary Structure*, trans. Yvonne Freccero (Baltimore: Johns Hopkins University Press, 1965), 81.

4. René Girard, *Evolution and Conversion: Dialogues on the Origins of Culture with Pierpaolo Antonello and João Cezar de Castro Rocha* (London: Continuum, 2008), 25.

5. Of an original cluster of phenomenological terms in Girard's early work—perception, sensory impression, material bridge, affective memory—only "perception" is retained in Girard's later work and then only in *Things Hidden since the Foundation of the World*, research undertaken in collaboration with with J.-M. Oughourlian and G. Lefort, trans. Stephen Bann and Michael Metteer (Stanford, CA: Stanford University Press, 1987), 130. Where "perception" is found, its phenomenological meaning is largely absent. For example, "perception" (*la perception*) is associated with hallucinatory phenomena in ritual trances (35). Perception is used analogically by Girard to compare meanings derived through ethnological interpretations with those associated with the figures that Gestalt psychology produces (61). Girard's post-1960s discussions of spiritual conversion—*I See Satan Fall Like Lightning*, trans. James G. Williams (Maryknoll, NY: Orbis, 2001); *Evolution and Conversion*, 175, 198, 212; "Conversion in Literature and Christianity," in *Mimesis and Theory: Essays on Literature and Criticism, 1953–2005*, ed. Robert Doran (Stanford, CA: Stanford University Press, 2008), 263–73—do not include a role for affect and sensation in conversion.

6. An earlier version of the argument explored in this section appears in Martha J. Reineke, "After the Scapegoat: René Girard's Apocalyptic Vision and the Legacy of Mimetic Theory," *Philosophy Today* 55, no. 3 (2011): 63–75.

7. Girard, *Evolution and Conversion*, 235.

8. Matthew 24:28; Girard, *Evolution and Conversion*, 234.
9. René Girard, *Battling to the End: Conversations with Benoît Chantre*, trans. Mary Baker (East Lansing: Michigan State University Press, 2010), x.
10. Girard, *Things Hidden since the Foundation of the World*, 254.
11. Girard, *Battling to the End*, 118.
12. Ibid.
13. Ibid., 119.
14. Ibid., 120.
15. Ibid., 133, 205.
16. Girard, *I See Satan Fall Like Lightning*, 15.
17. Ibid.
18. Ibid., 40.
19. As Gardner insightfully notes, Girard's denial of a natural order of desire is at odds with classical distinctions in philosophy. The philosophical tradition distinguishes reflexive passions (i.e., Girard's negative mimesis) from intrinsic ends—that which is desired for its own sake as a final end. Education shapes desire, but not because desire is aimless in the absence of such tutoring. There are objects that are intrinsically desirable, and we should desire them "with some acquired intuition of why they are intrinsically desirable, what makes them good." Stephen Gardner, "René Girard's Apocalyptic Critique of Historical Reason: Limiting Politics to Make Room for Faith," *Society* 47, no. 5 (2010): 458–59. Below, I account for that process as I discuss Proust.
20. Girard, *Things Hidden since the Foundation of the World*, 216–17.
21. Girard, *I See Satan Fall Like Lightning*, 15.
22. Ibid., 189.
23. Girard, *Evolution and Conversion*, 207.
24. Girard, *I See Satan Fall Like Lightning*, 13.
25. Ibid., 13, 14.
26. Girard, *Battling to the End*, 50, 120.
27. Ibid., 125.
28. Ibid., 122.
29. Ibid., 134.
30. Ibid., xvii.
31. Ibid., 44–45.
32. Ibid., 51.
33. Ibid., 112, 134.
34. Ibid., 130.
35. Ibid.

36. Paul Ricoeur, *The Symbolism of Evil*, trans. Emerson Buchanan (Boston: Beacon Press, 1986), 250, cited in Stephen J. Duffy, *The Dynamics of Grace: Perspectives in Theological Anthropology* (Eugene, OR: Wipf & Stock, 2007), 390.

37. Duffy, *The Dynamics of Grace*, 391.

38. Rebecca Adams, "Loving Mimesis and Girard's 'Scapegoat of the Text': A Creative Reassessment of Mimetic Desire," in *Violence Renounced*, ed. Willard Swartley (Telford, PA: Pandora Press, 2000), 289.

39. Julia Kristeva, *Proust and the Sense of Time*, trans. Stephen Bann (New York: Columbia University Press, 1993), 53.

40. Ibid., 57.

41. Ibid., 77.

42. Ibid.

43. Ibid., 79–81.

44. Ibid., 82.

45. Julia Kristeva, *Time and Sense: Proust and the Experience of Literature*, trans. Ross Guberman (New York: Columbia University Press, 1996), 308.

46. Ibid., 319.

47. Ibid.

48. Girard, *Battling to the End*, 205, 133.

49. Ibid., 131–32.

50. Cecilia Sjöholm, "Fear of Intimacy? Psychoanalysis and the Resistance to Commodification," in *Psychoanalysis, Aesthetics, and Politics in the Work of Julia Kristeva*, ed. Kelly Oliver and S. K. Keltner (Albany: State University of New York Press, 2009), 191.

51. Ibid.

52. Julia Kristeva, *Revolt, She Said*, trans. Brian O'Keeffe (Los Angeles: Semiotext(e), 2002), 120; Julia Kristeva, "The Revolt of Mallarmé," in *Mallarmé in the Twentieth Century*, ed. Robert Greer Cohn, trans. Louise Burchill (Cranbury, NJ: Associated University Presses, 1998), 31.

53. Kristeva, "The Revolt of Mallarmé," 36.

54. In her commentary on Kristeva's notion of intimate revolt, Kelly Oliver notes the juxtaposition of transgression with displacement. Kelly Oliver, *The Colonization of Psychic Space: A Psychoanalytic Social Theory of Oppression* (Minneapolis: University of Minnesota Press, 2004), 143.

55. Sjöholm, "Fear of Intimacy?," 188, 192–93.

56. Julia Kristeva, "Women's Time," in *New Maladies of the Soul*, trans. Ross Guberman (New York: Columbia University Press, 1997), 216n12.

57. Kristeva, *Intimate Revolt*, 47.

58. Ibid.

59. William W. Meissner, *To the Greater Glory: A Psychological Study of Ignatian Spirituality* (Milwaukee: Marquette University Press, 1999), 582.

60. Kristeva, *Intimate Revolt*, 101.

61. Ignatius of Loyola, "Journal des motions intérieures," in *Ecrits*, ed. and trans. M. Guiliani (Paris: Desclée de Brouwer, 1991), 76:368; As cited in Kristeva, *Intimate Revolt*, 104.

62. Kristeva, *Intimate Revolt*, 105.

63. Ibid., 109.

64. Ibid., 110–11.

65. W. W. Meissner, *Ignatius of Loyola: The Psychology of a Saint* (New Haven, CT: Yale University Press, 1994), 85.

PART 2

Mimetic Theory, Christianity, and Interfaith (Interreligious) Dialogue

Girard and World Religions: The State of the Question

Robert J. Daly

Presumably, I have this assignment primarily because I was the program convener for the 2000 COV&R meeting at Boston College under the title "Violence and Institution in Christianity, Judaism, Hinduism, Buddhism, and Islam," and eventual editor of its papers in *Contagion* 9 (2002). When, to begin this task, I asked the major presenters from that conference how their thinking on this subject had developed over the past decade, Francis Clooney, SJ,[1] helpfully informed me that the 1898 work of Silvain Lévi (on whom Girard relied in his recent book, *Sacrifice*)[2] was now considered to be a classic in the field. In addition, Sandor Goodhart sent me an electronic copy of the in-the-press *Sacrifice, Scripture, and Substitution*.[3] But all the rest could only wish me luck. Next, I became embarrassingly aware that if I were to do justice to this topic, it might be after, but definitely not before, hearing and studying the results of this symposium. For, after checking my own meager knowledge, and searching the university library and the Internet, as well as reviewing what we had learned at COV&R 2000, I find myself unable to produce what I would consider a satisfactory state-of-the-question report. Finally, the author of this report really should be Michael Kirwan whose 2009 *Girard and Theology*, esp. its chapter 9, "Girard and the Religions" (basically a commentary on the 2000 COV&R meeting that he characterized as a "stammering conversation"), already includes most of what my report attempts to summarize.[4] In the end, focusing primarily on just the past decade, I must content myself—hoping also not to disappoint you too badly—with pointing out some questions that have been raised and not yet satisfactorily answered.

The Evidentiary Value of Mimetic Theory

One notable world religions scholar whom I consulted described mimetic theory as "a broad theory based on flimsy anthropological evidence."[5] Such a dismissal, while in one sense true, also misses the point: there is no theory of human cultural and religious origins that can draw on more than "flimsy anthropological evidence" to support it. The real supporting evidence for mimetic theory, as James Williams and so many others have pointed out, is its heuristic value in helping us make sense of so much human history and experience. But notice how Eugene Webb nuances this situation:

> No group of experimentalists has directly taken up Girard's hypothesis for testing, and his theory of society (and language, religion, and even human consciousness as such) as founded on victimization is so broad and speculative that it is hard to imagine how all of it could be tested—although the twentieth century offered plenty of evidence that scapegoating does take place on a massive scale and at least circumstantial evidence that it can play an important role in generating class, party, or national solidarity.
>
> Girard's hypothesis about mimesis as a fundamental human motive, on the other hand, has received considerable indirect experimental support in the work of people studying imitative behavior among children (and in the recent neurological discovery of "mirror neurons."[6]

Mimetic theory is not supported by—and indeed has not yet been examined for—the kind of evidence that a "group of experimentalists" might assemble. But if it "works," if it explains human experience and behavior, that is surely enough to make it the basis for committed programmatic human activity. For example, in the nineteenth century, doctors began to discover that medical hygiene "worked." It saved lives long before biology provided the bacteriological evidence to support what used to be called just a theory.

Mimetic Theory and Christianity

René Girard was a Roman Catholic Christian. As has become increasingly clear, at the core of his mimetic theory is a specifically Christian understanding of the role of Jesus Christ in "unveiling" for us the scapegoating sacrificial mechanism. There is paradox here: for while mimetic theory seems to be intimately connected with a massive theological, even Christological, insight, Girard himself is not a member of the theological guild. But paradoxically, if mimetic theory basically wins the day—something on which our future probably depends—René Girard will have become the most influential Christian thinker of the past century, one about whom Christian theologians will have to do a lot of work. For if mimetic theory has us on the way to a more adequate understanding of who and what and how we are, then every article of the Christian creed, every Christian doctrine, teaching, and practice needs to be rethought in the light of mimetic theory. I am now realizing that that is what I myself have begun to do in my own *Sacrifice Unveiled*, in the section: "Sacrifice and Girardian Mimetic Theory: The End of Sacrifice?" and also in my contribution to the Girard Festschrift: "A Phenomenology of Redemption?"[7]

Thus, while making the claim that mimetic theory is profoundly true, I have to insist that this is so only, or at least precisely, in the "transcendental" sense that Bernard Lonergan uses when he insists that his philosophical and theological "method" is transcendental. That is, it claims to describe the processes of the human mind at work in each and every field of knowledge and understanding, and thus the processes that are present and working in each and every culture and religion. Is mimetic theory transcendental in that sense? That seems to be one of the basic questions—or assumptions—behind this symposium.

Mimetic Theory and Judaism

This seems to be the logical place to begin to answer this question. On the "no-brainer" level, the theory is obviously Judeo-Christian, and congenial to Jewish as well as Christian thought. Just read Sandy Goodhart's eloquent and moving account of his lifelong encounter with René Girard in the Girard Festschrift. Goodhart writes:

> Girard does not offer us—at least in my view—either an ethics or a theology. His own personal beliefs about Christianity are separable from his professional articulation of an anthropological reading that he identifies with that Gospel Scripture. One can be a Jew, a Christian, a Muslim, a Hindu, or a Buddhist and still be a Girardian. For me personally, the renewalist path of Buber-Rosenzweig and their inheritors (principally Levinas) offers the way to "refuse violence," to give up the sacrificial behavior that has led us to this impasse. But it is Girard who has taught us that refusing violence is our task, who has articulated the dimensions of the sacrificial crisis to which all such prophetic logics are a response. . . .
>
> For me personally, Girard offers the vocabulary for a return to Judaism, to the Judaism that is at the origin of the Christianity he so powerfully explains to us.[8]

This raises a question at the heart of mimetic theory's claim to be a transcendental theory: Is it—that is, in theory as well as in the obviously proven practice to which Goodhart gives witness—really separable from Christianity? Will living and acting in the light of and according to the insights of mimetic theory—even though it may be, as Goodhart says, neither an ethics nor a theology, and whether or not one is consciously a Girardian—make one a better Christian, a better Jew, a better Hindu, Buddhist, or Muslim, and in doing that give the world inhabited by these religions and cultures a less violent, more viable future? And if mimetic theory is truly "transcendental," then the other half of the "and" in the title of our symposium becomes not just "world religions," but also "world order" and "world peace." But is our task to try to find in the religions of the world correspondences to the Girardian (i.e. Western and ultimately Christian) formulation of mimetic theory, that is, using that formulation as our hermeneutic key? Or is it not rather to search in the other religions for ways in which, in their terms and in their language, they try to deal with violence and related issues?

As this report was being finished, I received a copy of the manuscripts being published in *Sacrifice, Scripture, and Substitution*. There Stuart Robertson writes:

> Although Girard's personal faith is Christian, his anthropological views and his views about the potential of scripture as anthropological reading have been accepted by non-Christians as well.[9]

In reading this volume one is impressed with the number of Jewish scholars who, in their sometimes critical engagement with mimetic theory, find it, as do Goodhart and Robertson, separable from Christianity.

Mimetic Theory and Hinduism

Our obvious starting point has to be Girard's recent book, *Sacrifice*. Based on three lectures to what must have been a general audience, this little jewel offers in Girard's own words a handy introduction to mimetic theory. It is also a handy introduction to Girard's "cheerful interdisciplinarity" and "multidisciplinary promiscuity,"[10] and his at times alienatingly frank excoriation of modern scholarship's reluctance to attend to the big picture (anthropology is the most frequently mentioned culprit). But in terms of our "state of the question," this book is also doing two things: First, it is implicitly spelling out the implications of mimetic theory's claim to be a transcendental theory. Second, it is doing this by way of a marvelously readable and accessible search into ancient Hindu literature for evidence to support mimetic theory.

Recalling my remarks above about the evidentiary value of mimetic theory, it is notable that Girard focuses not on mimetic theory's heuristic value in helping us make sense of things, but rather on the much more challenging search for actual evidence to support his theory that violent sacrifice is at the origins of human religion and culture. Not an Indologist and unable to work with the primary Sanskrit texts, he has astutely chosen to piggyback on the work of Sylvain Lévi whose 1898 work,[11] at first controversial because of his against-the-grain insistence on the coherence of the Brahmanas, has since (so Francis Clooney) become recognized as a classic. Early in *Sacrifice* Girard bluntly states that for which he is searching for supporting evidence:

> When we attentively examine archaic religions, we can see that, far from being a Platonic innovation, the concern with dissimulating or minimizing violence is already present at the center of ritual sacrifice. It belongs to the religious itself. Vedic sacrifice, for example, tries hard to minimize its own violence. The rites are organized so as to render the murder of victims as inconspicuous as possible.[12]

With the help of Lévi, Girard searches in the Vedic literature for the evidential "smoking gun" that will support his claim for the universality of mimetic theory by proving its presence in the origins of Hindu religion. What he seeks is significant traces of the single-victim scapegoat mechanism in the Vedic founding myths. He fails to find that clear evidence in the sacrifice that is at the heart of the *Hymn to Purusha* (number 90 in the tenth and final book of the Rig Veda). In his words:

> The genesis of myth is always a group of persecutors who transform their scapegoat, at first perceived as purely malevolent, into a benevolent divinity because of his reconciling power. To satisfy me entirely, and to verify mimetic theory, the *Hymn to Purusha* would need to contain a few more traces of the scapegoat mechanism in operation, in the form of a false yet indispensable accusation against the victim which, unfortunately, is no longer present in the example that occupies us.

But a few pages later, Girard exults:

> Fortunately for me, there is something other than Purusha. There is a second founding myth of sacrifice in the Vedas, as I indicated a short while ago, and I shall turn to it now. The accusation we vainly seek in the *Hymn to Purusha* we shall find in the texts of the Brahmanas on Prajâpati, texts that are likely an amended and enriched reprise of the hymn.[13]

Much of the rest of the book is simply dotting the "i's" and crossing the "t's" of Girard's claim that mimetic theory—or at least an essential fundamental component of it—is present in the founding myths of Vedic sacrifice, and thus at play in the subsequent distancing of the Brahmanas from sacrifice, and the subsequent rejection of it in Buddhism.

Mimetic Theory and Buddhism

Apart from its unique relationship with Judaism and Western Christianity, it is with Buddhism that mimetic theory's conversation with the other world religions seems to be the most advanced. Girard's recent *Sacrifice* indicates that the distancing of the Brahmanas (and of Hinduism in general?) from sacrifice was focused specifically on a distancing from the violence connected with sacrifice that seems obviously to be what was at play in, and that led to, the Buddhist rejection of sacrifice. Assuming the hypothesis of mimetic theory as a transcendental theory, how does that contribute to the conversation of mimetic theory with Buddhism? Our main guides in answering this are Leo Lefebure and Eugene Webb.[14]

In "Mimesis, Violence, and Socially Engaged Buddhism," before he began to engage Girardian mimetic theory, Lefebure had pointed out that the area of "social engagement" would be fruitful for Buddhist–Christian dialogue. In *Revelation, the Religions, and Violence* he makes some general observations, first, relevant to mimetic theory's evidentiary value:

> Girard has proposed a hypothesis that is most intriguing, but it has by no means reached the stage of empirical verification, and in many cases it is difficult to see how an affirmative judgment could be made.[15]

Other observations are relevant to mimetic theory as a transcendental theory:

> While the expressions of Zen and Christian experiences are very different, both [Masao] Abe and [Karl] Rahner nonetheless assume the strict universality of the pre-reflexive horizon of experience and thus allow for the possibility of analogous experiences and expressions in other traditions: Abe's *shunyata* is the universal process of emptying which is the dynamic movement of all beings just as they are, whether people use Buddhist categories

> or not; Rahner's God is the horizon of all finite reality, universally present whether people use Christian categories or not.[16]

But in "Buddhism and Mimetic Theory" Lefebure offers the beginning of a systematic discussion of the relationship between Buddhism and mimetic theory:

> The encounter between Buddhist perspectives and mimetic theory poses interesting challenges for both partners to the discussion. Mimetic theory offers Buddhism an analysis of the construction of desire and the self that in many ways complements traditional Buddhist perspectives. It also offers a naming of the mechanisms of violence in the formation of societies that may be helpful for Buddhists' social analyses. Buddhism for its part offers mimetic theory a centuries-old tradition of reflection on the role of desire in the construction of an illusory self as well as a body of practical wisdom on non-violence that, even if it has not always been put into practice, challenges and instructs the human community today.[17]
>
> The Buddhist teaching of no-self stresses the interdependence and impermanence of all beings. . . . Buddhists could well accept Girard's term "interdividual" to interpret the ancient teaching of interdependence.[18]
>
> Theravada Buddhist meditation practice, even though not based on as detailed a description of the scapegoat mechanism, does offer precise techniques for overcoming the problem. From the perspective of practical implications, one of Buddhism's greatest contributions to Girard's agenda lies in the tradition's concrete strategies of accepting responsibility for one's own feelings and desires, acknowledging envy and jealousy, and overcoming the urge to strike back in anger and vengeance.[19]

Then, after a discussion of the "four classical Buddhist virtues of loving-kindness (*metta*), compassion (*karuna*), appreciative joy (*muditha*), and equanimity (*upekkha*), known as the *Brahma-viharas* or the Dwelling Place of the Buddha, Lefebure concludes:

> Taken together and practiced over time, the Four Dwelling Places of the Buddha structure a conversation of consciousness, thought, feeling, and behavior that corresponds in many ways to the conversions that Girard describes in the Bible or in modern Western novels.[20]

Very much in continuity with Lefebure's analyses—although apparently independently of them—Eugene Webb points out "the ways in which Girard's thought might compare with Buddhist thinking on the psychology of desire."[21] His key text is, significantly, the very early *Mensonge romantique et vérité Romanesque*, "romantic lying and novelistic truth" (given the English title *Deceit, Desire, and the Novel*). Webb writes:

> The really deep connection lies in the fact that for Buddhism, as for Girard, desire is understood as fundamentally metaphysical. . . . What Buddhism is actually concerned with in its doctrine of *anatman* ["no-self"] is closely parallel to what Girard and his psychiatrist colleague, Jean-Michel Oughourlian, speak of when they talk about the "moi du désir," the "self of desire," as being not a substantial entity but a particular configuration of memory and desire.[22]

Webb sums up his analysis of this point by claiming that "Buddhist thought connects on a deep level with Girard's" and that "on this level Girard and Buddhism turn out to be allies."[23] What then, are the differences between them? Webb suggests

> that Buddhism's critique of desire, even if it does not talk quite explicitly about the rivalrous violence that desire can lead to, does not put special emphasis on its mimetic character, nor does it take up the themes of "sacrificial crisis" and the scapegoat as Girard conceives them. This may not, however, be because Buddhist thinkers have been evading this insight (as Girard thinks "sacrificial" Christianity has tended to do); it may rather be because the phenomena in question did not manifest dramatically enough in the Asian societies where Buddhism flourished to call special attention to themselves. Girard himself makes the point in *Deceit, Desire, and the Novel* that it was the breakdown of social boundaries after the revolutions of the eighteenth century and the consequent increase in social mobility that caused nineteenth-century novelists to begin reflecting so explicitly on the "novelistic truth" that Girard analyzes in that volume.[24]

This is a critical insight, a critical element in "the state of the question." It was a unique "Western" historical-cultural experience that enabled the articulation of—that was, in Karl Rahner's terms, the condition of the possibility of the articulation of—mimetic theory. Mimetic theory is a specifically Western articulation of a "transcendental"—in the Lonerganian sense—"universal" human condition.

Mimetic Theory and Islam

I saved this for last, in the hope that what came before might facilitate my treatment of this most difficult topic. The complicated and tense relationships East/West, Judaism/Islam, Christianity/Islam, Western culture/Islamic culture, etc., made all the more complicated since 9/11, make any attempt at a "state of the question" report seem rash indeed.

Our "stammering" discussion of this in our COV&R 2000 meeting in Boston—and that was before 9/11—illustrates this difficulty. Qamar-ul Huda was, Kirwan reports,

> trying to work within the dichotomy of descriptive and normative, to envisage a normative version of liberative Islam which is certainly compatible with mimetic theory. He underlines the point by using the word *islâm* in the lower case, meaning "the personal piety of surrendering to the divine and the journey of making one's faith meaningful" as distinct from a capitalized Islam which denotes the impersonal institutional, political and cultural dimensions.[25]

In the response and the discussion that followed, we were unwilling, or unable, to accept Qamar-ul Huda's invitation to discuss the issues on that normative level. Robert Hamerton-Kelly noted that one of the marks of the greatness of the great religions is "the candor with which they address the problem of the residual sacred violence in themselves."[26] The discussion never moved comfortably onto that level. Kirwan summed it up: "In the wide-ranging discussion which follows Huda's clarifications, at least one voice expressed the uncomfortable possibility that the COV&R group is instinctively 'scapegoating' Islam, though there appears to be at least the beginnings of a genuine dialogue."[27]

In the past decade, Girard himself has on repeated occasions attempted to wrestle with this challenge. But he, and we with him, seem to be still struggling to find a breakthrough to a hoped-for constructive dialogue. In his words:

> terrorism is something new that exploits Islamic codes but does not at all belong to classical Islamic theory. Today's terrorism is new, even from an Islamic point of view. It is a modern effort to counter the most powerful and refined tool of the Western world: technology. It counters technology in a way that we do not understand and *that classical Islam may not understand either* [my emphasis].
>
> Clausewitz is easier to integrate into a historical development. He gives us the intellectual tools to understand the violent escalation. But where do we find such ideas in Islam? Modern resentment never leads all the way to suicide. Thus, *we do not have the analogical structures that could help us understand* [my emphasis]. I am not saying that they are not possible, that they will not appear, but I admit my inability to grasp them. This is why our explanations often belong to the province of fraudulent propaganda against Muslims.[28]

I have, for emphasis, italicized phrases that suggest that terrorism may be as much a threat to Islam as to Christianity or the West. In a perversely paradoxical twist, do we need to band together with Islam in scapegoating terrorism?

To conclude, I can only "bullet" a number of issues/challenges that, taken together, and with so many more that can be added, are searching for a coherent solution:

- *Archaic religion*? Is that any help in understanding Islam, or aspects of it? Or is this just patronizingly alienating?
- *Fundamentalism*. Common elements in Christian and Islamic fundamentalism?
- *"Superiority" of Christianity*? Girard has been willing to speak in these terms. Does even raising the question tend to alienate, exclude, etc.?
- *Martyrdom*. All the great religions have actual or historical practices and teachings on martyrdom. Does, or in what way does, the suicide bomber relate to these?

- *History*. Whose story is being told? Generally it is only the stories of the winners and/or survivors that get to be told. Is there anything in Islam that corresponds to the attention to the voice of victims we find in Judaism and Christianity?
- *Religious/secular, church/state distinctions*. How recent these are in the Western world! There did not even exist any code of civil law until the sixth-century Justinian code. Definitely to be kept in mind when talking about Sharia or Islamism.

NOTES

1. Currently the director of the Center for the Study of World Religions at Harvard Divinity School, Clooney is considered by many to be the "Father" of the modern discipline of comparative theology.
2. René Girard, *Sacrifice*, trans. Matthew Pattillo and David Dawson (East Lansing: Michigan State University Press, 2011).
3. Ann W. Astell and Sandor Goodhart, eds., *Sacrifice, Scripture, and Substitution: Readings in Ancient Judaism and Christianity* (Notre Dame, IN: University of Notre Dame Press, 2011). This book includes papers from the 2002 COV&R meeting at Purdue, augmented by other related papers.
4. Michael Kirwan, *Girard and Theology* (London: T&T Clark, 2009), 120–31.
5. This quote is part of a personal communication from Prof. Wesley Wildman of Boston University. In this report, I am taking "mimetic theory" and "René Girard" to be basically synonymous.
6. Eugene Webb, "Mimetic Theory," in *Worldview and Mind: Religious Thought and Psychological Development* (Columbia: University of Missouri Press, 2009), 87–88. Webb refers to William Hurlbut, "Mimesis and Empathy in Human Biology," *Contagion* 4 (1997): 14–25. See also Scott R. Garrels, "Imitation, Mirror Neurons, and Mimetic Desire: Convergence between the Mimetic Theory of René Girard and Empirical Research on Imitation," *Contagion* 12/13 (2006): 47–86.
7. Robert J. Daly, *Sacrifice Unveiled: The True Meaning of Christian Sacrifice* (New York: T&T Clark, 2009), 203–22; Daly, "A Phenomenology of Redemption?," in *For René Girard: Essays in Friendship and in Truth*, ed. Sandor Goodhart et al. (East Lansing: Michigan State University Press, 2009), 101–9. I am continuing to work on the question "Is there a phenomenology of redemption?" Recent discussions suggest that what I am working toward might better be called a "theory of sanctification."
8. Sandor Goodhart, "Literature, Myth, and Prophecy: Encountering René Girard," in Goodhart et al., *For René Girard*, 94, 95.
9. Stuart D. Robertson, "Mimesis, Scapegoating, and Philo-Semitism: Reading Feldman and Girard," in Astell and Goodhart, *Sacrifice, Scripture, and Substitution*, 235–36.
10. Kirwan, *Girard and Theology*, 4, 5.
11. Sylvain Lévi, *La doctrine du sacrifice dans les Brahmanas* (Paris: Ernest Leroux, 1898; repr. Paris: Presses Universitaires de France, 1966).

12. Girard, *Sacrifice*, 5.
13. Ibid., 46–47.
14. (1) Leo D. Lefebure, "Mimesis, Violence, and Socially Engaged Buddhism: Overture to a Dialogue," *Contagion* 3 (1996): 121–40; (2) Lefebure, *Revelation, the Religions, and Violence* (Maryknoll, NY: Orbis, 2000); (3) Lefebure, "Buddhism and Mimetic Theory: A Response to Christopher Ives," *Contagion* 9 (2002): 175–84; (4) Eugene Webb, "René Girard and the Symbolism of Religious Sacrifice," *Anthropoetics* 11, no. 1 (Spring/Summer 2005); (5) Webb, "Girard, Buddhism, and the Psychology of Desire," in Goodhart et al., *For René Girard*, 147–57.
15. Lefebure, *Revelation*, 21.
16. Ibid., 199.
17. Lefebure, "Buddhism and Mimetic Theory," 175.
18. Ibid., 179.
19. Ibid., 182.
20. Ibid., 183.
21. Webb, "Girard, Buddhism," 147.
22. Ibid., 152–53.
23. Ibid., 154.
24. Ibid.
25. Kirwan, *Girard and Theology*, 124.
26. Robert Hamerton-Kelly, "Response to Qamar-ul Huda," *Contagion* 9 (2002): 99.
27. Kirwan, *Girard and Theology*, 124.
28. René Girard, "On War and Apocalypse," *First Things*, August 2009.

René Girard and World Religions

Michael Kirwan

Mimetic theory's encounter with world religions may be pictured as a tension between two powerful vectors or currents. The mainstream is the openness to the truth to be found in non-Christian religions, which we find articulated by the Second Vatican Council in 1965 (within a few years of the publication of *Deceit, Desire, and the Novel*), and taken forward in a series of official Roman Catholic pronouncements. I trace these developments not with a sectarian intent, but because these declarations comprise a legitimate heuristic: René Girard himself is a committed Catholic Christian, and among mimetic theorists exploring the implications of mimetic theory for other religious traditions there is a predominance of Catholic commentators. It seems appropriate, heuristically, to explore this distinctive trajectory. I do so while recognizing that "mimetic theory" is not coterminous with the thought of Girard and that alternative theological approaches are of course possible.

In *Nostra aetate* the council made its groundbreaking pronouncement that the church acknowledges the possibility of truth in other faith traditions:

> The Catholic Church rejects nothing that is true and holy in these religions. She regards with sincere reverence those ways of conduct and of life,

> those precepts and teachings which, though differing in many aspects from the ones she holds and sets forth, nonetheless often reflect a ray of that Truth which enlightens all men.[1]

This formula, however generous in intention, seems to be rather grudging and noncommittal. Nevertheless, it opens the door just wide enough for a steadily more explicit appreciation of other faith traditions, and the importance of engagement with them, to the extent that *Nostra aetate* is justly celebrated as a landmark document—an "inter-faith charter"—for the subsequent fifty years of reflection on this theme. Worth noting here is the opening of the decree, which states why interreligious dialogue is both desirable and unavoidable:

> In our time, when day by day mankind is being drawn closer together, and the ties between different peoples are becoming stronger, the Church examines more closely her relationship to non-Christian religions. In her task of promoting unity and love among men, indeed among nations, she considers above all in this declaration what men have in common and what draws them to fellowship. One is the community of all peoples, one their origin, for God made the whole human race to live over the face of the earth. One also is their final goal, God. His providence, His manifestations of goodness, His saving design extended to all men, until that time when the elect will be united in the Holy City, the city ablaze with the glory of God, where the nations will walk in His light. (NA 1)

It is the proximity of the peoples, an unmistakable "sign of the times," that makes opportune a close examination of what unites them. Girardian antennae are twitching at this point, of course, at the presupposition that "what men have in common" and "what draws them to fellowship" are unproblematic; the decree does not suggest anything unstable or dangerous in the closer proximity of peoples. We will return to this.

With *Nostra aetate*'s tentative opening of the door, a theological trajectory has been initiated. It finds further articulation in Pope John Paul II's encyclical *Redemptoris Missio*, promulgated in 1990, that affirms the missionary nature of the church and offers a renewed understanding of mission as comprising "dialogue" and "proclamation." There are also various attempts at inclusivist descriptions and more recent theological developments, which we will examine below.

At the risk of further sectarian self-indulgence, I would like to cite a document from one of the recent Society of Jesus (Jesuit) General Congregations. The *Decree on Mission* (GC34, held in 1995) seeks to articulate the Society's evangelizing mission in terms of a fourfold matrix of integral features, "without confusion, without separation." The service of faith, the promotion of justice, the evangelization of culture, and interreligious dialogue are "branches growing from one tree."

This is at odds, to say the least, with the tentativeness of *Nostra aetate*, and certainly contrary to the second cross-current, in tension with the mainstream. This current has for its most explicit source the catastrophic events of September 11, 2001; these and other actions of militant Islamists have undoubtedly challenged any easy optimism with regard to interfaith harmony. For many people, indeed, the atrocity has merely made plausible or even validated the hypothesis of a clash of civilizations, according to which the values of Christian and Islamic cultures are fundamentally incompatible. Even if such a hypothesis is rejected, dialogue can no longer proceed innocent of its own limits and difficulties, these being all too evident in a new climate of fear and suspicion toward the religious other.

Mimetic theory finds itself at the meeting point of these two currents. Its emergence fifty years ago is coincident with the council's remarkable articulation of a new openness toward other religious traditions; at the same time, mimetic theory's acknowledgement of the deep-seated complicity between religion, culture, and violence—emblematically demonstrated in the 9/11 crisis—gives the lie to any optimistic or facile sense of easy dialogue between religions, much less their harmonious convergence.

The encounter between mimetic theory and experts in non-Christian religions can be charted according to two phases. To begin with, meetings of COV&R (Colloquium on Violence and Religion) have swum with the mainstream tendency, in what has been described by me as a "stammering conversation" (not in any way to disparage what was said or written, but rather to affirm the authenticity of this theological dialogue, in its admittedly tentative beginnings).[2] The 2000 meeting in Boston College, and the 2002 colloquium in Purdue, Indiana, sought respectively to explore resonances and convergences between mimetic theory and major world religions, and then specifically between Christianity and Judaism.[3] The Boston Colloquium, "Violence and Institution in Christianity, Judaism, Hinduism, Buddhism, and Islam," was organized around Robert Daly's distinction between "normative" and "descriptive" accounts in order to get at what religions aspire to, by way of nonviolence or critique of violence ideals (normative), and what in actual fact has occurred in history. In 2002 it was Sandor Goodhart's turn to host COV&R, at the University of Purdue, with the specific theme of "Judaism, Christianity, and the Ancient World, Mimesis, Sacrifice, and Culture," including presentations from scholars such as Bruce Chilton and Michael Fishbane.

The second, post-9/11, phase includes the colloquia that took place later in the decade, and reflects something of the darker undertow. Meetings in Amsterdam (2007), Riverside (2008), and London (2009) addressed the vulnerability of tolerance and coexistence in multifaith and multicultural societies. In 2008, in the wake of Girard's book *Achever Clausewitz* (in English, *Battling to the End*, 2010), the language of catastrophe is used, as the apocalyptic implications of a post-9/11 "escalation to extremes," a globalized civil war, become more manifest (Girard, 2010, 198). Unsurprisingly the threat of militant Islam has attracted much of the attention at these meetings.

It is of course not true to say that interfaith dialogue began in 1965. From its inception Christianity has confronted its religious other, Judaism, as its adherents sought to reconcile their Jewish heritage and traditions with the unquestionably new revelation received in Jesus Christ. It is for this reason that *Nostra aetate* gives special attention to the relationship between Christians and Jews, initiating a theological rapprochement: catalyzed no doubt by the events of the Shoah, but given concrete expression in the explicit repudiation by the council of the doctrine that Jews bear collective responsibility for the death of Christ, the so-called blood libel. Subsequent scholarship on the Jewish identity of Jesus, the background of the earliest Christian communities, and nuanced scholarship on Paul have all confirmed the inescapable requirement for Christianity to acknowledge and affirm its Jewish origins, and for both traditions to confront their sibling relationship, burdened as it is with a nightmarish history of antagonism. The engagement of Christianity and Judaism has both chronological and existential priority, therefore, and in what follows, and at the risk of confusion, I will consider the issues arising from the Purdue colloquium of 2002 before tracking back to look at the Boston colloquium of 2000.

The Conversation Begins: Boston and Purdue

As host of the 2002 colloquium, and in his work more generally, Sandor Goodhart is guided by the conviction that one can be a Jew, a Christian, a Muslim, a Hindu, or a Buddhist and still be a Girardian. He draws attention to the renewalist path of Martin Buber, Franz Rosenzweig, and Emmanuel Levinas as the way to a Girardian reading of Judaism and its tasks, principally the refusal of violence and sacrificial behavior. "Girard offers the vocabulary for a return to Judaism, to the Judaism that is at the origin of the Christianity he so powerfully explains to us" (Goodhart, 2009, 95). He notes affinities between mimetic theory and the relational, ethicizing thought of Buber and Levinas, especially where the link between idolatry and violence is so clearly present in these thinkers. One might add that the importance of Simone Weil as an influence on Girard should also be noted here, though her antipathetic relationship to her own Jewish roots makes her a highly problematic figure, as Levinas has remarked.

Of these renewalist authors, Franz Rosenzweig offers in *Star of Redemption* a classic expression of Jewish-Christian "interdividuality" (Rosenzweig, 2005 [1921]). According to Rosenzweig, Judaism and Christianity have clearly differentiated tasks or modes of witnessing to the transcendent, making the traditions complementary rather than rivalrous or antagonistic. A similar approach underlies the biblical hermeneutics of James Williams, considered at the colloquium by Anthony Bartlett. For Goodhart and Williams, reading the Bible with a mimetic lens is an ecumenical act, affirming the biblical origins of both Judaism and Christianity and denying either one superiority. For each, it is rather the interpretive description of a single self-radicalizing tradition.

The colloquium at Boston two years earlier saw the first attempt by COV&R to facilitate authentic dialogue among the great religious traditions, an event owing something to the vision of comparative theology advanced by the Boston Theological Institute in the years preceding. Participants identified a shared area of concern between mimetic theory and the world religions: the need for transformation or conversion from the mimetic trap of scapegoating and violence, toward relations of spiritual connection and peace. Equally evident, however, was the sense that finding a way to articulate this concern in language that is not Western or ethnocentric is a major challenge.

A dialogue that proceeds with an a priori assumption that faith traditions can be interrogated and judged wanting, insofar as they lack a clear conceptualization of scapegoating or mimetic desire, is clearly inadequate. Francis X. Clooney (2011), speaking at Boston on behalf of Hindu traditions, warns against reading too much into this kind of lexical deficit; individual deficiencies are rarely significant, though they may point to larger differences between traditions. Nevertheless, Girard himself, in his book *Sacrifice* (2011), has found, to his satisfaction at least, significant traces of the single-victim scapegoat mechanism. Using Sylvain Lévi as his guide, Girard reads the *Hymn to Purusha* and the Brahmanas on Prajâpati and feels able to affirm that the subsequent distancing of the Brahmanas from sacrifice, and Buddhism's rejection of sacrifice, are comprehensible in terms of mimetic theory.

With regard to the latter tradition, Robert Daly has identified Leo D. Lefebure and Eugene Webb as mimetic theory's principal interlocutors. As with Clooney, so Lefebure issues a warning about overzealous "application" of mimetic theory, which can too easily proceed on the orientalist assumption that "only Western concepts are capable of understanding Asia's experience." The conversation must be two-way: the core themes of mimetic theory are allowed to provoke and challenge Buddhists, who must then be allowed to respond from their own resources. Lefebure (1996) notes affinities in Buddhism and mimetic theory, each denying an autonomous independent self, and in their concern for awakening from illusions of selfhood and desire. Elsewhere, he proposes dialogue around the areas of "social engagement," around the meaning of "revelation," and around transcendental approaches (comparing Maseo Abe and Karl Rahner). Eugene Webb similarly juxtaposes a Girardian understanding of the psychology of desire with Buddhist conceptions. Interestingly, for both Lefebure and Webb, it is the interdividual construction of false desire expounded in Girard's earliest book, *Deceit, Desire, and the Novel*, that is their point of departure. Webb concludes that Buddhist thought connects on a deep level with Girard's, though the connection between mimetic desire and scapegoating violence remains implicit within Buddhism.

The particular challenges with regard to Islam will be considered below, but it is worth noting here the proposition that the appropriate vehicle for mimetic theory and interfaith dialogue is that of the Abrahamic or monotheistic revolution. Insofar as it is precisely the monotheistic religions that are allegedly most prone to religious violence (Richard Dawkins after the 9/11 atrocity castigated "religions of the Abrahamic kind"[4]), then this framework needs to be explored. Wolfgang Palaver has drawn attention to the challenge of Elias Canetti, who identifies a special temptation for the Abrahamic faiths, or what he calls "religions of lament." The capacity of these traditions to give articulation to the cry of the oppressed lays them open to being overcome by righteous anger, so that the lamenting crowd quickly becomes a baying mob.

For Palaver, the Abrahamic legacy is centered in the understanding of divine revelation, pulling its adherents away from a sacrificial culture generated by the scapegoat mechanism. In particular, only a commitment to forgiveness, as an essential concomitant of the uncovering of the scapegoat mechanism, can counteract this temptation. Without this commitment, it is hard for the righteous holy to resist "hunting down the scapegoaters."

Can Islam recognize the inseparability of forgiveness and solidarity with victims? The connection is explicit in the Gospels, whereas the Qur'an lacks an equivalent of the Sermon on the Mount. Nevertheless, Palaver notes the condemnation of scapegoating in sura 4:112, "And whoso commits a delinquency or crime, then throws the blame of it upon the innocent, has burdened himself with falsehood and a flagrant crime," and sura 12, the story of Yusuf or Joseph. As in Genesis, chapters 37–50, the story of Yusuf represents the monotheistic rejection of scapegoating and the divinization of the victim. It may be, indeed, that a renewed paradigm for dialogue between Jews, Christians, and Muslims might be centered around the Josephine narrative as an alternative focus to the figure of Abraham.

Second Phase: Amsterdam and London

Despite the pacific resources of an "Abrahamic revolution," it is the atrocity of 9/11 and its aftermath, demonstrating the violent potential of political Islam and of religion more generally, that has held attention over the past decade. Mimetic theory's engagement with world faiths has inevitably been reshaped by it, to the extent that we can speak of a second phase in this conversation.

It is worth noting how Girard himself has altered his own appraisal of 9/11. His original reaction, in the 2001 interview in *Le Monde*, was to allege an outbreak of "mimetic rivalry on a global scale" (Girard 2001). He later draws attention to the specifically religious features of Islam that make the threat both unique and immense: a different attitude to death on the part of combatants, understood as a return to the "archaic sacred." To this extent, modern Islamist violence is as alien, and perhaps even as incomprehensible, to classical Islam as it is to the West. There is a breakdown in analogy; we are forced to recognize that we have moved beyond the humanist paradigm that held sway, even during the darkest moments of the Cold War (such that Girard could speak of Nikita Khrushchev's "turning the other cheek" as the resolution of the Cuban missile crisis).

This new unpredictability, baffling to Girard, has contributed to the sense of an "apocalyptic turn" in the recent writings of mimetic theorists, including Girard himself. The combination of an escalation to extremes, in terms of the technology of warfare, coupled with a militarized faith ideology that exceeds the bounds of humanistic rationality and instincts for self-preservation, makes 9/11 a highly significant marker. September 11 is a strange return of the archaic within the secularism of our time (Girard 2008, 25) For Robert Hamerton-Kelly, Islam's challenge is the same as for all the great religions: a struggle against the generative violence of the "pagan sacred." All religions are prone to regression and need to cope with the problem of the residual sacred violence in themselves. In a later essay, Hamerton-Kelly even suggests that being in the vanguard of this struggle, Islam has reached "a new extreme of this process and by destroying itself as a religion is ultimately saving itself as a faith, if indeed it is the true faith. If not, it is simply destroying itself" (Hamerton-Kelly 2007, 19).

This note of bafflement has to some extent pervaded recent COV&R meetings, notably Amsterdam and London. These colloquia sought to address issues of religious coexistence within a highly problematic context: secularized societies where a reigning orthodoxy of multiculturalism and tolerance is proving increasingly inadequate in the face of resurgent and to some extent hostile religious groups. In each case, recent acts of religiously inspired violence—the murder of Theo van Gogh in 2004, the London bombings of 2005—provided a somber backdrop.

The colloquium entitled "Vulnerability and Tolerance" (Amsterdam, 2007) included a presentation from Ian Buruma, the author of *Murder in Amsterdam: The Death of Theo van Gogh and the Limits of Tolerance*. As James Williams has pointed out, Buruma's analysis was highly compatible with mimetic theory in its recognition of patterns of imitation and resentment. The conference as a whole, as the title implied, sought to identify the shortcomings of Dutch traditions of tolerance in the wake of Islamic extremism, alienation, and the secularist backlash to it. Even something as apparently noncontroversial as the renunciation of violence cannot be the whole story, since acquiescence in the model of "tolerance" proposed to us by the state is, paradoxically, to hand ourselves over to an entity whose only possible sanctions are violence (a case argued at the colloquium by Joel Hodge, using the work of Charles Taylor and William T. Cavanaugh).

With this in mind, not only religious believers but also their dogmatic secularist critics need to beware of mimetic entrapment. Palaver advances once again the claims of the Abrahamic revolution: the overcoming of the scapegoat mechanism (which he identifies as the Abrahamic achievement) is also the true spirit of the Enlightenment. This would include the Voltairean insistence on defending and protecting even those with whom one disagrees, an attitude that finds poignant example in Buruma's lament concerning the fate of Ayaan Hirsi Ali, no longer able to live safely in Holland.

"Vulnerability and Tolerance" sought to address a culture of liberality and tolerance that, for complex historical and cultural reasons, has found itself in crisis. "Fearful Symmetries" (London, 2009) addressed the same issue, in the light of multiculturalism's failure to prevent alienation and disaffection among Muslims living and being radicalized in the UK. In both the Netherlands and in Britain, the background is a comparatively rapid process of secularization, with more or less spectacular collapse of confidence in and of Christian institutions. The secular paradigms intended to replace their previous hegemony are now themselves found wanting. There is by no means full agreement among mimetic theorists about how to move forward, and it is appropriate that some of the exchanges and presentations at these two colloquia have been edgy; nevertheless, a question emerges, to be addressed to believers and secularists alike. It is formulated thus by Gil

Bailie: how to honor the historic commitment to cultural openness and generosity without eviscerating the religious and moral sources of that very generosity. Williams (2012, 189) points out the irony that in a letter sent by Gil Bailie to a Dutch newspaper, the editors omitted this rather crucial question.

A number of Islamic speakers presented at the London colloquium, though with varying degrees of engagement with mimetic theory. Professor Tariq Ramadan (delivering the Raymund Schwager Lecture) called for intellectual empathy and a rejection of stereotypes of Islam. Reza Shah-Kazemi has acknowledged the presence of a Christic dimension within Islam and has collaborated, in the spirit of comparative theology, with the discussion of pacific texts and traditions in Islam and Christianity. The Qur'anic texts most cited by these scholars include the passages referred to above (sura 12, the Yusuf narrative) and sura 4:112 (protection of the innocent). Also important here is sura 5:48:

> Had Allah willed He could have made you one community. But that he may try you by that which he has given you, He has made you as you are. So vie one with another in good works. To Allah you will all return, and he will then inform you of that in which you differ.

Palaver reads this sura as a call to all believers to outdo each other in positive mimesis, a direction of our deepest desires toward the one God in whom all rivalry is overcome. This Qur'anic acceptance of diversity and pluralism as God-given is important in itself: it is also interesting, however, to juxtapose it with the view of the German political theorist Carl Schmitt (on whom Palaver has written extensively). Schmitt's political theology likewise affirms the importance of preserving differences, which he even claims to have been God-given (he cites the biblical story of the tower of Babel, where God introduces linguistic diversity among human beings in order to sabotage their cooperation on the building of the tower), but in a way that promotes conflict and hostility, rather than friendly emulation.

The wordplay of the 2009 conference title, "Fearful Symmetries," should by now be apparent. "Fearful," as in William Blake's poem "The Tyger," implies the wondrous admiration that the celebration of difference and plurality can inspire. But for a Girardian, the term also implies the frightening escalation of mimetic doubling, of difference gone wrong: whether in the antagonistic mirroring of rival religions, or as a defensive shrinking from a virulent secularizing modernity, insistent on unraveling difference in the name of "tolerance." James Alison's paper at the 2009 colloquium, "Brokeheart Mountain: Reflections on Monotheism, Idolatry, and the Kingdom," reminded us of further complexity: namely, the vulnerable position of sexual minorities who have too often found themselves scapegoated and excluded within each of these two faith traditions.

It is probably fair to say that in this second phase of conversation, there is less optimism among mimetic theorists that positive mimetic elements can be found in other religions. This needs to be set in the context of the discussion initiated at Riverside (2008) by Robert Hamerton-Kelly, who argued that mimetic theory does not allow for positive mimesis at all. His claim generated much debate, but if he is correct, then a fortiori the basis for constructive engagement with other religions is thin.

Finally, as the violent return of religion as such, and not just the individual faith traditions, has come into sharper focus, the role of the modern state as the arbiter and broker of peace has come to be increasingly scrutinized. We have noted that one Girardian scholar, Joel Hodge, has drawn on the work of William T. Cavanaugh in this regard. Essays in the *Blackwell Companion to Religion and Violence* (Murphy 2011) attempt to cover the ground; Cavanaugh's *The Myth of Religious Violence* (2009) is the fullest treatment from him of the secular state's founding myth, namely the narrative of a period of religious conflict at the dawn of modernity (the "wars of religion"), whose resolution is the emergence of the modern nation-state, with its monopoly of violence and apparent neutrality with regard to religious allegiance.

By focusing upon religion as the alleged primary cause of violence, the myth at once occludes the sacral nature of the state's own violence and deflects hard questions about it. At the same time, the myth marginalizes the capacity of religious traditions, especially Christianity, to generate a prophetic critique of this idolatry and to imagine a peaceful alternative. Mimetic theory is incompatible with this myth, because the theory posits an inherent connection, not between violence and religion, but between violence and mimetic desire; Cavanaugh's critique appears, therefore, to be an essential complement to mimetic theory in this phase of its development.

Theological Resources

We can point to one important asymmetry in Girard's work. He understands his hermeneutical method as a kind of recovery of the venerable practice of figural interpretation. The figure of Christ, crucified and risen from the dead, was understood in the patristic and medieval periods as the *figura* or hermeneutical key for interpreting the Old Testament passages, whether these refer to Adam, Moses, Abraham, or specific events, for example, the crossing of the Red Sea. In Girard's thought, by extension, the *figura*—the Lamb of God—interprets not just other scripture passages, but the whole of human reality. The death and resurrection of Christ shows forth the destruction of the scapegoat mechanism and the apotheosis of the victim, which reverberate throughout subsequent history: "the stone which the builders rejected has become the corner stone" (Psalm 118:22).

The figural approach clearly excites and interests Girard, though its dangers need to be acknowledged: of a kind of Christian exclusivism, devaluing the content of all religious traditions except insofar as they can be shown to point to Christ. Such a hermeneutic can be troubling enough with regard to the Christian–Jewish relations. When we move beyond, into the various theologies of interreligious dialogue more generally, the claims made by mimetic theory with regard to the uniquely revelatory power of the scriptures look even more problematic.

There are, on the other hand, misgivings from the perspective of Christian orthodoxy, if and when it seems that the uniqueness of Christ for salvation is not being acknowledged. My representation of the mainstream Catholic doctrinal position on other faiths would be seriously misleading if it did not also draw attention to the statements throughout on the necessity of Christ:

> Indeed, [the Church] proclaims, and ever must proclaim Christ "the way, the truth, and the life" (John 14:6), in whom men may find the fullness of religious life, in whom God has reconciled all things to Himself. (NA 4)

Hence the necessity of including in all dialogue a moment of proclamation; hence, also, the significance of the official declaration *Dominus Jesu* (2000), which sees itself as a corrective of alleged relativistic strategies of dialogue, in which the uniqueness of Christ and the importance of the church are downplayed or even denied outright.

The need to balance these imperatives is addressed by various theologians under the rubric of comparative theology. As Ulrich Winkler (2011) has pointed out, "comparative theology," understood as a "history of difference and interaction between religions and cultures," is as old as Christianity itself (234). In its present phase, however, a number of methodological issues are apparent, such as the need to move beyond a paradigm of "normative pluralism." Attempts at a neutral standpoint, above the fray, merely flatten out specificities of belief and practice on either side of the dialogue. They also fail to do justice to the lived complexity of actual religious communities, not least in their fraught and even destructive relations with one another. More recent initiatives considered here aim at a "dialogical non-reductive pluralism, which takes the truths and values of different faith communities with the utmost seriousness and seeks always to *learn* from them" (Barnes 2010, 438).

On the other hand, Keith Ward's version of comparative theology is intended as a counterprogram to denominational apologetics; theology must be held accountable in the face of the entire history of religions. The "Cross Cultural Religious Ideas Project" at Boston University (1995–99) was led by Robert C. Neville and resulted in a three-volume series of findings. Francis X. Clooney (2011), the foremost practitioner of comparative theology, has developed a method that consists in reading familiar Christian texts alongside unfamiliar non-Christian ones; a parallel approach is that of Scriptural Reasoning, in which Christians, Jews, and Muslims together read each other's texts with a view to attaining the inherited prudential wisdom in the respective traditions. The aim here is not simply to ensure a fair and accurate representation of the other, but to initiate a creative interplay of texts from the perspectives of the participants.

The pertinent image is that of theological subjects who act as hosts and guests, alternately taking the initiative or responding, in an exercise of responsible attention to the other—what is not-self—in the process of faith formation. From the Boston College website:

> Comparative theology takes time; its project of understanding, with the involved challenges regarding experience and scripture, proceeds only in

> time, over time, in a back and forth process of movement from one's own theological texts to those of the other tradition, and back to one's own tradition—again and again. Comparative theology is the acquisition of a new literacy, in which one's theology is enriched and complicated by reception of the vocabulary, methods, choices of the other tradition, and by one's assimilation of these into one's home tradition. While the elements of one's own tradition may individually remain stable, they "mean differently," because located in new context.[5]

Compare René Girard:

> There is no choice but to keep shuttling back and forth between alpha and omega. This constant movement, back and forth, imposes a form of composition resembling a snail, or a volute, or a spiral—a form that the reader is liable to find disconcerting, and in the worst case incomprehensible. . . . The best way to approach the book [my work], I think, is as a thriller. All of the pieces of the puzzle are given at the beginning, but it is only at the end that it becomes clear how they fit together. (Girard 2014, 50–51)

Conclusion

We have seen how the participants at COV&R 2002 explored Judaism and Christianity as a single self-radicalizing tradition. The essays that have emerged from this conference, published as *Sacrifice, Scripture, and Substitution*, represent sustained, high-quality scholarship on ancient Judaism and Christianity, through the lens of mimetic theory. Could this work provide a template, as it were, of what this conversation might look like more widely? Two factors need to be mentioned here. One, surely, is the presence of Sandor Goodhart, as the initiator of this colloquium but also as a major guiding presence of COV&R more generally. It seems fair to suggest that mimetic theory will make only limited progress with other religious traditions until scholars from those faiths commit themselves to the mimetic model in a comparable way.

The second factor concerns the dimension mentioned above, of self-radicalization, self-critique etc., which is a prerequisite for mimetic conversion.

Examples in Judaism and Christianity abound: Sandor Goodhart and James Alison show how, in the figures of Jonah and Peter respectively, ostensibly settled religious identities are challenged and overturned, according to a Möbius strip logic that reverses the roles of outsiders and insiders. By clinging idolatrously to his identity as a pious Jew, Jonah "becomes a pagan," that is, idolater, even as the pagans of Nineveh convert and thereby "become Israelites" (Goodhart 1996). In the same way, Alison shows the significance of Peter's vision in Acts 10, where he is presented three times with the command to "kill and eat" the food that, for a pious Jew, is unclean. His struggle with this command requires of him another conversion, as painful as his reconciliation after his threefold denial of Christ.

What remains inescapable, and at the heart of the Judeo-Christian paradigm, is the logic of overturning and reversal: of losing one's life in order to save it, the paradox of *kenosis*, of not clinging to status. The host/guest paradigm implicit in comparative theology recognizes the importance of role reversal: of being prepared to be received as a humble guest, as well as play the expansive and generous host. I would argue that the "dramatic theology" model developed by the Innsbruck theologians relies precisely on such an experience of conversion. The dramatic model turns on the shock of discovery on the part of the godly, who "did not know what they are doing" (Lk 23:24), only to find that "the Kingdom of Heaven has overtaken you" (Mt. 12:28)! In short, what James Alison has termed "the joy of being wrong" (Alison, 1998).

Are there similar resources within other religious traditions, including Islam, for articulating the overthrow of religious identity as well as its assertion, for the dismantling of mimetically compacted patterns of belonging? It is a commonplace of interfaith dialogue that partners must be ready to risk their identity, if dialogue is to flourish. What, precisely, does this risk involve?

René Girard's Christocentric claims need not, and should not, be understood in rigorously Christian exclusivist terms. Girard has clarified this in the discussion at the 2000 Colloquium: the truth of sacred violence and its overcoming is not the unique possession of any faith tradition, even if, at present, the language we have for talking about this happens to be Western in origin. The task in hand is to expand and improve our linguistic capability, just as the Enlightenment was not, despite appearances, an exclusion of

Christian perspectives, but their broadening out. As we have seen, Girard claims to find rich material in the Indian Vedas to illustrate the phenomena of mimetic rivalry and its relation to sacrifice; nevertheless, he continues to assert that as a matter of historical fact it is Christianity that has attained the fullest lucidity:

> All these religions are fully aware, from a normative standpoint, of the injustice of violence. . . . They know what sacrifice is and they progressively try to forbid it. The difference that I see between them and Christianity is that the latter was able to formulate in the Gospels and unmask in a full light the anthropological mechanism of mimetic scapegoating and sacrifice. (Girard 2008, 214)

Mimetic theory has something to offer non-Western cultures, provided it is not applied in a Procrustean manner. There is, nevertheless, a tension between the clean, streamlined attractiveness of mimetic theory and the more painstaking reality of authentic interreligious dialogue. What the latter requires is a patient search for analogies, rather than a triumphant demonstration of straight correspondences. The lexical challenge goes further than simply interrogating a given tradition about its words for "mimetic desire" and "scapegoat." Some of the key vocabulary of mimetic theory is value-laden; terms such as "primitive society" and the "archaic sacred," while clear enough in the context of mimetic theory, seem to have a needlessly provocative tone to them and leave mimetic theorists open to the charge of cultural superiority.

This is of especial relevance to mimetic theory's reading of Islam. At times Islam is presented as nothing other than a reconstruction of archaic religion, whose fundamental identity and dynamics are rooted in sacred taboo and prohibition. It is hard to see how this can be reconciled with an understanding of Islam as a part of the "Abrahamic revolution," as described by Palaver. What does it mean to anticipate, as does Robert Hamerton-Kelly, the "self-destruction of Islam as a religion and its rebirth as a faith"; and how, practically, would such a description be embodied in dialogue with actual Muslims? Again, what is required is a Muslim equivalent of Sandor Goodhart: a scholar committed to mimetic theory as well as to a non-Christian faith tradition.

We are reminded, in any case, that nowhere does mimetic theory encounter world faiths in some purified, essential form, but always in the throes of powerful and unsettling processes of modernization, and under the shadow of apocalyptic threats and challenges. There is no pure dialogue, outside of and apart from this context. If discussion is not to be carried off course by strong and dangerous crosscurrent, as much sociological and political as they are religious, then there is a need for a robust theoretical articulation of what we are doing and why.

To this end I have offered a Catholic paradigm, in terms of the basic trajectory of theology of religions since the Second Vatican Council's groundbreaking recognition of the possibility of truth outside of Christianity. It is offered here as one possible hermeneutic, though arguably a privileged one, given Girard's own Catholic allegiance, and that of a large number of his interlocutors. This hermeneutic finds modern expression in *Nostra aetate*; its origins lie, however, in the biblical revelation itself (in its openness to wisdom cultures outside Israel), flowering in the theological tradition of Justin Martyr in the second century, and reemerging in the twentieth century, with Karl Rahner, Jacques Dupuis, and inclusivist descriptions of varying degrees of adequacy.

A more recent example is the image of the "Court of the Gentiles," which has been a theme for Pope Benedict since 2009. For Pope Benedict, there should be, in addition to interreligious dialogue, a space of dialogue, "in front of the church," for those to whom religion is something foreign, but who nevertheless do not want to be left merely Godless. The forecourt of the cathedral of Notre Dame in Paris was opened up as precisely such a space of encounter in March 2011. One might conclude, of course, that this is yet one more example of a Christian appropriation of Jewish religious genius. Nevertheless, its aspiration to a form of religious hospitality, as integral and not superfluous to faith identity and mission, is clearly comprehensible within an interdividual mimetic framework.

Most recently, we arrive at the possibilities being opened up by comparative theology for genuine partnerships of theological exploration. This paradigm seems to be the most promising methodological development for the kind of dialogue that mimetic theory has initiated and seeks to continue. As with interfaith dialogue itself, the conversation will be two-way: even a cursory reading of *Nostra aetate* through a Girardian lens reveals areas of limitation. The document notes the increased proximity of the world religions, and implicitly celebrates this closeness as a catalyst for greater understanding and harmony. It does not in any way register this proximity as itself a possible cause of conflict.

I have also drawn attention to the second vector, the post-9/11 concern and alarm with regard to extremist forms of adherence. The problematic of religious violence appears to be an unavoidable hermeneutic for our present age; its hegemony—W. T. Cavanaugh calls it a "myth"—also needs to be challenged, however. Cavanaugh has begun its dismantling by demonstrating how our selective denunciation of religious violence serves to mask and perpetuate the sacralized violence of the modern, allegedly secular state. His analysis complements that of mimetic theory, in discerning the true nature of the crisis that confronts us. The presence of this undertow, with its dangerous eddies, must be recognized; but without the careful distinctions urged upon us by Cavanaugh and by Girard, it will draw us all too easily to an abandonment of genuine, pacific religious transcendence (from whichever tradition), to pessimism with regard to dialogue, and to an inevitable clash of civilizations.

As such, this undertow is, finally, incompatible with the insights of mimetic theory; it should not be allowed to divert or overwhelm the mainstream. Taken together, however, these currents comprise our apocalyptic situation, with its stark alternatives of life or death. We must either opt for openness and submission to the true sacred, wherein lies redemption, or we will acquiesce in the false sacred that entails our destruction.

NOTES

1. "Declaration on the Relation of the Church to Non-Christian Religions, *Nostra aetate*, Proclaimed by His Holiness Pope Paul VI on October 28, 1965," The Holy See, http://www.vatican.va/archive/hist_councils/ii_vatican_council/documents/vat-ii_decl_19651028_nostra-aetate_en.html.
2. Kirwan 2009, chap. 9, "Girard and the Religions," 120–31.
3. The papers, responses, and plenary discussions of the Boston colloquium were recorded in Daly (2002); for the proceedings of the Purdue conference, see Astell and Goodhart 2011. In my summary of these and other colloquia, I have drawn in part on James Williams's history of COV&R (2012).
4. Richard Dawkins, "Religion's Misguided Missiles," *The Guardian* September 15, 2001. https://www.theguardian.com/world/2001/sep/15/september11.politicsphilosophyandsociety1.
5. "Comparative Theology," Boston College, Morrissey College of Arts and Sciences, http://www.bc.edu/schools/cas/theology/comparative/resources/articles/ct.html.

WORKS CITED

Alison, James. 1998. *The Joy of Being Wrong: Original Sin through Easter Eyes*. New York: Crossroad.

Astell, Ann W., and Sandor Goodhart, eds. 2011. *Sacrifice, Scripture, and Substitution: Readings in Ancient Judaism and Christianity*. Notre Dame, IN: University of Notre Dame Press.

Barnes, Michael. 2010. "Religious Pluralism." In *Routledge Companion to the Study of Religion*, 2nd ed., ed. John R. Hinnells, 426–41. London: Routledge.

Cavanaugh, William T. 2009. *The Myth of Religious Violence*. Oxford: Oxford University Press.

Clooney, Francis X. 2011. "Comparative Theology—as Theology." In *Interreligious Hermeneutics in Pluralistic Europe: Between Texts and People*, ed. David Cheetham et al., 131–48. Amsterdam: Rodopi.

Daly, Robert, ed. *Contagion: Journal of Religion, Mimesis and Culture* 9 (Spring 2002).

Girard, René. 2014. *The One by Whom Scandal Comes*. Translated by M. B. DeBevoise, East Lansing: Michigan State University Press.

———. 2008. *Evolution and Conversion: Dialogues on the Origin of Culture with Pierpaolo Antonello and João Cezar de Castro Rocha*. London: T&T Clark Continuum.

———. 2010. *Battling to the End: Conversations with Benoît Chantre*. Translated by Mary Baker. East Lansing: Michigan State University Press.

———. 2011. *Sacrifice*. Translated by Matthew Pattillo and David Dawson. East Lansing: Michigan State University Press.

Girard, René, and Henri Tincq. 2002. "What Is Happening Today Is Mimetic Rivalry on a Global Scale." Interview. Translated by Thomas C. Hilde, *South Central Review* 19, nos. 2–3: 22–27.

Goodhart, Sandor. 1996. *Sacrificing Commentary: Reading the End of Literature*. Baltimore: Johns Hopkins University Press.

———. 2009. "Literature, Myth, and Prophecy: Encountering René Girard." In *For René Girard: Essays in Friendship and in Truth*, edited by Sandor Goodhart et al., 87–100. East Lansing: Michigan State University Press.

Hamerton-Kelly, Robert. 2007. "Introduction." In *Politics and Apocalypse*, ed. Robert Hamerton-Kelly. East Lansing: Michigan State University Press.

Kirwan, Michael. 2009. *Girard and Theology*. London: T&T Clark.

Lefebure, Leo D. 1996. "Mimesis, Violence and Socially Engaged Buddhism: Overture to a Dialogue." *Contagion* 3:121–40.

Murphy, Andrew, ed. 2011. *The Blackwell Companion to Religion and Violence*. London: Wiley-Blackwell.

Rosenzweig, Franz. 2005 [1921]. *The Star of Redemption*. Madison: University of Wisconsin Press.

Williams, James. 2012. *Girardians: The Colloquium on Violence and Religion, 1990–2010*. Münster: LIT Verlag.

Winkler, Ulrich. 2011. "What Is Comparative Theology?" In *Interreligious Hermeneutics in Pluralistic Europe: Between Texts and People*, ed. David Cheetham et al., 231–64. Amsterdam: Rodopi.

The Ambivalence of Interreligious Historiography: Foreign and Domestic Narratives

Richard Schenk

Whatever the charges of imprecision that might be raised against the concept of "world religions," there is one feature that religions claiming this title will necessarily share with one another: an explicit sense of their relation to several other religions with prima facie rights to this same claim. The self-understanding of each world religion is constituted in part by its understanding of other world religions. Precisely for Girardian theory, the perceived initial commonality that makes interrelationality and differentiation unavoidable also makes it likely from the start that world religions are not only expressions of how competitive processes internal to each religious community gradually developed into identifiable characteristics and shapes, but also that the identity of any world religion is completed and maintained by a kind of mimetic rivalry with other religions identified by it as "foreign" or "strange," even perhaps as the province of alien gods. Each religion will have developed a narrative of its distantiation and superiority vis-à-vis one or more, or often all, "foreign religions." In terms that can be elucidated with the help of Bernhard Waldenfels's *Studien zur Phänomenologie des Fremden*,[1] the constitution of the religious self or community corresponds to its constitution of the others as foreign. The argumentative goal of the present paper is to show that Girard's theory suggests that the more likely way of diminishing violence growing from such mimetic rivalry between religions is not to minimize the strangeness of the other but to identify and acknowledge the abiding strangeness within one's own religion or one's own stance toward religions.

Domestication and Estrangement in Interreligious Historiography: From Girard to Medieval Schemata

Girard's writings seem to suggest at least at times a kind of reversal of Ernst Troeltsch's thesis about the impossibility of establishing the absoluteness of Christianity on experiential grounds.[2] By Girard's account, the biblical writings of the older and especially the newer covenant would for the first time question and then in Christ's Passion and death unmask the scapegoat mechanism, thereby depriving it of its power.[3] The question of whether this assertion must qualify as a confession of faith or as an experiential fact of intellectual history need not concern us here. Nor do we want to explore yet the passages in Girard's opus that—increasingly—nuance, or even retract, this apparent claim that the Jewish-Christian Bible would merely and exclusively be able to reveal sacrificial structures as wholly negative. The leitmotif is frequently thematized: As a feature of "false religion,"

> Mythology falsifies this mechanism [of victimization] to the detriment of victims and to the advantage of persecutors of the victim. The Hebrew Bible frequently suggests the truth, evokes it, and even partially represents it, but never perfectly and completely. The Gospels, taken in their totality, *are* this representation, precisely and perfectly. . . .
>
> Before Christ and the Gospels the satanic accusation was always victorious by virtue of the violent contagion that imprisoned human beings within systems of myth and ritual.[4]

Girard's claim has a parallel, and perhaps a source, in a salvific-historical schematic that enjoyed prominence throughout much of the ancient and medieval history of Christian theology. By recalling the adventures and misadventures of that schematic, we can provide something of a map on which to follow the direction of Girard's progress in his treatment of biblical versus nonbiblical religions. For the purposes of this paper, we will limit the medieval treatment of the schematic here to its use by Augustine, Hugh of St. Victor, and Robert Kilwardby.

In his unfinished commentary on the Epistle to the Romans, Augustine (†430) had proposed a schematic of world history, portraying eternity ("in pace") as preceded by three temporal epochs of increasing perfection: *ante legem, sub lege, sub gratia*.[5] Augustine inscribes the historiological function of this distinction into a broader moral or existential status; indeed, he speaks at first not of epochs but of levels or "grades": "Prior to the Law, we pursue fleshly concupiscence; under the law, we are pulled by it; under grace, we neither pursue nor are pulled by it; *in pace*, there is no concupiscence of the flesh."[6] Augustine's characterization of these three salvific-historical grades of what "we" do or suffer already suggested that their correspondence to existential characteristics or moral states was more literal than their distribution into discrete epochs of world history. The imagination of their epochal distribution soon became secondary, but it continued to provide a basis for theological historicization.

In the early twelfth century, the famous Augustinian canon of St. Victor's in Paris, Hugh of St. Victor (†1141), would develop this schema in his *De sacramentis christianae fidei* into names and descriptions of the threefold division of history, while keeping the sense that they referred not just to discrete epochs but also to existential states characteristic of each epoch:

> in the time of the natural law, man was left entirely to himself; afterwards in the time of the written law, counsel was given to him, when he realized his ignorance; finally in the time of grace, help was furnished him when he confessed his lack. Counsel was offered in the very idea of satisfaction. Help was provided in the effect of redemption.[7]

Hugh tells us that, in one sense, the divisions refer to salvific-historical epochs, albeit porous ones:

> Wherefore it is clear that from the beginning there were Christians, if not in name, yet in fact. For there are three periods of time through which the space of the world runs. The first is the period of the natural law, the second the period of the written law, the third the period of grace. The first

> is from Adam even unto Moses, the second from Moses even unto Christ, the third from Christ even unto the end of the world.[8]

With even greater emphasis than Augustine, Hugh interprets the distinctions as moral and existential qualifications, all three sets of which are found in each of the three epochs:

> Similarly, there are three kinds of human beings, those of the natural law, those of the written law, and those of grace. Those can be called human beings of the natural law who direct their lives by natural reason alone; or rather, they are said to be of the natural law who walk according to the concupiscence in which they were born. Human beings of the written law are those who by exterior precepts are instructed unto right living. Graced human beings are those who, breathed upon by the inspiration of the Holy Ghost, are illumined to recognize the good that must be done and are inflamed as they love and strengthened to accomplish good. And that we may mark this with a clearer distinction, human beings of the natural law are openly evil, those of the written law are fictitiously good, while those of grace are truly good.... These three kinds of human beings have never been wanting at any time from the beginning of humanity.[9]

While Hugh sees the three types as roughly characteristic of the three ages named after them, and while he loosely associates the distinctions with the most common practices of religion by pagans, Jews, and Christians respectively, there is little detail about the implications for a phenomenology of religions (with the partial exception of matrimony). The existential meanings take predominance over the historical ones, in that each age knows all three sets of characteristics.[10] Within the loose unity provided by the patristic notion of the *ecclesia ab Abel*, the alterity of other religions is significantly relativized, especially with regard to the good manifested in them.[11]

A good century later, the Dominican Robert Kilwardby (†1279), a contemporary and increasingly a critic of the writings of his Dominican confrere Thomas Aquinas (†1274), will continue to interpret the threefold division taken from Augustine and Hugh as referring both to salvific-historical epochs and to the existential states found in persons of every epoch, but now these traits are used to identify and—at least initially—to praise the distinct kinds of religion that began in each epoch as being largely in continuity with the Christian religion. The standard debate had been whether to compare or contrast the chief initiation sacrament of the older and newer covenants; the rites of pre-Abrahamic religions had been considered by nearly all as of little use at best, often as idolatrous. Kilwardby breaks with this tradition to assume the divine inspiration and graceful workings of the rites of every age, which only deepened with the first covenant and its divinely offered pact.[12] While recognizing the gracious effects of many non-Christian rituals, the tendency is also strengthened here to play down the otherness of non-Christian religions vis-à-vis the Christian community. Where Augustine and Hugh had used the schema of the three temporal epochs and states to argue, not without an explicit ambivalence, for the toleration of Judaism,[13] while dismissing broadly the religions of the Gentiles, Kilwardby would develop a theology of religions far more optimistic in its evaluation not only of the first covenant, but even of pre-Abrahamic religions.[14] Their age was characteristically the *tempus simulationis*, when God feigned anger with and silence toward humanity, or likewise the *tempus dissimulationis*, when God by the same measure hid his ongoing care, providence, and grace, not revealing or instituting religious rites, but all the while inspiring human beings inwardly to live by hope in a merciful God and so to develop external rites of their own invention, rites that the God who inspired them also filled with effective grace. Kilwardby seeks to acknowledge the profound workings of grace mediated by the oblations, sacrifices, and tithings of this epoch. It was followed by the *tempus promissionis*, also called a time of expectation and waiting, with the explicit covenantal or even contractual establishment of rites that made sense and conferred grace in the God-given context of their own day, even while promising a still future context and a yet fuller grace for the future. The graceful workings of grace in all the God-given rites of the first covenant—not just in the ceremonial initiation into the rites[15]—are all the more certain for Kilwardby, as he sees them as having been promised and pledged by God's own word. Finally, this was followed by a third era, described by contrast to the earlier ones as the *tempus exhibitionis sive liberationis*, a term that arguably should have been reserved for the posttemporal state of blessed eternity, *in pace*.[16] For the third epoch remains one that requires faith in what is not yet completely manifest or "exhibited" and that imposes on many the continued existential burden of the yokes of the earlier two epochs or states as well, so that the greater sanctity often belongs to those of earlier epochs and of more ancient religions,[17] just as, conversely, genuine Christian existence requires elements of invention and waiting characteristic of earlier ages.

Kilwardby's work was remarkable on several accounts. One of the longest and most sustained works of the Middle Ages to develop a Christian theology of non-Christian religions, these systematically focused questions on the opening distinctions of Peter Lombard's *Liber Quartus Sententiarum* seem at first to constitute one of the friendliest treatments of non-Christian religions. Their ultimate failure is due not only to an unresolved contradiction, an unexplained reversal, but also because of what might be called a lack of "disciplined ambiguity," an initial loss of that moment of otherness that Kilwardby was trying to match with a moment of sameness, followed by a sense of urgency to reintroduce the kind of alterity that would necessitate a better covenant. Kilwardby had successfully avoided the narrow identity of faith (the "eadem fides") suggested by Robert Grosseteste (†1253) to span and unite the religious rites of the two biblical epochs.[18] Grosseteste's attempts to have the Jewish cult declared heretical were not founded upon its alien character but upon its unity with the Christian faith. By distinguishing between the proper context for the meaning and graciousness of first covenant rites and their prophetic reference to Christ, Kilwardby also could avoid the repressive policies toward the continued practice of Judaism that Grosseteste argued followed from the obligation to develop that one, common faith in its common, Christian trajectory. Kilwardby argued that alongside its promise of future religious and eschatological realities, the religious ritual of each epoch made sense and mediated grace in the proper context of its own day. The uncommon or "foreign" element proper to each religion, while similar in form to the others, served as a basis of its relative tolerance.

However, Kilwardby is forced to acknowledge two particular challenges to his otherwise impressive theology of religions, both stemming from what he thought the religious epochs shared in common. Having stressed the gracious character of the religious rites of each "status," both before and after Abraham, the assumption of an implicitly Christian dynamic and faith alongside and behind the thoroughgoing graciousness of all these pre-Christian rituals, while not as dominant as for Grosseteste, still overshadows in the end the non-Christian otherness of the rites described, so that Kilwardby is left with little basis for the distinct identities associated with the three epochs.

Kilwardby is particularly at pains to say why such a common and abundant grace had not been more fruitful from the start and why therefore some still better economy was required to redress the failures of preceding ages. The unmediated and therefore surprising claims about the abject status of the religionists of the pre-Christian epochs stand in unexplained contrast to the much lauded graciousness of their religious practices. Since the differences between epochs and states can hardly be explained by the minimal disparity of the religious practices and beliefs themselves, Kilwardby must exaggerate the moral differences of the average communities. Without preparation, he characterizes the general community prior to Abraham as idolatrous (a position that Peter Manducator had already borrowed from Jewish historians) and the community prior to Christ as *superbissimi, invidissimi, avarissimi, infidelissimi,* and as glorying only in external shows of worship.[19] In Girardian terms, the initial sense of similarity leads to a drastic resurgence of rivalry.

The second challenge stemming from Kilwardby's attempt to relativize the differences between religious systems is the very lack of perceptible difference between the mores of the average communities in the different epochs. Kilwardby admits that pride, jealousy, avarice, infidelity, and vainglory are not unknown qualities among those who belong to the *tempus exhibitionis sive liberationis*, but, unlike, say, a William of Auvergne, Kilwardby characterizes them as merely tangential to the third temporal epoch and its existential status.[20] Arguably Kilwardby was misled by the portrayal of the third epoch as a time of epiphany and liberty. In failing to stress the remaining distance to the eschaton "in pace," in failing to identify the presence of the "alien in the familiar," in overlooking what remains opaque and recalcitrant in Christian existence, Kilwardby compromises what had been a good beginning on the path to reducing the mimetic rivalry among the religions of his day.

The Dialectic of the Familiar and the Foreign in Girard's Interreligious Historiography: From Medieval to Girardian Schemata

In the first of his four *Studies Toward a Phenomenology of the Alien/the Foreign/the Other*, Bernhard Waldenfels recalled in 1997 both the dangers that can face those portrayed as foreign or alien by xenophobic forces and the relief that minority communities threatened with the loss of their identity can seek and find in patterns of life that appear alien to a centralizing majority. "Das Fremde"—the status of the stranger—can be both a threat and a refuge. Aware of the necessity of acknowledged alterity, *The Topography of the Alien* anticipated regional resistance to the centripetal and homogenizing forces of globalization.[21] Translated into interreligious dynamics, Waldenfels's studies remind us of the dual threat that can arise for a world religion either from the minimization or from the maximization of its religious distinctiveness.

Applied to Kilwardby's reception of the model of three salvific-historical ages, Kilwardby's minimalization of the differences in the religious intentions, the ritual dynamics, and the gifts of divine favor, despite the initial differences of the three epochs, might still have avoided the need to exaggerate the distinctions of moral achievement in the disparate ages, if he had been more willing to acknowledge what Waldenfels has called the "alien element in oneself," here the limitations to self-evidence and liberty in that third epoch. Waldenfels identifies not just moments of what is foreign in the individual self or in "intercultural" comparisons, but also in collective forms of "intracultural" strangeness, areas in our collective existence, say in our own religion, that remain opaque and recalcitrant. Waldenfels might easily have recalled here Martin Heidegger's sense of "Unheimlichkeit."[22] Admittedly, Waldenfels is concerned here above all to avoid what he sees as the exaggeration of an all too appropriative sense of the "alterity of the ego," such that every sense of alterity would be domesticated, a danger he sees in Julia Kristeva's work: "What is foreign and alien is in me, so we are all foreigners and alien. If I myself am foreign and alien, then there are no more foreigners, no more aliens."[23] Waldenfels takes up the dual task of overcoming both xenophobia and the loss of that sense of the alien that can provide protection for the stranger. His project is paralleled by those who know that the loss of identity can result from the rivalry of the part or the rivalry of the whole, for example, from the clash of civilizations or from a monolithic "Weltethos."[24] The validity of Waldenfels's concern to avoid a flight from and a flight into what remains strange to us does not invalidate the need to acknowledge as the proper limits of what remains foreign in us. Religions will be judged—not entirely, but in no small part—by their capacity for self-critique.

The implicit ambivalence toward sacrifice has become more pronounced in the late work of René Girard. Is the reason for his growing acknowledgement of some, limited good in the sacrifices of non-Christian religions perhaps the result of his perception of this strange reality in Christianity itself? Girard had long since begun to criticize the impression created by his own early work that we should already be seeking a religion completely without sacrifice, "a non-sacrificial space,"[25] and especially "A Non-Sacrificial Reading of the Gospel Text," including "The Non-Sacrificial Death of Christ" and a nonsacrificial view of Christian discipleship and existence.[26] As early as 1993, Girard would admit in conversation—perhaps too boldly—that he had "scapegoated [the Epistle to the] Hebrews and . . . scapegoated the word *sacrifice*," reserving the word "just for the primitive" and indeed "really trying to get rid of it."[27] Now calling his earlier dismissal of the portrayal in Hebrews of Christ's death as sacrifice "completely wrong" and "just plain ridiculous,"[28] Girard made the distance to his earlier statements clearer than the—legitimate—continuity of his earlier work with his more developed thought. To be fairer to Girard than he was to himself, his earlier work already had implied the need for an ongoing readiness to share the lot of victimage. The scapegoating mechanisms would remain—a consequence of the mystery called original sin—and the much needed attempts to unmask them would not be taken kindly (a consideration that later Girard will thematize under the heading of the "unavoidability of scandal").[29] Girard came to describe the call to imitate many of the saints' imitations of Christ's imitation of the Father's generosity as the necessary path of redeemed mimesis, but one that will not be possible without bearing the animosity of those inside or outside the church who have yet to recognize in themselves the "contagion of rivalry." What is new in Girard's later works is his willingness to name this cost of discipleship "sacrifice." The desire to avoid the "ambivalence" by divorcing completely the Passion of Christ from all sacrificial imagery points to a still legitimate "concern," but, as he later said, it should not be regarded as "absolute."[30] The flight into clear-cut differentiation, the declaration of a simple equivocation between archaic sacrifice and the death of Christ, leading to the complete avoidance of the use of sacrificial imagery to understand Christ's Passion, would come at too high a price:

> The accomplishment of his mission therefore doomed Christ to a death that he scarcely desired, but one that he could not avoid without submitting to the law of the world, the law of scapegoats. . . . It was not in order to

> play the game of his enemies that he gave himself up to be sacrificed, but in order to put an end to sacrifice.[31]

Of greater theological importance, if also of greater subtlety, than the continuity of Girard's earlier and later writings regarding the continued necessity of sacrifice is, however, the continuity of the later sense of sacrifice with the earlier one regarding the abiding negativity of sacrifice. Despite the increasingly explicit openness to a positive sense of sacrifice and its necessity, Girard never loses sight of the need to maintain a sensitivity for the destructive, antidivine dimensions of basic sacrificial mechanisms. He sometimes will speak of two types of sacrifice and

> the difference between the archaic sacrifice, which turns against a third victim the violence of those who are fighting, and the Christian sacrifice which is the renunciation of all egoistic claiming, even to life if needed, in order not to kill. This is the crucial point. . . . No greater difference can be found: on the one hand, sacrifice as murder; on the other hand, sacrifice as the readiness to die in order not to participate in sacrifice as murder.[32]

Even where it grants increasingly a more positive point to the language of Christ's "sacrifice," Girard's later work is keen to keep alive our sense of the negativity implied by even the metaphorical recollection of sacrifice, underscoring the ambivalent attitude toward sacrifice that Girard shares with much of the Western tradition. He criticizes as "sterile formalism" and "a systematic concealment of violence" the attempt to abstract from sacrifice a pattern of gift and countergift that would focus exclusively on the positive aspects of re-ligio, the binding-back of gifts received. Even for the late work of Girard, sacrifice never becomes an unqualified good.[33] Is it not likely Girard's growing acknowledgement of the strange presence in Christianity of a sacrifice both necessary and negative that opens Girardian theory to a greater familiarity with and recognition of non-Christian religions, allowing them a similar access, at times even a competitive access, to this familiarly alien reality in our lives?

NOTES

1. See especially Bernhard Waldenfels, *Studien zur Phänomenologie des Fremden*, vol. 1, *Topographie des Fremden* (Frankfurt am Main: Suhrkamp, 1997).

2. See Ernst Troeltsch, *Die Absolutheit des Christentums und die Religionsgeschichte: Vortrag, gehalten auf der versammlung der Freunde der Schrislichen welt zu Mühlaker am 3. Oktober 1901, erweitert und mit einem Vorwort versehen* (Tübingen: Mohr, 1902; 2nd ed., 1911; 3rd ed., 1929); now also as *Die Absolutheit des Christentums und die Religionsgeschichte* (Munich, 1969; 2nd ed., Gütersloh, 1985); in English translation as *The Absoluteness of Christianity and the History of Religions*, trans. David Reid (Richmond, VA: John Knox, 1971).

3. See René Girard, *I See Satan Fall Like Lightning*, trans. James G. Williams (Maryknoll, NY: Orbis, 2001), especially 106, 107, and 139.

4. Ibid., 137, 138.

5. See Paula Fredriksen Landes, ed., *Augustine on Romans: Propositions from the Epistle to the Romans; Unfinished Commentary on the Epistle to the Romans* (Chico, CA: Scholars Press 1982); Fredriksen, "*Excaecati Occulta Justitia Dei*: Augustine on Jews and Judaism," *Journal of Early Christian Studies* 3, no. 3 (1995): 299–334.

6. See Landes, *Augustine on Romans*, 13.

7. For the Latin text see Hugonis de Sancto Victore, *De sacramentis Christiane fidei*, ed. Rainer Berndt (Münster: Aschendorff, 2008), libri prioris pars octava (196).

8. *De sacramentis Christiane fidei*, ed. Berndt 203.

9. *De sacramentis Christiane fidei*, ed. Berndt 203.

10. *De sacramentis Christiane fidei*, ed. Berndt 203–4.

11. See Yves Congar, "*Ecclesia ab Abel*," in *Abhandlungen über Theologie und Kirche: Festschrift für Karl Adam*, ed. Marcel Reding (Düsseldorf: Patmos, 1952), 139–67.

12. See R. Schenk, "Covenant Initiation: Thomas Aquinas and Robert Kilwardby on the Sacrament of Circumcision," in *Ordo sapientiae et amoris: Hommage au Professeur J.-P. Torrell*, ed. Carlos-Josaphat Pinto de Oliveira (Fribourg: Éditions Universitaires, 1993), 555–93.

13. See Jeremy Cohen, *Living Letters of the Law: Ideas of the Jew in Medieval Christianity* (Berkeley: University of California Press, 1999) for the history of this Augustinian ambivalence as an enduring source of relative Christian tolerance in contrast to more univocal expressions of intolerance.

14. See R. Schenk, "'Divina simulatio irae et dissimulatio pietatis': Divine Providence and Natural Religion in Robert Kilwardby's Quaestiones in librum IV Sententiarum," in *Mensch und Natur im Mittelalter*, ed. A. Zimmermann (Berlin: De Gruyter, 1991), 431–55; Schenk, "Christ, Christianity, and Non-Christian Religions: Their Relationship in the Thought of Robert Kilwardby," in *Christ among the Medieval Dominicans: Representations of Christ in the Texts and Images of the Order of Preachers*, ed. K. Emery Jr. and J. Wawrykow (Notre Dame, IN: University of Notre Dame Press, 1988), 344–63.

15. See Schenk, "Covenant Initiation."

16. Robert Kilwardby, *Quaestiones in librum quartum Sententiarum*, ed. Richard Schenk (Munich: Bayerische Akademie der Wissenschaften, 1993).

17. Ibid., Q4, ad 4: "Quamvis autem sit distincta sic fides secundum status, tamen creditur semper in omni tempore viros spirituales fuisse, qui notitiam habuerint magnam et lucidam humanae liberationis et fidem, spem et caritatem eminenter valde, in quibus forte stetit ecclesia et profecit. Unde non est inconveniens aliquos electorum primi temporis plus abundasse in fide, spe et caritate quam multos secundi temporis, et aliquos electorum secundi temporis plus quam multos tertii temporis."

18. See R. Schenk, "Views of the Two Covenants in Medieval Theology," *Nova et Vetera* 4 (2006): 891–916.

19. Kilwardby, *Quaestiones*, Q 4.

20. In *De fide et legibus*, William of Auvergne (†1249) had appropriated Maimonides' moral critiques of sacrifice for his contemporary sermons on Catholic life.

21. Waldenfels, *Studien zur Phänomenologie des Fremden*, 161–64.

22. See Martin Heidegger, *Sein und Zeit*, 19th ed. (Tübingen: Niemeyer 2006), §40 and §57, 189–90 and 277.

23. Bernhard Waldenfels, *Der Stachel des Fremden* (Frankfurt: Suhrkamp 1990), 209.

24. Robert Spaemann, "Weltethos als 'Projekt' [1996], in Robert Spaemann, *Grenzen: Zur ethischen Dimension des Handelns* (Stuttgart: Klett-Cotta, 2002), 525–38, esp. 525–31; and R. Schenk, "Zwischen 'Projekt Weltethos' und 'The Clash of Civilizations': Religioese Identitaet im Zeitalter der Globalisierung," in *Nationale und kulturelle Identität im Zeitalter der Globalisierung*, ed. A. Rauscher (Berlin: Duncker & Humblot, 2006), 111–24.

25. René Girard, *Evolution and Conversion: Dialogues on the Origins of Culture with Pierpaolo Antonello and João Cezar de Castro Rocha* (London: Continuum, 2008), e.g. 217: "To put it bluntly, we cannot have a perfectly non-sacrificial space. In writing *Violence and the Sacred* and *Things Hidden* I was trying to find that non-sacrificial space from which to understand and explain everything without personal involvement. Now I think that this attempt cannot be successful." Girard explains his older and newer positions, notably his reluctant but growing willingness to accept R. Schwager's characterization of Christ as a sacrifice and a scapegoat, in R. Girard, René Girard. "Mimetic Theory and Theology," in *The One by Whom Scandal Comes* (East Lansing: Michigan State University Press, 2014), 33–44.

26. Formulations from the late 1970s, in René Girard, *Things Hidden since the Foundation of the World*, research undertaken in collaboration with with J.-M. Oughourlian and G. Lefort, trans. Stephen Bann and Michael Metteer (Stanford, CA: Stanford University Press, 1987), 180–223 (esp. 205–15), 224–62; Girard now refers to his earlier work as tending toward "a non-sacrificial Christianity": Girard, "Mimetic Theory and Theology," 42.

27. Rebecca Adams and René Girard, "Violence, Difference, Sacrifice: A Conversation with René Girard," *Religion & Literature* 25, no. 2 (1993): 29.

28. Ibid., 28.

29. Girard, *I See Satan Fall Like Lightning*, 7–18. For a Girardian reading of the theme of scandal, see Jeremiah Alberg, *A Reinterpretation of Rousseau: A Religious System* (New York: Palgrave Macmillan, 2007).

30. Girard, "Mimetic Theory and Theology," 42–43.

31. Ibid., 41.

32. Girard, *Evolution and Conversion*, 215, with reference to the story of Solomon's judgment and the dissimilar "sacrifices" of the two claimants; see Girard, "Mimetic Theory and Theology," especially 43–44, with reference to the at best "paradoxical unity of religion," mirrored in the need to use the one word "sacrifice"—but not without irony—for sacral violence and the death of Christ, as the latter aims at overcoming sacrifice.

33. Girard, "Mimetische Theorie und Theologie," 25.

Sacrifice as a Contested Concept between R. Schwager and R. Girard and Its Significance for Interreligious Dialogue

Nikolaus Wandinger

The purpose of this article is to sketch the development of the concept of sacrifice in René Girard's thinking, as it developed especially in discussion with Innsbruck systematic theologian and founder of the School of Dramatic Theology there, Raymund Schwager, to briefly reflect on this development in the light of Bernard Lonergan's theological method (this will show that we are dealing with "religious conversion" understood in a certain sense), and to make some suggestions as to how this can ground interreligious dialogue and provide it with additional significance.

Discussing the Concept of "Sacrifice"

Girard's Early Concept of "Sacrifice"

In 1978 René Girard confronted his previously developed theory of sacrifice[1] with the Passion of Jesus of Nazareth, as recorded in the New Testament's Gospels, and with its interpretation as a sacrifice in the letter to the Hebrews.[2] There Girard comes to the conclusion that Christ's Passion should not be called a "sacrifice" because the concept implies a violent deity that demands killing and—in the case of a person voluntarily sacrificing him/herself—a masochistic tendency in the victim. Since he excludes both preconditions with respect to Jesus's divine Father and Jesus himself, Girard rejects calling the Passion a "sacrifice," even at the cost of contradicting the letter to the Hebrews. He is convinced that interpreting Jesus's death as a sacrifice is a consequence of Christianity misunderstanding itself.

Girard had developed his concept of sacrifice from his discovery of the scapegoat mechanism. According to Girard, the institution of sacrifice developed from mimetically induced violence contagiously spreading throughout a human group or society thereby endangering the very existence of that society by throwing it into a war of all against all. In a mimetically structured human society only the scapegoat mechanism can prevent self-destruction because it is itself mimetically structured, yet focuses the dissipating violence on a single victim. If, during the fight of all against all, a particularly successful combatant is observed to fight a person who might be distinguished by certain peculiarities that make him/her somehow different from the others and possibly weaker,[3] mimetic contagion will make the other combatants emulate this strong fighter, and they will convene on the selected victim and collectively kill him/her. The result of this killing will be a sudden and surprising onset of peace. The target of the common aggression has been killed; the aggression subsides. This, however, is inexplicable unless the killed person had some superhuman power—the power to destabilize the whole society driving it to the brink of destruction, and the power to bring sudden peace back again. As a consequence the victim of the discharge of violence is divinized and revered as a god. Girard succinctly puts it later: "The peoples of the world do not invent their gods. They deify their victims."[4] Religious cults spring from the primordial experience of all-out violence and its inexplicable pacification in the killing of the god/dess. Whenever symptoms of mimetic contagion recur, the original spontaneous killing is ritually enacted as sacrifice. The strict rules and taboos that rituals must follow stem from the exact imitation of the original murder. This accounts for the variability and plurality of sacrificial rites, and their common properties of rigid rules and violent killings. Sacrifices do, however, serve a real purpose; they "contain"—in the double sense of the word—the violence of that particular society: they restrain and limit it, so that it cannot destroy the whole society but only one member of it; they also encompass it and channel it toward that member.

Girard was convinced that Jewish and Christian scripture, in a long and complicated process, uncovered the truth of the victim, namely that societies stabilize themselves by projecting their—mimetically induced—violence and aggression on a common enemy, whom they deem guilty of all their ills, and they kill him/her in deference to a "divine" will. The biblical writings thus reveal that the persecuted victim is not a justly condemned culprit but an innocent scapegoat. Moreover, they more and more come to the conclusion that God sides with that victim, is on the side of the innocent scapegoat and wants to protect him/her. While many biblical passages see this divine protection also as an act of violence, the high points of the biblical development depict God as nonviolent, and his taking sides with the victim then consists in affirming the victim's innocence and finally in the restoration of the victim's life. This occurs in utmost clarity in the Hebrew Bible with the character of the Suffering Servant (Isaiah 42:1–7, 49:1–9, 50:4–9, 52:13–53:12) and in the Christian New Testament with Jesus of Nazareth.

Girard argues that the death of Jesus of Nazareth can be construed according to the scapegoat mechanism: humans gang up and unite against an innocent victim, accuse him of grave crimes, and finally bring him to death. According to the Gospel of John, the High Priest Caiaphas even states the logic of the scapegoat mechanism when he says that it is better that one man die for the people (cf. John 11:49–50, 18:14).[5] Contrary to mythic texts, however, the New Testament unambiguously depicts Jesus as innocent and in accordance with the divine will, and his persecutors on the other hand as perpetrators of violence and trespassers of God's will. It reveals that Jesus in fact is a scapegoat and thus it destroys the scapegoat mechanism because "the scapegoat cannot appear as scapegoat, . . . without losing all credibility. . . . [The concept of the scapegoat is] a principle of illusion whose efficacy requires complete ignorance of it. To have a scapegoat is not to know that one has one. As soon as the scapegoat is revealed and named as such, it loses its power."[6]

Thus the gospel, according to Girard, reveals that sacrifice is a human—not a divine—institution that is against God's will because it projects guilt and violence on an innocent victim. It furthermore reveals that there is a way to stabilize human society without resorting to sacrifice, namely by emulating the Christ and having one's mimetic desire directed by Christ. Thus Girard sees a clear divide between myths and the Bible: while the former hide the scapegoat mechanism, see God on the side of the persecutors, and view the victim as guilty, the latter sees God on the side of the victim, who is recognized as innocent, and thus unveils the scapegoat mechanism and renders it inefficacious. In short: the myths endorse sacrifice, the Bible criticizes it.

It is clear that in this context, the fact that one biblical book, the letter to the Hebrews, and in its wake a strong Christian tradition interpret Jesus's death as a sacrificial death did not bode well with Girard. He therefore interpreted it as already belonging to "sacrificial Christianity," meaning a Christianity that misunderstood its own founding event and therefore relapsed into the scapegoat mechanism:

> The Christian sons have repeated, even aggravated the errors of their Judaic fathers. The Christians have condemned the Jews, but they themselves are condemned by Paul's statement in the Epistle to the Romans: "In passing judgment upon him you condemn yourself, because you, the judge, are doing the very same things" (Romans 2,1). In a remarkable paradox, but one that accords well with the sacrificial course of mankind, the sacrificial reading (that is, the logic of the violent Logos) refashions the mechanism that has been revealed and thus of necessity annihilated—if the revelation were genuinely accepted—into a kind of sacrificial cultural foundation. This is the foundation that both "Christianity" and the modern world have rested upon, right up to our own time. . . . I believe it is possible to demonstrate that historical Christianity took on a persecutory character as a result of the sacrificial reading of the Passion and the Redemption. . . . The very fact that the deity is reinfused with violence has consequences for the entire system, since it partially absolves mankind from a responsibility that ought to be equal and identical for all. Reducing the responsibility enables one to particularize the Christian event, to diminish its universality, and to search for the guilty men who would absolve humankind of guilt—the role the Jews fulfill. At the same time, violence continues to have repercussions, as we have seen, in the apocalyptic destruction that traditional readings still project upon the deity. What turns Christianity in on itself, so that it presents a hostile face to all that is not Christian, is inextricably bound up with the sacrificial reading. That reading cannot possibly be *innocent*. It is not difficult to demonstrate the close connections between resacralization and the historical development of Christianity—which is structurally parallel to that of all cultures being characterized, like them, by the gradual

> exhaustion of sacrificial resources, amid the increasing disintegration of all cultural formations.[7]

Girard considered the Epistle to the Hebrews as the beginning of this development because it "interprets Christ's death on the basis of the sacrifices under the Old Law."[8] While Hebrews acknowledges a difference between the old sacrifices and Christ's, "this difference is still defined within the context of the sacrificial, and consequently the real essence of the sacrificial is never examined."[9] Moreover by its emphasis on the positive value and the necessity of suffering, Christianity developed a kind of masochistic tendency toward self-sacrifice that, according to Girard, has nothing to do with Christ's attitude in his passion because his intention was not self-destruction at all.

Girard famously illustrates this by referring to the story of King Solomon's Judgment.[10] Two "harlots" demand a judgment from King Solomon. Each of them makes the same claim: "The other one has accidentally killed her own child and then has exchanged his corpse with my living child." What is clear is that one child has been killed and one is alive, and that each woman claims that the living baby is hers and the dead one her opponent's. But how is the king to decide that question? He makes a gruesome suggestion: By cutting the living baby apart, each woman could have her share of the child and a compromise would be found. Of course, this procedure would mean that this child is killed, too. That prospect, however, elicits two different reactions from the two women. One accepts Solomon's plan; it would satisfy her. The other one begs that she would be willing to give up the living child and hand it over to the other woman, if only the child's life were spared that way. Subsequently the king declares this woman the true mother of the child and returns him to her.

Girard analyzes this episode as a mimetic conflict between the two mothers, both resembling each other exactly with their initial claim. The king's suggestion follows this logic, which is also the logic of sacrifice: The conflict between the two women could be ended by sacrificing the child.[11] Peace could be restored by deferring the violence onto the weakest member of the community. The woman who approves of this suggestion shows that she adheres to that logic, the logic of sacrifice. It is all right with her that her interest is fulfilled at the expense of another person's life. The woman who opposes the king's plan and instead is willing to give up her claim to the child follows a different logic, which is, of course, what the king had had in mind.

Girard explains that the king's suggestion brings out which of the two women feels real motherly love for the child; even more: the mother, by agreeing to give the child away, risks her own life, because "she can have no advance knowledge of how things will turn out. She cannot be sure that her sudden decision to renounce the child will not be interpreted *unfavourably to her*, as if she were incapable of keeping up her daring lie any longer in the presence of his majesty. She has no means of anticipating the monarch's 'divine wisdom.' So she risks her own life."[12] Girard acknowledges that this behavior of the woman is characterized as a "sacrifice" by many interpreters, because she is giving up her right as a mother (with everything this entailed in society in those days) and she is even putting her life at risk. Girard, however, disagrees with this terminology:

> I believe that this vocabulary misses the essential point and introduces confusion where there is most need of clear distinctions. Not only does it play down the difference between the ways in which the two women behave, but—for the second woman—it also transfers to the foreground what is of secondary importance: that is, the act of renunciation and the personal risk to which it exposes the real mother. The sacrificial definition relegates to the secondary level what is most important for the real mother—that her child should live. The sacrificial definition always emphasizes renunciation, death, and split subjectivity; that is to say, it emphasises the values that belong to the bad mother. Sacrificial language can only betray the values of the second woman, which are not directed toward suffering and death, . . . and instead directed positively toward her neighbour and toward life. Sacrificial discourse cannot do justice to the crucial importance of life and the living in the very language of the text—to the fact that the child over whom the two women are quarrelling is always described as *the living child*. The good mother has absolutely no inclination to "sacrifice herself" in the abstract. She wishes to go on living to take care of her child. But she is ready to renounce her child for ever, even to renounce her own life if necessary, *in order to save his life*. This is her only motive and there is nothing "sacrificial" about it.[13]

Girard then moves on to compare the motivation and action of the real mother to that of Christ in his Passion:

> Christ's conduct parallels at every point that of the good harlot. She offers the most perfect *figura Christi* that can be imagined. Christ agrees to die so that mankind will live. We must beware of calling his action sacrificial, even if we then have no words or categories to convey its meaning. The very lack of appropriate language suggests that we are dealing with a type of conduct for which there is no precedent in the realm of mythology or philosophy, or indeed in the pragmatic sphere.[14]

So at this stage of his development, Girard makes a sharp distinction between sacrificial behavior, which he attributes to the egotistical woman, and a willingness to give up something freely out of love, as the real mother does, and he sees the two types of behavior as radically opposed to each other. He attributes the second type of behavior also to Christ in his Passion, which excludes the possibility of calling it a "sacrifice." There are two important features that distinguish the two kinds of behavior from one another. First, the direction of the violence: the mother of the dead child wants to direct violence away from herself to the living child, while the mother of the living child wants to avoid violence—yet, if this is impossible, she would rather direct this violence toward herself than to anybody else. Second, the motivation involved: the first woman wants to be equals with her opponent; her motivation is mimetically induced and is a relationship of mimetic doubles; the true mother's motivation is love and respect for life, which means that her motivation is neither any masochistic nor self-destructive tendency,[15] nor any subordination under an abstract command of duty; it is love for the child and his life—nothing else. Girard sees the same features at work in Christ's motivation to accept his death nonviolently, and for him that excludes the possibility of calling this a "sacrifice"

Schwager's Objection

Raymund Schwager objected to this standpoint very early on and for various reasons, the most obvious being that he, as a Roman Catholic professor of dogmatic theology, did not want to contradict a canonical biblical book, namely the Epistle to the Hebrews, and a strong church tradition that characterized Christ's death as a sacrifice. However, this most obvious reason might not be the most important one, as the correspondence between Schwager and Girard and M. Moosbrugger's doctoral thesis on the topic suggest.[16]

Moosbrugger shows convincingly that Schwager had an intuition for mimetic mechanisms, and what he calls "collectivist" or "military" sacrifice,[17] some years before Girard had even published *La violence et le sacré* in 1972. Schwager rejected "military" or "collective" sacrifice for Christianity, even criticizing the founder of his own order, Ignatius of Loyola, for advocating it.[18] Instead, Moosbrugger explains, Schwager insisted that the greater fruit for the ecclesial community never stood in contradiction to the greater fruit for the single person. Thus it seems that Schwager thinks in the same vein as Girard, rejecting "sacrifice" as a Christian form of life. Yet Moosbrugger also shows that from the beginning an opposite current can be seen. The focal point of Schwager's critique of Ignatius is not that his idea involves sacrifice as such; it is a perceived lack in giving humility its appropriate role in Christian life. Ignatius did see humility as important for individual believers but did not apply it to the community, neither his newly founded order nor the church as a whole. Schwager argues against this by invoking the "foolishness of the cross" and the "law of the grain of wheat."[19] Both have to be applied to the community as well. What is Schwager's reason for that? Moosbrugger explains: Where hopeful trust in such a law, whose logic resists all human planning and oversight, is lacking, the sacrificing of individuals for society at large is accepted as inevitable. Where there is no hope against all hope, hope in salvation history's law of the wheat grain, a different logic becomes effective: the logic of the military sacrifice, which Christianity should reject.

So far, we have encountered great parallels between Girard and Schwager (at a time when they hadn't heard of each other, Girard had not yet published his theory of sacrifice, and Schwager did not know Girard's work on the modern novel): both reject the kind of sacrifice that saves society at the expense of an individual; both do so arguing from the gospel; both see collective (mimetic) mechanisms at play; both argue that Christ's Passion did not follow that sacrificial logic; and both agree that the sacrificial logic has exerted strong influence in historic Christianity, even in great saints such as Ignatius of Loyola.

Still, Moosbrugger emphasizes that there are differences between Schwager and Girard, which already appear in Schwager's pointing to the two biblical passages mentioned, which have also been construed in a sacrificial manner. Furthermore, Schwager does not recoil from using the term "sacrifice" for Christ's behavior, although giving his own criteria for distinguishing Christian sacrifice from military sacrifice: "In the military, if circumstances demand, individuals or even units may be 'sacrificed' for the benefit of the whole army. In the church such a 'sacrificing' would mean that power rather than spiritual fruits were sought. In the church, sacrifice only makes sense when it is accepted in complete freedom and thus also seeks the 'greater fruit' for the individual person."[20] Moosbrugger rightly points out that at this stage in his development Schwager does not yet even consider the question of whether Christ's Passion should be called a sacrifice. He simply accepts this usage as a given; however, he senses its proneness to misunderstanding and tries to clarify it. Thus he takes a different approach than Girard: while the latter avoids the term in order to avoid a misunderstanding and to emphasize the huge difference between the two attitudes, Schwager wants to qualify the term, thereby not completely ruling out a misunderstanding. In *Jesus-Nachfolge*, which Schwager also wrote before knowing Girard, Schwager uses the term "Hingabe" and calls it "Jesus' new sacrifice."[21] So again, he clearly intends a qualification, not an abolition of the term. At this stage Schwager could probably not have answered the question of why he wouldn't let go of the term. This is corroborated by the fact that in the first book he wrote after reading *Violence and the Sacred* he avoided the term himself,[22] approaching the use Girard advocates although not completely dropping the word. Schwager discusses *Violence and the Sacred* and clearly agrees with its analysis of sacrificial Christianity:[23] "Two-thousand years ago general consciousness was not yet mature enough to comprehend the truth of the New Testament in all its consequences. The new wine was partly filled into old wineskins, and Christ's deed was ever again in danger of being misunderstood according to the sacrificial mechanism. The church herself came to a considerable degree under the spell of the idol of violence."[24] But again, even though Schwager sees the grave danger of misinterpretation even in a reformed concept of sacrifice, he does not renounce its usage, as a note at the very place makes clear: "Christ's action indeed can also be understood as a sacrifice, if this concept is defined completely anew—not anymore as a discharge onto another but as self-giving. However, it remains ambiguous to call this self-giving a sacrifice because this brings the whole problem of masochism into play as well."[25] Again Schwager sees all the problems Girard sees (cf. above) but he does not completely abandon the terminology.

From the correspondence of the two we learn that this was by no means accidental.[26] While Schwager's early letters to Girard are full of praise for his work in general, Schwager objects to Girard's abolition of the concept of sacrifice very soon. In a letter from March 29, 1978, Schwager writes to Girard after reading the largest part of *Des choses cachées*:

> I am absolutely in agreement with your anti-sacrificial interpretation of the death of Jesus. I can only underline what you say of the nonviolence of the Father, and of human responsibility. I sensed all this before discovering your theory, and your thinking helped me to *understand*. . . . One last point then I'll finish: your interpretation of the Epistle to the Hebrews. There is certainly a sacrificial *vocabulary* in this epistle; but I think that we can demonstrate that it is only the *vocabulary* that remains sacrificial, and that the *content* is quite other than this. I am supported by the following facts: (1) the epistle underlines at great length the difference between *the* sacrifices and the death of Jesus. (2) the same epistle shows a *continuity* between the Old and the New Testament, but this continuity does not appear under the *name* of sacrifice, but under the name of *faith* (11:1–12:4). And the epistle says clearly that the *believer* is one who withstands persecution. Jesus is the one who "persevered against such opposition from sinners" (12:3). His "*sacrifice*" was that he had learnt obedience, and this obedience was his *faithfulness* to the message of nonviolence at the time of his greatest persecution. Your interpretation certainly remains possible when we look at the Epistle to the Hebrews in isolation. But I assume that each text of the NT should be interpreted in the *context* of all the other New Testament writings. And I think that the Epistle to the Hebrews is—despite the sacrificial vocabulary—sufficiently clear to allow an anti-sacrificial interpretation. . . . Your interpretation of the Epistle to the Hebrews will create some problems [in that] it will serve as an argument for those who defend a sacrificial interpretation. *They will use your own argument against you.* I think, however, that this difficulty can be avoided. In any event, I will defend your anti-sacrificial interpretation against any arguments to the contrary that

can be drawn out of the epistle. The sacrificial vocabulary certainly affords one an opportunity to pursue a sacrificial interpretation—but the problem is the same with the apocalyptic texts. The apocalyptic vocabulary can be interpreted in the sense of divine anger. But, as you have well shown, the [nonviolent] *content* is nevertheless clear. . . . Thank you once again, for all that you have given me. I reiterate that I am completely in agreement with your anti-sacrificial interpretation. Consequently I'm very interested in what you have to say about my comments.[27]

Girard replies to that on April 17, 1978:

For the moment, I think what's essential is to explain and unpack all that which is concealed in the notion of sacrifice, while allowing for the evolution of this term in the direction that you indicate. It may be that at this stage of my work I'm being too adamant about the term itself, but I also maintain that the term isn't important, provided one can see the gulf between the perspective of the gospels and the perspective of the persecutors; a rift that, paradoxically, doesn't preclude a continuity—not just between the Old and the New Testament, but across all the religions on the planet—a strictly mediated continuity, in respect of humanity [*une continuite, sous le rapport de l'homme, qui est proprement mediatrice*], yet without any implication of complicity with the religions of violence. . . . [O]ne has to assume, I think, that what is great and good in the anti-sacrificial tenor of modern thought, [is] that which goes in the direction of the most profound kind of biblical inspiration. [28]

Again, Schwager reacts to this on April 22, 1978:

The only point that continues to worry me is your judgment on the Epistle to the Hebrews. Frankly, here I see a trace of sacrificial thinking. To *unify* the NT, *you throw out a text*. The Epistle to the Hebrews . . . your scapegoat?!? One could say that it is a minor point, but I attach a great importance to it, with respect to the reception of your thought in the theological world and in the church. I can already see theologians totally accepting your interpretation of the Epistle to the Hebrews, saying [*mais eux, ils diront*] that this is the true interpretation of the cross. From this

> position, they will go and collect all the other words that have sacrificial connotations in the other writings of the NT. They will construct an antagonistic position, which will pull you against your will into a position of rivalry, and behold, once again, the famous doubles. I think that we can and should avoid this difficulty. My interpretation of the epistle remains entirely in line with your thinking (pp. 205–9 of my book) and I could add further arguments. . . . (The main difficulties will come from those who—in the world of politics—will defend counterviolence as a requirement of good sense.)[29]

We do not have the space here to adequately analyze these rich passages. It should suffice to just draw together Schwager's arguments. He invokes a principle of biblical interpretation (that he has also used in arguments with historical exegesis), namely that one biblical book should not be interpreted in isolation; he gives a tactical reason: opponents who want to adhere to a sacrificial interpretation of the cross will use Girard's reading of Hebrews as support for their understanding of the cross and they will use Girard's criticism of Hebrews as an argument against his acceptability to orthodox Christian discourse. Then we have two arguments from mimetic theory itself, both questioning whether Girard is applying his own theory stringently enough. First, it might be with Hebrews, as it is with apocalyptic texts: both seem to talk of divine violence but in fact they do not. Second, for the sake of biblical unity Girard might be scapegoating a single biblical text. And there is what I would consider the main focus of Schwager's attention, an argument from content: Schwager claims that Hebrews uses sacrificial vocabulary but not sacrificial thinking. I consider this the main thrust of Schwager's concern because it is the one argument that recurs in his later book and main work, *Jesus in the Drama of Salvation*.[30]

But before we attend to this, what are the most important elements in Girard's response? On the one hand there is again his emphasis that the gospel perspective and the persecutor perspective are absolutely different ("gulf"), but on the other hand there is the admission that his stance might be too rigid and is due to a certain stage of his thinking; and there is the analysis that despite the gulf there is also a continuity between all religions of the planet. We will see that Girard will basically not give up this standpoint. He also says that the terminology is less important than the meaning. It is this remark that allows him later to accede to Schwager's terminology without really giving up his earlier insights, but still shifting his emphasis and thereby adding some new insights.

In *Jesus in the Drama of Salvation* Schwager reminds the reader that the Old Testament as a whole is very ambiguous with respect to sacrifice. Although the rules and regulations for sacrifice take up huge portions of Leviticus, critique of sacrifice also plays a role, especially in the prophets and the psalms. Schwager explicitly refers to Psalm 40:7–9, which Hebrews also quotes, saying that God does not demand any sacrifice but obedience to his will.[31] Schwager now argues that it is exactly the critique that is positively taken up by Hebrews:

> The letter to the Hebrews resolves the contradictory evidence of the Old Testament by relating the criticism of sacrifice directly to Christ, who with these words abolished the existing order and set up over against it obedience. The *continuity of content* between the Old and New Testament runs *not through the cultic line, but through the line of criticism of the cult*, which emphasizes obedience. The letter to the Hebrews is able, through a *massive hermeneutical reinterpretation*, to take up on the one hand the whole metaphorical and symbolic meaning of the cult, but on the other hand to express something which is *completely new in content*. Through the confrontation of the cultic tradition with the tradition critical of sacrifice, it succeeds in creating, out of a problematic at the heart of the Old Testament, a complex symbol for the divine action and the divine will: God by the law commanded something which he himself did not specifically want, but which—in awakening consciousness of sin—was temporarily needed for humankind. This command to offer sacrifices was promulgated by the law because of its pedagogic and linguistic function and not because of its atoning effect. The new teaching is tied in with the cult only as an illustration, whereas the criticism of sacrifice is spelled out as Christ's own words (Heb. 10:8ff.). What was a tradition competing with the cult in the Old Testament becomes in the letter to the Hebrews an authoritative pronouncement about this whole past practice of sacrifice.[32]

It is hard to say at the moment which of Schwager's arguments finally convinced Girard. For now it suffices to see the result of Girard's development.

Girard's Developed Concept of "Sacrifice"

In an interview with Rebecca Adams, which was published in 1993,[33] Girard revises his stance on sacrifice. Adams suggests to Girard, as Schwager had in his letter, that Girard might have been scapegoating the letter to the Hebrews, and Girard agrees with this.[34] This interview already contains many of the thoughts Girard then brings into a Festschrift for Schwager in 1995.[35] Because we are dealing here with the continuing discussion between Schwager and Girard, I am attending to this article now.

In his contribution to the Festschrift for Schwager's sixtieth birthday, Girard lays out his change as follows. He reiterates that he rejected the concept "sacrifice" for the Passion because it blurs and undoes the difference between the conduct of the two harlots in 1 Kings.[36] He then explains that he never wanted to contradict orthodox Christian doctrine (including the Epistle to the Hebrews) but tried to avoid the ambiguities that often characterize the use of the concept by Christians and non-Christians alike.[37] This caution is still legitimate and necessary, "but it must not be regarded as overriding or in any sense absolute."[38] Girard goes on to argue that using the same term for the two different types of conduct is legitimate and even important because it "suggests something essential, namely, the paradoxical unity of religion in all its forms throughout human history."[39] This in no way denies the fundamental difference, he argues, but adequately expresses that something common underlies and transcends that difference.

> It is commonly said that the good prostitute *sacrificed* rivalry for the sake of her child, whereas the bad prostitute agreed to *sacrifice* the child for the sake of the rivalry. What the biblical account says is that one can renounce sacrifice in one sense—sacrifice of another, violence against another—only by assuming the risk of sacrifice in another sense—the sacrifice of Christ, who died for all who were dear to him. Use of the same word in each case dispels the illusion of a neutral ground where violence is nowhere to be seen.[40]

Girard even goes as far as to reason that in the Passion, God was utilizing the scapegoat mechanism in order to overcome it, thus completing "the religious unity of mankind. It may perhaps be thought of as a slow and terrible voyage from the first sort of sacrifice toward the second."[41] Thus it is above all the unity of all religions that for Girard permits and even advocates using the same term for the opposed types of behavior. Girard had already acknowledged this unity in his letter from 1978; now he concurs with Schwager that this unity is best expressed by using the same term "sacrifice" for the deed of each of the two harlots, for the view on the Passion of Christ that the Gospels take, and for that which Caiaphas expressed. But Girard still emphasizes that this unity should not cloud the fact of the fundamental difference between the two perspectives.

In the past years, Girard has revised the French and German editions of *Things Hidden*, so that they now contain a footnote qualifying his earlier, critical, statements on Hebrews. This footnote contains the following important qualifications.[42] Girard now considers his emphasis on the strong opposition between a sacrificial and a nonsacrificial reading his last humanistic or progressivist illusion. He now regards the true opposition between a Christian and an archaic sacrifice to be the difference between sacrificing oneself and sacrificing another. The giving up of oneself is not necessarily neurotic. This difference is exemplified by the two harlots in the story of Solomon's Judgment. The motivation for the sacrifice of the real mother and of Christ is engagement for the life or the salvation of others, not any wish for self-harm. Girard explicitly retracts his earlier criticism of the Epistle to the Hebrews and has removed some of these passages from the new edition, although he left most of the text untouched because, as he says in the footnote mentioned, he does not want to hide the development he has gone through.

We can thus summarize that the story of Solomon's Judgment can now be used exactly to illustrate the difference between the archaic sacrifice (sacrificing another for one's own gain) and the sacrifice of self-giving (sacrificing oneself for an important value). Both can and should be referred to by the term "sacrifice" because both amount to the ultimate decision that one is faced with in the situation of grave peril and even the threat of death. This common anthropological theme provides the unity of all religions, even across the line of the Judeo-Christian revelation. However, all the signifiers that Girard used in his earlier phase to distinguish archaic sacrifice from a nonsacrificial attitude remain intact and serve now as points of distinction between an archaic and a Christian sacrifice. Among those the different motivation has to be seen as a very important signifier. Also Girard's cautioning against a masochistic interpretation of the sacrifice of self-giving remains intact, a fact that, I think, he should have emphasized more in his revision of *Des choses cachées*. Since it still contains these warnings against masochism,[43] they should be included in the definition of the sacrifice of self-giving. Sacrificing oneself instead of another is one element of the description; the other—equally necessary—elements are the positive motivation for an absolute value and free acceptance of death that is not neurotic in a masochistic or any other way.

In his most recent explanations on the matter,[44] Girard emphasizes the unity between archaic and Christian sacrifice even more, seeing the one as the precursor and prophecy of the latter, and he acknowledges that the change of terminology is not merely that, but is the consequence of new insights:

> The archaic sacrifice . . . turns against a third victim the violence of those who are fighting, and the Christian sacrifice . . . is the renunciation of all egoistic claiming, even to life if needed, in order not to kill. . . . Today I would write from the point of view of the Gospels, showing that the Gospels read the bad woman and the bad sacrifice as a metaphor of the old humanity, unable to escape violence without sacrificing others. Christ, through his own sacrifice, frees us from this necessity. We have then to use the word "sacrifice" as self-sacrifice, in the sense of Christ. Then it becomes viable to say that the primitive, the archaic, is prophetic of Christ in its own imperfect way. No greater difference can be found: on the one hand, sacrifice as murder, on the other hand, sacrifice as the readiness to die in order not to participate in sacrifice as murder. These two forms are radically opposed to one another, and yet they are inseparable. There is no non-sacrificial space in between, from which everything could be described from a neutral viewpoint. The moral history of humanity is the shifting from the first to the second meaning. . . .
>
> . . . [A]rchaic religions are the real educators of mankind, which they lead out of archaic violence. Then God becomes victim in order to free man of the illusion of a violent God, which must be abolished in favour of Christ's knowledge of his Father. One can regard archaic religions as a prior moment in a progressive revelation that culminates in Christ. . . . To put it bluntly, we cannot have a perfectly non-sacrificial space. In writing *Violence*

> *and the Sacred* and *Things Hidden* I was trying to find that non-sacrificial space from which to understand and explain everything without personal involvement. Now I think that this attempt cannot be successful.[45]

The new insight is the acknowledgement that there is no nonsacrificial space, that the humanistic standpoint that one could stand outside the sacrificial order and therefore take an antisacrificial standpoint is illusory. An antisacrificial standpoint is, in fact, a mimetically antagonistic standpoint of a sacrificial one, and thus is itself sacrificial.[46]

Further Criteria for a Christian Concept of "Sacrifice" according to Dramatic Theology

These are already important criteria for a Christian concept of sacrifice. New considerations and new problems have led to some additional criteria in the discussions dramatic theologians in Innsbruck have conducted.

In considering the concept of sacrifice in context with the *Harry Potter* novels, it occurred to me that Christ's sacrifice is distinguished by an important difference even from the good harlot's, namely that Christ's act of loving self-giving is also for the benefit of his adversaries, while the mother's is only for her own son. This does not contradict Girard's analysis that the good harlot is a *figura Christi*, but it clarifies that the *figurae Christi* might still lack something of the uniqueness of Christ's deed. Christ not only died for his friends, he even lived the love of enemies that he preached to the very end and died for his enemies. He could do so because of his "close union with his divine Father, . . . [which enabled him to] see even his enemies as his brothers, and . . . [to realize] that actually all sinful humans were subject to the same mimetic mechanisms as his persecutors."[47] Or in other words: Christ was able to see his adversaries more as victims of sin than as its perpetrators; and as victims of sin he identified with them and thus was able to live this love of enemies.[48] So, one additional criterion for a Christian sacrifice in the highest sense is that it is not only out of love for friends but even for enemies, who have been recognized as brothers and sisters, although they might see their victim as their enemy.

Another criterion, which has been elaborated on by Roman Siebenrock in his analysis of Christian martyrdom, is the difference between Christian sacrifice and heroism.[49] Because Christian sacrifice is accepted in discipleship to Christ, and because Christ did not behave hero-like but voiced his anguish and even prayed to be spared, Christian sacrifice and martyrdom must do without the attitude of heroism (which, according to Siebenrock, tainted the Christian martyr cult very early, coming, however, not from Christian sources but from Greek sources and the Maccabees). Christian martyrs need not be free of fear and anguish; if they experience them, they are very much on the way of Christian discipleship.

Finally, a new question arose with the advent of suicide bombers. They too give their lives, and they too claim that they do so for an overriding positive value, the freedom of their people or justice for their kin or something like that. Suicide attackers, however, cannot qualify for a sacrifice of free self-giving. They may act according to a military logic, something Schwager has already ruled out as a sacrifice in the truly Christian sense in his earliest writings, as we have seen. Even if they come of their own accord and of their own free choice, they still do not fulfill the criterion of love of enemies. The intended purpose of a suicide attack is the destruction of one's enemies. This cannot qualify as a sacrifice in the Christian sense because the element of love of enemies is not only lacking but is plainly counteracted.[50]

Methodological Reflection with the Help of B. Lonergan's Tools: The Development as a Process of "Dialectic" and "Foundations" and as Religious Conversion

I have already argued elsewhere that Raymund Schwager's dramatic theology can be understood as working on the levels of dialectic and foundations in B. Lonergan's methodology.[51] Here I can only briefly summarize this.

Schwager reads Jesus of Nazareth's life, among other things, as an attempt to clarify the image of God that humans have. Jesus does this by latching on to his Jewish faith and tradition, trying to transform the notions of God and his workings. This process of transformation takes up the Jewish Holy Scriptures (what Christian later came to call the Old Testament) and their understanding at the time and relates to it in a positive way. Nevertheless Jesus tries to clarify and purify that tradition and to transform it thus. In doing so, Jesus is not revolutionary or unique, he is merely continuing a process that the Old Testament writings had engaged in in their own development. In this process, however, Jesus meets the resistance of the religious authorities of his day. What started as a dispute about the right image of God (angry and vengeful or completely loving and merciful) turns into a dispute as to who rightly speaks in the name of God and—conversely—who is ruled by satanic forces. In the end, before Christ's conviction and death, "two completely opposite visions of reality confronted each other."[52] Jesus's adversaries hoped to resolve this opposition by killing their opponent and thus overcoming his view of reality. The Gospels, however, portray not the killing but the Resurrection of Jesus as the final moment of truth that shows that Jesus's adversaries' view on reality was ultimately wrong and Jesus's was correct. The Resurrection thus decides between two completely different views of reality, culminating in the image of God and, depending on that, of everything else, especially theologically important concepts, such as sacrifice. Consequently any Christian theology must undergo a similar process (albeit it will, of course, not start from the Old Testament perspective but from a later one, but the image of God is always in danger of being misunderstood; therefore no theological enterprise will be spared this process).

Lonergan places this type of choice "about one's horizon, one's outlook, one's world-view" in his functional specialty "foundations."[53] In foundations a theologian must make a choice between two opposing views, after s/he has exhausted the possibility of dissolving the opposition by explaining them as misunderstandings or just based on different terminologies (a task performed in the specialty of "dialectic").[54] What is the basis for that foundational decision?

Lonergan argues that in the realm of theology (and one might add in the humanities in general) recognizing the truth is always dependent on the authenticity of the subject making these judgments, or in his own words, "genuine objectivity is the fruit of authentic subjectivity,"[55] and this authenticity is attained through a threefold conversion: intellectual, moral, and religious. Intellectual conversion basically means to abandon the view that gaining knowledge is merely like looking at something; it is to acknowledge that gaining knowledge is a fourfold process "of experiencing, of understanding, of judging, and of believing."[56] "Moral conversion changes the criterion of one's decisions and choices from satisfactions to values."[57]

> Religious conversion is being grasped by ultimate concern. It is other-worldly falling in love. . . . [It is] a dynamic state that is prior to and principle of subsequent acts. It is revealed in retrospect as an under-tow of existential consciousness, as a fated acceptance of a vocation to holiness. . . . It is interpreted differently in the context of different religious traditions. For Christians it is God's love flooding our hearts through the Holy Spirit given to us. . . . Religious conversion is to a total being-in-love as the efficacious ground of all self-transcendence, whether in the pursuit of truth, or in the realization of human values, or in the orientation man adopts to the universe, its ground, and its goal.[58]

One should not get the impression, however, that Lonergan espouses some idealistic naïveté of human perfection. He is well aware that this process "consists in a withdrawal from unauthenticity, and the withdrawal is never a permanent achievement. It is ever precarious, ever to be achieved afresh, ever in great part a matter of uncovering still more oversights, acknowledging still further failures to understand, correcting still more mistakes, repenting more and more deeply hidden sins."[59] But this ongoing process for the theologian is also the basis for working out "general and special categories."[60]

Thus,

> for Schwager Jesus' death and resurrection provides that horizon and offers the Christian church and its theology that criterion. It is here that the image of the merciful, all-forgiving God was vindicated; consequently from here all other conceptions of God and all related concepts have to be transformatively re-interpreted, whereby categories are generated. This re-interpretation is not an exegesis. It is the conversion of the terminology and the notions behind it by putting it into the new context. . . . Christianity believes that Christ did offer a sacrifice by his willingness to die on the cross. But what does "sacrifice" mean in a context in which God is willing to forgive unconditionally and without reservation?[61]

It was exactly what we have witnessed above in the discussion of the concept of sacrifice by Girard and Schwager: They transformed the archaic concept of sacrifice into the Christian concept,[62] arguing about the difference and unity between the two and finally coming to a common standpoint.[63]

Our brief synthesis of Lonergan's analysis has helped us to recognize this process as a process of conversion that was definitely informed by religious conversion—certainly also by intellectual and moral conversion—but let us concentrate on the religious one and let us now consider what it could mean for interreligious dialogue.

Significance for Interreligious Dialogue

I want to examine this significance in a twofold way that we could call material and formal. By formal I mean the process of conversion that resulted in the advanced concept of sacrifice. This approach prescinds from the content of the concept of sacrifice and just looks at the structure of the conversion process and what it can mean for interreligious dialogue. But in a first step we will return to the material content of the concept of sacrifice and see what it can contribute to interreligious dialogue.

Material: Girard's Developed Concept of Sacrifice as a Point of Orientation for Interreligious Criteria

It might seem rather difficult to apply the material concept of sacrifice to interreligious dialogue, different religions having different notions of sacrifice—or maybe none at all. However, if Girard is right that archaic sacrifice is at the heart of all human religions and is the first means of "containing" violence, and that all further developments are variations of that, then this concept actually could facilitate interreligious dialogue.

From the beginning Girard has acknowledged that there is a unity of all religions; he has come to emphasize this even more lately and he is convinced that this unity can be expressed in the term "sacrifice." Therefore all religions are likely to be able to somehow relate to that concept. From the point of view of Girard's theory, there could even be criteria, as to how "advanced" a religious tradition is on the path from archaic sacrifice to the sacrifice of free self-giving. However, a serious objection arises: since Girard freely admits that his insights were inspired by biblical tradition, this tradition seems to be set up as an ideal against which all the others are measured. This would amount to a patronizing view of all other religions. It looks more like another attempt to claim superiority for Judeo-Christian tradition and to place other traditions below them. Admittedly, this could be construed like this. However, it need not be so for several reasons.

For one, it has been shown that Judeo-Christian tradition has not unequivocally achieved a nonsacrificial standpoint but has done so only in a dramatic struggle that involved many relapses into an archaic viewpoint, even bringing about a "sacrificial Christianity." So employing criteria gained from the most advanced form of the Judeo-Christian tradition does not imply necessarily placing that tradition above others; it merely means sharpening one's attention to see similar developments when they occur elsewhere. It is not Christianity (or Judeo-Christian tradition) versus all others, it is nonsacrificial interpretations (wherever they occur) in comparison to sacrificial ones.

Secondly, the development of an idea in a certain tradition, place, and time does not preclude its universal validity and applicability. Sometimes, of course, this is claimed. In this view, even universal human rights are not universal but historically limited ideas of a certain culture that cannot be applied beyond that culture. It is noteworthy, however, that the argument of the colonial and chauvinistic nature of human rights is mostly used by dictators and oligarchs who are loath to respect those rights; it is very rare that the victims agree with that. It is true, however, that even the appeal to universal rights can be abused in a usurpatory manner to justify coercion and even war, as has been done in the horrible instances of the history of "Christian" Europe and its behavior toward other continents and their peoples. However, this merely corroborates the logic developed here: It was exactly *sacrificial* Christianity that behaved like this, a Christianity that had not fully grasped, much less heeded, what its founding event, the Passion and Resurrection of Christ, had brought about. As a consequence it did not merely have a concept of sacrifice that was still modeled on the archaic, it also believed in a violent deity and behaved accordingly in its quest to "convert" others to this belief.

If Christians became able to engage in interreligious dialogue in the attitude of their founder, which "is the renunciation of all egoistic claiming, even to life if needed, in order not to kill,"[64] their way of engaging in interreligious dialogue would also have to be converted fundamentally—which will not entail giving up their claims of having found a universal truth.

We can clearly see that it is not the claim to have found a universal truth that necessarily engenders violence; rather it is the nature of that truth or whether the "truth" is appreciated by an authentic subject (Lonergan), that is, a subject that is able to take the perspective of the victim (Girard) in a way consistent with Christ's attitude of identification with all victims of sin (Schwager). For Christians, Christ is not just an accidental instance of that attitude but its epitome and even the one enabling others to abide by it. For non-Christians, as for mimetic theory as such, this can be suspended and Jesus of Nazareth can be taken as one example of what humanity is capable of and then one can look into one's own tradition for these attitudes and see whether they are there.

In that perspective, the sacrifice of free self-giving is not the "Christian" type of sacrifice, but it is the type of sacrifice consistent with a nonviolent God. Within each religious tradition, including the Christian, there might be strains that adhere to this high standard and others that do not but are more compatible with an angry and violent God. Here, a process of conversion is needed within each tradition, similar to the one exemplified by the way from archaic sacrifice to the sacrifice of free self-giving. Interreligious dialogue can facilitate a closer, critical look at one's own tradition, and thus advance that process. Lonergan's analysis of conversion helps to see that more clearly.

Formal: Interreligious Dialogue as Occasion for Religious Conversion within One's Own Religious Tradition

We have seen in Lonergan's description of religious conversion that he does not construe "conversion" in the colloquial sense of changing one's religious affiliation. Lonergan explicitly stated that different religious traditions interpret that very same religious conversion differently. For that reason I interpret his "religious conversion" to mean something else. It is not about converting non-Christians to Christianity but about converting within one's own religious tradition. When looking at this process within the Christian tradition, it can be described as

> different horizons within a Christianity in which opposing groups have referred and still refer to the same sentences but give them completely different meanings. In the most extreme case the same sentence could be used

> to express two opposed doctrines, depending on the background against which the sentence is understood, i.e. the horizon within which it is placed. Many conflicts in the history of Christianity can be explained that way as conflicts between authentic and unauthentic Christianity, between explicitly professed Christianity and an implicit, yet practically lived paganism, between non-sacrificial or sacrificial Christianity.[65]

"Jesus's Passion is a sacrifice" means very different things when the term "sacrifice" is understood as "archaic sacrifice" or as "sacrifice of free self-giving"; the latter, of course, could only have been developed by a close analysis of the event of the Passion.

So what we encountered in Schwager's and Girard's discussion is a process of dialectic and foundations that led the two thinkers to (more or less) the same conclusion and the same transformation of their terminology. It was a process of conversion within the Judeo-Christian tradition, within Christianity in the form of Catholic tradition, since both thinkers are professed Catholics. Nothing, however, would preclude a similarly structured process from occurring within another religious tradition—and the dialogue with another tradition could be supportive of that. We can see from this process that it has nothing to do with imposing one's conviction on another person but everything with a respectful, though sometimes controversial, exchange of views leading up to modifications in each thinker and to moving each of them beyond their original disagreement. It seems especially noteworthy that the movement went from the early archaic understanding (held by none of the two thinkers but by archaic religion) via an antisacrificial standpoint (which was stronger in Girard because of his humanistic leanings at the time) to a nonsacrificial standpoint that can encompass both the insights from the antisacrificial and the acknowledgment of the unity of all religions plus the insight that there is no neutral ground. This shows that, of course, the Judeo-Christian tradition is not an isolated strain of experience and thought but is embedded in the development of the religions of the world.

Therefore there is no insurmountable obstacle to do this also in an interreligious manner: One religious tradition can question another one in the same controversial but respectful way and can thus challenge it to rethink the horizon from which it makes its statements of faith and develops its terminology—and vice versa. The direction of learning is unlikely to be a one-way street. The transformation of the horizon—and this seems especially significant—need not result in different statements of faith; in fact the wording of religious sentences may remain unchanged. But their meaning will have been transformed nevertheless, as with the "sacrifice" of Jesus's Passion. Thus interreligious dialogue could facilitate conversion within a tradition or a religion, not prompting adherents of one religion to change their affiliation or even their religious terminology but prompting them to take new, maybe hence unthought of, looks at their own religion and thus go a further step in the ever precarious and fragmentary process of religious conversion.[66]

Of course, the danger of misunderstanding that Girard deemed so grave in *Things Hidden* is a given and should not be underestimated. However, since language develops and since religious traditions tend to span long periods of history, every terminology would be subject to this danger. It cannot be avoided completely; it can only be watched for and, if necessary, counteracted.

Thus, one goal of interreligious dialogue could be to sharpen the participants' alertness for actual or possible transformations in their own religious tradition, and to try to find out how far they have come in the process of religious conversion—not seen as a process of changing one's religious affiliation but of understanding one's own religion better from a standpoint of authentic subjectivity.

NOTES

1. See René Girard, *De la violence à la divinité* (Paris: Grasset, 2007), 293–699.
2. See René Girard, *Things Hidden since the Foundation of the World*, research undertaken in collaboration with J.-M. Oughourlian and G. Lefort, trans. Stephen Bann and Michael Metteer (Stanford, CA: Stanford University Press, 1987), esp. 224–53.
3. Girard later comes to call the peculiarities that make a person likely to be selected as a victim "marks of a victim"; in primitive societies these might be physical deformities or other kinds of abnormality; see René Girard, *The Scapegoat*, trans. Yvonne Freccero (Baltimore: Johns Hopkins University Press, 1986), 17–21.
4. René Girard, *I See Satan Fall Like Lightning*, trans. James G. Williams (Maryknoll, NY: Orbis, 2001), 70.
5. See Girard, *The Scapegoat*, 112–24. "Caiaphas is stating the same political reason we have given for the scapegoat: to limit violence as much as possible but to turn to it, if necessary, as a last resort to avoid an even greater violence. Caiaphas is the incarnation of politics at its best, not its worst. No one has ever been a better politician" (113).

6. René Girard, *Sacrifice*, trans. Matthew Pattillo and David Dawson (East Lansing: Michigan State University Press, 2011), 72.

7. Girard, *Things Hidden since the Foundation of the World*, 224–25.

8. Ibid., 227. See Hebrews 9:22–26, 10:11–14.

9. Girard, *Things Hidden since the Foundation of the World*, 228.

10. See 1 Kings 3:16–28 and Girard, *Things Hidden since the Foundation of the World*, 237–45.

11. Girard emphasizes that this is relevant for the understanding of ritual sacrifice, too, because the story can be read as an allusion to the inner-biblical conflicts surrounding the religious practice of child sacrifice (see Girard, *Things Hidden since the Foundation of the World*, 239). For the prophetic critique of these practices see Leviticus 20:1–5; Jeremiah 3:24, 19:5, 32:26; 2 Kings 23:10 (Girard explicitly refers to this last passage).

12. Girard, *Things Hidden since the Foundation of the World*, 240.

13. Ibid., 241.

14. Ibid., 241–42.

15. "In the light of our analyses, we are bound to conclude that any procedure involving sacrifice, even and indeed especially when it turns against the self, is at variance with the true spirit of the gospel text. The Gospels never present the rule of the Kingdom under the negative aspect of *self-sacrifice*. Far from being an exclusively Christian concept, which would form the summit of 'altruism' by contrast with an 'egoism' prone to sacrifice the other with gay abandon, self-sacrifice can serve to camouflage the forms of slavery brought into being by mimetic desire. 'Masochism' can also find expression in self-sacrifice, even if a person has no knowledge of this, and no wish to reveal it" (ibid., 236).

16. The correspondence covers the years 1974–91 and has been published in a bilingual edition of a research project directed by Józef Niewiadomski in Innsbruck and funded by the Austrian Science Fund: Raymund Schwager, *Briefwechsel mit René Girard*, ed. N. Wandinger and K. Peter (Freiburg: Herder 2014); for an English translation see René Girard and Raymund Schwager, *Correspondence 1974–1991*, ed. S. Cowdell, C. Fleming, J. Hodge, and M. Moosbrugger, trans. C. Fleming and S. Treflé Hidden (New York: Bloomsbury, 2016). Mathias Moosbrugger, *Die Rehabilitierung des Opfers: Zum Dialog zwischen René Girard und Raymund Schwager über die Angemessenheit der Rede vom Opfer im christlichen Kontext* (Innsbruck: Tyrolia, 2014). I am indebted to the author for allowing me a look at the chapter on Schwager in its draft stage, which greatly enriched my understanding of Schwager's development.

17. According to Moosbrugger, *Die Rehabilitierung des Opfers*, 172–89. Schwager did so already in his 1969 doctoral thesis, which was published a year later: Raymund Schwager, *Das dramatische Kirchenverständnis bei Ignatius von Loyola: Historisch-pastoraltheologische Studie über die Stellung der Kirche in den Exerzitien und im Leben des Ignatius* (Zürich: Benzinger, 1970), esp. 186–88.

18. Ibid., 165, 173–88.

19. Ibid., 173, 183; cf. 1 Corinthians 1:18; John 12:24.

20. Schwager, *Das dramatische Kirchenverständnis*, 188, my own translation.

21. Raymund Schwager, *Jesus-Nachfolge: Woraus lebt der Glaube?* (Freiburg: Herder, 1973), 177, my translation. Unfortunately there is no direct English translation for the German "Hingabe." It is dedication, commitment, and devotion, but also self-abandonment and self-giving. I will

henceforth use "self-giving" but the other meanings should still be in the background of the readers' minds as intended connotations.

22. Moosbrugger, *Die Rehabilitierung des Opfers*, 220–21 notes that before reading this book, Schwager had already encountered Girard's ideas on the Judeo-Christian tradition as contained in "Discussion avec René Girard," *Esprit* 41 (November 1973): 528–63. Therefore it was not too difficult for him to see that Girard was not an atheistic thinker, as many still supposed at that time.

23. Raymund Schwager, *Glaube, der die Welt verwandelt* (Mainz: Matthias-Grünewald-Verlag, 1976), esp. 137–56.

24. Ibid., 141, my translation.

25. Ibid., 173n99, my translation.

26. This correspondence is held at the Raymund-Schwager-Archive in Innsbruck, catalogue number RSA II. 12b, and have been published in the meantime. All emphases in the quotations from these letters are by the original authors.

27. Girard and Schwager, *Correspondence 1974–1991*, 51–54.

28. Ibid., 56.

29. Ibid., 59–60. Schwager is referring here to the first edition of *Brauchen wir einen Sündenbock? Gewalt und Erlösung in den biblischen Schriften*, (München: Kösel, 1978). It has since appeared in English: Raymund Schwager, *Must There Be Scapegoats? Violence and Redemption in the Bible*, 2nd ed., trans. Maria L. Assad (New York: Crossroad, 2000).

30. See Raymund Schwager, *Jesus in the Drama of Salvation: Toward a Biblical Doctrine of Redemption*, trans. James G. Williams and Paul Haddon (New York: Crossroad, 1999), 182–88.

31. Another prominent passage, to which Schwager, however, does not refer here, is Jeremiah 7:22. It is very striking because it does not merely link the validity of sacrifice to the right social conduct (as do Amos 5:21–25; Hosea 6:6; Jeremiah 6:20; Micah 6:6–8; Isaiah 1:1–11) but explicitly denies any divine command of sacrifices despite the contrary descriptions in Leviticus.

32. Schwager, *Jesus in the Drama of Salvation*, 183, emphasis mine.

33. See Rebecca Adams and René Girard, "Violence, Difference, Sacrifice: A Conversation with René Girard," *Religion & Literature* 25, no. 2 (1993): 9–33.

34. See ibid., 28–29.

35. For the English translation, see René Girard, "Mimetic Theory and Theology," in *The One by Whom Scandal Comes* (East Lansing: Michigan State University Press, 2014), 33–44.

36. See ibid., 42.

37. See ibid., 42–43.

38. Ibid., 42.

39. Ibid., 43.

40. Ibid., 43.

41. Ibid., 44.

42. For the following see Girard, *De la violence à la divinité*, 1001n1. Since I am not proficient in French and since the English version has not been revised, I am working from the German

translation: René Girard, *Das Ende der Gewalt: Erkundungen zu Mimesis und Gewalt mit Jean Michel Oughourlian und Guy Lefort*, trans. Elisabeth Mainberger-Ruh (Freiburg: Herder, 2009), 301n26. I hope that it adequately transposes the original text.

43. See Girard, *De la violence à la divinité*, 991–92; also Girard, *Das Ende der Gewalt*, 292.

44. See René Girard, *Evolution and Conversion: Dialogues on the Origins of Culture with Pierpaolo Antonello and João Cezar de Castro Rocha* (London: Continuum, 2008), esp. 214–20.

45. Ibid., 215–17.

46. See ibid., 230n28. This refers to Hugo Assmann, *René Girard com téologos da libertaçâo: Um dialogo sobre idolos e sacrificios* (Petropólis: Editoria Vozes, 1991), 42.

47. Nikolaus Wandinger, "'Sacrifice' in the Harry Potter Series from a Girardian Perspective," *Contagion* 17 (2010): 40.

48. See Schwager, *Jesus in the Drama of Salvation*, 195–96. For an analysis of the transforming power of sacrifice, which also enables the victim not to be determined by his persecutors but referring him/herself to the higher transcendence that we call God, see Niewiadomski's investigation into the modern martyr Janusz Korczak: Józef Niewiadomski, "Victima versus sacrificium: Nuancen der spannungsreichen Beziehung zwischen Liebe und Opfer," in *Lieben: Provokationen. Salzburger Hochschulwochen 2008*, ed. Gregor M. Hoff (Innsbruck: Tyrolia, 2008), 176–209.

49. See esp. Roman A. Siebenrock, *Christliches Martyrium: Worum es geht* (Innsbruck: Tyrolia, 2009); Siebenrock, "Zeichen der Erlösung in einer Welt der Gewalt: Eine systematisch-theologische Kriteriologie des christlichen Martyriums," in *Opfer—Helden—Märtyrer: Das Martyrium als religionspolitologische Herausforderung*, ed. Józef Niewiadomski and Roman A. Siebenrock (Innsbruck: Tyrolia, 2011), 153–72.

50. For a close analysis of the differences between suicide attackers, martyrs, and Christian sacrifice, see Józef Niewiadomski, "Märtyrer, Selbstopfer, Selbstmordattentäter," in Niewiadomski and Siebenrock, *Opfer—Helden—Märtyrer*, 275–91.

51. For the methodical steps see Bernard Lonergan, *Method in Theology* (Toronto: University of Toronto Press, 1971; repr., 2003), respectively 235–66, 267–93. For my interpretation of Schwager and Lonergan, see Nikolaus Wandinger, "Drama and Conversion: Raymund Schwager's Dramatic Theology as an Exercise of Bernard Lonergan's Functional Specialty of Foundations," *Revista Portuguesa de Filosofia* 63, no. 4 (2007): 1203–22.

52. Schwager, *Jesus in the Drama of Salvation*, 68.

53. Lonergan, *Method in Theology*, 268.

54. A functional specialty is a step in the methodical progress from gathering data to a result. Lonergan suggests eight such specialties for theology, ordered on four levels. On the fourth level he places the two we are concerned with: dialectic and foundations (see ibid., 125–51, esp. 127–33).

55. Ibid., 292.

56. Ibid., 238.

57. Ibid., 240.

58. Ibid., 240–41.

59. Ibid., 252.

60. Ibid., 282.

61. Wandinger, "Drama and Conversion," 1219.

62. I want to remind the readers that "Christian concept" does not mean that all Christians have actually attained this—as Girard's and Schwager's analyses of misunderstandings in historical Christianity attest to. It means that it should be the concept of a Christianity understanding itself adequately. Neither should the description "Christian concept" be taken to mean "exclusively Christian concept." Whether it is unique to Christianity or common to several religions is a matter to be decided exactly by interreligious dialogue.

63. The discussion between Girard and Schwager about the proper terminology may well belong in the specialty of dialectic, although the change of terminology did produce some factual insight as well. Yet the foundational conversion was certainly the insight on which both agreed from the beginning, namely that Christ's Passion must be seen as different from archaic sacrifice.

64. Girard, *Evolution and Conversion*, 215.

65. Wandinger, "Drama and Conversion," 1219–20.

66. See Raymund Schwager, Józef Niewiadomski, and Gerhard Larcher, "Dramatisches Konzept für die Begegnung der Religionen," in *Christus allein? Der Streit um die pluralistische Religionstheologie*, ed. Raymund Schwager (Freiburg: Herder, 1996), 83–117.

The Abrahamic Revolution

Wolfgang Palaver

Among scholars dedicated to mimetic theory recent debates raised the question of how Islam is related to Judaism and Christianity. One frequently mentioned starting point is the "Epilogue" in René Girard's book *Battling to the End*, in which he claims that Islam is a religion that "has used the Bible as a support to rebuild an archaic religion that is more powerful than all the others" (Girard 2010, 214). Could one draw from this and similar remarks the conclusion that Islam is an archaic religion and not at all comparable with Judaism and Christianity, even going as far as rejecting any notion that addresses these three religions together as "Abrahamic religions"? This question is much more complicated than it seems at first sight. First of all, René Girard is very careful when he addresses Islam, always telling the people with whom he discusses this religion that he is not an expert in this field and has never studied Islam or the Qur'an thoroughly. He is also very much aware of the danger to be mimetically drawn into a Western opposition against Islam without really coming to an understanding of it. Girard therefore warns of the danger to find explanations that "often belong to the province of fraudulent propaganda against Muslims" (Girard 2010, 215). His claim that there is a "return to the archaic" coming along with Islam is also clearly in need of some further clarification, because Girard at the same time maintains that there are "no longer any archaic religions" in today's modern world (Girard 2010, 212, 214).

In the following I will show that there happened an Abrahamic revolution meaning the exodus from archaic religion that comprises Judaism, Christianity, and also Islam.[1] We can justly use the term "Abrahamic religions" to address these three religions in their common distinction from archaic religion. A first step will focus on the story of Abraham who replaced his own son whom he was going to sacrifice with a ram. This is an important step out of the archaic practice of human sacrifice. A second story that deserves closer attention in this regard is the story of Joseph that emphasizes the Abrahamic rehabilitation of the victim overcoming by this the archaic pattern of scapegoating. A final part of my essay will emphasize the broader perspective that characterizes the Abrahamic concern for victims helping us to prevent the distortions that often follow this legacy and haunts us especially today. We will realize how important it is that the concern for victims is accompanied by reconciliation and that this attitude depends again on our awareness of our own weaknesses.

The Story of the Binding of Isaac: Overcoming Human Sacrifice

In the akedah the Bible narrates a decisive breakaway from the archaic tradition of human sacrifice. The archaic tradition demanded human sacrifice, and Abraham was consequently forced to offer his son as a sacrifice to God. But this tradition is replaced with a religion in which, instead of humans, only animals are allowed as sacrificial victims: "Do not lay your hand on the boy or do anything to him!" (Genesis 22:12). God prohibits the sacrifice of Isaac, and Abraham decides instead to sacrifice a ram discovered in bushes nearby. This substitution of a human sacrifice by an animal is, according to Girard, part of the biblical difference that he characterizes as "a single, dynamic movement away from sacrifice" (Girard 1987, 239). According to Girard, "the great scene of Abraham's sacrifice is the renunciation of the sacrifice of infants (which is latent in the biblical beginning) and its replacement with animal sacrifice" (2008, 203). It is not by chance that also Michel Serres emphasized this story in his speech at the reception of René Girard into the Académie française in 2005. Abraham's "first new truth" consists, according to Serres, in the "arresting of human sacrifice" (Serres 2009, 10). The German novelist and Nobel Prize laureate Thomas Mann reflected over a long time—during which he wrote his tetralogy *Joseph and His Brothers* (1933–43)—on the relationship between archaic religion and the biblical legacy. In a speech at the Library of Congress in 1942 Mann summarized the Abrahamic revolution as a significant shift from the "stupidity before God" (*Gottesdummheit*) to an "intelligence before God" (*Gottesklugheit*) (2008, 15–16):

> The original and only actual sacrifice was human sacrifice. At what moment did this practice become horrible and insane? It is in Genesis, this moment, in the image of the denied sacrifice of Isaac, the substitution of the animal. Man, advanced in God, frees himself from his stagnant ritual, from that beyond which God wants to take us—and already has. (Mann 1996, 199 [trans. by G. Borrud])

Does Islam belong also to this Abrahamic revolution that is so dramatically expressed in the story of the binding of Isaac? If we do not focus on marginal differences like the fact that the name of the spared son is not mentioned in the Qur'an and that the Muslim tradition usually identifies him with Ishmael, the basic story regarding human sacrifice is the same in the Bible and the Qur'an (Crook 2005a, 86–105). Girard himself referred in his book *Violence and the Sacred* to the fact that the Muslim tradition even linked the story of the spared son of Abraham with the sacrifice of Abel:

> According to Moslem tradition, God delivered to Abraham the ram previously sacrificed by Abel. This ram was to take the place of Abraham's son Isaac; having already saved one human life, the same animal would now save another. What we have here is no mystical hocuspocus, but an intuitive insight into the essential function of sacrifice, gleaned exclusively from the scant references in the Bible. (Girard 1977, 4–5; cf. Girard and Tincq 2002, 26)

In sura 37:107 we can find the passage about the substitution of an animal instead of Abraham's son: "We ransomed him with a momentous sacrifice."[2]

The text in the Qur'an even goes slightly beyond its biblical predecessor because it no longer mentions a direct commandment by God to sacrifice the son but records that Abraham was dreaming that he has to do so.[3] Bruce Chilton refers to sura 37:106 ("For this was obviously a trial") to show that the Qur'an detached the vision of God from the violent sacred of paganism. Muhammad's vision was, according to Chilton, that "violence is never God's requirement, but only an obvious trial" (2008, 170).

We find a parallel to this story about Abraham in the traditional biography of Muhammad. This biography includes a moving story about the grandfather of Muhammad, Abd al-Muttalib, who once vowed to sacrifice one of his sons if God would bless him with ten sons that would all grow up to manhood. This vow forced him into deep troubles when he finally had ten grown-up sons. In the end, however, he did not sacrifice his son but a hundred camels instead, saving by this the life of 'Abd Allāh who became later the father of Muhammad (Guillaume 2006, 66–68; Lings 2006, 12–14).

The most important difference between the Bible and the Qur'an regarding the akedah is a de-dramatization of the story. Abraham is no longer evading his son's question about the lamb that should be offered,[4] but both Abraham and his son are willingly cooperating, both in complete obedience to the will of God.[5] Close to the emphasis on obedience over against sacrifice in the Hebrew Bible (1 Samuel 15:22, "to obey is better than sacrifice") also the Qur'an emphasizes obedience and demythologizes archaic sacrifice. According to Angelika Neuwirth, a German Arabist and Qur'an scholar, the Qur'an does not recognize atonement through sacrifice (2010, 554–57; cf. 633–52). Despite the traditional Muslim Festival of Sacrifice that is closely linked to the story of the akedah, the Qur'an represents a critique of archaic cults very similar to the critique of bloody sacrifices by the Hebrew prophets (Neuwirth 2010, 536–37):[6]

> The sacrificial camels we have made for you as among the symbols from Allah, in them is (much) good for you: then pronounce the name of Allah over them as they line up (for sacrifice): when they are down on their sides (after slaughter), eat ye thereof, and feed such as (beg not but) live in contentment, and such as beg with due humility: thus have We made animals subject to you, that ye may be grateful. It is not their meat nor their blood, that reaches Allah; it is your piety that reaches Him: He has thus made

> them subject to you, that ye may glorify Allah for His Guidance to you and proclaim the good news to all who do right. (sura 22:36–37)

Exactly these verses in the Qur'an lead the Tunisian Muslim scholar Mohamed Talbi to the conclusion that God rejects human sacrifice (Richter-Bernburg 2007, 253).

The Story of Joseph: Rehabilitating the Scapegoat, Renouncing Idolatry, and Seeking Forgiveness

In the Hebrew Bible it is the story of Joseph that most clearly illustrates the difference between archaic religion and the perspective of the Bible.[7] Girard again and again refers to the Genesis account of Joseph and his brothers (Genesis 37–50) to illustrate this difference (Girard 2004, 107–13; 1987, 149–53; 2014, 28–29, 77; 2001, 107–15; 2008, 199–203; cf. Goodhart 1996, 106–21; Williams 1991, 54–60; Golsan 1993, 92–94). The Oedipus myth provides an enlightening contrast here, as the two texts also show numerous points of convergence. From childhood onward, Joseph and Oedipus are both branded as scapegoats. Oedipus is abandoned by his parents, while Joseph is sold into slavery by his brothers. Once again, however, the differences between these two texts outweigh the similarities. Contrary to Oedipus who remains a scapegoat, Joseph is a "rehabilitated scapegoat" (Girard 2008, 199). While Oedipus is made responsible for the plague in Thebes on account of his incestuous relationship with his mother, the biblical text is free of any comparable accusations against Joseph. It is not he who raped the wife of his adoptive father, Potiphar, but rather she who attempted to seduce him.[8] The Bible is unequivocally on the side of the victim Joseph, as it shows no solidarity with Joseph's envious brothers or with his accusers. Also, whereas Oedipus is exalted to quasi-divine heights after his expulsion from Thebes, Joseph expressly rejects similar attempts by his brothers who had persecuted him: "Then his brothers also wept, fell down before him, and said, 'We are here as your slaves.' But Joseph said to them, 'Do not be afraid! Am I in the place of God?'" (Genesis 50:18–19). According to Girard, archaic religion is characterized by the divinization of its victims. It is not an invention of priests to deceive their people but the result of an unconscious act of collective violence to overcome a dangerous internal crisis. Girard justly claims therefore that "the peoples of the world do not invent their gods" but "deify their victims" (Girard 2001, 70). In contrast to archaic religion the Bible rejects idolatry separating therefore the divine and collective violence. Girard emphasizes the renunciation of idolatry as an essential aspect of the Bible's divergence from archaic myth:

> The then brothers resist the temptation to idolatry. They are Israelites, and so they don't deify human beings. Mythic heroes typically have something rigid and stylized about them. They are first demonized, then deified. Joseph is humanized. The narrator bathes him in a warm luminosity that would be unthinkable in mythology. But this is not basically due to "literary talent," for the genius of the text is its renunciation of idolatry. (Girard 2001, 119)[9]

The story of Joseph is also part of the Qur'an. It is one of its very few narratives and the only biblical narrative that is nearly completely included in this religious text (Crook 2005b, 25; Gnilka 2007, 126–27). It is presented as "the most beautiful of stories," as "no less than a message for all creatures," as an "instruction for men endued with understanding," "a detailed exposition of all things, and a guide and a mercy to any such as believe" (sura 12:3, 104, 111). Like the story in the Bible it sides with the scapegoat Joseph and rejects all idolatry. In the Qur'an it is even Potiphar's wife herself—according to the Muslim tradition her name is Zulaikhá—that pronounces the innocence of Joseph: "I did seek to seduce him from his (true) self but he did firmly save himself guiltless!" (sura 12:32). This proclamation, however, did not prevent her from forcing Joseph into prison. But later she repeated his innocence when she was interrogated by the king who finally released Joseph from the prison: "Now is the truth manifest (to all): it was I who sought to seduce him from his (true) self: He is indeed of those who are (ever) true (and virtuous)" (sura 12:51). The Qur'an also shares with the Bible the reversal of scapegoating visible in Judah's willingness to take the place of Benjamin after the youngest son was caught as an apparent thief.[10] Judah anticipates to some degree the Suffering Servant of the Second Isaiah and Jesus in the Passion narratives of the New Testament (Williams 1991, 58). The version in the Qur'an is less dramatic and less personal but narrates the willingness of all the brothers to step in for Benjamin: "So take one of us in his place; for we see that thou art (gracious) in doing good" (sura 12:78). Joseph's immediate response to his brothers also emphasizes the breakaway from archaic patterns of scapegoating that would choose anyone to carry the burden of blame without further investigations: "Allah forbid that we take other than him with whom we found our property: indeed (if we did so), we should be acting wrongfully" (sura 12:79). Like a prophet, Joseph also represents the Muslim rejection of idolatry: "And I follow the ways of my fathers,—Abraham, Isaac, and Jacob; and never could we attribute any partners whatever to Allah. . . . He hath commanded that ye worship none but Him: that is the right religion" (sura 12:38–40).

The story of Joseph not only represents the biblical perspective of the victim but also emphasizes forgiveness as the proper response to overcome violence, be it the collective violence of scapegoaters or any kind of retaliation that would only prolong persecution.[11] This story powerfully emphasizes forgiveness because Joseph does not seek revenge but pardons all his brothers (Williams 1994, 82):

> "Even though you intended to do harm to me, God intended it for good, in order to preserve a numerous people, as he is doing today. So have no fear; I myself will provide for you and your little ones." In this way he reassured them, speaking kindly to them. (Genesis 50:20–21)[12]

Joseph's forgiveness is perhaps even more powerfully expressed in the Qur'an by especially emphasizing God's mercy: "This day let no reproach be (cast) on you: Allah will forgive you, and He is the Most Merciful of those who show mercy!" (sura 12:92). Forgiveness and God's mercy are also underlined in the Qur'an in the relationship between Jacob and his remorseful sons seeking pardon: "They said: 'O our father! ask for us forgiveness for our sins, for we were truly at fault.' He said: 'Soon will I ask my Lord for forgiveness for you: for he is indeed Oft-Forgiving, Most Merciful'" (sura 12:97–98). Islam in general as well as the Qur'an particularly are deeply characterized by an "ontological mercy" as it was especially highlighted by the medieval Sufi mystic and philosopher Ibn Arabi who referred for this reason to sura 7:156 "My mercy extendeth to all things" (Izutsu 1984, 116–40; Shah-Kazemi 2007). The contemporary Muslim scholar Reza Shah-Kazemi shows how this ontology of mercy relates to the Qur'anic understanding of Jesus and how it also characterizes the interpretation of jihad (Shah-Kazemi 2006; 2009, 123–25).

As in the case of the akedah we also find significant parallels between the story of Joseph and Muhammad's traditional biography. Like Joseph who out of envy was scapegoated by his brothers also Muhammad was expelled by his family from his hometown Mecca, and also like Joseph Muhammad forgave the Meccans when he conquered Mecca some years later uttering even the same words with which Joseph forgave his brothers (Lings 2006, 314; Shah-Kazemi 2007, 50–51).

Comparing the biblical with the Qur'anic version of the story of Joseph we realize again a de-dramatization of the story and a much stronger emphasis on the spiritual dimension in the Qur'an (Ben Nabi 1983, 147–48; Crook 2005b, 129–31; Körner 2008, 172). In the Qur'an, both Jacob and Joseph are presented as prophets trusting strongly and patiently in God's providence. When Joseph was thrown down to the bottom of a well he already received a message from God that helped him to remain trustful:

> So they did take him away, and they all agreed to throw him down to the bottom of the well: and We put into his heart (this Message): "Of a surety thou shalt (one day) tell them the truth of this their affair while they know (thee) not." (sura 12:15)

And the Qur'anic Jacob never lost trust in God, always patiently awaiting the reappearance of his son Joseph.[13] When his sons presented to Jacob the bloody robe of Joseph, the Bible reports the deep despair into which he was thrown:

> He recognized it, and said, "It is my son's robe! A wild animal has devoured him; Joseph is without doubt torn to pieces." Then Jacob tore his garments, and put sackcloth on his loins, and mourned for his son many days. (Genesis 37:33–34)

The same event in the Qur'an, to the contrary, highlights Jacob's patient trust in God:

> They stained his shirt with false blood. He said: "Nay, but your minds have made up a tale (that may pass) with you, (for me) patience is most fitting: Against that which ye assert, it is Allah (alone) Whose help can be sought." (sura 12:18)

The Dangerous Cult of the Victim and How It Can be Healed by Becoming Aware of Our Common Weakness

Interpreting the Abrahamic revolution as the overcoming of the archaic religion of human sacrifice, however, does not really help us to explain contemporary threats of religiously motivated violence. We most likely would not discuss the relationship of religion and violence today if we were not trying to find explanations for the dangers we are facing today. How can it happen that we find people in our contemporary world who view themselves as belonging to one of the Abrahamic religions and who nevertheless are legitimating violence in a way that seems to contradict the commitment to peace and forgiveness that belongs to my understanding of the Abrahamic revolution? In order to answer this question we have to be aware of new dangers that may go along with the Abrahamic revolution.

The exposure of the scapegoat mechanism does not automatically lead to a more peaceful world but has often terribly increased the amount of violence by distorted understandings of it. To a certain degree such fragmented and distorted interpretations of the Abrahamic revelation help us to explain some of the temptations toward violence in our contemporary world. The most intriguing example of such a distortion of the Abrahamic tradition is connected with its siding with the victims. The Abrahamic concern for victims has led to the best and worst in our world. On the one hand it is one of the strongest sources that led to the still ongoing increase of the value of human beings resulting in our strong emphasis on human rights. On the other hand, however, we also recognize an increase of violence that follows any concern for victims that does not go together with forgiveness and reconciliation. The Abrahamic solidarity with the victims easily turns into an aggressive weapon if taking the side of the victim is not connected with forgiveness. We can underline both these tendencies by referring to Elias Canetti's concept of the "religions of lament" (Palaver 2008; 2010a). Referring especially to Christians and Shiite Muslims Canetti called those religions "religions of lament" whose members are siding with a persecuted victim in order to expiate their own guilt as persecutors (Canetti 1984, 143–45). Canetti refers to two consequences stemming from the legacy of religions of lament. First and more directly, he mentions the tremendous increase of the value of each human individual going along with the spread of Christianity (Canetti 1984, 467). A second, much more indirect consequence going along with the religions of lament is, according to Canetti, a certain tendency to legitimate violent and revengeful actions by siding with a persecuted victim. Lament can easily turn into war.

The temptation of vengeful religious lamenting has accompanied Abrahamic monotheism from its very beginning. It has remained, of course, a permanent temptation throughout Jewish, Christian, and Muslim history. Many secularized versions of it are also contributing to our contemporary culture of a radical victimology often turning the concern for victims into a dangerous weapon. Contemporary terrorism is especially characterized by legitimating all violence as a defense of persecuted victims (Hoffman 1998, 95–127; Juergensmeyer 2001, 12; Taylor 2004, 36; Richardson 2006, 65).The Canadian philosopher Charles Taylor has taken up basic insights of Girard's mimetic theory explaining with its help also the dangers coming along with our modern cult of the victim that he calls a "powerful cachet of victimhood" (Taylor 2004, 36; cf. Palaver 2010b). With Girard, Taylor maintains that the Gospel shows the innocence of the victim referring, however, at the same time to the abuse of the concept:

> The Gospel "points toward the raising up of victims, of the despised and rejected. Various religious reforms involve taking the idea of reversal farther. The Reformation itself is one such example, as also is modern humanism, which defends ordinary human life against persecution in the name of "higher" modes of spirituality. So this élan becomes part of the ethic of our time, the political ethic. . . . This becomes on one hand, a great force for battling against injustices. But it also becomes a way of drawing lines, denouncing enemies, the evil ones. . . . Because my being the victim means that you are the victimizer, I am pure. Claiming victimhood is an assertion of our purity; we are all right. Moreover, our cause is good, so we can fight,

> inflict a violence that is righteous: a holy violence. Hence we have a right to do terrible things, which others have not. Here is the logic of modern terrorism. (Taylor 2004, 36)

Also Girard himself has addressed again and again this dangerous cult of the victim. According to him, we often "practice a hunt for scapegoats to the second degree, a hunt for hunters of scapegoats" (Girard 2001, 158). This perversion of the concern for victims is the reign of the Antichrist, in which fighting persecution leads to even more cruel acts of violence (Girard 2014, 38; 2001, 181).

What are the remedies against these dangers coming along with a perverse cult of the victim and can we find them in the Abrahamic religions? The most important remedy against this temptation is forgiveness that must not at all be separated from the Abrahamic concern for victims. Let's take the Christian New Testament as an example. Contrary to all temptations of a vengeful lament the New Testament's solidarity with the victims does not at all legitimate retribution. Jesus's heavenly father personifies the love for enemies and the rejection of revenge: "Love your enemies and pray for those who persecute you, so that you may be children of your Father in heaven; for he makes his sun rise on the evil and on the good, and sends rain on the righteous and on the unrighteous" (Matthew 5:44–45). In accordance with his father Jesus forgave his enemies when he was murdered on the cross: "Father, forgive them; for they do not know what they are doing" (Luke 23:34). And when he met his disciples again after his resurrection he offered them his peace without blaming them for their weakness and cowardliness (Schwager 1999, 146, 152, 207): "Peace be with you" (John 20:19). The true Christian spirit contradicts vengeful lamenting and is beyond all resentment.

We already underlined the importance of forgiveness in the story of Joseph, in the Hebrew Bible as well as in the Qur'an. In this key story of the Abrahamic revolution the concern for victims and forgiveness are not separated but closely connected to each other. Jacques Derrida is right when he refers to an Abrahamic tradition of forgiveness (2001, 28, 42).

The separation of the concern for victims from reconciliation is one of the most dangerous temptations that can follow the Abrahamic revolution as its perverted legacy. It comes along with a type of puritanical attitude that exempts itself from all evil identifying oneself solely with the completely pure and good side. The Canadian philosopher Charles Taylor, who follows to a growing degree Girard's mimetic theory, recognizes a special danger in all attempts seeking a stance of purity that easily results in scapegoating. Drawing on the work of Fyodor Dostoyevsky he contrasts the slogan "no one is to blame" with its dangerous consequences to an attitude that characterizes all the redemptive characters in the works of the Russian novelist who know that "we are all to blame." According to Taylor, only those who do not exempt themselves from all evil are able to forgive others and find "a new footing of co-responsibility to the erstwhile enemy" (2004, 39). Forgiveness is based on a "recognition of common, flawed humanity" (Taylor 2007, 709). Thomas Merton shows in his introduction to a selection of texts on nonviolence from Mahatma Gandhi how strongly this insight is part of the Christian tradition by referring to the church fathers and to Thomas Aquinas's reflections on mercy. Humanity's situation is "a common relationship in a common complex of sins" (Merton 2007, 23). Realizing this situation enables us to forgive nonviolently without being forced to wipe out all sinners, setting ourselves completely apart from them. Taylor's insight that forgiveness depends on the recognition of our own faults refers indirectly to the concept of original sin that despite its many abuses and distortions throughout history helps us to overcome attempts to blame all evil on the other by adopting a violent moralism typical of crusaders (Taylor 2007, 651–53, 698, 709). This liberating dimension of original sin is also highlighted in Girard's interpretation of William Shakespeare's *Winter's Tale* that refers to humanity's inclination to purify oneself at the expense of scapegoats (Girard 1991, 284–87). Girard, furthermore, again and again emphasized strongly the conversion of the apostles Peter and Paul in this regard (Girard 1986, 149–64; 2014, 103–4; 2001, 19–20, 190–91). It is especially the story of Peter's denial that shows how much the overcoming of one's own inclination to scapegoating is the precondition to side with the victim and forgive the perpetrators. That the Gospel authors depict Peter's failure in such painstaking detail with the intention of preserving it for posterity belongs to one of the more outstanding aspects of biblical revelation. In stark contrast to the mythical perspective, we find a text that does not place the blame on others, but rather focuses in on man's own weakness and inexorable entanglement in conflict. This conversion, however, is not achieved through Peter's own moral strength and power but is the result of grace. It is the work of the Holy Spirit, especially Peter's recognition of the resurrected Christ.

Talking about original sin, grace, the Holy Ghost, and Jesus's Resurrection seems to suggest that we now finally have arrived at a point where we no longer can find any common ground between this important Christian legacy and Islam. Such a conclusion, however, is not really true because it is superficially seeking difference where we still can find similarities. Of course, Islam does not share a concept of original sin with Christianity. But it is also aware how much human beings are prone to sin (Platti 2008, 140). To illustrate this claim we can again turn to the Qur'anic story of Joseph. In it we find a Joseph who does not boast to be innocent and morally capable to resist all temptations by himself but a humble prophet who knows his weaknesses and also how strongly he relies on being helped by God: "Nor do I absolve my own self (of blame): the (human) soul is certainly prone to evil, unless my Lord do bestow His Mercy: but surely my Lord is Oft-forgiving, Most Merciful" (sura 12:53).[14] The example of Joseph shows us how much forgiveness relies on being humbly aware of our own inclination toward evil.[15] And it is not only Joseph with whom we can identify in this regard. Also the story of his brothers is not told to strengthen our own righteousness but to recognize in them our own weakness. At least the Persian Sufi poet Attar of Nishapur writing in the twelfth century read this story in such a way:

> These brothers who had come to beg for bread
> Stood speechless, faint with apprehensive dread:
> When they gave Joseph for the merchant's gold,
> It was themselves, and all the world, they sold—
> And when they threw their brother in that well,
> They threw themselves in the abyss of hell.
> Whoever hears these words and cannot find
> How they apply to him is truly blind. (Attar 1984, 139)

This insight that we human beings are never completely free from entanglements in the common complex of sins applies also toward the relationship between the Abrahamic revolution and archaic religion. The more we think we can completely break free from the bloody past the more we are in danger to increase our dependency on scapegoating. According to Taylor, the "recreation of scapegoating violence both in Christendom . . . and in the modern secular world" results from attempts of reform that try to break entirely with the past: "It is precisely these claims fully to supersede the problematic past which blinds us to the ways in which we are repeating some of its horrors in our own way" (Taylor 2007, 772). Girard's book on Clausewitz is fully aware of this danger and therefore, in probably the most important chapter of this book, he follows Friedrich Hölderlin's insight that there is not only a "fundamental discontinuity" but also a "continuity between the Passion and archaic religion" (Girard 2010, xv; cf. 129). Whereas the earlier Girard only emphasized the fundamental difference between Dionysus and the Crucified in reversing Nietzsche, the mature Girard complements this important insight with Hölderlin's emphasis on the connection between Dionysus and Christ—"you are the brother also of Evius". That does not, however, hide the truth that "Dionysus is violence and Christ is peace" (Girard 2010, 127, 130). There is always the possibility of either slowly transforming the archaic world toward the perspective of the Kingdom of God or of cutting short a long and difficult path by violently eradicating the archaic past. Modern terrorism and many types of fundamentalism—including secular forms—represent attitudes that want to break completely free from the past. We are, however, in need of transformative attitudes that are ready to deal with our own involvement in violence and search for a common attempt to overcome it.

If there is a temptation that possibly accompanies Islam, it is not so much a return of the archaic sacred but rather a tendency of breaking completely away from it.[16] The de-dramatization of the biblical stories in the Qur'an possibly contributes to a puritanical reformist temptation typical of our modern world that tends to overlook all remaining continuities between the archaic past and the Abrahamic tradition.[17] Also violent Islamism has to be understood as a primarily modern phenomenon and not so much as an offspring of Islam itself. Modern jihadism is a modern phenomenon that lacks a proper connection to the tradition of Islam (Lumbard 2009).

We can find a tendency toward a too strong separation between archaic religion and the Bible also in the early stage of Girard's unfolding of mimetic theory. Girard, however, has justly turned to a broader more "catholic" approach—in the best sense of the word catholic—in recent years. Girard emphasizes today that there is both "a break and a continuity between the archaic, sacrificial religions and the biblical revelation" (Girard 2008, 218).

To overlook this continuity remains connected to the false and dangerous assumption that we are "by nature strangers to violence" (218). We know we are not and we know also how much we are in need of repentance. Such a more self-critical attitude may allow us to come to a deeper understanding of the Abrahamic revolution with all its potentials and temptations.

NOTES

1. On the term "revolution" see Girard's remark that the "small evangelic minority" that claimed Jesus as an innocent victim has set in motion "the greatest cultural revolution in history" and Taylor's discussion of the "Axial Revolution" (Girard 2011, 76; Taylor 2011, 367–79).
2. The quotations from the Qur'an are taken from Ali 2008.
3. Genesis 22:2: "He said, 'Take your son, your only son Isaac, whom you love, and go to the land of Moriah, and offer him there as a burnt offering on one of the mountains that I shall show you.'" Sura 37:102: "Then, when (the son) reached (the age of) (serious) work with him, he said: 'O my son! I see in vision that I offer thee in sacrifice: Now see what is thy view!' (The son) said: 'O my father! Do as thou art commanded: thou will find me, if God so wills one practicing Patience and Constancy!'"
4. Genesis 22:7–8. "Isaac said to his father Abraham, 'Father!' And he said, 'Here I am, my son.' He said, 'The fire and the wood are here, but where is the lamb for a burnt offering?' Abraham said, 'God himself will provide the lamb for a burnt offering, my son.' So the two of them walked on together."
5. Tariq Ramadan claims that the Qur'an is superior to the biblical account of the akedah that is "tragic" and full of "tension" (Ramadan 2008, 211–13).
6. Girard too, emphasizes the fact that compared to the akedah the prophetic texts go a step further telling us that even animal sacrifices no longer work (cf. Psalm 40). The Bible aims at the "end of the sacrificial order in its entirety" and will reach this goal through the "consenting victim who is Jesus Christ" (Girard 2008b, 203).
7. The story of Joseph is, of course, also a powerful story to illustrate how mimetic rivalry causes violence between human beings. The Hebrew Bible talks about the envious brothers of Joseph: "His brothers were jealous of him" (Genesis 37:11). In the Qur'anic version we find several metaphors that point toward mimetic rivalry. A first image is "Satan"—a typical mimetic figure—who "had sown enmity between me and my brothers" (sura 12:100; cf. 12:5). A second image is a wolf that is mentioned by Joseph's brothers as the cause of his apparent death: "O our father! We went racing with one another, and left Joseph with our things; and the wolf devoured him" (sura 12:17). It was the Persian Sufi mystic Rumi in the thirteenth century who understood the mimetic meaning of this reference to the wolf. According to Rumi, "envy is like a huge wolf in disguise": "The outward wolf did not harm his [Jacob's] fine son; / The wolf of jealousy surpassed that one: / This wolf attacked instead in that wolf's place, / With the excuse: '*We had gone out to race.*' / A thousand wolves don't know such trickery; / This wolf will be disgraced eventually: / Without a doubt the envious will transform / On Judgment Day into a vile wolf's form." (Rumi 2007, 83, lines 1411, 1413–16) The image of a race between the brothers also strongly points toward mimetic rivalry.
8. Genesis 39:7 "And after a time his master's wife cast her eyes on Joseph and said, 'Lie with me.'"

9. In a more recent interview Girard claims that the Gospels surpass the story of Joseph: "Christ defines himself as the Son of God, who accepts death in order to reveal to mankind what they are doing. I do not think there is anything equivalent anywhere, even in the Bible. So, if it is only in the Gospel, we can be sure that there is something quite special about the New Testament that goes even beyond the story of Joseph. The story of Joseph is splendid in the same sense. Joseph is repeatedly scapegoated, and each time his innocence is revealed. And he never really scapegoats his brothers in return. The 'deconstruction' of scapegoating is the quintessence of the whole Bible from Genesis to the Gospels. If you have the Joseph story and the Gospels as a pointcounterpoint, you have the whole Bible, its whole truth, its whole beauty. And, the fact that this truth, present in the Old Testament, is not quite as fully expressed means to me that Jesus must be the perfect revelation" (Girard and Palaver 2008, 63).

10. Genesis 44:33: "Please let your servant remain as a slave to my lord in place of the boy." In the Bible it is this readiness of Judah to step in for his brother that moves Joseph so much that he reveals himself to his brothers: "Then Joseph could no longer control himself before all those who stood by him, and he cried out, 'Send everyone away from me.' So no one stayed with him when Joseph made himself known to his brothers. And he wept so loudly that the Egyptians heard it, and the household of Pharaoh heard it. Joseph said to his brothers, 'I am Joseph. Is my father still alive?' But his brothers could not answer him, so dismayed were they at his presence. Then Joseph said to his brothers, 'Come closer to me.' And they came closer. He said, 'I am your brother, Joseph, whom you sold into Egypt. And now do not be distressed, or angry with yourselves, because you sold me here; for God sent me before you to preserve life'" (Genesis 45:1–5).

11. Leo Lefebure overlooks this part of the story of Joseph in his criticism of Girard's contrasting of the biblical revelation with other religions. According to Lefebure, the Egyptian *Tale of the Two Brothers* anticipates the rehabilitation of the scapegoat in the story of Joseph: "The Egyptian tales anticipates point by point Girard's analysis of rivalry, incest, and violence; but it directly contradicts Girard's claim that only biblical revelation takes the side of the victim. The Egyptian tale had vindicated the scapegoat long before the birth of Israel" (Lefebure 2000, 31). Lefebure, however, does not narrate the conclusion of the Egyptian story that ends with the killing of the woman that seduced the younger brother. "From this point on the Bible and the Egyptian stories diverge considerably. In the Egyptian tale, the two brothers confront each other and the younger swears his innocence, finally cutting off his own phallus and throwing it to a fish. This drastic measure convinces the elder brother and he returns home where he kills his wife and throws her body to the dogs" (Crook 2005b, 77).

12. According the account in the book of Genesis it was Jacob who asked Joseph to forgive his brothers: "Realizing that their father was dead, Joseph's brothers said, 'What if Joseph still bears a grudge against us and pays us back in full for all the wrong that we did to him?' So they approached Joseph, saying, 'Your father gave this instruction before he died, "Say to Joseph: I beg you, forgive the crime of your brothers and the wrong they did in harming you." Now therefore please forgive the crime of the servants of the God of your father.' Joseph wept when they spoke to him" (Genesis 50:15–17).

13. The Persian Sufi poet Attar, however, clearly expresses the despair of Jacob that he suffered through the loss of Joseph (Attar 1984, 50–51).

14. According to Abdullah Yusuf Ali it is not Joseph who blames himself with these words but Potiphar's wife Zulaikhá (Ali 2008, 570–71). To exempt Joseph in this way, however, may take away an important insight of the Qur'an, making the story less dramatic and less realistic. Most translators and commentators attribute these words to Joseph. It is not necessary to keep a prophet free from faults, temptations, and the need for forgiveness. Even Muhammad has to

ask for forgiveness for his faults: "Patiently, then, persevere: for the Promise of Allah is true: and ask forgiveness for thy fault, and celebrate the Praises of thy Lord in the evening and in the morning" (sura 40:55). Abdullah Yusuf Ali does not exempt Muhammad from being a sinner in his comment to this verse: "Every mortal according to his nature and degree of spiritual enlightenment falls short of the perfect standard of God (16.61), and should therefore ask God for forgiveness" (Ali 2008, 1277). I am grateful to Adam Ericksen for referring me to this verse.

15. We can find a somewhat similar awareness of our need to be helped by God in the writings of Mahatma Gandhi: "If one has that pride and egoism, there is no non-violence. Non-violence is impossible without humility. My own experience is that whenever I have acted non-violently I have been led to it and sustained in it by the higher promptings of an unseen power. Through my own will I should have miserably failed" (Merton 2007, 50).

16. One can find Asian types of Islam resulting from an inculturation that slowly transformed older religions leading to a type of Islam that is not at all prone to violence or aggression. And there are also variants of Islam puritanically aiming at the eradication of the religious past. What we face today, for instance, in Pakistan is a bloody battle of radical reformers who fight with "puritanical severity" against those types of Islam that, as a result of its inculturation, remained closer to the indigenous religions. The prize-winning historian and travel writer William Dalrymple describes the war of iconoclastic Taliban against Sufi shrines in Pakistan as a type of aggressive Puritanism in his marvelous narration "The Red Fairy": "Here in the deserts of Sindh it seems that Sufi Islam, and the deeply rooted cult of the saints, with all its borrowings from the indigenous religious traditions of the area, may yet be able to act as a powerful home-grown resistance movement to the Wahhabis and their jihadi intolerance of all other faiths" (Dalrymple 2009, 141).

17. We should, however, be aware that there exists also the opposite danger, that is, to overlook the difference between archaic religion and the Abrahamic legacy. According to Girard, "sacrificial Christianity" is an example in this direction (Girard 1987, 224).

WORKS CITED

Ali, Abdullah Yusuf. 2008. *The Holy Qur'an: Text, Translation and Commentary*. Elmhurst, NY: Tahrike Tarsile Quran.

Attar, Farid ud-Din. 1984. *The Conference of the Birds*. Translated by A. Darabandi and D. Davis. Harmondsworth: Penguin.

Ben Nabi, Malik. 1983. *The Qu'ranic Phenomenon: An Attempt at a Theory of Understanding the Holy Koran*. Translated by A. b. Kirkari. Indianapolis: American Trust Publications.

Canetti, Elias. 1984. *Crowds and Power*. Translated by C. Stewart. New York: Farrar Straus Giroux.

Chilton, Bruce. 2008. *Abraham's Curse: Child Sacrifice in the Legacies of the West*. New York: Doubleday.

Crook, Jay R. 2005a. *The Bible: An Islamic Perspective; Abraham*. Chicago: ABC International Group.

———. 2005b. *The Bible: An Islamic Perspective; Jacob and Joseph*. Chicago: ABC International Group.

Dalrymple, William. 2009. *Nine Lives: In Search of the Sacred in Modern India*. London: Bloomsbury.

Derrida, Jacques. 2001. *On Cosmopolitanism and Forgiveness*. Translated by M. Dooley and M. Hughes. London: Routledge.

Girard, René. 1977. *Violence and the Sacred*. Translated by Patrick Gregory. Baltimore: Johns Hopkins University Press.

———. 1986. *The Scapegoat*. Translated by Yvonne Freccero. Baltimore: Johns Hopkins University Press.

———. 1987. *Things Hidden since the Foundation of the World*. Research undertaken in collaboration with with J.-M. Oughourlian and G. Lefort. Translated by Stephen Bann and Michael Metteer. Stanford, CA: Stanford University Press.

———. 1991. *A Theater of Envy: William Shakespeare*. Oxford: Oxford University Press.

———. 2001. *I See Satan Fall Like Lightning*. Translated by J. G. Williams. Maryknoll, NY: Orbis.

———. 2004. *Oedipus Unbound: Selected Writings on Rivalry and Desire*. Stanford, CA: Stanford University Press.

———. 2008. *Evolution and Conversion: Dialogues on the Origin of Culture with Pierpaolo Antonello and João Cezar de Castro Rocha*. London: Continuum.

———. 2010. *Battling to the End: Conversations with Benoît Chantre*. Translated by Mary Baker. East Lansing: Michigan State University Press.

———. 2011. *Sacrifice*. Translated by Matthew Pattillo and David Dawson. East Lansing: Michigan State University Press.

———. 2014. *When These Things Begin: Conversations with Michel Treguer*. Translated by Trevor Cribben Merrill. East Lansing: Michigan State University Press.

Girard, René, and Wolfgang Palaver. 2008. "The Bloody Skin of the Victim." In *The New Visibility of Religion: Studies in Religion and Cultural Hermeneutics*, edited by Michael Hoelzl and Graham Ward, 59–67. London: Continuum.

Girard, René, and Henri Tincq. 2002. "What Is Happening Today Is Mimetic Rivalry on a Global Scale." Translated by Thomas C. Hilde.*South Central Review* 19, nos. 2–3: 22–27.

Gnilka, Joachim. 2007. *Die Nazarener und der Koran: Eine Spurensuche*. Freiburg im Breisgau: Herder.

Golsan, Richard J. 1993. *René Girard and Myth: An Introduction*. New York: Garland.

Goodhart, Sandor. 1996. *Sacrificing Commentary: Reading the End of Literature*. Baltimore: Johns Hopkins University Press.

Guillaume, Alfred, ed. 2006. *The Life of Muhammad: A Translation of Ishaq's Sirat Rasul Allah*. Oxford: Oxford University Press.

Hoffman, Bruce. 1998. *Inside Terrorism*. London: Gollancz.

Izutsu, Toshihiko. 1984. *Sufism and Taoism: A Comparative Study of Key Philosophical Concepts*. Berkeley: University of California Press.

Juergensmeyer, Mark. 2001. *Terror in the Mind of God: The Global Rise of Religious Violence*. Berkeley: University of California Press.

Körner, Felix. 2008. *Kirche im Angesicht des Islam: Theologie des interreligiösen Zeugnisses*. Stuttgart: Kohlhammer.

Lefebure, Leo D. 2000. *Revelation, the Religions, and Violence*. Maryknoll, NY: Orbis.

Lings, Martin. 2006. *Muhammad: His Life Based on the Earliest Sources*. Rochester, VT: Inner Traditions.

Lumbard, Joseph E. B., ed. 2009. *Islam, Fundamentalism, and the Betrayal of Tradition: Essays by Western Muslim Scholars*. Bloomington, IN: World Wisdom.

Mann, Thomas. 1996. *Essays*. Vol. 5, *Deutschland und die Deutschen 1938–1945*. Frankfurt am Main: Fischer Taschenbuch Verlag.

———. 2008. *Thomas Mann's Addresses Delivered at the Library of Congress, 1942–1949*. Rockville, MD: Wildside Press.

Merton, Thomas, ed. 2007. *Gandhi on Non-Violence: Selected Texts from Mohandas K. Gandhi's Non-Violence in Peace and War*. New York: New Directions Paperbook.

Neuwirth, Angelika. 2010. *Der Koran als Text der Spätantike: Ein europäischer Zugang*. Berlin: Verlag der Weltreligionen.

Palaver, Wolfgang. 2008. "The Ambiguous Cachet of Victimhood: On Violence and Monotheism." In *The New Visibility of Religion: Studies in Religion and Cultural Hermeneutics*, edited by Michael Hoelzl and Graham Ward, 68–87. London: Continuum.

———. 2010a. "The Ambiguous Cachet of Victimhood: Elias Canetti's 'Religions of Lament' and Abrahamic Monotheism." *Forum Bosnae* 49:19–31.

———. 2010b. "Religion und Gewalt: René Girards und Charles Taylors komplementäre Beiträge zu einer zeitgemäßen Theorie." In *Kommunitarismus und Religion*, edited by M. Kühnlein, 319–28. Berlin: Akademie Verlag.

Platti, Emilio. 2008. *Islam, Friend or Foe?* Translated by B. Doyle. Leuven: Peeters.

Ramadan, Tariq. 2008. *Islam, the West and the Challenges of Modernity*. Translated by S. Amghar. Leicester: Islamic Foundation.

Richardson, Louise. 2006. *What Terrorists Want: Understanding the Terrorist Threat*. London: John Murray.

Richter-Bernburg, Lutz. 2007. "Göttliche gegen menschliche Gerechtigkeit: Abrahams Opferwilligkeit in der islamischen Tradition." In *Opfere deinen Sohn! Das "Isaak-Opfer" in Judentum, Christentum und Islam*, edited by B. Greiner, B. Janowski and H. Lichtenberger, 243–55. Tübingen: Francke.

Rumi, Jalal al-Din. 2007. *The Masnavi. Book Two*. Translated by J. Mojaddedi. Oxford: Oxford University Press.

Schwager, Raymund. 1999. *Jesus in the Drama of Salvation: Toward a Biblical Doctrine of Redemption*. Translated by J. G. Williams and P. Haddon. New York: Crossroad.

Serres, Michel. 2009. "Receiving René Girard into the Académie Française." In *For René Girard: Essays in Friendship and in Truth*, edited by Sandor Goodhart et al., 1–17. East Lansing: Michigan State University Press.

Shah-Kazemi, Reza. 2006. "Jesus in the Qur'an: Selfhood and Compassion—An Akbari Perspective." In *Sufism: Love & Wisdom*, edited by J.-L. Michon and R. Gaetani, 217–35. Bloomington, IN: World Wisdom.

———. 2007. *My Mercy Encompasses All: The Koran's Teachings on Compassion, Peace & Love*. Emeryville, CA: Shoemaker & Hoard.

———. 2009. "From the Spirituality of *Jihād* to the Ideology of Jihadism." In Lumbard, *Islam, Fundamentalism, and the Betrayal of Tradition*, 119–48.

Taylor, Charles. 2004. "Notes on the Sources of Violence: Perennial and Modern." In *Beyond Violence:*

Religious Sources for Social Transformation in Judaism, Christianity and Islam, edited by J. L. Heft, 15–42. Ashland: Fordham University Press.

———. 2007. *A Secular Age*. Cambridge, MA: Belknap Press.

———. 2011. *Dilemmas and Connections: Selected Essays*. Cambridge, MA: Belknap Press.

Williams, James G. 1991. *The Bible, Violence, and the Sacred: Liberation from the Myth of Sanctioned Violence*. San Francisco: HarperSanFrancisco.

———. 1994. "'Steadfast Love and Not Sacrifice': A Nonsacrificial Reading of the Hebrew Scriptures." In *Curing Violence*, edited by M. I. Wallace and T. H. Smith, 71–99. Sonoma: Polebridge Press.

The "Hellenic" Rationality of Interreligious Dialogue: René Girard, Simone Weil, and Pope Benedict XVI

Ann Astell

Simone Weil's *The Need for Roots* (*L'Enracinement*), written during the last months of her life (1909–43) and with her dying strength, is a fitting companion piece to *Battling to the End* (*Achever Clausewitz*), the last book by René Girard (b. 1923). Compatriots, Weil and Girard each retell the long story of French history from the Middle Ages, beginning in medias res and dwelling upon many of the same modern turning points—1789, 1815, 1914, 1940. Girard explicitly links his own childhood memories of the war years with the Free French radio broadcasts from London and the names of Maurice Schumann and Simone Weil.[1] Elsewhere Girard has openly acknowledged Weil's influence upon him from the start of his career.[2] Known to have exerted a strong influence upon Pope John XXIII and Pope Paul VI,[3] and, through them, upon *Nostra aetate*, Vatican Council II's Declaration on the Relationship of the Church to Non-Christian Religions,[4] Weil's thought has also contributed to Pope Benedict's idea of a Christian Europe.[5] (His published 2004 correspondence with Marcello Pera, president of the Italian Senate, on the subject of Europe's Christian identity is entitled *Without Roots*—an obvious allusion to Weil's work.)[6]

By triangulating Pope Benedict's famous 2006 Regensburg Lecture, "Faith, Reason, and the University—Memories and Reflections,"[7] with *The*

Need for Roots and *Battling to the End*, I hope to underscore the meaning of the "Hellenic" for Pope Benedict, Weil, and Girard as a necessary condition for the Christian reading of the sacred texts of the world religions. In their Christian interpretations of non-Christian scriptures, Weil and Girard perform a Hellenic allegoresis that is geared toward the refusal of violence and the honoring of religious truth in its various revelations. Interpreting non-Christian texts in a Christian way, they set an example of interreligious hermeneutics that would, mutatis mutandi, allow non-Christians to discover the gospel in their own scriptures, and vice versa, to find their own scriptures in the Gospels. Strikingly, Weil, Girard, and Pope Benedict XVI all see the "Hellenic" dialogue between religion and science as crucial to the dialogue between and among the world religions.

Pope Benedict XVI's Diagnosis of Dehellenization

What is meant, then, by the word "Hellenic" in this discussion? Narrowly defined, the word has often been set in opposition both to the "Hebraic" and to the authentically Christian,[8] but, as Michel Gitton points out, the historical record of cultural contact (dating back at least to Alexander the Great's conquest of Palestine in the fourth century BC) is such that "any juxtaposition of a pure Hellenism and a Palestinian Judeo-Christianity that was itself allegedly intact and free from outside influence is bound to produce misinterpretation."[9] In his influential 1967 essay, "Jerusalem and Athens: Some Preliminary Reflections," Jewish philosopher Leo Strauss (1899–1973) argues for a necessary, historical, and cultural relationship between the two: "Western man became what he is and is what he is through the coming together of Biblical faith and Greek thought."[10] For his part, in the Regensburg Lecture, Pope Benedict insists: "I believe that here [namely, in the 'conviction that acting unreasonably contradicts God's nature'] we can see the profound harmony between what is Greek in the best sense of the word and the Biblical understanding of faith in God" (*RL* 134–35, par. 17).

To prove his point, Benedict cites the echo of Genesis 1:1 in the first verse of the Gospel according to St. John, "In the beginning was the Word," the Logos, "and the Word was with God, and the Word was God" (1:1). This "encounter between the Biblical message and Greek thought did not happen by chance," Benedict avers, recalling that St. Paul found the "roads to Asia barred and in a dream saw a Macedonian man plead with him, 'Come over to Macedonia and help us!'" (*RL* 135, par. 19; Acts 16:6–10). The pope interprets this dream-vision as "a 'distillation' of the intrinsic necessity of a rapprochement between Biblical faith and Greek inquiry" (*RL* 135, par. 19), a "rapprochement" that had, "in point of fact, . . . [already] been going on for some time" (*RL* 135, par. 20), as the Hebrew scriptures themselves, especially the Wisdom literature and the later prophets, bear witness. Emphasizing the providential character of "this inner rapprochement between Biblical faith and Greek philosophical inquiry," Benedict calls it "an event of decisive importance not only from the standpoint of the history of religions, but also from that of world history" (*RL* 138, par. 29), adding, "this convergence, with the subsequent addition of the Roman heritage, created Europe and remains the foundation of what can rightly be called Europe" (*RL* 138, par. 30).

In the Regensburg Lecture, the "Hellenic," positively understood, is an adjective more than it is a noun. Its meaning is never stated outright, but emerges contextually as Benedict meditates on human reason and language in its relationship to the divine Logos, on human cooperation with the goodness and wisdom of the divine plan, and on the analogy between the rational powers of the creature and those of the creator, in whose image and likeness humankind has been created. Its positive meaning emerges also contrastively, as Benedict outlines the process of the dehellenization of Christianity in three interconnected stages.

In the first of these, according to Benedict, the Protestant reformers of the sixteenth century, taking *sola scriptura* as their motto, sought to distinguish between the purity of biblical faith and the philosophically Greek, conceptual language of the dogmatic formulations of the patristic and medieval periods. Reacting alike against an Aristotelian scholasticism and a mystical Christian Platonism, they drove a wedge between faith and reason that would widen over time in ways unforeseen and unintended by them. In the second stage, associated with the technological developments in science and with the liberal theology of the nineteenth and twentieth centuries, both faith and reason—cut off from each other—were increasingly reduced. As Benedict describes the process, "reason," on the one hand, narrowed its province—namely, to the empirically provable and technologically practical, a realm from which God, by definition, is excluded. Indeed, "questions of religion and ethics no longer concern" a "reason so reduced" (*RL* 143, par. 49). The Jesus of "faith," on the one hand, became at this second stage the shining example of a properly human, commonsensical morality, rather than the Incarnate Word, while the Bible became, not the inspired Word of God, but the scientific object of the formal-critical method. At a third stage of dehellenization, according to the pontiff, other "Christianities" are imagined in the global economy whose inculturated forms would take their beginning from a Jesus such as never existed historically in an already Hellenized Palestine. "This thesis is not only false; it is coarse and lacking in precision," Benedict asserts, noting: "The New Testament was written in Greek and bears the imprint of the Greek spirit, which had already come to maturity as the Old Testament developed" (*RL* 143–44, par. 52). The pope readily admits that "there are elements in the evolution of the early Church which do not have to be integrated into all cultures," but he insists: "the fundamental decisions made about the relationship between faith and the use of human reason are part of the faith itself" (*RL* 144, par. 53).

After analyzing the process and the cultural effect of the historical dehellenization of Christian Europe, Pope Benedict, at the conclusion of his Regensburg Lecture, calls upon the scientific community to broaden its conception of reason and its application, out of fidelity to the genuine "scientific ethos," which is "the will to be obedient to the truth" (*RL* 144, par. 55), and in honest recognition of its own unanswered questions, which point "beyond [modern science] itself and beyond the possibilities of its methodology" toward religious faith and, in particular, toward "theology, as inquiry into the rationality of faith" (*RL* 145, par. 59, 57). The West, he concludes, cannot afford to avoid "the questions which underlie its rationality" and must summon "the courage to engage the whole breadth of reason" (*RL* 146, par. 62), in the context of which (and only there) "the dialogue of cultures"—interreligious, as well as religious and scientific—can take place (*RL* 146, par. 63).

Historically important for the responses it elicited from the worldwide Muslim community—both the violent public protests that erupted in September 2006, and the thoughtful, constructive reply given to the pope by 138 Muslim scholars in their open letter of October 11, 2007, titled *A Common Word between Us and You*—the Regensburg Lecture remains enigmatic to interpreters.[11] They puzzle over Benedict's motive in choosing to quote in it, from an obscure medieval source, in speech dated post-9/11, the "brusque" challenge that the fourteenth-century Byzantine emperor Manuel II Paleologus had posed to his Persian interlocutor: "Show me just what Mohammed brought that was new, and there you will find things only evil and inhuman, such as his command to spread by the sword the faith he preached."[12] They struggle, too, to see a connection between the pope's two urgent invitations issued in the lecture: the first, calling for interreligious and ecumenical dialogue; the second, for a vital scientific and religious exchange. What can the cited medieval dialogue possibly have in common with these contemporary conversations? And how does the church's dialogue with science and scientists relate to interreligious concerns?

Responding to the Regensburg Lecture: The "Hellenic" in the Thought of Weil and Girard

In this essay I read the last writings of Simone Weil and of René Girard as a response (in Weil's case, an anachronistic one) to the plea of Pope Benedict XVI for the sort of "Hellenic," interreligious dialogue that can and should take place, first and foremost, in and through Europe, a continent whose cultural roots are and remain Christian. Girard explicitly praises the pope's 2006 Regensburg Lecture in *Battling to the End*. There can be no doubt that Simone Weil, the French Jewish philosopher and mystic, would also have praised it. Her final writings from wartime London, published posthumously under the title *The Need for Roots*, bear an uncanny resemblance to the pope's own analysis of the effects of the dehellenization of Europe, on the one hand, and to Girard's account of mimetic desire, on the other.

Girard has often and self-consciously characterized his mimetic theory as a scientific hypothesis, subject to empirical testing, but also as a theory precisely of religion and of culture as shaped by religion—its prohibitions, rituals, and mythic narratives. Unlike most cultural anthropologists, moreover, he has recognized and encouraged others to pursue the specifically theological questions raised by his theory, making the dialogues between science and faith, and those between the social science and literature, intrinsic to the dynamic refinement of mimetic theory through its application across scholarly disciplines.[13] Given his own broad understanding of rationality (as opposed to the narrower view espoused by the Enlightenment), it is not surprising that he responds favorably to the Regensburg Lecture in *Battling to the End*. Indeed, he identifies that lecture's clarion call for "a certain kind of reasoning" with the aim of his own mimetic theory: "The goal of mimetic theory is to bring this rationality to the forefront" (*BTE* 197).

Acknowledging that critics of the Regensburg Lecture have seen it as a "declaration of war against Islam and Protestants," Girard expresses puzzlement about this: "I see it instead as first a plea for reason" (*BTE* 176). Later in the book, Girard devotes an entire section to a discussion of the Regensburg controversy. There he writes: "The pope is alerting us to the fact that Greek reason is disappearing. . . . Rationalism's disdain of religion not only turns reason into a religion, but [also] makes for a corrupted religion" (*BTE* 207). Seeing Christianity as a third way between rationalism, on the one hand, and fideism, on the other, Girard identifies his own stance with the pope's in urgent opposition to the sacrificial "'pathologies' of religion and reason" that occur when the two become completely separated, one from the other (*BTE* 209).[14] For Girard, the concern voiced by the pope over a dehellenization of Christianity can already be heard, albeit in a complex and self-contradictory way, in the poetry of Friedrich Hölderlin (1770–1843): "Hölderlin is much less haunted by Greece than we have been led to believe. I see him instead as frightened by the return to paganism that infused the classicism of his time" (*BTE* 121).

As this last sentence shows, Girard's own attitude toward Hellenism frequently betrays a similar distrust. Girard's vigorous defense of Greek reason in *Battling to the End* has therefore surprised some of his friends and students (Robert Hamerton-Kelly, for example), who point to Girard's own strongly drawn distinction in *Things Hidden since the Foundation of the World* (*Des choses cachées depuis la fondation du monde*, 1978) between "the Johannine Logos," which is "foreign to any kind of violence," and the "Heraclitean Logos, the Logos of expulsion, the Logos of violence, which, if it is not recognized, can provide the foundation of a culture."[15] In this important theoretical work, Girard asserts that "the first centuries of Christianity betrayed a great mistrust for Greek thought" (*THSFW* 263), that the Greek philosophical contribution to Christian theology was "only admitted very gradually" (*THSFW* 263), and that that Greek philosophical element—epitomized in modern times in the Hellenism of G. W. F. Hegel, Friedrich

Nietzsche, and Martin Heidegger—has ultimately dared to articulate a rival logic that would usurp and displace the Judeo-Christian.

What are we to make of this apparent self-contradiction on the part of Girard? His account in *Things Hidden* of the historical relationship between nascent Christianity and Hellenism is admittedly less positive than Pope Benedict's in the Regensburg Lecture (although the pope's address, it must be noted, also refers explicitly to the persecution of Christians by Hellenistic rulers and to "the customs and idolatrous cult of the Greeks," from which Jews and Christians alike distanced themselves) (*RL* 136, par. 22). Reading closely, however, one can easily see that Girard's attitude toward Greek thought and culture, even in *Things Hidden*, is complex (as is the pope's in his address at Regensburg).[16] Understood in proper context, things "Greek" also have a high value for Girard. What is crucial for Girard, Benedict, and Weil alike is that philosophy be understood "in the light of religion" (*THSFW* 15), and not the reverse. For his part, Girard seeks to find a middle course between two possible errors: that of many "Christian thinkers" who "regard Greek philosophers as unconscious [Christian] theologians" (and thus run the risk of reducing Jesus to a superior sage) and that of "post-Christians," who find an originally Greek philosophical "Logos" superior to its belated Christian imitation—both of which camps miss the wisdom of Christ's cross, which is "scandalous to Jews and a folly to the Greeks" (cf. 1 Corinthians 1:22–23) (*THSFW* 264). This rational middle path between extremes, spelled out in *Things Hidden*, is arguably the same middle path between "rationalism" and "fideism" to which he adheres in *Battling to the End*. For Girard, a cruciform rationality alone can make sense of, endure, and ultimately triumph over the violent order of things.

For Simone Weil, too (as Palle Yourgrau puts it), "the true intersection, the centre of the cross, lies where the road from Athens meets the one from Jerusalem."[17] In *The Need for Roots*, written in London for the Free French in the midst of World War II, Weil similarly argues in defense both of a broad, Hellenic rationality, capable of combining scientific inquiry differentially with religious faith, and of a Judeo-Christian moral identity with the afflicted. Envisioning France in the light of an eventual Allied victory, *The Need for Roots* makes a series of social, economic, and educational recommendations, based not on human rights (the guiding idea of the French Revolution), but rather on human needs—material and spiritual—and the moral and societal obligations entailed by them. The question of dehellenization arises, for Weil, precisely in the context of education, scientific and religious. Like Pope Benedict and René Girard, Weil sees a broadly defined rationality and the ability to draw analogies as crucial to the dialogues between science and religion, on the one hand, and between and among the world religions, past and present, on the other.

Weil is insistent that participants in any meaningful dialogue must be rooted in a given culture as a primary point of orientation. "Uprootedness breeds idolatry," she writes, because "relations being cut, each thing is looked upon as an end in itself" (*NFR* 69). Noting the violent, socially and psychologically uprooting results of European colonization, as it has affected the colonized and the colonizers alike, and deploring the irretrievable loss of a cultural past that is no longer the content of a living tradition, Weil calls for the growing again of local roots in postwar Europe as the firm basis for hospitality and global exchange: intercultural, interreligious, and economic. In the case of France, its "genius," she writes, "is a Christian and Hellenic genius" (*NFR* 236). Girard concurs: "There is an essential Catholicism in European culture" (*BTE* 176). The "convergence" of the Hebraic and the Hellenic in Christianity, he writes, "created Europe and remains the foundation of what can rightly be called Europe" (*BTE* 208).

Within a French European setting, Weil urges, the Bible and Christian thought should find an appropriate place in the public schools, as a protection against a narrowing of rationality, whether in a purely secular, "laical" setting or in a marginalized, "clerical" environment:

> The soul of a child, as it reaches out toward understanding, has need of the treasures accumulated by the human species through the centuries. We do injury to a child if we bring it up in a narrow Christianity, which prevents it from ever becoming capable of perceiving that there are treasures of purest gold to be found in non-Christian civilizations. Laical education does an even greater injury to children. It covers up these treasures, and those of Christianity as well. (*NFR* 91)

"Future professional teachers and schoolmasters should simply be told that religion has at all times and in all countries, save quite recently in certain parts of Europe, played a dominant role in the development of human culture, thought, and civilization," she opines, adding, "being in Europe, when you talk about religion, you should refer primarily to Christianity" (*NFR* 92).

Even as Weil's diagnosis of the dehellenization of Christianity anticipates that of Pope Benedict, so too does her analysis of the dehellenization of science. She points out that, for the Greeks, whose science "was as scientific as our own, if not more so," the study of the cosmos "was not a subject of profane study. The Greeks regarded it as a religious subject" (*NFR* 245). Since "the second half of the Renaissance," however, "the very conception of science has been that of a branch of study whose object is . . . viewed without any relation either to good or evil, but especially without any relation to good. Science only studies the facts as such, and the mathematicians themselves regard mathematical relations simply as facts of the mind. Facts, force, matter, isolated, considered singly, without reference to anything else—there is nothing here that a human mind can love" (*NFR* 254).

For Weil, as for Pope Benedict and Girard, this narrowing of scientific rationality has had enormous consequences. She goes so far as to charge "the modern conception of science" (along with that of history and art) with responsibility "for the monstrous conditions under which we live" (*NFR* 237). Noting the lack of moral concern in the scientific community about technological application (*NFR* 237), the absence of any connection in scientific theory between natural and divine laws,[18] and the idolatry of savants in manufacturing science in order to obtain material and temporal rewards for themselves,[19] she writes: "Scientists . . . are possibly guiltier of Hitler's crimes than Hitler himself" (*NFR* 240).

Not only the scientists themselves are guilty, however. In Weil's analysis, the modern separation of science from religion has placed science increasingly in a position of rivalry with religion, with idolatrous consequences: "So far as the prestige of science is concerned, there are no such people nowadays as unbelievers" (*NFR* 239). Christians, too, may be said to "believe" in science, in its explanatory and salvific powers. According to Weil, "Among [modern] Christians, the absolute incompatibility between the spirit of religion and that of science, to both of which they cling, leaves the soul in a permanent state of secret, unacknowledged uneasiness" (*NFR* 246). Indeed, "the modern phenomenon of irreligion among the population can be explained almost entirely by the incompatibility between science and religion" (*NFR* 247). Citing the inadequacy of the church's pastoral and theological response and its apparent "inferiority complex" vis-à-vis science as a modern institution of knowledge and manufacture (*NFR* 239), Weil concludes: "We are really and truly suffering from the disease of idolatry, and it is so deeply rooted that it takes away from Christians the power to bear witness to the truth" (*NFR* 259). The "remedy" Weil proposes—and here she anticipates Benedict's plea for dialogue in the Regensburg Lecture—"is to bring back again among us the spirit of truth, and to start within religion and science; which implies that the two of them should become reconciled" (*NFR* 261).

She calls upon theologians, in particular, to broaden their doctrine of Divine Providence to include an "impersonal" understanding of it as "the regulating principle of this universe . . . eternal Wisdom, unique, spread across the whole universe in a sovereign network of relations" (*NFR* 263, 285). "The order of the world is to be loved," she writes, "because it is pure obedience to God" (*NFR* 289). She challenges theologians and scientists alike to recognize that the human soul and human spiritual relationships are governed by laws, even as the physical universe is. "The ever greater and greater methodological control, which men have exercised over matter since the sixteenth century, has led them to believe, by way of contrast, that the things of the soul are either arbitrary or else bound up with some form of magic, with the immediate efficacy of intentions and words" (*NFR* 188), she writes, objecting that

> such is not the case. Everything in creation is dependent on method, including the points of intersection between this world and the next. That is what the word *logos* indicates, signifying connection even more than word. The method merely differs according to the different sphere. The higher one goes, the more rigorous and precise it becomes. It would be strange, indeed, if the order of material things were to reflect more of divine wisdom than that of spiritual things. The contrary is true. (*NFR* 188)

Interpreting the *logos*, as she does here, as "signifying connection," Weil certainly refers—as Pope Benedict does in the Regensburg Lecture—to Christ, the Incarnate Word (John 1:1), the "one Mediator" or *metaxu* between heaven and earth (1 Timothy 2:5).[20] There is an analogy in Christ, the Logos, Weil argues, that connects the laws of matter and the scientific method, at one level, to the laws of the soul and the discipline of the spiritual life, at another—so much so that one may discover in the Gospels "a supernatural physics of the human soul" (*NFR* 265). Properly understood, Weil insists, "Scientific investigation is simply a form of religious contemplation" (*NFR* 262).

Lest misunderstanding arise, it must be noted that Weil is no Luddite, imagining a return to premodern science in her quest for a spiritualization of modern science, education, and labor. To the contrary, in *The Need for Roots*, she calls explicitly for advances in technological science, with the aim of producing machinery that would assist people (rather than hinder them) in the enhancement of their humanity, the growing of their "roots" (a metaphor she uses to point to the capacity for spiritually nourishing relationships with places, local traditions, people, and work, physical and intellectual). In this respect, the word of René Girard about Weil can be paraphrased. "She held," writes Girard approvingly, "that even before presenting a 'theory of God,' a *theology*, the Gospels offer a 'theory of man,' an *anthropology*."[21] Drawing lessons from the dehumanizing experience of factory work (she herself having worked on an assembly line in 1934–35) and of war (both the Spanish Civil War and World War II), Weil similarly upheld in the realm of applied science the priority, in theory and practice, of an anthropology, an ethics attentive to the afflicted, the social outcast, and opening upon a mysticism of wonder at the law-bound beauty of the world.

Placing Girard in conversation with Weil, one cannot help but think of his scientific delineation of the mimetic principles governing interpersonal relationships and group dynamics, of his analysis of mediated desire (mediation being one definition of *logos*), of his predilection for the language of mechanism, of his idea of a contagious violence (which, as Marie Cabaud Meaney has shown, parallels in many respects Weil's idea of force),[22] and of his meditations on the scapegoated Johannine Logos. Like Weil, whose search for truth crossed different fields of study (religion, mathematics, physics, politics, education, economics, literature, and language), Girard finds a logical consistency in his mimetic theory that has allowed him and his students to apply it across disciplines (literature, anthropology, sociology, biblical criticism, philosophy, psychology, politics, economics, cognition studies, and history, among others).

Given the breadth of this rationality and its cultural consequences, Girard seems to have heard in Pope Benedict's call in the Regensburg

Lecture for a broad (as distinct from a narrow) rationality an echo of his own fundamental distinction in *Things Hidden since the Foundation of the World* between a Heraclitean Logos of sacrificial violence and a Johannine Logos of love and nonviolence. Like Weil's characteristic principle of the counterbalance whereby "gravity" and "grace" are opposed to and interactive with each other, Girard's mimetic theory holds these two *logoi* (constitutive of the respective orders of the city of humans and the city of God) in coexistent, principled opposition to each other until the end of time. Martin Heidegger (1889–1976), by contrast, in his *Introduction to Metaphysics*, also distinguishes two kinds of *logoi*, biblical and Greek, but he does so (Girard explains) in a vastly different way that actually undoes the true distinction between them and works effectively to support the secularist expulsion of the Johannine Logos as the supposed communication of a tyrannical God, the Hegelian "master" who is himself the invention of Judeo-Christian "slaves" (*THSFW* 265).

Like Pope Benedict, who in the Regensburg Lecture criticizes the liberal, Hegelian theology of Adolf von Harnack (1851–1930) (*RL* 140, par. 36–39), Girard sees in Heidegger the product of a rationalist, theological, and philosophical tradition that has failed to hold in sufficient tension the distinction between the Heraclitean and the Johannine *logoi*. The problem is not that the Bible is lacking in rationality, according to Girard, or that the New Testament should never have been written and read in Greek, but that its revealed truth cannot be reduced to a Greek philosophical wisdom that would refashion it into its own likeness. What Heidegger and others have done is to attempt to domesticate the biblical Logos, removing it from the cross (the transcendent meeting point of Jerusalem and Athens, the very means historically for the reconciliation of Greeks and Jews, circumcised and uncircumcised; cf. Colossians 3:11), and transferring it instead into a newly religionless realm.

When taken from the cross, the reconciliation of Greek and Jew accomplished there by Christ represents for Pope Benedict and Girard alike a fragile synthesis that is repeatedly undone either by a "Greek" expulsion of the Hebraic from Christianity (à la Heidegger) or by a "Hebraic" rejection of the Greek (à la the Protestant reformers). If and only if the Heraclitean Logos of violence is sufficiently distinguished from the nonviolent Johannine Logos can the truth disclosed by Christ's death be seen as heralded "since the foundation of the world" (Matthew 13:35; Revelation 13:8) by a new line of prophets, the innocent victims of the scapegoat mechanism, Jew and Gentile alike.[23] Following the practice of the fathers of the church and influenced by the writing of Erich Auerbach (1892–1952),[24] Girard finds figures of Christ in a host of Old Testament figures—Abel, slain by Cain; Joseph, sold into slavery; Job, rejected by his people; the psalmist in complaint; the Suffering Servant of Isaiah 52:13–53:12—but also depicted in Greek tragedy and other nonbiblical texts.[25] In this, too, he follows the fathers. Girard reads Sophocles' *Oedipus Rex* interreligiously, for example, as a kind of Greek prophecy of the scapegoat mechanism through which an arguably innocent Oedipus is singled out for blame, blinding, and exile as the putative cause of the plague.[26]

Weil similarly finds intimations of Christianity among the ancient Greeks (to echo the title of one of her books), discovering in Sophocles' heroine of love, Antigone, someone who is (in Girard's words) "the most perfect *figura Christi* of the ancient world" (*THSFW* 244).[27] Indeed, Weil's notebooks and essays, including *The Need for Roots*, are filled with references to folktales and legends from Chinese, Greek, Egyptian, Persian, and Indian sources, all of which she reads as referring symbolically, in one way or another, to biblical revelation. In her New York notebooks, filled with entries during her brief stay in the United States as an émigré, she records with approval the Augustinian doctrine that "before Christ, and outside Israel, there were 'spiritual members' of Israel among other peoples, and to each of them the unique Mediator and his future coming was divinely revealed."[28] Her sustained interest in Vedic literature—especially the Bhagavad Gita—almost certainly has encouraged Girard's own, somewhat belated study of Hindu sources: the Gita, the Upanishads, and the Brahmanas. Weil's interreligious writings, which have been justly criticized for their syncretism, their lack of historical grounding, and (most obviously) their disturbing, anti-Judaic bias,[29] have also been praised—indeed, often by the same critics—for their beauty, their saintly passion, and the depth of their philosophical and theological insights. Girard's work, when compared to, and contrasted with, Weil's Christian commentaries on non-Christian texts,[30] can be seen to possess features that scholars today associate with interreligious hermeneutics and its dialogical forms.

The Christian Interreligious Hermeneutics of Girard and Weil

In her introduction to the essays collected in *Song Divine: Christian Commentaries on the Bhagavad Gita*, Catherine Cornille first discusses the history of Christian reception of the Gita, which, "from the time of its earliest translation, more than two centuries ago, . . . has exercised a powerful fascination upon the Christian imagination, inspiring missionaries, poets, and philosophers alike."[31] Cornille then proceeds to make more general comments about present-day religious pluralism and "inter-religious hermeneutics, whereby the sacred texts of one religious tradition may be understood—consciously or unconsciously—from within the philosophical and religious framework of an entirely different religious tradition" (4). The act of commenting "on a sacred text belonging to a tradition other than one's own," she observes, "raises a series of hermeneutical and ethical questions" (4).

Cornille highlights two in particular. The "first among these," according to Cornille, "concerns 'ownership,' or what we might call *hermeneutical privilege* in relation to a text" (4). Acknowledging that a classical Hindu text like the Gita belongs, first, to Hindus, before it belongs "to all the world" (to echo Bede Griffiths)[32] may lead some Christian exegetes, for example, to incorporate Hindu commentaries into their own as a sign of their dialogism. (This is the practice, I would add, in the Scriptural Reasoning groups, where the participants who belong to the religious tradition from which the text being studied together originates are given primacy in its "plain sense" or "literal" exposition, but yield freedom to respectful participants from other traditions to interpret the same passage spiritually, in keeping with their own contextual understanding.)[33] Both Girard and Weil read non-Christian scriptures "Christianly," and thus as possessing a universal truth, to the extent that the texts conform to biblical revelation. Unlike contemporary practitioners in interreligious dialogue, however, Weil and Girard do not typically allow other commentators to mediate between the text and their own interpretation of it.

In this respect, Weil, a "catastrophe Jew" and a confessed Christian who renounced sacramental baptism into the church,[34] is more stubbornly independent than Girard, whose suspicion of myth has kept him ever on guard against the majority report, ever attentive to the cry of the concealed victim. In mythic accounts of historical lynchings, past and present, according to

Girard, "there are only false witnesses."[35] Weil similarly worries that "History . . . is nothing but a compilation of the depositions made by assassins with respect to their victims and themselves." (*NFR* 225). Her distrust of ideologies and of group-think cut her off from needed corrective guidance—for example, that which she might have received concerning Judaism both from Jewish rabbis and from her spiritual director, Fr. Perrin, had she been willing to accept it. Her attitude toward Israel and toward her own Jewish identity remains ambivalent throughout her writings and helps to explain her conflicted view of the church. As a "religion of slaves," Judaism and Christianity alike are at the heart of her ethos of compassion and of her own personal experience of affliction.[36] As colonizing and tyrannical forces, by contrast, Israel and Rome stand as the respective objects of her sharp rebuke.[37]

In Weil's case, her interreligious hermeneutics is most convincing when the ever poetic connections she makes between non-Christian texts and the Christian Bible are motivated by her own mystical experiences, her attentive observation, and her strong philosophical insights—for example, those concerning the nature of "force" as a mimetic contagion, the causes and effects of idolatry, the meaning of affliction and of beauty. Girard, for his part, has similarly brought familiar texts to new life through his scientific discovery in them of an anthropology that is deservedly open to a theological characterization, complementation, critique, and development. "For Weil," however, as Cyril O'Regan notes, "the theological dimension is basic in a way it is not for Girard,"[38] who sees in Christ primarily the innocent victim, in solidarity with all the victims.

The second issue mentioned by Cornille concerning interreligious hermeneutics is a specifically theological one that "concerns the *religious status* of sacred texts of other religions,"[39] the divinely inspired nature of such texts, and the truth to be found in them. Catholics instructed by the Vatican II document *Nostra aetate* are prepared to find "seeds" or "rays" of truth in sources other than the Bible,[40] while discovering the fullness of revelation only in the canonical scriptures as they have been interpreted within the church's tradition. That openness allows, importantly, also for the possibility that the encounter with an other's sacred text and its "rays" of truth might illumine, enrich, or transform one's understanding of one's own.

When Girard reads the sacred Vedic texts searching for evidence in support of his mimetic theory, which finds the genesis of ritual sacrifice in communal violence directed against a single victim, he seeks and finds in the Brahmanas "a repudiation of blood sacrifice," "a revelation that discredits sacrifice," a revelation that possesses "comparable but never truly identical traits" to those of the Judeo-Christian tradition, in which alone, for Girard, the scapegoat mechanism is completely exposed.[41] Weil similarly reads the Vedic literature, as well as the sacred texts of other cultic traditions, vis-à-vis the Bible, giving a Christian interpretation to an amazing array of ancient tales. As her bewildered spiritual director, Fr. Perrin, recalls: "Simone connects the testimony of John, present at Calvary, with an esoteric Thibetan doctrine! She compares the baptistery, on account of its shape, with the ritual basin of antiquity and even with the sea itself. She links together Dionysius, Noah, and Melchisedech because of the vine . . . we might make a long list of these associations of words or names."[42] One is tempted to see represented in Girard and Weil, as "Hellenic" thinkers, the exegetical propensities of Antioch and Alexandria—Girard, as the latter-day Antiochene, demonstrating a metonymic gift for literal and typological narrative, standing next to Weil, as the metaphoric Alexandrian.[43]

Such a distinction, however, might obscure what their Judeo-Christian Hellenism has in common: namely, a broadly defined rationality, capacious enough to bridge the gap between the sciences and religious faith and between and among the world religions. In support of a rationality broadly conceived, Weil calls for the practice of the "transposition" of truth from one conceptual context or sociocultural milieu to another, adding that the kinetic "art of transposing truth is one of the most essential and the least known" (*NFR* 68). Explaining that "there is three-dimensional space" in the mind, Weil invites her readers to imagine truth as an object that can be viewed from different positions or perspectives (*NFR* 68). The differences in appearance that result from transposition (that is, from moving from one perspectival position to another vis-à-vis the object) prove the reality of the thing itself, as it exists in different dimensions. In this way, "transposition is a criterion of the truth," according to Weil; "a truth which cannot be transposed isn't a truth" (*NFR* 68). "It is [also] impossible for us," she writes in her *Notebooks*, "to think without movement."[44]

The reason that the transposition of truth is so difficult in practice, according to Weil, is that it demands detachment from one's ego, a going forth from it. The successful practitioner has first "to have placed oneself at the center of a truth and possessed it in all its nakedness, behind the particular form in which it happens to have found expression" (*NFR* 68). Only then can he or she find the same truth expressed in another form. To do so is not to succumb to relativism (another name for a Girardian mimeticism), but to live in a singular relationship to a unifying and universal (that is, catholic) Truth, the Johannine Logos that is has been cast out from this world, the "city of man," but which finds its home in the city of God.[45]

In Weil's philosophy, only a desire, a hunger, that is awakened by supernatural grace allows for such a placement at the naked center of a truth—that form of mediation that Girard calls "innermost," and that he identifies with the imitation of Christ through identification with the other in the other's suffering, "a special aptitude for empathy" (*BTE* 133). "No philosophical thought will master the shift to charity," Girard writes; indeed, "Given the extent of its growing control, escaping from mimeticism is something only geniuses and saints can do" (*BTE* 133).

Like philosophy, science has reasons that fall short of the Pascalian reasons of the heart,[46] but scientific discovery and religious insight each have their place within the continuum of a graduated, "Hellenic" rationality. The related exercises of transposition in the intellectual order and of an empathetic analogizing in the moral order together prepare the way for, and help to perform, the deep-reaching dialogue of cultures between science and religion and among the world religions for which Pope Benedict, Weil, and Girard have all called.[47]

NOTES

1. René Girard, *Battling to the End: Conversations with Benoît Chantre*, trans. Mary Baker (East Lansing: Michigan State University Press, 2010) (hereafter cited as *BTE* by page), 193: "The Free French were hanging by a thread at the time when Gaulism consisted only in Radio London. When Simone Weil spoke of 'radio education' [in *The Need for Roots*], she was thinking about Maurice Schumann's Free French chronicles that were broadcast from London. A good third of France was Schumannist. I listened to Schumann religiously, and I was very moved to meet him later." On the use of the radio, see Simone Weil, *The Need for Roots: Prelude to a Declaration of Duties Toward Mankind*, trans. Arthur Wills (New York: G. P. Putnam's, 1952) (hereafter cited as *NFR* by page), 191.

2. See René Girard and Christian de Maussion, "Simone Weil vue par René Girard," *Cahiers Simone Weil* 11 (1988): 201–2; René Girard, *Evolution and Conversion: Dialogues on the Origins of Culture with Pierpaolo Antonello and João Cezar de Castro Rocha* (London: Continuum, 2008), 150–51.

3. See P. Hebblethwaite, *John XXIII, Pope of the Council* (London: HarperCollins, 1984), 57, quoted in David McClennan, *Utopian Pessimist: The Life and Thought of Simone Weil* (New York: Poseidon Press, 1990), 268; P. Hebblethwaite, *The Year of the Three Popes* (London: Collins, 1978), 2.

4. See Louis Salleron, "Simone Weil et Vatican II," *Itinéraires* 125 (July–August 1968): 271–92. For the text of *Nostra aetate*, see Walter M. Abbott, ed., *The Documents of Vatican II, with Notes and Comments by Catholic, Protestant, and Orthodox Authorities* (Baltimore: America Press, 1966), 660–68.

5. On this topic, see Joseph Cardinal Ratzinger (Pope Benedict XVI), *Europe: Today and Tomorrow* (San Francisco: Ignatius Press, 2007); Joseph Cardinal Ratzinger (Pope Benedict XVI), *Christianity and the Crisis of Cultures* (San Francisco: Ignatius Press, 2006); Joseph Cardinal Ratzinger (Pope Benedict XVI), *Truth and Tolerance: Christian Belief and World Religions* (San Francisco: Ignatius Press, 2007).

6. See Joseph Ratzinger and Marcello Pera, *Without Roots: The West, Relativism, Christianity, Islam* (New York: Basic Books, 2007). In at least one of his speeches, Pope Benedict quotes from "the French Jew Simone Weil, who said that 'we experience good only by doing it . . . When we do evil we do not know it, because evil flies from light.'" See John F. Thornton and Susan B. Varenne, ed., *The Essential Pope Benedict XVI: His Central Writings and Speeches* (New York: HarperCollins, 2007), 260–61.

7. See James V. Schall, *The Regensburg Lecture* (South Bend, IN: St. Augustine's Press, 2007). This text includes in an appendix (130–48) the complete translated text of the lecture, from which I quote in the following paragraphs, giving abbreviated title (*RL*), page, and paragraph.

8. As expressed in Martin Luther's "theology of the cross" and in G. Budé's *De Transitu Hellenismi ad Christianismum* (Paris, 1535), the hypothesis of a falsification of Christianity by Greek metaphysics has remained current, especially in Protestant theological circles, since the Reformation. See Jean-Louis Vieillard-Baron, "Platonisme et paganisme au XVIIIe siècle," *Archives de Philosophie* 42 (1979): 439–56. Adolf von Harnack (1851–1930) famously speaks of Christian dogma as a "creation of the Greek mind on the gospel's land" (*Lehrbuch der Dogmengeschichte: Der Entwickelung des kirchlichen Dogmas*, 4th ed. [Tübingen: J.C.B. Mohr, 1909]).

9. Michel Gitton, "Hellenization of Christianity," in *Encyclopedia of Christian Theology*, ed. Jean-Yves Lacoste (New York: Routledge, 2004), 1:686.

10. Leo Strauss, "Jerusalem and Athens: Some Preliminary Reflections" [1967], in *Jewish Philosophy and the Crisis of Modernity: Essays and Lectures in Modern Jewish Thought*, ed. Kenneth Hart Green (New York: SUNY Press, 1997), 377.

11. Schall notes: "In the months after the lecture was first given, an almost infinite number of comments, analyses, recriminations, encomia, and reactions have been printed throughout the world" (*The Regensburg Lecture*, 9–10).

12. *RL* 133 (par. 12). In quoting this passage, the pope explicitly cites the "seventh conversation . . . edited by Professor Khoury" (*RL* 133, par. 11), that is, Manuel II Paléologue, *Entretiens avec un Musulman. 7e Controverse*, ed. Theodore Khoury, Sources Chrétiennes n. 115 (Paris: Cerf, 1966).

13. For these extended engagements of mimetic theory with theology and science, see especially Michael Kirwan, *Girard and Theology* (London: T & T Clark, 2009), and Scott R. Garrels, ed., *Mimesis and Science: Empirical Research on Imitation and the Mimetic Theory of Culture and Religion* (East Lansing: Michigan State University Press, 2011).

14. Extending this analysis, "Islamicism"—understood as a political and economic corruption of Islam—is a mimetic product of the East's competition with a "rationalistic," antireligious, modern West. After the 9/11 terrorist attack on the Twin Towers in New York, Girard spoke in an interview published in *Le Monde* about Al Qaeda's imitation of the Western culture it purports to oppose. See Robert Doran, "Apocalyptic Thinking after 9/11: An Interview with René Girard," *SubStance* 37, no.1 (2008): 20–32.

15. René Girard, *Things Hidden since the Foundation of the World*, research undertaken in collaboration with with J.-M. Oughourlian and G. Lefort, trans. Stephen Bann and Michael Metteer (Stanford, CA: Stanford University Press, 1987), 271. Hereafter *THSFW*.

16. Girard, for example, praises Plato for his "fear of mimesis," for being "closer than anyone to what is essential, closer than primitive religion itself," even as he faults Plato (*THSFW*, 15). Pope Benedict, appreciative of "the Platonic element" in the scientific grasp of "the mathematical structure of matter," similarly recognizes dangers in the "synthesis between Platonism (Cartesianism) and empiricism" (*RL* 141, par. 40–41).

17. Palle Yourgrau, *Simone Weil* (London: Reaktion Books, 2011), 136.

18. By contrast, according to Weil, Greek scientific and mathematical language was double-coded to refer both to material and spiritual truth. Citing the example of Pythagoras, who "offered up a sacrifice in his joy at having discovered the possibility of drawing a right-angled triangle inside a semicircle," she explains that the circle symbolized God in his perfection and eternity, and the mean proportion referred to the divine mediation between God and his creatures, with the result that "geometry thus becomes a double language, which at the same time provides information concerning the forces that are in action in matter and talks about the supernatural relations between God and his creatures" (*NFR* 291–92).

19. According to Weil, "Savants are people who are paid to manufacture science; they are expected to manufacture some; they feel it their duty to manufacture some. But that is insufficient for them as a stimulant. Professional advancement, professorships, rewards of all kinds, honors and money, receptions abroad, the esteem and admiration of colleagues, reputation, fame, and titles—all that counts for a great deal" (*NFR* 256–57). The "acquisition of fresh knowledge is not a sufficient stimulus to encourage savants in their efforts" (*NFR* 254).

20. On Weil's Christological understanding, see Eric O. Springsted, *Christus Mediator: Platonic Mediation in the Thought of Simone Weil* (Chico, CA: Scholars Press, 1983). See also E. Jane Doering and Eric Springsted, eds., *The Christian Platonism of Simone Weil* (Notre Dame, IN: University of Notre Dame Press, 2004).

21. René Girard, *I See Satan Fall Like Lightning*, trans. James G. Williams (Maryknoll, NY: Orbis, 2001), 44.

22. Marie Cabaud Meaney, "Simone Weil and René Girard: Violence and the Sacred," *American Catholic Philosophical Quarterly* 84, no. 3 (2010): 565–88. For other comparative studies of Weil and Girard, see Georges Charot, "Le Refus de la violence chez René Girard: Rencontre avec la pensée de Simone Weil," *Cahiers Simone Weil* 3 (1980): 179–202; Jean-Marie Muller, *Simone Weil: L'Exigence de non-violence* (Paris: Éditions du Témoignage Chrétien, 1999), 185–99; Ann W. Astell, "Saintly Mimesis, Contagion, and Empathy in the Thought of René Girard, Edith Stein, and Simone Weil," *Shofar* 22, no. 2 (2004): 116–31; Cyril O'Regan, "Countermimesis and Simone Weil's Christian Platonism," in Doering and Springsted, ed., *The Christian Platonism of Simone Weil*, 181–208; Wolfgang Palaver, "Die Frage des Opfers im Spannungsfeld von West und Ost: René Girard, Simone Weil und Mahatma Gandhi über Gewalt und Gewaltfreiheit," *Zeitschrift für katholische Theologie* 132 (2010): 462–81.

23. According to Girard, "the two types of Logos have never been sufficiently distinguished" from each other (*THSFW* 264).

24. Auerbach published his famous essay "Figura" in 1944. After the war, he published *Mimesis: The Representation of Reality in Western Literature*, the remarkable book he had composed as a refugee in Istanbul.

25. On the topic of Girard's use of figural interpretation, see Kirwan, *Girard and Theology*, 87–92.

26. Girard's student Sandor Goodhart goes so far as to find an innocent victim in *Oedipus Rex*, pointing to Sophocles' deliberate ambiguity concerning Oedipus's actual guilt of parricide and incest. See Goodhart, *Sacrificing Commentary: Reading the End of Literature* (Baltimore: Johns Hopkins University Press, 1996).

27. Girard calls this "one of [Weil's] amazing insights" (*THSFW* 244). For an excellent study of Weil's Christological hermeneutics, see Marie Cabaud Meaney, *Simone Weil's Apologetic Use of Literature: Her Christological Interpretations of Ancient Greek Texts* (Oxford: Oxford University Press, 2007).

28. Simone Weil, *First and Last Notebooks*, trans. Richard Rees (London: Oxford University Press, 1970), 120–21.

29. For these critiques, see, for example, Joseph-Marie Perrin, "Syncretism and Catholicity," in M. Perrin and G. Thibon, *Simone Weil as We Knew Her*, trans. Emma Craufurd (London: Routledge, 2003), 52–66. The best defense of Weil's attitude toward Judaism has been offered by Palle Yourgrau on philosophical grounds. See his *Simone Weil*, 117–35.

30. For an insightful study of Weil's Christian exegesis of a Hindu text, see Maria Clara Bingmeier, "War, Suffering, and Detachment: Reading the *Bhagavad Gita* with Simone Weil," in *Song Divine: Christian Commentaries on the Bhagavad Gita*, ed. Catherine Cornille (Leuven: Peeters, 2006), 69–89.

31. Catherine Cornille, introduction to Cornille, *Song Divine*, 1. Subsequent citations parenthetical.

32. Bede Griffiths, *River of Compassion: A Christian Commentary on the Bhagavad Gita* (New York: Continuum, 1995), 1. As Griffiths explains, "I only want to show how it can be a practical guide to a Christian and to anyone who is in search of a guide on the spiritual path" (1).

33. For an introduction to Scriptural Reasoning, an international movement of interreligious hermeneutics founded by the Jewish semiotician Peter Ochs, see the website of the *Journal of Scriptural Reasoning* at http://etext.lib.virginia.edu/journals/jsrforum/gateways.html.

34. The term "catastrophe Jew" was coined by Jean Améry. See Jean Améry, *At the Mind's Limits: Contemplation by a Survivor on Auschwitz and Its Realities*, trans. Sidney Rosenfeld and Stella P. Rosenfeld (Bloomington: Indiana University Press, 2009).

35. René Girard, *Sacrifice*, trans. Matthew Pattillo and David Dawson (East Lansing: Michigan State University Press, 2011), 77.

36. Simone Weil, *Waiting for God*, trans. Emma Craufurd (New York: G. P. Putnam, 1951; repr. 1973), 67.

37. In one such rebuke, Weil writes: "Rome and Israel introduced into Christianity, mixed with the spirit of Christ, the spirit of the Beast. . . . The Beast is social idolatry" (*First and Last Notebooks*, 120).

38. O'Regan, "Countermimesis and Simone Weil's Christian Platonism," 206n32.

39. Cornille, introduction to *Song Divine*, 5.

40. Abbott, *Documents of Vatican II*, 662, par. 2.

41. Girard, *Sacrifice*, xii.

42. Perrin and Thibon, *Simone Weil as We Knew Her*, 53–54.

43. On the subject of these exegetical schools in the context of Jewish-Christian biblical exegesis, see Michael A. Signer, "Searching the Scriptures: Jews, Christians, and the Book," in *Christianity in Jewish Terms*, ed. Tikva Frymer-Kensky et al. (Boulder: Westview Press, 2000), 85–98.

44. Simone Weil, *The Notebooks of Simone Weil*, trans. Arthur Wills, 2 vols. (New York: Putnam's, 1951), 1:52.

45. John Milbank was perhaps the first to characterize Girard as an Augustinian political theologian. See his *Theology and Social Theory: Beyond Secular Reason* (Oxford: Blackwell, 1990). Since then Girard's Augustinianism has been increasingly accepted. See, for example, Cyril O'Regan, "Girard and the Spaces of Apocalyptic," *Modern Theology* 28, no. 1 (2012): 112–40.

46. The French mystic, mathematician, and philosopher Blaise Pascal (1623–62) famously wrote in his *Pensées* (iv.277), "The heart has reasons that reason knows not of."

47. On empathy as a form of ethical analogy and as a transposition, see Astell, "Saintly Mimesis."

PART 3

Rivalry, Sacrifice, and World Religions

Burning Desires, Burning Corpses: Girardian Reflections on Fire in Hinduism and Buddhism

Brian Collins

Monks, everything is on fire.
—Ādittapariyāya Sutta

The subject of this essay is the role of fire and its explicit and implicit understandings in the Hindu and Buddhist traditions. At first glance, this appears to be a useful way of narrowing the scope of an essay that began with the impossible task of producing a mimetic analysis of Indian religions. But the scope thus narrowed is still much too broad to be manageable. As in Christianity, Islam, Zoroastrianism, and Judaism, the understanding of fire in the Hindu and Buddhist traditions is in equal measure heterogeneous, historically contingent, and (in some senses) foundational, which makes for a wide variety of interpretations. Even if it is limited to the insights provided by an engagement with mimetic theory, a systematic analysis of the role of fire in Hinduism and Buddhism is far too large a project for an essay like this. Fire is one of the central elements of the ancient Indian ritual system of śrauta sacrifices ("solemn" rites conducted on a large scale in public like the *agnicayana*) and *gṛhya* sacrifices ("household" rites like the *agnihotra*, to be performed twice daily). In mythology, the blaze (*tejas*) of fire comes to refer both to the fame of a warrior that outlasts his physical body and to the puissance that enables him to win that fame. In the form of inner heat generated by ascetic practices (*tapas*) fire underlies the esoteric physiology-cosmology of the systems of yoga. The Buddha asks his followers to extinguish the metaphorical fires of hatred, delusion, and greed. Finally, fire generates one of the most striking visual representations of the Hindu life cycle—the funeral pyre and the related image (used by colonial British missionaries as a fundraiser to great effect) of the widow who throws herself onto the burning body of her husband.[1] To attempt a systematic exposition of all of these interrelated forms and functions of fire (which are but a small part of the totality) in an essay would be impossible. Instead, I will present an unsystematic series of reflections on the role of fire in episodes from the Vedas, the Brāhmaṇas, the epic *Mahābhārata*, and the Buddhist Ādittapariyāya and *Aggi-Vacchagotta Sutta*s in hopes of throwing some light on the intersections between mimetic theory and Indian religions.

Agni Vaiśvānara and the Indo-European Fire God

> Men always follow: it is Agni who conquers.
>
> —Roberto Calasso, *Ardor*

Calling themselves Āryans, the nomadic Vedic people split off from the ancient Indo-Iranian culture and moved into India around 1500 B.C.E. They brought with them the cult of fire, connected especially to the practices of the priestly clans called the Āṅgirasas and the Bhṛgus, along with the orally transmitted Vedic texts. In the *Ṛg Veda*, the oldest of these, the fire god Agni is addressed in some two hundred hymns, making him second only to the divine warrior and storm god Indra in popularity. And while, of the four hierarchical estates that develop in ancient India (i.e., Brahmin priests, warriors, producers, and servants or laborers), Indra becomes identified with the warrior class, Agni is identified with the Brahmin priesthood. He is referred to as the divine priest, the one who intercedes between gods and men just as Brahmin priests do. And like the Brahmin priests, who are the only class of Vedic society able to accept gifts without incurring the debts that act as social glue in a gift economy, he is also ever hungry and all-devouring.

Agni is the "first-born" and sometimes even the "self-born" of the gods (and the first god invoked in the *Ṛg Veda*). He is the paragon of manhood, leading the Vedic warrior bands into battle and protecting them as long as they keep him burning in their hearths and sacrificial enclosures. He represents the kinship of the Vedic people and their conquest of their foes. He is the center of the world, holding it up like a pillar.[2] But despite his centrality, as Stephanie Jamison and Joel Brereton observe, "Agni participates in almost no narrative mythology, in strong contrast to Indra."[3] However, what little narrative mythology there is tells us some important things about Agni. In Ṛg Veda 10.124 Indra calls Agni to leave the side of the enemies of the gods (called the Asuras, or demons) and asks him to join the gods as oblation-bearer. Agni agrees to defect from the side of the demons in favor of the gods, which is probably a variant of Agni's major myth motif in Ṛg Veda 10.51, in which he is coaxed out of the waters by the gods, where he has hidden out of fear for his life after his three brothers have been killed in the gods' previous sacrifices.[4]

Freud observes that the acquisition of fire in myth is always a theft (e.g., Prometheus)[5] that comes with a burden of guilt. He puts forward the hypothesis that "in order to gain control over fire, men had to renounce the homosexually-tinged desire to put it out with a stream of urine."[6] The concrete example he uses may be a bit too literal, but Freud's point is that early humans, unable to cultivate fire, had to conserve a naturally occurring flame for as long as possible in order to benefit from its heat and light.[7] Maintenance of a fire that would be gone forever once it went out and, on the other hand, would engulf the environs if left untended, must have indeed required a measure of, if not renunciation, then discipline. In Girardian terms, this uncultivated fire is analogous to the spontaneous lynchings in the early human communities that stopped the spread of contagious violence for as long as people were able to renounce or at least control their mimetic instincts. The cultivated fire, which must have carried the memory of the destructive possibility of wildfire, is analogous to the sacrificial ritual instituted to recapture the social cohesion born out of the earlier impulsive killings.

To be eligible to participate in the solemn rites, such as the *agnicayana* (the "piling up of the fire"), one must be an ātihāgni, a "three-fire sacrificer," and keep burning in one's home at all times the three fires: the āhavanīya (offering fire), the *gārhapatya* (household fire), and the *dakṣināgni* (protective southern fire).[8] Every morning and evening, the householder offers the *agnihotra*, which is a repetition of the original sacrifice that created the universe as well as a reestablishment of the link between gods and humans. Most importantly, the *agnihotra* serves to keep fire in its proper place, either under control inside the ritual-social structure of the Vedic world or far away from the community in the form of the sun. According to the *Jaiminīya Brāhmaṇa*, in the time before people understood the truth they believed that the sun went away at night.[9] But the Vedic ritualists know better: they know that it does not go away but breaks into six pieces that are deposited for the night into the Brahmins, the cattle, the fire, the plants, the waters, and the trees. With the fire of the sun, which is also Death,[10] thus dispersed and diffused, all is safe. But every morning, the *agnihotra* has to be performed to put it back together that it can rise up whole in the east and be kept at a safe distance while in its reconstituted, unmediated form.

In the *agnihotra*, the texts tell us, the first oblation is the *sthāṇu*, the Sanskrit equivalent of *skandalon* or "stumbling block." Translator H. W. Bodewitz discusses the mysterious nature of this "stumbling-block" in a lengthy footnote,[11] but Girard's reading of the sacrifice allows us to identify the *sthāṇu* in the twice-daily *agnihotra* as the model-rival in the mimetic triangle, represented in its most ritualized and least dangerous form. The discipline of fire maintenance with its minimization of the stumbling block gives rise to the rites of ascetic renunciation, which take the partial abandonment of desire that comes with householder life and its attendant ritual obligations to the extreme. When a man is preparing to become an ascetic, he extinguishes his fires and "deposits" them in himself, where they then reside permanently. As Patrick Olivelle explains,

> The internalized ritual is more permanent and more sublime. The renouncer's internal fires are permanently lit; he kindles them with every breath. His eating becomes a sacrificial offering. His body and bodily functions are transformed into a long sacrificial session. The renouncer's body thus becomes a sacred object; it is equal to the fire altar where the Vedic rites are performed.[12]

Fire represents both creative destruction and quietistic withdrawal. Reflecting these two modes, Proto-Indo-European, the hypothetical reconstructed language that is the supposed source for the liturgical languages of Vedic religion, classical Hinduism,[13] and Buddhism (i.e., Vedic, Sanskrit, and Pali, respectively) has two distinct word-types for fire, one active or masculine and the other passive or neuter. The first of these gives us name of the fire god, cognate with the English words "ignite" and "igneous." In the early Vedic period the divine figure of Agni emerges from this active fire principle as the god of the sacrificial fire and has cognate deities in Greek, Norse, Iranian, and other Indo-European cultures. Ellison Banks Findley also links Agni to a still more ancient strata of Indo-European myth in the figure *Ak/gnis*, "a god of devastation and annihilation" mentioned in the fourteenth-century B.C.E. Hittite treaty recorded in an inscription at the site of the ancient city of Hattusa near Boğazkale, Turkey.[14]

But, as M. L. West notes, even in cultures whose common word for fire comes from the same active word-type as does *agni*, the gods of fire themselves often go by different names. Why? "[In] the case of such a dangerous entity," West observes, "it is only to be expected that its primary name should often have become taboo and ordinary names substituted. So we should keep an open mind, and be alert for points of contact that go beyond the simple association with fire."[15] To take two instructive examples, Agni shares many attributes with the technologically oriented Greek smith-god Hephaestus, whose name is also synonymous with the sacrificial and funeral fires in the Homeric epics,[16] and with the Norse Logi ("Blaze") who disguises himself as a human and beats the trickster god Loki in an eating contest.[17]

Like Logi in the eating contest, Agni is eternally hungry. And the story that best illustrates his insatiable appetite is the burning of the Khāṇḍava forest in the *Mahābhārata* epic. In this episode Agni comes to the heroes Arjuna and Kṛṣṇa disguised as a Brahmin priest and asks for food. When they assent, the ersatz Brahmin takes on his true form and reveals that the food he wants is the entire Khāṇḍava forest, home of the snake king Takṣaka. He has not been able to consume it because Indra, as a friend of Takṣaka, protects the forest by sending down rain whenever it starts to burn. And so, to feed Agni, Arjuna and Kṛṣṇa set fire to the forest, ward off Indra's rain with arrows, and kill any creature that tries to escape.[18] The story has an Oedipal aspect, since Arjuna is in fact the son of Indra, whom he defeats on behalf of Agni. Jamison and Brereton describe some of the Promethean-Oedipal aspects of Agni's personality:

> The creation or birth of the ritual fire from the kindling sticks, his parents, is a major subject in Agni hymns, with intricate descriptions of the first stirrings of flame and smoke as the friction of the kindling sticks produces sparks that finally catch. The just-born Agni is depicted as a tender babe, who quickly grows to become stronger than his parents and to devour the plants from which he was born.[19]

All sacrificial offerings must be *pakvā* or "cooked," before they are put into the fire. The fire must be controlled carefully and only allowed to consume that which is already made sacred and not tainted by violence. In the Vedic fire sacrifice and the ascetic and esoteric traditions that proceed from it, a fire out of control means unstoppable spreading violence, but a fire brought under control means freedom from death. This connection is well illustrated in the word śamī, the name of the wood used to kindle the sacrificial fire. It derives from the root śam-, meaning, "to make a (ritual) effort," "to be at peace," "to die," and "to extinguish." The root also gives us the word śamitar, the one who immolates the sacrificial victim, in which case it carries the double meaning of "the one who kills" and "the one who is appeased." As Madeleine Biardeau observes:

> This deep ambiguity of the term joins the ambivalence of the sacrificial fire, the source of all prosperity, but also of mortal danger. On the one hand, by burning the offered substances or cooking the flesh of the victims, it is associated with death, but also with the fecundity of sacrificial death. On the other hand, if it is not properly handled according to the rules, it can exceed the prescribed bounds and destroy what does not belong to it.[20]

The destructive-creative and contemplative-self-abnegating aspects of fire are combined in the figure of Agni Vaiśvānara, an epithet that can be translated as "Agni Common to All Men," who "sweetened" the untamed lands that the early Vedic kingdoms brought under their dominion.[21] Fire pacifies; it forbids violence, standing as a constant reminder of the potential conflagration that violence can unleash. In a Vedic verse that represents a ritualized verbal contest called the *brahmodya*, two Brahmins are posing a series of questions to one another about the nature of Agni Vaiśvānara that concludes with the questioning priest denying that his queries have had any hostile intent. This denial implies that the questioning of the *brahmodya* typically *does* have hostile intent, but this hostility is to be avoided in the discussion of Agni Vaiśvānara.[22] In the later commentarial tradition of the Śatapatha Brāhmaṇa, Agni Vaiśvānara is identified with Puruṣa, the victim of the primordial sacrifice that creates the world in the Ṛg Veda,[23] and the author proclaims that, "whosoever thus knows . . . Agni Vaiśvānara as Puruṣa-like, as established within the Puruṣa, repels death, and attains all life."[24]

While it does not fully exhaust all the functions of fire in Vedic religion, this complex of ideas surrounding Agni—eternally hungry and all-consuming, fed by sacrifice, firstborn of the gods, ruling humankind, present in all people, the pillar of human society, identical with the sacrificial victim, defusing conflict, whose proper understanding grants victory over death—all strongly suggest Girard's understanding of the violent sacred as the source of human community. But at the same time, the violence of the fire and its subsequent internalization in the ascetic tradition seems to create a smokescreen that hides the real violence of the sacrifice. The oblations that Agni accepts are typically not blood or flesh, but ghee or clarified butter, the most refined animal product and the farthest conceptually from slaughter. In the Vedic rite, as Girard points out, the killing of the sacrificial victim quietly happens away from the sacred enclosure at the killing post or *yupa* while all the spectacle of dramatic flames and smoke happens at the fire altar.[25] And as ritual increasingly gives way to the mystical and speculative reflections of the Upaniṣads in the late Vedic period, Brahmins eschew any association with killing, adopting vegetarianism as the mark of the ritual purity. When the *agnicayana* ritual was revived under the auspices of Harvard University in the southern state of Kerala in 1975, the Brahmin officiants decided to replace the animal victims with vegetable substitutes. The human heads that were once buried under the altar had long been replaced by head-shaped pots.[26]

The Submarine Fire and the Churning of the Ocean

> Whether the fire dies down or whether it blazes up, its caprice means disaster.
>
> —Paul Valéry, "On the Pre-Eminent Dignity of the Arts of Fire"

As we have seen, the only narrative myth in the Ṛg Veda concerning Agni has him going into hiding and having to be coaxed out by the gods. His hiding place is the water, whence he gets the epithet Apām Napāt ("Child of the Waters"). The theme of the fire-in-the-water is a central one to Indo-Iranian religion.[27] We find it in the destruction by fire and water of both the cosmos and the corpse: conflagration and flood in the case of the (mythical) destruction of the cosmos, the funeral pyre and immersion in the sacred Ganges in the case of the (ritual) destruction of the corpse.[28] In the Iranian version of the fire-in-the-water or submarine fire motif, the benevolent demigod Spenta Mainyu and the malevolent demigod Aingra Mainyu are engaged in a tug-of-war over the *xvarənah*,[29] the fiery signifier of sacred sovereignty, when it escapes and is hidden under the waters by Apām Napāt, at which point the supreme god Ahura Mazda declares that any *airya* ("noble," cognate with Āryan) who can dive under the waters and retrieve the *xvarənah* can claim the sovereignty its possession entails. And for the *airya* who can retrieve the *xvarənah* from under the waters, there will also be victory, wealth, and strength.[30]

In classical Indian mythology, a variant of this myth exists that is typically not connected to the idea of the submarine fire[31] but that, based on its striking parallels with the Iranian myth, should be: the churning of the ocean as told in the *Mahābhārata*. The episode begins as the gods have assembled to hatch a plan to obtain the *amṛta*, the elixir of life. The *amṛta*, like the *xvarənah*, will grant sovereignty to the gods. It is also contained in the ocean and can only be obtained by churning it. The method of churning is not the up-and-down motion of a plunger, but rather a back-and-forth sawing motion that rotates a central stick in exactly the same way a fire drill is used to kindle the sacred flame of the fire sacrifice. The gods are "kindling" the ocean. They choose Mount Mandara to serve as the churning rod, the giant tortoise Akūpāra to use his shell as the base, and the cosmic snake Ananta ("Endless") to drive the motion of the churning rod. But the gods alone are not capable of doing the deed, so they have to enlist the help of their rivals the demons to pull from the other side of the snake. The image presented here is something like a gigantic tug-of-war with the gods pulling Ananta's tail and the demons pulling his head, whipping up the ocean into froth.

As they begin churning the ocean, every creature that lives in the sea is crushed to death by the motion of the mountain. Large trees on the mountainside crash into one another and cause forest fires with their friction, burning all the forest creatures alive. Then the raging fire is doused with rain sent by Indra and flooded with the sap of the burning trees that, along with the molten gold that flows from the superheated mountain, pour into the ocean to create the draught of *amṛta*.[32] As the gods and the demons continue to churn, the ocean soon turns to milk, and cream begins to rise to the top, along with the sun, the moon, a magical wish-bestowing cow, and the goddess Śrī (Victory). Finally, Dhanvantari, the physician of the gods, rises out of the ocean bearing a white gourd filled with the *amṛta*, and the short-lived truce between the gods and demons comes to an abrupt end. The demons scream out, "It is mine!" and take hold of it. But the god Viṣṇu quickly takes the form of a beautiful woman and seduces the demons, tricking them into handing over the *amṛta*. As soon as they do, the gods attack the demons and slaughter them wholesale, driving the survivors under the ocean.[33]

The violent mixing of fire and water and the presence of gold under the water (the form the submarine fire takes in *Das Rheingold*)[34] is more evidence that the churning of the ocean is a myth about the fire-in-the-water, identified now with *amṛta*, the elixir that gives freedom from death. This is an easy enough identification to make since in the classical and epic myth of the churning of the ocean, *amṛta* has taken the place of *soma* (whose name, like Agni's, when capitalized can also refer to the god that is the deified form of the substance), the "fiery liquid"[35] of the Vedic myths and rituals drunk by the gods (especially Indra) and by earthly sacrificers and poets. The immersion of fire in water is also the means of producing the draught of *amṛta* in the Indian alchemical traditions. In the alchemical myths connected to the legendary mercury well (and possibly the fire-belching Candrakūpa, or "Moon Well,"[36] at the shrine of the goddess Hiṅglāj in northeastern India), we see an inversion of the churning-of-the-ocean story. Rather than the gods and the demons fighting over the elixir and Viṣṇu turning into a beautiful woman to get it back, the elixir itself (in the form of mercury) is tempted by a beautiful woman, as this set of alchemical instructions illustrates:

> Upon seeing a well-adorned maiden who, having bathed after first coming into season, [rides by] mounted upon a horse, mercury, which is found in wells, [becomes] possessed of a desire to seize her, [and] rushes up out [of its well]. Upon seeing it, she gallops away. The mercury pursues her for the distance of one yojana [eight to nine miles]. [When] that [mercury that is] born of Śiva then quickly returns to the well, it is caught in troughs dug in its path. That mercury, because of its heaviness, fell from the mouth of Agni in Darada-deśa. That mercury, absorbed into the surface of the earth there, came to remain in that country.[37]

Alchemy, in its exoteric form, is the transformation of a base substance into something of value. Mimetic desire also transforms a base substance into something of value by making it the object of another's desire. The key to understanding all of these myths is the actions the gods take in the churning of the ocean, because it is in this story that the myth structure is laid bare: There is no object of desire, no *amṛta/soma/xvarənah*/submarine fire/mercury, *until the gods enter into rivalry with the demons*. The object only exists when both parties desire it. And when it comes into existence as the inexhaustibly protean object of desire,[38] it immediately becomes a focal point of erotic desire as well; Viṣṇu wins it back from the demons by becoming a beautiful woman in the *Mahābhārata*, while the object is itself drawn to a beautiful woman in alchemical text. The object is nothing but what Girard calls *desir selon l'Autre*, as these mythic transformations indicate. The myth of the churning of the ocean also reveals the apocalyptic trajectory of mimetic desire with its violent depiction of the destruction of every living thing both on the fiery mountain and in the boiling ocean. In the practices of alchemical yoga, derived from Upaniṣadic doctrines of inner heat, this process is internalized; the practitioner uses his own inner fire to "cook," "ripen," or "perfect" himself (all meanings of the Sanskrit *pakvā*) and attain *amṛta*, "deathlessness," just like the gods. Control of the sacrificial fire and control of the inner fire of desire both result in deathlessness, which is *not* eternal life, but the absence of violent unnatural death like the kind that accompanies the sacrificial crisis. Fire kindled by oneself is free from danger and desire, but fire taken from a mimetic rival is more powerful. As Jan Heesterman concludes, "the churned [by oneself] fire is the most pure (*puṇya*), but by the same token it is least productive (*anardhuka*)."[39]

The Funeral Fire, the Buddha, and the Dead God

If there is a remnant left of a fire, a debt, or an enemy it will grow back again and again. Therefore you must leave no remnant.

—Sanskrit Proverb

Commenting on the story of Empedocles jumping into Mount Etna, Bachelard writes, "Death in the flame is the least lonely of deaths. It is truly a cosmic death in which a whole universe is reduced to nothingness along with the thinker."[40] A certain strain of Hindu thought recognizes this correlation between personal and universal extinction in the idea of the *nityapralaya*, the constant cosmic dissolution constituted by the successive death of individuals. Mirroring one another, the destruction of the cosmos and the destruction of the self both begin with fire. At the famous Manikarnikā burning *ghat* in Varanasi where bodies are cremated day and night,[41] the sacred fire kept by the low-caste Doms is said to have been burning as long as anyone can remember.[42] It is used to light the pyres on which the deceased makes his "last sacrifice" (*antyeṣṭi*) and on which a form of Agni bearing the epithet Krāvyad, "The Corpse-Devourer," consumes his physical body.

As the Sanskrit proverb above suggests, fire in Indian thought is often imagined in ways that recall the obligation of a debt and the danger of an enemy, all of which—obligation, debt, danger, and enmity—are embedded in the deep structure of the Vedic economy of the sacred. The cremation of a body is the mechanism by which death pays for the next life in the system of rebirth. The corpse is an extremely polluted and polluting object in Hinduism, but is still ritually anointed, bathed, and blessed with mantras in the exact same way as a sacrificial victim. The modern Hindi word for corpse (śav) resembles the name of the god Śiva, lord of the cremation ground, a correspondence that forms part of the funeral liturgy. There is an inconsistency here: the body is supposed to be a corpse, since death is believed to occur when the last breath leaves the body, but it is treated like a sacrificial victim (i.e., like a god). Parry observes that mourners at the funeral ground treat the corpse as still alive, still containing one last breath (*prān*), until the moment when the deceased's son or some other relative strikes his head with a stave while he is engulfed in flames, causing the skull to split open and release the spirit. It is only after this, the *kapāl kriyā* or "skull rite," that the body becomes a polluting corpse.[43]

The French Indologist Charles Malamoud notes that at the end of a sacrifice, "[there] always remains a residue which, while ambiguous, is nevertheless always possessed of an active, rather than an inert character."[44] There is never simply nothing after a sacrifice: even if all of the offering has been consumed using one of the ritually prescribed methods, there is still the karmic reward that will come to the sacrificer in this life or the next. Out of this idea of ritual incompletion comes the later, Purāṇic idea of the remainder (śeṣa) at the end of each cosmic cycle of destruction that provides the seed for the next cycle, deified as the cosmic thousand-headed serpent Ananta Śeṣa ("Remainder without End").[45] In the later Hindu forms of temple worship, the remnant of food offered to a deity is the *prasād*, eaten by worshippers to attain the grace of the god or goddess. And in the individual *nityapralaya* that parallels the cosmic dissolution called *mahāpralaya*, the remainder takes the form of unspent karma, the results of which must be experienced in the next life.

For the Buddha, this fire that rekindles itself from a cinder again and again, from life to life, is not an image of renewal but of redeath: *punarmṛtyu*, a vicious cycle perpetuated by anger, greed, and delusion, above all the delusion of a permanent self. The Buddhist solution is to cultivate selflessness and good conduct and thereby extinguish the three fires of anger, greed, and delusion. When these three fires are extinguished, the enlightened one enters *nirvāṇa*. "Nirvana, the quenching of fire, is an irreducible image," argues Steven Collins, "a fundamental semantic device without which Buddhism in its historical expression would be impossible, quite literally unthinkable."[46] In the so-called "Fire Sermon," the Ādittapariyāya Sutta, the Buddha explains that all of the senses (sight, hearing, touch, taste, smell, and mind), the objects they apprehend, the consciousness that arises from the apprehension of the objects, and the sensations that arise as a result of that consciousness are all "burning" with the fires of hatred, greed, and delusion. In other words, our mediated experience of the world causes and is caused by the three poisons that keep us trapped in the endless cycle of redeath. In the *Aggi-Vacchagotta Sutta*, the "Discourse to Vacchagotta on Fire," the Buddha explains to the titular wandering ascetic that an enlightened one who has entered *nirvāṇa* is neither reborn, nor is not reborn, nor both is and is not reborn, nor is neither reborn nor not reborn (the so-called "fourfold negation"). Vacchagotta is understandably confused, so the Buddha asks the ascetic how he would answer someone who asked whether a fire that has burned itself out has gone north, south, east, or west. Vacchagotta responds that the question is meaningless (it is in fact what the philosopher Gilbert Ryle would have called a "category-mistake") because the fire has run out of fuel and is called "extinguished."[47]

Collins observes that European scholars tried to see behind this passage the older Indian notion that there is an invisible presence of fire inherent in wood—where, as we recall, Agni deposits himself overnight according to the liturgy of the *agnihotra*—that is conjured up by the kindling of flame and that returns to invisibility when the fire appears to go out. But, he argues, "[in] the majority of uses of fire-imagery in Buddhist texts, the fires that go out or go down like the sun, are—like the three fires of Greed, Hatred and Delusion—precisely what must be *wholly* eliminated for release to be possible."[48] In order to be released, one must be totally free of the three poisons. And when they are put out completely, the enlightened one can enter *nirvāṇa* where she is no more connected to the world of rebirth and redeath than the cold ashes of an extinguished fire are to the blaze it was before it burned out. The Buddhist conception of a fire that can be totally extinguished is much closer to the Sanskrit proverb than the argument for a pure potentiality of fire that exists even in its apparent absence.

In my reading of the Girardian "primal scene," God and religion,[49] along with culture, the symbolic, language, and the scapegoat mechanism, simultaneously come into being with the death of the sacrificial victim. These primary processes and structures do not come from the hypothetical moment in which a pack of proto-humans in the grip of a spreading conflagration of multiplying mimetic rivalries turn on one of their members and kill him, expending their aggression and bringing a feeling of peace and equilibrium. The founding moment of culture, as Girard shows us in *Violence and the Sacred*, is the second killing, the one that is performed in an effort to renew the salutary effects of the first spontaneous killing; it is the kindled fire, not the conserved one. Our language knows this: the Latin *victima* and the Modern English "victim" (as well as "witch") are both related to the Germanic word cluster derived from the Proto-Indo-European **weik*, "consecrate."[50] But, in the same way as "The Great War" only becomes "World War I" after the naming of World War II (paradoxically making World War II the actual first world war), the first "victim" is always-already the second victim because his death retroactively turns the luckless proto-human previously killed by the crowd spontaneously into a victim too. The death of the second victim is actually the resurrection of the first, bringing back to life one who has died outside of the symbolic order and therefore outside of space and time. The first victim, the transcendental signifier, has all the attributes of the monotheistic God. He preexists creation, since creation is the birth of the symbolic order (and thereby, human consciousness) through the death of the second victim. He has never lived, nor can he ever die, existing only as the undead corpse beyond space and time, incessantly calling for victims. The Iranian philosopher Reza Negrastani seems to grasp this point when he writes that "the Dead God is a God beyond judgment."[51] The morality of Christianity, nothing new at the time, would not have been nearly enough to end the reign of this God. Only the Passion and Resurrection could have done this. No wonder then, that St. Paul says in 1 Corinthians 15:14, "If Christ has not been raised, our preaching is useless and so is your faith." Only a God that truly lives, having been dragged into our order of existence, can truly die and allow us to be free of him.

The sacred, in this admittedly somewhat heterodox reading of Girard, is synonymous with the horror and fascination of undeath. Recall that in Vedic myth the word *amṛta*, usually applied to the gods, especially Agni, and identified as the elixir churned from the ocean, means "deathless" or "without death," which is quite different from eternal life. But to be without death is not only to be free from violent unnatural death, but also to be outside of death's domain, into which all humans are born. To pay the sacrificial debt that a man is born owing to the gods in the Vedic system is to "buy himself back from death," for which he requires the help of Agni Vaiśvānara. A Vedic sacrificer is born in and through the performance of his sacrifice, which is why those eligible to perform the sacrifice are called *dvija*, "twice-born." In a very different way, the Buddha's revelation promises freedom from death in the form of *nirvāṇa*. This is why the Māra, the god of death and desire, goes to such great lengths to prevent the Buddha's enlightenment, tempting him with sex and threatening him with violence. In Buddhist, yogic, and Vedic ideas of *amṛta*, we can see an awareness of the violent sacred as undeath—founded on a God that is dead and because he is dead, can never die and can only bring more death—as well as an awareness of the necessity of fire in any attempt to escape the pull of the violent sacred: extinguishing the fire in the

Buddhist case, internalizing it in the yogic-alchemical case, and employing it in the Vedic case.

"*Fire is no longer a reality for science*," concludes Bachelard, and as a result, prescientific ideas about fire, immune from the scrutiny of a scientific discourse that has already moved past them, have become deeply entrenched in our ways of thinking, shaping the questions we ask about the world.[52] In the wake of Albert Einstein's work on relativity, the world suddenly becomes post-Newtonian and post-Cartesian. But the revolution (or revelation) is incomplete in that folk beliefs still operate at the unconscious level and are made visible in poetic language rather than in the realm of theories and hypotheses. Chemists have relegated fire, once one of the four constituent elements of the world, to the status of an unimportant effect of processes at the molecular level. But scientific discourse, blind to its own mythmaking ("spontaneous combustion" and the like) is not adequately equipped to truly disenchant the world and so Bachelard turns to (largely Jungian) psychoanalysis to uncover the fire "complexes" regnant in our épistème. Girard has come to a similar conclusion as Bachelard's about fire with regard to the unreality of "sacrifice" in the study of religions.[53] In the Indian traditions, both fire and sacrifice remain central topics of contemplation and investigation. Does smoke reveal the presence of fire as the Indian Nyāya logicians say it does in the formalized logical relation of *vyapti*? Or do smoke and fire, stinging the eyes, choking the lungs, and singeing the eyebrows of anyone who gets too close, actually conceal the presence of something else altogether, hidden in plain sight on the edge of the enclosure surrounding the fire altar—the violent sacrifice?

NOTES

1. Some useful guides to the role of fire in Indian religion include V. S. Agarwal, "Fire in the Rigveda," *East and West* 1 (1960): 28–32; Chauncy Blair, *Heat in the Rig Veda and Atharva Veda* (Cambridge, MA: Harvard University Press, 1961); David M. Knipe, *In the Image of Fire: Vedic Experiences of Heat* (Delhi: Motilal Banarsidass, 1975); Ellison Banks Findly, "Aspects of Agni: Functions of the Ṛgvedic Fire" (PhD diss., Yale University, 1978); Uma Marina Vesci, *Heat and Sacrifice in the Vedas* (Delhi: Motilal Banarsidass, 1992); John Stratton Hawley, *Sati, the Blessing and the Curse: The Burning of Wives in India* (Oxford: Oxford University Press, 1994); Jonathan P. Parry, *Death in Benares* (Cambridge: Cambridge University Press, 1994); Lata Mani, *Contentious Traditions: The Debate on Sati in Colonial India* (Berkeley: University of California Press, 1998); Laurie L. Patton, *Bringing the Gods to Mind: Mantra and Ritual in Early Indian*

Sacrifice (Berkeley: University of California Press, 2005), chap. 4; and Frits Staal, *Agni: The Vedic Ritual of the Fire Altar*, 2 vols. (Delhi: Motilal Banarsidass, 2010).

2. See Jarrod Whitaker, *Strong Arms and Drinking Strength: Masculinity, Violence and the Body in Ancient India* (Oxford: Oxford University Press, 2011), 36–41.

3. Stephanie Jamison and Joel P. Brereton, trans., *The Rigveda: The Earliest Religious Poetry of India*, vol. 1, (Oxford: Oxford University Press, 2014), 42.

4. See Brian Collins, *The Head Beneath the Altar: Hindu Mythology and the Critique of Sacrifice* (East Lansing: Michigan State University Press, 2014), 66–67.

5. In Ṛg Veda 1.60.1, the Indian Prometheus, Mātariśvan, steals fire from heaven and gives it to the progenitor of the Bhṛgu Brahmin clan.

6. Sigmund Freud, "The Acquisition and Control of Fire," in *The Standard Edition of the Complete Psychological Works of Sigmund Freud*, vol. 22 (London: Hogarth Press, 1953–74), 183.

7. A naturally occurring fire could be caused by lightning, volcanoes, sparks from falling rocks striking one another, or exothermic internal reactions in piles of manure or other forms of compost.

8. Upon death, the ātihāgni performs the final sacrifice (*antyeṣṭi*) in which all three fires come together to form the fire that burns his corpse.

9. See H. W. Bodewitz, *The Daily Evening and Morning Offering (Agnihotra) According to the Brāhmaṇas* (Delhi: Motilal Banarsidass, 1976), 163.

10. See Roberto Calasso, *Ardor*, trans. Richard Dixon (New York: Farrar, Straus and Giroux, 2010), 195.

11. H. W. Bodewitz, *Jaiminīya Brāhmaṇa I, 1–65: Translation and Commentary* (Leiden: Brill, 1973), 70n5.

12. Patrick Olivelle, trans., *Saṃnyāsa Upaniṣads: Hindu Scriptures on Asceticism and Renunciation* (Oxford: Oxford University Press, 1992), 68–69.

13. The Vedic religion begins around 1500 BCE and is centered on the orally transmitted Vedic corpus, the institution of sacrifice, and the pantheon of gods led by Soma, Agni, Mitra-Varuṇa, and Indra, while classical Hinduism begins around 200 BCE and is centered on temple worship, the epics and Purāṇas, and the pantheon of gods led by Śiva, Viṣṇu, and Devī, the Goddess.

14. Ellison Banks Findley, "Agni," in *The Encyclopedia of Religion*, 2nd ed., vol. 1, *Aaron–Attention* (Farmington Hills, MI: Macmillan, 2005), 178–79.

15. M. L. West, *Indo-European Poetry and Myth* (Oxford: Oxford University Press, 2007), 266.

16. See Nick Allen, "Hephaestus and Agni: Gods and Men on the Battlefield in Greek and Sanskrit Epics," in *New Perspectives on Myth: Proceedings of the Second Annual Conference of the International Association for Comparative Mythology, Ravenstein (the Netherlands), 19–21 August, 2008*, ed. Wim M. J. van Binsbergen and Eric Venbrux (Haarlem: Shikanda, 2010), 357–72; and West, *Indo-European Poetry and Myth*, 267–68.

17. Logi, not Loki (as Wikipedia reports) is the source for Loge in *Das Rheingold*. See West, *Indo-European Poetry and Myth*, 268.

18. *The Mahābhārata: Text as Constituted in Its Critical Edition*, vol. 1, *Ādi-, Sabha-, Āraṇyaka-, and*

Virāṭa-Parvans (Poona: Bhandarkar Oriental Research Institute, 1976), 277–90. Hereafter, I will refer to passages from the *Mahābhārata* by citing the book, chapter, and verse.

19. Jamison and Brereton, *Rigveda*, 41.

20. Madeleine Biardeau, *Stories about Posts: Vedic Variations around the Hindu Goddess*, trans. Alf Hiltebeitel, Marie-Louise Reiniche, and James Walker, ed. Alf Hiltebeitel and Marie-Louise Reiniche (Chicago: University of Chicago Press, 2004), 54.

21. See Michael Witzel, "The Development of the Vedic Canon and Its Schools: The Social and Political Milieu," in *Inside the Texts, Beyond the Texts*, ed. Michael Witzel (Columbia, MO: South Asian Books, 1997), 260n14; and Brian Black, *The Character of the Self in Ancient India: Priest, Kings, and Women in the Early Upaniṣads* (Albany: State University of New York Press, 2007), 13.

22. George Thompson, "The Brahmodya and Vedic Discourse," *Journal of the American Oriental Society* 117, no. 1 (January–March 1997): 25.

23. Analyzing the description of the cosmic giant Puruṣa's willing dismemberment to create the universe as a scapegoat myth, Girard writes: "This is essential, and I shall summarize it once more: *somewhere in an indeterminate past there must have been a crime attributed to Purusha*. It was of course only a projection—imaginary but necessary for the fabrication of a really odious scapegoat. *If Purusha no longer appears guilty, it must be due to the extreme age of the myth, which has effaced everything that in the genesis of the religious order is unsettling*, anything that might potentially reveal the founding violence." René Girard, *Sacrifice*, trans. Matthew Patillo and David Dawson (East Lansing: Michigan State University Press, 2011), 45 (italics added).

24. Julius Eggeling, trans., *The Śatapatha Brāhmaṇa*, part 4, *Sacred Books of the East*, vol. 43 (Oxford: Clarendon Press, 1897), 398.

25. "Vedic India had no temples and so, before performing a sacrifice, priests would trace the boundaries of a site officially consecrated to this purpose, but *it was outside of these boundaries that the immolation was performed*. To better conceal the act and avoid the spectacle of bloodshed, they surreptitiously strangled the victim instead of cutting his throat as was once done." Girard, *Sacrifice*, 5–6.

26. See Robert Gardner and Frits Staal, *Altar of Fire*, VHS (Watertown, MA: Documentary Educational Resources, 2000).

27. See Jaan Puhvel, *Comparative Mythology* (Baltimore: Johns Hopkins University Press, 1987), 277–84; and West, *Indo-European Poetry and Myth*, 270–72.

28. Jonathan Parry, "Sacrificial Death and the Necrophagous Ascetic," in *Death and the Regeneration of Life*, ed. Maurice Bloch and Jonathan Parry (Cambridge: Cambridge University Press, 1982), 76.

29. For a dense philological argument about the meaning of *xvarənah*, see Alexander Lubotsky, "Avestan *Xvarənah-*: The Etymology and Concept," in *Sprache und Kultur, Akten der X. Fachtagung der Indogermanischen Gesellschaft*, ed. W. Meid (Innsbruck: IBS, 1998), 479–88.

30. James Darmesteter, trans., *The Zend Avesta*, part 2, *Sacred Books of the East*, vol. 23 (Oxford: Oxford University Press, 1882), 297–300; and Puhvel, *Comparative Mythology*, 278.

31. Biardeau, *Stories about Posts*, 82–83, is a possible exception, though she does not explicitly refer to Agni in the waters.

32. *Mahābhārata* 1.16.12–27.

33. One demon, Rahu, manages to get close enough to the *amṛta* to take a swallow, but Viṣṇu chops off his head before it passes through his throat, leaving Rahu as an immortal but disembodied head who periodically swallows the sun and moon, causing solar and lunar eclipses.

34. "Nichts weiss der Alp von des Goldes Auge, das wechselnd wacht und schläft? Von der Wassertiefe wonnigem Stern, der hehr die Wogen durchhellt?" Richard Wagner, *Das Rheingold (The Rhine-Gold): A Music-Drama in Four Scenes, Prelude to the Trilogy "Der Ring des Nibelungen" (The Nibelung's [sic.] Ring), The English Version by Charles Henry Meltzer* (New York: Fred Rullman, 1904), 10.

35. "The divine personality of Soma, it is true, is, even for Vedic imagery, of an extremely vague and shadowy character; but it is difficult to see what plastic conception there could be of a deity whose chief activity apparently consists in mingling his fiery male nature with the teeming waters of the sky, and the swelling sap of plants. The principal cause, however, of the vagueness of Soma's personality, and the source of considerable difficulties in explaining many of the Vedic conceptions of this deity, is his twofold nature as a fiery liquor, or liquid fire,—that is to say, his fluid and his fiery or luminous nature." Julius Eggeling, trans., *The Śatapatha Brāhmaṇa*, part 2, *Sacred Books of the East*, vol. 26 (Oxford: Clarendon Press, 1885), xii.

36. We should note here that the identification of *soma* and the moon is common in Indian literature from the Vedic period onward.

37. David Gordon White, *The Alchemical Body: Siddha Traditions in Medieval India* (Chicago: University of Chicago Press, 1996), 203.

38. For Girard's take on the mutability of the object that mediates the rivalry of the gods and the demons in Sanskrit myth, see Girard, *Sacrifice*, 11–22.

39. J. C. Heesterman, "Other Folk's Fire," in *Agni, the Vedic Ritual of the Fire Altar*, ed. Frits Staal et al., vol. 2 (Berkeley: Asian Humanities, 1983), 94.

40. Gaston Bachelard, *The Psychoanalysis of Fire* (Boston: Beacon Press, 1964), 19.

41. Death is a big business in Varanasi, since the city is sacred to Śiva and to die there is to attain instant liberation.

42. Diana Eck, *Banaras: City of Light* (Princeton, NJ: Princeton University Press, 1982), 340.

43. Parry, "Sacrificial Death and the Necrophagous Ascetic," 78–79.

44. Charles Malamoud, *Cooking the World: Ritual and Thought in Ancient India*, trans. David White (Delhi: Oxford University Press, 1996), 22.

45. Ananta Śeṣa, whom we have previously encountered as the rope used to churn the ocean, is the brother of the snake Takṣaka from the Khāṇḍava forest, the architect of the universe, and the archenemy of Agni. See Malamoud, *Cooking the World*, 19.

46. Steven Collins, *Nirvana: Concept, Imagery, Narrative* (Cambridge: Cambridge University Press, 2010), 81.

47. Bhikku Ñāṇamoli and Bhikku Bodhi, trans., *The Middle Length Discourses of the Buddha: A New Translation of the "Majjhima Nikāya"* (Boston: Wisdom Publications, 1995), 593; and Collins, *Nirvana*, 83.

48. Collins, *Nirvana*, 84.

49. I do not say "archaic God" and "archaic religion" to distinguish these terms from "Christian God" and "Christian religion" because in my reading of Girard, Christianity (not to be confused with

Christendom) can only be understood as the destruction of religion. From this, I understand "Christianity" to be a term that can be widened to include any ethical, political, scientific, or even literary practice that seeks to undermine the scapegoat mechanism and replace it with love and justice, something like Karl Rahner's idea of the "anonymous Christian" (see Karl Rahner, *Theological Investigations*, trans. David Bourke, vol. 14 [London: Darton, Longman & Todd, 1976], 283) but completely removed from any type of apologetics. I also understand "Christianity" to be completely dispensable.

50. J. P. Mallory, *The Oxford Introduction to Proto-Indo-European and the Proto-Indo-European World*, ed. Douglas Q. Adams (Oxford: Oxford University Press, 2006), 412.

51. Reza Negrastani, *Cyclonopedia: Complicity with Anonymous Materials* (Melbourne: Re-Press, 2008), 207.

52. Bachelard, *Psychoanalysis of Fire*, 2.

53. Let one example stand for many: In the words of Christopher A. Faraone and F. S. Naiden, "Forty years after the publication of [Walter Burkert's] *Homo Necans*, the notion of 'sacrifice' is a category of the thought of yesterday." *Greek and Roman Animal Sacrifice: Ancient Victims, Modern Observers* (Cambridge: Cambridge University Press, 2012), 10. I owe this observation to Roberto Calasso. See his "The Last Superstition," *RES: Anthropology and Aesthetics* 65/66 (2014/2015): 403. There are, of course, exceptions, such as Naphtali S. Meshel's provocative study *The Grammar of Sacrifice: A Generativist Study of the Israelite Sacrificial System in the Priestly Writings with a "Grammar" of* Σ (Oxford: Oxford University Press, 2014).

Girard and Hindu Sacrifice

Noel Sheth

In dealing with René Girard's ideas about Hindu sacrifice, I concentrate on his book *Sacrifice*[1] since it mostly deals with Vedic, that is, early Hindu, sacrifice.[2] My article is divided into three parts.[3]

Girard's Interpretation of Vedic Sacrifice and Its Basic Confirmation

In his book *Sacrifice* Girard pays special attention to sacrifice in the Brāhmaṇas. Although he deals with it later in his book, let me start, in chronological order, with the Puruṣa-Sūkta (Hymn of the [Cosmic] Person) (RV 10.90), in which creation or emanation takes place through the sacrifice, and even dismemberment, of the Cosmic Person.[4] Girard points out that in the last verse the Cosmic Person is not just a passive victim, but also takes part in the sacrificial activity, the active facet of sacrifice, which is further developed in the Brāhmaṇas.[5] But Girard is faced with a problem: although required by his mimetic theory,[6] the unanimous accusation of the Puruṣa by a mob is conspicuously absent in this hymn. Now Girard's mimetic theory is particularly applicable to archaic religions, and the RV is much older than the Brāhmaṇas, so the absence of any accusation is all the more problematic. Hence Girard speculates that there must have been earlier versions of this hymn, in which the accusation against the Puruṣa and making him a scapegoat must have been present. He thinks that the great number of sacrificers present is a hint that an earlier version may have existed.[7]

Be that as it may, Girard rejoices that his theory is amply confirmed in the Brāhmaṇas in the case of the god Prajāpati, who commits incest with his daughter, Dyaus (the Sky) or Uṣas (the Dawn). The other deities, considering this a transgression, ask Rudra to pierce him, which Rudra does.[8] This story is certainly supportive of Girard's theory of the lynching of a victim by a crowd. However Girard himself admits, on the basis of Lévi's book, on which he depends greatly, that there are other versions where there is neither incest nor punishment, for example, Prajāpati's sacrificial activity exhausts him and he dies.[9]

One of the recurrent themes in the Brāhmaṇas, which gives strong support to Girard's theory, is the repeated rivalries between the deities or *devas* and the demons or *asuras*. Girard analyzes these conflicts very well. Both groups are adversaries and do not wish to be reconciled or make a compromise. Both desire the same thing, the world, or the sun or the moon, etc.—the whole of creation.[10]

Even when the moon is divided (with its different phases) between the *devas* and the *asuras* by Prajāpati, the *devas* are in fact greedier and always ready to fight for what they desire. What provokes these quarrels is mimesis. The conflict is resolved by sacrifice, in favor of the deities; but again there are new desires, renewed rivalries, and more sacrifices.[11]

Based on the data that he had at his disposal, Girard concedes that, in the conflicts of the *devas* and *asuras*, humans are absent and yet, he says, they have much to do with these dramas between the *devas* and *asuras*: all humans as well as deities and demons are created by sacrifice, especially through Prajāpati, the greatest among the deities. There are conflicts galore between the deities and the demons in the Brāhmaṇas because they reflect the many rivalries in our human world.[12]

In the pressing of the soma plant, one is asked to think of one's enemy, or, in the absence of an enemy, a blade of grass (SB 3.9.4.17). The text asks the sacrificer to think of the one whom one really desires to kill, viz., one's enemy.

So the passage reveals that sacrifice is a strategy for preventing enemies from killing each other by supplying substitute victims. Girard asserts that this text is the best in revealing the intrinsic purpose of sacrifice, viz., to avert violence by performing a sacrifice. And he emphasizes that this essential significance of sacrifice is shown not only at the core of Vedic sacrifice, but also in the soma sacrifice, which, according to him, is at the periphery of sacrificial activity. He also mentions that there is even a substitution of the sacrificers who are actually purchasing and drinking the soma juice: the text states that a false buyer is proposed to the god Soma, that is, a man from a lower class, so that the anger of the god Soma would be directed against this man.[13] This again supports his scapegoat theory, Girard maintains.[14] We may give a further confirmation of this latter part by mentioning that in the Śyena (Falcon) Sacrifice, meant for destroying enemies, the offerings consist of nine groups (SadB 4.2.1–2, 23) that, according to the commentator Sāyaṇa, are defective, for example, a group of one-eyed animals or of lame animals, etc.[15]

Having briefly put forth Girard's understanding of the antagonism between the deities and the demons, I shall now offer further confirmations of Girard's thesis and also make some nuanced comments. One can give many more examples of rivalries between the deities and the demons in the Brāhmaṇas, and the deities ultimately always get the better of the demons. Here is an interesting example: The proud demons make offerings into their own mouth, but the deities make the offerings to one another. Hence Prajāpati, whose body was the sacrifice, gives himself to the deities (SB 5.1.1.1–2, 11.1.8.1–2). The Tānūnaptra (Bodily Covenant) rite, in which the deities deposit their bodies in the house of the deity Varuṇa, brings about unity among the deities so that their adversaries, the *asuras*, are defeated (AB 1.24).[16]

A direct rivalry between *devas* and human beings (not *asuras*) is found in both wanting to possess the same thing, viz., sacrifice itself. For example, the deities, after sucking the sap of the sacrifice, remove any telltale traces of it, so that human beings would not be able to sacrifice and attain heaven. However the seers (*ṛṣis*) catch wind of this and finally manage to find the sacrificial cake (*puroḍāśa*) and offer it as a sacrifice (SB 1.6.2.1–4).[17] Moreover, as a sort of further confirmation of Girard's mimetic theory, many sacrifices in the Brāhmaṇa texts have their origin in human beings imitating the deities in the manner of performing the sacrifices. In fact, Sylvain Lévi cites several texts to illustrate the law of sacrifice, viz., that one should perform the sacrifices in the manner in which the deities do them.[18]

There are many sacrifices mentioned in the Brāhmaṇas against enemies. Indra kills his enemy through the Vighana (Killing) Sacrifice (TMB 19.18.1–2); he also destroys the opposition of the Maruts by means of this sacrifice (TB 2.7.18.1). We have the Śyena (Falcon) Sacrifice for catching one's enemies, since it is the swiftest among the birds (SadB 4.2.1–3); the Saṁdaṁśa (Tongs) Sacrifice is for taking hold of one's enemy just as one seizes with a pair of tongs something that is difficult to hold (SadB 4.4.1–4).

Similarly, there are many sorcery rites that are intended to harm or gain victory over one's enemies. In some of these rites, one has to think of one's enemy; for example, at the time of uttering the *vaṣaṭ* call, which is interpreted as a thunderbolt, one thinks of one whom one hates (AB 3.6); one may also mention the enemy's clan, family (*gotra*), and mother (TMB 6.6.2). One of the sorcery sacrifices is called the Arrow (Iṣu) (SadB 4.3.2–3); another is the Thunderbolt (Vajra) (SadB 4.4.1–8). There are also rituals to defend and protect oneself from the sorcery of others (TB 1.7.7.5; TMB 22.17.3); still others combine defense as well as a counterimprecation (SB 5.2.4.20). It should be noted, however, that many of these sorcery (*abhicāra*) rites are optional and not prescribed: often the sacrifice is introduced by the words, "If one wishes to use sorcery (*yadyabhicaret*)" (SB 1.2.5.22).

These sacrifices, in a way, support the thesis of Girard. However, I would like to point out that here we have the slaying of enemies, and not a crowd of people ganging up against one scapegoat. These rites are believed to actually kill one's enemies, and not to resolve the enmity through a sacrifice. However, Girard's comment, in this context, is germane: the scapegoat understanding is unconscious. The expression scapegoat "is not an ordinary concept. Instead it is something paradoxical, a principle of illusion whose efficacy requires complete ignorance of it. To have a scapegoat is not to know that one has one. As soon as the scapegoat is revealed and named as such, it loses its power. . . . The persecutors of any scapegoat . . . hate him *without reason*, by virtue of an illusion."[19]

Girard mentions that, in consonance with the taboo against ritual violence in ancient religious traditions, the Vedic sacrifice often plays down or attempts to hide the violence against sacrificial victims, camouflaging the gory sight of blood by strangling the victim, rather than slitting its throat.[20]

We can offer further confirmation of this approach: water is sprinkled in order to "soothe" or "heal" the cruelty of killing (SB 3.8.2.8–11); the priests look away from the victim so that they may not be eyewitnesses of the slaying; often, instead of using words like "slay" or "kill," they employ the euphemistic expression "quieten," or the animal is said to "go near to the deities" (SB 3.8.1.15). The victim is not led to death but to sacrifice: there is no "death," but simply "sacrifice" (SB 3.8.1.10); in fact, some ritual actions and words are said to mystically instill life into the animals being slaughtered (SB 13.2.8.2), and the animals are also said to become "immortal" (SB 3.8.3.26).

Sylvain Lévi calls Prajāpati the sacrifice god; Girard goes further and calls him the god sacrifice.[21] It is true that sacrifice is frequently identified with Prajāpati (e.g., Kauṣītaki-brāhmaṇa, 10.1, 25.11, 26.3). But sacrifice is also identified with Agni (Fire) (SB 2.1.4.19, 3.7.1.16); in fact, all sacrifices are Agni, since they are performed in fire (SB 4.1.5.1.13). Indra is the self (ātman) of sacrifice (SB 9.5.1.33). Sacrifice is also identified with Viṣṇu (SB 14.1.1.6; TB 1.4.3.6; TMB 13.5.5).

A Critique of Girard's Thesis

I now undertake a brief critique of Girard's analysis and statements concerning the mimetic nature of Vedic sacrifice. I have already made a few nuanced statements and comments about certain aspects of Girard's understanding and interpretation of Vedic sacrifice. I now make some more remarks particularly in reference to what Girard has not said.

First, generally, only the three higher classes had the right to perform sacrifice. The lowest group or Śūdras were, with rare exceptions, not entitled to perform almost any sacrifice.[22] Now, since the lower classes and the outcastes far outnumber the higher classes and castes, the question is how do these people not destroy one another, when they are practically never permitted to perform sacrifice? Girard himself tells us that the Brahmins propose sacrifice as a solution to problems to the warrior or princely class (*kṣatriyas*), who are the main clients of the Brahmins because only they can afford to offer sacrifices,[23] but, from Girard's perspective, this makes the problem of resolving conflicts even more acute for the lower classes and castes.

Although in a sacrificial session (*sattra*) all the priests are themselves considered sacrificers, and they are all consecrated and shared in the fruits of the sacrifice,[24] it is rare to have more than one sacrificer in the Brāhmaṇas: in the Indrāgnyoḥ Kulāya there are two sacrificers (TMB 19.15.1–2), in the Marutstoma there are three (TMB 19.15.2–3), but generally there is only one sacrificer. So, though there are certainly sacrifices occasioned by the animosity of a crowd, most of the sacrifices have only one sacrificer. Similarly, in most sacrifices, only one person gets the result of the sacrifice, not a whole group of people, except in the case of a sacrificial session (*sattra*), where all the sacrificers share in the benefits of the sacrifice. In fact, it is mentioned that, in ancient times, in sacrificial sessions different people desired various things and their different desires were fulfilled.[25] In other words, most of the time we do not have a mob seeking to take revenge by a substitute scapegoat that is sacrificed.

We find texts in which the sacrificial victim is not the substitute of an enemy, but of the sacrificer. It is explicitly stated that the sacrificial victim is in essence the sacrificer (e.g., AB 2.11). This is further confirmed by the idea of the sacrificer's buying off or redeeming oneself (ātmaniṣkrayaṇa) through the sacrificial animal (SB 11.7.1.2–3; Kauṣītaki-brāhmaṇa, 10.3). Lévi, on whom Girard depends, also mentions this concept of buying off oneself by offering the animal as a substitute, and he also quotes texts to this effect.[26] Girard appears to have missed this through inadvertence.

In the context of the substitute victim or scapegoat, Girard also speaks of a generally unconscious heaping of blame on the scapegoat who is held responsible, subjected to lynching, and sacrificed.[27] However, we have the well-known case of Śunaḥśepa (AB 7.13–18), who is sold by his father Ajīgarta to be sacrificed as a substitute for the king's son. Since no one can be found to bind Śunaḥśepa and no one to slay him, his father offers to do both for additional remuneration. Just as his father is about to sacrifice him with the sharpened knife, Śunaḥśepa appeals to various deities, the last being Uṣas, and his bonds come loose. Later, Ajīgarta expresses remorse for the evil he had done (AB 7.17). There is no need to discuss the various details and interpretations of this story,[28] but what is relevant is to draw attention to the fact that not only does Ajīgarta proclaim the innocence of his scapegoat son, by expressing remorse for what he had done, but so does the sacrificial priest Viśvāmitra, who agrees with the son that Ajīgarta has done an irreparable and dreadful deed (AB 7.17). So here we have the clear declaration of the innocence of an intended victim, in some way similar to the cases of Job and Joseph in the Hebrew Bible and of Jesus Christ in the Gospels, which Girard thought was unique to Judaism and Christianity.[29] The story of Manu being duped to give away his wife to be sacrificed also implies the innocence of his wife, but not so forcefully as in the tale of Śunaḥśepa.[30] Elsewhere in his book, Girard reveals that he is aware of an antisacrificial or nonsacrificial stance in the Upaniṣads and in Buddhism,[31] and more recently he accepted that Orphism did proclaim the innocence of the victim and that Jainism was antisacrificial.[32] But I wish to draw attention to the at least occasional reference to the innocence of the victim in the early Vedic tradition, too.

With regard to Christianity, Girard declares, "Wherever the Gospels take root, blood sacrifices disappear forever."[33] But vegetarian offerings, such as various types of grains and the soma plant, and animal products (but not animals), such as milk, were already there in the Vedic period.[34] A vegetarian sacrificial cake (*puroḍāśa*) was offered in place of the animal, especially in certain sacrifices, and symbolized the sacrificial animal. For instance, it is said that the awns of the rice grains represent the hairs, the husks the skin, the chaff from polishings the blood, the ground rice the flesh, the substantial parts the bone (AB 2.9); or the ground rice is the hair and, when water is poured on it, it becomes skin, when it is mixed it becomes flesh, when it is baked it turns into bone, and when it is taken off the fire and sprinkled with butter, it changes into marrow (SB 1.2.3.8).

There are also some minor errors in Girard's book, which do not militate against his essential thesis. For example, he says that one cannot actually kill the god Soma because he is immortal.[35] But the early Vedic deities are not immortal (see SB 11.2.3.6). Referring to the deceiving of Soma by presenting an apparent buyer, Girard says, "How can one hope to conceal from a god, who is supposed to read the human conscience like an open book, a dissimulation as crude as this?"[36] Such an understanding, however, had not yet developed in reference to most of the deities at this stage in Hinduism; in fact, even at present there are minor deities (who are ignorant souls reborn in deity-bodies) and major or supreme deities,[37] and it is only the latter who can read our conscience.

Supplementary Information on Hindu Sacrifice

In this part I deal with further developments of Hindu sacrifice, generally not mentioned by Girard, but that also raise some questions about the universal applicability of his mimetic theory to Hinduism as a whole. This section is a further spelling out of one of the symposium's subthemes, "Beyond Archaic Religion," under which my paper was included.

Close to the beginning of his book, Girard says that some later texts of the Brāhmaṇas even strongly criticize sacrifice and thus go beyond themselves.[38] At the end of his book, even though Girard declares that he has neither the time nor the expertise to delve into such matters, he gives an example from the Brāhmaṇas, from Sylvain Lévi's book, of a comic, ironic satire of sacrifice, where the selfish priests exploit the sacrificers. And he concludes that both Vedic and biblical texts critique sacrifice.[39] Let me now go a little further.

Already in some Brāhmaṇa texts there is a reference to the later Upaniṣadic concept of Brahman as the highest Principle, which is the origin of everything (SB 11.2.3.1–6). Some texts assert that through knowledge one can ascend to the world where desires have gone away, and sacrificial gifts and rites without knowledge do not lead one to that world (SB 10.5.4.16). The relatively ancient and archaic JUB, apart from speaking at length about *sāmans* (metrical chants),[40] is more interested in metaphysical questions and on the sacred syllable om than in sacrifices and rituals. Also a couple of Upaniṣads are already included in the Brāhmaṇas: the Kena-upaniṣad is found in the JUB (starting from 10.1.1); the important Bṛhad-āraṇyaka-upaniṣad forms the last part of the SB (from 10.6.4.1 onwards).

In this section I wish to also deal with certain aspects of the later Vedic, and still later Hindu, understanding of sacrifice.[41]

Expanded Meaning of Sacrifice

Already the SB (11.5.6.1–3) and the Taittirīya-āraṇyaka (2.10) widened the scope of sacrifice. They spoke of the five daily Great Sacrifices (*mahā-yajña*):[42] (1) *Deva-yajña*: Sacrifice to Deities by making an oblation in the fire, even if it is just a fuel-stick; (2) *Pitṛ-yajña*: Sacrifice to the Ancestors, even if it is through mere libations of water; (3) *Bhūta-yajña*: Sacrifice to (supernatural) Beings by offering a *bali* or a morsel of food; (4) *Manuṣya-yajña*: Sacrifice to

Human Beings, by feeding Brahmins; (5) *Brahma-yajña*: Sacrifice to Scripture, even if one recites a verse from the RV, or a sacrificial formula from the Yajur-veda, or a stanza from the Sāma-veda.[43] These sacrifices were further elaborated in later medieval texts. For example, the Sacrifice to Beings now included the offering of food to outcastes and those inflicted with diseases, and to dogs, crows, and insects;[44] and the Sacrifice to Human Beings now included the honoring and feeding of guests, even of low castes and outcastes.[45] It will thus be seen that the concept of sacrifice was not confined merely to Ṛg-veda rituals anymore but also to social concern: to one's obligations not merely to the deities and ancestors, but also toward fellow human beings, particularly the needy, as well as to animals. In contrast to the goals of the earlier forms of sacrifice, the intentions of these five great sacrifices are more altruistic and spiritual, for they manifest faith, thanksgiving, happy remembrance, dependence, honor, benevolence, open-mindedness, and love for scripture. Sacrifice, therefore, included the whole of actual living and one's solidarity with, and concern for, the entire universe.[46]

Interiorization of Sacrifice

As a reaction to the excessive ritualism of the Brāhmaṇa texts, the Āraṇyakas and Upaniṣads moved toward the interiorization of sacrifice. Interest in the external world began to wane, and attention was concentrated on the knowledge of the interior Self. The emergence of a monistic philosophy made the deities and sacrifices unnecessary. Ritual and other action was even considered an obstacle in acquiring this inner knowledge of the Self, of ultimate Being. Action was replaced by knowledge, and so sacrifice was interiorized. Gradually the focus shifted from the external universe to the inner world of the human being. The purpose of sacrifice was not so much to maintain the macrocosm, but the microcosm: sacrifice was made to the immanent Divine Self. Human beings sacrificed even their empirical thoughts and desires and, in thus dying to their petty selves, they became one with the Absolute.[47]

The Muṇḍaka-upaniṣad strongly criticizes the ritualism of the Brāhmaṇas: those who practice ritualism, being full of desire, fall from the (temporary) heavens when their merit is exhausted, and they even sink to a world lower than earth. Only those who practice penance and faith in a forest, are calm, lead a life of knowledge, and live on alms will reach the immortal Self (ātman) (1.2.9–11). The Bṛhad-āraṇyaka-upaniṣad says that by rites one reaches the world of the ancestors (*pitṛloka*), but by knowledge one attains the world of the deities (*devaloka*), the best of the worlds (1.5.16).

In some Upaniṣads we notice some vacillation between the life of ritual and other action on the one hand, and the renunciation of action and the pursuit of knowledge on the other. The *Śvetāśvatara-upaniṣad* concedes, "Where the fire is kindled . . . where the soma juice overflows, there the mind is born" (2.6–7). The Īśāvāsya-upaniṣad gives some place to sacrifices, provided they are performed without selfish desire (1–2); and, on the other hand, it declares that those who worship ignorance enter into blind darkness, but those who take delight in knowledge enter into greater darkness (9).

The Bhagavad-gītā tried to steer a middle course between the early ritualism and the later Vedic renunciation of all actions. Sacrifices were still obligatory (18.5), but they, like all other nonritual actions, had to be performed without selfishly desiring the results for oneself (2.47, 18.6): in this way the Gītā modified the path of ritual and other action (*karma-mārga*). It also accepted the idea of interiorization by mystically extending the concept of sacrifice to include the control of the senses, penance, the study of scripture, and knowledge (4.26–30). However, it discouraged renunciation of action and retirement into the forest (3.4, 3.8) and recommended being active in the world, without being attached to it (3.26): in this manner it changed the way of knowledge (*jñāna-mārga*). To these two transformed paths of action and knowledge, the Gītā added a third road of loving devotion (*bhakti-mārga*). Surrendering oneself to God as one's only refuge (18.66), one should offer all actions, whether sacrificial ones or others, as an act of devotion (9.27) to a loving God (18.65).

New Forms of Sacrifice

In the devotional schools of Vaiṣṇavism and Śaivism, there developed new forms of sacrifice. These were partly Vedic, but also partly non-Vedic, being based on the important post-Vedic scriptures of these schools, viz., the Purāṇas, etc. Instead of being offered to the Vedic deities, the sacrifices were directed to the Major Gods Viṣṇu or Śiva, or, in Śaktism, to the Supreme Goddess called Śakti or Durgā. In order to distinguish these sacrifices of Devotional Hinduism from the Vedic sacrifices (*yajña*), they are called *yāga*.

While the Vedic sacrifices were meant for individual benefits, the sacrifices of Devotional Hinduism are theoretically always offered for the welfare of the world or for the good of the whole local community, but not for personal gains. So, theoretically, this understanding does not confirm Girard's earlier somewhat narrow and negative understanding of mimetic desire.[48] In practice, however, the sacrificer may seek some personal benefit or at least the acquisition of merit. With the exception of the oblations to the Great Goddess, the offerings in sacrifices performed by the higher castes are generally vegetarian and so are their priests.[49] So, in this case, as in Christianity, we do not have blood sacrifices.

Pūjā, which developed after the Vedic period, is the ritual honor of an image or aniconic form of a deity, or the ritual worship of a sacred or powerful person, animal, or object.[50] There is no need to go into various details of the *pūjā*. The purposes of the *pūjā* are both spiritual as well as material. They include salvation, the forgiveness of sins committed in the present and in past lives, the pleasing of the deity concerned, peace, happiness, health, wealth, protection from various evils, etc. There are three types of *pūjā*: daily, occasional, and optional. Theoretically, the devotee should not perform the daily and occasional *pūjās* for selfish reasons. Optional *pūjās* are generally intended for material gains or even to harm others through black magic.[51] So, in this latter case, Girard would find some support for his theory.

Tāntrism believes that, by symbolically or really joining the male and female aspects here on earth, one becomes united with the Supreme Being. Certain tāntric groups have five special offerings, viz., alcohol, meat, fish, an aphrodisiac grain, and sexual intercourse. This latter may be intercourse between a man and a woman or a community sexual congress between couples of men and women gathered together in a circle (*cakra-pūjā*).[52] The mental *pūjā* or internal sacrifice is very important and is preceded by Kuṇḍalinī Yoga, which has to do with yogic nerve centers (*cakra*), etc. The oblations could include an animal or even a human being.[53] Here again, while certain aspects of Girard's thesis, for example, regarding animal and human sacrifices, have some support, there are other elements, such as mental or internal sacrifice, that do not support his theory. Already in the Brāhmaṇas we do come across some rites that foreshadow the later tāntric development. Although in several sacrifices there are restrictions on sexual intercourse with any woman or even with all one's wives, still, for example, in the Gosava

Sacrifice, sexual intercourse with one's mother or sister or any woman of one's own family is obligatory (JB 2.113).

The practice of *pūjā* is very much on the decline, especially in the homes. However, in the temples the *pūjās* continue due to professional priests assigned to perform them. In modern times, *pūjā* has been interpreted in broader, nonritual, terms. For example, *pūjā* consists in honoring parents, teachers, guests, and one's spouse; or social service is a form of image-worship, because serving people is like serving God.[54]

Finally, there are the village or folk sacrifices of the lower castes, which generally consist of animal sacrifices to the lesser divinities.[55] In the Vedic sacrifices the spilling of the blood was reduced to a minimum since the animal was killed by strangulation, but this later folk animal sacrifice is very bloody since the animal's head is severed.[56] According to Whitehead, the priests generally belong to the lower castes or are even outcastes. These sacrifices are meant either to propitiate the angry village deities or to request them to ward off evil spirits that cause diseases and other calamities. Other purposes, such as thanksgiving and praise, are almost totally absent.[57] Biardeau is more charitable and grants that the animal sacrifice could have the same value as the āgamic. However, she is of the opinion that in reality earthly enjoyment generally prevails over, or probably even replaces, the desire for salvation.[58]

Let us now briefly consider the buffalo sacrifice.[59] The Vedic sacrificial victim was pure and was not an incarnation of evil. In this case, however, the buffalo is opposed to the Goddess: it is the incarnation of evil, the enemy of the deities and of righteousness (*dharma*).[60] What is remarkable in the region of the Deccan is that it is neither an individual nor a single caste that offers the buffalo sacrifice, but the entire village that does so, on the occasion of the feast of the Goddess or during an epidemic. It does not matter whether one is a vegetarian or not: everyone contributes toward the cost of the buffalo and the fees for the ritual, even if one does not participate in the ceremonies, since the benefit desired concerns the whole community.[61] So this buffalo sacrifice certainly supports Girard's theory to a large extent.

The solemn Vedic sacrifices are almost defunct, and of the domestic rites, generally only a few of the life-cycle rituals (*saṁskāras*), such as initiation into the higher classes (*upanayana*) and marriage, are celebrated nowadays. The sacrifices of Devotional Hinduism, however, continue to be performed in the temples, and the bloody village sacrifices are still popular. In modern times sacrifice has also been interpreted in broader terms. Vinoba Bhave, for instance, started a movement of donating land to the landless, and he called it a sacrifice (*bhūdān-yajña*).

In conclusion, I would say that, although Girard's theory of sacrifice is applicable to certain Vedic sacrifices, it does not seem to be universally applicable to all Vedic sacrifices. Furthermore, his concept needs to be broadened and expanded and also needs to be more nuanced especially when one considers the later developments in the understanding of sacrifice in Hinduism, where we discover that not all sacrifice is violent and that one can also have desires that are selfless and altruistic and that sacrifice includes the whole of actual living and one's solidarity with, and concern for, the entire cosmos. As we have mentioned, Girard is now open to at least some of the nuances highlighted in my article but, as far as I know, has not explicitly accepted all of them in the context of Vedic Hinduism, and especially in reference to later developments of the concept of sacrifice in Hinduism.

NOTES

1. René Girard, *Sacrifice*, trans. Matthew Pattillo and David Dawson (East Lansing: Michigan State University Press, 2011).
2. For a study of Hindu Sacrifice and a comparison with the Eucharist, see Noel Sheth, "Hindu Parallels to the Eucharist—I," *Vidyajyoti Journal of Theological Reflection* 62, no. 9 (September 1998): 679–99; Sheth, "Hindu Parallels to the Eucharist—II," *Vidyajyoti Journal of Theological Reflection* 62, no. 10 (October 1998): 753–68; and Sheth, "Hindu *Prasada*, and Its Reception," *The Examiner* 149, no. 18 (May 2, 1998): 12–15.
3. I have used these abbreviations for the following vulgate and critical editions of Vedic texts frequently mentioned in the article: AB (Aitareya-brāhmaṇa); JB (Jaiminīya-brāhmaṇa); JUB (Jaiminīya-upaniṣad-brāhmaṇa, in Jaiminīyārṣeya-Jaminīyopaniṣad-Brāhmaṇas, critically ed. by Bellikoth Ramachandra Sharma, Tirupati: Kendriya Sanskrit Vidyapeetha, 1967.); RV (Ṛg-veda); SadB (Ṣaḍviṁśa-brāhmaṇa, in Ṣaḍviṃśa Brāhmaṇa, with *Vedārthaprakāśa* of Sāyaṇa, ed. Bellikoth Ramachandra Sharma, Tirupati: Kendria Sanskrit Vidyapeetha, 1967); SB (Śatapatha-brāhmaṇa, Mādhyandina recension); TB (Taittirīya-brāhmaṇa); TMB (Tāṇḍya-mahā-brāhmaṇa).
4. Girard, *Sacrifice*, 38–39.
5. Ibid., 42–43.
6. In recent interviews with two interlocutors, he explains aspects of his mimetic theory. See René Girard, *Evolution and Conversion: Dialogues on the Origins of Culture with Pierpaolo Antonello and João Cezar de Castro Rocha* (London: Continuum International Publishing, 2010), 56–95.
7. Girard, *Sacrifice*, 43–46.
8. Ibid., 51–52.

9. Ibid., 53. Sylvain Lévi, *La doctrine du sacrifice dans les Brâhmaṇas* (Paris: Ernest Leroux, 1898), 22–24.

10. I may mention in passing a contrary example, viz., the well-known story of the churning of the ocean in later Hinduism (i.e., in the Epics and some Purāṇas), where the inimical deities and demons cooperate—because they need each other's help in the gigantic task of churning the ocean—in order to obtain the nectar of immortality (*amṛta*), which both of them desire.

11. Girard, *Sacrifice*, 15–18.

12. Ibid., 12, 23.

13. Lévi, *La doctrine du sacrifice*, 170.

14. Girard, *Sacrifice*, 55–59.

15. SadB, at 4.2.23; see also Alfred Hillebrandt, *Ritual-Litteratur, vedische Opfer und Zauber* (Graz, Austria: Akademische Druck- u. Verlagsanstalt, 1981), 139.

16. For a few more examples of conflicts between the deities and demons, see, for instance, JUB 1.15.4, 1.18.5.

17. However, the Brāhmaṇas also speak of mutual cooperation between the deities and human beings so that both may be able to live through sacrifice: see JB 1.258.

18. Lévi, *La doctrine du sacrifice*, 85–86.

19. Girard, *Sacrifice*, 72.

20. Ibid., 4–6.

21. Ibid., 47.

22. Arthur Berriedale Keith, *The Religion and Philosophy of the Veda and Upanishads*, 2 vols. (Cambridge, MA: Harvard University Press, 1925), 1:298–99.

23. Girard, *Sacrifice*, 24.

24. Keith, *Religion and Philosophy of the Veda*, 349; see, e.g., Gopatha-brāhmaṇa 1.4.1–6, where various priests in the sacrificial session are consecrated for the sacrifice.

25. JB 3.234.

26. Lévi, *La doctrine du sacrifice*, 130–34.

27. Girard, *Sacrifice*, 26–27, 80–83.

28. See, e.g., Georges Dumézil, *Flamen-Brahman*, vol. 51 (Paris: Librairie orientaliste Paul Geuthner, 1935), 19–32.

29. Girard, *Sacrifice*, 74–80.

30. Both these stories are referred to by Lévi, *La doctrine du sacrifice*, 118–20, 134–36.

31. Girard, *Sacrifice*, 88.

32. Girard, *Evolution and Conversion*, 211–14.

33. Girard, *Sacrifice*, 87.

34. Keith, *Religion and Philosophy of the Veda*, 1:278–79, 283–84.

35. Girard, *Sacrifice*, 55.

36. Ibid., 60.

37. Note, incidentally, that most Hindus believe in only one Supreme Being: a Hindu of one sect considers the Supreme Deity of another sect as a minor deity that is subordinate to one's own Supreme Being.

38. Girard, *Sacrifice*, 11.

39. Ibid., 87–93.

40. This it does understandably since it is linked with the Sāma-veda.

41. The term "Vedic" includes also the Upaniṣads, while the term "Hindu" applies more specifically, but not exclusively, to the later developments in Hinduism, after the period of the Upaniṣads.

42. For a detailed treatment of these sacrifices, bringing together earlier and later interpretations, see Pandurang Vaman Kane, *History of Dharmaśāstra: Ancient and Mediaeval Religious and Civil Law*, 2nd ed., 5 vols. (Poona: Bhandarkar Oriental Research Institute, 1968–77), 2.1:696–2.2:756.

43. The order and the brief explanation are in accordance with Taittirīya-āraṇyaka, 2.10.

44. Kane, *History of Dharmaśāstra*, 2.2:746–47.

45. Ibid., 2.2:749–56.

46. Ibid., 2.1:697–98.

47. Raimundo Panikkar, *The Vedic Experience—Mantramañjari: An Anthology of the Vedas for Modern Man and Contemporary Celebration* (Pondicherry: All India Books, 1977), 401–24, see esp. 402, 406–8, 417. However, I do not agree with all his interpretations. On the interiorization of sacrifice, see also Madeleine Biardeau, "Le sacrifice dans l'hindouisme," in *Le sacrifice dans l'Inde ancienne*, Madeleine Biardeau and Charles Malamoud (Paris: Presses Universitaires de France, 1976), 65–73.

48. More recently Girard has given further nuances to his mimetic theory, stating that some human beings do resist desire and mimetic rivalry; he also talks of good imitation, e.g., of Jesus Christ or the saints: Girard, *Evolution and Conversion*, 222–24.

49. Biardeau, "Le sacrifice dans l'hindouisme," 138–42.

50. Gudrun Bühnemann, *Pūjā: A Study in Smārta Ritual* (Vienna: De Nobili Research Library, 1988), 29.

51. Ibid., 84–85.

52. Agehananda Bharati, *The Tantric Tradition* (London: Rider, 1965), 244–67.

53. Sanjukta Gupta, "Modes of Worship and Meditation," in *Hindu Tantrism*, Sanjukta Gupta, Dirk Jan Hoens, and Teun Goudriaan, (Leiden: E. J. Brill, 1979), 128, 145–46, 153, 170–79.

54. Bühnemann, *Pūjā*, 93–94.

55. For a graphic description of animal sacrifices in Andhra, Karnataka, and Tamilnadu, see Henry Whitehead, *The Village Gods of South India* (Calcutta: Association Press and Oxford University Press, 1921), chaps. 4–6.

56. Biardeau, "Le sacrifice dans l'hindouisme," 141.

57. Whitehead, *Village Gods*, 43–47.

58. Biardeau, "Le sacrifice dans l'hindouisme," 152–53.

59. For a discussion of these buffalo sacrifices, see ibid., 146–52.

60. Ibid., 146–47, including n. 1. In this note, she points out that, since the bloody sacrifice is the characteristic of the impure castes, it is logical that the sacrificial victim too shares in this impurity.

61. Ibid., 149.

The Roots of Violence: Society and the Individual in Buddhism and Girard

Jacob Dalton and Alexander von Rospatt

René Girard's complex and sophisticated theory of sacrifice offers insights into the workings of human society that transcend culture and time and, while privileging Christianity and modernity, claim a certain universality. This invites scholars of other cultures and religions to consider the applicability of Girardian thought to their own fields of study. As scholars of Buddhism we take up this challenge by bringing Buddhism into conversation with Girard. Instead of concentrating on a particular text (Schlieter 2009) or genre (Hahn 2009) or practice (Arifuku 2009), we aim for a more comprehensive and general engagement with Girard by suggesting how Buddhism might be brought into conversation with his principal ideas. We build on the work of Leo Lefebure, whose response to Christopher Ives we find useful and insightful. We take as given Ives's own conclusions, namely that the history of Buddhism is not free from violence and that Buddhists have been involved in not only the perpetuation of violence but also its condoning and sanctioning. Our paper also expands upon Eugene Webb's efforts to read sacrifice into the Buddhist denial of a permanent, immutable self (ātman). Similarly we attempt to go beyond Jean-Claude Dussault's point that early Buddhism's liberative project disproves Girard's claim that the Christian revelation stands alone in unmasking and overcoming mimetic desire and rivalry and the dynamics of victimization.[1] While we basically agree with Dussault and even adduce further materials that support his larger point (i.e., from outside of the canonical scriptures of Pali Buddhism, which constitute his primary sources), we question whether Buddhist treatments of desire and Girard's schema of mimetic desire coincide in quite the way Dussault proposes.[2] Finally, our thinking benefits from Ilkwaen Chung's monograph on Girard and the "violent origins of Buddhist culture," though here again we take a somewhat different approach. Whereas Chung skillfully applies Girardian thought to Buddhism, we attempt the opposite: to apply Buddhism to Girard, to imagine what Buddhists might have to say about Girard's theories. As a result, we concur with Chung that Girard's more "social anthropological" approach to Buddhism yields many valuable insights, but we question whether such an approach might also miss certain aspects of Buddhist thought, particularly regarding the impossibility of a transcendence of the sacrificial framework at the social level.

We divide our essay into three parts: The first part addresses the psychology of the individual and the central role that desire, mimetic or otherwise, plays in the construction of the self. Then part two turns to the question of sacrifice and its role in the infamous "liberation rite" of tantric Buddhism. In this part we show how this rite lends itself on one level remarkably well to Girardian analysis. In the third part we complicate this interpretation by showing that on a different level this ritual can also be read as a critique of sacrificial violence. Toward this end, we introduce the figure of the bodhisattva, the ideal advocated by Mahāyāna Buddhism, and his role as the savior of sentient beings. The bodhisattva is said to pursue the quest of awakening (or "enlightenment," to use the term that is usually, though inaccurately, employed in English writings on Buddhism) not for the sake of his own liberation, but in order to alleviate the suffering of other sentient beings, to work for their welfare and, ultimately, their salvation. In the case of the liberation rite this means that the sacrificial priest performs the rite as a bodhisattva in order to spare the "killed" (we resist using the label "victim") from the disastrous karmic consequences his acts would entail. And it is the bodhisattva himself—and not the killed—who ultimately suffers the karmic consequences of this violent encounter. We conclude in part three by comparing and contrasting the Mahāyāna ideal of the bodhisattva and his somewhat more ambivalent role as the savior of sentient beings with Girard's reading of the Judeo-Christian revelation of the sacrificial framework and show that from a Buddhist perspective self-sacrifice and its revelation of the sacrificial framework cannot ever truly and permanently deliver society from the violence of sacrifice. Thus, while in part one we present Buddhism as a soteriology concerned with individual liberation and the complex processes of mental purification that are taught toward that end, we finish, in part three, with the Mahāyāna and its focus on the social arena and altruistic engagement with others.

The Psychological: Desire and the Construction of the Self

In order to present Buddhist thought as comprehensively as space here allows, we take the core teachings of mainstream Buddhism as our starting point. This entails that we begin by treating Buddhism as a soteriology and focus on the core doctrines shared by most Buddhist schools through history. In any conversation between Buddhism and Girard, it is significant that both place desire at the root of their models. Here we consider the three "evils" of early Buddhism—variously referred to as the three *kleśa*, *viṣa*, and *akuśala-mūla*, or desire, hatred, and ignorance—and examine how they can be aligned with mimetic desire, mimetic rivalry, and the ignorance implicit within the Girardian scheme.

Early Buddhist doctrine, like the contemporaneous Indian religious teachings of Jainism and the Upanisads, is grounded in the understanding that humans and all other sentient beings—this also includes animals, ghosts, and infernal, demonic, and divine beings—are bound to the cycle of birth, death, and rebirth, and that this bondage inevitably involves suffering. The principal concern of Buddhist soteriology is to end all suffering. While Buddhism does value the worldly mitigation and temporary suspension of suffering, its primary objective is the quest for complete and everlasting deliverance from suffering. This, in turn, requires liberation from the desire that lies at the root of our suffering—desire that traps us and drives us into perdition. A critical component of this liberation is the realization of the intrinsic unsatisfactoriness of conditioned existence, that is, the fact that the world we inhabit is impermanent by nature and does not allow for the lasting gratification of our desires. Just as the world of objects in which our desires are invested cannot satisfy those desires, neither is there any enduring self that can serve as the subject that would enjoy them. The self is a construct that is in truth nothing but a constant flow of impersonal events—the focus is on the mental events that constitute our mind stream. Realizing all this leads to an end of desire and hence too of suffering. Such a realization involves, of course, not a simple discursive understanding of a teaching, but a transformative realization that the Buddhist adept attains only after many, many years, and even lifetimes, of practice.

In addition to desire and the root ignorance that allows for desire to become operative in the first place, there is a third root evil that Buddhism identifies, namely the hatred and enmity that contribute to our bondage and suffering. The triad of these principal "evils" is depicted in animal form in the wheel of existence often found painted on the walls of vestibules of Tibetan (and Indian) monasteries as a comprehensive summary of existence and the laws that govern it. The hub of the revolving wheel is propelled by a pig, a cock, and a snake, which stand respectively for delusion/ignorance (*moha*), desire/craving (*rāga*), and hatred/enmity (*dveṣa*). They are joined to each other in a circular swirling motion, each animal holding in its mouth the tail of the animal preceding it, and in turn having its own tail held in the animal's mouth following upon it. The three animals thereby illustrate how the evils condition each other and keep the wheel of existence in motion. The individual is caught in the resulting dynamics since beginningless time. Conditioned by past acts (*karma*) of desire and hatred and the ignorance underlying these acts, the individual is propelled to commit further such acts, until patient and diligent Buddhist practice begins to recondition the individual and helps her, eventually, to break free of this vicious cycle.

The three root "evils" of Buddhism, as presented here in its earliest and doctrinally idealized form, may be aligned with the principal elements of the Girardian scheme. (1) Corresponding to desire/craving (*rāga*) is mimetic desire (arguably the fundamental element in Girardian thinking, according to which one desires that which is proper to the other); (2) corresponding to hatred/enmity is mimetic rivalry (i.e., the conflict that results from mimetic desire); and finally, (3) corresponding to delusion/ignorance (*moha*) is the ignorance, or deceit, that is inherent in mimetic desire and rivalry. In Buddhism, ignorance allows for *rāga* and *dveṣa* to become operative, just as in the Girardian scheme, ignorance allows for the operation of mimetic desire and rivalry.[3] Notwithstanding these structural parallels, however, there remains a crucial difference here: Buddhist *moha* refers specifically to the delusion about the true nature of self and existence, so that Buddhist desire requires this ignorance to veil the truth that desire can never be gratified due to the impermanent nature of existence. Meanwhile, Girard's mimetic desire requires a somewhat different form of ignorance (or "deceit," to use his term), namely the delusion that one's desires originate from oneself rather than from the other whom one is striving to emulate; the mimetic aspects of mimetic desire, in other words, must remain obscured:

> The romantic *vaniteux* always wants to convince himself that his desire is written into the nature of things, or, which amounts to the same thing, that it is the emanation of a serene subjectivity, the creation *ex nihilo* of a quasi-divine ego. Desire is no longer rooted in the object perhaps, but it is rooted in the subject; it is certainly not rooted in the Other.[4]

In short, where Buddhist ignorance is mistaken about the impermanent nature of the existence of both the self and the outer world, Girardian ignorance is deluded about the mimesis.

The Buddhist focus on the nature of existence rather than mimesis is also reflected in its treatment of desire. Early Buddhist accounts do not focus on desire as mimetic. Instead, the texts speak of two kinds of desire: the thirst for pleasures, in particular sexual desire (*kāmatṛṣṇā*), and the thirst for existence (*bhavatṛṣṇā*), that is, the clinging to existence, particularly as it manifests at the time of death causing rebirth.[5] While such a typology of desire does not preclude mimetic desire, particularly under the first category of thirst for pleasures, it tends to emphasize other forms of desire that draw our attention more to the existential status of the self and its objects of desire (usually as impermanent and intrinsically unsatisfactory).

The same difference in emphasis is seen again in Buddhist treatments of the second evil, hatred/enmity. Like Girard's mimetic rivalry, it is the ill will and negativity that underlies violence; however, while *dveṣa* by definition calls for another person to serve as the object of dislike and hatred, we are not aware of any statement within Buddhism that would explicitly identify the root of enmity as mimicry. On the other hand, it is clear that early Buddhists were not oblivious of the mechanisms of mimetic rivalry; indeed they developed elaborate practices to counteract it. Like Girard, they dwelt on the vicious cycle of reciprocal violence in which hatred traps its perpetuators. Their writings point to the pain suffered by the perpetrator of enmity and violence in the beyond, due to karmic retribution; they appeal to empathy and invoke the principle of the golden rule not to do unto others what one does not want to be subjected to oneself.[6] This approach comes to greatest prominence in a set of contemplative practices for cultivating four dispositions known as the "four immeasurables" (*apramāṇa*) or the "four Brahma abidings" (*brahmavihāra*). These dispositions are (1) friendliness and kindness (*maitrī*), (2) compassion (*karuṇa*), (3) sympathetic participatory joy (*muditā*) about the thriving of others, and (4) equanimity (*upekṣā*). These dispositions are to be fostered and expanded endlessly toward all sentient beings, hence their designation as immeasurable. Of particular interest for our purposes is *muditā*, as it is a direct antidote to the envy and mimicry that the successes of others commonly inspire. The fact that *muditā* is to be cultivated after friendliness and compassion confirms the difficulty of fostering this sentiment. On this point too, Buddhism shares common ground with Girard's theories and attests, at least indirectly, to the strength of the mimetic impulse and mimetic desire, and its universality in human nature.

There is a further parallel to note here: Whereas the two evils of desire and ignorance are identified as the prime cause for our bondage and suffering—in the four noble truths desire alone is mentioned, but the law of dependent origination (*pratītyasamutpāda*) in its fully evolved form accommodates both desire and ignorance—enmity contributes only indirectly, that is, by defiling the mind and facilitating ignorance and desire. Hence, Buddhist soteriology privileges the elimination of desire and ignorance, though there are also specific practices to tackle the evil of enmity, in particular the aforementioned "four immeasurables." The elimination of desire and ignorance is emphasized because ridding the mind of these two factors will automatically put an end to enmity. This indicates that enmity is grounded in desire and ignorance, just as Girardian mimetic rivalry is rooted in desire and the ignorance of its true object.

At this point the philosopher or the theologian might argue that really the different respective emphases of early Buddhism (the impermanent and unsatisfactory nature of existence) and Girard (mimesis) are not necessarily so very dissimilar. Even the Buddhist thirst for existence, which is normally treated as an innate drive rather than as mimetically constructed, one might suggest, is necessarily involved in mimetic desire, insofar as the self only comes into being precisely through the paradoxical assertion of its semblance, that it is something other than what it is.[7] And to be sure, the Buddhist "self" is relational, in that it requires an other as its foil. Nonetheless, there is no articulation of such a perspective here, in the earliest stratum of Buddhist doctrine. Buddhist discussions of desire are moreover missing any formulation of Girard's third element of the mediator, who intervenes between the desiring subject and its object. Mimetic desire requires all three elements, and its deceitful power lies precisely in its structure of triangulation, for while the subject is focused on the object, that focus is in large part defined by the mediator whom the subject seeks to emulate through that object. Without the mediator, the subject would have no desire for the object; the object would have no purchase on her. By contrast, an explanation of why the desiring subject chooses its particular object of desire remains relatively unexplored in early Buddhism.

The Social: The Liberation Rite as a Case of Girardian Sacrifice

Before we turn now to the next stage of Girard's analysis, that of sacrifice and scapegoating, we need to address a common misperception of Buddhism, which is apparently shared by Girard himself, namely the reductive view of Buddhism as a "world-escapist" religion. Though Buddhism's principal thrust with its focus on individual liberation differs from that of Girard, whose primary salvific concern is communal violence and its roots, Buddhism does not deal with enmity and violence solely as a personal, private psychological issue. Buddhism has always had a pragmatic orientation and, despite some of its doctrinal concerns, was deeply involved in society. Even within the monastic community, early Buddhists set forth rules and regulations that banned and punished violent acts. Indeed, the very first rule of practice (*śikṣāpada*) bans killing (*prāṇātipāta*), and the monastic rules of the *vinaya* make clear that homicide results in automatic expulsion from the order (*pārājika*). Moreover, Buddhism from early on was more than just a soteriology for the ascetic elite; it quickly grew into a universal religion that addresses all humanity, and hence also the laity. Buddhism's ban on violence is not an ascetic practice but a universal law that applies to all humans. In other words, the code of nonviolence (*ahiṃsā*) is not restricted to a religious elite but is valid for all. Thus Buddhism is vocal in its censorship of professions from butchery to soldiery, henchmen, judges, and even the king, insofar as they entail acts of violence, committed either directly or indirectly by order, as in the case of pronouncing the death sentence. The primary ban on killing is therefore focused on homicide, yet Buddhism also censors the slaughter of animals. (For an example, witness the famous edict of the great Buddhist king Aśoka in which he announces the reduction of animals slaughtered in his kitchen on a daily basis.) Finally we may note that at the heart of many Buddhist critiques of violence lies a categorical rejection of sacrificial practices that involve violence, in particular those that were central to the Brahmanical religious milieu in which Buddhism developed. It follows that Buddhism's rejection of violence cannot be reduced to the arena of individualized religious practices alone. Taken as a whole, then, Buddhism is not simply a religion of world-escapists, as Girard seems to suggest.[8]

This becomes particularly clear in the liberation rite we now want to introduce in order to engage Girard's analyses of sacrifice and scapegoating, both of which build on, and are in this sense subsequent to, mimetic desire and the construction of the self. Whereas the mechanisms of mimetic desire shape the individual and his desires, the sacrificial framework functions more to structure societies at large. Like his triangular scheme of mimetic desire, Girard's model of sacrifice and the scapegoating it entails represent a powerful hermeneutic. The relevance of its structures to Buddhism may be nowhere more obvious than in the ritual-myth pair of the notorious liberation rite and the mythic narrative of the subjugation of Rudra. The liberation rite is a ritual of tantric Mahāyāna Buddhism in which a person (usually an effigy of that person) is ritually killed in order to liberate him from his present existence and the disastrous consequences in future lives that threaten him. The corresponding myth tells of the Buddha's own original performance of the liberation rite, when he killed the demon Rudra, then resurrected him as a deified protector of the tantric mandala.

There are many versions of both the ritual and the myth. The ones presented here are unusually elaborate and share certain historical characteristics that allow them to be placed in conversation with one another.

In particular, both are written in Tibetan and both date from the earliest period of Tibetan Buddhist history. The liberation rite is described in what is likely a tenth-century manuscript discovered in the so-called "library cave" of Dunhuang on the old Silk Road, while the myth in question appears in a mid- to late ninth-century tantra called the *Compendium of Intentions* (Tib. *Dgongs pa 'dus pa'i mdo*). Both have their origins betwixt and between India and Tibet: Though the ritual was probably put into writing in the tenth century in Tibet, its forms reflect a slightly earlier period and are likely Indic in origin, while the myth appears to have been composed by a team of Indian, Nepalese, and Tibetan Buddhist scholars through a mixture of translation and invention.[9] Both, in other words, are Tibetan in origin but rooted in the tantric traditions of, roughly speaking, ninth-century India.

Liberation rites (*sgrol ba*), and compassionate violence more generally, appear throughout Tibetan Buddhism, depicted in art, reenacted through ritual dance, discussed in religious histories, and performed by tantric practitioners. In most if not all cases, they are directed against effigies, so that they are essentially rituals of sympathetic magic by which violent curses may be cast against one's enemies. The tenth-century manuscript from Dunhuang is somewhat unusual, for it does not mention an effigy. It is quite possible, however, that one was assumed; certainly most modern followers of Tibetan Buddhism would assume, if not insist, that one must have been. That said, other Buddhists do appear to have occasionally taken the ritual instructions of the liberation rite literally, the 1997 ritual killing of the monk Geshe Lobsang Gyatso in Dharamsala, India being, arguably, a particularly recent example.[10] Moreover, during precisely the same period to which our ritual manual dates, in the late tenth century, King Yeshe Ö of western Tibet released a royal edict famously condemning the *tāntrikas* of Tibet for their "corrupt" performances of the liberation rite upon live humans.[11] Perhaps in our ancient manuscript from Dunhuang, then, we have a ritual manual not unlike those that are said to have inspired such "corrupt" performances, one that has fortuitously resurfaced in the present. Whether Buddhists ever took the liberation rite literally or not, taken at face value, the ritual forms described in our tenth-century manual conform closely to those of a rite of human sacrifice and suggest fruitful comparison with the theories of Girard.

The rite begins with the officiating master entering an advanced meditative state. This is a crucial point. All of the proceedings that follow are to be accomplished while maintaining this same state. If the master is unable to achieve this, he is instructed not to continue. Otherwise, the text warns, an endless series of negative rebirths will result: "The performance of the activity (i.e., the killing) will not overpower the eight great terrors, whereby those who assemble [to perform the rite] will immediately become extremely unhappy, and (as a result) even if great compassion is felt, they will wander through the realms of samsara."[12] The master then prepares the ritual space, consecrates the site, and arranges the appropriate offerings upon a shrine. He initiates all those present into a wrathful mandala, possibly that of the *Guhyasamāja* ("Secret Gathering") ritual system, the *Guhyasamāja* being the primary tantra referenced elsewhere in the manuscript. Next, all the ritual officiants present generate themselves as deities from within that imagined mandala and recite the mantra of the central deity. The assembled then present to the deities of the mandala several offerings. They pray for protection against any possible obstructions and repair any past transgressions of their vows by means of confession and further prayers. Anyone present who has not received the necessary initiations is expelled from the ritual arena. The ritual space is sealed, and protective boundaries are established, a process that typically involves the visualized construction of an adamantine protective cage that encloses the ritual space. Now the "object of compassion" (be it the live person to be killed or an effigy representing him) is brought in and placed at the center of an altar platform that has been constructed at the heart of the ritual space. The "object of compassion" is positioned upon that platform, facing west, possibly with the intention that the "object of compassion's" consciousness will soon depart in that direction, to the realm of Sukhāvatī, the Buddha Amitābha's heavenly buddha field.

The "object of compassion" himself should represent a threat to the Buddhist teachings and, we are told, be guilty of one of five possible heinous crimes. He should be either (1) someone who has deprecated the Buddhist teachings, (2) one who insults an enlightened one, (3) one who practices the secret rites of the tantras without having received the proper initiations and sacraments, (4) one with false views, or (5) one who threatens the survival of the teachings. Having been identified as guilty of one of the five crimes, the "object of compassion" is determined to be an appropriate target for liberation. "The liberation of such a being," the text emphasizes, "should be undertaken with an attitude of great compassion."

Next come a series of purificatory rites. First, all those present imagine themselves being cleansed of all their karmic impurities, then the "object of compassion" is purified through the application of a white-mustard-seed paste at five key points on his body, "blocking the exits" through which his consciousness might depart the body for rebirth in each of the five possible realms of samsara.[13] As each daub is smeared upon the body, an associated syllable is recited: *oṃ* blocks the "object of compassion's" rebirth in the realm of the *asuras*, *hrīḥ* for the human realm, *hūṃ* for the animal realm, and so forth. Next a final purification of the "object of compassion's" mental impurities is performed by the ritual master who has imaginatively transformed himself into the wrathful buddha Ṭakkirāja. The *Guhyasamāja Tantra* includes a brief description of this deity: "The great wrathful Ṭakkirāja," it reads, "has three terrifying faces and four supremely terrifying arms." The mere appearance of this fearsome buddha, our Dunhuang manual explains, with his apocalyptic gaze and wild laughter, completes the cleansing of the "object of compassion's" karmic imprints. From his right eye burst flames that incinerate the impurities, from his left eye flood waters that wash them away, and the winds of his laughter blow away any that remain, leaving him thoroughly purified.

Now the goddess Kālarātrī is summoned. Ferocious in form, she appears in the space directly above the "object of compassion's" neck, riding a white mule. By means of the mantric syllable *krong*, she empowers and propels the liberating weapon, driving it with the force of many blades. Proclaiming Ṭakkirāja's mantra, the master then beheads the "object of compassion." As the "object of compassion's" consciousness emerges from his body, presumably from the severed neck, the master carefully directs it up to the mouth of the wrathful *heruka* buddha at the center of a mandala palace that is visualized in the space above the proceedings, and there the consciousness is consumed. Purified, the consciousness dissolves into the buddha's "jeweled stomach," and thus too, ideally, into enlightenment. According to tradition, this is the crucial moment that determines the success or failure of the liberative aspect of the rite, and it hinges entirely on the master's ability to link his consciousness to that of the "object of compassion" and guide it into enlightenment, or at least to a better rebirth. This key practice, of transferring a consciousness (Skt. *utkrānti* or *saṃkrānti*; Tib. *'pho ba*) into enlightenment, or at least a better rebirth, was common from an early date in both tantric Buddhism and Śaivism and can involve the transferal of either one's own consciousness or another's at the time of death.[14] It is notable that here this crucial moment is cast in terms of a bloody sacrificial feast.

Through the imagined buddha's feasting on the successfully transferred consciousness, it is said that the ten parts of the "object of compassion's" dead body—his four limbs, head, and five internal organs—are purified once more and transformed into the ten wrathful gods and goddesses. Finally, all lesser beings on the Buddhist path (that is, not those deities who dwell *within* the mandala, as they have already received the choicest share of the sacrifice in the form of the consciousness) are invited to feast upon the bodily remains and receive them as blessings. Now the master ejects the "object of compassion's" consciousness once more into the mandala. The prior transferal of the consciousness into the mouth and stomach of the central mandala deity led to the purificatory feast. This second ejection would appear to parallel the initiation of the "object of compassion" into the mandala. It is accompanied by a simultaneous hurling of the severed head—be it real, effigial, or imaginary—onto the altar platform. The position in which the head comes to rest is then interpreted to divine the "object of compassion's" rebirth, and thus the success or failure of the transferal of consciousness; if the head splits open, for example, the rebirth will be a good one; if it lands on its face, there have been some obstructions.

Many elements of this ritual lend themselves well to a Girardian reading. Foremost perhaps, the victim is deemed a criminal. The different offenses he may be found guilty of all boil down to hostility toward the Buddhist dharma in one form or another. They are so vague that they are perfectly suited to criminalize whomever the collective chooses to victimize, and they thus provide ideal conditions for the operation of scapegoating. In Girard's terms, the victim is believed to merit his punishment, so that the community does not notice "the purely mimetic and mechanical nature of their religious experience."[15] Moreover, there are telling fissures in the logic of the ritual. Thus before the "object of compassion" is killed it is, as just mentioned, purified of all negative karma. This raises the question why the killing liberating him from the consequences of his actual or potential acts should still be required. It may be that the rite is still needed to stop him from performing further negative karma, though why he would still be disposed to perform such acts once his karmic imprints have been cleansed remains a question. Here it could be relevant that in the Rudra myth summarized below, Rudra in a previous rebirth passes through a great conflagration at the end of an eon, the sufferings of which purify many beings, but not those stubbornly evil ones like Rudra. In other words, multiple purifications may be necessary in cases such as Rudra's. Still, it is clear that there are some unresolvable tensions between the claim that the victim is now purified and the continuation of the ritual, which is predicated on the victim's karmic pollution (and his proneness to commit evil acts). This speaks to the fact that the supposed purpose of the ritual, the liberation of the criminal victim, is on one level a ploy and subterfuge. In other words, the break in logic here is a potentially revelatory point that unmasks what is otherwise concealed by the rhetoric of performing the rite for the victim's sake. To be sure, unlike Girard's concealment of the sacrificial framework, this Buddhist rhetoric of "liberation" is not only a ploy. Rather, it is also to be taken seriously and at face value, as a critique, if not a repudiation, of sacrificial violence, as we argue below.

But what of the other aspects of Girard's sacrifice? Is there mimesis here? And rivalry? What of the mob, and its frenetic Dionysian violence? After his immolation, is the scapegoated victim deified somehow as a savior and a protector? Is there perceived, in other words, a creative side to this sacrificial act? In fact, the answer to every one of these questions is yes, and all these elements appear with remarkable clarity in the second text under discussion here—the myth of the buddhas' violent subjugation of the demon Rudra, the myth that is held to justify and explain the liberation rite just described.

In the *Compendium of Intentions*, we first meet Rudra in a previous lifetime, countless eons ago. Then a prince named Black Deliverance (Thar pa nag po), he and his personal attendant Denpak (Dan phag) are disciples of a Buddhist teacher named Invincible Youth (Thub dka' zhon nu). It soon becomes apparent that the master and his servant have radically divergent interpretations of their teacher's words. Black Deliverance grows angry at his servant's discord and banishes him from the country. Only then does he ask his teacher whose understanding was correct. When he hears that his servant had been right all along, Black Deliverance again becomes furious and exiles his teacher as well. He quickly plunges into a life of nihilistic hedonism and spends the rest of his days wearing human skins and eating human flesh, living in charnel grounds, conducting orgies, and performing other horrifying transgressive acts. After Black Deliverance dies, he descends into a series of violent and terrible rebirths that reach their nadir in the lowest of hells, where he is tortured incessantly.

After countless more rebirths, he is finally born into our world, on the island of Laṅka. The newborn's mother is a prostitute who dies in childbirth, and the locals leave the illegitimate child on his dead mother's body in the cemetery. There, the child subsists by devouring his mother's breasts and then her entire corpse (hence his name, "Rudra the Mother-Eater"). He moves on to the other corpses in the cemetery, growing ever stronger and gaining power over the other demonic beings living there. Eventually, having overwhelmed all the beasts and demons of Laṅka, he turns his sights on the various Hindu gods, killing the males from Brahmā to Indra and stealing their wives. Next he targets the peaceful Buddhist monks, who are unable to withstand the terrible austerities that Rudra demands of them. Now the most powerful god in the world, he transforms the entire universe into a realm of darkness, chaos, and violence. Even the Buddhist teachings themselves are threatened with extinction. Rudra, then, is a criminal in multiple ways, and from a Buddhist perspective well deserves his violent punishment.

In response to Rudra's many crimes, the Buddha emanates in the likeness of Rudra himself and appears before the demon's queen. Thus mimetically disguised, the Buddha seduces and impregnates her. Soon the avenging son, the wrathful Mahābhairava-buddha, is born, and the fight is on. The battle culminates in Rudra making a series of increasingly desperate attempts to destroy the Buddha. He pronounces his powerful mantras and mutates into ever-larger forms, but each is easily echoed, mirrored, and surpassed by the Buddha, until the defeated demon collapses in a stupor. From beginning to end, the battle between Buddha and Rudra is one of mimicry. Even after Rudra's defeat, we are told, the Buddha makes Rudra's bloody mandala-palace his own, "taking his skin [as a cloak], his skull as his cup, and even wearing Rudra's charnel ground ornaments as signs of his triumph." The mimesis is complete. Triumphant, the Buddha plunges a trident into Rudra's chest and swallows him whole. Within the Buddha's belly, Rudra is purified. Remember here that the same ingestive imagery is used in the liberation rite from Dunhuang, where the sacrificial victim is fed into the mouth of the presiding *heruka* buddha. In an orgy of sex and violence, all the bloodthirsty buddhas crowd around, "acting in the manner of vultures," as the manuscript says. A late ninth-century commentary to this mythic moment adds further details: "[The buddhas] ate the flesh," it says. "They drank the blood, arranged the bones, and ate the three poisons as offerings. They hacked and cut off the limbs, ripping out the heart and sense organs. Drawing out the internal organs, they swallowed them, and all was purified in their stomachs." Here, then, may be Girard's Dionysian frenzy of the mob. Finally the Buddha reconstitutes Rudra, now in a completely purified state. At last Rudra is ready to receive initiation into the newly converted Buddhist mandala. At the close of the initiation, a new name and identity is bestowed upon Rudra. Now called Black Excellence (Legs ldan nag po), he is appointed chief protector of the Buddhist mandala and bound by vow to remain at the mandala's periphery and assist all future practitioners of tantric Buddhism. A truly liminal figure, Rudra is now and forevermore transformed into a savior. Simultaneously dead and alive, worldly and enlightened, he is, in Girard's own prescient words, "simultaneously violent and peaceful, malevolent and benevolent." In all these ways, then, the Rudra myth—and by extension the liberation rite—is a wonderful example of Girardian sacrifice.

The Social Redux: The Liberation Rite as a Case of Girardian Self-Sacrifice

But this is only half the story. At the same time the liberation rite also includes the critique of sacrifice and reveals the wrongs of sacrificial violence. To understand this properly we need to introduce the figure of the bodhisattva and turn to the teachings of the Mahāyāna ("Greater Vehicle"), which arose around the beginning of the Common Era and took Buddhism in new directions. According to Mahāyāna polemics, followers of the early Buddhist traditions were too self-interested in their search for enlightenment, hence the derogatory characterization "Lesser Vehicle" (*hīna-yāna*) used for their tradition. Far better, claim the followers of the Great Vehicle (*mahā-yāna*), is the path of the bodhisattva, the heroic saint on the path to full and complete buddhahood, who sees no difference between nirvana and samsara and even postpones his own enlightenment—and sacrifices his immediate liberation—in order to help others gain their own. Here, then, is an explicit project of compassionate engagement with others, and in this way the Mahāyāna at once contradicts Girard's description of Buddhism and brings Buddhism still closer to Girard's own ideals, for the Mahāyāna bodhisattva, like Girard's Christ, is deeply involved in self-sacrifice.

The acts of the bodhisattva are best known from the tales of the Jātakas and Avadānas. There, the future Buddha Śākyamuni, in his previous lifetimes as a bodhisattva, or buddha-in-training, is described giving away his eyes, flesh, and so on to the most unworthy of recipients. As Reiko Ohnuma (2005, 115) writes, "The recipient of the bodhisattva's body is usually either someone pitiful (such as hungry animals, thirsty insects, blind beggars) or someone evil (such as evil brahmins, evil kinds, evil women)—but in either case, a poor field of merit that will produce little in the way of karmic returns. This is fully intentional, for the unworthy recipient thereby becomes proof of the pure, disinterested nature of the bodhisattva's bodily gift." The bodhisattva's gift is thus one of utter self-sacrifice: one who is purely innocent, giving of himself to save others from their own sinfulness. Though the defining virtue of this gift is its complete selflessness, it should be understood that its practice serves to perfect the bodhisattva's virtue of generosity (*dāna*), which is the first of a set of typically six or ten perfections (*pāramitā*) that the bodhisattva has to cultivate in his quest for buddhahood. Practicing generosity serves to "equip" the bodhisattva with the store of merit he employs for helping others, and it also brings him closer to buddhahood, which he aspires to in order to alleviate suffering and rescue sentient beings.

The narratives of the bodhisattva's self-sacrifice take on a ritual form in the Tibetan practice of "cutting" (*gcod*). In this practice, the meditator imagines himself being cooked and eaten by fearsome spirits and demons. Here, too, the purpose is for the meditator to accumulate the merit (and wisdom) necessary for enlightenment by offering his most precious possession—his own body—to demons who hunger for his blood, who chase him and demand repayment. The demons, in other words, are Girard's mob, bent on scapegoating the meditator for the wrongs they perceive him to have wrought, a mob to which the meditator willingly submits: "With the hook of compassion," writes Machik Labdrön (Ma gcig lab sgron), an eleventh-century founder of the cutting tradition, "I catch those evil spirits. Offering them my warm flesh and warm blood as food, through the kindness and compassion of bodhicitta I transform the way they see everything and make them my disciples. . . . The great adepts of Chö [i.e., cutting] of the future will boast of killing them [the demons], beating them and casting them out. That will be a sign that false doctrines of Chö, the teachings of demons, are spreading."[16] Here the reader is warned not to feel hatred for these demons. Even though they may, in their ignorance, scapegoat you for their own sufferings, they may only be tamed with the love and compassion of the bodhisattva. "To say, 'Eat me! Take me away!' once is a hundred times better than crying, 'Protect me! Save me!'"[17] Despite the violence of the imagined rites of cutting, these are acts of love. Indeed, precisely their violence is what makes cutting such a revolutionary act of compassion. Through self-sacrifice, violence becomes precisely the opposite of what we might normally expect: absolute love.

The eleventh-century *Bodhisattvāvadānakalpalatā* reflects the two opposing sides of compassionate violence. In his account of the bodhisattva Satyavrata's sacrifice of his body to a hungry tigress, the author, Kṣemendra, describes the act in terms that accentuate simultaneously its bloody violence and its compassionate beauty: "Then the tigress, stimulated by a desire for his blood, fell down upon his broad chest as he lay immobile, tearing into it with the glistening tips of her claws, which seemed to smile with joy, as if they were engraving into his chest the wonder of his noble conduct in this world. . . . And as his unblemished chest was torn apart by the sport of the tigress's rows of claws, it looked for a moment as if it were full of shooting rays of light whose purity was as bright as the moon" (Ohnuma 2007, 12). The wonderfully incongruous language of the account highlights the tensions that are inherent in the idea of the bodhisattva's self-sacrifice. The more excruciating and bloody the act, the more compassionate the gift. In this way the disjunction between the bloody violence and the bodhisattva's compassionate intention is both terrifying and beautiful.

We have followed this tangent on the logic of the bodhisattva's self-sacrifice for a reason, for the liberation rite, we want to suggest, may be understood similarly as an act of self-sacrifice on the part of the officiant. As the rite's name already implies, its purpose is to free the "object of compassion" from his samsaric cycles of suffering. Though the liberation rite appears to be an act of blood sacrifice, very much in line with Girard's model, its authors carefully frame it as a ritual of self-sacrifice. From this perspective, it seeks less to scapegoat and punish the "sacrificial victim," and more to liberate him from the binds of karma and desire. Thus the myth has Rudra, having been killed and "transferred" into the Buddha's stomach, exclaim: "I finally understand my karma. I understand how I took [so many] rebirths. I have seen my karma and seen my rebirths. My karma and rebirths have become evident!"[18] By means of the liberation rite, the bodhisattva Vajrapāṇi lifts the veil of ignorance that heretofore has obscured the endlessly vicious cycles of desire in a world defined by change and impermanence. Still from within the Buddha's belly, Rudra explains:

> If all the karmic propensities were put together, they would be unimaginable; words could not express. But despite all these repeated and constant births and deaths throughout the three realms [of samsara], my karmic activities have been utterly useless, every one a waste. . . . Due to the power of my ignorant and confused karma, I have wandered eternally within the darkness of misunderstanding. Will you not clear it with the light-rays from your lamp of wisdom? The effects of my karmic misdeeds are unbearable. Will you not perform the activities of great compassion? (Dalton 2011, 193)

Here we see how the liberation rite delivers its "beneficiary" by revealing to him the mechanisms of desire, impermanence, and the inevitable sufferings these engender. In Buddhism, desire (and thus *saṃsāric* violence) is uprooted through the revelation of its pointlessness, whereas Girard's Christ focuses not on eradicating (mimetic) desire, but on unveiling the mechanisms of the sacrificial framework. For Girard, it is the removal not of the illusion inherent in mimesis, but of the ignorance allowing for scapegoating that plays this critical role—the unveiling of the mechanisms of false victimization that renders them inoperative. Hence for both Buddhism and Girard, the removal of ignorance allows one to see through the forces that normally drive our actions, and thereby frees us from their coercive hold. But in Buddhism this is basically about revealing the mechanisms of desire, whereas in Girard's scheme it is more about scapegoating and less the mimetic rivalry In this regard, the liberation rite, which resembles so closely the sacrificial act, functions actually, ironically enough, as an act of self-sacrifice on the part of the saving bodhisattva. The bodhisattva's compassionate activities and self-sacrifice are performed as a revelation, not unlike Girard's description of Christ's crucifixion, but they function at a deeper level, serving to enlighten not just the ignorance inherent within scapegoating, but the even deeper (from a Buddhist perspective) ignorance of impermanence that makes desire operative. Like Girard's Christ, the bodhisattva turns the tables on the usual economy of desire and sacrifice, giving instead of taking, and sacrificing himself in the place of others. He sacrifices his own welfare for the sake of others, giving away his most valued possessions—even his own life and limb—to whomever desires them, accepting negative karma in order to save others from the painful consequences of their own immoral behaviors, and even postponing his own enlightenment indefinitely to help other beings gain enlightenment.

The Rudra myth—and by extension the liberation rite—is thus a wonderful example of Girardian sacrifice, while at the same time, we want to argue, it also represents a challenge to Girard's thought, for the liberation rite is framed as an instance of the bodhisattva's self-sacrifice and thus too of a Christlike revelation of the mechanisms of sacrifice. The tantric master who performs the rite is presented not as a sacrificant, but as a realized bodhisattva who acts not as the frenzied mob, but as a reluctant and highly rational savior. Hence the judicious instructions that open the text—on the master's required realization and his experience with selfless compassion. And as the Rudra myth makes clear, the decision to kill is reached only after all other options have been exhausted and a series of lengthy meetings have been held by the buddhas. Indeed, the myth's narrative follows the contours of the four activities of tantric ritual—pacification, enhancement, coercion, and violence—so that before the buddhas manifest before Rudra to destroy him, they first emanate a buddha in monk's robes who tries to reason with him, then another buddha who offers gifts. Only then, after still further exhaustive discussions, does the final *heruka* buddha appear. Theirs is a rational and well-considered sacrifice. And even then, having collectively recognized the need for the redemptive violence of the liberation rite, their manifestation in a wrathful form is carefully represented as play-acting: "The ocean of great poisons must be dried up by means of a wrathful intervention," proclaim the buddhas, "through a self-adaptation into abundantly heaping clouds of miracles *playing at appearing* in the costumes of the childish."[19] Despite the *heruka* buddha's violent exterior, inwardly he remains ever cool and compassionate.

The ritual injunctions and the mythological narratives thus at once emphasize the sacrificial violence and minimize it. They insist that the rite be performed in an utterly dispassionate manner and that it only proceed after all other options have been exhausted. The killed person is represented as the true beneficiary of the ritual killing (or "liberation"), while from a karmic perspective, the priest committing the act of killing is the true victim who will now suffer the consequences of his violent act. The killed is the priest's "object of compassion," whom the priest takes pity on and liberates from his present unfortunate existence and the negative karma he has committed and is sure to continue committing unless an end is put to his life. If the rite is successfully performed, the killed is not only spared the accumulation of further bad karma; he is also protected from the consequences of the bad karma he has already committed. Instead of descending into a hell, he is reborn in a Pure Land paradise, where he will find ideal conditions for practicing Buddhism and swiftly attain liberation from samsara. By contrast, the sacrificial priest sacrifices himself by voluntarily taking upon himself the negative karma of killing—an act that is still, despite all the attenuating circumstances and all the mitigating measures put into place, an inherently negative act of violence. In Christian terminology, one might say that the priest sacrifices himself in order to redeem the killed culprit.

This evaluation of killer and killed turns the tables on sacrificial violence and serves to cast the killing in an entirely different light than the usual sacrificial killings theorized by Girard. Even though the ritual and the mythological narrative do not overcome and do away with sacrificial violence, they reinterpret and transform it into an altruistic act of compassion. The paradoxical mechanisms of karmic reversal at work here are perhaps best understood through the famous story of the ship's captain recounted in the Skill-in-Means (Upāyakauśalya) Sūtra. There Mahākaruṇā ("Great Compassion"), a bodhisattva ship captain at sea on a long voyage, discovers a thief onboard who is about to murder his five hundred fellow passengers, all merchants. The captain finds himself in a moral quandary, for if he tells the merchants of the thief's plan, they will certainly kill the thief and thereby come to suffer terrible karmic consequences for their violent act. If he does nothing, five hundred will die and their murderer will suffer the karmic consequences. The only solution, he concludes, is for him to kill the thief himself and, in doing so, accept the karmic retribution that will follow his violent act, so as to save the thief from the much worse fate that would result from his own killing of five hundred men. Paradoxically (and not insignificantly), however, precisely in sacrificing himself for the good of another, the bodhisattva escapes the negative karma normally associated with killing and indeed, as we well know, eventually attains buddhahood. The thief, meanwhile, dies to be reborn in paradise.[20] Here the compassionate self-sacrifice of the ship captain, precisely in his killing of another, is laid bare, and the same basic mechanism is at work within the liberation rite.

Thus from the same normative Mahāyāna perspective, the person killed is carefully described not as a "victim" of the rite, but as an "object of compassion," one for whom the officiating priest feels nothing but love and forgiveness. Indeed, in terms of the rite being a bodhisattvic act, it is the priest who is sacrificed, by himself and for that object of compassion. On the surface, the liberation rite looks like a sacrifice of Rudra, but at a deeper level, the bodhisattva, by involving himself in killing, is sacrificing his own karmic well-being to save another. While this may seem like a forced or even a blindly optimistic reading of an extremely violent and sacrificial rite, one should remember that the tales of the bodhisattva's activities that appear in the Jātakas and Avadānas similarly cleave to the extreme. When the future Buddha Śākyamuni throws himself off a cliff to feed a starving tigress or gives away his children into slavery, the message is that even here, at the outer edges of the imaginable, the bodhisattva maintains his compassionate attitude of self-sacrifice; how much more so should we, who are faced with ordinary obstacles, practice compassionate self-sacrifice for others? Indeed, one might even suggest that precisely in depicting the liberation rite as a bloody, cultish sacrifice, the authors of the rite implicitly recognize that it is negative, that it will only enmesh one further within the vicious cycles of samsara, and that it therefore is in need of transcendence in the Girardian sense. Paradoxically, in this sense, it is precisely the sacrificial aspects of the rite that allow the bodhisattva to subject himself to them, in an act of ultimate self-sacrifice.

As we have noted above, there is an element of concealment in this reading of the liberation rite that is typical of scapegoating as defined by Girard: the victim is determined to be guilty, a threat to the religiously constituted order, and beyond any hope of betterment, even after the performance of a ritual that supposedly effected his purification. Only by casting the sacrificial victim as guilty and concealing the mechanisms of the collective victimization of the scapegoat can the perpetrators, Girard's "mob," be convinced to indulge in the killing. However, while in the Buddhist case discussed here there is indeed an element of such concealment, the nature of this concealment is different: Its central concern is to manage the ritual violence enacted. Casting it as justified is only one measure toward this end. More important is the insistence that the priest perform the killing with a perfectly pure mind in a state of absorption that is free from any enmity and motivated, by contrast with Girard's mob, solely by compassion for the "object of compassion." This, we insist, is an instruction that must be taken seriously. In short, while the sacrificial killing discussed here fits the Girardian model of sacrificial violence remarkably well, it also differs in fundamental ways and includes a critique of the very violence it unleashes. In this sense, the liberation rite represents at once a sacrifice and a critique of sacrifice.

The Buddhist tradition recognizes well that even in the most extreme circumstances, compassionate violence is highly problematic. Indeed, this is precisely why the bodhisattva's involvement in it represents an act of self-sacrifice. In later centuries, tales abound of highly realized Tibetan lamas suffering the karmic consequences of their involvements in such rituals. Even the great Fifth Dalai Lama, in his own autobiographical account of his rise to power in the seventeenth century, attributes a two-month-long illness to his previous performance of liberation.[21] Similarly too, in the Skill-in-Means Sūtra, the ship captain, in his subsequent and final lifetime as the Buddha Śākyamuni, is pricked by a thorn as a result of stabbing the thief on ship. The Mahāyāna interpretation of the liberation rite is not, in other words, total; there remains some lingering anxiety surrounding its doctrinal justifications of compassionate violence. In this sense, the bodhisattva involves himself in sacrificial violence only under duress, making the best of a bad situation (i.e., of samsara, with all its inherent negativities) and mitigating the inevitable suffering of another by performing a necessary sacrifice that can never be free from the taints of violence. Perhaps one might say that sacrifice, like samsara more generally, is specifically not Buddhist, but what is Buddhist is precisely the inner, psychological adaptation to this reality, an accommodation that does not overcome sacrificial violence but mitigates it to the greatest possible degree.

The liberation rite only contains and mitigates sacrificial violence without rejecting it outright. It should be realized that this and other rare cases of "compassionate killing" are the exception to the rule, namely that Buddhist doctrine categorically rejects any form of violence and explicitly extends this prohibition to sacrificial acts. It does so not only for soteriological purposes, for those elite "escapists" bent on renouncing life in this world, but also in order to shape the religious practices of the laity living within society. In the rare cases where Buddhism allows for sacrificial violence—and with the liberation rite we have deliberately chosen the most extreme example—this violence is not embraced with fervor, but as we have seen is carefully controlled and restricted without ever losing its stigmatization. We could add to this from other Buddhist cultures. In the Indic Buddhist tradition surviving in the Kathmandu Valley among its native population, the Newars, animal sacrifices are built into major public rituals. However, the recipients of these rites are not deities with an explicit Buddhist identity, but autochthonous deities. At times these autochthonous deities receive their sacrifices in close proximity to Buddhist deities, as for instance when their shrine is located at the precinct of a Buddhist temple. Arguably in such situations they function as sacrificial recipients instead of the Buddhist deities, to whom no sacrifices may be directly offered (see McCoy Owens 1995). In this way sacrifice is not completely rejected, but it is relegated to a domain outside, or at the very periphery, of the Buddhist orbit, demonstrating that sacrificial violence is in principle antithetical to Buddhism.

Our analysis here of Buddhist doctrine and ritual practice suggests that a renunciation of sacrificial violence can, and indeed did, also happen outside of (modern) societies rooted in Christianity.[22] This is at odds with Girard's well-known argument that the Christian cultures and the modern world that sprung from them are unique in having evolved beyond the sacrificial framework. In Girard's reading, Christ's self-sacrifice on the cross revealed the unconscious mechanisms of sacrifice and scapegoating and thereby ushered in a more enlightened approach to these perennial problems. With Christ's crucifixion, the victim is no longer guilty and the mob innocent; now he is innocent and the sacrificing mob guilty. By turning the tables on the mechanisms of sacrifice in this way, Girard argues, Christianity revealed their inner workings and thereby transcended them. This revolutionary step, according to Girard, has made Christianity exceptional among the religions of the world. This is why, according to Girard, "in the most diverse cultures, with the exception of the Christian and the modern world which issues from it, men have always immolated victims to their divinities."[23]

While this stark statement is contradicted by the case of Buddhism (and, one might argue, Jainism and other Indian religious traditions), it has to be acknowledged that the emancipation from sacrificial violence as claimed by Girard for Christian-grounded modernity differs from the renunciation of such violence in Buddhism (and related Indian religious traditions). Girard is addressing specifically sacrificial violence and the social dynamics unleashing this violence. By contrast, Buddhism's rejection of violence is categorical and does not restrict itself to socially engineered forms of violence. From the Buddhist perspective, violence—and sacrificial violence is no exception—cannot be divorced from the individuals committing it. It is grounded in human nature and the enmity, desire, and ignorance that drive us. It is hence not society that can rid itself of violence once and forever, but only individuals. There can, then, from a Buddhist vantage point, be no scope for the kind of intervention with which Girard credits Christianity when he writes "Wherever the Gospels take root sacrifices weaken and die out; archaic religion cannot reemerge."[24] Rather, for Buddhism violence has to be overcome by each individual, again and again, each working at the level of a fundamental desire that is rooted in the erroneous belief in a self and the fiction of a stable world that could satisfy the desires we project upon it. This alone allows one to contain and control violence also on the communal level, for violence is ultimately rooted in the minds of individuals, and it is there that it has to be tackled. A Girardian response might be that this precisely proves the uniqueness of the Christian revelation and the deliverance from the mechanisms of sacrificial violence that it bestowed upon mankind. Such a response would of course be legitimate, but it would also shift the debate onto the terrain of faith, and Buddhists might be forgiven were they not to follow Girard onto this terrain and instead to meet such claims of revelatory deliverance with skepticism.

NOTES

1. For a recent example, see Girard 2011, 87: "What I have just said about the Bible and the Gospels comes close to declaring the absolute superiority of the Judaic and Christian over other religions."
2. Pursuing such a line of thought, Jean-Claude Dussault arrives at the conclusion that Buddhist and Girardian mimetic desire in final analysis coincide. To start with, he maintains that mimetic desire culminates in the desire to exist, a desire that is ultimately directed toward "the Whole" or "the Nothing," leaving but "two possible outcomes: violence or renunciation" (Dussault 1981, 64–65: "le désir est ultimement le désir de l'être: on désire d'abord ce que l'Autre possede, puis selon l'Autre, puis finalement l'Autre lui-meme et au-delà de l'Autre, l'être, c'est-à-dire, selon la perspective où l'on se place, le Tout ou le Rien—ce qui dans la pratique revient exactement au même. Il n'existe que deux débouchés possible: la violence ou la renunciation"). He then argues that Buddhism speaks to the same dynamics when it analyzes existence as the enchainment in a vicious circle driven by desire and ignorance, a circle that can only be overcome by renunciation,

just as in the case of mimetic desire. In support he points to the teaching of the four noble truths and the law of dependent origination. However, the Buddhist materials he marshals do not speak to the role of mimicry and do not offer as detailed an analysis of the nature of desire as Girard does. Also, despite structural parallels, Girard's renunciation of desire and violence ultimately serves a different function than does renunciation in Buddhism. In our opinion, the two cannot be equated in the way Dussault proposes in support of his larger point, that is, that the insights Girard identifies as the exclusive and defining feature of Christianity were realized half a millennium earlier by Buddhism. Related to this, we do not see how Dussault's treatment takes care of Girard's claim that the renunciation in Buddhism (i.e., in this "great oriental religions") differs from the Christian one by its escapist nature ("absolute renunciation of all worldly concerns, a kind of living death"). Rather, to counter such a claim it is necessary to point—as we do below—to the way Buddhism operated within society and to the way in which the development of Mahāyāna Buddhism shifted the focus from individual salvation to the compassionate working for the well-being and weal of other sentient beings.

3. It is in this sense that Girard writes of the illusoriness of the value that is conferred upon the object, an illusion that "is a living being whose conception demands a male and a female element. The poet's imagination is the female which remains sterile as long as it is not fertilized by the mediator" (Girard 1965, 17).

4. Girard 1965, 15–16.

5. In addition there is a third form of thirst, namely the thirst for annihilation (*vibhavatṛṣṇā*), that is, the thirst for deliverance from suffering. The identification of this form of thirst is a somewhat later development that is largely restricted to the Pali tradition and does not play the same role as the other two forms of thirst. Cf. Vetter 1988, 14–15 and n. 4.

6. A good example for the application of the golden rule in Buddhist scriptures is the *Veḷudvāreyyasutta* (Pali Text Society edition, *Saṃyuttanikāya* vol. 5, 352–56). Here the Buddha makes sense of the first four rules of conduct binding monks and nuns and the committed laity by appealing to the golden rule. Since one does not like oneself to be killed, be robbed, be exposed to sexual misconduct, or be harmed by lies, slander, and other forms of hurtful speech, one should not engage in killing, theft, sexual misconduct, and hurtful speech oneself. For each of these four rules the Buddha repeats the same formula: "The matter that for myself is not likeable and pleasing, that matter is also for somebody else not likeable and pleasing. How could I bring a matter that is not likeable and pleasing for myself upon somebody else?"

7. In using the word *semblance*, we here follow Lacoue-Labarthe in his chapter, "Diderot: Paradox and Mimesis." There, Lacoue-Labarthe deploys the term in the context of highlighting the paradoxical interdependence of the nothingness of the subject, on the one hand, and the mimetic appropriation of the other, on the other. In order for mimetic desire to function, in other words, the subject must lack its own center. "The paradox states a *law of impropriety*," Lacoue-Labarthe writes, "which is also the very law of mimesis: only the 'man without qualities,' the being without properties or specificity, the subjectless subject . . . is able to present or produce in general" (*Typography*, 258–59). The self comes into being, in other words, by becoming that which it is not.

8. See, for example, Girard's *Things Hidden* (1987, 400) where he explains that the "kind of (conversion) experience (overcoming mimetic desire and victimization) can be found in the great oriental religions. But there the aim is to allow the individual to escape completely from the world and its cycles of violence by an absolute renunciation of all worldly concerns, a kind of living death." Cf. Webb (2005, 1–2) and Dussault (1981, 61), who both cite this passage when assessing Girard's engagement with Buddhism.

9. On the dates and origins of the *Compendium of Intentions*, see Dalton 2016, 30–47. For an extensive study and translation of both the myth and ritual in question, see Dalton 2011.

10. Whether this killing was authentically "Buddhist" is, however, a highly contentious question, and in this regard it is notable how the liberation rite works at the very edges of what may be called "Buddhism" (on this idea, see Dalton 2011, 4–5). On the Indian side, one may also point to the regular reports of tantric ritual killings that appear in the newspapers and are tried in the courts, though there the murders are performed by Hindu rather than Buddhist *tāntrikas*.

11. See Karmay 1998, 3–16; and Dalton 2011, 95–109.

12. For further details on the meditative state required, see Dalton 2011, 81–83.

13. Elsewhere, both in Dunhuang (see, e.g., IOL Tib J 841, fol. 4r; note that "IOL Tib J" is an abbreviation of "India Office Library, Tibetan, J" and is used as the shelf mark for the Dunhuang manuscripts now held at the British Library) and throughout India (Edgerton 1953, 2:208–9), the five rebirths are listed as the realms of the gods, humans, animals, ghosts, and hell-beings. In such lists we see a reduced list of the six realms that are somewhat better known today, less that of the *asuras* (the "jealous gods"). Such fivefold lists seem well suited to the present ritual context, wherein five (and not six) realms are blocked. Nonetheless, the present manuscript includes the *asura* realm among the five realms being blocked and excludes that of the gods, implying that the path to the god realm remains open. This appears somewhat anomalous because, from a normative Buddhist perspective, the god realm is still situated within samsara and is therefore not an ideal place for the consciousness of the "object of compassion" to end up. One might account for this, however, by equating rebirth as a deity with rebirth in a paradisiacal buddha field, such as Sukhāvatī. Existence in a realm such as Sukhāvatī is blissful and free of suffering just as rebirth in a divine realm is, with the added bonus that it provides the ideal conditions for the effortless practice of Buddhism and the realization of definite liberation from samsara. Given such an interpretation, the liberation ritual does not deliver the "object of compassion" immediately from samsara, but via a buddha field as a staging ground for final liberation. Such a scenario (for which we adduce supporting evidence below) would be more in keeping with the Buddhist teaching that liberation cannot simply be bestowed from outside but has to be realized and in a sense earned individually.

14. Péter Szántó (2012, I, 455–68 & II, 214–23) has written on an early example of utkrānti/saṃkrānti in the Catuṣpīṭhatantra, while Sakurai 1996 has observed elements of the rite in several later initiation manuals. Variations on the rite are also seen throughout a number of Dunhuang manuscripts (often those dealing with *gnas bstabs*, or "offering into the realm"), and the twenty-third chapter of the *Thabs kyi zhags pa* (see, e.g., IOL Tib J 321, fol. 66r, line 2–fol. 67v, line 1) represents a particularly clear example of a scriptural discussion of *gnas bstabs* that likely predates that *utkrānti* rite examined by Szántó. More work needs to be done on the history of the relationship between *gnas bstabs* and *utkrānti*, which is usually translated into Tibetan as 'pho ba, but here we are treating them as variations of the same basic ritual by which one transfers the consciousness (of oneself or of another) into a better realm. A similar practice is also found in tantric Śaivism, where it may be performed in connection with ritual suicide by a devotee who has attained "world weariness" (*nirveda*) and who seeks to abandon his body and merge his mind with Śiva. For a discussion of this practice, see Vasudeva 2004, 437–45.

15. Girard 2011, 44.

16. Rinpoche, 303.

17. Rinpoche, 305.

18. Dalton 2011, 191.

19. Dalton 2011, 175; our italics.

20. The entire story is translated in Tatz 1994, 73–77.

21. See Dalton 2011, 140–41.

22. And the same argument could be made in even stronger terms for Buddhism's sister religion Jainism. Jainism, which originated alongside Buddhism in northern India in the middle of the first millennium BCE, identifies violent action (*hiṃsā*) as the prime culprit behind our bondage to the samsaric cycle of existence. Hence in Jainism, liberation is achieved by purging (through austerities and self-mortification) the soul of all traces of past violent karma and by avoiding further new acts of violence. Accordingly, Jains take elaborate precautions to avoid accidental killing of any form, including covering their mouth with gauze to avoid the accidental intake of microorganisms in air, sweeping the ground to be walked upon, and only drinking sterilized water. Jainism's focus is thus on the violent acts themselves, rather than on the underlying intentions, as is the case in Buddhism.

23. Girard 2011, 2.

24. Girard 2011, 76.

WORKS CITED

Arifuku, Kogafu. 2009. "Der Bodhisattva-Weg und der Opfergeist im Buddhismus. Die Grundstellung des Mahāyāna-Buddhismus." In *Opfer in Leben und Tod = Sacrifice between Life and Death: Ergebnisse und Beiträge des Internationalen Symposiums der Hermann und Marianne Straniak Stiftung, Weingarten 2008*, ed. Walter Schweidler, 165–82. Sankt Augustin: Academia-Verlag.

Chung, Ilkwaen. 2010. *Paradoxie der weltgestaltenden Weltentsagung im Buddhismus. Ein Zugang aus der Sicht der mimetischen Theorie René Girards*. Münster: LIT.

Dalton, Jacob P. 2011. *The Taming of the Demons: Violence and Liberation in Tibetan Buddhism*. New Haven, CT: Yale University Press.

Dalton, Jacob P. 2016. *The Gathering of Intentions: A History of a Tibetan Tantra*. New York: Columbia University Press.

Dussault, Jean-Claude. 1981. "René Girard: La révélation évangélique et le bouddhisme." *Studies in Religion/Sciences Religieuses* 10, no. 1:59–66.

Edgerton, Franklin. 1953. *Buddhist Hybrid Sanskrit Grammar and Dictionary*. 2 vols. New Haven, CT: Yale University Press.

Girard, René. 1965. *Deceit, Desire, and the Novel: Self and Other in Literary Structure*. Translated by Yvonne Freccero. Baltimore: Johns Hopkins University Press.

———. 1987. *Things Hidden since the Foundation of the World*. Research undertaken in collaboration with with J.-M. Oughourlian and G. Lefort. Translated by Stephen Bann and Michael Metteer. Stanford, CA: Stanford University Press.

———. 2011. *Sacrifice*. Translated by Matthew Pattillo and David Dawson. East Lansing: Michigan State University Press.

Hahn, Michael. 2009. "Das Opfer als Bestandteil der buddhistischen Kardinaltugend der Wohltätigkeit und seine Darstellung in der einheimischen Theorie." In *Opfer in Leben und Tod = Sacrifice between Life and Death: Ergebnisse und Beiträge des Internationalen Symposiums der Hermann und Marianne Straniak Stiftung, Weingarten 2008*, ed. Walter Schweidler, 149–63. Sankt Augustin: Academia-Verlag.

Ives, Christopher. 2002. "Dharma and Destruction: Buddhist Institutions and Violence." *Contagion* 9:151–74.

Karmay, Samten Gyaltsen. 1998. *The Arrow and the Spindle: Studies in History, Myths, Rituals and Beliefs in Tibet.* Kathmandu: Mandala Book Point.

Lacoue-Labarthe, Philippe. 1989. *Typography: Mimesis, Philosophy, Politics.* Cambridge, MA: Harvard University Press.

Lefebure, Leo D. 2002. "Buddhism and Mimetic Theory: A Response to Christopher Ives." *Contagion* 9:175–84.

McCoy Owens, Bruce. 1995. "Human Agency and Divine Power: Transforming Images and Recreating Gods among the Newar." *History of Religions* 34, no. 3:201–40.

Ohnuma, Reiko. 2005. "Gift." In *Critical Terms for the Study of Buddhism*, edited by Donald S. Lopez Jr., 103–23. Chicago: University of Chicago Press.

Ohnuma, Reiko. 2007. *Head, Eyes, Flesh, Blood: Giving Away the Body in Indian Buddhist Literature.* New York: Columbia University Press.

Rinpoche, Patrul. 1994. *Words of My Perfect Teacher*. San Francisco: Harper Collins Publishers.

Sakurai, Munenobu. 1996. *Indo Mikkyō Girei Kenkyū: Kōki Indo Mikkyō no Kanchōshidai.* Kyoto.

Schlieter, Jens. 2009. "Die 'vollkommene Freigebigkeit' des Viśvāntara: gedeutet mit Hegel, Nietzsche und Bataille." In *Opfer in Leben und Tod = Sacrifice between Life and Death: Ergebnisse und Beiträge des Internationalen Symposiums der Hermann und Marianne Straniak Stiftung, Weingarten 2008*, ed. Walter Schweidler, 133–48. Sankt Augustin: Academia-Verlag.

Schmithausen, Lambert. 2003. "Zum Problem der Gewalt im Buddhismus." In *Krieg und Gewalt in den Weltreligionen. Fakten und Hintergründe*, edited by A. T. Khoury, E. Grundmann, and H.-P. Müller, 83–98. Freiburg im Breisgau: Verlag Herder.

Szántó, Péter-Dániel. 2012. "Selected Chapters from the Catuṣpīṭhatantra: Introductory Study with the Annotated Translation of Selected Chapters; 2 vols." PhD diss., Oxford University.

Tatz, Mark. 1994. *The Skill in Means (Upāyakauśalya) Sūtra.* Delhi: Motilal Banarsidass.

Vasudeva, Somadeva. 2004. *The Yoga of the Mālinīvijayottaratantra.* Pondicherry, India: Institut Français de Pondichéry.

Vetter, Tilmann. 1988. *The Ideas and Meditative Practices of Early Buddhism.* Leiden: E. J. Brill.

Webb, Eugene. 2005. "René Girard and the Symbolism of Religious Sacrifice." *Anthropoetics* 11, no. 1 (Spring/Summer). http://www.anthropoetics.ucla.edu/ap1101/ap1101.htm.

Religious Sacrifice, Social Scapegoating, and Self-Justification

Ted Peters

When the term *sacrifice* is used to designate practices common to various world religions and used to designate a historical scapegoat at the founding of a social order, are we referring to the same thing? Perhaps not. The sacrifice of which the Girard school speaks applies to any social order—whether a political order, an ideological organization, a social movement, or such—not merely to an established religious tradition.[1] So, let us pose the question: What is the value of Girardian theory? Is it to illuminate the religious concept of sacrifice or to illuminate human nature in general? I believe it is the latter.

I think Girard offers us an interpretation of human nature broadly speaking, not merely describing sacrifice as it appears in religious rituals. Even in a secular or avowedly nonreligious society, the mechanism of scapegoating still obtains, even if less recognizable than ritual sacrifice. I would not expect the Girardian account of scapegoating to fit like a glove over the hand of religious sacrifice.

Religion replete with ritual and even ritual sacrifice is one human institution among many, at least in our modern pluralistic global community. For most of us, religions and their rituals do not provide a single sealed worldview or horizon of self-understanding, at least not in the comprehensive manner they might have in isolated archaic societies. Yet, I plan to argue, René Girard's theory of the scapegoat remains as an illuminating description of human being-in-the-world regardless of which social order or even multiple orders we live in.

According to Girard's insightful theory, human violence is ubiquitous and it is ubiquitously feared. The first stage of violence is precipitated by mimetic desire, where each desires what the other desires. A competition ensues and violence gets out of control. Fearing the loss of control, the contenders unite all against one, against the scapegoat. Once the scapegoat is lynched or crucified or destroyed, the previous enemies find themselves united in peace and community.[2] A social order is established around the once hated scapegoat who is now becoming a god. The social order then tries to perpetuate the peace-bringing effect of this original scapegoating by commemorating it ritually and sacrificially. This ritualized violence becomes the basis for mythology, religion, kingship, and traditional social orders.

"The community unites against a victim in an act of spontaneous killing," Girard summarizes. "This act unites rivals and restores peace and leaves a powerful impression that results in the establishment of sacrificial religion."[3] It appears that what we have here is an explanation for the founding of sacrificial religious practices.

Girard presses forward. He advances the view that the scapegoating mechanism has shackled the human race in a prison of its own making, a prison that requires sacred violence combined with lying about this violence in order to maintain an uneasy communal peace. The shackles begin to fall, adds Girard, when we view the death of Jesus Christ. Why? Because the classical scapegoat myth is broken. By remembering the victim rather than the victor, we realize that our community is founded on a gratuitous murder. Our social order is founded on untruth. The cross stands in judgment over the human condition. "But Christ, the son of God, is the ultimate scapegoat—precisely because he is the son of God, and since he is innocent, he exposes all the myths of scapegoating and shows that the victims were innocent and the communities guilty."[4]

In what follows I plan to fabricate a four-step argument for the unique insight into human nature that can be gained through the revelation in Jesus Christ, an insight routinely missed in the ritual sacrifices of the world's religious traditions. I will then press the matter of what is common and what is distinctive about the Christian insight when compared to scholarly interpretations of religious practice. The greatest value of Girardian theory for Christian theology, I will then argue, is not found in its ability to analyze religious ritual but rather in its illuminative power for understanding the human condition overall. My recommendation will be that theological anthropology would do well to incorporate Girard's insights into its explication of sin.

Despite the overlap between religious sacrifice and social scapegoating, I will distinguish them. Girard's theory shines light on the latter more than the former. Still, what Girard reveals regarding scapegoating indirectly applies to ritual sacrifice too, namely, the structure of self-justification works in both. Characteristic of the human condition is our inclination to draw the line between good and evil and place ourselves on the good side of the line. Religious sacrifice is erroneously assumed to provide a mechanism whereby we are cleansed or somehow made good in the eyes of the deity. Social scapegoating similarly declares that we the scapegoaters are good; but the price we pay for this goodness is self-deceit. If the gospel of Jesus Christ reveals that God accepts no sacrifices and judges scapegoating from the side of the victim, then the mechanism of self-justification is broken. It will no longer work. Once our trust in the mechanism of self-justification through either sacrifice or scapegoating is broken, then we are ready to drop the lie and accept the truth: our justification comes from God, not from ourselves.

A Girardian Argument for the Uniqueness of the Gospel of Jesus Christ

As a test hypothesis, let us assume that Girard's scapegoat theory summarizes and represents the Christian understanding of sacrifice. What would this look like? What might be its theological implications? Follow me as we take four steps.

Step 1: Acknowledge the place of Christianity among the plurality of world religions. Founding myths and sacrificial practices characterize religion in general, and some ancient religious myths look like the Christian founding story. Girardian interpreter S. Mark Heim of Andover Newton acknowledges this. "An awareness of world religions and mythology has put

Jesus' death in an unavoidably comparative context. . . . Tales of dying and rising gods are commonplace. . . . We are told that these dying and rising gods express symbolic truths about the cycles of nature, the quest for psychic wholeness, the healing of inner wounds. . . . In sum the Christian story of the cross is exactly like all the others and perversely, uniquely worse than all of them."[5] On the surface, it appears that the Jesus story is just one among others. What might a closer look uncover?

Step 2: A closer look uncovers that myths are disguised accounts of a founding violence, remembered by the perpetrators of the violence, in order to establish and preserve the social order. Myths are not what they appear to be. More than merely personifying forces of nature, myths are told to justify a hidden history that includes the scapegoating of a victim by the prevailing power structure. "Girard maintains that central human myths are in fact transcriptions of a consistent kind of violence that he calls the 'founding murder.' . . . It makes human community possible."[6]

Step 3: Distinguish the history of Jesus from founding myths in other religious communities. The Gospels of the New Testament, "appear to be myth because the death of Christ is presented as a sacrifice, and sacrifice of the scapegoat is the origin and theme of all mythology. The Gospels may *appear* to be myth, but they actually deconstruct other myths. The death of Jesus is a sacrifice that refutes the whole principle of violence and sacrifice. God is revealed as the 'arch-scapegoat,' the completely innocent one who dies in order to give life. And his way of giving life is to overthrow the religion of scapegoating and sacrifice—which is the essence of myth."[7] Heim adds, "When mythical sacrifice succeeds, peace descends, true memory is erased, and the way is smoothed for the next scapegoat. . . . But in the case of Jesus' death, something else happens. . . . Instead, an odd new counter-community arises, dedicated both to the innocent victim whom God has vindicated by resurrection and to a new life through him that requires no further such sacrifice. As Girard sees it, this is the good news, the inexplicable revelation, that is found in the Bible."[8]

Yet, one might object, the Christian religion distorts this originating insight by becoming itself a religion of ritual sacrifice, the religion of the Eucharist. Is the Eucharist not ritual sacrifice for the Christian Church? No, not necessarily. If the Christian Church properly interprets the Sacrament of the Altar, human sacrifice can be avoided. What is the proper interpretation?[9]

To see the Eucharist as God's sacrifice on our behalf, not a sacrifice we offer to God.[10] In the original cross event remembered and made present in the sacrament, the mechanism of sacrifice, as well as the mechanism of the scapegoat, is broken by God's gift to us.

Step 4: Apply the scapegoat mechanism to human nature universally, including judgment against the Christian Church. Does the remembrance of the revelatory history of Jesus accrue to the affirmation that Christianity is the best religion? No. The tendency to scapegoat and to cover communal violence with justifying myths can be found wherever there is human community, even Christian community. Followers of Jesus have been known to remythologize and to twist the otherwise revelatory history of Jesus into a justification for scapegoating. Christian anti-Semitism provides perhaps the most dreadful example. "Christians are as susceptible as others to scapegoating, and have often turned their tradition to sacrificial ends," writes Heim. "Christian history is a struggle between a redemptive resistance to sacrifice and a remythologizing of the gospel."[11]

Feminist theologian Rita Nakashima Brock is condemnatory. "Killing in the name of Christ became a holy act, preached by bishops, supported by taxes, celebrated by poets and artists, institutionalized as penance enacted by ritual, legalized by canon law, and legitimated by theologians."[12] The practice of redemptive violence became for the Christian pious a substitute for internal regeneration. "Committing violence substitutes for spiritual rebirth as the route to paradise."[13]

Ritual sacrifice within a specific religious tradition or the redemptive sacrifice of a scapegoat establish the delusion that our particular religion or our particular social order is justified. Appeal to what is revealed in the death of Jesus, however, shatters this delusion. Unless, of course, we insist on living in the delusion despite the criticism of revelation.

Factors in Connecting or Disconnecting the Scapegoat with Religious Sacrifice

In this chapter we are posing this question: When the term *sacrifice* is used to designate practices common to various world religions and used to designate a historical scapegoat at the founding of a social order, are we referring to the same thing? Perhaps the scapegoat mechanism and traditional ritual sacrifice overlap, but I do not believe they are identical. The sacrifice of which the Girard school speaks applies to any social order, not merely to an established religious tradition. What, then, is the value of Girardian theory: is it to illuminate the religious concept of sacrifice or to illuminate human nature in general? As I have said, I believe it is the latter. Common to both religious sacrifice and scapegoating in the social order—even in a secular social order—is the human propensity to declare itself good, to justify itself. Ritual cleansing or blaming the scapegoat declare that we are good, clean, right, or powerful.

We have just taken four steps to make the argument that Girard's theory applies to human nature universally. Now, let us turn to four factors or components in contemporary scholarly discussion that provide additional support to this observation: (1) the nature of sacrifice in religious tradition; (2) the distinction between sacrifice and scapegoat; (3) the internalization or spiritualization of sacrifice; and (4) the elimination of the practice of sacrifice in religious and secular communities.

What is the nature of ritual sacrifice as practiced in religious traditions? Does sacrifice contribute to the social order? Yes, indeed. Still, the presumptions at work in the practice of sacrifice suggest belief in a mechanism for harnessing suprahuman power. Commenting on the ancient Vedic practice of sacrifice, A. L. Basham writes, "The chief purpose of the sacrifice was the gratification of the gods in order to obtain boons from them . . . success in war, progeny, increase of cattle, and long life, on a *quid pro quo* basis."[14] Human sacrifice to the deities is a mechanism for obtaining the goods of prosperity.

"Sacrifice is found in most of the religions known to us," contends Joseph Henninger.[15] Sacrificial rites include an offering. Bloodless offerings, especially among food-gatherers, will include vegetative foodstuffs they have collected. The offerings may also include inanimate objects such as clothing, jewelry, weapons, precious stones, and such. Motives for sacrificial offerings include homage and thanksgiving to the divine source of life, performed in such a way as to participate in the power of life that transcends us.

Sharing in the transcendent power of life becomes even more intense with blood offerings. Blood offerings are usually identified with food cultivators. One might think that blood offerings belong to hunter cultures, but curiously, this does not seem to be the case. Hunters tend to offer a small but symbolically important part of the animal slain; so the slaying itself is not part of the sacrificial action but precedes it. Among the cultivators, on the other hand, blood seems to have fertility power. By sprinkling the blood of a sacrificed animal or human person in the fields, cultivators believe that they can promote fertile crop yields.

Fertility and femininity come together. Feminist interpretations of religious structures focus on power relations in the social order. Sacrifices give to males the mysterious powers that are akin to those that women have in childbirth. Patrilineal descent through males is not naturally given but socially achieved through ritual violence.[16] One might argue that a patrilineal hierarchy scapegoats women, and one might look for signs of this scapegoating in a given religion's myths. Yet feminist scholars focus on the power transaction, not on scapegoating.

Is there an *esse* or heart or center to the practice of sacrifice? The essence of sacrifice, argues one pioneer in the field of the history of religions, Joachim Wach, is the gift. We human beings give to the gods, and the gods give to us. "There are three major reasons for making gifts to God: propitiation, expiation, and gratitude."[17] Each of these results in a cleansing, in an identification of the sacrificer with what is sacred or good. When the sacrifice becomes internalized, what we give are intangibles; we give ourselves. "The sacrifice of intangibles is symbolic in a double sense, representing in the offered 'heart' the person of the giver and symbolizing as well this person's total surrender to God."[18] To offer such a gift-sacrifice testifies that we have a clean heart, or at least our heart will be cleansed once the sacrifice is accepted.

Another pioneer in the study of archaic religious sensibilities is Adolf Jensen, who would not place the gift at the center of sacrificial practice, especially blood sacrifice. Jensen like others believes that the earliest human communities—the hunter-gatherers that gave way to the development of agriculture—did not sacrifice animals. Blood sacrifice came later. What accounts for this cultural change? "The act of killing was not a gift to the deity. [Rather, sacrifice] is a religiously founded ethical action."[19] The function of sacrificial ritual is to provide the paradigm and sustain communal taboos and customs. Sacrifice accompanied by myth and ritual portray and support communal practices. "*To act 'ethically' means to live by the universal order*. Not to subordinate the self to the divine code or to act counter to it would be sacrilege and therefore unethical."[20] Jensen's view that the function of ritual sacrifice is to maintain the community's customs through ethics might be a place of overlap with Girard's view that the scapegoat creates and maintains the social order. Yet we may ask whether ritual sacrifice is in all cases structured according to the scapegoat mechanism. This does not seem to be the case for the interpreters of sacrifice I've noted above.[21]

Is Jesus a sacrifice or a scapegoat? Scholarly readers of the ancient Hebrew Scriptures technically distinguish between a ritual sacrifice and a scapegoat, at least within the context of the Pentateuch. In Leviticus 16 the scapegoat is driven out into the wilderness, into *Azazel.* Another goat is sacrificed for Yahweh, while the scapegoat bears the sins of the people to *Azazel.* Fordham University biblical studies professor Stephen Finlan contends that the "scapegoat ritual is to be distinguished from sacrifice . . . the scapegoat ritual is surrounded by the regime of sacrificial cleansings (Lev. 16), yet retains its distinctive character: an expulsion ritual, not a sacrifice."[22] Whereas ritual sacrifice includes worshipful facts such as holiness, pollution, cleansing, and obeisance, the "scapegoat ritual is not an act of worship but a violent act of self-defense based on the most primitive metaphysics."[23]

Now, which applies to Jesus: the sacrifice or the scapegoat? The Leviticus 16 template does not exactly fit Jesus, argues one scholar. The scapegoat's blood is not shed, nor is it sacrificed. "Unlike the scapegoat, he [Jesus] does suffer a sacrificial death. . . . But as the scapegoat was never regarded as an offering to anyone, least of all to God, the notion of the scapegoat was not developed in the New Testament and later Christian doctrines of atonement and salvation through Christ."[24]

The early Girard did not like applying the term "sacrifice" to the death of Jesus, even though Jesus's destiny certainly fits the model of the scapegoat. "There is nothing in the Gospels to suggest that the death of Jesus is a sacrifice."[25] Yet, a critic might ask, how then will Girard deal with Hebrews 9:26: "He has appeared once for all at the end of the age to remove sin by the sacrifice of himself." On Girard's behalf, it seems to me that the theological meaning of this passage is clear: Jesus's sacrifice is the sacrifice to put an end to all sacrifices. It could even mean that the mechanism of sacrifice had never been embraced by God.

Girard certainly affirms this interpretation. So, in the later Girard, we find a reluctant willingness to apply the word "sacrifice" to the cross with the caveat that in this case we receive God's gift to us and not the reverse. Girard uses the term "bad sacrifice" for traditional religious ritual.[26] Our point here is that Girard recognizes the difference between ritual sacrifice in religion and the deconstruction of the scapegoat mechanism in the revelation of the cross.

Heim summarizes Girard. "Christ has ended sacrifice. The one approach emphasizes that the cross has revealed what was always wrong with sacred violence. The other emphasizes that Christ's sacrifice is better than all the others. It is the one truly effective offering and accomplishes what all the others never could. But these are not really opposed to each other. They are more like two sides of the same thing."[27] Or, more succinctly: "a koan-like conclusion. If you believe in sacrifice, then you can't practice it anymore, because it has been done completely, perfectly, once for all. This was the sacrifice to end sacrifice."[28]

The conflation of sacrifice with scapegoat has led to a widely shared criticism of Girard, namely, his scapegoat theory falls short of universal application. "Girard's concept of sacrifice is too narrow," complains Joseph Henninger, "for he supports it by reference solely to stratified societies and high cultures. It could at most explain blood sacrifices involving killing, but not sacrifice as such and certainly not the sacred as such, since the idea of the sacred exists even among peoples . . . who do not practice sacrifice. . . . Firstlings sacrifices (of which Girard does not speak) have intellectual and emotional presuppositions far removed from Girard's key concepts of primal murder and scapegoat mechanism."[29]

I do not take this to be a critique of Girard's theory of sacred violence. Rather, it suggests that the Girardian paradigm does not apply to the full range of religious sacrificial practices. Rituals associated with the annual agricultural cycle, for example, may rely upon a metaphysical mechanism whereby human offerings help to insure fair weather and a bountiful harvest.

Similarly, Finlan criticizes Girardian theory on the grounds that it is not universally applicable to either religious communities or other communities. "The fatal flaw in Girard's proposal is the reductionist insistence that all culture and religion are founded on one thing, the scapegoating mechanism. . . . In fact, there are numerous (but less thrilling) reasons for the formation of human societies: the advantages of coordinating efforts at securing food, shelter, and defense."[30] Even though Girard's theory falls short of explaining every phenomenon including ritual sacrifice, Finlan grants how it illuminates the blame game in political rhetoric. "There is an ugly human inclination to focus blame and to take revenge. There is no difference in method, only in details, between Hutu leaders vilifying the Tutsi, Hitler's systematic blaming of the Jews for Germany's defeat in World War I, and Russian Socialists' discussion of which groups were to be blamed and punished . . . [or] radical Islam's blaming of Zionism for every problem."[31] We blame others—we blame those who are evil—so that we can ascribe contrasting goodness to ourselves. To my mind, this application to large political movements in the twentieth century reveals its illuminative value when asking about human nature in the broad sense.

What happens when sacrifice becomes meditation or prayer through internalization? The third factor is the phenomenon of internalization or spiritualization of the sacrifice. In the Vedic period of ancient India, for example, the fire sacrifice ritual was a communal event. In this case, the Vedic deity Agni, the god of fire, would consume the plant sacrifice, and its smoke would wend its way aloft until it reached heaven. Agni united earth with heaven. The priests of Agni facilitated this marriage of earth with heaven through the fire sacrifice over which they presided with their sacred utterance, the mantra.[32]

As we move into the period of the Brāhmanas and Aranyakas (forest books), we find commentaries on the fire sacrifice and its meaning. The commentators begin to internalize the ritual so that it becomes an inaudible meditative practice, a silent mantra. It becomes individualized. The repetition of the once communal ritual within the individual mind gives rise to a complex inner consciousness and the yogic pursuit of saving knowledge or saving awareness. By the time we arrive at the end of the Vedic period with the Upanishads, the pantheistic and monistic metaphysics that will characterize later Hinduism have been established.[33] What has gradually replaced the mechanistic assumptions of ritual sacrifice is a new vision of the transcendent, of Brahman. If the divine Brahman is pure Being, then the divine cannot be conceived in the form of an image before which sacrifices might be efficacious. The value of sacrifice, then, becomes an internal one—that is, sacrifice takes place within one's meditative psyche as a means for cultivating spiritual devotion. "This can be called 'interiorized' or 'internal' sacrifice," writes Finlan. "In this kind of spiritualization motive is everything: the *true* sacrifice is not the ritual act but the inward disposition."[34]

Internalization of sacrifice was anticipated in ancient Israel with the great prophets who distinguished between a righteous heart committed to social justice and merely external communal rituals. Hosea 6:6: "For I desire steadfast love and not sacrifice, the knowledge of God rather than burnt offerings." Or Psalm 51:16–17: "For you have no delight in sacrifice; if I were to give a burnt offering, you would not be pleased. The sacrifice acceptable to God is a broken spirit; a broken and contrite heart, O God, you will not despise." Whether this spiritualization implied the elimination of cultic sacrifice entirely or merely a nonhypocritical approach is less than fully clear. Henninger makes the ambiguous point: "prophetic criticism of sacrifice was directed at an outward cult unaccompanied by interior dispositions and ethical behavior."[35]

This ethical internalization manifests itself even in Islam, at points where Islamic theology opposes ritual sacrifice. "It is not their flesh and blood [i.e., that of sacrificial animals] that reaches God but the piety of your heart" (Qur'an, sura 22:38). This sura suggests that Islam reveres the internalization; the pure heart of the devotee is more important than the public or communal ritual.

Might we think of contemporary Christian practices such as petitionary prayer and especially confession as internalizations of ritual sacrifice? It looked this way to William James. "Not nearly as widespread as sacrifice, it corresponds to a more inward and moral stage of sentiment. It is part of the general system of purgation and cleansing which one feels one's self in need of, in order to be in right relations to one's deity."[36]

In sum, the internalization or spiritualization of sacrifice turns religious ritual toward human subjectivity, the subjectivity of the individual. The external ritual no longer provides the means for establishing or preserving the social order. Enlisting the heartfelt commitment of devotees or citizens so that they live ethically might be required for communal maintenance, to be sure; but the sacrificial ritual itself no longer plays the intervidual or communal role. In short, to postulate that the scapegoat mechanism allegedly at work in ritual sacrifice is what establishes and maintains the social order does not seem to fit the phenomenon of internalized spiritualization.

With internalization or spiritualization and the rise of private meditation and private prayer, we turn away from communal or intervidual practice toward individual subjectivity. Is the social order still at stake?

What happens when ritual sacrifice is eliminated in a religious or secular community? The fourth factor is that nonreligious persons and some religious practitioners find they can get along quite well without ritual sacrifice at all. This seems to be the case in modern secular society, especially modern pluralistic society. Modern consciousness no longer relies upon sacrifice. "The symbolical links with the spirit world, which sacrifice regulated and normalized, have been broken."[37] Yet, one might argue, mimetic rivalry and scapegoating still abound. If we look solely in the direction of ritual sacrifice, we may not see the presence of scapegoating or its influence.

Adam, Eve, and Jesus

Let us turn to theological anthropology. Karl Rahner reminds us that a distinctively theological anthropology attempts to get at an understanding of human nature beneath or more broadly than scientific or other forms of anthropology. "Theology is a science which is concerned with the interpretation of human existence, a field which is existentially and ontologically prior to man's interpretation of himself at the level of the natural sciences."[38] Theological anthropology will require, among other things, an appeal to distinctively Christian resources carefully interpreted. This is where Girard's value to theology can be best demonstrated.

The universal value of Girardian theory, I contend, is that it illuminates the human condition. By this I mean Girard's description of the scapegoat mechanism replete with its lie shines light into a dark human secret, namely, we human beings justify ourselves while scapegoating others. This is the human psyche at work.

Let us return for a moment to the Garden of Eden in Genesis 2–3, to the conversation between God and his newly minted human creatures. Once the sin of eating the forbidden fruit was discovered, a chain of self-justification ensued. Adam blamed Eve, thereby implying that he was innocent. Eve blamed the serpent, thereby implying that she was innocent. So, the reader asks: who made the serpent? God did, of course. This means that God indirectly becomes the author of sin for creating the serpent and putting the temptation into the garden in the first place. Adam and Eve have learned to draw the line between good and evil. With this knowledge they draw a line between good and evil and place themselves on the good side of the line. We are so intent on placing ourselves on the good side of the line that we will do so even if it means placing God on the evil side. In his exegesis of this story, Martin Luther concludes, "This is the last step of sin, to insult God and charge Him with being the originator of sin."[39]

We lie. We lie individually and intervidually. We draw the line between good and evil and place ourselves on the good side of the line, an act that itself is evil because it justifies violence against the scapegoat. Girardian James Alison sees this in ritual sacrifice. "All these forms of sacrifice, from big bullocks all the way down to grains of incense, are part of a pattern of desire by which people form themselves in their own image, lock themselves into projections of themselves, and then proceed to call good, to delight in, things which are not good at all."[40] The key insight here is drawn not from the mechanism of sacrifice but rather the apparent human desire to self-justify, to perform a ritual that declares: we are good.

This compulsion to self-justify suggests bondage. Perhaps it is a symptom of original sin. Systematic theologian Wolfhart Pannenberg sees this in human nature in general. "Only the power of the lie that says that good is evil and evil good and deceptively offers us life as the reward for sin [explains how] human beings can nonetheless choose what is objectively evil, and choose it not through negligence but by compulsion. This is the bondage of the will."[41] In order to declare ourselves as good, we are driven toward self-deception.

We get so wrapped up in our distortions that we can "no longer see the lies," writes Raymund Schwager.[42] Gregory Love holds that "the problem is not merely that we do not see the truth, *but that we also do not want to see the truth*."[43] The chief lie is that God is to blame. God becomes our scapegoat. This is the human condition in general, perhaps even universally according to the Christian perspective on human nature. Girard helps us to see through the lie with his exegesis of Jesus as the final scapegoat.

One of Girard's chief theological concerns is that we avoid scapegoating God. Even if Adam and Eve scapegoated God, we can avoid it because of what we have learned from the cross. God does not demand sacrifice, even if we do. The sacrificial death of Jesus on the cross does not turn God's wrath into love, because God's love is prior and is the motive for the divine action of atonement. John Calvin reminds us this way: "The fact that we were reconciled through Christ's death must not be understood as if his Son reconciled us to him that he might now begin to love those whom he had hated. Rather, we have already been reconciled to him who loves us. . . . 'God shows his love for us in that while we were yet sinners Christ died for us' [Romans 5:8]."[44] For those within the Christian tradition who insist that atonement consists of appeasing a wrathful God with a human sacrifice, a great reversal is in store. "We have a complete reversal—God does not receive a sacrifice, but becomes it. Instead of us reaching up to God, God reached down to us. The reversal of the sacrifice from man-to-God to God-to-man is extremely significant."[45] It is God who is good, not us. And divine goodness comes to us as a gift, not through acts of self-justification such as ritual sacrifice let alone scapegoating.

At least two theological implications come to mind. The first is for those of us who scapegoat. If the cross of Christ is indeed a revelation from God, then it means that our justification comes from God and not from our scapegoating. Whatever need we might have previously felt—a need to draw a line between good and evil with ourselves on the good side—has been mitigated. God has placed the divine self on the evil side of the line. To be godly means to accept ourselves as scapegoaters justified by God rather than by ourselves. We do not need to continue the practice of either ritual sacrifice or scapegoating.

Nor do we who are victims need to internalize the evil heaped upon us by our scapegoaters. This leads to the second implication. The revelation in Jesus Christ regarding human nature should result in liberation from false consciousness, from a loss of dignity. The gospel can elicit a sense of self-love and self-worth for those previously victimized by scapegoating. African American Womanist theologian JoAnne Marie Terrell celebrates this insight for those in her social location. "Because God desires mercy and not sacrifice, there should never really be any reason for the act of sacrifice. . . . Contrary to the church's historical attempts to impose the hermeneutics of sacrifice on any people whom it or the state would subjugate, this is not sanction for anyone's or any group's victimization. . . . When black women can see the truth of this revelation, self-love becomes imminently possible."[46]

Conclusion

From the point of view of the Christian systematic theologian, we are dealing here with the concept of sin within anthropology. "Scapegoating is one of the deepest structures of human sin, built into our religion and our politics. It is demonic because it is endlessly flexible in its choice of victims and because it can truly deliver the good that it advertises. Satan can cast out Satan, and is the more powerful for it. Its hold is stronger where it is most invisible. Victims are called criminals, gods, or both. So long as we are in the grip of sin, we do not see our victims as scapegoats. Texts that hide scapegoating foster it. Texts that show it for what it is undermine it."[47]

What we have done here is distinguish between the ritual of sacrifice within religious traditions, on the one hand, and scapegoating for the purpose of establishing and maintaining the social order, on the other. Girard's theory illuminates the latter more than the former. Nevertheless, what Girard uncovers regarding scapegoating indirectly applies to ritual sacrifice, namely, the structure of self-justification works in both. It is common to us in the human condition to draw the line between good and evil and place ourselves on the good side of the line. Religious sacrifice is erroneously assumed to provide a mechanism whereby we are cleansed or somehow made good. Social scapegoating similarly declares that we the scapegoaters are good, but the price we pay for this goodness is self-deceit. If the gospel of Jesus Christ reveals that God accepts no sacrifices and judges scapegoating from the side of the victim, then the mechanism of self-justification is broken. It will no longer work. This realization may lead to a further awareness that it is the goodness of God's gift that provides us with our justification.

NOTES

"René Girard and World Religions." GTU Symposium, Graduate Theological Union, Dominican School of Philosophy and Theology, April 14–16, 2011.

1. When I initiated an attempt to appropriate the scapegoat theory of René Girard for theology, I was attracted to his partial model for atonement, one that revealed to humanity our sinful state. Ted Peters, "Atonement and the Final Scapegoat," *Perspectives in Religious Studies* 19, no. 2 (Summer 1992): 151–81; and Peters, *God—The World's Future* (Minneapolis: Fortress Press, 1992), 162–63. More astutely than others, Girard helps us to unmask the lie we tell ourselves when engaging in self-justification. Peters, *Sin: Radical Evil in Soul and Society* (Grand Rapids: Eerdmans, 1994), chap. 6.

2. "The role of sacrifice is to stem this rising tide of indiscriminate substitutions and redirect violence into proper channels." René Girard, *Violence and the Sacred*, trans. Patrick Gregory (Baltimore: Johns Hopkins University Press, 1977), 10.

3. Brian McDonald, "Violence & the Lamb Slain: An Interview with René Girard," *Touchstone*, December 2003, http://www.touchstonemag.com.

4. Ibid.

5. S. Mark Heim, "Saved by What Shouldn't Happen: The Anti-Sacrificial Meaning of the Cross," in *Cross Examinations: Readings on the Meaning of the Cross Today*, ed. Marit Trelstad (Minneapolis: Fortress Press, 2006), 212.

6. Ibid., 215.

7. McDonald, "Violence & the Lamb Slain."

8. Heim, "Saved by What Shouldn't Happen," 220.

9. "Die Eucharistiefeier bildet immer aufs Neue den heilbringenden Opfertod Christi ab, sie repräsentiert (vergegenwärtigt) ihn realistisch. In diesem Sinn is das Opfer der Kirche nach Augustin similitudo des Opfers Christi." Christof Gestrich, "Opfer," in *Religion in Geschichte und Gegenwart*, 4th ed., ed. Hans Dieter Betz et al., 8 vols. (Tübingen: Mohr Siebeck, 1998–2005), 6:587.

10. The post-Tridentine assumption that a sacrifice takes place on the Eucharistic altar could be misleading. Richard Schenk uncovers a pre-Tridentine ambivalence toward the concept of sacrifice. Contemporary ambivalence toward sacrificial imagery and the critique of such imagery has a systematic foundation. "Opfer und Opferkritik aus der Sicht römisch-katholischer Theologie," in *Zur Theorie des Opfers: ein interdisziplinäres Gespräch*, ed. Richard Schenk (Stuttgart: Frommann-Holzboog, 1995), 193–250.

11. Heim, "Saved by What Shouldn't Happen," 221.

12. Rita Nakashima Brock, "The Cross of Resurrection and Communal Redemption," in Trelstad, *Cross Examinations*, 246.

13. Ibid., 247.

14. A. L. Basham, *The Wonder That Was India* (New York: Grove Press, 1984), 239.

15. Joseph Henninger, "Sacrifice," in *Encyclopedia of Religion*, 2nd ed., ed. Lindsay Jones, 15 vols. (New York: MacMillan, 2005), 12:8005.

16. See Nancy Jay, *Throughout Your Generations Forever: Sacrifice, Religion, and Paternity* (Chicago: University of Chicago Press, 1992).

17. Joachim Wach, *The Comparative Study of Religions* (New York: Columbia University Press, 1958), 108.

18. Ibid., 109.

19. Adolf E. Jensen, *Myth and Cult Among Primitive Peoples*, trans. Marianna Tax Choldin and Wolfgang Weissleder (Chicago: University of Chicago Press, 1963), 165.

20. Ibid., 198.

21. Girard might object to my somewhat bland conclusion here on the grounds that a closer look would reveal what history of religions scholars and ethnologists cannot see, namely, that

persecution of victims is universal in the world's societies and religious traditions. Scholars miss this point "*because we do not know how to decipher the documents we do possess.*" René Girard, *The Scapegoat*, trans. Yvonne Freccero (Baltimore: Johns Hopkins University Press, 1986), 25. Be that as it may, what such scholars report they see is relevant to this argument.

22. Stephen Finlan, *Options on Atonement in Christian Thought* (Collegeville, MN: Liturgical Press, 2007), 13.
23. Ibid., 14.
24. David Phillips, "Scapegoat," in *Man, Myth, and Magic: An Illustrated Encyclopedia of the Supernatural*, ed. Richard Cavendish, 24 vols. (New York: Marshall Cavendish, 1970), 18:2488.
25. René Girard, *Things Hidden since the Foundation of the World*, research undertaken in collaboration with with J.-M. Oughourlian and G. Lefort, trans. Stephen Bann and Michael Metteer (Stanford, CA: Stanford University Press, 1987), 180.
26. McDonald, "Violence & the Lamb Slain."
27. S. Mark Heim, *Saved from Sacrifice: A Theology of the Cross* (Grand Rapids: Eerdmans, 2006), 157.
28. Ibid., 180.
29. Henninger, "Sacrifice," 8005.
30. Finlan, *Options on Atonement in Christian Thought*, 106.
31. Ibid., 107–8.
32. See R. C. Zaehner, *Hinduism* (Oxford: Oxford University Press, 1962), 19–20.
33. Ibid., 38. The move from external sacrifice to internal meditation can be recapitulated today by the individual Hindu. "Sacrifice in the temple, a self-offering which is still external, is later internalized step-by-step in meditation." Michael von Brück, *The Unity of Reality: God, God-Experience, and Meditation in the Hindu-Christian Dialogue*, trans. James Zeitz (New York: Paulist Press, 1990), 65.
34. Finlan, *Options on Atonement in Christian Thought*, 38.
35. Henninger, "Sacrifice," 8007.
36. William James, *The Varieties of Religious Experience*, Gifford Lectures, 1901–1902 (New York: Fontana, 1960), 443.
37. Eric J. Sharpe, "Sacrifice," in Cavendish, *Man, Myth, and Magic*, 18:2458.
38. Karl Rahner, "Theological Observations on the Concept of Time," in *Theological Investigations*, 22 vols. (London: Darton, Longman, and Todd, 1961–76; New York: Seabury, 1974–76; New York: Crossroad, 1976–88), 11:289.
39. Martin Luther, *Luther's Works*, ed. Jaroslav Pelikan, vols. 1–30 (St. Louis: Concordia, 1955–67); ed. Helmut T. Lehmann, vols. 31–55 (Minneapolis: Fortress Press, 1955–86), 1:179.
40. James Alison, *Broken Hearts and New Creations: Intimations of a Great Reversal* (New York: Continuum, 2010), xv.
41. Wolfhart Pannenberg, *Anthropology in Theological Perspective*, trans. Matthew J. O'Connell (Louisville: Westminster John Knox Press, 1985), 118.

42. Raymund Schwager, *Jesus in the Drama of Salvation: Toward a Biblical Doctrine of Redemption*, trans. James G. Williams and Paul Haddon (New York: Crossroad, 1999), 91.

43. Gregory Anderson Love, *Love, Violence, and the Cross* (Eugene, OR: Cascade Books, 2010), 214.

44. John Calvin, *Institutes of the Christian Religion*, II.xvi.4 (1559), ed. John T. McNeill (Louisville: Westminster John Knox Press, 1960), 1:506–7.

45. Derek Flood, "The Rebel God: Understanding the Cross and the Radical Love of God" (master's thesis, Graduate Theological Union, 2011), 59–60.

46. JoAnne Marie Terrell, "Our Mother's Gardens: Rethinking Sacrifice," in Trelstad, *Cross Examinations*, 45–46.

47. Heim, "Saved by What Shouldn't Happen," 217.

Judaism and the Exodus from Archaic Religion: Reading René Girard among the World Religions

Sandor Goodhart

> To what purpose is the multitude of your sacrifices unto Me? saith the LORD.
>
> —Isaiah 1:11

> We did esteem him stricken, smitten of God, and afflicted. But he was wounded because of our transgressions; he was crushed because of our iniquities: the chastisement of our welfare was upon him, and with his stripes we were healed. . . . He was cut off out of the land of the living, for the transgression of my people to whom the stroke was due. And they made his grave with the wicked, . . . although he had done no violence, neither was any deceit in his mouth.
>
> —Isaiah 53:4–9

We are coming upon the week when in Judaism we tell the story of the Exodus, the passage from Egypt to the desert where the people led by Moses will gather at the "foot of the mountain" in Rashi's translation (*b'tachtiyt hahar* in Exodus 19:17[1])—some say "beneath the mountain"—ready to receive the *aseret hadibrot*, the ten utterances or commandments. What has always been of special interest to me in the seder (that Jews hold in the diaspora on the first and second night of Pesach or Passover) is the extent to which we are asked (when we read the story in the Haggadah) to respond as if we ourselves were there in Egypt when these events occurred, to describe these events that occurred "when we were in Egypt" rather than events described in a fictional scriptural text, to act in other words as if the text is a performative, as if in reading it or saying it we are doing something rather than just invoking it, as if the act of reading is a site of instruction.

All of Judaism, I would like to suggest to you, is a site of instruction. Perhaps all of Christianity as well. Perhaps, if we push this idea to the extreme, all of the world's so-called revealed religions are sites of instruction, places or loci where what is being taught inside is being enacted outside, where the outside is in fact an extension of the inside rather than its representation. That may be, in my view, the most important lesson to be garnered from today's conference on "René Girard and World Religions."

Prologue

It is not without good reason that the theme of exodus and the religious practice known historically and on the contemporary scene as Judaism have long been associated with each other. Judaism is nothing if not the exodus from archaic religion, the systematic removal of its practitioners from all traces of the behavior that in the communities from which they have come have led them into difficulty. The name for this exodus is the law of anti-idolatry, the recognition of the moment at which the sacrificial and violence—to use the Girardian vocabulary—have become indistinguishable from each other, when the way out is the way back in, when every effort to remove one from the sacrificial crisis are the very efforts that insure its uninterrupted continuation. The law of anti-idolatry recognizes this moment precisely (and not unexpectedly) as "idolatry," as the moment of the confusion of the divine with the human, the substitution of what is not God for God. Judaism has arrived at this assessment from within the logic of what I have called—and I am not the first one to do so—the prophetic, which is to say, the recognition of the dramas in which human beings are engaged and the naming in advance of the end of those dramas in order that they may decide whether to proceed to that end or not, or, to use a less Greek and more Hebraic structure, an "if/

then" structure, a structure recognizable for example in the Book of Jonah: "Forty days more, and Ninevah will be destroyed," the reluctant prophet is admonished to proclaim. And we are to understand by that proclamation not that God may change his mind, or that such is the inevitable outcome of your behavior no matter what you do, but rather *if* you do not change your evil ways, if you continue down the path you have been traveling, then here is what will happen. On the other hand, if you change your ways, if you give up the destructive path you are on, *then* who knows what creative possibilities may occur; God may relent the planned destruction he has in mind for you and you may not in fact be destroyed. The logic of the prophetic appeared in Judaism around the time of the overrunning of the Temple in Jerusalem by the Babylonians in 586 BCE—before the collapse, during the exile, and during the return (in 530 under the aegis of the Persian Empire) and the building of the Second Temple during the subsequent century—and is reflected most famously in texts like those of Isaiah and Jeremiah. It is within the context of this prophetic Judaism—and not the cultic sacrificial practices that opposed it internally—that Rabbinic Judaism and the Judaism of the classical rabbis emerged (after the destruction of the Second Temple). And it is within the context of this prophetic rabbinic thinking that the law of anti-idolatry came to be formulated, and with its formulation, to reread the entire tradition: the sacrificial priestly cult (known historically in the first century of the modern era as the Sadducees), the literary, historical, legal, and autobiographical narratives (known collectively as Chumash or "five books of Moses"), the prophetic texts proper, and everything else that went into the subsequent writings.

Judaism teaches classical rabbinic thinking. Classical thinking is prophetic thinking. And the manifestation of this prophetic thinking is the law of anti-idolatry, the exodus from the surrounding cultural communities that we designate today as archaic. Judaism is already "Girardianism before the fact," so to speak, a systemic antisacrificial critique built in to the very fabric of the religious orientation preceding Christianity. So what, then, has this seeming "Johnny-come-lately" to add to classical Judaism? What has this post-Holocaust thinker and the extraordinary body of work he has compiled over the last fifty years—from *Mensonge romantique* in 1961 to *Achever Clausewitz* in 2007—to add to this ancient classical Judaic body of prophetic scriptural writing?

A great deal, I would like to argue. What Girard does for us, which no other thinker on the contemporary scene does for us, is make explicit the prophetic sacrificial critique, or tragic prophetic critique, at the root of classical post-exilic Judaism, and therefore (since Christianity is an extension of this particular Judaism) at the root of Christianity. Girard's three big ideas—mimetic desire, the logic of the sacrificial and the scapegoat mechanism, the exposure of all of this in Christian scriptural writings—are the articulation of that to which Judaism is already above all and primarily a response, a response, that is to say, constructed along the ethical lines that a thinker like Emmanuel Levinas has articulated as infinite responsibility for the other individual, for other members of the community in which we happen to be living. Girard articulates the core of the crisis, the collapse of the sacrificial structuration that he, along with Judaism and Christianity, sees as the motor force behind all cultures worldwide, and Judaism and later Christianity articulate and refine the ethical possibilities that derive from this prophetic antisacrificial critique.

In order to demonstrate what I mean, to give you a concrete example of it, in the context of a recent book published in France in 2003, I want to turn to a passage of *Le sacrifice*.[2] In that book, more so than in any other to my knowledge, Girard undertakes to place his theories regarding sacrifice within the context of the world's revealed religions other than Judaism and Christianity, in particular those of the Vedic tradition and others of the Indian subcontinent. In my final sections, I will return to this idea that I have begun to develop, that Girard articulates the sacrificial crisis behind Judaism.

Part One: The Frazerians and the Durkheimians

The nineteenth century had two very different ways of viewing sacrifice, both forms of dismissal. On the one hand, it was viewed within the province of superstition. This view is that of Sir James Frazer and those around him in England who congregated to his insights—the so-called "armchair philosophers," the Cambridge anthropologists or ritualists—Gilbert Murray, Jane Ellen Harrison, and Francis Cornford among others. In *The Golden Bough*, Frazer laid out an entire panorama of rites, rituals, customs, and behaviors of primitive peoples, all of whom were deemed childlike in their inspiration, and not to be taken seriously in comparison to the reason-governed institutions populating the modern English and European cultural scene.

On the other hand, starting with Émile Durkheim, and later pursued at the turn of the century by Marcel Mauss, and more recently in our own century by Claude Lévi-Strauss, an understanding was formulated that founded itself upon pure differences, systematic oppositions. From this point of view, primitive peoples and modern European peoples were on an equal playing field, so to speak, solving the problems that all cultures faced albeit in different ways. This later tradition was as much reflective of French culture as the former was of English culture, the hyper-Cartesianism of the latter echoing in opposition the importance of an appreciation of the quaint and eccentric in cultural life in the former, in the ongoing discourse in each other's eyes of divergent national character.

But from a Girardian point of view, both rejected sacrifice as a reality. Surprisingly, in Girard's view, Sigmund Freud alone notices something real in the sacrificial; something murderous and distinctly exclusionary in its import when he writes about the primal horde in *Totem and Taboo* (and later again in *Moses and Monotheism*). This is somewhat surprising for Girard since in his more mainstream writings he relegated all such behaviors to the psychological category of illusion (although in the case of Freud personal illusion prevails over social illusion). The English version thus served to bolster cultural supersessionism and triumphalism, a secular version of the old religious idea, while the French position supported an ecumenism and cultural relativism that could be seen as its inverse.

In the middle of these formalist and interpretative readings, Girard inserts mimetic desire. The mimetic hypothesis explains ritual behavior on the level of real human relations (unlike the explanation of the Frazerians for whom it is one more species of the imaginary) and offers a reading of enigmatic phenomena like sacrifice (which can appear at one moment as the cause of all the worst violence in the community and at another as its salvation), a phenomenon that in the purview of the French formalists is reducible to purely formal categories. The Bible and the Christian scriptural make their appearance in Girard's scenario as the source of the understanding of culture's foundational and generative sacrificial mechanisms. Like the Frazerians, Girard takes seriously the idea of sacrifice (although for him it operates in both the primitive universe and modern universe), and like the

Durkheimians he reads it systematically and structurally, although he gives a generative understanding to sacrifice in relation to the category of the sacred. Both the reality of sacrificial behaviors and their systematic importance are the legacy of Jewish and Christian scriptural writings.

Part Two: The Bible, the Gospels, and the Vedic Texts

How so? The Bible and the Gospels reveal the mechanism of mimesis and sacrifice, and that revelation undoes their efficacy. And this revelation (and consequent repudiation) is present in other cultural writings as well: for example, in the Vedic Indian scriptures.

> One thus finds in the Bible and the Gospels the explanation of the sacrificial process. . . . The revelation and repudiation of sacrifice go hand in hand, and all of this is found, up to a certain point, in the Vedanta and in the Buddhist refusal of sacrifices.
>
> By recognizing that the Vedic tradition can also lead to a revelation that discredits sacrifice, mimetic theory locates within sacrifice itself a paradoxical power of quiet reflection that leads, in the long run, to the eclipse of this violent institution that is, nevertheless, fundamental for the development of humanity. (xi–xii)

Later in the same book, Girard suggests that the Vedic texts are also antisacrificial.

> We will not have time to complete our study, but I cannot conclude these lectures without mentioning certain developments essential to our theme, even if we are unable to treat them at great length. They have to do of course—my audience suspects it—with the presence of an anti-sacrificial and even nonsacrificial inspiration in the most advanced parts of the Vedic tradition, those which announce the great Indian mysticism of the Upanisheds, as well as those which, leaving India, ultimately give rise to Buddhism. (87–88)

The existence of these "anti-sacrificial and even nonsacrificial" texts in the Vedic tradition in fact leads Girard to question the purported superiority of Western knowledge over other traditions in a new way. "Far from unduly privileging the Western tradition and awarding it a monopoly on the knowledge and repudiation of blood sacrifice," Girard notes, "mimetic analysis recognizes the comparable but never truly identical traits in the Indian tradition" (xii).

And after comparing the appearance of the Vedic texts to the appearance of the texts of the Hebrew prophets in Israel (Micah, for example), he concludes:

> In the end, the two texts, the Vedic and the Biblical, formulate the same critique of sacrifice which is presented to divert men from violence but actually encourages it. There is the same understanding on both sides, but in India it is expressed in an ironic and satirical fashion. (83)

The "same critique of sacrifice." In other words, ethnocentrism is a mistake. The nineteenth-century anthropological thinkers who saw the West as superior before a superstition-driven and myth-driven universe in archaic culture were rationalizing their own cultural egos, projecting the narcissistic image they saw in the mirror rather than making independent, realistic, and verifiable claims about the nature of the structure of planetary communities. But so is antiethnocentrism, the dogmatic and intolerant antidogmatism that arose in response to such ethnocentrism and assumed in the late twentieth century, under the banner of "deconstruction" in Girard's view, alternative prominence, ironically, a new dogmatism, an intolerant and triumphalist regard for ethnocentric cultures. And the same for the inverse. If absolute differences among cultures are not to be rewarded (whether positive or negative), neither are absolute identicalities, as if culture were a system of pure differences, and all cultures participated in a kind of planetary soup or bouillabaisse, a universal humanism or ecumenism spanning the full range of mathematical options.

The only viable approach, in Girard's view, is the one the scriptural texts of both traditions teach: both the biblical and Gospel on one side, and the Vedic on the other. Mimetic analysis teaches that the Vedic is "comparable" if not identical to Western approaches, the "same critique of sacrifice" as the prophetic critique from which the Hebrew Bible, the Israelitic scriptural texts, have emerged.

Part Three: Comparable but Never Truly Identical

But that idea has unexpected consequences. For if the Vedic texts are comparable, the "same critique" of sacrifice, a number of conclusions follow.

The first is that we now understand in a new way what it means to say that Girard is not a theologian but an anthropologist. Whatever the dynamics of his personal faith, whatever Girard's individual religious orientation, "Girardianism" as an intellectual movement is a scientific hypothesis, a theory of the origins and ongoing structure of human community in the ancient and modern universe. The "mimetic hypothesis" is a hypothesis, a view to be verified or counterverified, revealed as intellectually useful and powerful, or revealed as flawed and partial in its usefulness. If the Vedic is "comparable" to the Christian and to the postexilic Hebraic, then neither the Judaic nor the Christian can be primary, superior to all the rest.

But there is a second and it is more tricky. If the Vedic texts are comparable, the "same critique" of sacrifice, what does that say about our own Jewish and/or Christian orientation? What does it say, for example, about God? Or about the Christian scriptural revelation of the truth of sacrificial violence?

Let me elaborate. Girard claims that the Christian Gospel is a reading of primitive archaic religion. He says that his reading of sacrifice and of the mimetic hypothesis is not original with him but that he is just finding it within the scriptural writings, that the theory of sacrifice as the origin and ongoing motor structure of human community is an anthropological perspective he has located in the scriptural writings. It is not entirely surprising then that his understanding of the Gospel has been compared to that of Karl Rahner and Bernard Lonergan.

How does he know that? He finds it there and it is effective. He can show it, demonstrate its presence in passages like Jesus's "reference to the stone that the builders rejected," or John the Baptist's reference to the "lamb of God" (xi). And the proof is in the proverbial pudding. The theory works. Cultural life is an elaborate management machine for the control of mimetic desire in order that its work get done. Sacrifice insures its survival and regenerates its distinctions at moments of its breakdown through the identification of an arbitrarily chosen sacrificial victim. Violence is kept removed from the city as the sacred, segregated, sequestered, and commemorative ritual repetition keeps the process in check. The theory and its four stages (the effective operation of differences, the sacrificial crisis and "undifferentiation," the scapegoating mechanism and its engendering of a difference to end all differences, and ritual commemoration of the whole process up to a point) explain all we need to explain. It is a better explanation than others that have been proposed.

And its appearance in scripture—which suggests that it is no longer effective—allows us to pose a new problem: how do we go on in a universe in which sacrifice no longer works (or no longer works with the efficacy of bygone days), the problem of the ethical.

But how does Girard know it does not come from elsewhere? For example, from Judaism? What if, in other words, Christian scripture derives necessarily from Jewish scripture? If we ask, where does Christian scripture come from, we get ourselves quickly into a tight corner. We get answers like the church fathers—Augustine, Origen, Ambrose, other writers of the early church who collected and decided what Gospels would count as the key four. Or we turn to the Gospel writers—Matthew, Mark, Luke, John. Or to the apostles: Peter, for example, and especially Paul. Or, ultimately, we invoke the inspiration of Jesus himself. The apostles, the writers of the Gospels, the subsequent church fathers (East and West) emulate Jesus himself.

Let us, for the sake of argument, accept all of these answers. Let us say, the church fathers are emulating Gospel writers or the apostles or Paul or others preceding them. And let us say that these earlier generations of writers are getting the insights that populate their writings from Jesus himself. Where does Jesus get it? Do we not have to say either that he gets it by direct divine intervention (or divine origin) or that he gets it from the Jewish community in which he learned and grew from childhood on?

And what if we do say he gets it from God, the God whom he identifies as his father and whose firstborn male son he is by virtue of Christian theology? What are we to make of the fact that what he gets from God turns out to be exactly what Judaism is saying? In other words, even if he gets it from God, and even we accept that he gets it from God, by divine intervention or divine origin, then what God says to him in effect is that the Jews are right. If everything that comes out of his mouth, everything that Jesus says, is absolutely compatible with the way in which we have been describing Judaism, the Judaic position, the law of anti-idolatry, the midrashic deconstruction of all positions that would posit themselves within the mythic and sacrificial system, does it matter if he gets that understanding from God or from Judaism? For all intents and purposes they are one and the same.

And if René Girard then comes along in the latter half of the twentieth century (and first decade of the twenty-first) and finds within that Christian perspective the foundation for his own theories, are we not led, after all is said and done, to an unexpected conclusion: namely, that Girard and Girardianism are Jewish?

Part Four: Judaism and Girardianism

In the spirit of Passover, we are suddenly prompted to ask: why is this conference different from all other conferences in which Girardians gather? And the answer is suddenly apparent. All other conferences have been "for" René Girard. This conference is "about" René Girard.

What would it mean to say that Girard is a Jewish thinker, that Girard (or more precisely his work) participates, not in spite of but precisely through its affiliation with Christian scriptural insights, in the tradition of Hebraic prophetic thinking?

To say that René Girard is a Jewish thinker is a characterization that at first glance beggars description. Although Girard has enormous respect for Judaism, he has very little professional interest in Judaism proper, either in the ancient rabbis (except for passing references made by some continental thinkers like Emmanuel Levinas) or in liturgical practice of Judaism in either its ancient or modern incarnations. It is simply not his topic.

And yet I want to make the claim that Girard's work is fundamentally Jewish, that it is Jewish not in spite of its relation to Christianity but because of it, that what his thinking discovers through Christianity is its Jewish strain, a strain or line of thought he gets, again, not in spite of the Jewish origin of its founder but because of that origin, a founder, Jesus of Nazareth, for whom Judaism is, and in particular prophetic Judaism is, the be-all and end-all of religious thinking. Finally, if Girard, or Girardianism, is to be afforded a place in the series of strategies mounting a critique of religions, it is above all because of its affinities to Jewish thinking and through Judaism to the prophetic structure of which it is a reflection.

In what sense then is he Jewish?

Girard is Jewish insofar as he is writing from the point of view of Jesus and Jesus is writing (teaching, speaking) from the point of view of Judaism. Girard elaborates the dynamics Judaism identifies as the pre-Judaic dynamics, the dynamics to which Judaism is already a response: the dynamics of sacrificial violence and scapegoating, the antisacrificial dynamics that rose to the surface in Isaiah 1–39 but especially in 40–65. Isaiah is the prooftext for Jesus as it is for Judaism at large. And he does what all the rabbis do: enact the text, live "a life of Torah," perform the text in a manner that is known as oral tradition or oral Torah.[3]

There are many ideas in this compact set of assertions and no time to expand them in any but the most elliptical manner. The argument I am making has in effect four prongs or planks.

One, Girard's mediator is Jesus. Thus Girard says repeatedly he is not a theologian. He is not. He reads Jesus as Jesus reads, just as when he turns to Greek tragedy, he reads not from the point of view of any critical position but from the text itself, as it identifies a coherent "tragic prophetic" reading. He reads "before" the theologians who come along later in the process.

Two, Jesus's mediator is Isaiah. Isaiah is the text in context of which Jesus actively structures his life and ministry. Isaiah is not just one more text for Jesus. It is one of the—if not in fact "the"—texts for him, as Isaiah is not just one prophet among others but "The Prophet." There are others: the Joseph story, in which the one expelled becomes the right-hand man of Pharaoh who dispenses the daily grain, and the *akeidah*, in which the one to be sacrificed emerges from the sacrificial altar and the place of that event is memorialized as *yiru-shalem*, which becomes Jerusalem. But Isaiah is the key text.

Three, Isaiah is the "proof text" in the foundation of Judaism, the text that along with a few others reflects the climate in which the ancient texts were assembled. Isaiah (especially Deutero-Isaiah) is part of the community immediately preceding the catastrophe of 587, during the exile, and immediately following the return. Its language echoes the language in the latter half of the book of Job and examines all the themes engaged by the book of Job: namely, the mythic thinking of the Adversary, the institutional thinking of the friends, the social justice thinking of Job, and the creation-centered thinking of the divine. It includes all we recognize through Girard as the critique of the sacrificial: namely, the antisacrificial as a program, the scapegoat mechanism (with its innocent victim of community violence whose "stripes" heal the community) as the expression of its failure, anti-idolatry as the solution, and creation and suffering (or social injustice) as its themes.

Four, Jesus responds to this text in a way that is characteristic of the rabbis of his time—the rabbis of the Talmudic tractates, for example. He takes the act of reading the text (or more properly studying the text, which the rabbis say is equivalent to doing all of the commandments) as a site of instruction. And in particular he takes his body and his life as a "teaching tool" with regard to it. "I am going to live a 'life of Torah'" he says in effect as it has not been lived to this point. He constructs his life to perform the text, to enact it, to display it in a particularly spectacular fashion as a means of teaching it. He sacrifices his life, in effect, to the text, to Torah, to Jewish instruction. Enacting the text of Isaiah, taking it as his own life story, Jesus makes not only reading but his own life into a site of instruction.

As a consequence, we understand René Girard's reading in a new way. Girard's appropriation of Jesus, of Jesus's appropriation of Isaiah, of Isaiah's reading of the antisacrificial and the anti-idolatrous, is the appropriation of a prophetic Jewish reading. Girard articulates what is at the core of Isaiah's reading of Judaism, which is at the core of Jesus's reading, which is thus at the core of Judaism itself.[4]

Thus the long tradition that perceives Isaiah 52–53 as foretelling the history of Jesus has it both profoundly right and profoundly wrong. It is right because it recognizes the link between that narrative and the life of Jesus. But it is wrong because it reverses the priority. In the shadow of this Jewish text, a text at the heart of his tradition, Jesus takes on the project of living it, takes it on as his own. He could have done otherwise. He chooses to give his life to make this Jewish text alive for others. As such, the fortune-telling reading of Isaiah 52:13 to 53:12 that identifies a historical prediction about an event six hundred years down the line is wrong in another sense. It is just such a historical reading that Jesus rejects. What Jesus opposes in choosing to enact the text (rather than see it as a remote intellectual formulation that he reads from the outside and over which he has no control) is just such a reading that divorces the text from history, that separates it from human choice and sacrificial drama. The fortune-telling reading is wrong not because it is literal, but because it is not literal enough, because it is in fact a ground-level metaphorical reading, one that wrests control of the text and its experience away from the community it reflects. Judaic readers, like Jesus, undertake to read the text in a way that recognizes the continuity between the inside and the outside, the duplication of the inside in the outside or more precisely "as" the outside.

Does the interpretation I am proposing—of Girard, or of Jesus, or of Isaiah and its relation to Judaism, or of Jesus and his relation to the reading of texts—challenge transcendental understandings of Jesus? In fact, I would suggest rather that it strengthens them. Jesus is only effectively transcendent if he is at the same time also fully human, if his message appears within and as a reflection of the community into which he is born.

Conclusion

Born on December 25, 1923, René Noël Théophile Girard, iconoclastic son of Avignon, reads the Gospel as the Gospel reads, namely through its central figure, Jesus, who reads, we have suggested, Jewishly, and in particular through Isaiah and in a performative manner the rabbis would recognize as oral Torah.

The exodus from archaic societies is at the heart of what Judaism is doing—in the face of which it develops the link between creation and suffering known as anti-idolatry, which it takes then as the law of the universe—is at the heart of René Girard's work as it is at the heart of the work or ministry of Jesus of Nazareth who is his model or mediator or mentor. Whether or not the rabbis have perceived the prophetic antisacrificial reading at the heart of Torah, and whether or not the Christian church fathers have perceived this prophetic antisacrificial reading of Jesus at the heart of the gospel, is another matter, another discussion for another time.

Suffice it to say for the present that Judaism, Jesus, Christianity, and Girard's thought about the scapegoat mechanism and the innocent victim, the victim innocent of all the crimes with which he has been charged—above all, of being the one responsible for all the violence—are profoundly linked. Any understanding of Judaism, Christianity, Jesus, or Girardian thinking that eschews this linkage is bound to be partial.

To read Judaism as an exodus from archaic religion is to read Girard as expressing insights buried within Judaism, insights from which Judaism emerged. If we accept Girard's analysis as accurate for the understanding of world religions and world culture (and I do), and if we take seriously his claim that his insights come specifically from Christian scripture (and I accept that claim as well), then the Jewish understanding of Girard has to be that Jesus gets it from Judaism: that Jesus is "Girardianism before the fact," and, to the extent that Jesus's view is a legitimate expression of Judaism (and I think it is), that Judaism is "Girardianism before the fact."

This is not a conclusion we might have predicted. But it is one to which we must be committed, I would suggest, if we are to take the texts before us seriously, both the scriptural texts and the secular texts, a prospect that, however daunting, may yield unexpected rewards.

NOTES

A shorter version of this paper was delivered at a meeting on April 15, 2011, at the Berkeley Symposium on "René Girard and World Religions," which was held April 14–16 in Berkeley, California.

1. *The Holy Scriptures According to the Masoretic Text: A New Translation* (Philadelphia: The Jewish Publication Society of America, 1917). All subsequent scriptural citations from the Hebrew bible are from this translation unless otherwise indicated.
2. René Girard, *Le sacrifice* (Paris: Bibliothèque nationale de France, 2003); translated as *Sacrifice*, by Matthew Pattillo and David Dawson (East Lansing: Michigan State University Press, 2011). All page references in this paper are to the English edition and will appear in the text.
3. My colleague, Charles Mabee, would argue that the figure in the text we know as Jesus is Paul's creation so that it would be Paul who identifies Jesus with Isaiah, and Paul, who would certainly be aware of the common rabbinic practice of "oral Torah," of reading Torah in such a way that recognizes the site of reading as a site of instruction, who would identify Jesus as reading in such a way. Although I am not in a position to evaluate this view theologically or historically, it seems to me that Mabee's view is entirely compatible with the view expressed in this paper and adds an additional (and welcome) layer of complexity to it.
4. Here is one text from Isaiah 1:4–13 on the antisacrificial: "4 Ah sinful nation, a people laden with iniquity, a seed of evil-doers, children that deal corruptly; they have forsaken the LORD, they have contemned the Holy One of Israel, they are turned away backward. . . . 11 To what purpose is the multitude of your sacrifices unto Me? saith the LORD; I am full of the burnt-offerings of rams, and the fat of fed beasts; and I delight not in the blood of bullocks, or of lambs, or of he-goats. . . . 13 Bring no more vain oblations; it is an offering of abomination unto Me; new moon and sabbath, the holding of convocations—I cannot endure iniquity along with the solemn assembly."

   And here is another on the scapegoat: Isaiah 52:13–53:12: "13 Behold, My servant shall prosper, he shall be exalted and lifted up, and shall be very high. 14 According as many were appalled at thee—so marred was his visage unlike that of a man, and his form unlike that of the sons of men—15 So shall he startle many nations, kings shall shut their mouths because of him; for that which had not been told them shall they see, and that which they had not heard shall they perceive." Isaiah 53: "1 'Who would have believed our report? And to whom hath the arm of the

LORD been revealed? 2 For he shot up right forth as a sapling, and as a root out of a dry ground; he had no form nor comeliness, that we should look upon him, nor beauty that we should delight in him. 3 He was despised, and forsaken of men, a man of pains, and acquainted with disease, and as one from whom men hide their face: he was despised, and we esteemed him not. 4 Surely our diseases he did bear, and our pains he carried; whereas we did esteem him stricken, smitten of God, and afflicted. 5 But he was wounded because of our transgressions, he was crushed because of our iniquities: the chastisement of our welfare was upon him, and with his stripes we were healed. 6 All we like sheep did go astray, we turned every one to his own way; and the LORD hath made to light on him the iniquity of us all. 7 He was oppressed, though he humbled himself and opened not his mouth; as a lamb that is led to the slaughter, and as a sheep that before her shearers is dumb; yea, he opened not his mouth. 8 By oppression and judgment he was taken away, and with his generation who did reason? for he was cut off out of the land of the living, for the transgression of my people to whom the stroke was due. 9 And they made his grave with the wicked, and with the rich his tomb; although he had done no violence, neither was any deceit in his mouth.' 10 Yet it pleased the LORD to crush him by disease; to see if his soul would offer itself in restitution, that he might see his seed, prolong his days, and that the purpose of the LORD might prosper by his hand: 11 Of the travail of his soul he shall see to the full, even My servant, who by his knowledge did justify the Righteous One to the many, and their iniquities he did bear. 12 Therefore will I divide him a portion among the great, and he shall divide the spoil with the mighty; because he bared his soul unto death, and was numbered with the transgressors; yet he bore the sin of many, and made intercession for the transgressors."

Tawhid: The Oneness of God and the Desire for the Good

Adam Ericksen

In the epilogue of his book *Battling to the End*, René Girard articulates his growing anxiety concerning the West and Islam since September 11, 2001. He states that "We are witnessing a new stage in the escalation to extremes."[1] As an escalation of mimetic rivalry, both Islam and the West are responsible for their participation in the current global crisis of violence. Indeed, Girard claims in the same book, "When violence is involved, wrongs are always shared."[2] But it might seem as though violence is endemic to Islam in a way that it is not to the West. Girard invokes Islamic history, claiming that the 9/11 attacks are "a clear sign of the return to the archaic, a return to seventh, eighth and ninth centuries."[3] This reference to the first centuries of Islam situates violence at the very heart of the religion, and at the heart of the Prophet Muhammad's mission. Islam, Girard seems to assume, is a religion built on conquest, indeed, built on archaic sacred violence. "Personally," he claims, "I have the impression that this religion has used the Bible as a support to rebuild an archaic religion that is more powerful than all the others. It threatens to become . . . the new face of the escalations to extremes. . . . It would be an archaic religion strengthened by aspects of the Bible and Christianity."[4]

Girard's growing concern since 9/11 that Islam could be a regression to archaic religions, which are necessarily connected to sacrificial violence, is shared by many. Of course, that horrific day wasn't the first time people used religion to justify horrendous acts of terror, but it made the question of violence and Islam one of the most pressing issues of our time. The religious motivation behind 9/11 was undeniably demonstrated by a letter full of violent religious language found in the luggage of one of the hijackers. The document evokes a liturgy, as if that violent attack was an act of worship:

> Purify your soul from all unclean things.
>
> Tame your soul. Convince it. Make it understand. Completely forget something called "this world."
>
> Pray the supplication as you leave your hotel. Pray the supplication when riding in the taxi, when entering the airport. Before you step aboard the plane, pray the supplication. At the moment of death, pray.
>
> Bless your body with verses of scripture. Rub the verses on your luggage, your clothes, your passport. Polish your knife with the verses, and be sure the blade is sharp; you must not discomfort your sacrifice.
>
> Remember, they may be stronger than you, but their equipment, their security, their technology—nothing will keep you from your task. How many small groups have defeated big groups by the will of God?
>
> Remember, this is a battle for the sake of God. The enemy are the allies of Satan, the brothers of the Devil. Do not fear them, for the believer fears only God.
>
> And when the hour approaches, welcome death for the sake of God. With your last breath remember God. Make your final words "There is no god but God."[5]

This letter is cause for great concern, as it seems to bolster Girard's contention that Islam engenders a return to the archaic sacred. This analysis admits that violence is easily found in the Qur'an and in Islamic history. Indeed, all of human history and all sacred texts contain justifications for sacred violence against an other. The question that mimetic theory poses is whether or not Islam contains within it the necessary elements to critique that violence.[6] Using Islamic theology, Islamic anthropology, and the tools of mimetic theory, I will argue that, instead of inducting its followers into a return to archaic violence, Islam is itself a critique of archaic religion.

According to Girard, mimetic violence has infected human beings from the foundation of human culture. The first culture was born out of scapegoating violence, and out of that violence, archaic religion was also birthed. Before the murder, the victimizers demonized their scapegoat by transferring "the disorder and the offenses producing it to the victim." After the sacrifice, when peace was temporarily restored, the victimizers transferred "their newly found peace to the victim."[7] Girard calls this process "double transference." A god and a mythology were soon birthed, but it was a god and a mythology of paradoxical effect. The mythological gods are simultaneously violent and peaceful. In this system, peace is only temporary. Whenever violence and conflict again threatens the community's survival, a new scapegoat is blamed and then sacrificed, once again bringing temporary peace and unity. The demand for the sacrifice is projected upon the gods. The intoxicating sense of unity and peace that comes from uniting over and against the sacrificial victim blinds the community to its own violence. As Girard claims, "The celebrants do not and must not comprehend the true role of the sacrificial act. The theological basis of the sacrifice has a crucial role in fostering this misunderstanding. It is the god who supposedly demands the victims."[8] This misunderstanding means that it is impossible to critique our own violence, for the gods demand it. Within the sacrificial system of the archaic, we are by definition blind to our own violence.

The Islamic Critique of Archaic Theology: Tawhid

In its historical context, pre-Islamic Arabia is known to Muslims as the *Jahaliyah*, or the "Age of Ignorance." Muslims claim that pre-Islamic Arabians were ignorant about God because they had not received a revelation from God.[9] It is often assumed today that this was a polytheistic culture, but that is not quite right. Arabian archaic religions evolved into henotheism, the belief in a high, transcendent God with lesser divinities between that God and the world.[10] Pre-Islamic Arabians called the high God *al-Lah*, or the God. This high God was entirely transcendent and had very little concern for the world. People would pray to the lesser divinities, hoping that those divinities might act as intermediaries between them and *al-Lah*. Unfortunately, *al-Lah* remained largely uncaring. Farid Esack claims that in the religious worldview of pre-Islamic Arabia, one's political, economic, and social position in life was determined by the mystery of Time. "Time had pre-arranged the four fundamentals of existence: food, the sex of children, happiness or misery, and one's life span."[11]

The pre-Islamic Arabian understanding that God is transcendent and not at all concerned about the world or human affairs contributed to a lack of concern for the victims of culture. There was little desire to care for victims of poverty or hunger because the connection between cultural practices, assumptions, roles, and institutions that led to the creation of victims remained unknown. Time was in control; thus, there were no victims, no scapegoats.

Islam's fundamental theological concept, known as *tawhid*, critiques both archaic religions' ambivalent gods and its evolution into the indifferent high God of pre-Islamic henotheism. Tawhid refers to the oneness of God. Islamic scholar Michael Sells claims that tawhid refers to the "interior unity of the deity, that in God all the attributes—such as seeing, hearing, knowing, and *willing*—are in some sense one."[12] Tawhid thus critiques the ambivalent nature of the archaic gods. For God to have paradoxical effects or conflicting wills would break God's tawhid. This means there can be no paradox of violence and peace within God's tawhid. In addition, the Muslim theologian Tariq Ramadan claims that "the concept of tawhid expresses first and essentially the fact of the absolute oneness of God: the first Principle, Creator of all, eternally present in history and at each moment."[13] Far from being the aloof and uncaring God of pre-Islamic henotheism, the Islamic doctrine of tawhid means that God has always been radically present in the world and cares deeply about human affairs.

The essence of God's oneness, according to the Islamic doctrine of tawhid, is not associated with violence or conquest. Rather, the essence of God's oneness is Grace and Mercy.[14] This is revealed in the formulaic prayer that introduces 113 of 114 suras of the Qur'an.[15] Muslims refer to this payer as the "*basmalah*." The *basmalah* has been translated in various ways, but the formula is essentially, "In the name of God, Most Gracious, Most Merciful."[16] In his commentary on the Qur'an, Abdullah Yusuf Ali explains the implications of God's Grace and Mercy, stating that God's

> Mercy may imply pity, long suffering, patience, and forgiveness, all of which the sinner needs and God Most Merciful bestows in abundant

> measure. But there is a Mercy that goes before even the need arises, the Grace which is ever watchful, and flows from God Most Gracious to all His creatures, protecting them, preserving them, guiding them, and leading them to clearer light and higher life.[17]

The *basmalah* is essential to understanding God's tawhid of Grace and Mercy, and thus is essential for interpreting the Qur'an. By placing the *basmalah* at the beginning of these chapters, the Qur'an provides its own interpretive lens of Grace and Mercy. As Ali suggests above, God's Grace and Mercy are pure gift. The *basmalah* reveals God's desire to offer Grace and Mercy before we even need it, indeed, before we even ask for it. Reza Shah-Kazemi supports Ali's statement when he writes, "The Koran describes the divine Mercy in a manner that is as inspiring as it is overwhelming: God's love is infinite and thus His Mercy is given to us 'beyond all reckoning,' beyond anything 'deserved by us.'"[18]

The great sin within Islam is to forget the essential Oneness of God, and thus associate something to God other than God's Grace and Mercy.[19] Forgetting the Oneness of God is sinful, but not because it harms God. The Qur'an is a reminder of God's tawhid and states to Muhammad about those who have forgotten or don't believe in the reminder, "[Prophet], do not be grieved by those who disbelieve. They will not harm God in the least" (3:176). Humans only harm themselves, as God gives us the freedom to cultivate sinful practices, as sura 3:178 states: "The disbelievers should not think that it is better for them that We give them more time: when We give them more time they become more sinful." But sinning is not something that just "disbelievers" do. The Qur'an even states that the Prophet Muhammad should ask for forgiveness. "So be patient, Prophet, for what God has promised is sure to come. Ask forgiveness for your sins" (40:55). Humans are solely responsible for sin and oppression, while God is, as the Qur'an claims, "self-sufficient and full of mercy" (6:133).

Qur'anic Anthropology: The Desire for the Good

As Islamic theology must begin and end with the tawhid of God, Islamic anthropology must begin and end with the tawhid of being human. Islam asserts that God's desire for humans is consistent with God's Grace and Mercy. The Arabic word *islam* partly means "submission." The goal of a Muslim is to submit to God's Grace and Mercy and participate in that Grace and Mercy.[20] *Islam* also has strong connotations of "peace" and "self-giving."[21] One's submission to God is not an act of capitulation to a tyrannical divinity. Rather, submission to God is an act of receiving one's identity from God's self-giving Grace, Mercy, and Peace. The goal is peace, as Mohammad Abu-Nimer claims: "Peace, not war or violence, is God's true purpose for humanity."[22]

According to the Qur'an, God created all humans "in the finest state" (95:4). The Qur'an also reveals that humans were created from "one soul" (7:189) and that God "gave everything its form" (20:50). These verses reveal the oneness, or tawhid, of being human, which is, according to Shah-Kazemi, "a reflection of the oneness of God."[23] When we submit to God and openly receive our identity from God, we freely receive the finest state that God mercifully bestows upon all humans. Receiving our being from God frees us from having to fight with one another to obtain that "finest state" of being. It frees us from what mimetic theory refers to as a mimetic rivalry.

Although humans are created in the finest state, there is diversity among humans. The Qur'an claims that God intended that diversity and that diversity is not a justification to make accusations of difference. "O Mankind!" says the Qur'an. "We created you from a single (pair) of male and female and made you into nations and tribes that you may know each other (not that you may despise each other) (49:13).

But the Qur'an is very clear that we don't have to submit to God. We don't have to acknowledge the tawhid of being human. We can choose to submit to other models. Ultimately, claims the Qur'an, we have two choices: God or Satan. We will submit to one or the other. The Qur'an states, "You who believe, enter wholeheartedly into submission to God and do not follow in Satan's footsteps, for he is your sworn enemy" (2:208). In sura 4:119, Satan tells God what he will do to humans: "I will mislead them and incite vain desires in them; I will command them to slit the ears of cattle; I will command them to tamper with God's creation." The verse goes on to say, "Whoever chooses Satan as a patron instead of God is utterly ruined." According to the Qur'an, no matter how much we justify violence and war, these are false human realities rooted in a satanic desire to cause enmity, hatred, and destruction. Satan's spell is so strong that if left to our own desires, we will be seduced by Satan. The Qur'an warns against Satan's spell, but also points to the solution. In sura 7:26–27 God tells the "Children of Adam, We have given you garments to cover your nakedness and as adornment for you; the garment of God-consciousness is the best of all garments—this is one of God's signs so that people may take heed. Children of Adam, do not let Satan seduce you." God's consciousness is the tawhid of Grace and Mercy. It's a consciousness that God has given to all humanity, all of Adam's children.

Whereas God graciously bestows the "finest form" upon humans, Satan mimetically incites vain desires in all humans. Following in the footsteps of Satan, we easily forget the tawhid of being human. When we forget this, we fall into rivalry with one another. The rivalry is thrilling, but ultimately leaves us searching for more. The Qur'an acknowledges this mimetic principle, saying, "Bear in mind that the present life is just a game, a diversion, an attraction, a cause of boasting among you, of rivalry in wealth and children. It is like plants that spring up after the rain: their growth at first delights the sower, but then you see them wither away, turn yellow, and become stubble. There is terrible punishment in the next life as well as forgiveness and approval from God; the life of this world is only an illusory pleasure. So race for your Lord's forgiveness" (57:20–21).

The Qur'an insists upon the threat of hell. It describes hell in very mimetic terms. Hell is a place where humans no longer participate in the goodness of God's Mercy. More specifically, hell is a place where we forget the tawhid of being human and we fall into a cycle of accusation and blame. The Qur'an claims that to the inhabitants of hell "[It will be said], 'Here is another crowd of people rushing headlong to join you.' [The response will be], 'They are not welcome! They will burn in the Fire.' They will say to them, 'You are not welcome! It was you who brought this on us, an evil place to stay.' . . . This is how they will be. The inhabitants of the Fire will blame one another in this way" (38:55–64).

Islam seeks to reorient our desires away from the hell of accusations and toward the Grace and Mercy of God by acknowledging the tawhid of being human. Once we acknowledge that anthropological truth, all scapegoating categories are no longer valid and we desire the good for all humans. There is an ethical component to desiring the good. As Reza Shah-Kazemi states, "The human participation in the divine quality of compassion is made crystal clear in the Koran."[24] The essence of that participation is found in 2:177:

> Goodness does not consist in turning your face towards East or West. The truly good are those who believe in God and the Last Day, in the angels, the Scripture, and the prophets; who give away some of their wealth, however much they cherish it, to their relatives, to orphans, the needy, travelers and beggars, and to liberate those in bondage; those who keep up the prayer and pay the prescribed alms; who keep pledges whenever they make them; who are steadfast in misfortune, adversity, and times of danger. These are the ones who are true, and it is they who are aware of God.

Participating in the Mercy and Compassion of God means that we desire the good for the other, especially the other who is a scapegoat of culture. As stated previously, the henotheism of pre-Islamic Arabia allowed the rich to neglect the cultural practices, assumptions, and institutions that fostered the scapegoats of their society, specifically orphans, the poor, and widows. Islam's message challenged those practices, assumptions, and institutions. As Mohammad Abu-Nimer claims in his book *Nonviolence and Peace Building in Islam*, "A major call of Islamic religion is to establish a just social reality. . . . It is a Muslim's duty to work for justice and reject oppression on both interpersonal and structural levels."[25] This message of social justice put Muhammad in conflict with his own tribe, the Quraysh. The Quraysh tribe was the political, religious, and economic powerhouse of Arabia, and the powerful members of the Quraysh had little concern for the poor and vulnerable members of society. Reza Aslan points out that "The Shaykhs of Quraysh had become far more interested in maintaining the apparatus of trade than in caring for the dispossessed."[26] Muhammad challenged his tribe's victimization of the marginalized, but the Quraysh would not listen. Sura 7:28 states "Yet, when [these people] do something disgraceful they say, 'We found our fathers doing this,' and 'God has commanded us to do this.' Say [Prophet], 'God does not command disgraceful deeds.'" The Qur'an called for a radical transformation in the cultural understanding of God: This is a God who stands with the victims of culture. It was a message that would necessarily put Muhammad into conflict with the powerful elite of Mecca, indeed, with his own tribe.

The Quraysh sought to violently thwart Muhammad's message; while living in Mecca, Muhammad responded with nonviolence. Many Muslims emphasize this period of Muhammad's life and see in him a model of nonviolence. For example, internationally known Islamic scholar Maulana Wahiddudin Khan has produced over one hundred books that have been translated into numerous languages. His audience "includes Muslim professionals and secular educators and intellectuals, as well as graduates of the *madrasah* (Islamic seminary) system and other religiously minded Muslims."[27] He claims that "of the twenty-three-year period of prophethood, the initial thirteen years were spent by the Prophet in Mecca. The Prophet fully adopted the way of pacifism or non-violence during this time. There were many such issues in Mecca at the time which could have been the subject of clash and confrontation. But, by avoiding all such issues, the Prophet of Islam strictly limited his sphere to peaceful propagation of the word of God."[28] Wahiddudin Khan also looks to the Qur'an to argue for an Islamic theology of nonviolence. "According to the Qur'an, God 'abhors violence' (*Surat al-Baqarah*, 2:205) and encourages one to be patient, which in turn dissipates violence."[29] He also claims:

> [In the Qur'an], . . . patience is set above all other Islamic virtues with the exceptional promise of reward beyond measure (39:10). . . . Patience implies a peaceful response, whereas impatience implies a violent response. The word *sabr* [patience] exactly expresses the notion of non-violence as it is understood in modern times. That patient action is non-violent action has been clearly expressed in the Qur'an.[30]

During the mid-twentieth century, the renowned Muslim pacifist Abdul Ghaffar Khan referred to Muhammad's nonviolent action while in Mecca to persuade one hundred thousand of his fellow Pathans to join him in nonviolent resistance to the British Raj. He claimed that "There is nothing surprising in a Muslim or a Pathan like me subscribing to the creed of nonviolence. It is not a new creed. It was followed fourteen hundred years ago by the Prophet all the time he was in Mecca, and it has since been followed by all those who wanted to throw off an oppressor's yoke."[31] Muhammad Abu-Nimer lists seven Islamic scholars who each look to "the new global realities, including advanced weaponry systems and increasingly destructive forms of warfare" and claim that they "oblige Muslims—indeed, all people—to abandon violence since there can no longer be assured limits to its extent."[32] Syrian Islamic scholar Jawdat Sai'd critiques violence by noting "a famous Hadith that has been widely quoted in Islamic literature and is often hung as a calligraphic adornment in Muslim homes: 'Whenever violence enters into something, it disgraces it, and whenever "gentle-civility" enters into something it graces it. Truly, God bestows on account of gentle conduct what he does not bestow on account of violent conduct.'"[33]

Conclusion

In conclusion, Girard is correct that we need to try to understand the relationship between Islam and violence "without any presuppositions and [by] using all the resources available from the study of Islam." Indeed, "The work to be done is immense."[34] That immensity of work requires us to explore violence in the Qur'an, Muhammad's violence in Medina, as well as the violence found in Islamic history, theology, philosophy, and law. I wonder, though, just how honest our exploration can be if we take Girard's concern as our starting place. Does this blind us to new discoveries? Does it condemn us to find exactly what we predicted we would find?

Most importantly, if mimetic theory is to make any inroads into Islamic studies, it is imperative that Islamic scholars take the lead in that endeavor. As I demonstrated, Muslim scholars are engaged in a vigorous critique of the religious justifications for violence. Any sweeping accusation against Islam from within mimetic theory will alienate those potentially sympathetic Islamic scholars from collaborating with us. The best way to move forward in the study of Islam, violence, and mimetic theory is in the spirit of openness and the humility that starts with a willingness to learn from and be influenced by one another.

NOTES

1. René Girard, *Battling to the End: Conversations with Benoît Chantre*, trans. Mary Baker (East Lansing: Michigan State University Press, 2010), 212.
2. Ibid., 16.
3. Ibid., 212.
4. Ibid., 214.
5. Reza Aslan, *How to Win a Cosmic War* (New York: Random House, 2009), 3–4.

6. Mimetic theory claims that the Bible contains sacred violence, but also critiques that violence. Mimetic theory calls the Bible a "text in travail" as it struggles against its sacred violence. See Gil Bailie, *Violence Unveiled* (New York: Crossroad, 1996), 133–52.

7. René Girard, *Girard Reader*, ed. James Williams (New York: Crossroad, 1996), 293.

8. René Girard, *Violence and the Sacred*, trans. Patrick Gregory (Baltimore: Johns Hopkins University Press, 1979), 7.

9. See Karen Armstrong, *Muhammad: A Biography of the Prophet* (New York: Harper Collins, 1992), 55–71.

10. Henotheism is a term coined by Friedrich Max Müller and can be found in a book called *Lectures on the Origin and Growth of Religion as Illustrated by the Religions of India* (London: Longmans, Green, 1878), 290. For its relationship to pre-Islamic Arabia, see Reza Aslan's *No God but God* (New York: Random House, 2005), 8, 40.

11. Farid Esack, *The Qur'an: A User's Guide* (Oxford: Oneworld Publications, 2005), 34.

12. Michael Sells, *Approaching the Qur'an* (Ashland, OR: White Cloud Printing, 1999), 19. Italics added.

13. Tariq Ramadan, *Western Muslims* (New York: Oxford University Press, 2004), 12.

14. When associating God with Grace and Mercy, the Qur'an capitalizes Grace and Mercy. I will follow the Qur'an's lead throughout this essay.

15. Sura 9 does not begin with the *basmalah*. For a brief discussion of the multiple theories about the missing *basmalah*, see Esack, *The Qur'an*, 60–61. Many scholars believe that sura 9 is the continuation of sura 8, which explains the missing *basmalah*.

16. This is how Abdullah Yusuf Ali translates the *basmalah* in his book *The Qur'an: Text, Translation, and Commentary*, 4th ed. (Elmhurst, NY: Tahrike Tarsile Qur'an, 2002).

17. Ibid., 14n19.

18. Reza Shah-Kazemi, *My Mercy Encompasses All: The Koran's Teachings on Compassion, Peace, & Love* (Emeryville, CA: Shoemaker & Hoard, 2007), 8.

19. See Seyyed Hossein Nasr, *The Heart of Islam: Enduring Values for Humanity* (New York: Harper Collins, 2002), 6–7.

20. See Shah-Kazemi, *My Mercy Encompasses All*, 6.

21. Tariq Ramadan, *In the Footsteps of the Prophet* (New York: Oxford University Press, 2007), 1.

22. Mohammed Abu-Nimer, *Nonviolence and Peace Building in Islam: Theory and Practice* (Gainesville: University Press of Florida, 2003), 27.

23. Shah-Kazemi, *My Mercy Encompasses All*, 4.

24. Ibid., 7.

25. Abu-Nimer, *Nonviolence and Peace Building in Islam*, 49.

26. Aslan, *No God but God*, 31.

27. See Irfan A. Omar, "Towards an Islamic Theology of Nonviolence," *Vidyajyoti Journal of Theological Reflection* 72, no. 9 (2008): 671–72.

28. Quoted in Abu-Nimer, *Nonviolence and Peace Building in Islam*, 42.

29. Omar, "Towards an Islamic Theology of Nonviolence," 677.

30. Ibid.

31. Eknath Easwaran, *Nonviolent Soldier of Islam*, 2nd ed. (Tomales, CA: Nilgiri Press, 1999), 103.

32. Abu-Nimer, *Nonviolence and Peace Building in Islam*, 39–40. He refers to Chaiwat Satha-Anand, "Core Values for Peacemaking in Islam: The Prophets Practice as Paradigm," in *Building Peace in the Middle East*, ed. Elise Boulding (Boulder, CO: Lynne Reiner, 1993); Maulana Wahiddudin Khan, "Nonviolence and Islam" Address to the Forum on Islam and Peace in the Twenty-First Century, American University, Washington, D.C., 1998; Jawdat Saiʿd, "Peace—or Nonviolence—in History and with the Prophets," paper presented at the Forum on Islam and Peace in the Twenty-First Century, American University, Washington, D.C., 1997; John Kelsay, *Islam and War: A Study in Comparative Ethics* (Louisville: Westminster/John Knox Press, 1993); Eknath Easwaran, *A Man to Match His Mountains: Badshah Khan, Nonviolent Soldier of Islam* (Petaluma, CA: Nilgiri Press, 1984); Glenn Paige, Chaiwat Satha-Anand, and Sarah Gilliatt, eds., *Islam and Nonviolence* (Honolulu: Center for Global Nonviolence Planning Project, Matsunaga Institute for Peace, University of Hawaii, 1993).

33. Quoted in Abu-Nimer, *Nonviolence and Peace Building in Islam*, 42.

34. Girard, *Battling to the End*, 214.

Islam: Law and Violence (and Nonviolence)

Rüdiger Lohlker

I have to apologize—being not a Girardian—when starting with an idea introduced in the text on "Violence and Religion: Cause or Effect?": "The question of religious violence is first and foremost a human question, . . . and not a directly religious question" (Girard 2004).

This leads me to some remarks on the concept of law in Islam or law relative to Islam (see Lohlker 2011). If we think about law in an Islamic context we are often conflating two concepts: law, called *fiqh*, and Sharia. Talking about *law* as *fiqh* we mean a complex web of rules elaborated by Muslim scholars and derived from Qur'anic verses, from the narratives on the prophet (or the Imams, for the Shiites), and from discussions of Islamic scholars aiming at an evaluation of the deeds of men. *Sharia* means the rules only known to god, which human scholars try to understand when interpreting the scriptures. We will find material law, but to a large extent the problems discussed are ethical considerations or rules concerning questions like prayer, purity, pilgrimage, etc., not to be judged in this world, but in the hereafter. There are other areas concerning the law of Muslim societies: the law proclaimed by rulers or customary law. All form the complex structure we may call the law of Muslim or Islamicate (Humphreys) societies.

To cope with this complexity I will present a twofold argument. I will examine the legalistic thought concerning violence and especially the use of legalistic arguments by jihadists.

One other remark: the ongoing transformation processes in predominantly Muslim societies in North Africa and the Middle East, and even in South Asia, demonstrate that the assumption that Muslims are solely focused on martyrdom is no longer acceptable. To analyze the relation of Islam and violence we have to refer to *fiqh*, man-made reasoning about what god may have intended and how we are to apply his intended will in this world, in our case: jihad. So it is the "human question" we have to turn to.

The current religious interpretation of jihad as the practice of violently fighting enemies that are understood as anti-Islamic forces, even as forces of a new era of ignorance, similar to pre-Islamic times, is deeply influenced by the thoughts of Muslim jurisprudents throughout history, justifying wars and enlarging the Qur'anic conception of jihad. But these views are looked upon as isolated ideological memes fit to be recombinated at the whim of the jihadists ignoring the complex structure of older scholarly discussions.

Older Discourses on Jihad

The ways older scholars of Islamic law interpreted the Qur'an on jihad precepts can be explained by political circumstances furthering the use of violence legitimated religiously as jihad and is much more a "human question" not a religious one. We may think of jihad against crusaders in the Near East, jihad in South Asia for the expansion of the Delhi Sultanate, jihad against the Portuguese at the Mappila Coast, jihad against Muslim rulers in West Africa, etc. (Lohlker 2009).

The older law developed in the context of an expanding (Arabo-)Islamic empire, a set of frontier societies. As the dynamics of expansion stopped at the end of the ninth century CE, the conquering society existed only as a kind of fantasy. And at that time the doctrines of jihad were elaborated by scholars. In the first two Islamic centuries there are no proofs for a preeminence of jihad over other duties. A closer scrutiny of the traditions of the Prophet Muhammad, the Hadiths, shows jihad as the most important duty was supported only by a group of pious Muslims in Syria, at the Byzantine-Muslim frontier; in other regions other duties were much more valued.

On a pragmatic level the question if every Muslim is obliged to fight in a jihad was solved by declaring it a collective duty to be performed by enough Muslims, the army of the caliph, or the ruler in general. An individual effort is restricted to self-defense against enemies or to follow the call of the ruler if necessary.

On a more collective level "war was definitely seen as a valid, indeed even necessary, means of dealing with non-Muslims, at least when non-Muslims are attacking Muslims and perhaps in more general terms" (Donner 1991, 47).

> The dual meaning of Jihad is also captured by Khadduri in the use of Jihad as a valued instrument with which Muslims sought to achieve their objectives. "But the *Jihad*, though often described as a holy war, did not necessarily call for fighting, even though a state of war existed" in theory "between the two *dars—dar al-salam* and *dar al-harb*—since Islam's ultimate goals might be achieved by peaceful as well as by violent means." (Khadduri 1984, 164)

Khadduri also recognizes jihad as a just war but, again, the only type of war permitted in Islam. Jihad is considered a collective duty in the sense that believers have a duty to participate in fighting when they are so called upon by appropriate religious authorities. Due to changes in Islamic political and territorial boundaries, particularly with the concern that internal security and Muslim unity was at risk, Islamic scholars began revising their notion of jihad. Thus emerged a conventional acceptance of jihad as a defensive war instead of a constant state of war with the unbelievers (Khadduri 1984, 169; Abu-Nimer 2003, 30).

The system of rules of jihad, the *fiqh* of jihad, includes rules about the legitimate declaration of war, leadership in war, distribution of the spoils of war, regulations about treating prisoners of war, the relations to non-Muslim powers, treaties to be concluded or not, rules of warfare in general, treating noncombatants (a set of rules jihadists reinterpreted to allow attacking civilians), and others.

We may think this theory of jihad developed by Islamic scholars has been uncontested by other concepts in Muslim societies. We cannot delve into these questions but should bear in mind that an isolated analysis of jihad will not understand its implications in the history of Muslim societies. I will come back to it.

But we can make up a specific list of situations in which the use of violence is permitted by scholars: "A just cause, which can also be understood as the imperative to extend the boundaries of the territory of Islam; an invitation/declaration of Muslim intentions, in which the ruler of the Muslims communicates with enemy authorities to either accept Islam or pay tribute as an acceptance of the state of Islam; the requirement of right authority to declare such war or armed conflict; conduct of war in accordance with Islamic values, because Muslims are to fight for the just cause and straight path and not for the destruction and spoils of war or personal glory" (Kelsay 1993, qtd. by Abu-Nimer 2003, 34).

This summarizes very aptly some of the basic rules of jihad Islamic scholars wrote about. The requirement of having a right authority to declare jihad has been widely understood as hindering the declaration of jihad without a proper caliph in charge or—for the Twelve Shiite scholars—without the presence of an imam (Lambton 1970).

But coming back to my introductory remark that Islamic law or the law of Muslim communities is a very complex phenomenon we may mention that Muslim rulers—very credible regarding their piety—very often broke with the requirements the scholars put up; for example, the necessity of the payment of tribute by non-Muslim rulers was no more practiced in al-Andalus, the Muslim ruled part of the Iberian Peninsula. Non-Muslim rulers were accepted as equals by their Muslim counterparts (Lohlker 2006). Other examples can be found for a nonacceptance of the scholarly rules. The situation is different when we come to modern times.

Interestingly the first prominent case of jihad in the twentieth century occurred when the Germans in World War I used an Islamic scholar to write a religious ruling, a fatwa, calling for jihad against the United Kingdom and France.

In 1973 Egypt was the first modern Muslim state to invoke Islamic law to wage war. President Sadat asked the religious scholars for a religious ruling, a fatwa, for his war against Israel. Six years later he asked again for a fatwa, this time for his peace agreement with Israel.

Islamic arguments were used again in 1991 and 2003 during the wars against Iraq. Saudi Arabia was in need of these arguments to justify the presence of non-Muslims on Saudi soil. Another question to be answered was whether waging war against other Muslim nations is allowed.

But the use of the concept of jihad is not restricted to states: organizations like Hamas, Hizbollah, or al-Qaeda use Islamic arguments to defend their political and military actions. One example is Hamas's use of the term *hudna* for a cessation of hostilities with Israel. This resulted in confusion since nobody seems to understand the real nature of *hudna*. Another example is the definition of Palestinian territory, including Israel, as a religious endowment, a *waqf*, thus sacralizing their enmity against Israel.

The most belligerent interpretation of older Islamic law is brought forth by al-Qaeda or transnational jihadism in general.

These views are encouraged by certain scholarly discussions, for example, by Ibn Nuhhas, and as such may be seen fit to interpret social conflicts as to be solved through violence—and nothing else. This kind of interpretation, this kind of speaking eases the move to the use of violence, a relation to be noted in several religious communities turning to violence (Kippenberg 2008). The most notorious community in contemporary Islam in this respect is the jihadist subculture.

Jihadism

If we read the documents jihadists write, listen to audiotapes, or watch videos they publish, there is a disturbing element: it is much less an archaic religion we are confronting; it's a true globalist view of the conflicts arising in our world and the idea that on a global scale jihadist Islam is the way to save not only Muslims but humankind in general. The mission of jihadi operations is, as Faisal Devji puts it, a humanitarian mission and as such a product of the globalized world. Or to quote Girard on the reasons for the rise of jihadist terrorism:

> To the contrary, it lies in an exacerbated desire for convergence and resemblance. Human relations are essentially relations of imitation, of rivalry. What is experienced now is a form of mimetic rivalry on a planetary scale.
>
> When I read the first documents of Bin Laden and verified his allusions to the American bombing of Japan, I felt at first that I was in a

> dimension that transcends Islam, a dimension of the entire planet. Under the label of Islam, we find a will to rally and mobilize an entire third world of those frustrated victims in their relations of mimetic rivalry with the West. But the towers destroyed had as many foreigners as Americans. By their effectiveness, by the sophistication of the means employed, by the knowledge that they had of the United States, by their training, were not the authors of the attack at least somewhat American? Here we are in the middle of mimetic contagion. (Girard 2001)

How are we to understand the difference between the older Islamic law and jihadist usage of Sharia? Let's say, it's the "human question" again. Muhammad Khalid Masud wrote in his general treatment of Hadith and violence (Masud 2002) that the fragmentary structure of Hadith literature facilitates a decontextualized reading of the traditions from the prophet thus making it possible to legitimize the use of violence. The same can be said about the jihadist use of Qur'anic verses and of Shariatic discourses.

To illustrate a discursive strategy referring to Sharia discussions very similar to this usage of Qur'an and Hadith, I will look into a treatise on the legitimacy of using weapons of mass destruction (WMDs). This treatise as a fatwa, a jurisconsults recommendation, was written by a Saudi scholar once very popular in jihadist circles, now less popular since he returned to the camp of the Wahhabi establishment, Nasir Hamad al-Fahd (al-Fahd 2003). The treatise is called *Treatise on the Legal Assessment on the Use of Weapons of Mass Destruction against the Unbelievers*.

Al-Fahd starts with a twofold strategy: He explains the double standards used by Western powers when justifying their own use of WMDs and denying the right to use these weapons to anybody else, especially Muslims, we may assume. Stating that under these circumstances it is allowed for Muslims and Mujahidin, that is, jihadists, to use WMDs, he turns to the legitimation of the use of WMDs as self-defense against Western aggression. No religious argument is brought forth at this stage. Having stated the legitimacy of using WMDs al-Fahd now turns to religious justifications.

He begins with one Qur'anic verse urging Muslims to speak the truth, thus saying that he will obey the commandment of god and what he, al-Fahd, writes is plain truth. Coming to the issues interesting for him in this treatise he quotes two Hadiths about the legitimacy of burning down everything in the land of the enemies without discussing the context these Hadiths are referring to. He then turns to the Islamic scholarly literature on international law, quoting the renowned author al-Sarakhsi. Interestingly he ends his quotations when al-Sarakhsi himself turns to a very precise discussion of the peculiarities of the indiscriminate use of violence in war. A juridical discussion of technical questions of the *ius in bello* is reduced to a mere proof legitimizing the use of WMDs by jihadists, thus distorting the whole structure of older Islamic scholarly discussions.

The general approach of jihadists to legitimizing their choice of violent jihad may be illustrated by referring to the first theoretician and foremost propagandist for the Afghan jihad and its transnational elements. ʿAbdallah ʿAzzam wrote several treatises on the *fiqh* of jihad. The main points are that military jihad is an individual duty for every Muslim and the foremost of all religious duties (ʿAzzam 2); it's an age old tradition (8); if ʿAzzam is talking about defensive jihad, in other places he is frank about the offensive character of his jihad, saying it is to be fought in every region the unbelievers control if it has ever been under Muslim rule at any time in history.

The jihadist worldview as expressed by ʿAzzam is characterized by a stress on violent jihad that may be—at first glance—very similar to the propagation of jihad in former times of crisis. But today jihad is seen as the one and only marker of Muslim identity giving it a preeminence it never had before. This change can be understood if we accept that jihadism is really part of modernity, and jihadists and all other people on earth, Muslim and non-Muslim, share "a dimension of the entire planet."

Ways Out of Violence

But the legitimization of violence is only one part of the picture. There is compared to, for example, the Egyptian experience (Jackson 2009) a very elaborated approach to criticize jihadism from a Muslim point of view developed in Singapore by the Religious Rehabilitation Group and scholars like Muhammad Haniff Hassan. The latter published several books and booklets on these issues pointing at the necessity to develop a counterideology (Hassan and Bin Ali 2008) based on a thorough understanding of the traditions of Islamic scholarship on Jihad, thus delegitimizing Jihadist thought (Hassan

2009). Abou El Fadl puts in a different way when he says we have to look into theology and law if we are to deal with jihadists when he writes that common social, sociopsychological, or political explanations of the radicalization into violence of Muslims "do not adequately explain the theological positions adopted by radical Islamic groups, or how violence can be legitimated in the modern age. Further, none of these perspectives engage the classical tradition in Islamic thought regarding the employment of political violence, and how contemporary Muslims reconstruct the classical tradition. How might the classical or contemporary doctrines of Islamic theology contribute to the use of terrorism by modern Islamic movements?" (Abou El Fadl 2001, 29). And so we might look into "the classical and contemporary doctrines of Islamic theology" to find ways out of violence.

Qur'an and Sacrifice

The perspective we have to bear in mind is what Toshihiko Izutsu told us about the ethico-religious concepts in the Qur'an in general. Izutsu stresses that despite the difference between the system of old Arab virtues and Islam—understood as a community—Islam revived and adopted, "in a new form suitable to the needs of monotheism, many of the outstanding virtues of Paganism" (2002, 74). These virtues were transformed, adopted, and assimilated into the new Islamic system of moral teachings; we could talk about generosity, loyalty, or patience.

In this context we may look at the Qur'anic view of sacrificial rituals. Angelika Neuwirth in her seminal work on the Qur'an as a text of late antiquity (Neuwirth 2010) hints at an ambivalence of the early Islamic community concerning sacrifice. Sacrificial rituals continue the ancient pagan sacrifices performed during the pre-Islamic pilgrimages at Mecca. They do not refer to biblical models. Sacrifice of animals in Islam means following the Abrahamic example, slaughtering during *'id al adha*, the festival of sacrifice, is an *imitatio* of Abraham by the Muslim believer and nothing else. It is a kind of demythologizing of the sacrifice. In the Qur'an we find verses explicitly negating sacrifice (22, *al-hajj*: 36–37):

> (36) And the camels! We have appointed them among the ceremonies of Allah. Therein ye have much good. So mention the name of Allah over

> them when they are drawn up in lines. Then when their flanks fall (dead), eat thereof and feed the beggar and the suppliant. Thus have We made them subject unto you, that haply ye may give thanks. (37) Their flesh and their blood reach not Allah, but the devotion from you reacheth Him. Thus have We made them subject unto you that ye may magnify Allah that He hath guided you. And give well tidings (O Muhammad) to the good.

Sacrifice as such is transformed into an act of fearing god; piety is enforced instead of sacrifice. This transformation is crucial for a thorough understanding of martyrdom in the Qur'an.

Martyrdom

After moving/fleeing to Medina from Mecca the early Islamic community became, reluctantly, a community of fighters using—according to the practice of the pre-Islamic Arabs—force against their Meccan enemies (see Neuwirth 2010: 548–52). Looking into the Qur'an the fact may be surprising that fighting is nowhere connected with salvation; no former messenger of god we are told about is related to fighting. The new concept of jihad is—in the beginning—not understood as military practice. It is understood as an ascetic ideal, to fight one's own desires, appetite, self-control, for instance in Qur'an 29, *al-'ankabut*: 6 ("And whosoever striveth, striveth only for himself," "wa man jahada, yajhidu li-nafsihi") and Qur'an 29:69 ("As for those who strive in Us, We surely guide them to Our paths," "wa-alladhina jahadu fina la-nahdiyannahum subulana") in the late Meccan period. This aspect of self-restraint is still to be found later when jihad has become synonymous with military action.

But much more significant is the word *qital*, "fight," known from pre-Islamic times. This concept is transformed into the militant support of the new community of believers, no longer the fight for the glory of the tribal community. There is one Qur'anic verse hinting at a recompense other than the mere solidarity of the community of the believers. We read in 3, *al 'imran*: 169–70:

> Think not of those who are killed in the Way of god as dead. Nay, they are alive, with their Lord, and they have provision. (170) They rejoice in what

> god has bestowed upon them of His Bounty, rejoice for the sake of those who have not yet joined them, but are left behind (not yet martyred) that on them no fear shall come, nor shall they grieve.

This verse is read in later Islamic scholarly literature as the most important Qur'anic proof of the legitimacy of the concept of martyrdom (Cook 2007). But is there really a Qur'anic idea of martyrdom? If we understand the development of the revelation of the Qur'an as an ongoing process reflecting also the religious situation in late antiquity in the Near and Middle East we might expect a certain reflection on the Christian concept of martyrdom in the Qur'an. But there is no reflection of this kind. The concept of *shahid*, very famous today, is to be understood in the Qur'an to occur in a juridical sense, that is, as a witness. In certain verses, for example, Qur'an 3, *al 'imran*: 140, there may be possible an interpretation of *shahid* as martyr, but it is not clear. But there is in this verse, however, no hint at any eschatological dimension of the *shahada* of the *shahids*. And the verse Qur'an 3, *al 'imran*: 169 is left as the only, singular indication of martyrdom, where *shahids* are not mentioned. So we are still left without any concept in the Qur'an. *Shahida*, the verb related to *shahid*, is a central concept in the Qur'an. When not used in a juridical sense *shahid* is meant as witnessing the truth of monotheism. To put it simply: no Qur'anic verse when talking about violent death mentions witnessing. Death is not seen as a witness for the truth of god. So consequently Jesus is not dying at the cross to expiate the sins of humanity (and to break the circle of sacrificial traditions); he calls for a unitarian, monotheistic religion and is saved by god like other prophets mentioned in the Qur'an.

This may be seen as an example for the Islamic "concern for antagonism and separation from Judaism and Christianity" René Girard spoke of, but I think it should be seen much more as an outcome of the rivalry between Islam as an emerging religion in the Arabic peninsula and other religions, monotheistic and nonmonotheistic, a fact to be recognized when reading the Qur'an in its precanonical form as a document of an intense reflection and debate with other religions. It is not a proof of an ongoing antagonism.

Earlier we heard about the demythologized concept of the sacrifice of animals as an act of imitating the example of Abraham. And, looking at

Qur'an 37, *al-saffat*, we see a redefinition or reenactment of the act of sacrifice—very similar to the story in Midrash Ben Ish Hai on the binding of Isaac (*'aqedath Ishaq*)—as an action performed by father and son together, and Isaac at last being saved by god, a sheep put in his place. This documents from another point of view the demythologizing tendency in the Qur'an.

Notwithstanding this overwhelming tendency to demythologize, Qur'an 3, *al 'imran*: 169 marks a fundamental difference, breaking with the Qur'anic eschatological paradigm claiming that all humans will be resurrected at the day of resurrection and not before. That there is no other indication of a coherent idea of martyrdom in the Qur'an might indicate that this verse is meant as propagating dedication for the Islamic community and the cause of god, but not as the foundation of a martyrology legitimated by theological reasoning.

This verse may be the starting point for the sacralization of death "for the sake of god" (*fi sabil allah*), but no collective expiation is intended; it is just an individual act, to say it in juridical terms: it's an individual duty, *fard 'ayn*. Turning it into a collective act hints the origin of modern concepts of *shahid* in nationalism, that is, dying for the fatherland, or in globalized movement, dying for all humans (or nature, animals, etc.). And the revival of the concept of *shahid* as an individual duty in modern times by jihadists is the result of a twofold process: community building in jihadist groups and the jihadist subcultures in general, and jihad and becoming *shahid* becoming a standardized marker of identity for every member of the jihadist subcultures. It's a modern paradox: the individualization of commodified—symbolic—goods, not a true revival of the ancient concept.

But there are ways of contemporary Islamic thinking that confront this martyrological turn. The Qur'anic ideas I described are expounded further by scholars arguing "although the use of force is prescribed in the Qur'an under specific and strict conditions, nevertheless, Islamic values systematically give higher ground to forgiveness than to revenge or violence" (Abu-Nimer 2003, 43). These scholars tend to quote Qur'anic verses like 42, *al-shura*: 39: "The recompense of an ill-deed is an ill the like thereof. But whosoever forgives and makes reconciliation, his reward is due from Allah. Lo! He loves not wrong-doers." There are many Hadiths quoted by these scholars "to illustrate the importance of peace building and patience" (Abu-Nimer 2003, 44).

Abel and Cain

The most interesting parable from the Qur'an hinting at this interpretation is the story of Habel (Abel) and Qabil (Cain). Some contemporary South Asian authors see Abel as the representative of justice and righteousness, who refuses to soil his hands with blood. Cain is the representative of aggression, ready to kill on any pretext. This story is to be found in Qur'an 5, *al-ma'ida*: 26–27:

> (26) But recite unto them with truth the tale of the two sons of Adam, how they offered each a sacrifice, and it was accepted from the one of them and it was not accepted from the other. (The one) said: I will surely kill you. (The other) answered: Allah accepts only from those who are righteous. (27) Even if you stretch out thy hand against me to kill me, I shall not stretch out my hand against thee to kill you! I fear Allah, the Lord of the Worlds.

This story shows a willingness to break with "the mimetic contagion" that is at the same level with the demythologizing tendency described before.

The Syrian writer Jawdat Sa'id[1] summarized this story and the conclusions for creating an Islamic theory in his books *Madhhab Ibn Adam al-awwal* (The school of the first son of Adam) and *Kun ka-Ibn Adam* (Be as the son of Adam). Criticizing his fellow Muslims he says in an attempt to substantiate the pacifist nature of Islam (Abu-Nimer 2003, 44):

> I don't see anyone in this world who has clearly explained when it is incumbent upon a Muslim to behave like (Abel) the son of Adam! Nor does anyone teach the Muslims that the Messenger of God said to his companion Sa'd ibn abi Waqqas "*Kun ka-Ibn Adam* (Be as the son of Adam)!" at the time when Muslims turned to fight each other. The Prophet said to his companion Abu Dharr al-Ghifari in a similar situation, when Abu Dharr asked him: "But what if someone entered into my home (to kill me)?" The Prophet replied: "If you fear to look upon the gleam of the sword raised to strike you, then cover your face with your robe. Thus will he bear the sin of killing you as well as his own sin." And in the same situation the Prophet told his companion Abu Musa al-Ash'ari:

> "Break your bows, sever your strings, beat stones on your swords (to break the blades), and when infringed upon by one of the perpetrators, be as the best of Adam's two sons."

NOTE

1. I have to thank Wolfgang Palaver for reminding me of the importance of Jawdat Sa'id.

WORKS CITED

Abou El Fadl, Khaled. 2001. "Islam and the Theology of Power." *Middle East Report* 221:28–33.

Abu-Nimer, Mohammed. 2003. *Nonviolence and Peace Building in Islam: Theory and Practice.* Gainesville: University Press of Florida.

'Azzam, 'Abdallah. Undated. *Fi'l-Jihad: fiqh wa-ijtihad.* Peshawar. http://www.tawhed.ws.

Cook, David. 2007. *Martyrdom in Islam.* Cambridge: Cambridge University Press.

Donner, Fred. 1991. "The Sources of Islamic Conceptions of War." In *Just War and Jihad: Historical and Theoretical Perspectives on War and Peace in Western and Islamic Traditions,* edited by J. Kelsay and J. T. Johnson, 31–69. Westport, CT: Greenwood Press.

Fahd, Nasir Hamad al-. 2003. *Risala fi hukm istikhdam asliha al-damar al-shamil didda al-kuffar.* http://www.tawhed.ws.

Girard, René. 2001. "What Is Occurring Today Is a Mimetic Rivalry on a Planetary Scale: An Interview by Henri Tincq." Translated by Jim Williams. *Le Monde,* November 6, http://www.uibk.ac.at/theol/cover/girard/le_monde_interview.html.

———. 2004. "Violence and Religion: Cause or Effect?" *The Hedgehog Review* 6, no. 1 (Spring).

Hassan, Muhammad Haniff. 2009. *Unlicensed to Kill: Countering Imam Samudra's Justification for the Bali Bombing.* 2nd ed. Singapore: Nature Media.

Hassan, Muhammad Haniff, and Mohamed Bin Ali. 2008. *Don't Be Extreme in Your Religion.* Singapore: MUIS/Perdaus.

Izutsu, Toshihiko. 2002. *Ethico-Religious Concepts in the Qur'ān.* Montreal: McGill-Queen's University Press.

Jackson, Sherman A. 2009. "Beyond Jihad: The New Thought of Gama'a Islamiyya." *Journal of Islamic Law and Culture* 11, no. 1:52–68.

Kelsay, John. 1993. *Islam and War: A Study in Comparative Ethics.* Louisville: Westminster/John Knox Press.

Khadduri, Majid. 1984. *The Islamic Conception of Justice.* Baltimore: Johns Hopkins University Press.

Kippenberg, Hans. 2008. *Gewalt als Gottesdienst: Religionskriege im Zeitalter der Globalisierung.* Munich: C. H. Beck Verlag.

Lambton, Ann K. S. 1970. "A Nineteenth Century View of Jihād," *Studia Islamica* 32:181–92.

Lohlker, Rüdiger. 2006. *Islamisches Völkerrecht: Studien am Beispiel Granada*. Bremen: Kleio Humanities.

———. 2009. *Dschihadismus: Materialien*. Vienna: facultas/wuv.

———. 2011. *Islamisches Recht*. Vienna: facultas/wuv.

Masud, Muhammad Khalid. 2002. "Hadith and Violence." *Oriente Moderno* 21, no. 1:5–18.

Neuwirth, Angelika. 2010. *Der Koran als Text der Spätantike: ein europäischer Zugang*. Berlin: Verlag der Weltreligionen.

Sa'id, Jawdat. Undated a. *Madhab Ibn Adam al-awwal*. http://www.jawdatsaid.net.

———. Undated b. *Kun ka-ibn Adam*. http://www.jawdatsaid.net.

Girard and the Analogy of Desire

James Alison

If the devil is in the details, then God is in the prepositions, and I want today to look at one such preposition: the little word "for." I think this to be the most difficult and delicate word to parse in the whole of theology. Let me explain why. As St. Thomas Aquinas taught us, we cannot say of God what God is, only what God is not. This very properly negative approach to God is vital if we are to avoid idolatry. Idolatry is where whatever passes as "god" is in fact a function of our group dynamics and the patterns of desire that they produce in us, a bit player within a thoroughly human imaginary projection. Yet in Christian theology the whole purpose of the *via negativa*, as it is called, is not to leave us with nothing that we can affirm, but rather to set our minds and hearts free from the interferences by which we block God who is not-a-thing, from showing Godself to us as affirming *us*. In other words, the pruning, which certainly feels negative, is part of a purely positive movement toward us.

Now here is the problem: if God is not a "being" in any normal sense of the word, not something that "is" within the order of everything that exists; if God is much more like nothing at all than like something that is, is much more like no-god-at-all than like one-of-the-gods, then in principle we have no reason at all to conceive of God as in any way either for or against us.

God really would be so much other than anything that we can imagine that there would be quite simply no hook, no criterion by which this other could have incidence in our world. If you are a chocolate pudding, a Beethoven string quartet exists in a sense that you cannot possibly pick up. It is not in any way in rivalry with you, does not occupy the same space as you, floats by in an entirely different sphere from you, and has no incidence in your life or existence. Even if it had in fact inspired a cook in a kitchen to make you, and even if its sound does in fact envelope you completely while you are being cooked, none of this is available to you. Neither can you hear it, nor can it smell or taste you. You pass each other by indifferently like ships in the night.

And of course, some people have tended to see the *via negativa* as making of God something indifferent. Indeed, I have read material by some who subscribe to the *via negativa* that has left me with a sense of horror: all that emphasis on unknowability can lead to the emotional correlate of a sense of lostness before a completely arbitrary other. Those, among whom I include myself, who strongly defend the *via negativa* as indispensable if we are to avoid idolatry have a real task on our hands if we wish to defend both the utter otherness of God, and, yet, while holding onto that otherness, a sense of there being in, and as a nonarbitrary part of, that otherness, a "for" us.

The difficulty with this is that the moment you have a sense of a "for," some hint of a movement toward or benefiting you, you are by definition talking of the incidence of the totally other in your reality, and therefore of something that in principle cannot be understood only negatively, but has to have some positive content that is available to you from within your frame of reference.

It may be that a tiger in a game reserve in India is hunted down by the warden of the reserve and shot with a tranquilizer dart. This puts it to sleep so that it can be moved with comparative ease to another reserve where there is a better ecosystem for its survival and potential mates for its reproduction. As a member of the film crew accompanying this, you can see quite clearly that the whole exercise is *for* the benefit of this tiger in particular and is being conducted by people who are in favour of the survival of tigers in general. All of this is entirely unavailable to the tiger, which can only relate to the unfolding events from within the framework of invincible tigritude. The tiger is quite unable to distinguish between wardens armed with tranquilizer darts and hunters armed with guns. No attempt by the warden to parlay with the tiger and explain why he was going to shoot a tranquilizer dart into it would have the slightest effect. When the exercise is finished, something has indeed happened *for* the tiger, but the tiger cannot talk about what happened being either for it or for tigers in general. For the tiger this was an arbitrary part of a kill-or-be-killed world in which, as it happened, it lived to prowl another day.

So when humans talk about the "for" in God we are actually saying that we are marginally different from the tigers, in that there has been some form of communication that does not totally pass us by; that there are some hooks in our cultural framework by which a "forness" that is entirely from outside our way of being, is able to be understood, and responded to, by us as having incidence within our way of being.

Now the easy way of coping with this is to say "Yes, in principle we can know nothing about God, but God has communicated to us in this or that way—by means of a cataclysm, or a book, or a prophet, or a law, or a sacrifice—so a perfectly straightforward positive knowledge of what God wants of us is now available to us." Nevertheless, I hope you can see that any straightforward positive communication of a "for" us will always be interpreted by us, put to use by us, entirely within the preexisting social and cultural framework that forms us. In other words the sense of the word "for" is as liable to idolatry as the word "is," or even more liable. By definition, the sense of "for" is partial—partial to us, to me. So part of the problem of any claim that a communication of God is "for" us or "for" me is that it it seems to be saying "OK, we've got all that negative stuff about God's 'being' out of the way, so now we can go back to a purely positive account of God's partiality, one that meshes with our preexisting sense of what being 'for,' or being 'me,' or being 'us' means. And, whoops, although we're convinced that we are right, because we have a positive communication, in fact, for all practical purposes, we've fallen straight back into idolatry."

It's as if the tiger, recovering from anesthetic in its new wildlife reserve and discovering a gun left planted nearby, were somehow to have associated the gun with it being brought to this new place. So, along with other tigers, it worships the gun as a totem, entirely blind to the distinction between wardens with tranquilizer darts and hunters with bullets, and with no alteration at all in its kill-or-be-killed attitude to its general surroundings. It would be an entirely futile form of worship because the tigers would not, in any way at all, be having the structure of their engagement with their own way of life altered from within such that they could begin to share, with a degree of equality of understanding, in the network of human relations that had done something *for* them. The gun-totem, bereft of the tigers being given from within the terms of reference of their own tigritude the wherewithal to interpret what it was about, including making sense of its potential ambivalence, would be worse than useless: it would be misleading, a false source of security.

It is rather the same with a word that is often bandied about by people of different religious backgrounds as associated with God. This is the word "mercy." The human claim that God is merciful is entirely useless unless accompanied by a self-interpretation by God of what God's mercy looks like within human interaction. That is to say, unless it offers us an anthropological criterion and the wherewithal for us to be taken inside the criterion's own interpretation of itself, we are left within the equivalent of our invincible tigritude. After all, the "mercy of god" can be invoked and thanked by a group of people for whom it reveals itself in having shown them which defiler was disturbing their unity, and must thus be cast out. God's mercy can also be invoked by the defiler, who may or may not have done anything wrong, as he is led to the gallows. In his invocation of mercy he is begging protection from, and a way out of, what looks to him like crowd violence, rather than God's mercy. God's mercy can even be invoked by an entirely innocent person in the process of being thrown out. She is invoking it upon those who are engaged in throwing her out—while they are thinking that this is how they receive mercy—as an act of her not holding their tigritude against them. But there is nothing in the word itself to say which of these uses is true. And since the uses are completely opposed to each other in meaning, then the word either means far too much or nothing at all. It means whatever it means entirely within the preexisting human framework, nothing more. There is nothing in the word itself that requires us to engage in any self-criticism, any *via negativa* concerning what the words "for" and "us" might mean.

All of this has been to bring us to the place where I would like to highlight how Girard can help us. Let us take the phrase: "God is for us." It seems to me that where traditionally the negative approach to God has hinted at a sense of God who is not in rivalry with anything that is, and thus saved us from the danger of worshiping a god within the order of things that are, it has done so by problematizing the word "is." It doesn't offer much help in problematizing either the "for" or the "us"—which are inseparably bound together. It seems to me that Girard's insight into the mimetic nature of desire, which some people accuse of being far too negative, actually gives us a chance to problematize the "for" and the "us" in very helpful ways. Or to put it in a nutshell: when we say that "God is not in rivalry with anything that is," the phrase "not in rivalry" might be a very useful starting place for working toward a sense of a "for" that is not part of our cultural framework, and yet that has a positive incidence in it. So I'd like here to set out some hints of what I might call the Girardian analogy—the *via negativa* of rivalistic desire.

Traversing Hostility

Let me illustrate what I'm talking about—my parameters if you like—from scripture. I'm taking two apparently unconnected texts, and what I will hope to discuss is how Girard's insight helps us traverse between what is unsaid in the one and what is said in the other.

The first is from St. Matthew's Gospel:[1]

> You have heard that it was said "You shall love your neighbour and hate your enemy." But I say to you, Love your enemies and pray for those who persecute you, so that you may be sons of your Father who is in heaven; for he makes his sun rise on the evil and on the good, and sends rain on the just and on the unjust.

The second is from St. Paul, writing to the Galatians:[2]

> I have been crucified with Christ; it is no longer I who live, but it is Christ who lives in me. The life in the flesh which I am living now, I am living in the faith of the Son of God who loved me and gave himself *for me*. (emphasis added)

When I called your attention to the word "for" earlier, it was its appearance here in Galatians, where it translates the Greek uper, ὑπὲρ that most strongly impressed itself upon my mind. I have deliberately chosen this passage, where the word "for" is linked to "me" rather than one of the occasions where "for" is linked to "us" (for instance, Ephesians 5:2 or Titus 2:14).

My choice is because it is, I think, much more difficult to come up with a satisfactory way of interpreting the "for" when it points not to a general collective but to a historical individual, and to one with whom, as it happens, Jesus had no personal contact at all during the course of his life and ministry. It is also true that, at the personal level of any of us, it is a much less demanding exercise to imagine God loving "us" than it is to imagine God loving "me." It is too easy to have recourse to lazily idolatrous pictures of what it is for someone to love an "us," whereas to glimpse what is meant by talk of someone who is both historical and invisible loving *me* is a real stretch and a challenge.

So let me explain the parameters of what I would like to bring out. In the quotation from St. Matthew we are given something approaching a characterization of the otherness of God: "your Father who is in heaven . . . [who] makes his sun rise on the evil and on the good, and sends rain on the just and on the unjust." Alongside this we have an indication that the one speaking thinks that his characterization is not so removed from the earthly sphere that it is simply inconceivable that humans might be in some way like God: "love . . . pray . . . *so that you may be* sons of your Father." We also have an indication of precisely what criteria, in the anthropological sphere, constitutes the sort of human activity by which some degree of similitude to God becomes possible: "love *your enemies* and pray for *those who persecute you*." In other words, the similitude is to be found in the sphere of desire stretched by the presence of some well-specified social interactions.

So here in the Matthean text there is an astonishing mixture: We have an apparent Divine indifference or impartiality—being for everybody regardless of their moral status rather than partisan in being for this person and against that; we have a guarantor of overall cosmological benevolence who is in some way personal, since it is not merely "the" sun, but "his" sun that God causes to rise; and yet we also have striking hints, attributed to God, of an entirely particular sense of being *for* that is both personal and yet doesn't include any sort of *over against*. It is this latter sense that, I would suggest, is typically massively mysterious to us, such that it is very difficult for us to imagine any positive content to it at all. How can being *for* my enemies and those who are out to get me include any positive sense of being for *me*? Jesus presupposes both the complete otherness of God to our ways of thinking and yet insists that this otherness not only does not disclude, but actively includes, a potential similitude, though one that is a huge stretch for us: being for our enemies.

It is in the context of this stretch that St. Paul's understanding of God being *for* him becomes especially interesting. St. Paul's starting point here is that he was an enemy of God—for that is who he had discovered himself to be on the road to Damascus. The sort of *for* that Jesus describes in St. Matthew's Gospel was experienced by St. Paul. However, not in the first place as a moral injunction telling him to do something toward an enemy, but rather as an accurate description of what he, Paul, as an enemy, found himself undergoing at the hands of someone who was *for* him. There was a definite shape to the *for* of God, and it involved God's occupying a specific place in the human scheme of things: as one vulnerable to hatred and persecution at the hands of enemies. It involved a human movement toward voluntarily occupying the space created by enmity before anybody realized the importance to them of that space, indeed while they were entirely blind to its importance for them personally. The blindness to its importance is absolutely part of the enmity from which the enemy is being, unbeknownst to him/herself, set free.

If I may use yet another inadequate image: it looks as though in the Matthew text, Jesus is describing a somewhat shapeless glove—the outer shape of a movement of an as-yet-contentless benevolence from God pointing toward humans, who are seen as hostile and persecuting, a benevolence that Jesus's listeners are being urged to fill out, to enflesh. St. Paul is describing exactly the same glove but from the receiving end. Now this glove has been tightly stretched by a living hand, a thoroughly content-ful human acting out by Jesus, pointing toward him, Paul, as just such a hostile and persecuting human.

Now the phrase "just such a hostile and persecuting human" doesn't yet make it personal to a "me"; it leaves Paul as a typical member of a collective. So I'd like to go further than this, since in the passage in question, St. Paul problematizes the "me" who is on the receiving end of this "for," and the way he problematizes it yields, I hope, some insight into the nature of the "for."

As far as I can see there is a genuinely detectable mimetic anthropology at work in St. Paul's very mysterious-seeming utterances here, and I wish to express my gratitude and indebtedness to Robert Hamerton-Kelly for his insistence on something that hadn't been at all obvious to me. And that is the importance of the occasions when Paul talks of the faith *of* Jesus Christ or *of* Christ, or *of* Jesus,[3] alongside the occasions when he talks about faith *in* Christ.[4] I have come to see that given that St. Paul is talking not simply about a historical being who is an object of faith, but about one who has become a life-giving spirit, to use his own language,[5] then what he is bringing out is the sense in which the "life-giving spirit" in question is an active protagonist of faith. In other words, this life-giving spirit believed in him, Paul. And the strength and force of this person's passionate belief in him is what has completely taken him over from within. It is because this person's—Christ's—passionate belief in him has taken him over that he finds himself coming to believe on the inside of this person's—Christ's—belief. So when he talks about believing *in* Christ he is expressing both the sense of being on the inside of someone's belief, within their subjectivity, as it were, and their being a completely permeable, and nongraspable, "object" of belief.

Now let me quote to you a little more from that Galatians passage:

> For through the law I died to the law, so that I might live to God. I have been crucified with Christ; and it is no longer I who live, but it is Christ who lives in me. The life in the flesh which I am living now, I am living in the faith of the Son of God who loved me and gave himself for me. I do not nullify the grace of God; for if justification comes through the law, then Christ died for nothing.

At first glance the phrase "for through the law I died to the law" seems odd, since it makes it sound as though Paul somehow considers himself the victim of the law. Yet I think it very important that there is nothing victimary in his thinking here, but a very clear mimetic anthropology. Paul's understanding of the self is always reflexive, interdividual to use Girard's only neologism: your only access to your self is in your relation to another. As you do to your neighbor so you do to yourself. If you are complicit in killing someone, you have consented to killing yourself. Thus when Saul was driven by his investment in the law to persecute Jesus's Way and consent to the killing of Stephen, the law was actually killing him in making of him a murderer of his neighbour. But please notice he is not using this realization as some sort of special pleading, to mitigate the circumstances in his defense: "Sorry Officer, it was the Law made me do it." On the contrary, he seems glad of the state in which this has left him: he's not complaining about it at all. It was as someone who was a dead "self," and therefore beyond any of the reaches of the law, which is entirely moot among the dead, that he was reached by the one whose enemy he had been.

The appearance to him of Jesus on the road to Damascus as "YHWH Jesus whom you are persecuting" was the appearance of someone who believed in him. And let us not double-guess the English language here: it is quite right that believing in someone can be both a relationship toward someone that ends in them as an object of one's belief; and it can also be a powerful attitude of yours that enters into the person as subject such that they, knowing themselves believed in, can do much more than they might have done. It can be both on the one hand, "I believe in X, my candidate for mayor," or "I believe in Y, my bright hope for saving Manchester United from dropping down the league tables," and on the other hand it can also be "Go on, girl, you can do it; I believe in you!"

I think this points to a perfectly normal, and healthy, human experience: I, who am not very sure of who I am, of my strengths and weaknesses, of what I dare to aspire to or not, have the good fortune to be met by someone who believes in me, even when I don't. They can clearly see more to me than I can myself. They can imagine me doing things that I can't, can see some of the pitfalls to which I am prone, and which I will interpret as dead ends by which I will be discouraged. But they can envision these apparent dead ends as crucibles through which I may be turned into something much bigger than I could have imagined. And as I take on board that they believe in me, it is in fact their imagination, their vision, their pattern of desire that will come to run my relationship to the events, the people, and the situations in which I find myself. I will start to look at these situations through their eyes. I will start to think my way through such and such a situation as if they were thinking inside me, as if it were their mind thinking through me. However, it will not be their mind thinking through me *instead* of me. It will be their mind thinking in me *as* me. I will be in the process of receiving a new "I" that is in principle inseparable from the "I" of the one believing in me.

Thus Paul's former self—Saul—was dead, because of its consenting complicity, via legally enflamed persecution, in the murder of Christ. So, what the appearance of "YHWH Jesus who you are persecuting" opened up for him was how he was both an enemy to God and actually dead "in his sins" at the time he was approached. He was approached by someone who believed in him even though he was both dead and an enemy—that is what being *called*, given a vocation and a new name, actually means. The One who called him, in the very act of doing so, was showing that he believed in him, that there was a someone whom he, Paul, was called to become, and would become in the degree in which he took on board that impelling belief of Jesus in him. The source of his "I" is the one who believes in him, and so his "I" is interchangeably his current historical fleshly life, and yet run from within by the "I" of the one who believes in him.

Paul says, "The life in the flesh which I am living now, I am living in the faith of the Son of God who loved me and gave himself for me." I propose that the last phrase "I am living in the faith of the Son of God who loved me and gave himself for me" be read in a slightly unfamiliar way. In this reading it is not that there is a subject, "the Son of God," and then a couple of more or less emotionally charged qualifications tacked on—"who loved me and gave himself for me." Rather there is one subject: "The Son-of-God-who-loved-me-and-gave-himself-for-me." The purpose of this whole is to indicate the nature, the full richness of anthropological content, of the protagonism toward him, Paul, that included a human longing and trusting of the sort that can get alongside, and thus within, another human being—believing in them.

Please notice the extraordinary combination of power and of powerlessness that this suggests. The power consists in being able to make of a grotesque and awful human death not only a one-off act of standing in for someone else, but in fact a gift outside any possibility of reciprocity, an act of communication of a huge love of passion and longing for those trapped in the self-demeaning cycles of enmity. But there is something of even greater power than this present. By losing to his enemies, Jesus is not secretly winning through some hidden ruse. Rather, one dimension of the power of the act of communication, the appeal, is in the loss, the occupying and remaining in the place of loss.

The loss, and the powerlessness, is appealing to Saul, saying to him "Here is where my being not out to get you, but for you, leaves me. It leaves me beneath your feet, as it were, under you, powerless before you. It is as one who is dead before you that I am for you. Only thus could I be *toward* you, for you, in a way that is not *over against* you in any way at all, for the dead are in no way at all over against the living. What God being *for* you looks like is unimaginable except in as far as you learn to see a dead enemy as having in fact been *for* you. It is only available to you as you begin to glimpse how *your* sense of God being 'for' 'us' was in fact driven by hostility, such that you were the enemy of what was authentically for you. But it is genuinely as one who has allowed himself to be defined by all the worldly helplessness of the dead before you that I am for you—that is the content of my being a life-giving spirit. From now on, it really will be *you* who takes this somewhere new. I am entrusting myself to *you* to do with as you will. I want to show you that I don't do the 'God' thing separately from you and independently of you. But I believe in you, and so I will come to be all that I will come to be with you, and in you, and not independently of you. The gentleness of my belief in you is such that I don't invade you, but come on board without displacing you; this happens in the degree to which you, discovering yourself believed-in are able to let go of that 'I' built in self-destructive enmity. I know of no richer way to say that I love you than to say that I am overjoyed to be in this apparently dead-end place for you, since I know that by my being in this place I can get it across to you that I believe in you. My occupying this space was not, and is not, a juddering to a helpless halt before you, it is an act of communication toward you, a sign of how much I want to come out to play with you, my completely irrevocable statement of trust and belief in you: that I know you have potential for a much much richer way of being than you yet know. Where will you take this? What will you make of me-who-am-entrusting-myself-to-you? I am psyched about what you are going to make of this!"

The Negative Analogy from Desire

Well, I hope you can see that this discussion might fit in with conversations that we have been having among those who have taken on board René Girard's mimetic insight, as also with some classical theological discussions, and even with some modern discussions concerning desire and religion in the wider sphere.

The *via negativa* of mimetic desire turns out to offer us a way in which the word "for" can have a non-idolatrous but genuinely human meaning from a place just outside our ken, our understanding, our being able to grasp it. It is sealed off from our grasp by its apparent powerlessness in the place of death. However, it has come to have a non-idolatrous meaning only through traversing an anthropological space that is entirely familiar to us: the space of one being driven out to death, and facing us from that driven-out space, invisibly, as it were, except in as far as we find ourselves being let go of our hostility to it. In other words, the inexhaustibly rich positive sense of God's "for" begins to show itself among us only in and as a pruning of all our senses of "for" derived from within rivalry, vengeance, and over-against.

I hope that it becomes clear how this might illumine one of the most difficult discussions concerning the place of human desire in relation to the things of God. If I may give some slightly cartoonish characterizations: there are those for whom human desire is so negative, so corrupt, that grace is extrinsic to us. It can reveal, and then forgive and cover over, our wickedness; however, if we are to be given the chance of a genuinely new human culture it is one that does not start here, but in heaven, and is not in organic continuity with what we know here. So there is no analogy between our sense of "for us" and God's. Fear of idolatry is such that all we're left with is idolatry, since there's no criterion in our midst by which we might recognize what isn't idolatry.

Then there are those for whom human desire is not so negative, such that the kingdom of heaven starts here and is very much in continuity with what we know here. God's sense of "for us" and ours are not so different, which is another way of having no criterion in our midst for recognizing our idolatry, since we simply idolatrize our criteria.

What it seems to me that Girard's understanding offers is the anthropological shape of our idolatry as offered to us by someone outside it who is offering us to be stretched beyond it through empowering us to traverse our own hostility. Grace perfects nature through a very specific social shape: having our hostility undone by One who has approached us from within the centre of our hostility.

I don't have time in this conference to develop this in all the ways I would like—the radical blossoming of the personal, the flowering of creativity that begins to show through from the other side of the *via negativa* of desire. However I would like to end by sharing with you a passage in the gospel that brings out all that I have been trying to say here with such clarity that it is blinding.

In St. John's Gospel,[6] there is a meeting of concerned parties to try and work out what to do about Jesus: he is creating such waves that they fear that the colonial power, the Romans, will take advantage of the disruption as an excuse to destroy the Temple and their nation. Caiaphas, who was acting High Priest, says to the meeting: "You understand nothing at all. You do not conceive that it's expedient *for* you that one man should die *for* the people, and that the whole nation should not perish."

Well, we've all heard this before: in fact it is the classic statement of sacrificial political ethics. In my terms of reference, it is the word "for" used with invincible tigritude. What we rarely remember is the verse immediately following: "He did not say this from himself, but being high priest that year he prophesied that Jesus should die *for* the nation, and not for the nation only, but to gather into one the children of God who are scattered abroad."

Here there is a positive sense both of priesthood and of prophecy, even if one entirely unknown to, and working despite, its placeholder. Using the hook of a strikingly ambivalent human dynamic, a hugely positive act of communication, with an abundance of fruit way beyond what the ambivalent dynamic could possibly imagine, was unfurling itself in our midst as a "for" that is in no way run on our terms.

NOTES

Presentation for the Symposium on René Girard and World Religions Graduate Theological Union Berkeley, April 14–16, 2011.

1. Matthew 6:43–45.
2. Galatians 2:19b–20.
3. For example, Romans 3:22, 26 as well as this Galatians passage.
4. For example, Galatians 2:16.
5. 1 Corinthians 15:45.
6. John 11:49–52.

Contributors

Jeremiah Alberg is a professor in the humanities department at the International Christian University, Tokyo, where he teaches philosophy. His research interests include Rousseau, Kant, and German Idealism. He has written extensively on Rousseau and scandal. He has also developed a "hermeneutics of forgiveness" in his book, *Beneath the Veil: Reading Scandalous Texts*. At present he is writing on Kant's reception of Rousseau's thought. He is currently serving as president of the Colloquium on Violence & Religion, the deputy chief editor of *Tetsugaku: International Journal of the Philosophical Association of Japan*, and the director of the University's Center for Teaching and Learning and the Library.

James Alison is a priest, theologian, and author. Currently a fellow of Imitatio, he resides in Madrid, from where he teaches courses and accompanies retreats in a variety of countries each year. His published works include *The Joy of Being Wrong*, *Faith Beyond Resentment: Fragments Catholic and Gay*, and most recently *Jesus the Forgiving Victim*, a DVD- and text-based course of introduction to the Christian faith for adults.

Ann Astell is professor of theology at the University of Notre Dame and past president of the Colloquium on Violence and Religion. She was professor of English and medieval studies at Purdue University from 1988 until 2007. She is the author of six books: *The Song of Songs in the Middle Ages* (1990), *Job, Boethius, and Epic Truth* (1994), *Chaucer and the Universe of Learning* (1996), *Political Allegory in Late Medieval England* (1999), *Joan of Arc and Sacrificial Authorship* (2003), and *Eating Beauty: The Eucharist and the Spiritual Arts of the Middle Ages* (2006). She is also the editor or coeditor of six collections of essays, including *Lay Sanctity, Medieval and Modern: The Search for Models* (2000), *Joan of Arc and Spirituality* (2003), *Levinas and Medieval Literature: The "Difficult Reading" of English and Rabbinic Texts* (2009), *Sacrifice, Scripture, and Substitution: Readings in Ancient Judaism and Christianity* (2011), and *Magistra Doctissima: Essays in Honor of Bonnie Wheeler* (2013).

Benoît Chantre is a publisher in the social sciences, an associate member of the Centre international d'études de la philosophie française contemporaine, a fellow of Imitatio, and president of the Association Recherches Mimétiques. He has written books of interviews (*La Divine Comédie*, with Philippe Sollers; *Le Choix de Pascal*, with Jacques Julliard; *Achever Clausewitz*, with René Girard), an essay on Charles Péguy (*Péguy point final*), a tribute to René Girard (*Les Derniers Jours de René Girard*), and numerous articles on Bergson, Girard, Levinas, and Simone Weil (for *Artpress*, *Cahiers Simone Weil*, *Esprit*, *L'Infini*, *La Revue des deux mondes*, etc.) He has directed three stagings (*Le Naufragé* by Thomas Bernhard, Festival d'Avignon; *The Messiah* by Handel and *Il Re Pastore* by Mozart, Théâtre du Châtelet), two films of interviews with René Girard (*La Violence et le sacré* and *Le Sens de l'histoire*), and organized numerous seminars, lectures, and conferences in France and in Italy (Académie de France à Rome). He is preparing Girard's biography.

Brian Collins is the Drs. Ram and Sushila Gawande Chair in Indian Religion and Philosophy at Ohio University and the author of *The Head Beneath the Altar: Hindu Mythology and the Critique of Sacrifice* (2014).

Jacob Dalton, Khyentse Foundation Distinguished University Professor in Tibetan Buddhism, holds a joint appointment in South and Southeast

Asian Studies and East Asian Languages and Cultures at the University of California, Berkeley. He works on tantric ritual, Nyingma religious history, paleography, and the Dunhuang manuscripts. He is the author of *The Taming of the Demons: Violence and Liberation in Tibetan Buddhism* (2011), *The Gathering of Intentions: A History of a Tibetan Tantra* (2016), and coauthor of *Tibetan Tantric Manuscripts from Dunhuang: A Descriptive Catalogue of the Stein Collection at the British Library* (2006).

Robert J. Daly, SJ, is professor emeritus of theology at Boston College. A former editor of *Theological Studies*, his interest in mimetic theory began with his foreword to Maria Assad's 1987 translation of Raymund Schwager's *Must There Be Scapegoats?* He subsequently organized the 2000 meeting of COV&R at Boston College on "Violence and Institution in Christianity, Judaism, Hinduism, Buddhism, and Islam" and edited its proceedings for the 2002 (vol. 9) issue of *Contagion*. He sums up his theological view of mimetic theory in the section "Sacrifice and Girardian Mimetic Theory: The End of Sacrifice?" toward the end of his 2009 magnum opus: *Sacrifice Unveiled: The True Meaning of Christian Sacrifice* (2009).

Jean-Pierre Dupuy is professor emeritus of social and political philosophy, Ecole Polytechnique, Paris, and professor of political science, Stanford University. He is a member of the French Academy of Technology, a spinoff of the Academy of Sciences, and of the Conseil Général des Mines, the French High Magistracy that oversees and regulates industry, energy, and the environment. He chairs the Ethics Committee of the French High Authority on Nuclear Safety and Security. He is the director of the research program of Imitatio, a San Francisco foundation devoted to the dissemination and discussion of René Girard's mimetic theory. His most recent work has dealt with the topic of catastrophe. Among his publications in English are the following: *The Mechanization of the Mind* (2000); *On the Origins of Cognitive Science* (2009); *The Mark of the Sacred* (2013); *Economy and the Future: A Crisis of Faith* (2014); and *A Short Treatise on the Metaphysics of Tsunamis* (2015).

Adam Ericksen is a graduate of Linfield College and Garrett Evangelical Theological Seminary. At Linfield, he received his BA in religious studies, with a minor in history. The title of his senior thesis was "The Divine in

Disguise: How Judaism Deals with Suffering and Death." He continued this theme with his honors thesis, which was titled "The Divine in Disguise: How Christianity Deals with Suffering and Death." He received his masters in theological studies from Garrett, with an emphasis in theology and ethics. His master's thesis was titled "Love and Nonviolence in Christianity and Islam." Adam writes blogs and films vlogs for the *Raven ReView* and *Teaching Nonviolent Atonement* websites. He explores the intersections of mimetic theory, current events, religion, and popular culture. Adam is a frequent public speaker at conferences and churches and his writing has been featured in *Time* magazine. He is the minister of Faith Development at Lake Oswego United Church of Christ in Lake Oswego, Oregon.

Sandor Goodhart is a professor of English and Jewish studies at Purdue University's Department of English, and author of six books on literature, philosophy, and Jewish studies: *Möbian Nights: Reading Literature and Darkness* (2017), *The Prophetic Law: Essays in Judaism, Girardianism, Literary Studies, and the Ethical* (2014), *Sacrifice, Scripture, and Substitution* (2011; coedited with Ann Astell), *For René Girard: Essays in Friendship and Truth* (2009; coedited with J. Williams, T. Ryba, and J. Jørgensen), *Reading Stephen Sondheim* (2000), and *Sacrificing Commentary: Reading the End of Literature* (1996). He directed the Jewish Studies Program at Purdue (1997–2002), the Philosophy and Literature Program (2005), and the Classical Studies Program (2007–11). He served as guest editor for a special issue of *Shofar* 26, no. 4 (Summer 2008) on Emmanuel Levinas, as the coeditor (with Monica Osborne) of a special issue of *Modern Fiction Studies* 54, no. 1 (Spring 2008) on Emmanuel Levinas, and as the editor of a special issue of *Religion* 37, no. 1 (March 2007) on René Girard. He is a founding board member of the North American Levinas Society, the former president of the Colloquium on Violence and Religion (2004–7), and the author of over ninety essays.

Otto Kallscheuer is a philosopher and political scientist and a former member of the Institute of Advanced Study in Princeton and of the Italian Academy for Advanced Study at Columbia University (New York). Kallscheuer has taught political science and philosophy at several universities in Germany, Switzerland, and Italy, including the Free University Berlin.

His research fellowships include *inter alia* the IWM (Institute for Human Sciences, Vienna), the Käte Hamburger Kolleg "Dynamics in the History of Religion" at the University of Bochum (Germany), and the ZRWP (Center for Religion, Economy and Politics) of the Universities of Basel, Zürich, and Lucerne (Switzerland). His book publications include the following: *Gottes Wort und Volkes Stimme* (1994); *Das Europa der Religionen* (1996); *Die Wissenschaft vom Lieben Gott* (2006); and *Zur Zukunft des Abendlandes* (2009). Otto Kallscheuer is a regular contributor to major German and Swiss newspapers.

Michael Kirwan is a British Jesuit priest, lecturing in systematic and pastoral theology at Heythrop College (University of London), where he is also the director of the Heythrop Institute for Religion and Society. His doctoral thesis, completed in 1998, explored theologies of martyrdom in the light of Girard's mimetic theory. He is the author of *Discovering Girard* (2004), *Political Theology: A New Introduction* (2008), and *Girard and Theology* (2009). He is also coeditor (with Sheelah Treflé Hidden) of *Mimesis and Atonement: René* Girard and the Doctrine of Salvation (2017). As well as Girardian mimetic theory, his research interests include contemporary political theology and the conversation between theology and literature.

Rüdiger Lohlker is professor of Islamic studies at the Oriental Institute, University of Vienna (Austria). His areas of interest are the history of Islamic ideas, Islam and the Arab world online, modern Islamic extremist movements, and Jihadism. He is the author of "Syrian Electronic Army: Propaganda Warfare and Cyber Espionage," *Journal for Intelligence, Propaganda and Security Studies* 9 (2015); *Theologie der Gewalt: Das Beispiel IS* (2016); "Theology Matters: The Case of Jihadi Islam," *Strategic Review* (2016); and "Die Salafisten: Der Aufstand der Frommen, Saudi-Arabien und der Islam."

Wolfgang Palaver, a Catholic theologian from Austria, is currently professor of Catholic social thought at the School of Catholic Theology at the University of Innsbruck, where he was also dean from 2013 until 2017. From 2007 to 2011, he was president of the "Colloquium on Violence & Religion" and became an honorary member of its board in 2016. He is a member of the advisory board of Imitatio, a nonprofit organization dedicated to René

Girard's mimetic theory. He has published books and articles on violence and religion, Thomas Hobbes, Carl Schmitt, René Girard, and Simone Weil. His books include *Politische Philosophie versus Politische Theologie? Die Frage der Gewalt im Spannungsfeld von Politik und Religion* (edited with A. Oberprantacher and D. Regensburger, 2011), *René Girard's Mimetic Theory* (2013), *The European Wars of Religion* (edited with H. Rudolph and D. Regensburger, 2016), *Eskalation zum Äußersten? Girards Clausewitz interdisziplinär kommentiert* (edited with W. Guggenberger, 2016), and *The Palgrave Handbook of Mimetic Theory and Religion* (edited with J. Alison, 2017).

Ted Peters is Distinguished Research Professor Emeritus of Systematic Theology and Ethics at Pacific Lutheran Theological Seminary and the Graduate Theological Union in Berkeley, California, and coeditor with Robert John Russell of the journal *Theology and Science* at the Center for Theology and the Natural Sciences. He has just published the third edition of his systematic theology, *God—The World's Future* (2015). He is also author of *Sin Boldly! Justifying Faith for Fragile and Broken Souls* (2015), which employs Girardian scapegoat theory.

Anselm Tilman Ramelow is professor of philosophy at the Dominican School of Philosophy and Theology in Berkeley, chair of the philosophy department, and a member of the Order of Preachers. He is also a member of the Core Doctoral Faculty at the Graduate Theological Union in Berkeley and the Academy of Catholic Theology. Ramelow received his doctorate in Munich under the direction of Robert Spaemann in 1996. His areas of research and teaching include free will, the history of philosophy, and philosophical aesthetics. Most recently he has worked on a philosophical approach to miracles. He is author of *Gott, Freiheit, Weltenwahl: Die Metaphysik der Willensfreiheit zwischen Antonio Perez, S. J. (1599–1649) und G.W. Leibniz (1646–1716)* (1997) and *Beyond Modernism?—George Lindbeck and the Linguistic Turn in Theology* (2005), as well as *Thomas Aquinas: De veritate Q. 21–24; Translation and Commentary* (2013) and *God: Reason and Reality (Basic Philosophical Concepts)* (2014), as editor and contributor. His articles have appeared in *Historisches Wörterbuch der Philosophie*, *Archiv für Begriffsgeschichte*, *Nova et Vetera*, *American Catholic Philosophical Quarterly*, and *Angelicum*.

John Ranieri is a graduate of Columbia University and Boston College. He is a professor of philosophy and the director of the University Honors Program at Seton Hall University in South Orange, New Jersey. The relationship between the Abrahamic traditions and political philosophy has been an ongoing focus of his work. He is currently working on a project exploring the relationship between mimetic theory and the Qur'an. Another area of interest is the political thought of Chinese Neo-Confucian thinkers.

Martha Reineke is professor of religion in the Department of Philosophy and World Religions at the University of Northern Iowa. A specialist in the thought of René Girard and Julia Kristeva, she is the author of *Sacrificed Lives: Kristeva on Women and Violence* (1997). Her book *Intimate Domain: Desire, Trauma, and Mimetic Theory* (2014) draws on Kristeva, trauma studies, and Girard's early work on sensory experience. She is coeditor, with David Goodman, of *Ana-María Rizzuto and the Psychoanalysis of Religion: The Road to the Living God* (2017).

Richard Schenk is a retired professor of philosophy and theology and a Roman Catholic priest of the Order of Preachers, currently in chaplaincy to the University of Freiburg im Breisgau. He served as professor of philosophy and theology at the Graduate Theological Union in Berkeley 1990–2011 as well as director of the Hannover Institute of Philosophical Research from 1991–2000 and of the Intercultural Forum for Studies in Faith and Culture (Washington, D.C.) 2004–6. He was president of the Catholic University of Eichstaett-Ingolstadt 2011–14. In 2004 he was named Master of Sacred Theology (S.T.M.) in the Dominican Order. In 2007–8 Schenk served as the founding president of the Academy of Catholic Theology. He has been a member of the European Academy of Sciences and Arts since 1991. He edited *Zur Theorie des Opfers* (Collegium Philosophicum, vol. 1), Stuttgart-Bad Cannstatt, Frommann-Holzboog 1995) and authored *Soundings in the History of a Hope* (Washington, D.C., Catholic University of America/ Sapientia 2016).

Noel Sheth, SJ (1943–2017), was professor of Indian and Asian religions in the Department of Interreligious Studies at St. Xavier's College (Autonomous), Mumbai, and was adviser to its Heras Research Institute. He was president emeritus of Jnana-Deepa Vidyapeeth, Pontifical Institute of Philosophy and Religion, Pune, India. Holding a doctorate in Sanskrit from Harvard University, his publications are on the exegesis of Sanskrit and Pali texts, on Indian-Asian religions, and on comparative theology and philosophy. He received many awards, was a member of various international learned societies and administrative bodies, and was on the board of advisers of some international journals. He was an adviser to the Jesuit General for interreligious dialogue with Hinduism and a member of the International Secretariat for Ecumenical and Interreligious Relations for the worldwide Society of Jesus.

Alexander von Rospatt is professor of Buddhist and South Asian studies at the University of California, Berkeley. He specializes in the doctrinal history of Indian Buddhism and in Nepalese Buddhism, the only Indic Mahayana tradition that persists in its original South Asian setting, the Kathmandu valley. His publications include a monograph on the development and early history of the Buddhist doctrine of momentariness, and numerous essays in which he treats particular aspects of the Nepalese Buddhist tradition, including its narrative literature and its rituals and their origins and evolution. Von Rospatt was trained at the universities of Hamburg and London. Prior to his appointment at Berkeley, he served as assistant professor at the University of Leipzig and taught on visiting appointments at the universities of Oxford and Vienna.

Nikolaus Wandinger, associate professor of systematic theology at the University of Innsbruck, Austria, has been active in the field of theological anthropology, employing mimetic theory and dramatic theology. He is coeditor of *Gesammelte Schriften* by Raymund Schwager (2014–17), the first theological dialogue partner of René Girard, has also published on Karl Rahner's theology and its compatibility with mimetic theory, and has worked on the interpretation of popular culture with the help of Girard's theory.

Index

T